Urban Economics

THIRD EDITION Urban Economics

Arthur O'Sullivan
Department of Economics
Oregon State University

IRWIN

Chicago • Bogotá • Boston • Buenos Aires • Caracas
London • Madrid • Mexico City • Sydney • Toronto

IRWIN   **Concerned about Our Environment**
In recognition of the fact that our company is a large end-user of fragile yet replenishable resources, we at IRWIN can assure you that every effort is made to meet or exceed Environmental Protection Agency (EPA) recommendations and requirements for a "greener" workplace.

To preserve these natural assets, a number of environmental policies, both companywide and department-specific, have been implemented. From the use of 50% recycled paper in our textbooks to the printing of promotional materials with recycled stock and soy inks to our office paper recycling program, we are committed to reducing waste and replacing environmentally unsafe products with safer alternatives.

© Richard D. Irwin, a Times Mirror Higher Education Group, Inc. company, 1990, 1992, and 1996

Irwin Book Team

Senior sponsoring editor: *Gary Nelson*
Editorial assistant: *Tracey Klein Douglas*
Senior marketing manager: *Ron Bloecher*
Production supervisor: *Pat Frederickson*
Project editor: *Waivah Clement*
Designer: *Crispin Prebys*
Compositor: *Publication Services, Inc.*
Typeface: *10/12 Times Roman*
Printer: *Quebecor Printing Book Group*

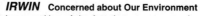
Times Mirror
Higher Education Group

Library of Congress Cataloging-in-Publication Data
O'Sullivan, Arthur.
    Urban economics / Arthur O'Sullivan.—3rd ed.
      p.   cm. — (The Irwin series in economics)
    Includes index.
    ISBN 0-256-16072-4
    1. Urban economics. I. Title. II. Series.
HT321.088 1996
330.9173′2—dc20   95–37278

Printed in the United States of America
2 3 4 5 6 7 8 9 0 Q–K 2 1 0 9 8 7 6

To Babe

Preface

This book uses economic analysis to explain why cities exist, where they develop, how they grow, and how different activities are arranged within cities. It also explores the economics of urban problems such as poverty, inadequate housing, segregation, congestion, pollution, and crime.

The text is designed for use in undergraduate courses in urban economics and urban affairs. It could also be used for graduate courses in urban planning, public policy, and public administration. All of the economic concepts used in the book are covered in the typical intermediate microeconomics course, so students who have completed such a course will be able to move through the book at a rapid pace. Students whose exposure to microeconomics is limited to an introductory course will require more time and effort to move through the book. The book uses several concepts that are not covered in most introductory courses, including the consumer-choice model (indifference curves and budget lines), monopolistic competition, the input choice model (isoquants and isocosts), short-run and long-run curves, and interactions among markets.

The instructor's manual that accompanies this text contains a primer on indifference-curve analysis. It is written for students whose exposure to microeconomics is limited to an introductory course, but could also be used as a refresher for students who covered the consumer-choice model in an intermediate microeconomics course. The overview is produced in a format suitable for reproduction and distribution to students.

The book covers more topics than the typical urban economics text, giving instructors several options for a one-semester course in urban economics. A course that emphasizes interurban location analysis would cover all five chapters in Part I (Market Forces in the Development of Cities), while other courses might omit some of these chapters. The prime candidates for omission are Chapter 3 (Where Do Cities Develop?), Chapter 4 (The History of Western Urbanization), and Chapter 5 (How Many Cities?). A course emphasizing intraurban location analysis would cover all five chapters in Part II (Land Rent and Urban Land-Use Patterns), while other courses might omit Chapter 9 (General-Equilibrium Land Use) or Chapter 11 (Land-Use Controls and Zoning). A course emphasizing urban problems would cover all four chapters in Part III (The Federal Response to Urban Problems) and several of the chapters in Part IV (Urban Problems and Local Government). The three chapters on local government (Chapters 16 through 18) could be omitted in a course emphasizing traditional urban problems, but would be an integral part of a course emphasizing urban public finance. The last two chapters deal with education and crime, two urban problems that receive less attention in other urban texts.

Changes for the Third Edition

For the Third Edition, I updated many of the tables and charts with the most recent data. In addition, I added an Appendix that reviews some of the key tools of microeconomic analysis, including supply and demand analysis, the theory of consumer choice, and marginal analysis. These tools are used in different parts of the book, and a quick review will be helpful for many students.

The instructor's manual for the book has two features that will be useful for many instructors.

1. Model answers to end-of-chapter exercises. The book has exercises and discussion questions at the end of each chapter (an average of 13 per chapter), and the instructor's manual provides a complete set of model answers.

2. Chapter outlines and suggested in-class exercises. Each chapter outline refers to several exercises and discussion questions that could be integrated into a lecture on the relevant material. I ask my students to develop a group answer to a particular question, and then I collect the answers and discuss some of the alternatives. This approach breaks up the lecture into more manageable sections and gives students an opportunity to become engaged in the learning process. It also gives the instructor some feedback on what students are learning.

Arthur O'Sullivan

Acknowledgments

I am greatly indebted to my two mentors in urban economics. As an undergraduate at the University of Oregon, I was taught by Ed Whitelaw, whose enthusiasm for urban economics is apparently contagious. He used a number of innovative teaching techniques that made economics understandable, relevant, and even fun. As a graduate student at Princeton University, I was taught by Edwin Mills, one of the founding fathers of urban economics. He refined my mathematical and analytical skills and also provided a steady stream of perceptive insights into urban phenomena. I hope that some of what I learned from these two outstanding teachers is reflected in this book.

I am also indebted to many people who read the book and suggested ways to improve the coverage and the exposition.

Arthur O'Sullivan

Contents in Brief

Contents

4 The History of Western Urbanization 71

5 How Many Cities? 91

9 General-Equilibrium Land Use   233

10 Suburbanization and Modern Cities   251

15   Housing Policies   409

APPENDIX

Tools of Microeconomics   695

Tools of Microeconomics   697

CHAPTER 1 Introduction

Cities have always been the fireplaces of civilization, whence light and heat radiated out into the dark.
Theodore Parker

I'd rather wake up in the middle of nowhere than in any city on earth.
Steve McQueen

This book explores the economics of cities and urban problems. The quotes from Parker and McQueen reflect our mixed feelings about cities. On the positive side, cities facilitate production and trade, so they increase our standard of living. In addition, they provide consumers with a wide variety of goods and services. Unfortunately, cities also have serious problems such as poverty, congestion, pollution, and crime. Although these problems are truly urban in nature, they could be solved without abandoning our cities. One of the purposes of this book is to show that policies that solve urban problems will increase the vitality of cities, causing cities to grow, not shrink.

Another purpose of the book is to explain some broad changes in the size of cities and the fraction of the population living in cities. In 1990, over 75 percent of the U.S. population lived in urban areas, up from only 6 percent in 1800. This rapid urbanization resulted in large part from the technological changes of the industrial revolution. A number of innovations in production and transportation increased industrial output and trade. Since most firms locate in cities, the increases in output and trade increased the size and number of cities. More recently, however, many northeastern and north-central U.S. cities have actually lost population, a result of migration to the West and the South and a shift away from the traditional manufacturing economy.

The book also explains some changes in the internal spatial structure of cities. In the 19th century, the typical large metropolitan area was monocentric, with the bulk

1

of the city's employment in its central core area. In the typical modern metropolitan area, about half of the jobs are in suburban areas, and many of the suburban jobs are in suburban subcenters. The suburbanization of employment was caused by a number of factors, including changes in transportation and communications technology, the building of highways, and other government policies.

As mentioned in the opening paragraph, this book explores the economics of urban problems. The conventional list of urban problems includes poverty, segregation, inadequate housing, congestion, pollution, inferior education, and crime. This text provides three insights into the analysis of these problems. First, most of these urban problems are related: many of the problems have common roots, and some of the problems are exacerbated by the other problems. For example, poverty contributes to the problems of inadequate housing and crime, and crime contributes to neighborhood deterioration and thus worsens the problem of inadequate housing. Given the common roots and interdependencies of many urban problems, a comprehensive approach to the problems may be more effective than a piecemeal one.

The second insight about urban problems is that the economic approach to these problems often differs from the approaches adopted by policymakers. For example, the problems of congestion and pollution occur because some resources (roads and air) are improperly priced; the economic approach is to force travelers and polluters to pay for the resources they use. In contrast, the policy response to these problems often involves regulation or subsidization.

The third insight into urban problems is that most of the problems are affected by land-use patterns and also influence land-use patterns. An understanding of the spatial dimension of a particular urban problem is necessary to (1) fully understand the reasons for the problem and (2) predict the spatial responses to a particular public policy.

The remainder of this brief introductory chapter addresses two questions. First, what is urban economics? The answers to this question provide a preview of the material covered in the book. Second, what is a city? The economist's definition of a city differs from the definition used by the U.S. Census Bureau.

What Is Urban Economics?

Urban economics is the study of the location choices of firms and households. Other branches of economics ignore spatial aspects of decision making, adopting the convenient but unrealistic assumption that all production and consumption take place at a single point. In contrast, urban economics examines the *where* of economic activities. In urban economics, a household chooses where to work and where to live. Similarly, a firm chooses where to locate its factory, office, or retail outlet.

Urban economics explores the spatial aspects of urban problems and public policy. Urban problems such as poverty, segregation, urban decay, crime, congestion, and pollution are intertwined with the location decisions of households and firms: location decisions contribute to urban problems, and urban problems influence location decisions. For example, the suburbanization of employment opportunities contributes to central-city poverty, which causes further suburbanization as wealthy households flee the fiscal problems of the central city. An informed discussion of alternative policy options must take these spatial effects into account.

If urban economics is the study of location choices, why isn't it called *location economics* or *spatial economics?* There are three reasons for the *urban* in urban economics. First, most location decisions involve an urban choice: over three fourths of the U.S. work force live in cities, meaning that much of location analysis involves urban areas. Second, urban economics is also concerned with location choices within cities. Finally, the most important problems caused by location choices occur in urban areas.

Urban economics can be divided into four related areas, which correspond to the four parts of this book. These are (1) market forces in the development of cities, (2) land rent and land use within cities, (3) spatial aspects of poverty and housing, and (4) local government expenditures and taxes.

Market Forces in the Development of Cities

The first part of the book shows how the location decisions of firms and households cause the development of cities. A firm chooses the location within a region that maximizes its profit, and a household chooses the location that maximizes its utility. These location decisions generate clusters of activity (cities) that differ in size and economic structure. The questions addressed in this part of the book include the following:

1. Why do cities exist?
2. What is the role of trade in the development of cities?
3. Where do urban areas develop?
4. Why did the first cities develop?
5. What is the connection between industrialization and urbanization?
6. Why do cities differ in size and scope?
7. What causes urban economic growth and decline?
8. How do local governments encourage economic growth?
9. How does employment growth affect a city's per capita income?

Land Rent and Land Use within Cities

The second part of the book discusses the spatial organization of activities within cities. In contrast to the first part, which examines location choices from the regional perspective, the second part examines the location choices of firms and households within cities. It shows how land-use patterns are shaped by the interactions between different urban activities. The questions addressed in the second part include the following:

1. What determines the price of land, and why does the price vary across space?
2. How does public policy affect the price of land and land-use patterns?
3. Why does the price of housing vary across space?

4. Why are households in U.S. cities segregated with respect to income and race?
5. Do the location decisions of households affect the location decisions of firms?
6. What factors caused the suburbanization of employment and population?
7. Why was the monocentric city of the 19th century replaced by the multicentric city of the 20th century?
8. Why do local governments use zoning and other land-use controls to restrict location choices?
9. How does zoning affect the equilibrium price of land?

Spatial Aspects of Poverty and Housing

The third part of the book examines the spatial aspects of two related urban problems, poverty and housing. Urban poverty has a distinct spatial dimension: the poor are typically concentrated in the central city, far from the expanding employment opportunities in the suburbs. The discussion of poverty addresses the following questions:

1. Who are the poor, and where do they live?
2. What causes poverty?
3. To what extent do market forces diminish racial discrimination in employment?
4. Does residential segregation contribute to poverty?
5. How does the federal government combat poverty?
6. What are the merits of reform proposals such as the negative income tax, workfare, earned-income tax credits, and mandated child support?

The third part of the book also examines the spatial aspects of urban housing problems. Housing choices are linked to location choices because housing is immobile: when a household chooses a dwelling, it also chooses a location. The most important urban housing problems are segregation and the decay of dwellings and neighborhoods in the central city. The two housing chapters address the following questions:

1. What makes housing different from other commodities?
2. Why do the poor occupy used housing?
3. What causes racial segregation in housing?
4. Under what conditions will a neighborhood switch from being mostly white to mostly black?
5. How does public policy affect the supply of low-income housing and its price?
6. Should the government build new low-income housing or give money to the poor?
7. How does rent control affect the supply of low-income housing?

Local Government Expenditures and Taxes

The last part of the book explores the spatial aspects of local government policies. Under the fragmented system of local governments, most large metropolitan areas have dozens of local governments, including municipalities, school districts, and special districts. These local governments provide a wide variety of goods, including transportation systems, education, and crime protection. Firms and households "shop" for the jurisdiction that provides the best combination of services and taxes: citizens vote with their feet. Therefore, tax and spending policies affect location choices, thus influencing the spatial distribution of activity within and between cities.

The process of shopping for a local government raises five questions about the fragmented system of local government:

1. Is the fragmented system of government efficient?
2. What is the role of intergovernmental grants in the fragmented system?
3. How do taxpayers respond to local taxes on property, income, and sales?
4. Is the local property tax regressive or progressive?
5. Does the property tax encourage segregation with respect to income and race?

One of the responsibilities of local government is to provide a transportation system. Most cities combine an auto-based highway system with some form of mass transit (bus, light rail, or heavy rail). Since activities are arranged within cities to facilitate interactions between different activities, changes in the transportation system that affect the relative accessibility of different sites affect land-use patterns. The chapters on transportation address the following questions:

1. What causes congestion, and what are the alternative policy responses?
2. How does congestion affect land-use patterns?
3. What are the alternative policies for dealing with auto pollution?
4. Under what circumstances is a bus system more efficient than a fixed-rail system such as San Francisco's BART or Washington's Metro?
5. What are the costs and benefits of light-rail systems?
6. Should transit be deregulated to allow private firms to compete with transit authorities?

The last two chapters of the book deal with two local public goods: education and crime control. The study of education fits naturally into the scheme of urban economics because education affects location decisions: a household's choice of residence depends in part on the quality of local schools and the taxes required to support the schools. In addition, location choices affect the provision of education: if households segregate themselves with respect to income, per pupil spending is likely to be relatively low in poor districts, so poor children may receive inferior education. In addition, a child's achievement level depends on (*a*) the income and education level of his or her parents and (*b*) the achievement level of classmates. Therefore, a child in a poor community may receive an inferior education even if all schools spend the same amount per pupil.

The chapter on education addresses the following questions:

1. Which of the inputs to the education production function are most productive? How do the home environment and the peer group affect educational achievement? Do class size and teachers' qualifications matter?
2. Why does spending per pupil vary across school districts?
3. To what extent do intergovernmental grants decrease spending inequalities?
4. Why does educational achievement vary across school districts?
5. What are the effects of desegregation policies on enrollment in public schools and educational achievement?
6. What are the merits of proposals to use vouchers or tax credits to subsidize education in private schools?

The final chapter of the book explores the economics of crime. Like education, crime affects location decisions: a household's choice of residence depends in part on the local crime rate and the taxes required to support the criminal-justice system. Location decisions affect the provision of crime protection: if households segregate themselves with respect to income, spending on crime protection may be lower in poor areas. In addition, because there is often a relatively large number of potential criminals in poor areas, citizens in poor communities would experience higher crime rates even if spending on crime protection were the same in all communities.

The crime chapter addresses the following questions:

1. Are criminals rational? Is it possible to decrease crime by changing the expected benefits and costs of crime?
2. Why are crime rates relatively high in central cities?
3. What is the optimum amount of crime?
4. How do the police, the courts, and the prison system deter crime?
5. Do policies that control illegal drugs increase property crime?

What Is an Urban Area?

To an urban economist, a geographical area is considered *urban* if it contains a large number of people in a relatively small area. In other words, an **urban area** is defined as an area with a relatively high population density. For example, suppose that the average population density of a particular county is 20 people per acre. If part of the county contains 50,000 people in a 20-square-mile area (i.e., the population density is 2,500 people per square mile), it is considered an urban area because it has a relatively high population density. This definition accommodates urban areas of vastly different size, from a small town to a large metropolitan area. The economist's definition is stated in terms of population density because the urban economy is based on frequent contact between different economic activities, and such contact is feasible only if firms and households are packed into a relatively small area.

Census Definitions

The Census Bureau defines a number of geographical areas. Since most empirical work in urban economics is based on census data, a clear understanding of these definitions is important.

Municipality or City.   A **municipality** is defined as an area over which a municipal corporation provides local government services such as sewerage, crime protection, and fire protection. Another census term for municipality is **city**. In this case, *city* refers to the area over which a municipal government exercises political authority. When a census document refers to a *city*, it is referring to the political city, not the economic city. To define the economic city, we would draw boundaries to include all the activities that are an integral part of the area's economy. When using census data, it's important to remember the distinction between the political city and the economic city.

Urbanized Area.   An **urbanized area** includes at least one large central city (a municipality) and the surrounding area with population density exceeding 1,000 people per acre. To be an urbanized area, the total population of the area must be at least 50,000. Figure 1–1 shows an urbanized area as the large circle centered on a municipality. The urbanized area outside the central city is called the **urban fringe**. In 1990, there were 396 urbanized areas in the United States, containing 63.6 percent of the nation's population.

Metropolitan Area.   A **metropolitan area (MA)** is defined as the area containing a large population nucleus and the nearby communities that are integrated, in an economic sense, with the nucleus. Each metropolitan area contains either (1) a central city with at least 50,000 people or (2) an urbanized area. In the census definition, the nucleus of a metropolitan area is either the central city or the urbanized area, and the

---

FIGURE 1–1   Urbanized Area and Metropolitan Area

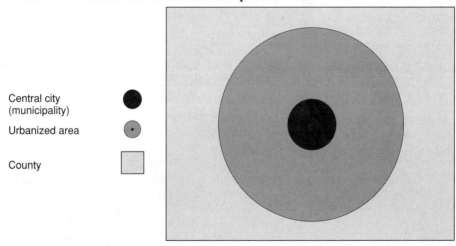

Central city
(municipality)

Urbanized area

County

integrated communities are the surrounding counties from which a relatively large number of people commute to the nucleus. To be designated a metropolitan area, the area in and around an urbanized area must have either a central city with population greater than 50,000 or a total population (including the integrated communities) of at least 100,000 (75,000 in New England). This means that some small urbanized areas are not metropolitan areas. For example, consider an urbanized area with 40,000 people in its central city, 60,000 people in the urbanized area, and another 30,000 people in the integrated counties, for a total of 90,000. Because the central city has fewer than 50,000 residents and the entire area has fewer than 100,000 people, the urbanized area is not considered a metropolitan area. In 1990, there were 284 metropolitan areas in the United States, ranging in population from just over 50,000 to just over 18 million.

Figure 1–1 shows the simplest possible arrangement of a metropolitan area. The MA is the county containing the urbanized area. This simple case shows one of the problems with the MA concept. To form a metropolitan area, the Census Bureau takes an urbanized area (or a central city) and tacks on the rest of the county, so the MA includes areas that are essentially rural. Metropolitan areas are defined by counties because the county is the smallest geographical unit for which a wide range of data is collected. In New England, where counties are relatively unimportant, metropolitan areas include the urbanized area and towns that are sufficiently integrated with the urban area.

Most metropolitan areas include more than one county. A **central county** is defined as one in which (1) the majority of the population lives in the urbanized area or (2) at least 2,500 of its residents live in the central municipality. An adjacent county is included in the metropolitan area if it is sufficiently integrated with the central county or counties. The degree of integration is measured in terms of commuting flows and population density. For example, the county is included in the MA if over 50 percent of its work force commutes to a central county and its population density exceeds 25 people per square mile. As the commuting percentage drops, the threshold population density increases. For the minimum commuting percentage (15 percent), the county is included if the population density exceeds 50 people per square mile.

Consolidated Metropolitan Statistical Area (CMSA).   There are two types of metropolitan areas: consolidated metropolitan statistical areas (CMSAs) and metropolitan statistical areas (MSAs). If the population of a metropolitan area exceeds 1 million, the metropolitan area may be divided into two or more primary metropolitan statistical areas (PMSAs). A **PMSA** consists of a large urbanized county (or a cluster of counties) that is integrated, in an economic sense, with other portions of the larger metropolitan area. When a metropolitan area is divided into two or more PMSAs, the metropolitan area is called a **CMSA**.

In 1990, there were 20 of these large metropolitan complexes, ranging in population from just over 1 million (Hartford–New Britain–Middletown) to just over 18 million (New York–Northern New Jersey–Long Island). Figure 1–2 shows the maps of two CMSAs, Chicago–Gary–Lake County and San Francisco–Oakland–San Jose. Each of these CMSAs has six PMSAs.

FIGURE 1–2   Consolidated Metropolitan Statistical Areas

Chicago-Gary-Lake County CMSA

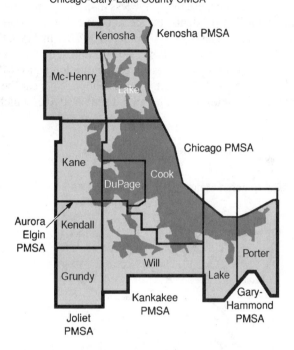

San Francisco-Oakland-San Jose CMSA

Metropolitan Statistical Area (MSA).   A **metropolitan statistical area (MSA)** is defined as a metropolitan area that does not qualify as a CMSA. Most MSAs are designated as such because they have less than a million residents. Other MSAs have more than a million residents, but do not have distinct areas within the metropolitan area that can be classified as separate PMSAs. In 1990, there were 264 MSAs, ranging in population from just over 50,000 to just under 2.4 million (Baltimore).

Figure 1–3 shows the maps of two multiple-county MSAs, Sacramento and Atlanta. The urbanized areas are the darkened areas near the centers of the MSAs. There are four counties in the Sacramento MSA, two of which stretch far to the east

FIGURE 1–3   Metropolitan Statistical Areas

Sacramento Metropolitan Statistical Area

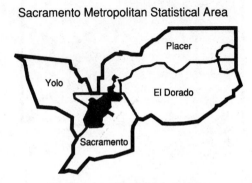

Atlanta Metropolitan Statistical Area

TABLE 1–1   **Urbanization of U.S. Population under Different Census Definitions**

Area Definition	*Percent of U.S. Population in Area in 1990*
Urbanized areas: central cities and surrounding dense areas	63.6%
Metropolitan areas: CMSAs and MSAs	77.5
Urban areas: urbanized areas and smaller urban places	75.2

through rural areas to the Nevada border, about 90 miles from the city of Sacramento. The Atlanta MSA is more compact, with 18 counties surrounding an urbanized area centered on the city of Atlanta.

The Census Bureau recently changed its terminology for metropolitan areas. Before 1983, metropolitan areas were called *Standard Metropolitan Statistical Areas* (*SMSAs*), and groups of related SMSAs were called *Standard Consolidated Statistical Areas* (*SCSAs*).

Urban Place and Urban versus Rural.   An **urban place** is defined as a geographical area with at least 2,500 inhabitants in a relatively small area. The Census Bureau defines the nation's **urban population** as all people living in urbanized areas plus people outside urbanized areas who live in urban places. According to this definition, in 1990, about three fourths of the U.S. population lived in urban areas.

Summary: What Is Urban?   In collecting and reporting data, the Census Bureau uses several definitions of *urban*. Table 1–1 shows, for three different urban definitions, the percentage of the U.S. population that is considered "urban." The percentage living in urban areas (75.2 percent) exceeds the percentage in urbanized areas (63.6 percent) because the urban-area definition includes people who live in relatively small places (urban places with populations between 2,500 and 50,000). The percentage living in metropolitan areas differs from the percentage in urbanized areas for two reasons. First, the metropolitan-area definition excludes people who live in urbanized areas with either a relatively small central city (less than 50,000) or a relatively small total population (less than 100,000 in the urbanized area and the integrated counties). Second, the metropolitan-area definition includes people who live outside urbanized areas (in the county containing the urbanized area or a county adjacent to it). The exclusion of people in small urbanized areas is outweighed by the inclusion of people outside urbanized areas, so the percentage of the population living in metropolitan areas exceeds the percentage in urbanized areas.

Definitions Used in This Book

This book uses three terms to refer to spatial concentrations of economic activity: *urban area, metropolitan area,* and *city*. These three terms, which will be used interchangeably, refer to the economic city (an area with a relatively high population density that contains a set of closely related activities), not the political city. When referring to a political city, the book will use the term *central city* or *municipality*.

Discussion Questions

1. Suppose that you have the power to develop a new set of census definitions for urban and metropolitan areas. How would you define (*a*) a metropolitan area, (*b*) an urban resident, (*c*) a central city, and (*d*) a suburban area?

2. Consider a region in which all urbanized areas have populations of at least 100,000. Will the percentage of the region's population living in urbanized areas be less than or greater than the percentage living in metropolitan areas?

3. Between 1980 and 1990, the gap between the percentage of the population living in urbanized areas and the percentage of the population living in metropolitan areas decreased, from 14.8 percentage points (76.2% − 61.4%) to 13.9 percentage points (77.5% − 63.6%). Provide an explanation for the narrowing of the gap.

4. Which of the three urban definitions used by the Census Bureau (urbanized area, urban place, metropolitan area) is closest to the economist's definition of a city?

5. In 1990, 86 percent of the population in the western states lived in urbanized areas, and 85 percent lived in metropolitan areas. In the same year, 79 percent of the population in the northeastern states lived in urbanized areas, and 88 percent lived in metropolitan areas. Why is the West more urbanized than the Northeast under the urbanized-area definition but less urbanized under the metropolitan-area definition?

References

U.S. Department of Commerce. "Appendix A: Area Classifications." In *1990 Census of Population and Housing: Summary of Population and Housing Characteristics.* Washington, D.C.: U.S. Government Printing Office, 1990. Defines all the geographical entities and concepts that are used in the 1990 census. See pages A-8 to A-13 for definitions of cities and metropolitan areas.

PART I Market Forces in the Development of Cities

In a market economy, individuals exchange their labor for wage income, which is then used to buy other goods and services. How do these market transactions affect cities? Chapter 2 discusses the fundamental reasons for centralized production and marketing and explores the implications for the development of cities. Chapter 3 shows how the location decisions of firms cause the development of cities in particular locations. Chapter 4 provides a brief historical sketch of urbanization, using the concepts developed in chapters 2 and 3 to explain the history of cities. Chapter 5 takes a regional perspective, showing how competition among firms leads to the development of a hierarchical system of cities. Chapter 6 explores the reasons for urban economic growth.

CHAPTER 2 Why Do Cities Exist?

Man is the only animal that makes bargains; one dog does not change bones with another dog.

Adam Smith

Cities exist because individuals are not self-sufficient. If each of us produced everything we consumed and we didn't want much company, there would be no need to live in cities. We aren't self-sufficient, however, so we exchange our labor for other goods. Most of us live in cities because that's where most of the jobs are. Cities also provide a rich mixture of consumer goods and services, so even people who are not gainfully employed are attracted to cities. By living in cities, we achieve a higher standard of living, but we also must put up with more pollution, crime, noise, and congestion.

This chapter explores three reasons for the concentration of jobs in cities. **Comparative advantage** makes trade between regions advantageous, and interregional trade causes the development of market cities. **Internal scale economies** in production allow factories to produce goods more efficiently than individuals, and the production of goods in factories causes the development of industrial cities. **Agglomerative economies** in production and marketing cause firms to cluster in cities, and this clustering causes the development of large cities. This chapter focuses on the market forces that generate cities, ignoring the social reasons for cities (e.g., religion, companionship, and politics). Some of these nonmarket reasons for cities will be discussed later in the book.

A Model of a Rural Region

Under what conditions would there be no cities in a particular region? In other words, what set of assumptions guarantees a uniform distribution of population? This section develops a model of a region that has a uniform distribution of population and thus has no cities. The model of the rural region provides a list of assumptions that together preclude the development of cities. When these assumptions are relaxed, cities will develop.

The model of the rural economy captures some of the essential features of England before the Norman Conquest of the 11th century. The economy was essentially rural, with only a few small market towns serving the local population. Later in the chapter, the model will be used to explain the market forces behind the development of English cities after the Norman Conquest.

Consider a region where only two commodities (wheat and wool cloth) are produced and consumed. The regional economy has the following characteristics:

1. **Inputs**. Wheat and cloth are produced with labor and land. Land is used to grow wheat and raise sheep. Residents spin the raw wool into yarn and then weave the yarn into cloth.
2. **Equal productivity**. All residents are equally productive at making cloth and producing wheat. In one hour, every person can produce either one bushel of wheat or one yard of cloth. Similarly, all land is equally productive in the production of wheat and raw wool.
3. **No scale economies**. Production is subject to **constant returns to scale**: a worker produces one yard of cloth per hour, regardless of how much cloth is produced. Similarly, wheat production per hour is independent of the volume produced.
4. **Travel time**. Travel within the region is by foot: residents walk at a speed of four round-trip miles per hour.

These assumptions are strong enough to prevent trade. Every household in the region will produce its own wheat and cloth. Because every household is equally productive in producing both goods, there are no advantages from trade between households. Because productivity is independent of the volume produced, there are no advantages from centralized production. A factory worker would be no more productive than a person working at home. The disadvantage of factory cloth is that travel to the factory takes time, making the net cost of the factory cloth (price plus travel cost) greater than the cost of homemade cloth. To summarize, there are no advantages from trade or centralized production, so every household in the region is self-sufficient.

The population will be distributed uniformly throughout the region. Every household will pick a plot of land and make its own wheat and cloth. Since all land is equally productive, the distribution of population will be uniform. Since a *city* is defined as a place with relatively high population density, a region with a uniform distribution of population has no cities. There are no cities because the model's assumptions are strong enough to eliminate the possibility of trade.

Comparative Advantage and Urban Development

One factor in the development of cities is comparative advantage. The model of the rural region assumes that all households are equally productive in the production of cloth and wheat. If this assumption is relaxed, one part of the region may have a comparative advantage in cloth production, and the other part may have a comparative advantage in wheat production. Under certain circumstances, comparative advantage causes trade and the development of cities.

Comparative Advantage

The notion of comparative advantage can be explained with a simple model of trade between two parts of the region. Suppose that the western half of the region is more productive than the eastern half. In Table 2–1, the West has an **absolute advantage** in producing both wheat and cloth: western residents produce twice as much wheat per hour and six times as much cloth per hour. The differences in productivity could be caused by differences in labor skills, weather, or soil quality.

The notion of **comparative advantage** is based on the principle of opportunity cost. In a one-hour period, a western worker can produce either six yards of cloth or two bushels of wheat. Therefore, the opportunity cost of cloth is one third of a bushel of wheat, and the opportunity cost of wheat is three yards of cloth. An eastern worker can produce either one bushel of wheat or one yard of cloth, so the opportunity cost of wheat is one yard of cloth, and vice versa. The West has a comparative advantage in the production of cloth because the opportunity cost of cloth is one third of a bushel of wheat, compared to one bushel of wheat in the East. Similarly, the East has a comparative advantage in wheat because the opportunity cost is one yard of cloth instead of three.

Trade and Transportation Cost

Comparative advantage may lead to trade between East and West. To explain the possible advantages of trade, suppose that all households in the region are initially self-sufficient. Suppose that two households, one in the East and one in the West, agree to exchange two yards of cloth for one bushel of wheat; that is, the price of wheat is two yards of cloth. If the western household switches one hour of work from wheat production to cloth production, it sacrifices two bushels of wheat to produce six additional yards of cloth. If it exchanges the extra cloth for three bushels of wheat from an eastern household, its net gain from trade is one bushel of wheat. If the eastern household switches one hour of work from cloth to wheat production and exchanges the extra bushel of wheat for two yards of cloth, its net gain from trade is one yard of cloth.

TABLE 2–1   Comparative Advantage

	Output per Labor Hour		Opportunity Cost of Production	
	East	*West*	*East*	*West*
Wheat	1	2	1 Cloth	3 Cloth
Cloth	1	6	1 Wheat	$1/3$ Wheat

What about transportation costs? Trade between the two households is beneficial only if the differences in productivity are large enough to offset the costs of shipping wheat and cloth between the two areas. To continue the numerical example, suppose that it takes 2 hours of travel time for the western household to execute the trade of cloth for wheat. Is trade still beneficial? The net gain from trade is the gross gain (one bushel of wheat) less the opportunity cost of the 2 hours spent executing the trade. Since the western household could use the 2 hours to produce 4 bushels of wheat for itself, trade is not beneficial.

Trade will be beneficial if transportation costs are small relative to the differences in productivity. If the net gains from trade are positive, western households will specialize in cloth production and eastern households will specialize in wheat production. For example, suppose that it takes only six minutes (1/10 of an hour) to execute a trade, so the opportunity cost of the transaction for the western household is only 0.20 bushels of wheat. In this case, the net gain is 0.80 bushels (1.0 − 0.20), so households trade to exploit their comparative advantages.

Trading Cities

Trade will cause the development of a trading city if there are scale economies in transportation. To explain the importance of scale economies in transportation, suppose that there are no scale economies: the transport cost per bushel of wheat (or yard of cloth) per mile is independent of the volume shipped. In this case, households in the two regions engage in direct trade: each eastern household links up with a western household to exchange cloth and wheat. If there are scale economies in transportation, however, the cost per unit per mile decreases as the volume transported increases, so it is cheaper to transport wheat and cloth in bulk. By exploiting these scale economies, trading firms can collect, transport, and distribute the goods at a lower cost than would be incurred by households engaged in direct trade. The trading firms locate at places convenient for the collection and distribution of the goods, causing the development of marketplaces at crossroads, ports, river junctions, and other transshipment points.

The location decisions of traders cause the development of market cities. People employed by the trading firms live near the marketplace to economize on commuting costs, and bid up the price of land. As the price of land increases, residents economize on land by occupying relatively small lots. In other words, the population density around the marketplace is higher than the population density in the rest of the region. Since a *city* is defined as a place with a relatively high population density, the combination of comparative advantage and scale economies in transportation causes the development of a market city.

The market city develops because three conditions are satisfied. First, agricultural productivity is high enough that agricultural workers produce enough wheat and cloth for themselves and the urban traders. The agricultural surplus feeds and clothes the urban workers. Second, the differences in productivity that generate comparative advantage are large enough to offset transportation costs, so trade occurs. Third, there are scale economies in transportation, making large-scale trade and central marketplaces efficient.

Internal Scale Economies in Production

A second factor in the development of cities is scale economies in production. One of the assumptions of the model of the rural region is that there are constant returns to scale in the production of both wheat and cloth. Therefore, there are no advantages from centralized production in factories, and all goods are produced in the home. If this assumption is dropped, factory production may replace home production, causing the development of industrial cities.

Scale Economies and the Cloth Factory

Suppose that there are advantages from the large-scale production of cloth. In other words, as the volume of production increases, the labor required to produce one yard of cloth decreases. Figure 2–1 shows the average labor requirements for different amounts of factory cloth. The average labor time decreases from 1 hour for 1 yard of cloth (the same time as home production) to 15 minutes for an output of 400 yards. These scale economies arise for two reasons:

1. **Factor specialization**. In a large operation, each worker is assigned a single task. The specialization of labor increases productivity because (*a*) workers' skills increase with repetition and (*b*) workers spend less time switching from task to task. The making of woolen cloth has several steps: the raw wool is spun into yarn, the yarn is woven into cloth, and the raw cloth is finished (cleaned, thickened, and dyed). One reason for

FIGURE 2–1   Scale Economies in Clothmaking

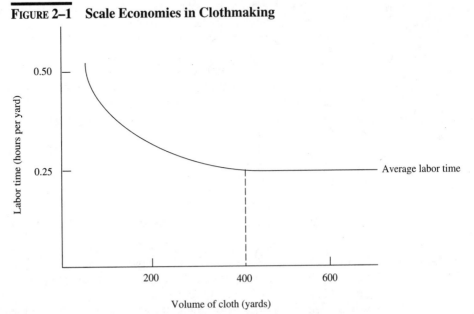

If there are scale economies in clothmaking, the average time required to make a yard of cloth decreases as the volume produced increases.

scale economies in cloth production is that individual workers can specialize in different tasks. A group of 10 specialized workers can produce more than 10 times as much as 10 individuals working in isolation (each of whom performs all the production tasks).

2. **Indivisible inputs**. An input to the production process is indivisible if the input has a minimum efficient scale. If an indivisible input is cut in half, the total output of the two halves is less than the output of the whole. The cloth factory uses equipment (spinning machines, power looms, thickening machines, dyeing vats) that cannot be efficiently scaled down for use by individual clothmakers. As output increases, the factory uses more indivisible inputs, increasing productivity.

If the cloth factory produces 400 yards of cloth per hour, it employs 100 workers (400 times 0.25 hours of labor per yard of cloth).

What is the wage of factory workers? The wage must be high enough to make cloth workers indifferent between working in the factory and working at home. If consumers pay the factory workers 0.25 bushels of wheat for one yard of cloth, the factory worker earns one bushel of wheat per hour of factory work. At this wage, the worker is indifferent between working in the factory (earning one bushel of wheat per hour) and producing his or her own wheat (at one bushel per hour).

A household buys factory cloth if the net cost of factory cloth is less than the cost of home production. There are two components to the net cost of factory cloth. The first is the time required to produce enough wheat to pay the factory worker (0.25 bushels of wheat requires 0.25 hours of wheat production). The second is the time required to travel to and from the cloth factory. If the trip to the factory takes less than 0.75 hours, the net time cost of factory cloth is less than the time required to produce cloth at home, so the household will buy the factory cloth. To pay for the factory cloth, the household stops making homemade cloth and uses the extra time to produce more wheat.

Figure 2–2 shows the **market area** of the cloth factory. The *market area* is defined as the area over which the factory underprices home production. The vertical axis measures the net cost of cloth, the sum of the factory price (0.25 hours of wheat production) and travel time to the factory. The horizontal axis measures the distance to the factory in miles. If walking time is four round-trip miles per hour, the factory will underprice homemade cloth for residents within three miles of the factory (within 0.75 hours walking time). Therefore, the factory's market area is a circle with a radius of three miles.

Scale Economies and an Urban Area

A small urban area develops around the cloth factory. If the output of the factory is 400 yards of cloth, it employs 100 people. The workers live near the factory to economize on commuting costs, and bid up the price of land near the factory. As the price of land increases, workers economize on land by occupying small lots. In other words, the population density around the cloth factory is higher than the population density in the rest of the region. Since a *city* is defined as a place with a relatively high population density, the factory causes the development of a small factory city.

FIGURE 2–2   Market Area of Cloth Factory

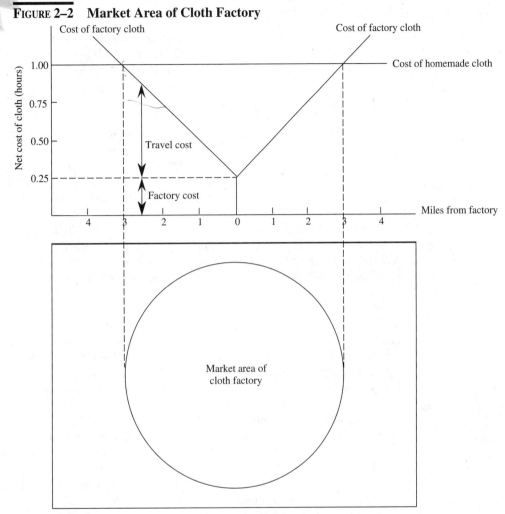

The market area of the cloth factory is the area over which the net cost of factory cloth (production time plus travel time) is less than the production time of homemade cloth (1 hour).

The factory city develops because two conditions are satisfied. First, the productivity of agricultural workers (wheat growers) is high enough that they can feed themselves and have enough left over to feed the cloth workers in the city. In other words, the agricultural surplus feeds city workers. Second, scale economies are large relative to travel costs, so the cloth factory can underprice homemade cloth.

The size of the city is determined by the number of factory workers, which in turn depends on the total output of the factory. The factory can increase its output if it manages to underprice more home producers. Therefore, output increases as scale economies increase (decreasing the factory price) and transportation costs decrease (decreasing the net cost of factory cloth). Chapter 5 (How Many Cities?) provides a more complete analysis of the factors that determine the firm's market area.

Examples of Urban Development

This section discusses the role of comparative advantage and scale economies in the development of cities in England and the United States. It uses the concepts of this chapter to explain the timing and the location of urban development.

The English Woolen Industry

Before the Norman Conquest in 1066, the making of wool cloth in England was an entirely local affair. Individual households and villas raised their own sheep, spun the raw wool into yarn, and wove the yarn into cloth. In other words, households were self-sufficient in cloth production, and no cities were involved in the production or trade of wool cloth. A small number of towns and small cities were involved in local trade.

The Norman Conquest increased the interaction between England and the continent, setting the stage for the development of the woolen cloth trade. The barriers to trade fell, and England was able to exploit its comparative advantage in the production of wool cloth. Exports to the continent rose, causing the development of small cities and towns based on the cloth trade.

In the 12th century, there was a flourishing cloth industry in several English cities, including Lincoln, Northampton, York, and Bristol. These cities developed as both commercial and production centers. Although spinning, weaving, and finishing were still performed by hand, there were some small scale economies associated with labor specialization, so centralized production in cities was efficient.

Starting in the 13th century, the clothmaking industry moved from cities to rural areas with water power. The fulling process involves cleaning and thickening the wool cloth. Before the development of the fulling mill, workers stomped on wet cloth to clean and thicken it. The water-powered fulling mill replaced foot-stomping, causing producers to move their finishing operations to sites along fast-moving streams.

The move to rural fulling sites caused the replacement of urban spinners and weavers by rural workers organized under the **putting-out system**. The clothier distributed raw wool to rural households for spinning and weaving. The making of cloth (using primitive spinning wheels and hand looms) was a part-time activity, typically performed by the women of the rural household. The clothier collected the raw cloth from his rural workers, brought it to fulling mills for cleaning and thickening, and then shipped the cloth to his customers in other regions and countries.

The shift to fulling mills and a rural work force caused the decline of the traditional clothmaking cities and the development of new villages and small cities. The fulling mills provided a convenient collection point for the cloth produced by the rural households and caused the development of many small villages. Since most of the production activity was performed by rural households, most of the cities involved in the cloth industry served primarily as commercial centers. They differed from the traditional clothmaking cities, which served as both commercial and production centers.

The industrial revolution of the 19th century produced a number of innovations that increased the scale economies associated with the production of wool cloth.

Mechanized spinning replaced hand spinning in the early 1800s, and power looms replaced hand looms about 1830. When the coal-fired steam engine was modified to power the spinning and weaving machinery, large factories developed on sites accessible to coal deposits (e.g., the West Riding of Yorkshire). The cloth factory integrated the production process, performing the tasks of spinning, weaving, and finishing under a single roof. The scale economies in production allowed the factory to produce wool cloth at a lower cost than home producers, so the putting-out system was replaced by factory production. The development of large factories caused the development of relatively large factory cities. The leading cities in the production of wool cloth were Bradford, Halifax, Leeds, Huddersfield, and Wakefield.

This brief history of English clothmaking cities shows how changes in trade and scale economies transformed rural areas into highly urbanized ones. The opening of the European markets following the Norman Conquest allowed England to exploit its comparative advantage in clothmaking, and the traditional clothmaking cities developed. The industrial revolution increased scale economies in clothmaking, causing the development of clothing factories and large factory cities.

The Sewing Machine and U.S. Urbanization

The sewing machine, which was developed in the middle of the 19th century, increased scale economies in the making of clothing and contributed to the development of cities. Around the beginning of the 19th century, about four fifths of the clothing worn in the United States was hand-sewn in the home for a member of the household. The other fifth was hand-sewn by tailors. The sewing machine allowed factory producers to underprice home producers, and, by 1890, nine tenths of U.S. clothing was being made in factories. As clothing factories sprung up in the United States, new cities developed around the factories.

The sewing machine also contributed to the development of U.S. cities around shoe factories. Before 1700, most shoes were produced in the home or the local village. The cost of transportation was so high that local production was efficient. Over time, transportation costs decreased, allowing the exploitation of comparative advantage in shoe production. The putting-out system was implemented in the 1700s: shoe producers distributed raw materials to cottage workers, collected their output, and finished the shoes in a central shop. As new shoemaking machines were developed, the number of operations performed in the central shop increased. The McKay sewing machine, which mechanized the process of sewing the soles to the uppers, increased scale economies in shoe production to the point that the central shop became a genuine factory. Cities developed around the new shoe factories.

Agglomerative Economies in Production

This section explores some of the reasons why cities are large. The analysis of scale economies earlier in the chapter suggests that a city develops around a factory. This section explains why most cities have more than one factory; that is, it explains the development of large industrial cities.

The large industrial city develops because of agglomerative economies in production. By locating close to one another, firms can produce at a lower cost. This is an example of a **positive externality** in production: the production cost of a particular firm decreases as the production of other firms increases. There are two types of agglomerative economies: localization economies and urbanization economies.

Localization Economies

Localization economies occur if the production costs of firms in a particular industry decrease as the total output of the industry increases. The positive externalities underlying localization economies are realized by firms in a particular industry. To realize the localization economies, a firm must be located close to other firms in the industry, so firms cluster to decrease their production costs. Localization economies occur for three principal reasons: scale economies in the production of intermediate inputs, labor-market economies, and communication economies.

Scale Economies in Intermediate Inputs.   Some clusters occur because firms in a particular industry buy an intermediate input from the same supplier. Firms cluster around a common input supplier if two conditions are satisfied:

1. The input demand of an individual firm is not large enough to exploit the scale economies in the production of the intermediate input.
2. Transportation costs are relatively high. If demanders and supplier interact in the design or fabrication of the intermediate input, face-to-face contact between buyer and seller is necessary, and proximity to the input supplier is important. Similarly, if the intermediate input is bulky, fragile, or must be delivered quickly, proximity is important.

Vernon (1972) uses the Manhattan dressmaking industry as an example of a cluster that resulted from scale economies in the production of intermediate inputs. Because the demand for high-fashion dresses is unpredictable, a dressmaking firm cannot commit itself to large-scale production of a given type of dress, but must be prepared to quickly change to another type of dress if the first dress is a bomb. The firm must employ inputs (capital and labor) that can (1) produce a wide variety of dresses and (2) make the transition from one dress to another quickly. Specialized labor and machinery are not feasible. The manager of the firm must carefully monitor the dress market, the design process, and the production process. The operation must be kept small enough that the manager can be involved in most decisions.

One of the intermediate inputs to dressmaking is buttons. Suppose that there are scale economies in the production of buttons, and it takes 10 dressmakers to generate sufficient button demand to exhaust the scale economies in button production. By sharing a buttonmaker, the 10 dressmakers can get buttons at a lower cost. Because the scale economies in buttonmaking are large *relative* to the scale economies in dressmaking, the dressmakers share a buttonmaker.

Why should dressmakers cluster around the button firm? They locate near the button producer because they must supervise the production of buttons. Because the buttons for a high-fashion dress are not standardized, they cannot be ordered out of a catalogue. The buttons are designed to complement the other features of the dress and the dressmaker participates in the design and fabrication of buttons to ensure that the buttons match the dress. Given the importance of face-to-face contact, dressmakers locate close to the buttonmaker.

There are many other examples of clusters that result from scale economies in the provision of intermediate inputs.

1. **Corporate headquarters**. The corporate headquarters produces a wide variety of outputs. The executive may design an advertising campaign one week, pick a location for a new plant the next week, and develop a strategy to fend off a lawsuit the following week. Most corporations use outside advertising firms because scale economies in the production of advertising campaigns are large relative to the advertising demand of an individual corporation. Corporate executives need to be close to the advertising firm because the executives assist in the design of the advertising campaign; that is, face-to-face contact is important. In general, the clustering of corporate headquarters (usually in central business districts) allows corporations to exploit scale economies in the production of intermediate goods (advertising, economic consultants, legal services) for which face-to-face contact is an important part of the production process.

2. **High-technology firms**. Firms producing new high-technology goods face uncertain demand for their products. Instead of producing all of their own components, they purchase electronic parts from firms that can exploit scale economies in production. The firms interact with their suppliers in the design and fabrication of the components, and must locate close enough to facilitate frequent face-to-face contact. Although the high-technology firm need not locate close to its supplier of nuts and bolts (standardized inputs that can be ordered from a catalogue), it needs to locate closer to the supplier of nonstandardized electronic parts. In addition, high-technology firms exploit scale economies in product testing by sharing firms that provide testing facilities. They locate close enough to tap the testing facilities at top speed.

3. **Publishing**. Newspapers and magazines produce outputs (text and illustrations) that change in unpredictable ways from day to day. In producing their products, publishers call on a wide variety of experts, including information sources and illustrators. If each publisher uses an expert on Armenian history for one story per year, it would be inefficient for each publisher to hire a full-time Armenian expert. Instead, the publishers may share a single expert, sharing the cost of specialized information. Similarly, publishers occasionally need special illustrations, and call on graphic design firms to do the illustrations. Publishers cluster around organizations that provide expert information (libraries, research institutes, universities) and illustrations (graphic design firms).

What is the role of business services in the development of firm clusters? Some industries require specialized financial services such as specialized banking and insurance. There are scale economies in the provision of these services, and firms in a cluster can exploit these scale economies by sharing banks and insurance agencies. Similarly, there are scale economies in the provision of transportation services, and firms can share a transportation firm. For example, a small firm can hire trucks from a trucking firm instead of providing its own truck fleet.

Public services also play a role in the development of firm clusters. The public sector is responsible for the development of the transportation network and the sewage system. If firms in an industry require specialized transport networks or sewage services, public-service costs are lower if the firms cluster. The provision of public education has also played a role in the development of firm clusters. In England, some towns established spinning schools to provide specialized laborers for the textile industry. More recently, the universities and colleges in the Silicon Valley have been turning out a large number of engineers and computer scientists for the computer industry.

Labor-Market Economies.   A second reason for localization economies is that a cluster increases the efficiency of the labor market. Consider an industry with rapidly changing production processes and product demands, such as the computer industry. Every year, computer firms introduce new products; some are big sellers, and others fail. Eventually, the workers in the unsuccessful firms move to the successful ones. A cluster facilitates the transfer of workers between computer firms for two reasons. First, workers in the cluster have relatively low search costs because (1) information about job openings is spread through informal channels (casual conversation at restaurants, bowling alleys, and baseball games) and (2) prospective employers are nearby, making formal job searches relatively easy. Second, because of the physical proximity of employers, moving costs are relatively low: workers can easily switch to a different firm in the same city. Because search costs and moving costs are relatively low, firms in the cluster of computer firms can quickly fill their job vacancies and quickly increase production.

The television industry also benefits from labor-market economies. In a given season, some television programs are hits, and others are failures. When it becomes clear which programs will continue to be produced, actors and technicians move from the unsuccessful programs to the successful ones. The concentrations of the television industry in Los Angeles and New York facilitate the transfer of laborers from one firm to another.

Communication Economies.   A third benefit of a cluster is that the cluster facilitates the rapid exchange of information and diffusion of technology. Workers from different firms exchange ideas about new products and new production techniques; the larger the number of workers in an industry, the greater the opportunity to exchange ideas. The opportunity to exchange ideas occurs in both formal and informal settings. A cluster of computer makers produces a large concentration of computer scientists and engineers, who can exchange ideas while they work (e.g., the suppliers of intermediate inputs interact with the designers of new products) and play (e.g., the workers from unrelated firms "talk shop" while eating or jogging).

Where Do the Clusters Develop?   Localization economies cause the firms in some industries to locate close to one another. Most of these clusters are not isolated from other activities, but are typically in cities. As explained later in the chapter, some intermediate inputs are shared by firms in different industries, causing firms from different industries to cluster in cities. For example, the dressmaker cluster (around the buttonmaker) occurs in Manhattan because dressmakers also use business services (machine repair, banking, transportation services) utilized by nearby firms in other industries.

The Incubator Process.   Localization economies are responsible for the **incubator process**. A cluster of firms supplies a rich set of intermediate inputs, providing a nurturing environment where firms in an immature industry "incubate," developing new products and production technologies. In the early life of many industries, demand is unpredictable and production techniques are unsettled, so firms cluster to (1) exploit scale economies in the production of intermediate goods, (2) realize labor-market economies, and (3) exploit the opportunities to exchange ideas about products and production processes. As the industry matures, it develops standardized products and production processes, allowing large-scale production. Firms internalize most of the production process, and move to locations that provide lower labor and land costs. This is also known as the **product cycle theory** of industrial location: products are developed by small firms in clusters; when the product is standardized and produced on a larger scale, firms move to sites with lower labor and land costs.

As pointed out by Vernon (1972), one example of incubation comes from the radio industry. In the 1920s, the market for radios was unpredictable, and firms were experimenting with alternative production processes. Mass production was impractical: the firms didn't know what kind of radio consumers wanted, and hadn't developed efficient production techniques. Radio firms were small, agile, and nervous, and clustered in New York City to exploit scale economies in the production of intermediate goods. In the 1930s and 1940s, products were standardized, and firms developed efficient methods of mass production. Firms moved their assembly facilities to the Midwest, which had lower wages and better access to the national markets. Tube producers migrated to the Northeast and the South, where labor costs were lower.

The computer industry is also subject to the incubation process. In the 1970s and early 1980s, the demand for computers was unpredictable, and production techniques were being developed. Small computer firms clustered in the Silicon Valley in California and along Route 128 in Boston to exploit localization economies. The standardization of products and production processes allowed firms to set up large production facilities outside the clusters. Why did the clusters survive the exodus of production facilities? New products continue to be developed, and firms continue to cluster to exploit localization economies. Most firms maintain their research and development facilities in the clusters and set up branch plants for manufacturing and assembly.

Urbanization Economies

Urbanization economies, a second type of agglomerative economy in production, occur if the production cost of an individual firm decreases as the total output of the urban area increases. Urbanization economies differ from localization economies in two ways. First, urbanization economies result from the scale of the entire urban economy, not simply the scale of a particular industry. Second, urbanization economies generate benefits for firms throughout the city, not just firms in a particular industry.

Urbanization economies occur for the same reasons as localization economies. Firms from different industries share common input suppliers, allowing the realization of scale economies in the provision of business services (banking, insurance, real estate, hotels, building maintenance, printing, transportation) and public services (highways, mass transit, schools, fire protection). Large cities also provide citywide labor-market economies. If fluctuations in the labor demands of different industries are not correlated, the large city provides a stable level of total employment. When a job disappears in one industry, it is likely to be replaced by a new job in another industry. Search costs and moving costs are lower in large cities, so firms are able to increase or decrease their work forces more easily.

As explained by Jacobs (1960), the urban environment also encourages innovation. Urban areas contain people with diverse backgrounds and interests. In such an environment, the exchange of ideas between people with different perspectives can lead to innovations in product design and production methods.

Empirical Estimates of Agglomerative Economies

How important are localization economies and urbanization economies? One approach to measuring agglomerative economies is to estimate the effects of changes in industry output and city size on labor productivity. The hypothesized relationship is

$$q = f(k, e, Q, N) \qquad (2\text{--}1)$$

where

q = Output per worker in a particular industry
k = Capital equipment per worker
e = Education level of workers (a measure of labor skill and productivity)
Q = Total output of the industry
N = Total population of the metropolitan area

Output per worker should increase with capital per worker and the education level of the work force. If localization economies exist, output per worker also increases with Q (industry output), and if urbanization economies exist, output per worker increases with N (population). Statistical analysis can be used to estimate the independent effect of changes in Q (industry output) on output per worker, that is, the increase in output per worker per unit change in Q, holding constant the other determinants of labor productivity (k, e, and N). Similarly, one can estimate the independent effect of changes in N (city size) on output per worker.

Henderson (1988) uses this approach to estimate both localization and urbanization economies. He measures localization economies as the elasticity of output per worker with respect to industry output, defined as the percentage change in output per worker divided by the percentage change in industry output. For the electrical machinery industry, the localization elasticity is 0.05, meaning that a 10 percent increase in the output of the electrical machinery industry increases output per worker by about 0.50 percent. His elasticity estimates for other U.S. industries range from 0.02 for the pulp and paper industry to 0.11 for the petroleum industry. In contrast, Henderson's results suggest that urbanization economies are very small: the elasticity of labor productivity with respect to city size is close to zero.

Henderson's results have important implications for urban development. It appears that an increase in city size, by itself, does not increase productivity. Larger cities are more productive because they have large concentrations of specific industries (localization economies), not simply because they are large (urbanization economies). The results of O'hUallachain and Satterthwaite (1992) are consistent with the view that localization economies are more important than urbanization economies.

In another study, Segal (1976) uses 1967 data on manufacturers in 58 metropolitan areas to estimate the magnitude of urbanization economies. His hypothesized relationship is

$$G = f\,(K, L, N) \tag{2--2}$$

where

G = Total output of the metropolitan area
K = Total capital in the metropolitan area
L = Total labor in metropolitan area (adjusted for quality)
N = Total population of metropolitan area

In other words, he estimates a metropolitan production function, including city size in the production function to estimate the magnitude of urbanization economies. Segal concludes that large metropolitan areas (population exceeding 2 million) are 8 percent more productive than smaller cities, meaning that urbanization economies are relatively large.

The results of Henderson and Segal are inconsistent. Henderson concludes that urbanization economies are very small, and Segal concludes that they're relatively large. Can the different results be reconciled? It's possible that the Segal estimate of large urbanization economies is actually the result of localization economies: the larger cities in his sample may have large concentrations of industries subject to localization economies. If so, it is localization economies, not urbanization economies, that make these larger cities more productive. Another explanation for the different results is that the two researchers used different statistical methods. Additional empirical work is needed to resolve this issue of the size of localization and urbanization economies.

Agglomerative Economies in Marketing: Shopping Externalities

This section explains how agglomerative economies in marketing affect the development of cities. The previous section of the chapter explains how agglomerative economies in production cause industrial firms to cluster, resulting in the development of large industrial cities. This section explains how agglomerative economies in marketing cause trading firms to cluster, resulting in the development of small market-based cities and retail concentrations within cities.

A **shopping externality** occurs if the sales of one store are affected by the location of other stores. Suppose that an isolated drugstore relocates next to a grocery store. If both stores experience an increase in sales, they generate shopping externalities: each store attracts consumers to the retail cluster, generating benefits for the other store. These shopping externalities cause firms selling related products to form retail clusters. Some retail clusters cause the development of market cities. Other clusters occur within large cities, generating downtown shopping areas, malls, and shopping centers. There are two types of products that generate shopping externalities: imperfect substitutes and complements.

Imperfect Substitutes

Two goods are imperfect substitutes if they are similar but not identical. Suppose that you've decided to buy a new sports car, but haven't decided whether to buy a Ford, a Chevy, or a Honda. The sports cars offered by the three companies are similar, but differ in performance, shape, color, and gadgetry. Because the differences between the cars are subtle, you must do your comparison shopping in person, spending time and money traveling to the three car dealers. If the three dealers form a cluster, they decrease the cost of comparison shopping, attracting consumers to the cluster.

There are many goods that are imperfect substitutes. Some examples are clothes, shoes, jewelry, and electronic equipment. For these goods, the clustering of firms selling similar products decreases shopping costs and attracts potential buyers. Some retailers cluster in the city center, while others cluster in shopping centers and malls.

Figure 2–3 illustrates the notion of agglomerative economies from comparison shopping. Suppose that there are two auto dealers in a particular city, and they are initially located far from one another. Each dealer has a fixed supply of 50 cars per week, so the supply curves at each location are vertical at 50 cars. In the initial equilibrium, each dealer faces the demand curve D' and sells its 50 cars at a price of $8,000. Suppose that dealer M moves to a site next to the other dealer. The total supply of cars at the location of the original dealer doubles, from 50 cars per week to 100 cars. If the customers of dealer M follow the dealer to its new location, the demand for cars also doubles: the demand curve shifts to the right by 50, from D' to D''. If the demand and supply curves shift to the right by the same amount, the relocation of dealer M does not affect the market price of cars.

The shift of the demand curve from D'' to D^* incorporates shopping externalities. The clustering of auto sellers decreases the shopping costs of consumers who engage

FIGURE 2–3   Agglomerative Economies from Comparison Shopping

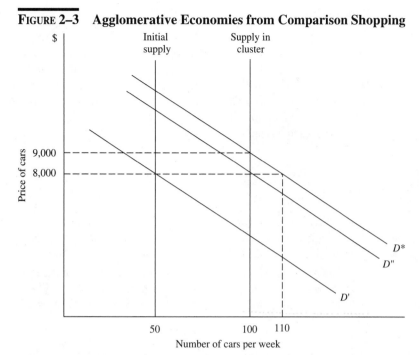

In the initial equilibrium with two auto dealers located far from one another, each dealer supplies 50 cars at a price of $8,000. If dealer M relocates next to dealer S, the supply of cars at location S doubles, from 50 to 100. The demand more than doubles because the cluster attracts comparison shoppers who would otherwise not patronize either dealer.

in comparison shopping. Therefore, the cluster attracts consumers who would otherwise not patronize either of the dealers. These additional consumers cause another rightward shift of the demand curve, from D'' to D^*. In this example, an additional 10 consumers patronize the two dealers. If the dealers continue to supply only 50 cars each, the equilibrium price increases from $8,000 to $9,000. Of course, another option is to increase the number of cars sold. In either case, the extra shift of the demand curve from comparison shoppers generates benefits for the dealers in the cluster, resulting in a higher price or a larger volume.

Complementary Goods

Clustering also occurs when firms sell complementary goods. Complementary goods are often purchased on the same shopping trip. For example, if a consumer purchases pants and shoes on the same trip, his travel cost will be lower if the pants store is near the shoe store. The shoe store will benefit from the presence of the pants store because together they provide one-stop shopping for consumers. Because of the benefits of one-stop shopping, firms selling complementary goods cluster in shopping centers, malls, and city centers.

Retail Clusters

The agglomerative economies associated with shopping generate several types of retail clusters. For some goods, retailers form retail strips along arterial streets, for example, auto rows. Other retailers cluster in shopping centers, malls, and city centers. These clusters provide both a mix of imperfect substitutes (different jewelry stores) and complements (food and drugs, clothing and shoes), allowing both comparison shopping and one-stop shopping. Retailers that choose isolated locations instead of clusters sell goods that are not subject to shopping externalities.

Summary

1. Employment opportunities are concentrated in cities for four reasons: comparative advantage, scale economies in transportation, internal scale economies in production, and agglomerative economies.
2. Comparative advantage results from differences in productivity. Trade occurs if the differences in productivity are large enough to offset transport costs. Trading firms (and urban areas) develop if there are scale economies in transportation.
3. Internal scale economies, which result from factor specialization and indivisible inputs, generate a negatively sloped long-run average-cost curve.
   a. If scale economies are large relative to transport costs, goods are produced in factories.
   b. Factory workers economize on travel costs by locating near factories, causing the development of factory cities.
4. The English wool cloth industry illustrates the role of comparative advantage and scale economies in the development of cities.
   a. The opening of England to the continent allowed the country to exploit its comparative advantage in clothmaking, causing the development of cities involved in the production and trade of cloth.
   b. The development of the water-powered fulling mill shifted production to rural areas and caused the development of villages and small trading cities.
   c. The industrial revolution produced mechanized spinning and weaving, generating scale economies that caused the development of large factories and factory cities.
5. The sewing machine increased scale economies in the production of clothing and shoes, causing home production of clothes and shoes to be replaced by factory production. Cities developed around the clothing factories and shoe factories.
6. Localization economies occur if the production cost of a particular firm decreases as industrywide output increases. There are three sources of localization economies.

a. If there are scale economies in the production of an intermediate good for which transportation costs are relatively high, several firms share a supplier of the intermediate input and form a cluster around the input supplier.

b. If output per firm varies from year to year, a cluster of firms facilitates the transfer of workers from one firm to another (labor-market economies).

c. A cluster of firms improves communication, facilitating the rapid exchange of information and the diffusion of innovations (communication economies).

7. Urban areas, with their rich set of intermediate inputs, provide a nurturing environment for immature industries (the incubator process).

Early Radio Firms in New York

8. Urbanization economies occur if the production cost of a particular firm decreases as the total output of the urban area increases. Urbanization economies result from the sharing of input suppliers (business services and public services), labor-market economies, and communication economies.

9. A shopping externality occurs if the sales of a particular store increase as other retailers move closer to the store. These agglomerative economies in marketing cause the clustering of retailers.

a. Comparison shopping causes the clustering of firms selling imperfect substitutes.

b. One-stop shopping causes the clustering of firms selling complementary goods.

c. Retail clusters occur in downtowns, shopping centers, malls, and retail strips.

Exercises and Discussion Questions

1. The table below summarizes the productivity of workers in wheat and cloth production in two parts of a region.

	Output per Labor Hour		Opportunity Cost of Production	
	East	*West*	*East*	*West*
Wheat	1	12		
Cloth	1	3		

a. Complete the table by providing the opportunity costs of producing wheat and cloth in the East and the West.

b. Assume that transport costs are zero and that the exchange rate is two bushels of wheat for one yard of cloth. If a western household switches one hour from cloth production to wheat production and exchanges half of its additional wheat for cloth, will the household be better off?

    c. Suppose that the time required to execute the trade in (*b*) is two thirds of an hour. Is trade still beneficial? At what transaction cost (time per trade) would the net gain from trade be zero?

    d. Under what conditions will the differences in labor productivity cause the development of cities?

2. Consider a region that has a single trading city (a city that developed as a result of comparative advantage and scale economies in transportation). There are no shopping externalities (no imperfect substitutes or complementary goods), and communication between households is costless. Suppose that a matter transmitter is introduced into the region. The transmitter costlessly transports goods, but cannot be used to transport people. The transmitter is cheap enough that every household can purchase one at a relatively low cost.

    a. Explain the effects of the matter transmitter on urban development. Specifically, will the region's trading city grow, shrink, or disappear?

    b. How would your answer to (*a*) change if cloth from one household is not a perfect substitute for cloth from other households?

3. Consider a country with two regions that are separated by a mountain range. Initially, there are no cities in the country. Suppose that a tunnel is bored through the mountain, decreasing travel costs between the two regions. Under what conditions will the tunnel cause the development of trading cities?

4. Consider a region that has a single factory city (a city that developed as a result of scale economies in production). Suppose that the introduction of pump sneakers increases the walking speed from four round-trip miles per hour to eight. Assume that the new type of shoes sells for the same price as the old type. How will the new footwear affect the size of the region's city? Will its population increase or decrease?

5. Region F has a single factory city (a city that developed as a result of scale economies in production). Suppose that a matter transmitter is introduced into the region. The transmitter can costlessly transport goods, but cannot be used to transport people. The transmitter is cheap enough that every household can purchase one at a relatively low cost. Explain the effects of the matter transmitter on urban development in the region. Specifically, will the city grow, shrink, or disappear?

6. Consider a region that produces and consumes fruit and ice. All resources are distributed uniformly throughout the region, and all people are equally productive in producing fruit and ice. There are scale economies in the production of ice, causing the development of an ice factory and a factory city. Suppose that a small refrigerator is introduced and imported into the region, providing an alternative to the ice purchased from ice factories. Explain the effects of the refrigerator on (*a*) the market area of the ice factory and (*b*) the size of the city surrounding the ice factory.

7. Consider Retireland, a region where most residents are retired. Residents of the region consume a single good (food), which is imported from another

region and sold in vending machines. Will there be any cities in Retireland? If so, how will they differ from cities in regions where most people work?

8. Most of the dresses made in the United States are produced by large firms in suburban areas, not by small firms in city centers. Is this consistent with the notion of industry externalities and clusters? Hint: Is there a difference between a Kmart dress and a dress produced by a small dressmaker?

9. The conventional wisdom for urban economic development is: "Don't put all your eggs in one basket. Diversify the economy." To explain the idea of diversification, consider old McDonald, who must carry a dozen eggs from the barn to the house. The ground between the barn and the house is slippery, so there is a 50 percent chance that McDonald will slip on a given trip and break all the eggs in his basket. Consider two strategies: a one-basket strategy (a single trip with all 12 eggs) and a two-basket strategy (two trips, with 6 eggs per trip).
   a. List all of the possible outcomes under each of the strategies.
   b. What is the expected number of delivered (unbroken) eggs under each strategy?
   c. What are the trade-offs between the two strategies? If you were McDonald, which strategy would you adopt?
   d. What are the lessons for economic development strategies?

10. According to the conventional wisdom concerning urban economic development, a city should develop a diverse economy, with a large number of industries. Evaluate the merits of the conventional wisdom in light of the empirical evidence concerning the magnitudes of localization and urbanization economies.

11. Consider a 10-firm industry that produces computer equipment, a set of goods with rapidly changing demand and production technology. The industry has the following characteristics:
   i. The 10 firms produce computer equipment using labor and raw materials.
   ii. Raw materials are ubiquitous (available at all locations at the same price).
   iii. Each firm produces one new product per year, and each product becomes obsolete after a year.
   iv. Only 3 of the 10 new products will be successful (sell more than a trivial amount).
   v. The monetary and time costs of switching a worker from one firm to another are zero, regardless of the spatial distribution of firms.
   a. Will the firms in the industry form a cluster? Why or why not?
   b. How would your answer to (*a*) change if workers incur moving costs when they switch from one firm to another?

12. Suppose that the outputs of beauty shops and pet-grooming salons are complementary, providing one-stop shopping for personal and pet maintenance. Betty Beehive is thinking about moving her beauty shop from an isolated location to a vacant building next to Peter's pet-grooming shop. In making her decision, she makes the following assumptions:

     i. If Betty moves, she will keep all of her current customers (20 people per week), and attract 25 percent of Peter's current customers.

     ii. Peter currently has 60 customers per week.

     iii. Excluding rent, Betty's profit per beauty treatment is $10.

     iv. The weekly rent at the new location is $200 higher than Betty's current rent.

  a. If Betty moves her beauty shop, will her profits increase or decrease?

  b. Suppose that if Betty makes the move, 50 percent of her original customers will switch from George's grooming salon to Peter's. If Peter's profit per treatment is $8, how much would he be willing to pay Betty to make the move? Will the payment be enough to induce Betty to make the move?

13. Consider a city with two auto sellers, a Toyota dealer and a Honda dealer. Initially, the distance between the two sellers is three miles. The Toyota dealer wants to relocate to a site adjacent to the Honda dealer and submits a rezoning request to the city council. The Honda dealer responds to the rezoning request with the following statement: "One of the lessons from Econ 100 is that an increase in supply will decrease price. If the Toyota dealer moves to the site adjacent to my dealership, the local supply of cars will increase and I'll have to cut my prices to sell the same quantity of cars." Critically appraise the Honda dealer's statement. If the statement is incorrect, what's wrong with the reasoning? Illustrate your answer with a graph.

References and Additional Readings

History of the English Woolmaking Industry

Jenkins, D. T. *The West Riding Wool Textile Industry, 1770–1835.* Leeds: Maney & Sons, 1975. Describes the transition of the clothmaking industry from the putting-out system to factory production.

Ponting, Kenneth G. *The Woolen Industry of South-West England.* Bath: Adams & Dart, 1971. Describes the early history of the English woolmaking industry.

Localization Economies

Clapp, J. M. "Endogenous Centers: A Simple Departure from the NUE Model." *Papers of the Regional Science Association* 54 (1984), pp. 13–24. Describes the process through which contacts between firms cause the development of a CBD and subcenters.

Hall, Peter, and Ann Markusen. *Silicon Landscapes.* Winchester, Mass.: Allen & Unwin, 1985. Discusses the role of external scale economies in the location of high-technology industries.

Hoover, Edgar M. *Location Theory and the Shoe and Leather Industries.* Cambridge, Mass.: Harvard University Press, 1937. Discusses the role of scale economies in the location of shoe and leather industries.

O'Hara, D. J. "Location of Firms within a Square Central Business District." *Journal of Political Economy* 85 (1977), pp. 1189–207. Discusses how interfirm contacts cause the development of a central business district.

Stephens, John D., and Brian Holly. "City System Behavior and Corporate Influences: The Headquarters Location of U.S. Industrial Firms 1955–1975." *Urban Studies* 18 (1981).

Tauchen, H., and Anne Witte. "An Equilibrium Model of Office Location and Contact Patterns." *Environment and Planning* 15 (1983), pp. 1311–26. Discusses how interfirm contacts cause the development of a central business district.

Vernon, Raymond. "External Economies." In *Readings in Urban Economics,* ed. M. Edel and J. Rothenberg. New York: Macmillan, 1972. A discussion of agglomerative economies for industry and clusters.

Urbanization Economies

Carlino, Gerald A. *Economies of Scale in Manufacturing Location.* Boston: Martinus Nijhoff, 1978.

Higgs, Robert. "American Inventiveness, 1870–1920." *Journal of Political Economy* 79 (1971), pp. 661–67.

Jacobs, Jane. *The Economy of Cities.* New York: Random House, 1960. Discusses why many innovations are developed in urban areas.

Noyelle, Thierry, and Thomas Stanback. *The Economic Transformation of American Cities.* Totawa, N.J.: Rowman and Allanheld, 1984.

Sveikauskas, L. "Interurban Differences in the Innovative Nature of Production." *Journal of Urban Economics* 6 (1979), pp. 216–27.

Empirical Estimates of Localization and Urbanization Economies

Henderson, J. V. "Efficiency of Resource Usage and City Size." *Journal of Urban Economics* 19 (1986), pp. 47–90. Estimates the magnitude of localization and urbanization economies.

———. *Urban Development: Theory, Fact, and Illusion.* New York: Oxford University Press, 1988. Chapter 5 provides estimates of localization economies and urbanization economies for the United States and Brazil. Other chapters discuss the theory of systems of cities and public policy implications.

Moomaw, Ronald L. "Productivity and City Size: A Critique of the Evidence." *Quarterly Journal of Economics* 96 (1981), pp. 675–88. Discusses statistical problems with the Segal and Sveikauskas analysis of urbanization economies.

O'hUallachain, Breandan, and Mark A. Satterthwaite. "Sectoral Growth Patterns at the Metropolitan Level." *Journal of Urban Economics* 31 (1992), pp. 25–58. Explores the clustering of firms in particular industries and provides evidence of localization economies.

Segal, David. "Are There Returns to Scale in City Size?" *Review of Economics and Statistics* 58 (July 1976), pp. 339–50. Estimates the magnitude of urbanization economies.

Sveikauskas, L. "The Productivity of Cities." *Quarterly Journal of Economics* 89 (1975), pp. 393–413.

Agglomerative Economies in Shopping

Eaton, B. Curtis, and Richard G. Lipsey. "Comparison Shopping and the Clustering of Homogeneous Firms." *Journal of Regional Science* 19 (1979), pp. 421–35. Discusses the role of comparison shopping in the location of retailers.

Stahl, Konrad. "Differentiated Products, Consumer Search, and Locational Oligopoly." *Journal of Industrial Economics* 31 (1982a), pp. 97–113. Discusses the effects of consumer search costs on the location of retailers.

———. "Location and Spatial Pricing Theory with Nonconvex Transportation Cost Schedules." *Bell Journal of Economics* 13 (1982b), pp. 575–82. Shows that consumers are attracted to retail sites providing many goods, explaining the clustering of retailers.

General

Toynbee, Arnold. *Cities on the Move.* New York: Oxford University Press, 1970a.

Where Do Cities Develop?

Let the river roll which way it will, cities will rise on its banks.
Ralph Waldo Emerson

Chapter 2 showed that cities develop because of comparative advantage, scale economies in transportation and production, and agglomerative economies. Cities develop around the concentrations of employment generated by firms, so the location choices of firms play a role in the location of cities. This chapter explores the location decisions of two types of firms: industrial firms and commercial firms. *Industrial firms* (e.g., sawmills, breweries, manufacturers, and bakeries) process raw materials and intermediate inputs into outputs. *Commercial firms* trade goods rather than producing them. The location decisions of industrial and commercial firms cause the development of various types of cities. This chapter also discusses the role of government in the location of cities.

Commercial Firms and Trading Cities

The location decisions of commercial firms cause the development of trading cities. Trading firms collect goods from suppliers and distribute the goods to consumers, providing employment for salespeople and other intermediaries. Trading firms typically locate at transshipment points (ports, crossroads, railroad junctions, river junctions) because such locations offer convenient points for the collection and distribution of goods. Transportation firms move goods from place to place, providing employment at transshipment points for truckers, sailors, and longshoremen. Firms providing business services (banking, insurance, bookkeeping, machine repair) locate close to the trading and transportation firms that use their services.

The American fur trade was an important force in the development of cities along the Mississippi River. New Orleans, located at the mouth of the Mississippi River, provided a convenient transshipment point for American furs destined for

European markets. In 1764, fur traders from New Orleans established St. Louis, located at the junction of the Missouri and Mississippi rivers, as a central substation for the fur trade. By 1800, there were over 1,000 people in St. Louis, living in the middle of an almost unpopulated continent.

The experience of New York City illustrates the importance of trade in the development of cities. The city, which began as a fur-trading post for the Dutch, was taken over by the British in 1664. The city grew rapidly, along with other eastern cities, as a result of the flour trade with the West Indies. At the time of the War of 1812, New York and Philadelphia were about the same size. Following the war, New York grew rapidly and became the country's dominant city. Why?

The rapid growth of New York was caused by increases in trading activity, which were caused by two factors. First, New York State built the Erie Canal, connecting New York City with the Great Lakes. The Erie Canal opened vast market areas to New York traders. Second, traders in New York developed innovative trading practices, one of which was the auction sale. A British manufacturer consigned his goods to a U.S. auctioneer, who then sold the goods to U.S. merchants. The auction sale decreased prices because it eliminated the British exporter and the traditional U.S. importer. While Philadelphia and Boston passed laws that discouraged auction sales, New York allowed them. U.S. merchants responded by buying more goods from New York traders, so the city grew at the expense of Philadelphia and Boston. New York traders were also the first to establish regularly scheduled shipping across the Atlantic, which attracted more traders and shippers to the city.

Cities also developed as a result of the railroad. The spread of the railroad after 1830 gave merchants in Boston, Philadelphia, and Baltimore access to midwestern markets, so these cities diverted some trading activity from New York. In 1868, Kansas land speculators chose a site for a new city along the Chisholm Trail (the route for cattle drives from Texas to Kansas railheads). They persuaded the railroad company to extend its tracks to the site. By 1872, thousands of carloads of cattle were being shipped from the city, and Wichita was a booming cow town.

Transfer-Oriented Industrial Firms

A **transfer-oriented firm** is defined as one for which transportation cost is the dominant factor in the location decision. The firm chooses the location that minimizes total transport costs, defined as the sum of **procurement cost** and **distribution cost**. *Procurement cost* is the cost of transporting raw materials from the input source to the factory. *Distribution cost* is the cost of transporting the firm's output from the factory to the consumer.

The classic model of a transfer-oriented firm has four assumptions:

1. **Single output**. The firm produces a fixed amount of a single good. The output is shipped from the factory to a marketplace at point M.
2. **Single transferable input**. The firm may use several inputs, but only one input is shipped from an input source (point F) to the factory. All other inputs are ubiquitous (available at all locations at the same price).

3. **Fixed-factor proportions**. The firm produces its fixed amount of output with a fixed amount of each input. In other words, firms do not substitute between inputs in response to changes in relative prices, but use a single recipe for producing the good.
4. **Fixed prices**. The firm is so small that it does not affect the prices of its inputs or outputs.

Under these four assumptions, the firm maximizes its profit by minimizing its transportation costs. The firm's profit equals total revenue (price times the quantity of output) less input costs and transport costs. Total revenue is the same at all locations because the firm sells a fixed amount of output at a fixed price. Input costs are the same at all locations because the firm buys a fixed amount of each input at fixed prices. The only costs that vary across space are procurement cost (input transport costs) and distribution cost (output transport costs). Therefore, the firm will choose the location that minimizes its total transport costs.

The firm's location choice is determined by the outcome of a tug-of-war. The firm is pulled toward the input source by low procurement costs, and pulled toward the market by low distribution costs. For the **resource-oriented firm,** the pull toward the input source is relatively strong, so the firm locates near its raw material source. For the **market-oriented firm,** the pull toward the market is relatively strong, so the firm locates near its marketplace.

Resource-Oriented Firms

Table 3–1 shows the transport characteristics of a resource-oriented firm. The firm makes baseball bats, using five tons of wood to produce three tons of bats. The firm is involved in a weight-losing activity in the sense that the output is lighter than the transferable input. The **monetary weight** of the input is defined as the physical weight of the input (five tons) times the transportation rate ($1 per ton per mile), or $5 per mile. Similarly, the monetary weight of the output is three tons times $1, or $3 per mile. The firm is considered a resource-oriented firm because the monetary weight of its transferable input exceeds the monetary weight of its output.

Figure 3–1 shows the firm's transportation costs. If x is the distance from the forest to the factory, procurement cost is

$$PC = w_i \cdot t_i \cdot x \tag{3–1}$$

TABLE 3–1   **Physical and Monetary Weights of a Resource-Oriented Firm**

	Input (wood)	Output (bats)
Physical weight (tons)	5	3
Transport rate (cost per ton per mile)	$1	$1
Monetary weight (physical weight times rate)	$5	$3

FIGURE 3–1   **Total Transport Costs for a Resource-Oriented Firm**

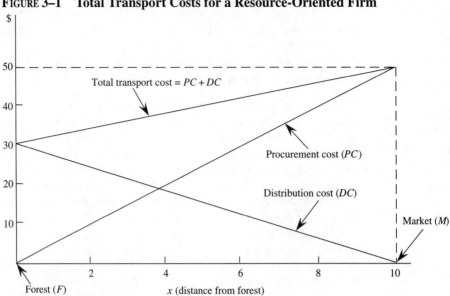

Total transport cost (the sum of procurement cost and distribution cost) is minimized at the forest because the monetary weight of the input ($5) exceeds the monetary weight of the output ($3). The weight-losing activity locates at its source of raw materials.

that is, the monetary weight of the input (weight w_i times rate t_i) times the distance between forest and factory. The slope of the procurement-cost curve is the monetary weight of the input, so PC rises by $5 per mile, from zero at the forest to $50 at the market 10 miles away. If x_M is the distance between the forest and the market, distribution cost is

$$DC = w_o \cdot t_o \cdot (x_M - x) \qquad (3\text{–}2)$$

that is, the monetary weight of the output (weight w_o times rate t_o) times the distance from the factory to the market. The slope of the distribution-cost curve is the monetary weight of the output, so DC decreases by $3 per mile, from $30 at the forest (10 miles from the market) to zero at the market.

Total transport cost is the sum of procurement cost and distribution cost, as shown in Figure 3–1. Total transport cost is minimized at the forest site ($30). If the firm moves one mile away from the forest toward the market, its distribution cost decreases by $3 (the monetary weight of the output) but procurement cost increases by $5 (the monetary weight of the input), so total transport cost increases by $2. Total cost is minimized at the forest site because the monetary weight of the input exceeds the monetary weight of the output. The resource-oriented firm locates near its input source.

Weight-Losing Activities.   The bat firm is resource-oriented because it is a **weight-losing activity,** using five tons of wood to produce only three tons of bats.

The cost of transporting wood is large relative to the cost of transporting the finished output, so the firm saves on transport costs by locating near the forest. In this case, the tug-of-war is won by the input source because there is more physical weight on the input side.

There are many other examples of weight-losing firms. Beet-sugar factories locate near sugar-beet farms because one pound of sugar beets generates only about 2.7 ounces of sugar. Onion dehydrators locate near onion fields because one pound of fresh onions becomes less than one pound of dried onions. Ore processors locate near mines because they use only a fraction of the materials extracted from the ground.

Other Resource-Oriented Activities.   Some firms locate near input sources because inputs are relatively expensive to ship. Suppose that the physical weight of the transferable input equals the physical weight of the output, but the unit cost of shipping the input exceeds the unit cost of shipping the output. The firm will locate near its input source because the monetary weight of the input will exceed the monetary weight of the output. The input will be more expensive to ship if it is more bulky, perishable, fragile, or hazardous than the output. Hoover (1975) provides several examples of such activities:

1. **Cotton baling**. The input (fluffy cotton) is more bulky than the output (baled cotton). Since the cost of shipping a ton of fluffy cotton exceeds the cost of shipping a ton of compacted cotton, the cotton baler is resource-oriented and locates near the cotton fields.
2. **Canning**. The input (raw fruit) is more perishable than the output (canned fruit). Since the cost of shipping one ton of perishable fruits (in refrigerated cars) exceeds the cost of shipping canned goods, canners locate near the fruit farms.
3. **Skunk deodorizing**. The input (fully armed skunks) is more fragile and hazardous than the output (disarmed skunks). Since the cost of shipping a ton of armed skunks exceeds the cost of shipping a ton of disarmed ones, the skunk deodorizer will locate near the skunk source.

A firm with a relatively bulky, perishable, fragile, or hazardous input will locate near its input source. The tug-of-war between input forces and output forces is won by the input source, not because the input is heavier, but because it is more expensive to ship.

Market-Oriented Firms

For a market-oriented firm, the cost of transporting output is relatively large, so the firm locates near its output market. Table 3–2 shows the transportation characteristics of a market-oriented firm. The bottling company uses one ton of sugar and three tons of water (a ubiquitous input) to produce four tons of soft drinks.

Figure 3–2 shows the firm's transportation costs. The monetary weight of the output exceeds the monetary weight of the input by $3. As the firm moves toward the market, total transport cost decreases by $3 per mile, dropping from $40 at the

TABLE 3–2   **Physical and Monetary Weights of a Market-Oriented Firm**

	Input (sugar)	*Output (soft drinks)*
Physical weight (tons)	1	4
Transport rate (cost per ton per mile)	$1	$1
Monetary weight (physical weight times rate)	$1	$4

sugar plantation (point F) to $10 at the market. The firm is market-oriented because the monetary weight of the output exceeds the monetary weight of the input.

The bottling firm is market-oriented because it is a **weight-gaining activity**. The firm adds three tons of local water to one ton of sugar to produce four tons of soft drinks, so output is heavier than the transferable input (sugar). In this case, the tug-of-war is won by the market because there is more physical weight on the output side.

Some firms locate near their markets because their output is relatively expensive to ship. If the physical weights are equal but the output is more costly to ship, the monetary weight of the output will exceed the monetary weight of the input, and the firm will locate near its market. The cost of shipping the output will be relatively high if the output is relatively bulky, perishable, fragile, or hazardous. Hoover (1975) provides several examples of such firms:

1. **Automobile assembly**. The output (assembled automobiles) is more bulky than the inputs (metal, plastic, and rubber parts). The cost of

FIGURE 3–2   **Total Transport Costs for a Market-Oriented Firm**

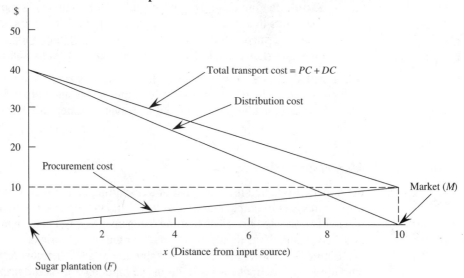

Sugar plantation (F)

Total transport cost ($PC + DC$) is minimized at the market because the monetary weight of the output ($4) exceeds the monetary weight of the transferable input ($1). The weight-gaining activity locates at its market.

shipping one ton of assembled automobiles exceeds the cost of shipping the ton of the metal, plastic, and rubber that goes into the automobiles.

2. **Bakery**. The bakery produces a relatively perishable output: although flour can be stored for months without spoiling, bread becomes stale after just a few days. A bakery locates near its market because it would be expensive to ship bread from a site near the flour mill to the marketplace in a timely manner.

3. **Weapons**. A weapons producer combines harmless inputs into a lethal output. The firm locates near its output market to avoid transporting the hazardous (or fragile) output long distances.

A firm with a relatively bulky, perishable, fragile, or hazardous output will locate near its market. The tug-of-war is won by the output, not because it is heavier, but because it is more expensive to ship.

Intermediate Location

The analysis of the transfer-oriented firm suggests that a firm will locate either at its input source (the resource-oriented firm) or its market (the market-oriented firm). Will a transfer-oriented firm ever choose a location between its input source and its market?

A firm will be indifferent among all the sites between the input source and the market if two conditions are met. First, the monetary weight of the input is equal to the monetary weight of the output. Second, unit transport costs are independent of the distance shipped. If these two conditions are met, the slope of the procurement-cost curve will be equal to the slope of the distribution-cost curve, and the total-cost curve will be a horizontal line. Total transport costs will be the same at all locations, so the firm will be indifferent among all locations between its input source and the market.

The possibility of an intermediate location is eliminated by scale economies in transportation. Scale economies arise for two reasons:

1. **Terminal costs**. The fixed costs of a shipment are the costs of loading and unloading the goods and the cost of paperwork for the shipment. Because these costs are independent of the distance shipped, the average shipping cost decreases as the distance shipped increases.

2. **Line-haul economies**. The shipping cost per mile decreases as the distance shipped increases, reflecting the efficiencies from using different modes. Firms use trucks (relatively high cost per mile) for short hauls, trains (lower costs per mile) for medium-length trips, and ships (low cost per mile) for long hauls.

Figure 3–3 shows procurement cost and distribution cost when there are scale economies in transportation. There is a fixed terminal cost per shipment, and the unit costs of shipping (t_i and t_o) decrease as the distance shipped increases. The slope of the procurement-cost curve decreases as the firm moves away from the input source, and the slope of the distribution-cost curve decreases as the firm moves

FIGURE 3–3   **Transport Cost with Declining Unit Costs**

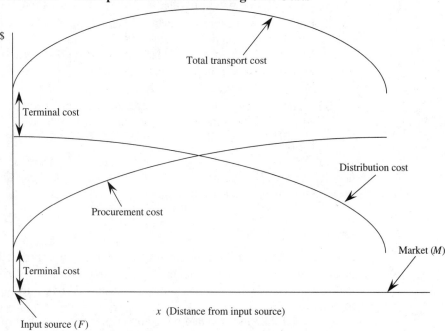

If there are terminal costs and declining unit transport costs, total transport cost ($PC + DC$) is minimized at either the input or the market. Although the monetary weight of the input equals the monetary weight of the output, the firm locates at either F or M, not somewhere between the two points.

away from the market. The total-cost curve is no longer a straight line, but is bowed outward in the middle, so total costs are lower at the endpoints (the input source or the market) than at intermediate locations.

The presence of scale economies reinforces the tendency for firms to locate at input sources and markets. If there are scale economies in transportation, it is more efficient to make one long trip (shipping the input or the output the entire 10 miles between the input source and the market) instead of two short trips (shipping the input 5 miles and the output 5 miles).

Implications for the Development of Cities

The analysis of the transfer-oriented firm provides a simple rule for predicting the location choices of firms. If the monetary weight of the input exceeds the monetary weight of the output, the firm will locate at its input source. If the reverse is true, the firm will locate at its market. Of course, this rule is based on a simple model in which the firm has only a single transferable input and a single output. What about location choices involving a firm with several input sources and markets? The general principles of this section apply to these more realistic cases. The higher the cost of shipping inputs or outputs to a particular location, the greater the pull toward that location.

The analysis of the transfer-oriented firm predicts the development of two types of cities. Resource-oriented firms locate near their raw material sources, causing the development of **resource-based cities**. Some examples are lumber towns, steel towns, and food-processing towns. The analysis also suggests that as a city grows, it will attract market-oriented firms. The location decisions of these market-oriented firms often generate cities that serve as regional **market centers**.

The Principle of Median Location

The classic model of the transfer-oriented firm assumes that the firm has a single input source and a single market. This section examines the location decisions of firms with several input sources and several markets. The most important concept is the **principle of median location**. According to this principle, the optimum location for a firm with several inputs and outputs is the **median transport location**, the location that splits the total monetary weight of the firm into two equal halves. At the median transport location, half the monetary weight comes from one direction, and half the monetary weight comes from the other direction.

Location Choice with Multiple Markets

To explain the location choice of a firm with several markets, consider Ann, who makes and delivers pizzas. In choosing a site for her pizza parlor, Ann must consider the following:

1. **Ubiquitous inputs**. All inputs (labor, dough, toppings) are ubiquitous (available at all locations for the same price), so input transport costs are zero.
2. **Pizza consumers**. Ann's customers are located along a highway. The price of pizzas is fixed, and every consumer demands one pizza per day.
3. **Delivery costs**. Ann delivers the pizzas to her customers at no charge, making one trip per customer per day. The delivery cost is 50 cents per pizza per mile.

Ann will choose the location that minimizes total delivery cost.

Figure 3–4 shows the distribution of consumers along the highway. Distances are measured from the western end of the highway (point W). There are 2 customers at point W, 8 customers at point X (one mile from W), 1 customer at Y (two miles from W), and 10 customers at Z (nine miles from W). Since each customer buys one pizza and the delivery cost is 50 cents per pizza per mile, the monetary weight of a particular location (the sales volume times the delivery cost per pizza per mile) is half the number of consumers at that location.

According to the principle of median location, Ann will minimize total transport costs at the median location. Since point Y divides the monetary weights into two equal halves, it is the median location. The monetary weight of locations to the west is $5 ($1 for W plus $4 for X), and the monetary weight of locations to the east is $5

FIGURE 3–4   **Pizza Delivery and the Principle of Median Location**

	W	X	Y	S		Z
Distance from W (miles)	0	1	2	3		9
Number of consumers	2	8	1			10
Monetary weight	$1	$4	$0.50			$5

Assumptions

1. Every customer purchases one pizza.
2. The delivery cost per pizza per mile is 50¢.
3. The firm delivers one pizza at a time.

Ann will locate her pizza parlor at point Y because it is the median location: she delivers 10 pizzas to consumers to the west of Y, and 10 to consumers to the east of Y. A move from Y to S would decrease delivery cost for the 10 consumers at point E (savings of $5), but would increase delivery costs for the 11 consumers at points W, X, and Y (increase in costs of $5.50). A move in the opposite direction would also increase total transport cost.

($5 for Z). The median location divides Ann's customers into two equal halves: she has 10 customers to the east, and 10 to the west.

To show that the median location minimizes total transport costs, suppose that Ann starts at the median location, and then moves to point S, one mile east of Y. As she moves to the east, there is good news and bad news. The good news is that she spends less on delivery to point Z: she saves 50 cents per trip to Z, saving a total of $5 in eastward delivery costs. The bad news is that westward delivery costs increase: she pays 50 cents more per trip to points W, X, and Y; since there are 11 customers to the west of S, her westward delivery costs increase by a total of $5.50 ($1 more for W, $4 more for X, and 50 cents more for Y). Since the increase in westward delivery costs exceeds the decrease in eastward costs, the move from Y to S increases total delivery costs. The same is true for a move in the opposite direction: if Ann moves from Y toward W, total delivery costs will increase.

Why does the median location minimize total transport costs? It is the minimum-cost location because it splits pizza consumers into two equal parts. At any location to the east of Y, there will be more consumers to the west of the pizza parlor than to the east. As Ann moves eastward away from Y, she moves further away from 11 customers, but moves closer to only 10 customers. Similarly, a westward move will cause her to move closer to 10 customers, but further from 11 customers. In general, any move away from the median location will increase delivery costs for the *majority* of consumers, so total costs increase.

It is important to note that the distance between the consumers is irrelevant to the firm's location choice. For example, if the Z consumers were located 100 miles from W instead of 9 miles from W, the median location would still be point Y. Total delivery costs would still be minimized (at a higher level, of course) at point Y.

FIGURE 3–5   Median Location in the Large City

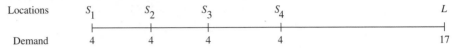

The median location is in the large city (*L*). Any move to the left of point *L* will increase travel costs for the majority of consumers, increasing total transportation costs.

Median Location and Growth of Cities

The principle of median location provides another explanation of why large cities become larger. Suppose that a firm delivers its product to consumers in five different cities. In Figure 3–5, there is a large city at location *L*, and four small cities at locations S_1, S_2, S_3, and S_4. The firm sells 4 units in each small city, and 17 units in the large city. The median location is in the large city, even though the large city is at the end of the line. A one-mile move westward from *L* would decrease transport costs by $16 (as the firm moved closer to consumers in the small cities), but would increase transport costs by $17 (as the firm moved away from consumers in the large city). The lesson from this example is that the concentration of demand in large cities causes large cities to grow.

Transshipment Points and Port Cities

The principle of median location also explains why some industrial firms locate at transshipment points. A *transshipment point* is defined as a point at which a good is transferred from one transport mode to another. At a port, goods are transferred from trucks or trains to ships. At a railroad terminal, goods are transferred from trucks to the train.

Figure 3–6 shows the location options for a sawmill. The firm harvests logs from locations *A* and *B*, processes the logs into lumber, and then sells the lumber in an overseas market at point *M*. Suppose that because of scale economies in production, a single sawmill is efficient. Highways connect points *A* and *B* to the port, and ships travel from the port to point *M*. The sawmill is a weight-losing activity: the monetary weights of the inputs are $15 for point *A* and $15 for point *B*, and the monetary weight of the output is $10.

Where will the firm locate its sawmill? Although there is no true median location, the port is the closest to a median location. If the firm starts at the port (*P*), it could move either toward one of its input sources or to its market.

1. **Toward input source *A* or *B***. A one-mile move from *P* toward point *A* will cause offsetting changes in the costs of transporting logs from *A* and *B*. Because output transport costs increase by $10, the port location is superior to locations between *P* and *A*. The same argument applies for a move from *P* toward *B*.

2. **To market (*M*)**. Unless the firm wants to operate a floating sawmill, it would not move to points between the port and the overseas market at *M*. It could, however, move all the way to the market. A move from *P* to

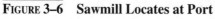

FIGURE 3–6   Sawmill Locates at Port

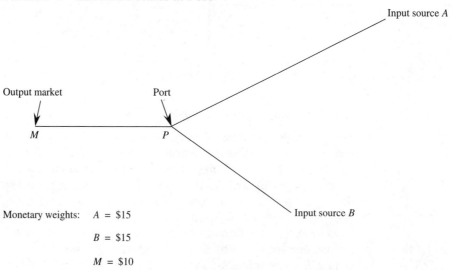

The firm locates its sawmill at the port (*P*) because it is the median transport location. A move from *P* toward either *A* or *B* would increase output transport costs by $10 without affecting input transport costs. A move from *P* toward *M* would increase input transport costs by $30 but decrease output transport costs by only $10.

M would decrease output transport costs by $10 (the monetary weight of output) per mile of distance between *M* and *P* and increase input transport costs by $30 per mile (the monetary weight of the inputs). Transport costs would increase by $20 per mile, so the port location is superior to the market location.

Although the sawmill is a weight-losing activity, it will locate at the port, not at one of its input sources. The port location is efficient because it provides a central collection point for the firm's inputs.

There are many examples of port cities that developed as a result of the location decisions of industrial firms. Seattle started in 1880 as a sawmill town: firms harvested trees in western Washington, processed the logs in Seattle sawmills, and then shipped the wood products to other states and countries. Baltimore was the nation's first boom town: flour mills processed wheat from the surrounding agricultural areas for export to the West Indies. Buffalo was the midwestern center for flour mills, providing consumers in eastern cities with flour produced from midwestern wheat. Wheat was shipped from midwestern states across the Great Lakes to Buffalo, where it was processed into flour for shipment, by rail, to cities in the eastern United States. In contrast with Baltimore, which exported its output (flour) by ship, Buffalo imported its input (wheat) by ship.

Median Location and Cities

The principle of median location explains the development of several types of cities. If the median transport location is an input source, a **resource-based city** will form around the input source. If the median location is in the center of the region, a **regional center** will develop. If the median location is the transshipment point, a **port city** will develop. If the median location is in an existing city, the city will grow.

Firms Oriented toward Local Inputs

An input is considered local if it cannot be efficiently transported from one location to another. Examples of local inputs are energy, labor, intermediate goods, and local public services. A firm that spends a large fraction of its total costs on a particular local input is pulled toward locations where the price of the local input is relatively low. For example, an energy-intensive firm is pulled toward a site with inexpensive energy, and will locate at a site with cheap energy if the savings in energy costs are large relative to any extra costs for other inputs and transportation.

Similarly, a labor-intensive firm is pulled toward a site with inexpensive labor, and will locate at the low-wage site if the savings in labor costs dominate any extra costs for other inputs and transportation.

Energy Inputs

In the first half of the 19th century, energy was a local input. The waterwheel was the first device used to generate nonanimal mechanical energy. The waterwheel was turned by waterfalls and fast-moving streams, providing power for production facilities located along rivers and streams. Textile manufacturers set up factories along small backcountry streams in New England and used waterwheels to power their machinery. Among the cities that developed as a result of the waterwheel are Lowell, Lawrence, Holyoke, and Lewiston.

The development of the steam engine in the second half of the 19th century made energy a transferable input. The steam engine could be operated anywhere, with the only constraint being the availability of coal to fuel the engine. Some energy-intensive manufacturers located near the coal mines in Pennsylvania. Others located along navigable waterways and shipped coal from the mines to their factories. The steam engine allowed New England textile firms to shift from the backcountry waterfall sites to sites along navigable waterways. Production shifted to the Fall River–New Bedford area along the south coast of New England. After the development of the railroad, firms were able to move to production sites connected to the coal fields by rail.

The development of electricity affected the location patterns of manufacturers. Because electricity can be transmitted over distances of several hundred miles, a firm can use the energy generated from water power without locating along a backcountry stream. Similarly, a firm can use coal resources without shipping the bulky fuel from the mine to its factory. In general, the development of electricity decreased the importance of energy considerations in location decisions. The activities for which energy considerations are still important are energy-intensive activities such as the production of aluminum and artificial abrasives. Such activities are attracted to regions that offer inexpensive energy. The Pacific Northwest, with its abundant and inexpensive hydroelectric power, attracts energy-intensive activities.

Labor

There are practical limits on how far laborers are willing to commute, so labor is a local input. A labor-intensive firm, defined as a firm in which labor costs are a large fraction of total cost, chooses a location with low labor costs. Note that the choice is based on labor costs, not simply wages. A high-wage location will be efficient if the labor productivity is high enough to justify the higher wages. In other words, the firm bases its location decision on labor cost *per unit of output*, not simply the hourly wage.

Labor costs differ across space for four reasons. First, firms must compensate their workers for any undesirable features of the local environment. If an area has relatively dirty air or foul weather, workers will demand relatively high wages. Second, areas with strong labor unions generally have higher wages. Third, because households are not perfectly mobile, some areas will have a plentiful supply of labor and thus relatively low wages. In other words, there is disequilibrium in the labor market. Fourth is the phenomenon of **joint labor supply:** households move to locations that provide a job for the household's primary worker, increasing the supply of secondary workers. In colonial Massachusetts, the area north of Boston attracted men to sailing and fishing jobs. The resulting surplus of female workers decreased the wages of jobs held by women. Shoemakers moved to the area to take advantage of its low wages.

There are many examples of firms that base their location decisions primarily on labor costs. When advances in energy technology reduced their dependence on local water power, many textile firms moved from the high-wage New England states to low-wage Southern states. More recently, apparel and shoe firms have moved overseas or to sites near the Mexican border to take advantage of inexpensive labor. The location decisions of these labor-intensive industries cause the development of cities in areas where labor is inexpensive.

Amenities, Migration, and Labor Costs

Some firms are indirectly attracted to sites that provide amenities such as good weather, high-quality schools, low crime rates, a clean environment, and cultural opportunities. If workers migrate to locations offering these amenities, the resulting excess supply of labor will decrease wages, attracting labor-oriented firms to the area. In this case, the firm's location choice depends on the location choice of its work force. Instead of workers following firms, firms follow workers. Graves (1979) and Porell (1982) provide empirical support for this phenomenon.

Amenities appear to be most important for firms that employ high-income workers. Since the demands for these amenities are income-elastic, high-income workers are attracted to locations with amenities, and the firms hiring these people follow. For example, research and development firms employ engineers and computer scientists, who place a high value on good weather, high-quality local schools, a clean environment, and cultural opportunities. One explanation for the shift of employment from northern states to the southern and western states is that rising income has increased the demand for certain amenities, causing workers to move to areas that provide these amenities.

Intermediate Inputs: Localization and Urbanization Economies

Some firms are drawn to locations that provide intermediate inputs. As explained in Chapter 2, localization economies generate clusters of firms in the same industry. By sharing the suppliers of intermediate inputs, firms in the cluster exploit scale economies in the production of specialized inputs. The cluster attracts both the demanders of intermediate inputs (dressmakers, corporate headquarters, research and development facilities) and the suppliers of the inputs (buttonmakers, advertising agencies, law firms, testing facilities). Firms in the cluster also exploit scale economies in the provision of specialized business services and local public services.

Urbanization economies cause firms from different industries to cluster in cities. The firms in cities exploit scale economies in the provision of business services (machine repair, banking, insurance, transportation, employment agencies) and local public services (transportation facilities, schools).

Local Public Services and Taxes

Local governments influence the location decisions of businesses by the provision of public services. The public sector provides some of the inputs used directly by firms (water, roads, ports, and sewers) and provides goods consumed by the city's work force (education, parks, roads, transit systems, public safety). A city can attract firms by providing a set of high-quality, efficient public services. In addition, industrial firms require production sites that (1) are accessible to the intracity and intercity transportation networks and (2) have a full set of public services (water, sewerage, electricity). By coordinating its land-use and infrastructure policies to ensure an adequate supply of industrial land, a city can attract new firms and encourage the expansion of existing firms.

The public sector also affects the location decisions of businesses through its tax policies. Taxes on businesses increase production costs and discourage firms from locating in the city. Taxes on residents increase the costs of living in the city and will ultimately result in higher wages and production costs.

Many cities try to attract export firms by offering special subsidies for new firms. Levy (1981) describes several types of subsidy programs, including the following:

1. **Tax abatement**. In some cities, new firms are exempt from local property taxes for a fixed period (e.g., 10 years). Some cities offer tax abatements to all new developments, while others offer abatements only to firms that are particularly sensitive to tax differentials.

2. **Industrial bonds**. Some cities issue tax-free industrial bonds to finance property developments. The local government uses the revenue from the bonds to purchase the land, and leases the property to a private firm. Because the interest income from industrial bonds is not subject to federal taxes, the bond buyer accepts a relatively low interest rate (e.g., 8 percent instead of 12 percent). Therefore, the lessee pays less than the market interest rate on the money borrowed to finance the project. The

use of industrial bonds was sharply curtailed by the Tax Reform Act of 1986.

3. **Government loans and loan guarantees**. Some cities loan money directly to developers, and others guarantee loans from private lenders. In both cases, developers borrow money at a relatively low interest rate: either the city charges an interest rate below the market rate, or the city decreases the risk associated with a private loan, allowing the developer to borrow private money at a relatively low interest rate.

4. **Site development**. Some cities subsidize the provision of land and public services for new development. The city purchases a site, clears the land, builds roads and sewers, and then sells the site to a developer at a fraction of the cost of acquiring and developing the site.

Several Local Inputs

How does a firm with several local inputs choose among the alternative locations? The location choice is determined by the outcome of a tug-of-war between forces pulling the firm toward its different local inputs (labor, energy, intermediate goods, local public services). The strength of the pull toward a particular input source depends on (1) the relative importance of the input to the firm and (2) the spatial variation in the input price. The greater the importance of the input and the price variation, the stronger the pull toward a particular input source.

Consider a firm that has two local inputs: labor and energy. The firm is pulled toward city L (which has low wages) and city E (which has inexpensive energy). The forces pulling the firm toward L will win the tug-of-war if (1) the firm's labor consumption is large relative to its energy consumption (the firm is labor-intensive) and (2) the difference in the wage (controlling for productivity differences) is large relative to the difference in the price of energy.

Location Choices and Land Rent

This section suggests that some types of firms choose locations that provide inexpensive local inputs. The labor-intensive firm chooses a location with relatively low labor costs. The firm in an industry subject to localization economies locates in a cluster of similar firms. The firm that is dependent on business services locates near banks, law firms, and advertising agencies. How do these location choices affect the land market?

If a particular location offers a desirable mix of local inputs, it will attract input-oriented firms. The resulting increase in the demand for land increases the equilibrium price of land. Therefore, the advantages of a particular site (inexpensive labor, access to intermediate inputs) will be offset, in part, by higher land costs. For example, a firm in the city center can economize on intermediate inputs by locating close to banks, law firms, and advertising agencies, but it also pays more for land. Later in the book, the factors that determine the equilibrium price of land will be examined in greater detail.

Transport Costs versus Local-Input Costs

This chapter divides industrial firms into two types: those that base their location decisions exclusively on transport costs (transfer-oriented firms) and those that base their location decisions exclusively on local input costs (input-oriented firms). Table 3–3 summarizes the results of the chapter, listing the various types of transfer-oriented and input-oriented firms.

In the real world, things are not so tidy. Most firms cannot be easily classified with respect to their locational orientation. For most firms, location decisions are based on both transport costs and local-input costs. Since transport costs and input costs vary across space, the typical location choice requires a trade-off between these two types of costs.

TABLE 3–3   Summary of Locational Orientation

Orientation	*Relevant Characteristic*	*Example*
Transfer Orientation	Transport costs are large fraction of total costs.	
Resource orientation	Weight loss Bulk loss Perishability loss Hazard (fragility) loss	Bat factory Cotton baling Canning Skunk deodorizing
Market orientation	Weight gain Bulk gain Perishability gain Hazard (fragility) gain	Bottling Auto assembly Baking Explosives
Local-Input Orientation	Transport costs are small fraction of total costs.	
Energy	Energy-intensive production	Aluminum
Labor	Labor-intensive operation	Textiles
Intermediate inputs		
Specialized inputs	Localization economies	Dressmakers
Business services	Urbanization economies	Corporate HQ
Amenity Orientation	Workers are sensitive to weather and recreation.	R&D

Trade-off between Transport Costs and Local-Input Costs

To explain the location choice of a firm that considers both transport and input costs in its location decision, consider a decision about where to locate an auto-assembly factory. In choosing a production site, the firm must consider the following:

1. **Inputs and output**. The input source is the same as the market: point *B* is the source of transferable inputs and the market.
2. **Transport costs**. The monetary weights of inputs and outputs sum to $6. As shown in Figure 3–7, total transport costs rise from zero at point *B* to $60 at point *M* (10 miles from point *B*).
3. **Local input**. Labor costs vary across space. As the firm moves away from *B,* labor costs decrease by $3 per mile, dropping from $40 at point *B* to $10 at point *M*.

Total cost (transport cost plus labor cost) is minimized at point *B* because transport costs are large *relative to* labor costs. As the firm moves from point *B* toward point

---

FIGURE 3–7   Transport Costs versus Labor Costs: Transfer Orientation

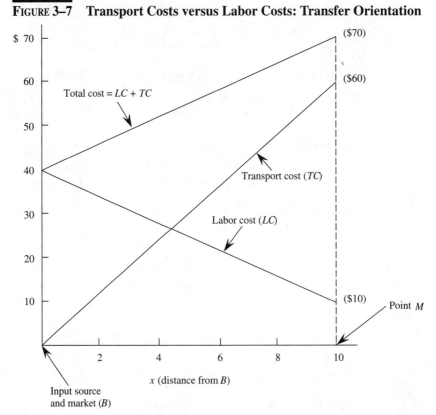

Total cost (the sum of transport cost and labor cost) is minimized at point *B* (the location of the input and the output market). The transfer-oriented firm locates at *B* because the spatial variation in transport costs is large relative to the variation in labor costs.

M, the savings in labor costs ($3 per mile) is less than the increase in transport costs ($6 per mile). Because the spatial variation in transport costs is relatively large, the firm chooses point *B,* close to its input sources and market.

Change in Orientation: Decrease in Transport Costs

Figure 3–8 shows the effect of a decrease in transport costs on the firm's location choice. Transport costs fall to one fourth of their original level (from $6 per mile to $1.50 per mile), decreasing the slope of the transport-cost curve from 6.0 to 1.5. The slope of the total-cost curve is negative instead of positive: a one-mile move away from point *B* generates a net savings of $1.50 (a $1.50 increase in transport costs is combined with a $3 decrease in labor cost), so the firm will move to the low-wage location. In other words, the decrease in transport costs transforms the firm from a transfer-oriented firm to an input-oriented firm.

In the last several decades, many industries have switched from a transfer orientation to an input orientation. Firms have moved from locations close to input sources and markets to locations with inexpensive local inputs. The changes in locational orientation resulted from innovations in transportation and production.

FIGURE 3–8   Switch from Transfer Orientation to Input Orientation

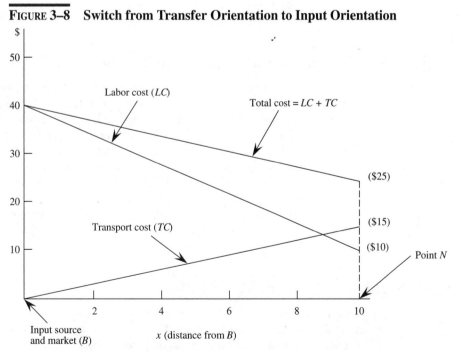

A decrease in transport costs causes the firm to switch from a transfer orientation to an input orientation. Total cost (*LC* + *TC*) is minimized at *x* = 10 because the spatial variation in labor cost is large relative to the spatial variation in transport cost.

Innovations in Transportation.   Improvements in transport technology decreased the cost of transporting both inputs and outputs. For example, the development of fast ocean ships and container technology (shipping freight in large, standardized containers instead of in small bundles) made ocean shipping more efficient, decreasing the unit cost of transportation (cost per ton per mile). Similarly, improvements in rail, trucks, and planes decreased unit freight costs. For some firms, the decrease in transport cost was large enough to cause a switch from a transfer orientation to a local-input orientation. These firms then based their location decisions on access to inexpensive local inputs rather than access to markets or inputs. A recent example is the movement of the assembly operations of many U.S. manufacturers to sites along the Mexican border.

Innovations in Production.   Improvements in production techniques decreased the physical weight of inputs. As the weight of inputs decreased, total transport cost decreased, and some transfer-oriented firms became local-input firms. These firms moved from sites with low transport costs to ones with inexpensive local inputs. An example is the U.S. steel industry. Over the last several decades, the amount of coal and ore required to produce one ton of steel has decreased steadily, a result of improved steelmaking methods and the use of scrap metal (a local input) instead of iron ore (a transferable input). As the physical weight of inputs decreased, transport costs decreased relative to labor costs, and some firms became oriented to local inputs. Many steel plants are now located in low-wage countries (Brazil, Korea, Mexico), far from both raw materials and steel markets.

Location Orientation and Growth Patterns

Changes in transport costs affect economic growth patterns. As transport costs decrease, the relative attractiveness of a resource-rich region decreases, causing firms to move to areas with inexpensive local inputs. The steel industry has moved from the eastern United States, with its rich coal and ore deposits, to Japan and Korea, which have neither coal nor ore deposits. The steel industry made the move because the relative importance of transport costs decreased: steel firms moved to areas with lower wages because the savings in labor costs exceeded the increase in transport costs (for ore, coal, and steel). Similarly, manufacturers have moved from the United States to Asia and Mexico, far from U.S. markets, because the savings in labor costs dominate the increase in transport costs.

Case Studies and Empirical Studies

This section discusses some of the facts on the location choices of firms. The first two parts discuss the location decisions of firms in two branches of the computer industry, semiconductor manufacturers and computer makers. The third part summarizes a case study of the decision to site GM's new Saturn plant near Nashville, Tennessee. The fourth part summarizes an empirical study of location decisions in the electronic components industry and also discusses some empirical evidence concerning the effects of taxes, public services, wages, and unions on firms' location decisions.

The Semiconductor Industry

The semiconductor industry illustrates some of the complexities of locational choices in modern industry. The industry's output is light and compact relative to its value (i.e., it has a low bulk-value ratio), so transport costs are relatively unimportant in location decisions. What matters are localization economies and access to different types of labor.

As explained by Castells (1988), the making of semiconductors involves several distinct operations, requiring three different types of labor:

1. **Research and development**. Engineers and scientists design new circuits and prepare the circuit for implantation into silicon chips.
2. **Wafer fabrication**. Skilled technicians and manual workers make the chips holding the circuits.
3. **Assembly into components**. Unskilled workers assemble the chips into electronic components.

Many semiconductor firms split their operations into three parts. Research and development occurs in the Silicon Valley to exploit localization economies generated by the large concentration of semiconductor firms. The Silicon Valley is also considered a desirable location by engineers and scientists. Advanced manufacturing (wafer production) is typically located outside the Silicon Valley. For example, National Semiconductor has manufacturing facilities in Utah, Arizona, and Washington State; Intel has plants in Oregon, Arizona, and Texas; Advanced Micro Devices has a plant in Texas. These facilities are located in areas that provide (1) a plentiful supply of skilled manual laborers, (2) an environment attractive to engineers and technicians, and (3) easy access, by air transportation, to the Silicon Valley. The firm's assembly facilities are typically overseas, in locations such as Southeast Asia that have a plentiful supply of low-skilled workers.

Computer Manufacturers

The splitting of manufacturing operations also occurs among computer makers. Hekman (1985) has studied the location decisions of firms producing large mainframe computers. The five largest firms, which control over 95 percent of the U.S. market, have their main research and design facilities in large metropolitan areas, one each in Boston, New York, and Philadelphia, and two in Minneapolis. Because of the frequent design changes in mainframe computers, there is a great deal of nonroutine communication between designers and manufacturers, so proximity between design and fabrication activities is important. Four of the five mainframe makers assemble their computers near their research and design facilities.

In contrast, peripheral equipment (terminals, tape drives, and printers) is produced in branch plants outside the home metropolitan area. Because peripherals are not subject to rapid design changes, they can be easily produced far from the design facilities, in Tennessee, Nebraska, South Dakota, Utah, North Carolina, Florida, and Michigan. Similarly, individual computer components are standardized inputs, and are produced in Mexico, Brazil, Hong Kong, Taiwan, and Puerto Rico.

A Case Study: The Location of GM's Saturn Plant

In 1985, General Motors announced that its new Saturn plant would be located in Spring Hill, Tennessee, a crossroads community about 30 miles from Nashville. The plant, which cost several billions of dollars to build, employs about 3,000 workers and supports thousands of jobs in the Nashville area. Why did GM choose Nashville over the dozens of other communities that sought the plant?

A case study by Bartik, Becker, Lake, and Bush (1987) suggests that the most important factor in the site choice was labor costs. Transportation costs and taxes also influenced the decision. A labor contract between GM and its unionized workers stipulates that the Saturn workers will be paid the same wage regardless of the plant's location, so GM will not decrease its own wage bill by locating in Tennessee, a state with low wages. However, GM will purchase a large fraction of its inputs from nearby suppliers, who will pay low wages and pass on the savings to GM.

The first step in the case study addressed the issue of transportation costs and market access. The authors estimated the costs of shipping finished cars from hundreds of alternative production sites to GM's markets in the continental United States. Based on 1984 sales figures, the cost-minimizing location (the location offering the best market access) was Indianapolis, Indiana. Based on the distribution of projected sales in 2000, the location offering the best market access was Terre Haute, Indiana. The shift from Indianapolis to Terre Haute reflects the shift in population and car consumers to the southern and western areas of the United States.

The second part of the study incorporated labor costs and taxes into the analysis. The authors estimated labor costs and taxes for production sites that provided reasonable access to GM's markets (a total of 130 sites in seven states). Table 3–4 shows the costs (expressed as costs per car) for one site in each of the seven states.

1. **Transportation costs**. The variation in transportation cost among the seven sites was relatively small. The gap between the lowest-cost site (Terre Haute) and the most expensive site (Kalamazoo) was only $17 per car. Nashville was ranked fifth, with transport costs only $13 per car higher than Terre Haute.

2. **Labor costs for local suppliers**. The variation in labor cost was relatively large. The difference between the lowest-cost site (Nashville) and the highest-cost site (Kalamazoo) was $85 per car.

3. **State and local taxes**. Table 3–4 shows the tax cost per car in the absence of special subsidies and exemptions. The difference between the highest-tax site (Marysville) and the lowest-tax site (Lexington) was $63 per car. Nashville was ranked third, with tax costs per car $12 higher than Lexington.

TABLE 3–4   **Case Study of GM's Saturn Plant**

	Estimated Cost (dollars per car)			
	Transport Costs	*Labor Costs for Local Suppliers*	*State and Local Taxes (before subsidy)*	*Total Measured Cost*
Nashville, TN	426	159	118	703
Lexington, KY	423	186	106	715
St. Louis, MO	419	172	134	725
Bloomington, IL	417	202	162	781
Kalamazoo, MI	430	244	116	790
Terre Haute, IN	413	209	168	790
Marysville, OH	427	219	169	815

SOURCE: Timothy J. Bartik, Charles Becker, Steve Lake, and John Bush, "Saturn and State Economic Development," *Forum for Applied Research and Public Policy,* Spring 1987, pp. 29–40.

The case study suggests that in the absence of special tax treatment, Nashville was the lowest-cost site. The sum of its transportation, local labor, and tax costs was $12 less per car than Lexington, the second-ranked site, and $87 less than Terre Haute, the site that minimizes transportation costs. Nashville's slight disadvantage in market access is offset by its lower labor costs.

Tennessee offered three types of inducements to GM. The first was a $30 million highway project that connected the plant with Interstate 65. The second was a subsidized job-training program for Saturn workers, worth about $4 per car. The third was a program of property tax subsidies, worth about $30 per car. Although these subsidies would not have been necessary in the absence of similar subsidies from other states, it appears that Tennessee offered them to stay competitive with other states bidding for the plant.

The Relative Importance of Local Inputs: Empirical Results

On a theoretical level, all local inputs (labor, energy, intermediate inputs) influence location choices. Which local inputs are the most important? A number of recent empirical studies of location decisions address this question.

Carlton Study: Birth Rates for Firms.   Carlton (1979) examines the location choices of firms in three input-oriented industries, plastics products, electronic transmitting equipment, and electronic components. These industries have relatively low transport costs, so they are oriented toward local inputs, not toward output markets or natural resources. Carlton hypothesizes the following relationship between the number of new firms in a particular metropolitan area (the number of "births") and the characteristics of the metropolitan area:

$$N = f(W, E, Q, G, T, I, U) \qquad (3\text{–}3)$$

where

N = Number of new firms in a particular industry
W = Metropolitan wage
E = Unit energy cost
Q = Metropolitanwide output of the industry
G = Number of engineers in the metropolitan area
T = The tax level of the metropolitan area
I = Measure of incentive programs offered by government to new
     business (revenue bonds, subsidized loans, tax exemptions)
U = Metropolitan unemployment rate

In other words, the number of births depends on the cost of local inputs (W and E), localization economies (as measured by Q, the total output of the industry), the technical expertise of the area (as measured by G, the number of engineers), government tax policy (T and I), and the health of the local economy (as measured by U, the unemployment rate).

Table 3–5 shows Carlton's results for the electronic components industry, reported as the elasticities of the number of births with respect to the various location factors. The elasticity of the number of births with respect to the wage is -1.07. A 10 percent increase in the SMSA wage decreases the number of births by 10.7 percent. The elasticity for energy cost is lower, from -0.38 for natural gas to -0.95 for electricity. The elasticity for industry output (0.43) suggests that localization economies are important: the number of births increases as the size of the industry increases. The technical expertise of the SMSA (measured by the number of engineers) also affects the number of new firms.

Carlton's results suggest that tax policies do not affect the location decisions of firms producing electronic components. The elasticities for the tax and incentive variables are close to zero, implying that SMSAs with low taxes and lucrative incentive packages do not experience higher birth rates. These results are consistent with earlier studies of the influence of taxes on location decisions.

**TABLE 3–5   Relative Strengths of
Location Factors**

	Elasticity of Births with Respect to Variable
Wage	-1.07
Energy cost	-0.38 to -0.95
Output of industry	0.43
Number of engineers	0.25
Taxes	Close to zero
Government incentives	Close to zero

SOURCE: Dennis W. Carlton, "The Location and Employment Choices of New Firms: An Econometric Model," in *Interregional Movements and Regional Growth,* ed. William C. Wheaton (Washington, D.C.: The Urban Institute, 1979).

Carlton's results for the other two industries (plastics products and electronic transmitting equipment) were similar. The most important location factors were wages, energy costs (less important for electronic transmitting equipment), industry output, and technical expertise.

Effects of Taxes and Public Services on Business Location Decisions

In the last 20 years, there have been dozens of empirical studies of firms' location choices. Bartik (1991) summarizes the results from many of these studies and draws some general conclusions about the effects of taxes and public services on firms' location choices.

There is solid evidence that local taxes have a strong negative effect on regional business growth. In other words, a high-tax city will grow at a slower rate than a low-tax city, everything else being equal. Similarly, if a city increases its taxes, it will grow at a slower rate, everything else being equal. It's important to note that one of the items included in *everything else* is public services: a high-tax city grows at a slower rate because firms pay higher taxes without receiving better public services in return. If a high-tax city were to use the extra tax revenue to provide better public services, the city might grow at a faster rate than a low-tax, low-service city.

Empirical studies of business location decisions distinguish between two types of decisions, intermetropolitan decisions (choosing a metropolitan area) and intrametropolitan decisions (choosing a site within a metropolitan area). One way to summarize the effects of taxes on location decisions is to compute the elasticity of business activity with respect to tax liabilities, defined as the percentage change (or percentage difference) in business activity divided by the percentage change (or percentage difference) in tax liabilities. For intermetropolitan location decisions, the elasticity is between -0.10 and -0.60: a 10 percent increase in taxes in a particular metropolitan area decreases business activity in the metropolitan area between 1 percent and 6 percent. For intrametropolitan location decisions, the elasticity is between -1.0 and -3.0. If an individual municipality increases its taxes by 10 percent, business activity in the municipality decreases between 10 percent and 30 percent. The elasticity for the intrametropolitan decision is larger because different locations within a metropolitan area are better substitutes than locations in different metropolitan areas.

Two other results from recent empirical studies are worth noting. First, it appears that manufacturers are more sensitive than other types of firms to tax differentials within and between metropolitan areas. This is sensible because manufacturers are likely to be oriented toward the national market and thus have a wider range of location options. Second, metropolitan areas with relatively high taxes on capital (in the form of taxes on business property) tend to repel capital-intensive industries and attract labor-intensive industries.

There is solid evidence that the provision of local public services has a strong positive effect on regional business growth. If two cities differ only in the quality of their local public services, the city with the better public services will grow at a faster rate. Similarly, if a city improves its public services, it will grow at a faster rate, everything else being equal. It's important to note that one of the items included in everything else is local taxes: the high-service city grows at a faster rate because firms receive better public services without paying higher taxes. The public services that have the largest positive effect on business growth are education and infrastructure.

How would simultaneous increases in taxes and spending on public services affect location choices and business activity? Studies by Helms (1985) and Munnell (1990) suggest that the effect of a tax increase depends on how the extra tax revenue is spent. If the extra tax revenue is spent on local public services (infrastructure, education, or public safety), the tax/expenditure program increases the relative attractiveness of the city and promotes economic growth. In contrast, if the extra tax revenue is spent on redistributional programs for the poor, the tax decreases the relative attractiveness of the jurisdiction and decreases the growth rate.

Effects of Wages and Unions on Business Location Choices

The recent evidence on the sensitivity of location decisions to wages is consistent with Carlton's results. Bartik (1991) examines and summarizes the results of dozens of studies and concludes that the long-run elasticity of business activity with respect to the wage is between -1.0 and -2.0. This means that a 10 percent decrease in the metropolitan wage will increase business activity between 10 percent and 20 percent.

How do unions affect location decisions and the volume of business activity? One of the effects of unions is to increase wages, so a highly unionized metropolitan area is likely to have relatively high wages. Since the elasticity of business activity with respect to the wage is relatively large, to the extent that unions increase wages, they decrease business activity. Unions may have other (nonwage) effects that influence business location decisions. For example, unions may affect labor productivity. According to Bartik (1991), the empirical studies of the nonwage effects of unions have generated mixed results: although most studies found that the presence of unions decreases business activity, many studies suggest that the negative effects are rather small.

The Role of Government in the Location of Cities

Not all cities develop as a result of the location decisions of profit-seeking firms. Some cities owe their existence to government policies. Government affects the location of cities in several ways. First, governments pick the sites for administrative offices, causing concentrations of government jobs in capital cities. In the United States, many state governments chose vacant sites for their capitol buildings, creating instant capital cities. Second, the siting of public facilities such as universities and prisons generates concentrations of jobs for guards and teachers.

Some cities develop as a result of differences in legal environments. During colonial times, several cities along the eastern seaboard thrived on illegal trade with the West Indies. Under the British Navigation Acts, trade with the French in the

West Indies was restricted. The British authorities made little effort to enforce the trade regulations in the colonies, so smuggling between the colonies and the West Indies flourished. British traders complained that because colonial traders ignored the Navigation Acts, they had an unfair advantage over their British competitors.

Some state governments have exploited differences in legal environments to stimulate growth. The state of Nevada has used liberal divorce laws and legalized gambling to stimulate the growth of its cities near the California border. In 1900, the state established itself as the state with the most liberal divorce laws and kept one step ahead of other states as they liberalized their divorce laws. The divorce industry was the primary force in the early development of Reno, 12 miles from the California border. When the divorce traffic slowed during the Depression, the state legalized gambling as a means of stimulating the state's economy. The gambling industry contributed to the growth of Reno, Las Vegas, and Lake Tahoe. The cities of Reno and Lake Tahoe cater to customers from Northern California, while Las Vegas caters to customers from Southern California.

Summary

1. Cities develop around the concentrations of employment generated by firms, so the location choices of firms play a role in the location of cities.
2. Trading firms collect goods from suppliers and distribute them to consumers, and locate at transshipment points. The location of trading and transportation firms explains the development of port cities and junction cities.
3. A transfer-oriented firm spends a relatively large amount on transport costs and chooses the location that minimizes total transport costs.
   a. A resource-oriented firm has relatively high transport costs for its inputs, so it locates near its input source. The location choices of resource-oriented firms cause the development of resource-based cities and port cities.
   b. A market-oriented firm has relatively high transport costs for its output, so it locates near its market. The location choices of market-oriented firms cause the development of port cities and the growth of existing cities.
4. According to the principle of median location, a market-oriented firm locates at its median transport location, defined as the location that splits its customers into two halves.
   a. This principle explains why big cities grow. The median location is often in a large city, so many market-oriented firms locate in large cities.
   b. This principle explains why some resource-oriented firms locate at transshipment points (ports). The port is often the median location for the firm because it provides a central collection point for inputs and a single distribution point for the output.

5. A *local input* is defined as an input that cannot be transported long distances. Examples are certain types of energy, labor, and intermediate goods.
   a. A firm is oriented toward a local input if (1) it uses a local input whose price varies across space and (2) it spends a large fraction of its budget on the local input.
   b. The input-oriented firm will locate near inexpensive local inputs, causing the development of cities and regions near sources of inexpensive energy, labor, and intermediate goods.

6. Firms that employ people who are sensitive to amenities (good weather, high-quality schools, low crime rates, a clean environment, cultural opportunities) are attracted to locations that offer these amenities. Instead of workers following firms, firms follow workers. Amenities are most important for firms that employ high-income workers.

7. One study of the location decisions of firms producing electronic components, plastics products, and electronic transmitting equipment suggests that the most important location factors are the wage, energy costs, industry output (a measure of localization economies), and technical expertise. Taxes and incentive programs do not seem to affect location decisions.

8. Until recently, most studies of location decisions suggested that taxes were not an important locational factor. Recent studies cast some doubt on this conclusion. One study suggests that the effect of a tax depends on how the tax revenue is spent: an increase in taxes increases the relative attractiveness of a jurisdiction if the money is spent on local public services (highways, education, public health and safety), but decreases the relative attractiveness of the jurisdiction if the money is spent on redistributional programs.

9. In the last several decades, the relative importance of transport costs has decreased, a result of innovations in transportation (which decreased unit transport costs) and production (which decreased the physical weight of inputs).
   a. Many resource-oriented and market-oriented firms have been transformed into firms oriented toward local inputs.
   b. The change in locational orientation provides one reason for the shift in economic growth from resource-rich regions (e.g., the United States) to places with low labor costs (e.g., Asia).

10. Government decisions cause the development of administrative cities and cities that host public facilities such as prisons and universities. Differences in legal environments cause the development of border cities.

Exercises and Discussion Questions

1. Comment on the following from the owner of a successful plywood mill: "Firms don't use location theory to make location decisions. I chose this location for my plywood mill because it is close to my favorite fishing spot."

2. Depict graphically the effects of the following changes on the bat firm's cost curves (shown in Figure 3–1). Explain any changes in the optimum location.
   a. The cost of shipping bats increases from $1 per ton to $4 per ton, while the cost of shipping wood remains at $1 per ton.
   b. The forest at point F burns down, forcing the firm to use wood from point G, which is 10 miles west of point F (20 miles from the market).
   c. The firm starts producing bats with wood and cork, using three tons of wood and two tons of cork to produce 3 tons of bats. Cork is ubiquitous (available at all locations for the same price).

3. Why do breweries typically locate near their markets (far from their input sources), while wineries typically locate near their input sources (far from their markets)?

4. The building of wooden ships was a weight-losing activity, as evidenced by the piles of scrap wood generated by shipbuilders. Yet shipbuilders located in ports, far from their input sources (inland forests). Why?

5. In the 1960s, the port of Oakland moved rapidly to develop facilities to take advantage of the new labor-saving containerization technology. As a result, it was able to take shipping business away from the San Francisco port (across the bay). Under what conditions will the adoption of containerization technology increase total employment in Oakland?

6. Consider a firm that delivers video rentals to its customers. The spatial distribution of customers is as follows: 10 videos are delivered to location W, 10 miles due west of the city center; 50 videos are delivered to the city center; 25 units are delivered to E, 1 mile due east of the city center; and 45 videos are delivered to point F, 2 miles east of the city center. Production costs are the same at all locations.
   a. Using a graph, show where the firm should locate. Explain your location choice.
   b. Suppose that point W is in a valley and point F is at the top of a mountain. Therefore, the unit cost of easterly transport (shipments from west to east) is twice the unit cost of westerly transport. If production costs are the same at all locations, where should the firm locate? Explain.

7. Figure 3–4 shows the location choice of Ann's pizza firm. Discuss the effects of the following changes on Ann's location choice.
   a. A tripling of the distance between Y and Z (from 7 miles to 21 miles).
   b. A tripling of the number of customers at point W. Instead of two customers at W, there are six.
   c. Ann stops delivery service, forcing consumers to travel to the pizza parlor.

8. In Figure 3–6, the weight-losing firm is located at point P (the port). If the monetary weight of location B is $27 instead of $15, will the firm still locate at point P?

9. There is some evidence that people have become more sensitive to air pollution. In other words, people are willing to pay more for clean air. If this is true, what influence will it have on the location decision of firms?

10. Consider a firm that uses one transferable input to produce one output. The monetary weight of the output is $4, and the monetary weight of the input is $3. The distance between M (the market) and F (the input source) is 10 miles.

   a. Suppose that production costs are the same at all locations. Using a diagram like the one in Figure 3–1, explain where the firm will locate.

   b. Suppose that the cost of land (a local input) increases as one approaches the market. Specifically, suppose that the cost of land is zero at F, but increases at a rate of $2 per mile as the firm approaches M. Depict graphically the location choice of the firm.

11. Chapter 2 discusses the incubator process. When industries mature, they move from single-activity clusters to areas with lower land and labor costs. Explain this process in terms of changes in the orientation of firms as they mature.

12. Suppose that country L has a plentiful supply of labor (and low wages) but a relatively low supply of raw materials. In contrast, H has a plentiful supply of raw materials, but a relatively low supply of labor (and high wages). The two countries are separated by a mountain range that makes travel between the two countries very costly. Suppose that a weight-losing product is initially produced in H (close to the supply of raw materials). Suppose that a tunnel is bored through the mountain, decreasing the costs of shipping raw materials and output between the two countries. Assume that laborers do not migrate from one country to the other.

   a. How will the tunnel affect the location choices of weight-losing firms?

   b. How will the tunnel affect wages in the two countries?

   c. How might this analysis be used to explain (1) the shift in manufacturing from the United States to East Asian countries and (2) the narrowing of the wage differential between the United States and East Asian countries?

References and Additional Readings

Location Theory of Firms

Alonso, William. "Location Theory." In *Readings in Urban Economics,* ed. M. Edel and J. Rothenberg. New York: Macmillan, 1972. Outlines the theory of firm location, focusing on the role of transport costs. Contains a brief bibliography of the seminal works in location theory.

Hoover, Edgar M. *The Location of Economic Activity.* New York: McGraw-Hill, 1963. Discusses the economics of industry location, urban structure, and regional development, focusing on the problems of locational change and adjustment.

——. *Regional Economics.* New York: Alfred A. Knopf, 1975. Chapters 2, 3, and 4 provide a concise analysis of the location decisions of firms.

Richardson, Harry W. *Regional Economics.* Urbana: University of Illinois Press, 1979, pp. 37–80.

Location of People: Migration and Amenities

Graves, Phillip E. "A Life-Cycle Empirical Analysis of Migration and Climate by Race." *Journal of Urban Economics* 6 (1979), pp. 135–47. Estimates the effect of climate variables on migration patterns in the 1960s.

Greenwood, Michael. "Human Migration: Theory, Models, and Empirical Studies." *Journal of Regional Science* 25 (1985), pp. 521–44. Survey of the theoretical and empirical literature on migration.

Porell, Frank W. "Intermetropolitan Migration and Quality of Life." *Journal of Regional Science* 22 (1982), pp. 137–58. Estimates the effects of economic and quality-of-life variables on migration patterns.

Applications of Location Theory

Levy, John M. *Economic Development Programs for Cities, Counties, and Towns*. New York: Praeger Publishers, 1981. Discusses the factors affecting the location choices of firms.

Schmenner, Roger. "Energy and Location." In *Energy Costs, Urban Development, and Housing,* ed. Anthony Downs and Katherine Bradbury. Washington, D.C.: Brookings Institution, 1984. Discusses the role of energy costs in location decisions.

Storper, Michael. "Toward a Structural Theory of Industrial Location." In *Industrial Location and Regional Systems*, ed. John Rees, Geoffrey J. D. Hewings, and Howard Stafford. Brooklyn, N.Y.: Bergin, 1981, pp. 17–40.

Industry and Case Studies of Location Decisions

Bartik, Timothy J.; Charles Becker; Steve Lake; and John Bush. "Saturn and State Economic Development." *Forum for Applied Research and Public Policy,* Spring 1987, pp. 29–40.

Castells, Manuel. "The New Industrial Space: Information Technology Manufacturing and Spatial Structure in the United States." In *America's New Market Geography,* ed. George Sternlieb and James Hughes. New Brunswick, N.J.: Center for Urban Policy Research, 1988. Examines the location patterns of information-technology industries (semiconductors, computers, communication equipment, electronic automated machines, and genetic engineering).

Hekman, John S. "Branch Plant Location and the Product Cycle in Computer Manufacturing." *Journal of Economics and Business* 37 (1985), pp. 89–102. Examines the influence of product development on the location decisions of computer manufacturers.

Schmenner, Roger W. *Making Business Location Decisions*. Englewood, N.J.: Prentice Hall, 1982. Discusses how firms make location decisions.

——. *The Manufacturing Location Decision: Evidence from Cincinnati and New England*. Cambridge, Mass.: Harvard–MIT Joint Center, 1981.

Empirical Studies of Business Location Decisions

Bartik, Timothy J. *Who Benefits from State and Local Economic Development Policies?* Kalamazoo, Mich.: W. E. Upjohn Institute, 1991. Chapter 2 summarizes the results from dozens of studies of firms' location decisions, focusing on the effect of public policy on location choices.

Carlton, Dennis W. "The Location and Employment Choices of New Firms: An Econometric Model." In *Interregional Movements and Regional Growth,* ed. William C. Wheaton. Washington, D.C.: The Urban Institute, 1979. Estimates the effects of wages, energy costs, industry output, and taxes on location decisions.

Helms, L. Jay. "The Effect of State and Local Taxes on Economic Growth: A Times Series-Cross Section Approach." *Review of Economics and Statistics* 68 (1985), pp. 574–82. Estimates effects of taxes on location decisions and growth rates; concludes that the effect of a tax increase depends on how the tax revenue is spent.

Munnell, Alicia H. "How Does Public Infrastructure Affect Regional Economic Performance?" *New England Economic Review,* 1990, pp. 11–33.

Urban and Regional Growth Patterns

Mieszkowski, Peter. "Recent Trends in Urban and Regional Development." In *Current Issues in Urban Economics,* ed. Peter Mieszkowski and Mahlon Straszheim. Baltimore: Johns Hopkins, 1979, pp. 3–39. Describes the broad patterns of urban and regional development since World War II, focusing on interregional migration, shifts in employment, and changes in regional income differentials.

Norton, R. D. *City Life Cycles and American Urban Public Policy.* New York: Academic Press, 1979. Explores the changes in the spatial pattern of growth in manufacturing and discusses the implications for public policy.

Norton, R. D., and J. Rees. "The Product Cycle and the Spatial Decentralization of American Manufacturing." *Regional Studies* 13 (1979), pp. 141–51. Analyzes changes in the spatial pattern of growth in manufacturing.

The Origins of American Cities

Boorstin, Daniel. *The Americans: The Democratic Experience.* New York: Vintage, 1974; and *The Americans: The National Experience.* New York: Vintage, 1965. American history. Discusses the influences of government on the location of cities (the siting of state capitals, county seats, and universities; the influence of divorce and gambling laws). Part Three, "The Upstarts: Boosters," of *The Americans: The National Experience* discusses some of the reasons for the development of U.S. cities, focusing on the role of local boosters.

Glaab, Charles, and A. Theodore Brown. *A History of Urban America.* 3rd ed. New York: Macmillan, 1983. A textbook on American urban history. Discusses the origins of many American cities.

Transport Costs and Industry Location

Chinitz, Benjamin. "The Effect of Transportation Forms on Regional Economic Growth." *Traffic Quarterly* 14 (1960a), pp. 129–42.

——. *Freight and the Metropolis.* Cambridge, Mass.: Harvard University Press, 1960b.

The History of Western Urbanization

"Dost thou know how to play the fiddle?"
"No," answered Themistocles, "but I understand the art of raising a little
village into a great city."
Motto on the masthead of the *Emigrant Aid Journal*

This chapter uses the concepts of chapters 2 and 3 to discuss the historical development of cities in the Western world. The earlier chapters explained that three factors contribute to the development of cities: comparative advantage, scale economies, and agglomerative economies. Together, these three factors explain why cities exist and where they develop. This chapter takes a historical perspective, discussing how changes in technology affected comparative advantage, scale economies, and agglomerative economies, and how these technological changes affected the development of cities. Changes in technology caused cities to grow and shrink, and eventually caused the transformation of the earth from a rural world into an urban one.

The First Cities

The first cities developed in the fertile river valleys in the Near East around 3000 B.C. The city-states that developed in the Mesopotamia Valley included Eiridu, Ur, Lagash, and Kish. Ur was the largest of these cities, with a land area of about 150 acres and a population of about 25,000. In 2000 B.C., the city of Babylon had a population of about 50,000. In the Nile River Valley, the leading cities were Memphis, Helipolis, and Thebes.

A necessary condition for the development of a city is an agricultural surplus. A number of agricultural breakthroughs preceded the development of cities in the Near East: grain was domesticated, irrigation systems were developed, and the plow replaced the hoe. Together, these innovations helped agricultural workers to produce a surplus of food, allowing some people to pursue nonagricultural activities in cities.

The food surplus was relatively small. According to Davis (1976), between 50 and 150 farmers were required to support a single city inhabitant.

Why did the first cities develop? There is some uncertainty about the social and economic features of early societies, so historians can only speculate about the origins of cities. Most agree that the first cities served both religious and defensive purposes. Can the development of defensive and religious cities be explained by the same factors that explain the development of market-based cities? If scale economies are responsible for the development of market-based cities, did the first cities develop as a result of scale economies in defense and religious services?

The Defensive City

A farmer who generates an agricultural surplus will eventually use the surplus, either consuming it himself or trading it for other goods. In either case, he must store the surplus food for some period of time. The stored food provides a lucrative target for thieves. If there are scale economies in food storage and protection, farmers may be better off storing their surpluses in a central storage facility. The people working in the fortified storage facility (managers and guards) will live near the facility, generating a place with a relatively high population density, a small city. This is the theory of the defensive city: the first cities developed because of scale economies in the storage of the agricultural surplus. Support for the theory comes from archaeologists, who have uncovered the remains of fortified storage facilities in the first cities.

How does this picture of the defensive city fit into the analysis of the market-based city in Chapter 2? The agricultural surplus generated a new economic activity: the storage and protection of the surplus. This activity is subject to scale economies, meaning that a single fortified storage facility is more efficient than a series of facilities, one for each farmer. Home storage was replaced by centralized storage, causing the development of a specialized labor force of managers and guards, who exchanged their services for a part of the agricultural surplus. In other words, cities developed because of scale economies in the provision of a new commodity, grain storage. Just as scale economies in cloth production caused the development of factory cities, scale economies in storage services caused the development of defensive cities.

The Religious City

According to Mumford (1961), the development of the first cities coincided with the development of large-scale religion. Before the development of cities, most people worshipped in small groups, either in the home or in the local village. Around the time that the first cities developed, the local earth gods were replaced by celestial gods, who apparently demanded worship on a grander scale. If adoration and supplication are more effective on a large scale, a doubling of the size of the shrine more than doubled the religious output. Large temples at central locations replaced the small shrines in homes and villages. The temples employed chieftains, priests, and religious workers, causing the development of a place with relatively high population density, a city. This is the theory of the religious city: the earliest cities developed because of scale economies in the provision of religion. Support for the theory comes from archaeologists, who have uncovered the remains of large temples in the first cities.

How does the theory of the religious city fit into the analysis of the market-based city in Chapter 2? The switch from earth gods to celestial gods caused home production of religion to be replaced by centralized production, and a specialized labor force of religious workers exchanged their labor for a part of the agricultural surplus. In other words, cities developed because of scale economies in the provision of religion. Just as scale economies in cloth production caused the development of factory cities, scale economies in religious services caused the development of religious cities.

The Defensive and Religious City

The most prominent feature of the early city was a large temple at the city center. The temple was a large monument, with thick walls and extravagant decorations. The thick walls were presumably used to both impress the gods and protect the agricultural surplus stored in the temple. In other words, the temple served both religious and defensive purposes, and early cities served as both religious and military centers.

What came first, the central storage facility or centralized religion? Perhaps the central storage facility made worship in the central temple more convenient, causing the switch to centralized religion. Alternatively, the development of a large temple could have provided a convenient and defensible storage facility for the agricultural surplus. In other words, there were economies of scope in the provision of religion and defense: the two services were provided more efficiently if they were provided together. A third possibility is that the local chieftains used centralized religion as a subterfuge to extract the agricultural surplus from local farmers.

The military played a major role in the early cities. The development of cities increased the frequency and severity of human conflict for two reasons. First, the cities worshipped different gods and fought wars to settle religious disputes. Second, the urban societies accumulated wealth, providing lucrative targets that encouraged materialistic wars. Although cities encouraged aggressive behavior, they also provided the most effective defense against aggression. Until the development of gunpowder in the 14th century, the most effective defensive maneuver was a large but simple wall. In addition, a city contained enough people to defend itself against attack from large forces. Once the simple wall was built, there was safety in numbers.

Greek Cities

The next stage of western urbanization occurred in Greece. In 500 B.C., there were hundreds of independent city-states, ranging in population from a few hundred to tens of thousands. Athens was the largest, with a population of about 150,000, and Sparta had a population of about 40,000. In contrast with earlier cities, which were controlled by chieftain-priests, most Greek cities were run by their citizens, using public assemblies to make policy.

Athens was a market city, with trading activity centered in the Agora. Early in its history, the city established independent colonies, and traded its household crafts and olive products for food and raw materials from the colonies. Trade was facilitated by the stamping of gold and silver coins in the seventh century B.C. In this early period, Athens fed itself through voluntary trade with other areas.

The Athenian empire developed in the aftermath of the successful war against Persia in the fifth century B.C. After the Greek city-states repelled the Persian invasion, they formed the Delian League to carry the war into Asia Minor. By the end of the successful campaign, Athens had assumed complete control of the league, dictating policy to the other city-states. Athens took control of the treasury, transforming the voluntary contributions of member city-states into payments of tribute to Athens.

The Peloponnesian War between the Athenian Empire and Sparta (431 to 404 B.C.) devastated Greece. Because Athens continued to use the Delian League to demand homage and tribute from the lesser cities, it appeared that war was inevitable. The war, which was precipitated by disputes between Athens and Corinth (an ally of Sparta) over two Corinthian cities, ended in 404 when Athens renounced control over its empire and demolished its defensive walls. The war caused large losses in manpower, and also caused many intellectuals to lose faith in the democratic system. Athens never regained its former power. Eventually, Philip of Macedonia was able to take advantage of the weakened city-states, and expanded his kingdom to include most of Greece.

Roman Cities

The next stage of western urban development occurred under the Roman Empire. By the third century A.D., Rome had a population exceeding 1 million. The Romans set up colonies to the north and west, establishing colonial cities throughout Europe. Rome fed its large population with a combination of trade and tribute, with tribute playing a relatively large role.

The Roman cities were eventually overrun by marauders from rural areas. According to Hohenberg and Lees (1985), the Roman economy emphasized the collection of the agricultural surplus and neglected production activity. Instead of exchanging urban goods for agricultural products, Rome used conquest and tribute to feed its population. In the fourth and fifth centuries, German tribes invaded from the north, disrupting the Roman collection system. It appears that there was little interest outside of Rome in restoring the "trade" routes, so the losses from successive invasions were cumulative. If Rome had relied to a greater extent on voluntary exchange, the colonies might have been more interested in maintaining the exchange network, and the Western empire might have recovered from the Germanic raids.

What are the lessons from the rise and fall of Athens and Rome? Early in its history, Athens engaged in voluntary trade with other areas, exchanging urban goods for food from the countryside. The city thrived under this system of voluntary exchange. The Athenians eventually switched to a system of conquest and tribute, resulting in war and the decline of the city. Mumford (1961) suggests that the city of Rome should have been called "Parasitopolis" to indicate the extent to which its population lived off the labors of outsiders. The decline of Rome was caused in part by the disruption of its collection system by the Germanic raids. Perhaps the lesson is that cities based on voluntary exchange are viable, but cities based on coercive transfer payments are not.

Feudal Cities

In the first few centuries following the fall of the Roman Empire, cities in the West declined. The Islamic conquest disrupted trading on the Mediterranean, causing the decline of port cities. Waves of marauding barbarians continued to sweep across Europe, making travel and trade dangerous. People sought safety inside city walls, where, once again, there was safety in numbers.

Table 4–1 shows the largest cities in Europe between 1000 and 1900. In 1000, most cities in western and central Europe were very small. The largest cities served the Byzantine Empire and the Muslim areas of Spain. Venice was one of the few large cities beyond the Byzantine and Muslim areas, but it was heavily dependent on trade with the Eastern empire.

Trade on the Mediterranean increased during the 11th and 12th centuries. The Italian city-states forged agreements with the Byzantine and Islamic rulers for trade with North Africa and the East. The Europeans traded wood, iron, grain, wine, and wool cloth for medicines, dyes, linen, cotton, leather, and precious metals. The increased trade contributed to the growth of Venice, Genoa, and Pisa.

The feudal economy of the 11th through the 14th centuries was based on manorial estates and small walled cities. On the manor, the lord inherited his serfs, who worked the lord's land and served in the military in exchange for the use of a small

TABLE 4–1   European Cities, 1000–1900

1000		1400		1700		1900	
City	Population (thousands)	City	Population (thousands)	City	Population (thousands)	City	Population (thousands)
Constantinople	450	Paris	275	Constantinople	700	London	6,480
Cordoba	450	Milan	125	London	550	Paris	3,330
Seville	90	Bruges	125	Paris	530	Berlin	2,424
Palermo	75	Venice	110	Naples	207	Vienna	1,662
Kiev	45	Granada	100	Lisbon	188	St. Petersburg	1,439
Venice	45	Genoa	100	Amsterdam	172	Manchester	1,255
Regensburg	40	Prague	95	Rome	149	Birmingham	1,248
Thessalonika	40	Caffa	58	Venice	144	Moscow	1,120
Amalfi	35	Seville	70	Moscow	130	Glasgow	1,072
Rome	35	Ghent	70	Milan	124	Liverpool	940

SOURCE: P. M. Hohenberg and L. H. Lees, *The Making of Urban Europe 1000–1950* (Cambridge, Mass.: Harvard University Press, 1985).

plot of land. In the small towns, workers produced handicrafts (cloth, leather goods, metal goods), which they exchanged for the agricultural surplus of the manor.

Cities in the feudal era were small and numerous. In the 11th century, London was the largest city in England, with a population of only 16,000. There were several other English cities with populations of around 5,000. The largest of the many German cities had a population of no more than 40,000.

Between the 11th and 14th centuries, the frequency of barbarian invasions decreased, and the small defensive cities gradually became market cities. The medieval cities specialized in commerce and handicrafts, and thus earned—rather than robbed—the agricultural surplus of their hinterlands. A small merchant class developed, and marketplaces were established just outside the city walls. The merchants were protected from plunder by the establishment of weekly market days: once a week, theft was outlawed in places marked by the market cross. The market peace was enforced by local chieftains, special courts with jurisdiction over traders, and the church. The markets flourished, and the city walls were extended to include the marketplaces. The urban market was primarily a place for the exchange of local agriculture and handicrafts. The producers of handicrafts made up a large fraction of the city's work force.

Hohenberg and Lees (1985) use Leicester, in the East Midlands of England, as an example of a medieval city in the 14th century. The city was surrounded by walls on three sides and a river on the fourth side. The town ditch was just outside the wall. The city was a regional marketplace, serving as a commercial center for the surrounding county. The city produced staples such as beer and bread for local consumption and produced woolen cloth for export. Occupations in the city included butchers, shoemakers, tailors, mercers, weavers, and bakers. Over half of the city's workers were employed in manufacturing, with the other half employed as foodmakers (25 percent), traders and merchants (10 percent), builders (5 percent), and other occupations. The merchant guild controlled most economic activity in the city.

According to Davis (1976), the first market-based cities developed for two reasons. First, power in the feudal system was decentralized. Unlike the Greek and Roman cities, medieval cities could not simply dominate their hinterlands and demand tribute, but had to produce something in exchange for agricultural goods. Second, agricultural productivity was relatively low, so a city could not survive on the output of its immediate hinterland, but had to trade with a relatively large area. As a result, the city had to develop products that could compete with homemade products in its hinterland *and* products produced in other cities.

Competition among the medieval cities caused innovations in production and commerce. Urban producers developed new production techniques, allowing them to underprice their competitors. Cities invested in secular education as a means of promoting literacy and developing commercial skills. These early efforts to improve the techniques of production and commerce set the stage for the industrial revolution of the 18th and 19th centuries.

Table 4–1 shows the top 10 European cities in 1400. Paris, the largest city, was a center for trade and education, and also the capital of the kingdom of France. Three of the top six European cities were Italian city-states. Bruges and Ghent, two cities in the Low Countries, grew rapidly in the 14th century, a result of the booming woolen cloth industry.

A series of famines and plagues between 1350 and 1450 decreased Europe's population by between one third and one half. Cities suffered more than rural areas because cities had less sanitary living conditions and higher population density (an urban sneeze transmits germs to more people). The associated disruptions of social and economic activities caused most cities to stagnate or decline.

Mercantile Cities

Starting in the 15th century, large mercantile cities developed in Europe. Two factors contributed to the development of large cities: the centralization of power and the growth of long-distance trade.

Centralization of Power

In the 15th century, political and economic power was transferred from a large number of feudal lords to a relatively small number of princes, queens, and kings. The shift in power was caused in large part by military advances that rendered the traditional feudal defense maneuvers obsolete.

Innovations in warmaking increased the seriousness and scale of conflict. The feudal lord used his serfs as part-time warriors. If the part-time warriors could not defeat the attackers in the field, the feudal lord could always hunker down behind his castle walls to wait out a siege. The professional army of the 15th century combined infantry (armed with pikes, crossbows, and muskets) with siege cannons and cavalry. The professional soldiers, with their sophisticated weapons, defeated the feudal lord's part-timers in the field. When the feudal lord retreated to the castle, the siege cannon blew holes in the castle walls. The professional armies defeated the feudal lords, centralizing power in the hands of princes, queens, and kings.

The mercantile cities developed defensive maneuvers appropriate to the new level of warfare. Defense was no longer a matter of building a simple wall and dumping hot oil on the attackers. It required the building of intricate fortifications and the hiring of professional soldiers. The larger cities were able to exploit the increased scale economies in defense.

The centralization of power caused the centralization of administrative and military functions in royal cities. After the 16th century, the most rapidly growing cities were the ones that harbored a royal court. In a short period of time, over a dozen cities grew to a size attained by only a few medieval cities: London had 250,000 people, Naples 240,000, Milan 200,000, and Paris 180,000; cities with around 100,000 inhabitants included Rome, Lisbon, Palermo, Seville, Antwerp, and Amsterdam.

Long-Distance Trade

Long-distance trade increased for two reasons. First, the consolidation of power caused a lifting of many restrictions on trade. When power was centralized, the local tariffs imposed by feudal lords disappeared and trade increased. Second, the development of ocean travel led to exploration and the discovery of new markets. Cities developed along trade routes and at transshipment points. While cities with river and sea ports flourished (Naples, Palermo, Lisbon, Liverpool), inland cities like Florence declined. In Table 4–1, four new seaports appeared among the top 10 European cities in 1700: London, Naples, Lisbon, and Amsterdam.

Urbanization during the Industrial Revolution

Despite the rapid spread of cities between 3000 B.C. and 1800 A.D., the world continued to be predominantly rural. Urbanization was limited by the relatively low productivity of agriculture, the high costs of transporting goods (which limited the volume of trade), and the relatively small advantages of centralized production. Until the early part of the 19th century, the fraction of the world's population living in cities was only about 3 percent. Between 1800 and 1970, the percentage of the population in urban areas increased to 39 percent. In the United States, the percentage of the population in urban areas increased from 6 percent in 1800 to over 75 percent in 1990.

The rapid urbanization of the last two centuries was caused by the industrial revolution, which started in the 19th century. The industrial revolution produced innovations in manufacturing and transportation that shifted production from the home and the small shop to large factories in industrial cities. Table 4–1 shows the effects of the industrial revolution on the top 10 cities in Europe. Between 1700 and 1900, Manchester, Birmingham, Glasgow, and Liverpool grew from tiny towns into giant industrial cities. Most of the other cities in the top 10 combined political functions with industrial development, causing dramatic growth. The innovations of the industrial revolution can be divided into four areas: agriculture, manufacturing, transportation, and construction.

Agriculture

The rapid urbanization of the industrial revolution was made possible by innovations that increased agricultural productivity. Farmers substituted machinery for muscle power and simple tools, increasing the output per farmer. For example, using a horse-drawn reaper, two people could harvest the same amount of grain as eight people using traditional harvesting methods. In addition, the development of agricultural science led to innovations in planting, growing, harvesting, and processing. As productivity increased, laborers were freed from food-raising responsibilities, allowing them to pursue other activities. In the United States, the share of employment in agriculture decreased from 69 percent in 1840 to 2.8 percent in 1988.

Manufacturing

Perhaps the most visible part of the industrial revolution involved innovations in manufacturing. New machines, made of iron instead of wood, were developed for the production of most goods. Manual production by skilled artisans was replaced by mechanized production using interchangeable parts, specialized labor, and steam-powered machines. Output per worker rose, and scale economies in production increased.

The innovations in manufacturing caused the development of large industrial cities. Mass production decreased the relative cost of factory goods, causing the centralization of production and employment. In addition, many of the new production processes were subject to agglomerative economies (localization economies and urbanization economies), increasing the advantages of urban locations.

Intercity Transportation

Innovations in intercity transportation contributed to industrialization and urbanization. The steamship and the railroad decreased the costs of moving goods between cities, decreasing the delivered price of factory goods. Production became more centralized, and factory cities grew. The new transportation modes also decreased the costs of moving agricultural goods, allowing greater regional specialization in agriculture. Agricultural regions were better able to exploit their comparative advantages, so agricultural productivity increased.

Before the railroad linked eastern cities with the western parts of the United States, a large fraction of the food consumed in New England was produced by the region's farmers. Similarly, a large fraction of the goods consumed in the West (e.g., shoes) were produced by local craftsmen. The coming of the railroad allowed eastern factories to underprice western craftsmen, and allowed western farmers to underprice eastern farmers. Trade increased because the railroad allowed both regions to exploit their comparative advantages.

Industrial cities developed at points accessible to the new intercity transportation network. During the steamship era, cities developed along the rivers and lakes served by the steamship. Firms that fueled their steam engines with coal located along rivers served by coal shippers. Later, the development of the railroad caused the development of cities along the rail lines. The cities that developed at transshipment points had commercial jobs (transportation, trade, business services) and manufacturing jobs.

Intracity Transportation

Innovations in intracity transportation increased the feasible size of cities. The size of a city is limited by the cost of traveling within the city. One rule of thumb is that the geographical area of the city should be small enough that the typical resident can travel from the edge of the city to the city center in an hour. Before the innovations in intracity transport, most people walked to workplaces and shops, so the radius of the city could be no more than two miles. During the last half of the 19th century, a series of innovations in public transit increased the speed of intracity travel, increasing the radius of the city.

The city of Boston provides a good example of the effects of transit innovations on city size. In 1850, Boston was a "walking" city with a radius of about two miles. In the 1860s, the horse-powered railroad (horses pulling cars along rails) was introduced, and the radius of the city increased to 2.5 miles in 1872 and 4.0 miles in 1887.

By the 1890s, the horse railroad was replaced by the electric trolley, which traveled at twice the speed and carried three times as many passengers. As a result, the radius of the city increased to about six miles. In the 40 years during which walking was replaced by the trolley, the radius of the city tripled and the land area increased ninefold.

The introduction of the internal-combustion engine had similar effects on the size of cities. This new engine allowed the development of relatively small vehicles for transporting people and goods. The development of the automobile decreased the cost of intracity travel, causing further increases in the feasible radius of the city. In addition, it freed travelers from the old fixed-rail systems that were designed to deliver people from the residential areas along the streetcar lines (the spokes) to the city center (the hub). The automobile increased the accessibility of locations throughout the city. Residents could live between the spokes, and firms could locate outside the hub. As the set of feasible locations for residents and firms increased, cities grew.

The introduction of the truck had similar effects. The truck decreased the cost of intercity transportation, increasing the advantages of centralized (urban) production. In addition, the truck freed firms from their dependence on the railroad terminal and the port, allowing firms to locate outside the central city. As the set of feasible production locations increased, the feasible population of the city increased. The development of the truck and the automobile also caused the suburbanization of population within the urban area, a topic to be covered in Chapter 10.

Construction Methods

Innovations in construction methods also increased city sizes. The first skyscraper, a 10-story building that housed the Home Insurance Company, appeared in 1885 in Chicago. The building was revolutionary because its frame was made of steel instead of bricks. Because the steel frame was relatively light, the steel-framed building could be taller than the traditional brick building. The development of the elevator decreased intrabuilding travel costs of tall buildings, increasing the feasibility of the skyscraper. The skyscraper increased the intensity of land use, increasing the city's productive capacity and its feasible population.

Urbanization in the United States

Figure 4–1 shows the trend in U.S. urbanization from 1800 to 1990. In 1800, only about 6 percent of the population lived in cities. The share of population in cities increased to 15 percent by 1850, 40 percent by 1900, 64 percent by 1950, and 75 percent by 1990. Urbanization in the United States can be divided into three periods. Between 1800 and 1930, the traditional port city eventually gave way to the industrial city. Urbanization was rapid during this period: the percentage of the population living in cities increased from 6 percent to 56 percent, and most metropolitan areas grew rapidly. The 1930s and 1940s were times of depression and war, and urbanization proceeded at a relatively slow pace: the percentage of the population in cities increased from 56 percent in 1930 to 59 percent in 1950. There are two figures for

FIGURE 4–1   **Percent of U.S. Population Living in Urban Areas,
1800–1990**

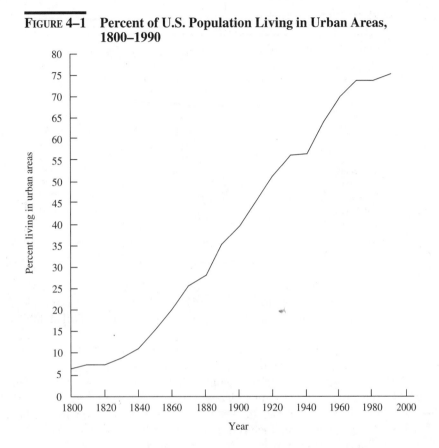

1950. Under the old, more restrictive, census definition of an urban area, 59 percent of the population lived in urban areas; under the new definition, the figure is 64 percent.

During the early part of the postwar period, urbanization proceeded at a moderate pace. The percentage of the population living in urban areas increased from 64 percent in 1950 to 73.6 percent in 1970. During the 1970s, there was a tiny increase in the percentage of the population in urban areas (73.6 percent to 73.7 percent). During the 1980s, the percentage of the population in urban areas increased by 1.5 percentage points, from 73.7 percent to 75.2 percent.

From Commercial to Industrial Cities

Table 4–2 shows the population trends for the 10 largest U.S. cities in 1930. In 1810, only four cities (New York, Philadelphia, Baltimore, and Boston) had more than 10,000 residents. The rapid growth of these cities around the turn of the century was caused in large part by the Napoleonic Wars, which tied up the English and French merchant marine and caused a boom in the American shipping industry. In 1850, the four seaports were still the dominant cities, with the population of the smallest one (Philadelphia) about 2.5 times the population of the next largest city (Pittsburgh).

TABLE 4–2   **Cities in the United States, 1810–1930**

City	Rank in 1930	Population in Year (thousands)			
		1810	1850	1890	1930
New York	1	120	696	2,507	6,930
Chicago	2	—	30	1,100	3,376
Philadelphia	3	54	121	1,047	1,951
Detroit	4	—	21	206	1,569
Los Angeles	5	—	2	50	1,238
Cleveland	6	—	17	261	900
Baltimore	7	47	169	434	805
Boston	8	34	137	448	781
Pittsburgh	9	5	47	239	670
Washington	10	8	40	189	487

SOURCE: U.S. Bureau of the Census, *Census of Population,* Washington, D.C., 1972.

The industrial revolution caused dramatic growth in U.S. cities. Between 1850 and 1890, the populations of New York and Boston more than tripled, the population of Baltimore more than doubled, and the population of Philadelphia increased more than eightfold. Lurking behind these changes were large increases in urban manufacturing activity. The share of employment in manufacturing more than doubled in all of these cities, from about 9 percent of total employment to about 19 percent.

The most dramatic urban growth between 1850 and 1890 occurred away from the eastern seaboard in Chicago, Detroit, Cleveland, Pittsburgh, and Los Angeles. On average, the populations of these cities increased over 18-fold between 1850 and 1890. Again, manufacturing growth led the way. In Chicago and Detroit, the percentage of employment in manufacturing almost quadrupled, from about 5 percent to around 19 percent. In Cleveland, the percentage in manufacturing more than doubled, from 8 percent to 19 percent. Pittsburgh was already an industrial city by 1860, so it experienced a relatively small increase in manufacturing employment (from 18 percent to 23 percent). Chicago was the first city to displace one of the eastern seaport cities from the top four positions, moving into the second spot by 1890.

Between 1890 and 1930, Philadelphia, Baltimore, and Boston were growing at relatively slow rates, allowing other cities to move ahead of them in the ranking. Detroit moved to number four; Los Angeles moved to number five; and Cleveland moved to number six. By 1930, most of the largest cities were industrial cities.

The Postwar Era

As shown in Figure 4–1, the pace of urbanization has slowed since 1950. Using the new definition of an urban area, the percentage of the population living in cities increased by 4.9 percentage points during the 1950s, 3.6 percentage points during the 1960s, 0.1 percentage points during the 1970s, and 1.5 percentage points during the 1980s.

Figure 4–2 shows the percentages of population living in urban areas for the United States as a whole and for four regions in 1990. The western region is the most

FIGURE 4–2   Percent of U.S. and Regional Populations in Urban Areas in 1990

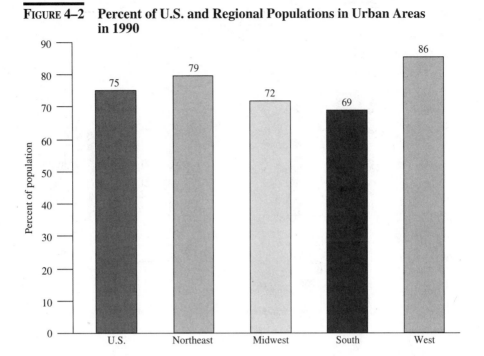

urbanized, with 86 percent of its population in urban areas. The western region has five of the six most urbanized states: California (93 percent), Hawaii (89 percent), Nevada (88 percent), Arizona (88 percent), and Utah (87 percent). The other highly urbanized states are New Jersey (89 percent), Florida (85 percent), Massachusetts (84 percent), and New York (84 percent). The southern region is the least urbanized, with 69 percent of its population in urban areas.

Metropolitan versus Nonmetropolitan Growth

Figure 4–3 provides a closer look at urbanization between 1960 and 1990. The figure shows the population growth rates for metropolitan areas (areas included in an MSA or a CMSA) and nonmetropolitan areas (counties that are not a part of an MSA or a CMSA). During the 1960s, metropolitan areas grew more than four times faster than nonmetropolitan areas (1.6 percent per year compared to 0.35 percent). In contrast, during the 1970s, nonmetropolitan areas grew about 25 percent faster than metropolitan areas (1.29 percent per year compared to 1.04 percent). During the 1980s, metropolitan areas grew more than three times faster than nonmetropolitan areas (1.29 percent per year compared to 0.39 percent).

Nonmetropolitan areas grew faster than metropolitan areas in the 1970s for a number of reasons.

1. **Dispersion of manufacturing employment**. Improvements in the intercity highway system increased the accessibility of nonmetropolitan

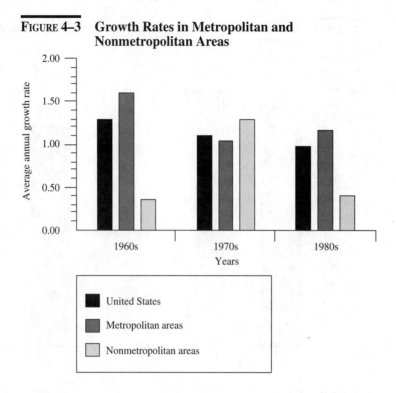

FIGURE 4–3   **Growth Rates in Metropolitan and Nonmetropolitan Areas**

locations. Some labor-intensive manufacturers moved from metropolitan areas to low-wage nonmetropolitan areas.

2. **Slow decline in farm employment**. Although total employment in agriculture decreased during the decade, it decreased at a relatively slow rate. Fewer people left farms to move to cities.

3. **Growth in extractive industries**. Increased prices for energy and raw materials increased employment in oil and mining industries. For example, total mining employment increased from 626,000 in 1969 to 957,000 in 1979.

4. **Growth in recreation and retirement activities.** A large number of elderly households moved to retirement communities in nonmetropolitan areas, pulling retail and service jobs to retirement areas. Other urban households moved to nonmetropolitan areas with outdoor recreational opportunities.

5. **Population spillovers**. Some households moved to counties that the Census Bureau inappropriately classifies as "nonmetropolitan." Some of these counties are integrated, in an economic sense, with a nearby MSA. Alonso (1980) suggests that this statistical problem causes a significant overestimate of the nonmetropolitan growth rate. During the 1970s, many of the fastest-growing areas were nonmetropolitan counties adjacent to metropolitan areas (MSAs and CMSAs).

During the 1980s, the growth rate for nonmetropolitan areas decreased and the growth rate for metropolitan areas increased, restoring the historical pattern of relatively rapid metropolitan growth. According to Garnick (1988), growth rates in nonmetropolitan areas decreased for three reasons. First, farm employment decreased more rapidly, a result of declining farm prices. Second, the employment in extractive industries decreased, a result of decreasing energy and resource prices. Third, labor-intensive manufacturing employment in nonmetropolitan areas decreased, a result of increased competition from abroad.

Population Losses in Some Metropolitan Areas

Another recent trend is the decline of some metropolitan areas. Table 4–3 shows the population growth rates for the 25 largest CMSAs and MSAs. During the 1970s, 7 of the top 25 metropolitan areas lost population: New York, Philadelphia, Detroit, Cleveland, St. Louis, Pittsburgh, and Milwaukee. The largest losses occurred in

TABLE 4–3   Population and Annual Growth Rates for 25 Largest Metropolitan Areas

Metropolitan Area: CMSA or MSA	Rank in 1990	Population in 1990 (thousands)	Average Annual Growth Rate (%) 1970s	Average Annual Growth Rate (%) 1980s
New York–Northern N.J.–Long Island CMSA	1	18,087	−0.36	0.31
Los Angeles–Anaheim–Riverside CMSA	2	14,532	1.42	2.37
Chicago–Gary–Lake County CMSA	3	8,066	0.20	0.16
San Francisco–Oakland–San Jose CMSA	4	6,253	1.22	1.54
Philadelphia–Wilmington–Trenton CMSA	5	5,899	−0.12	0.38
Detroit–Ann Arbor CMSA	6	4,665	−0.07	−0.19
Boston–Lawrence–Salem CMSA	7	4,172	0.08	0.49
Washington MSA	8	3,924	0.67	1.90
Dallas–Fort Worth CMSA	9	3,885	2.23	2.86
Houston–Galveston–Brazoria CMSA	10	3,711	3.64	1.82
Miami–Fort Lauderdale CMSA	11	3,193	3.43	1.90
Atlanta MSA	12	2,834	2.42	2.86
Cleveland–Akron–Lorain CMSA	13	2,760	−0.57	−0.26
Seattle–Tacoma CMSA	14	2,559	1.31	2.03
San Diego MSA	15	2,498	3.21	2.98
Minneapolis–St. Paul MSA	16	2,464	0.76	1.43
St. Louis MSA	17	2,444	−0.22	0.28
Baltimore MSA	18	2,382	0.51	0.80
Pittsburgh–Beaver Valley CMSA	19	2,243	−0.53	−0.77
Phoenix MSA	20	2,122	4.51	3.47
Tampa–St. Petersburg–Clearwater MSA	21	2,068	3.85	2.51
Denver–Boulder CMSA	22	1,848	2.71	1.34
Cincinnati–Hamilton CMSA	23	1,744	0.29	0.49
Milwaukee–Racine CMSA	24	1,607	−0.03	0.23
Kansas City MSA	25	1,566	0.43	0.89

SOURCE: U.S. Bureau of the Census, *Statistical Abstract of the United States: 1991,* Washington, D.C., 1991.

Cleveland (0.57 percent per year), Pittsburgh (0.53 percent per year), and New York (0.36 percent per year). In the 1980s, Detroit, Cleveland, and Pittsburgh continued to lose population.

Why have some metropolitan areas decreased in size? First, people migrated from the northern states to southern and western states, decreasing the growth rates of northeastern and north-central metropolitan areas. Between 1980 and 1990, the average annual growth rate was close to zero for northeastern and north-central metropolitan areas, compared to over 2 percent for southern and western metropolitan areas. Given this migration pattern, the best a northern metropolitan area could hope for was a small positive growth rate. In some northern metropolitan areas, large losses in manufacturing employment resulted in negative growth rates. Decreases in employment in primary metals, motor vehicles, rubber, and nonelectrical machinery industries caused population losses in Pittsburgh, Cleveland, and Detroit.

The Post-Industrial City

What does the future hold for cities? One economic trend that will affect cities and the urbanization process is the shift in employment from manufacturing to services. Table 4–4 shows the changes in the distribution of employment from 1947 to 1992, and Figure 4–4 shows the employment percentages for seven industries (retail and

TABLE 4–4   **Distribution of Employment by Industry, 1947–1992**

	Percent of Jobs in Activity				
	1947	*1959*	*1969*	*1979*	*1992*
Goods-Producing Sector					
Agriculture	11.60	7.40	4.00	3.66	2.96
Mining	1.70	1.20	0.80	1.03	0.57
Construction	5.20	5.50	5.40	4.80	4.02
Manufacturing	26.90	25.60	25.40	22.65	16.23
Total: Goods-producing sector	45.40	39.60	35.70	32.14	23.78
Service-Producing Sector					
Transportation	7.40	6.40	5.70	5.53	5.13
Wholesale trade	4.6	5.20	5.10	5.62	5.44
Retail trade	14.60	13.90	13.40	16.12	17.40
Finance, insurance, real estate	3.30	4.20	4.60	5.63	5.91
Services	13.00	14.70	16.90	18.06	25.56
Government	11.80	16.10	18.60	17.17	16.78
Total: Service-producing sector	54.60	60.40	64.30	67.86	76.22
Total	100.00	100.00	100.00	100.00	100.00

SOURCES: Daniel H. Garnick, "Local Area Economic Growth Patterns: A Comparison of the 1980s and Previous Decades," *Urban Change and Poverty,* ed. M. G. McGeary and L. E. Lynn (Washington, D.C.: National Academy Press, 1988); U.S. Bureau of the Census, *Statistical Abstract of the United States: 1991 and 1994,* Washington, D.C., 1991 and 1994.

FIGURE 4–4   Percentage of Employment by Industry, 1947, 1969, and 1988

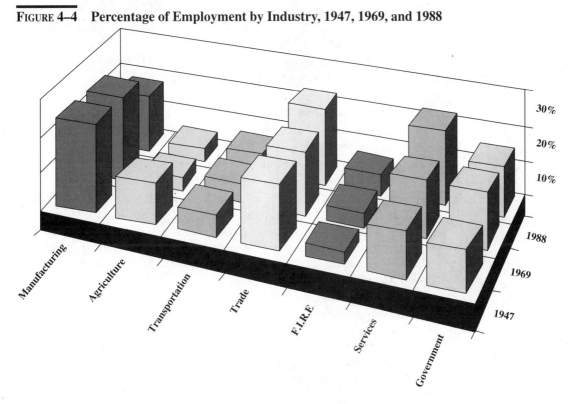

wholesale trade are combined into "trade") for 1947, 1969, and 1988. The percentage of jobs in the goods-producing sector (agriculture, mining, construction, and manufacturing) decreased from 45 percent in 1947 to 26 percent in 1988. The percentage in the service sector (transportation, wholesale and retail trade, finance, insurance, and real estate, services, and government) increased from 55 percent in 1947 to 74 percent in 1988. The largest percentage increases in employment occurred in retail trade, F.I.R.E. (finance, insurance, and real estate), services, and government.

How will the decrease in the relative importance of manufacturing affect cities? Most cities in the United States developed as manufacturing centers during the industrial revolution. The shift to a more service-oriented economy will certainly bring dramatic changes to some metropolitan areas. The cities that continue to be dependent on traditional manufacturing activity are likely to decline in population.

Summary

1. The first cities provided religious services and defense.
   a. Scale economies in the storage and protection of the agricultural surplus caused the development of centralized storage facilities and cities.

    b. According to some historians, cities appeared around the time that earth gods were replaced by celestial ones, suggesting that cities developed to exploit scale economies in the provision of religious services.

2. The development of cities encouraged aggression. Cities provided the best defense against aggression (simple walls).

3. Athens started out as a market-based city, but evolved into a city based on conquest and tribute. It declined after the Peloponnesian War with Sparta.

4. Roman cities were also based on conquest and tribute, and declined after the Germanic raids disrupted the collection system.

5. Feudal cities started as defensive cities, and eventually became market cities, specializing in commerce and handicrafts.

6. Mercantile cities developed as a result of the centralization of power caused by military innovations that eliminated the defensive advantages of the feudal castle. The centralization of power caused the development of administrative cities, and, by breaking down the barriers to trade, increased trade. The development of efficient ocean travel led to exploration and the development of new markets.

7. The rapid urbanization of the 19th and 20th centuries was caused by the industrial revolution and the associated innovations in agriculture, transportation, and manufacturing.

    a. Agricultural productivity increased as farmers substituted machines for laborers, freeing laborers to pursue nonagricultural activities. Transportation costs decreased, allowing greater regional specialization and greater productivity.

    b. The relative cost of factory goods decreased because transportation costs decreased and scale economies in production were realized. Factory employment increased and cities developed around the factories.

    c. Innovations in intracity transportation and construction techniques increased the feasible size of cities.

8. Between 1800 and 1930, the percentage of the U.S. population in cities increased from 6 percent to 56 percent. The pace of urbanization has slowed since World War II. The population in cities rose from 64 percent in 1950 to 75 percent in 1990.

9. In the 1970s, nonmetropolitan areas grew faster than metropolitan areas. In the 1980s, the growth rate for nonmetropolitan areas decreased, restoring the historical pattern of more rapid growth in metropolitan areas.

10. In the 1970s and 1980s, some northern metropolitan areas decreased in population.

Exercises and Discussion Questions

1. Critically appraise: "Innovation in agriculture during the industrial revolution was a necessary, but not sufficient, condition for the urbanization of society."

2. One of the reasons for the decline of the feudal system was the development of professional armies. If you were a feudal lord in the 14th century, would you have hired a professional army and equipped them with crossbows, pikes, muskets, and cannons? Would you have been able to defeat the princes and kings?

3. Some societies never developed any cities. Where did these societies develop? How did they differ from the societies that developed cities?

4. Suppose that you are a citizen of Rome when the first Germanic raid occurs. You have been asked to propose a strategy to respond to the raid (and the expectation that future raids are likely). What's your strategy?

5. The Romans auctioned off the rights to tax their colonies to commercial tax-collecting agencies. In other words, the Romans sold franchises to tax collectors. Might this auction scheme have contributed to the decline of Rome? If you were in charge of the franchising system, what restrictions would you place on the tax collectors?

References and Additional Reading

Alonso, William. "The Population Factor and Urban Structure." In *The Prospective City,* ed. Arthur Solomon. Cambridge, Mass.: MIT Press, 1980. A discussion of recent trends in urbanization.

Davis, Kingsley. "Urbanization." In *The Urban Economy,* ed. Harold Hochman. New York: W. W. Norton, 1976. A brief history of urbanization.

Garnick, Daniel H. "Local Area Economic Growth Patterns: A Comparison of the 1980s and Previous Decades." In *Urban Change and Poverty,* ed. Michael G. McGeary and Lawrence E. Lynn. Washington, D.C.: National Academy Press, 1988. Discusses growth trends in metropolitan and nonmetropolitan areas from 1959 to 1984, and examines the growth rates of the 50 largest metropolitan areas (MSAs and CMSAs) over this period.

Hohenberg, Paul M., and Lynn H. Lees. *The Making of Urban Europe 1000–1950.* Cambridge, Mass.: Harvard University Press, 1985. Discusses the reasons for the urbanization of Europe.

Hoselitz, Bert. "Generative and Parasitic Cities." *Economic Development and Cultural Change* 3 (1955), pp. 278–94. Discusses the effects of parasitic cities on their hinterlands.

Mumford, Lewis. *The City in History.* New York: Harcourt Brace Jovanovich, 1961. A lengthy discussion of the history of urbanization.

Olmstead, Alan, and Eugene Smolensky. *The Urbanization of the United States.* Morristown, N.J.: General Learning Press, 1973.

Pirenne, Henri. *Economic and Social History of Medieval Europe.* New York: Harcourt Brace Jovanovich, 1961. Discusses the role of trade in the rise and decline of medieval cities.

Rosenberg, Nathan, and L. E. Birdzell. *How the West Grew Rich.* New York: Basic Books, 1986. Discusses the transformation of the Western world from the anarchy and autarchy of the Dark Ages to its present state.

Sjoberg, Gideon. "The Origin and Evolution of Cities." In *Cities,* ed. Dennis Flanagan. New York: Alfred A. Knopf, 1965, pp. 25–39.

How Many Cities?

This chapter examines urban development from the regional perspective. In contrast with earlier chapters, which explore the development of individual cities in isolation, this chapter explains how cities develop as integral parts of a larger regional economy. A region supports cities of different size and scope, causing the development of a **regional system of cities.**

Table 5–1 shows the size distribution of urbanized areas in the United States in 1990. In general, the larger the size of the urbanized area, the fewer the urbanized areas of that size. There were three urbanized areas with populations exceeding 6.4 million (New York, Los Angeles, and Chicago), but 172 areas with populations between 50,000 and 100,000. Table 5–1 raises two questions about cities in a regional economy. First, what are the effects of market forces on the equilibrium number of cities? Second, why are some cities larger than others? The answers to these questions are provided by **central place theory.**

The chapter is divided into four sections. The first section shows how firms in a market-oriented industry carve a region into individual **market areas**, and the second shows why some industries have larger market areas than others. The third section uses central place theory to explain how the location patterns of different industries are merged to form a regional system of cities. The final section applies some of the principles of market-area analysis to decision making in the public sector, showing how policymakers could use the principles to choose the optimum number of fire stations, libraries, or hazardous-waste facilities.

The Analysis of Market Areas

Market-area analysis was developed by Christaller (translated in 1966) and refined by Losch (translated in 1954). A firm's *market area* is defined as the area over which the firm can underprice its competitors. The firm's net price is the sum of the price charged by the store and the travel costs incurred by consumers. To explain the notion

TABLE 5–1   **Size Distribution of U.S.**
             Urbanized Areas, 1990

Population of Urbanized Area	Number of Areas
More than 12.8 million	1
6.4 million to 12.8 million	2
3.2 million to 6.4 million	4
1.6 million to 3.2 million	14
800,000 to 1.6 million	19
400,000 to 800,000	33
200,000 to 400,000	52
100,000 to 200,000	99
50,000 to 100,000	172

SOURCE: U.S. Bureau of the Census, *Press Release,*
August 16, 1991.

of a market area, consider a region where consumers buy compact discs (CDs) from music stores. The region has the following characteristics:

1. **Common store price.** All music stores have the same production technology and face the same input prices, so they charge the same price for CDs.
2. **Travel costs.** Every consumer buys one CD per trip to the music store. The travel cost (the monetary and time costs of travel) is 50 cents per round-trip mile.
3. **Shape.** The region is rectangular, 60 miles long and 20 miles wide.

Because music stores sell the same product at the same price, they differ only in location.

Pricing with a Monopolist

Suppose that there is a single music store (owned by Bob) at the center of the region. The net price per CD is the sum of the store price and the consumer's travel cost. Figure 5–1 shows the net price of CDs for consumers living in different parts of the region. If Bob charges $8 per CD, the net price rises from $8 for a household living next to the music store, to $13 for a household living 10 miles from the music store, to $23 for a household 30 miles from the store.

Figure 5–2 shows how the monopolist chooses the profit-maximizing output. The monopolist's demand curve is negatively sloped: as the store price increases, people buy fewer CDs. The negatively sloped demand curve generates a negatively sloped marginal-revenue curve. Profit is maximized where marginal revenue equals marginal cost, so the monopolist produces q_m units of output. If the monopolist sells q_m CDs, the market-clearing price is P_m (the point on the demand curve above q_m). Total profit (revenue less cost) is indicated by the shaded area.

FIGURE 5–1   Net Price of CDs under a Monopoly

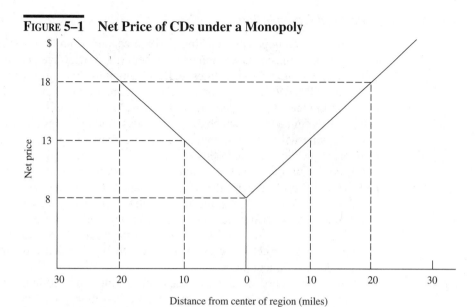

The net price of CDs is the sum of the store price ($8) and the cost of traveling to the music store (50 cents per round-trip mile per CD).

FIGURE 5–2   Price and Quantity with a Single Music Store

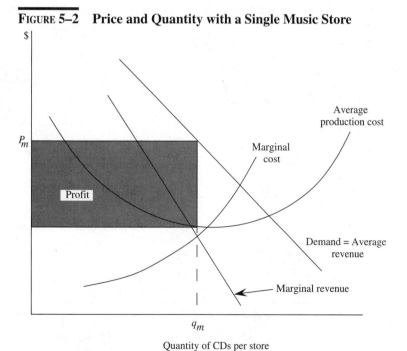

The profit-maximizing output (q_m) is the quantity at which marginal revenue equals marginal cost. The monopoly price is P_m, generating profit equal to the shaded area.

Entry and Competition

Since Bob the monopolist is making positive economic profit, other entrepreneurs will set up new music stores. Some consumers (those who live near the new music stores) will patronize the new stores, so Bob's demand curve shifts to the left: at every price, he will have fewer customers. As his demand curve and marginal-revenue curve shift to the left, his sales volume decreases and his profits fall. In other words, entry causes competition, which decreases sales volume and profit per firm.

How long will entry and the associated decreases in profit continue? Equilibrium occurs when two conditions are satisfied. First, every firm is maximizing its profit, producing the output at which marginal revenue equals marginal cost. Second, economic profit is zero: the store price equals the average total cost of production. Figure 5–3 shows the equilibrium situation. At an output q_e, marginal revenue equals marginal cost (firms are maximizing profit), and the store price P_e equals the average production cost (profits are zero). At the equilibrium output, the marginal revenue curve intersects the marginal-cost curve, and the demand curve is tangent to the average production-cost curve.

This is the theory of **monopolistic competition** (covered in most intermediate microeconomics textbooks). Each music store is a monopolist within its own territory, but its monopoly power is limited by entry and competition. Each store faces a

---

FIGURE 5–3   Equilibrium Price and Quantity of CDs with Entry

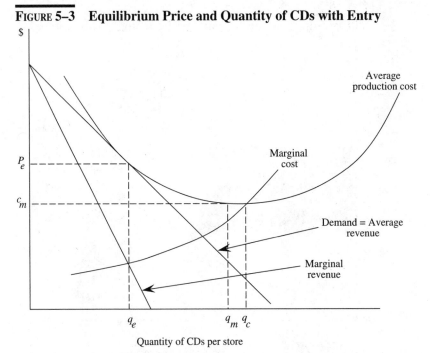

Entry shifts the demand curve of the individual store to the left, decreasing price and profit. Entry continues until profit is zero. The equilibrium output is q_e because marginal revenue = marginal cost (firms are maximizing profit) and profit = average production cost (profit equals zero).

negatively sloped demand curve, and entry shifts the demand curve to the point at which profits are zero. Like a perfectly competitive firm, a firm with a local monopoly earns zero economic profit.

Efficiency Trade-Offs

There are some efficiency trade-offs associated with entry and competition. On the one hand, entry decreases output per firm, so individual firms move upward along their average cost curves. Scale economies are lost since output is divided among a larger number of firms, each of which produces at a higher average cost. On the other hand, the increase in the number of stores decreases travel distances for consumers, decreasing travel costs.

Figure 5–4 shows the trade-offs between production and travel costs. The average total cost of CDs is defined as the sum of average production cost (from Figure 5–3) and average travel cost. Average travel cost is the travel cost incurred by the typical CD consumer. As the output of the music store increases, the market area increases and the typical consumer travels a longer distance to buy CDs. Therefore, the average travel cost increases with the output of the store. Average total cost (production cost plus travel cost) reaches its minimum point at q_t, far below the output that minimizes average production cost (q_c).

FIGURE 5–4   Trade-Offs with Entry: Production Cost versus Travel Cost

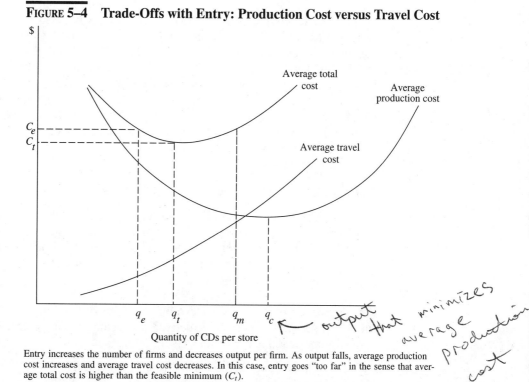

Entry increases the number of firms and decreases output per firm. As output falls, average production cost increases and average travel cost decreases. In this case, entry goes "too far" in the sense that average total cost is higher than the feasible minimum (C_t).

Entry decreases output per firm, generating bad news and good news. The bad news is that average production cost increases as firms move up the average production-cost curve. The good news is that average travel costs decrease as firms move down the average travel-cost curve. Starting from q_m in Figure 5–4, the good news dominates the bad news until output per firm reaches q_t. From that point on, further entry increases production costs by more than it decreases travel costs, so average total cost increases. In equilibrium, the output per firm drops to q_e, meaning that the entry process goes "too far" in the sense that average total cost is higher than the feasible minimum.

Figure 5–4 shows only one possible equilibrium outcome. For different sets of cost and demand curves, the equilibrium output per firm might be greater than q_t or equal to q_t. In other words, unless one knows something about the demand and cost curves, it's impossible to predict exactly where on the average total-cost curve the firm ends up. However, we do know that (1) entry decreases output per firm and (2) in equilibrium, the firm does *not* produce at the minimum point of its average production-cost curve, but at some point to the left of the minimum point.

Market Areas

Figure 5–5 shows the market areas for music stores under the assumption that there are three stores in equilibrium. Tammy and Dick set up music stores 20 miles from Bob and charge the same price for CDs ($6). Compared to Bob, Tammy has a lower net price in the western third of the region, and Dick has a lower net price in the eastern third of the region. The three music stores split the region into three equal market areas, so every store has a circular market area with a 10-mile radius.

The market arrangement in Figure 5–5 has two implications for CD consumers. First, if the spaces between the circular market areas are ignored, the maximum net price is $11, the sum of the price charged by music stores ($6) and the maximum travel cost ($5). Second, every household patronizes the music store closest to its home. All stores charge the same price for the same product, so a household will patronize the store with the lowest travel costs.

Determinants of the Market Area: Fixed Demand

What factors determine the market areas of market-oriented firms? The size of the market area depends on travel costs, per capita demand, population density, and scale economies. This section uses a simple algebraic model to identify the determinants of market areas. At first we assume that the demand for CDs is perfectly inelastic; later we drop this assumption.

An Algebraic Model of the Determinants of Market Area. An expression for the size of the market area can be derived with some simple algebra. The following symbols represent the market for CDs in a region:

d = Monthly per capita demand (number of CDs)
e = Population density (people per square mile)

FIGURE 5–5 Equilibrium Market Areas

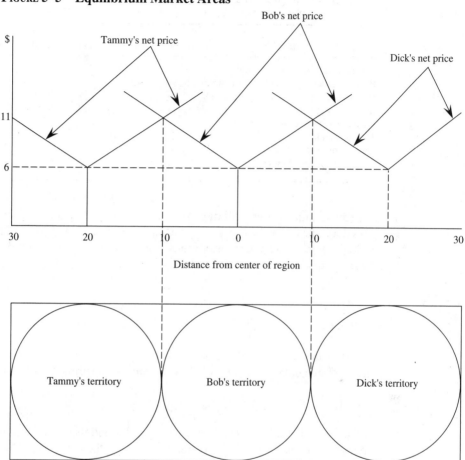

Each store's market area is the area over which its net price is less than the net prices of other stores. Each store has a circular territory with a 10-mile radius.

> A = Land area of the region (square miles)
> q = Output of the typical music store (CDs sold per month)

To simplify matters, per capita demand (d) is assumed to be independent of the net price of CDs: the individual consumer demands a fixed number of CDs, regardless of the net price. In other words, the individual demand curve is perfectly inelastic.

What is the equilibrium number of music stores? The total demand for CDs equals the product of per capita demand (d), population density (e), and the land area of the region (A):

$$Q = d \cdot e \cdot A \qquad (5–1)$$

Table 5–2 provides a numerical example that shows how to compute the equilibrium number of stores. Per capita demand is four CDs and population density is 50 people

TABLE 5–2   Numerical Example of Number of Stores and Market Area

Variable	Symbol	Numerical Example
Per capita demand (number of CDs)	d	4
Population density (people per square mile)	e	50
Demand density (CDs per square mile)	$d \cdot e$	200
Land area (square miles)	A	300
Output per store (CDs sold per month)	q	1,000
Total demand	$Q = d \cdot e \cdot A$	60,000
Number of stores	$N = Q/q$	60
Market area (square miles)	$M = q/(d \cdot e)$	5.0

per square mile, so **demand density** (CD demand per square mile, equal to d times e) is 200. The region has an area of 300 square miles, so total demand is 60,000 CDs (200 times 300). The number of music stores in the region is total demand divided by the output per firm:

$$N = \frac{Q}{q} \qquad (5\text{–}2)$$

Output per firm is 1,000 CDs, so there will be 60 stores in the region (60,000 divided by 1,000).

How large is the market area of music stores? The size of the market area equals the land area of the region divided by the number of firms:

$$M = \frac{A}{N} \qquad (5\text{–}3)$$

If the region has a land area of 300 square miles and there are 60 stores, the market area of the typical store is 5 square miles. Using the expressions for N and Q, the expression for M can be rewritten as

$$M = \frac{q}{d \cdot e} \qquad (5\text{–}4)$$

In other words, the size of the market area is determined by output per store (q), per capita demand (d), and population density (e). In Table 5–2, $q = 1,000$, $d = 4$, and $e = 50$, so the market area is 5.0 square miles.

The algebraic model identifies three factors that determine the size of the firm's market area: per capita demand, population density, and output per store. Output per store is affected by both scale economies and transportation costs. How do changes in each of these variables affect market areas?

Market Area and Scale Economies.   Figure 5–6 shows the effects of an increase in scale economies on the firm's cost curves. An increase in scale economies means that the average production-cost curve is negatively sloped over a larger range of output. Average production cost is minimized at q_4 instead of q_3. Since average total

---

FIGURE 5–6   Increase in Scale Economies Increases Output per Firm

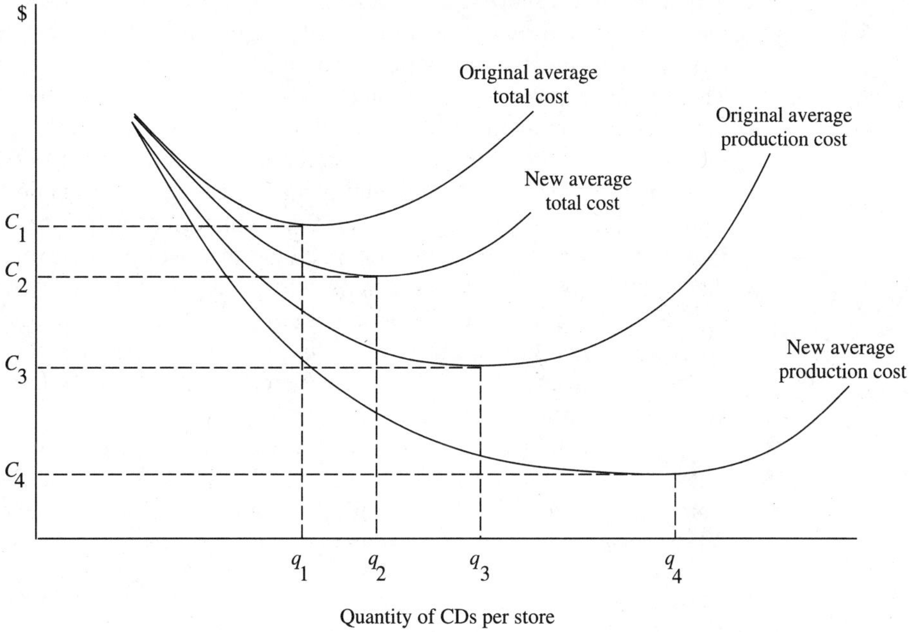

An increase in scale economies shifts the average production-cost curve downward, shifting the average total-cost curve downward. The minimum points of both curves move to the right. If the music store produces at the minimum point of its average total-cost curve, output per store increases from q_1 to q_2.

cost equals average production cost plus average travel cost, an increase in scale economies also shifts the average total-cost curve. Average total cost is minimized at q_2 instead of q_1.

The shift of the cost curves increases output per firm. Although it's impossible to predict exactly how much the firm will produce, it's safe to say its output will increase. One possibility is the firm starts at q_1 (the minimum point of the original average total-cost curve) and moves to q_2 (the new minimum point). If the firm starts with an output close to q_1, it is likely to switch to an output close to q_2. In general, an increase in scale economies increases the advantages of large-scale operations. Starting from q_1, the benefit of increasing output (savings in production costs) will exceed the costs (increase in travel costs), so output per firm will increase.

An increase in scale economies increases the market area of the typical music store. As output per store increases, fewer stores are required to serve the region. Using the numbers in Table 5–2, if output per store increases from 1,000 to 1,200, the number of stores will decrease from 60 to 50 (60,000/1,200). The decrease in the number of stores increases the market area from 5 square miles to 6 square miles (300 divided by 50). Because an increase in scale economies increases output per store, every store needs a larger market area to exploit its scale economies. Note that this result depends on the assumption that per capita demand is fixed, an assumption to be relaxed later in the chapter.

Market Area and Travel Costs.   How does a decrease in travel cost affect the output per store? Suppose the development of a faster, cheaper travel mode decreases the monetary and time costs of travel. In Figure 5–7, the gap between the average total cost and average production is cut in half because travel costs fall by one half. The minimum point of the average total-cost curve moves to the right, increasing the cost-minimizing output from q_5 to q_6. A decrease in travel costs decreases the relative importance of travel costs, so the minimum point of the average total-cost curve moves closer to the minimum point of the average production-cost curve.

The shift of the average total-cost curve increases output per firm. Again, it's impossible to predict exactly how much the firm will produce, but it's safe to say that output increases. If the firm starts with an output close to q_5 (the minimum point on the original average total-cost curve), it is likely to switch to an output close to q_6. In general, a decrease in transport costs increases the advantages of large-scale operations. Starting from q_5, the cost of increasing output will be less than the benefit, so output per firm will increase.

The decrease in travel costs increases the market area because every store needs a larger territory to sell its output. Using the numbers in Table 5–2, if output per store increases from 1,000 to 1,250, the number of stores will decrease from 60 to 48 (60,000/1,250). The decrease in the number of stores increases the market area

---

FIGURE 5–7   Decrease in Travel Costs Increases Output per Firm

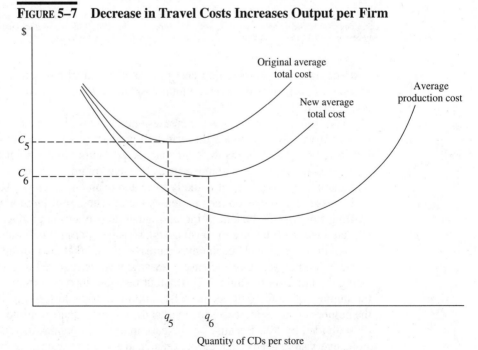

Quantity of CDs per store

A decrease in travel costs shifts the average travel-cost curve downward, shifting the average total-cost curve downward. The minimum point on the ATC curve moves to the right. If the music store produces at the minimum point of its ATC curve, output per store increases from q_5 to q_6.

per store from 5 square miles to 6.25 square miles (300 divided by 48). Because a decrease in travel cost increases output per store, every store needs a larger market area to exploit its scale economies. Again, this result depends on the assumption that per capita demand is fixed, an assumption to be relaxed later in the chapter.

Market Area and Per Capita Demand.   How does an increase in per capita demand affect the size of the market area? An increase in per capita demand increases the demand density (the number of CDs sold per square mile, or d times e). If output per store is fixed, each store needs a smaller market area to exhaust its scale economies. For example, a doubling of per capita demand doubles total demand, so it doubles the number of stores. If there are twice as many stores in the region, the market area per store will be cut in half (from 5 square miles to 2.5 square miles).

Market Area and Population Density.   How does an increase in population density affect the market area? Like an increase in per capita demand, it increases demand density. If output per store is fixed, each store needs a smaller market area to exhaust its scale economies. For example, a quadrupling of population density quadruples total demand for CDs, so it quadruples the number of stores. If there are four times as many stores in the region, the market area per store decreases to one fourth its original size (from 5 square miles to 1.25 square miles).

Market Area and Income.   How do differences in income affect the size of market areas? Consider a region with the following characteristics:

1. There are two cities, a poor one and a wealthy one.
2. A CD is a "normal" good (positive income elasticity of demand).
3. Land is a normal good (positive income elasticity).

The city with the larger demand density will have the smaller market area for music stores. Since both CDs and land are normal goods, the wealthy city has higher per capita demands for both CDs and land: its residents consume more CDs per capita, but also live in relatively low-density housing. For example, the wealthy may live in single-family homes and the poor may live in apartment buildings. In the wealthy city, the larger per capita demand for CDs (which increases demand density) is offset in part by a lower population density (which decreases demand density), so demand density may be either higher or lower. Therefore, the wealthy city may have a smaller or larger market area. The relationship between income and market area is ambiguous because income affects both per capita demand and population density.

Under what circumstances will the wealthy community have a larger market area? Suppose that the income elasticity of demand for land is large relative to the income elasticity of demand for CDs. If so, the density effect (increased income decreases population density) will dominate the demand effect (increased income increases per capita demand), and the wealthy city will have a lower demand density and a larger market area. Music stores will need a larger market area because although each household consumes more CDs, there are many fewer households per square mile.

TABLE 5–3   **Income and Market Area with Different Income Elasticities of Demand for Land**

| | **Poor City** | **Wealthy City** | |
		High Income Elasticity	*Low Income Elasticity*
Income elasticity for land	1.0	1.0	0.25
Per capita income	$1,000	$1,200	$1,200
Per capita demand for CDs (d)	4	4.4	4.4
Population density (e)	50	40	47.5
Demand density ($d \cdot e$)	200	176	209
Output per store (q)	1,000	1,000	1,000
Market area in square miles ($q/d \cdot e$)	5	5.68	4.78

Table 5–3 shows a simple example of how differences in income affect market areas. The income elasticity of demand for CDs is 0.50. In the wealthy city, where per capita income is 20 percent higher, the per capita demand for CDs is 10 percent higher. In the middle column, the income elasticity of demand for land is assumed to be 1.0. Therefore, the wealthy city has a 20 percent higher demand for land and a 20 percent lower population density (40 instead of 50). Given these assumptions, the wealthy city has a lower demand density, so music stores need a larger market area to exploit their scale economies (5.68 square miles instead of 5 square miles).

This result depends, of course, on the numerical assumptions. If the demand for land were relatively income-inelastic, the difference in population density would be relatively small. The demand effect would dominate the density effect, so the wealthy city would have a smaller market area. In the third column of Table 5–3, the income elasticity of demand for land is assumed to be 0.25: population density in the wealthy city is 47.5 (a 5 percent difference) instead of 40; demand density is 209 instead of 176; and the market area is 4.78 instead of 5.68. In general, if the income elasticity for land is small relative to the income elasticity for CDs, the wealthier city will have a smaller market area.

Market Areas and the Law of Demand

Up to this point, the discussion of the market area has assumed that per capita demand is fixed. In other words, the individual demand curve is perfectly inelastic. What happens if consumers obey the law of demand, increasing the quantity of CDs demanded as the net price decreases?

Travel Costs.   To explain the effect of the law of demand on market areas, suppose that travel costs decrease. As explained earlier in the chapter, a decrease in travel costs increases the output per store because the minimum point on the average total-cost curve moves to the right. The market area increases because each store needs a larger territory to sell its output. This is the output effect of a decrease in travel costs.

The decrease in travel costs also decreases the net price of CDs: in Figure 5–7, the net cost decreases from C_5 to C_6. If consumers obey the law of demand, per capita demand will increase, so each firm will need a smaller territory to sell a given output. This is the demand effect of a decrease in travel costs.

The net effect of a decrease in travel cost depends on the relative strengths of the output effect and the demand effect. The expression for the size of the market area is

$$M = \frac{q}{d \cdot e} \tag{5–5}$$

Suppose that the output effect increases q from 1,000 to 1,250 and population density (e) is 50. If the demand effect is relatively weak and d increases from 4 to 5, the market area will grow from 5 square miles (1,000/200) to 6 square miles (1,250/250). Alternatively, if the demand effect is relatively strong and d increases from 4 to 10, the market area will shrink from 5 square miles to 2.5 square miles (1,250/500). The strength of the demand effect depends on the price elasticity of demand for CDs: the more elastic the demand for CDs, the stronger the demand effect. Therefore, a decrease in travel cost is more likely to decrease the market area if the price elasticity is large.

For an example of the effects of changes in travel costs on market areas, consider the effects of parcel post on farm communities. Before the introduction of parcel post in 1913, most farmers purchased most of their goods, including clothing and tools, in general stores in small farm communities. The introduction of parcel post decreased the cost of shipping goods from big-city merchants to farmers. Mail-order houses (Sears Roebuck, Montgomery Ward) underpriced the local general store, and farmers started buying clothing and tools from the mail-order houses. In the year following the introduction of parcel post, the sales of Sears and Montgomery Ward quintupled, and many general stores disappeared.

The introduction of parcel post decreased the cost of transporting clothes and tools, increasing the market area of the typical firm. The general store, with its small market area, was replaced by Sears and Wards, with their large market areas. In this case, the output effect was stronger than the demand effect, so the market area grew. Although farmers consumed more trousers and shovels as the net prices fell, the increases in per capita demands were not large enough to offset the output effect.

Scale Economies.   If consumers obey the law of demand, an increase in scale economies has an ambiguous effect on the size of the market area. As explained earlier in the chapter, an increase in scale economies increases the output per store, increasing the market area required to exhaust scale economies (the output effect). If the net price falls as a result of the increased scale economies, the per capita demand for CDs will increase, generating a demand effect that provides downward pressure on the market area: the firm needs a smaller territory to sell a given output. The net effect of an increase in scale economies depends on the relative strengths of the output effect and the demand effect. If the demand for the good is relatively inelastic, an increase in scale economies will increase the market area.

The Demise of Small Stores

The demise of the small store illustrates the effects of changes in population density and transportation costs on market areas. Before the late 1800s, most goods in the United States were purchased in small stores. People bought food in small "mom and pop" grocery stores and purchased other goods in small general stores. The traditional merchant was involved in every transaction, playing two roles:

1. **Huckster.** The merchant assisted customers in their choice of goods, providing information on alternative products and persuading reluctant customers to buy the good. The merchant was an effective huckster because he knew the features of every good in the store and was a trusted source of information about his products.

2. **Haggler.** The merchant negotiated with each customer over the price of the good. The merchant was an effective haggler because she knew the cost of every good in her store, and could quickly compute her profit margin as she negotiated with the customer. In addition, the merchant was skillful in assessing her customers' willingness to pay for various goods.

Since huckster and haggler skills were not easily transferred to low-skilled employees, the merchant was involved in every transaction, and the traditional store was small.

The replacement of the small general store with larger stores suggests that the optimum store size increased. The optimum size increased for a number of reasons, two of which are related to transportation costs. First, in the late 1800s and early 1900s, innovations in urban transit increased the speed and decreased the monetary costs of intracity travel. Second, rapid urbanization during this same period increased population density, decreasing average travel distances (from home to store). As travel costs decreased, merchants expanded to exploit scale economies in marketing.

As merchants developed larger stores, they adopted new marketing techniques. New advertising and display techniques made the goods "sell themselves." Some stores, such as Macy's and Marshall Field's, used newspaper advertising to inform and persuade consumers. Woolworth's used plate-glass windows to display goods and attract customers. Grocery stores displayed their goods in such a way that consumers could do their own comparison shopping. A grocery store named Piggly Wiggly developed a floor plan that forced customers to walk through a maze from the entrance to the exit. By following the prescribed path from the entrance to the exit, customers were exposed to every commodity in the store, allowing them to make their own choices. These marketing techniques freed the merchant from acting as a huckster. Another new feature was the single-price policy, under which the merchant charged each customer the same price. The single-price policy freed the merchant from haggling.

These two new marketing techniques freed the merchant from being involved in every transaction, allowing an increase in the size of the store. The merchant hired low-skilled laborers to perform the simple tasks of stocking shelves, wrapping goods, and collecting money. A single merchant could run a self-service store with dozens of low-wage employees, and this store could underprice the small traditional store.

Market Areas of Different Industries

Market areas vary from industry to industry, reflecting differences in travel costs, per capita demand, and scale economies. If scale economies are large relative to per capita demand, the industry will have a small number of firms, each of which has a large market area. In contrast, if scale economies are small relative to per capita demand, there will be a large number of firms with small market areas.

Consider the market areas of pizza parlors and Tibetan restaurants. Suppose that both activities are subject to the same sort of scale economies, so the optimum output for both types of restaurants is 200 meals per day. If the total demand for pizza is 10,000 meals per day, the region will have 50 pizza parlors (10,000/200). If the total demand for Tibetan food is 200 meals per day, a single Tibetan restaurant will serve the entire region. The market area is not determined by scale economies per se, but by scale economies relative to per capita demand.

Central Place Theory

Central place theory, which was developed by Christaller (translated in 1966) and refined by Losch (translated in 1954), is used to predict the number, size, and scope of cities in a region. The theory is based on a simple extension of market-area analysis. Market areas vary from industry to industry, depending on scale economies and per capita demand, so every industry has a different location pattern. Central place theory shows how the location patterns of different industries are merged to form a regional system of cities. The theory answers two questions about cities in a regional economy:

1. How many cities will develop?
2. Why are some cities larger than others?

A Simple Central Place Model

Consider a region with three consumer products: CDs, pizzas, and jewelry. The region has the following characteristics:

1. **Population density.** The initial distribution of population is uniform. The total population of the region is 80,000.
2. **No shopping externalities.** As discussed in Chapter 2, shopping externalities normally occur with complementary goods (one-stop shopping) and imperfect substitutes (comparison shopping). The simple central place model assumes that there are no shopping externalities.
3. **Ubiquitous inputs.** All inputs are available at all locations at the same prices.
4. **Uniform demand.** For each product, per capita demand is the same throughout the region.

5. **Number of stores.** The three goods have different per capita demands and scale economies:
   a. **Jewelry.** Scale economies are large relative to per capita demand. Every jewelry store requires a population of 80,000, so a single jeweler will serve the entire region.
   b. **Compact discs.** Scale economies are moderate relative to per capita demand. Every music store requires a population of 20,000, so there will be four music stores in the region.
   c. **Pizza.** Scale economies are small relative to per capita demand. Every pizza parlor requires a population of 5,000, so there will be 16 pizza parlors in the region.

The central place model is a model of **market-oriented** firms, defined in Chapter 3 as firms that base their location decisions exclusively on access to their consumers. Because all inputs are ubiquitous, the firms ignore input costs in their location decisions.

The single jeweler will locate at the center of the region. Because production costs are the same at all locations (all inputs are ubiquitous), the jeweler will minimize its total costs by minimizing its travel costs. According to the principle of median location (discussed in Chapter 3), travel costs are minimized at the median location. Because population density is uniform, the median location is the center of the region. Therefore, the jeweler will locate at the center of the region.

A city will develop around the jewelry store. Jewelry workers will locate near the store to economize on commuting costs. The population density near the jeweler will increase, generating a city (a place of relatively high density) at the center of the region. In Figure 5–8, a city develops at point L.

The music stores will carve up the region into market areas, causing the development of additional cities. If the region's population density were uniform, music firms would carve out four equal market areas. However, because there is a city surrounding the jeweler in the center of the region, there will be enough demand to support more than one music store in city L. If city L along with the surrounding area has enough people to support two music stores, the two other music stores will split the rest of the region into two market areas. In Figure 5–8, two more cities develop at the locations marked with an M.

The pizza parlors will also carve up the region into market areas, causing the development of more cities. Because the population density is higher in the cities that develop around the jewelry store and the music stores, there will be more than one pizza parlor in L and the two M cities. Suppose that L will support four pizza parlors, and each of the M cities will support two pizza parlors. If so, a total of eight pizza parlors will locate in cities L and M. The remaining eight pizza parlors will divide the rest of the region into eight market areas, causing the development of eight additional cities (the places marked with an S in Figure 5–8).

The rectangular region has a total of 11 cities. The large city at the center of the region sells jewelry, CDs, and pizza. City L has a population of 20,000, meaning that it is large enough to support four pizza parlors (5,000 people per pizza parlor). The city sells CDs to consumers from the four surrounding S cities, so the total number of

FIGURE 5–8   The Central Place Hierarchy

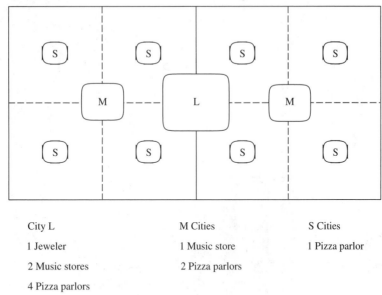

City L	M Cities	S Cities
1 Jeweler	1 Music store	1 Pizza parlor
2 Music stores	2 Pizza parlors	
4 Pizza parlors		

There are 11 cities in the region: one large city (L), two medium-sized cities (M), and eight small cities (S). The larger the city, the greater the variety of goods sold.

CD consumers is 40,000 (20,000 from L and 5,000 each from four S cities), enough to support two music stores. The two medium-sized cities sell CDs and pizza. Each of the M cities has a population of 10,000, meaning that each city is large enough to support two pizza parlors. Each city sells CDs to consumers from two nearby S cities, so the total number of CD consumers in each M city is 20,000 (10,000 from M and 5,000 each from two S cities), enough to support one music store per M city. The eight small cities sell only pizza. Each of the S cities has a population of 5,000, meaning that each city can support one pizza parlor.

Figure 5–9 shows the size distribution of cities in the region. The vertical axis measures city size (population), and the horizontal axis measures the rank of the city. The largest city (L) has a population of 20,000; the 2nd and 3rd largest cities (M cities) have populations of 10,000; and the 4th through the 11th largest cities have populations of 5,000.

The simple central place model generates a **hierarchical system of cities.** There are three distinct types of cities: L (high order), M (medium order), and S (low order). The larger the city, the greater the variety of goods sold. Each city imports goods from higher-order cities and exports goods to lower-order cities. Cities of the same order do not interact. For example, an M city imports jewelry from L and exports CDs to S cities, but does not interact with the other M city. Similarly, an S city imports jewelry from L and CDs from either L or an M city, but does not trade with other S cities. The system of cities is hierarchical in the sense that there are distinct types of cities and distinct patterns of trade dominance.

FIGURE 5–9   **Size Distribution of Cities with Simple Central Place Model**

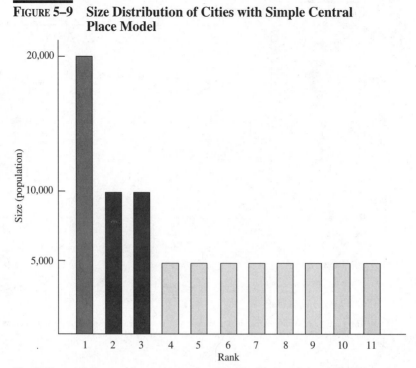

The simple central place model generates one large city (L) with a population of 20,000, two medium-sized cities (M), each of which has a population of 10,000, and eight small cities (S), each of which has a population of 5,000.

Three lessons can be learned from the simple central place model:

1. **Diversity and scale economies.** The region's cities differ in size and scope. This diversity occurs because the three consumer products have different scale economies relative to per capita demand, so they have different market areas. To explain the importance of differences in relative scale economies, suppose that the three goods have the same scale economies relative to per capita demand, so the region has 16 jewelers, 16 music stores, and 16 pizza parlors. The market areas of the three goods would coincide, so the region would have 16 identical cities, each of which provides all three goods. In other words, if there are no differences in scale economies relative to per capita demand, the region's cities will be identical.

2. **Large means few.** The region has a small number of large cities and a large number of small cities. Why isn't there a large number of large cities and a small number of small cities? A city is relatively large if it provides more goods than a smaller city. The extra goods provided by a large city are those goods that are subject to relatively large scale economies. Since there are relatively few stores selling the goods subject

to relatively large scale economies, few cities can be large. In the simple central place model, L is larger than an M city because L sells CDs, pizza, and jewelry. Since there is only one jewelry store in the region, there is only one city larger than the M cities.

3. **Shopping paths.** Consumers travel to bigger cities, not to smaller cities or cities of the same size. For example, consumers from an M city travel to L to buy jewelry, but do not travel to the other M city or an S city to consume CDs or pizza. Instead, they buy CDs and pizza in their own city. Similarly, consumers in S cities travel to larger cities for jewelry and CDs, but do not shop in other S cities.

Relaxing the Assumptions

Several of the assumptions of the simple central place model are unrealistic. This section relaxes some of the assumptions, addressing two questions. First, does a more realistic model generate the same hierarchical pattern of cities? Second, does a more realistic model have more or fewer cities?

Scale Economies, Market Areas, and the Number of Firms.   Suppose that the equilibrium number of pizza parlors decreases from 16 to 8. As explained earlier in the chapter, this would occur if scale economies increased relative to per capita demand, increasing the market area of pizza parlors. The decrease in the number of pizza parlors would decrease the equilibrium number of cities in the region: there would be two pizza parlors in city L and one parlor in each of the M cities, leaving four pizza parlors for the S cities. The equilibrium number of cities would decrease from 11 to 7 because there are fewer cities that provide only pizzas. The hierarchical pattern of cities persists: each city still provides a subset of the goods sold in larger cities.

Shopping Externalities: Imperfect Substitutes.   Suppose that consumers buy used CDs instead of new CDs. Used CDs are imperfect substitutes: consumers engage in comparison shopping, comparing the used CDs from several stores before buying. Therefore, music stores will cluster to facilitate comparison shopping. If the optimum cluster is four music stores, the stores will cluster at the center of the region. The region will have only two types of cities, large ones (with jewelers, music stores, and pizza parlors) and small ones (with pizza parlors). The presence of imperfect substitutes reduces the equilibrium number of cities from 11 to 9 because music stores compromise on their "ideal" (central place) locations to exploit the shopping externalities. Although comparison shopping decreases the number of cities, it does not disrupt the hierarchical pattern of cities.

Shopping Externalities: Complements.   Suppose that pizza and CDs are complementary goods, so that the typical consumer purchases a CD and a pizza on the same shopping trip. If so, music stores and pizza parlors will pair up to facilitate one-stop shopping. If pizza parlors cannot survive without a companion music store, there will be only two types of cities in the region: large (with jewelry, CDs, and pizza) and medium (with CDs and pizza). Pizza parlors compromise on their ideal (central place) locations to exploit the shopping externalities associated with one-stop shopping, so the equilibrium number of cities decreases from 11 to 3. The presence of complementary goods does not, however, disrupt the urban hierarchy.

Variation in Demand.   One of the assumptions of the simple central place model is that per capita demand does not vary with city size. Systematic variation in per capita demand may disrupt the urban hierarchy.

Consider first the possibility that the per capita demand for pizza decreases as city size increases. In other words, per capita demand is large in small cities, moderate in medium-sized cities, and zero in large cities. Alternatively, pizza could be replaced in the example with grits, a good for which per capita demand is higher in small cities. Since there will be no pizza parlors (grits restaurants) in the large city, the urban hierarchy will be disrupted: the medium-sized and the small cities supply goods that are not available in the large city. The variation in demand may also increase the equilibrium number of cities: if the region has the same total pizza demand, all 16 pizza parlors will be outside the largest city (instead of 12), so there will be more than 8 small (pizza-only) cities.

What if the per capita demand increases with city size? Pizza parlors will be more concentrated in medium and large cities: there may be 6 pizza parlors in L and 3 in each type-M city, leaving only 4 of the 16 pizza parlors for small cities. Therefore, there will be a total of 7 cities instead of 11. This type of variation in demand does not, however, disrupt the hierarchy of cities.

Other Types of Industry

Central place theory is applicable to market-oriented firms. The objective of a market-oriented firm is to minimize the travel costs of its consumers. The market-oriented firm is not concerned about (1) the cost of transporting its inputs or (2) the costs of local inputs. Central place theory predicts the pattern of cities that would result if all firms were market-oriented.

As explained in Chapter 3, there are two other types of firms, resource-oriented firms and input-oriented firms. For the resource-oriented firm (e.g., the producer of baseball bats), the cost of transporting raw materials is relatively high, so the firm locates near its input sources. For the input-oriented firm, the costs of local inputs vary across space, and the firm locates near sources of inexpensive labor, energy, or intermediate goods.

The location decisions of resource-oriented firms may disrupt the central place hierarchy. Suppose that a bat factory is located near the coastal forests of the region. Once the coastal city is established, it may attract some market-oriented firms (e.g., pizza parlors). In addition to the three types of cities described above (large, medium, and small) there will be a coastal city, with a bat factory and pizza parlors. The urban hierarchy is disrupted because the coastal city has one activity (bat production) not available in the largest city.

It is possible that the bat factory will not disrupt the region's urban hierarchy. Suppose that the coastal city becomes large enough that it becomes the median location for the jeweler. If so, the coastal city will have all four types of activities (jewelry, bats, CDs, and pizza). The medium-sized cities will have two activities (pizza and CDs), and the small cities will have only one activity (pizzas). In this case, the hierarchy is preserved because the coastal city takes the place of city L.

The same arguments apply to input-oriented activities such as textile firms (labor-oriented), aluminum producers (energy-oriented), corporate headquarters (oriented to intermediate inputs), and firms engaging in research and development (oriented to amenities valued by engineers and scientists). If the input-oriented firm locates near its input source, the resulting city will have some goods that are not available in the largest city. If, however, the resulting city becomes the median location in the region, it may replace city L as the largest city in the region.

Central Place Theory and the Real World

While central place theory is not literally true for many regions, it provides a useful way of thinking about a regional system of cities. The theory identifies the market forces that generate a hierarchical system of cities. It explains why some cities are larger than others, and why the set of goods sold in a particular city is typically a subset of the goods sold in a larger city. Exceptions to the hierarchical pattern result from (1) systematic variation in per capita demand and (2) the location decisions of firms oriented toward raw materials and local inputs.

Empirical Studies of Central Place Systems.   Table 5–4 shows the results of an empirical study of central place theory. Berry and Garrison (1958) examined the economic activities of urban places in Snohomish County, Washington. They concluded that the dozens of communities could be divided into three distinct types of urban places: town (high order), village (medium order), and hamlet (low order). The largest urban place, a town, was about twice as large as a village, which was in turn about twice as large as a hamlet. There were about half as many towns as villages, and about half as many villages as hamlets. As one moves down the hierarchy, the number of establishments and the number of functions decrease, which is exactly what is predicted by central place theory. Berry and Garrison concluded

TABLE 5–4   **The Urban Hierarchy in Snohomish County, Washington**

	Type of Place		
	Town	*Village*	*Hamlet*
Number of places	4	9	20
Average population	2,433	948	417
Average number of establishments per place	149	54.4	6.9
Average number of functions per place	59.8	32.1	5.9
Average number of establishments per function	2.5	1.7	1.2

SOURCE: Brian J. L. Berry and William Garrison, "The Functional Bases of the Central Place Hierarchy," *Economic Geography* 34 (1958), pp. 145–54.

that the system of urban places was indeed hierarchical, with individual communities exporting to lower-order places and importing from higher-order places.

Most of the empirical studies of central place theory examine systems of small towns in agricultural regions. Such regions have little industrial activity, so most firms are oriented toward the local market, not toward natural resources or local inputs. What about the national economy? As explained earlier, the central place hierarchy is disrupted by the location choices of resource-oriented firms and input-oriented firms. Since a large fraction of national employment comes from resource-oriented and input-oriented activities, it would be quite surprising if a study of the national economy provided much support for the simple central place model.

Size Distribution of Cities: The Rank-Size Rule.   Figure 5–10A shows the size distribution of the 25 largest urbanized areas in the United States in 1990. Population decreases from about 16 million in the largest U.S. urbanized area (New York) to 1.32 million in the 25th largest (Norfolk, Virginia). Figure 5–10B shows the size distribution for the 26th through the 396th largest U.S. urbanized areas. (Note that the vertical scale in Figure 5–10B is different from the scale in Figure 5–10A.) Pop-

FIGURE 5–10A   **Size Distribution of 25 Largest U.S. Urbanized Areas**

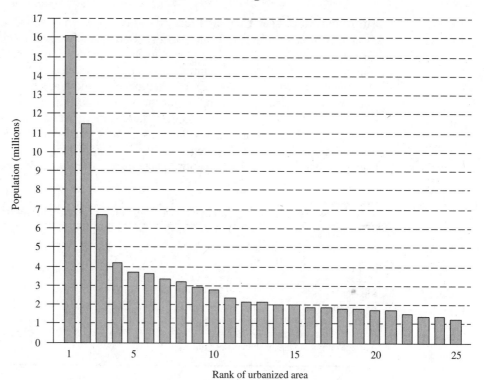

FIGURE 5–10B   **Size Distribution of 26th through 396th Largest U.S. Urbanized Areas**

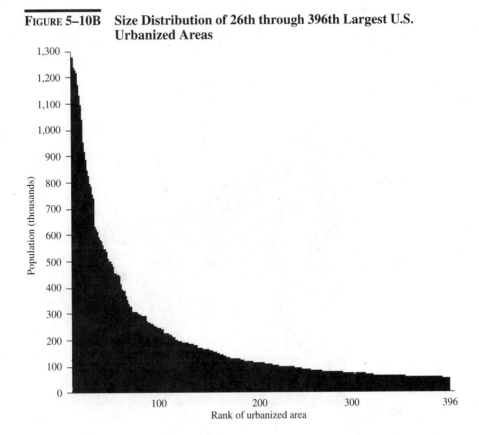

ulation decreases from 1.27 million in the 26th largest metropolitan area (Kansas City) to 50,066 in the smallest urbanized area (Brunswick, Georgia).

How does the U.S. size distribution of cities compare to the size distribution generated by the simple model of central place theory? To compare the two size distributions, compare Figure 5–9 to Figure 5–10. Both figures show a small number of large cities and a large number of small cities. In addition, as one moves down in the ranking (to smaller cities), the size difference between two successive cities decreases.

Geographers and economists have estimated the relationship between city size and rank. The relationship is approximated by the **rank-size rule:**

$$\text{Rank} \cdot \text{Size} = \text{Constant} \qquad (5\text{–}6)$$

This rule suggests that the product of rank and size is the same in all cities in a region. For example, if the largest metropolitan area has a population of 16 million, the rank-size rule suggests that the 2nd largest city has a population of 8 million, the 3rd largest city has a population of 5.33 million, and the 16th largest city has a population of 1 million. Figure 5–11 shows the rank-size relationship for U.S. urbanized areas in

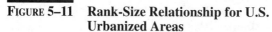

FIGURE 5–11   Rank-Size Relationship for U.S. Urbanized Areas

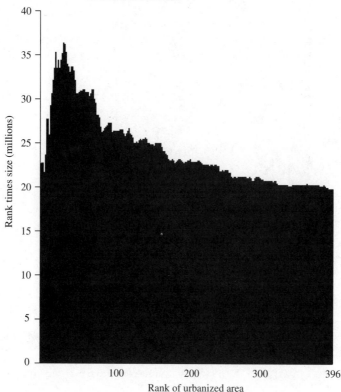

1990. The rank of the urbanized area is on the horizontal axis and the product of rank and size (in millions) is on the vertical axis. The largest deviation from the rank-size rule occurs in cities ranked 10th through 80th; these cities are much larger than would be predicted by the rank-size rule. In general, it does not appear that the size distribution of U.S. urbanized areas satisfies the rank-size rule.

Empirical evidence concerning the rank-size rule comes from statistical studies of city-size distributions. The hypothesized relationship between rank and size is

$$\text{Size} = \frac{\text{Constant}}{\text{Rank}^{\beta}} \qquad (5\text{--}7)$$

The rank-size rule is a good approximation of the relationship between rank and size if β (the exponent of rank) is close to 1.0. Rosen and Resnick (1980) estimated the rank-size relationship for 44 countries. They found substantial variation in β across countries, with an average value of 0.88. This result suggests that population is more evenly distributed between cities than would be predicted by the rank-size rule. Rosen and Resnick conclude that the rank-size rule is only a first approximation to the relationship between rank and size.

Application: Optimum Number of Fire Stations

This final section applies the concepts underlying market-area analysis to decision making in the public sector. A city government could use these concepts to determine the optimum number of public facilities (fire stations, police stations, schools, and public libraries) to provide.

The General Case

Figure 5–12 shows how a city government could use the concepts of market-area analysis to determine the optimum number of fire stations. The horizontal axis measures the number of fire stations, and the vertical axis measures the average cost of fire protection. The average production-cost curve is positively sloped: because of scale economies in fire fighting (indivisible inputs and labor specialization), a large number of small fire stations is more expensive, on average, than a small number of large stations. The average transportation-cost curve is negatively sloped: as the number of stations increases, travel time from the nearest station to a fire decreases, so the damage from fire decreases. The average total cost equals the sum of average production cost and average travel cost. As shown in Figure 5–12, the average total-cost curve is U-shaped.

Suppose that the city's objective is to minimize the average total cost of fire protection service. Starting from a single station, the city should increase the number

FIGURE 5–12   Optimum Number of Fire Stations

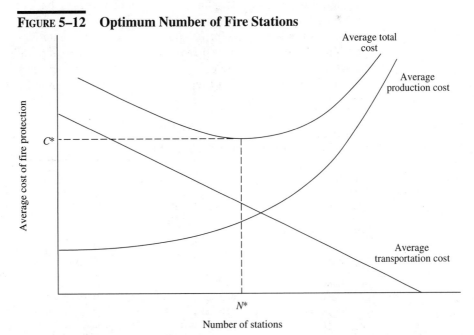

The average total cost of fire protection (the sum of average production cost and average transportation cost) is minimized with 15 facilities.

of stations as long as the decrease in average transportation cost exceeds the increase in average production cost. The city trades off scale economies in production (which favor a small number of large stations) and transportation costs (which favor a large number of small stations). In Figure 5–12, the cost-minimizing number of stations is N^*, and the average total cost of fire protection is C^*.

A Numerical Example

This section provides a numerical example of the use of market-area analysis for choosing the number of fire stations. Consider a city with the following character-istics:

1. **Frequency of fires.** The city expects 10 fires per year, distributed evenly throughout the city.
2. **Fire station options.** The city has three policy options: It will build 1, 4, or 10 fire stations.

The costs of three options are listed in Table 5–5. The total operating cost of the city's fire protection program increases with the number of fire stations, from $10,000 for 1 station to $40,000 for 10 stations. The average operating cost, equal to total operating cost divided by the expected number of fires, rises from $1,000 for 1 station to $4,000 for 10 stations.

Consider next the costs of property damage from fires. The response time of the fire department is the amount of time between the call for help and the arrival of the fire truck. An increase in the number of fire stations means that every house is closer to a fire station, so the average response time decreases. In Table 5–5, the response time drops from 11 minutes for 1 station to 2 minutes for 10 stations. Suppose that the typical fire generates property damage of $300 per minute of burning. If the city has a single station, the average property damage (property damage per fire) is $3,300 (11 minutes times $300). The average property damage drops to $1,500 for 4 stations and $600 for 10 stations.

TABLE 5–5   Costs of Different Fire Station Schemes

	1 Station	*4 Stations*	*10 Stations*
Total operating cost ($)	10,000	20,000	40,000
Average operating cost ($)	1,000	2,000	4,000
Response time (minutes)	11	5	2
Average damage per fire ($)	3,300	1,500	600
Average total cost ($)	4,300	3,500	4,600

Definitions:
1. Average operating cost = Total operating cost divided by 10 fires per year.
2. Average damage per fire = Response time times $300 property damage per minute.
3. Average total cost = Average operating cost + Average damage per fire.

Suppose that the city's objective is to minimize the average total cost of fires. The average total cost is the sum of the average operating cost and the average property damage. Given the assumptions about operating costs, response times, and property damage, the four-station option has the lowest average total cost ($3,500). As the city moves from the one-station option to the four-station option, there is good news and bad news. The good news is that the faster response time cuts property damage from $3,300 to $1,500, a savings of $1,800. The bad news is that the average operating cost increases by $1,000. Since the savings in property damage exceeds the increase in operating cost, the four-station option is more efficient than the one-station option. As the city moves from the four-station option to the 10-station option, the savings in property damage ($900) is smaller than the increase in operating cost ($2,000), so the four-station option is more efficient than the 10-station option.

Using Market-Area Analysis

Suppose that the policy analyst wanted to estimate the optimum number of other public facilities. How would the analyst compute the average transportation costs for other public services? For police services, the average transportation cost is determined by the response time of police: the larger the number of stations, the quicker the response and the lower the social costs of crime. In the case of libraries, the average transportation cost is the average travel costs for library patrons. As the number of libraries increases, the average distance from patrons' houses to libraries decreases, so travel costs decrease.

Do cities really base their facility decisions on this kind of formal analysis of average production costs and average transportation costs? Perhaps not. They do, however, consider the trade-offs between production costs and accessibility, usually in an informal way. The purpose of this section is to show how a formal analysis would proceed, providing a framework for addressing the issue of the optimum number of facilities.

Summary

1. The net price of a retail product is the sum of its price and consumers' travel costs. The market area is the area over which the firm offers the lowest net price.

2. Market-oriented firms are involved in monopolistic competition. Each has a local monopoly, but its monopoly power is limited by entry and competition from other firms.
   a. In equilibrium, every firm makes zero economic profit.
   b. The entry process decreases travel costs but increases average production costs.
   c. In equilibrium, each firm produces along the negatively sloped portion of its average production-cost curve.

3. The size of a firm's market area depends on output per firm, per capita demand, and population density. The market area increases as
   a. Output per firm increases.
   b. Per capita demand decreases.
   c. Population density decreases.

4. Because an increase in scale economies increases output per firm (the output effect) and per capita demand (demand effect), it has an ambiguous effect on market area.

5. A decrease in transportation costs increases output per firm and per capita demand. The market area will grow if the price elasticity of demand is relatively small.

6. Central place theory, which is based on market-area analysis, predicts that the regional system of cities will be hierarchical, with a small number of large cities and a large number of small cities. The set of goods sold in smaller cities will be a subset of the goods sold in larger cities.

7. If the assumptions of the simple central place theory are relaxed to allow imperfect substitutes (comparison shopping) and complements (one-stop shopping), the equilibrium number of cities may decrease, but the urban hierarchy will not be disrupted.

8. If the assumptions of the simple central place theory are relaxed to allow variation in per capita demand, the equilibrium number of cities may change and the urban hierarchy may be disrupted.

9. Central place theory is not applicable to resource-oriented firms and firms oriented toward local inputs. The introduction of such firms into the central place model may disrupt the urban hierarchy.

10. The rank-size rule suggests that the product of city rank and city size (population) is constant. A study of the rank-size relationship for 44 countries suggests that population is more evenly distributed between cities than would be predicted by the rank-size rule.

11. The concepts of market-area analysis could be used by policymakers to determine how many public facilities (fire stations, public libraries, schools, police stations) to provide. Market-area analysis shows the trade-offs between production costs and scale economies.

Exercises and Discussion Questions

1. The discussion of the market area of music stores assumed that Bob, Tammy, and Dick had the same production costs. As a result, each household patronized the store nearest its home. Suppose that Bob discovers a new way of marketing CDs that cuts his production cost (and store price) in half, from $6 to $3. Tammy and Dick continue to sell CDs for $6.
   a. How does the decrease in production cost affect Bob's market area?

   b. What is the net price at the border between Bob's and Tammy's market area?

   c. Will each household still patronize the firm closest to its residence?

2. Consider the market area of food stores in a region described by the following assumptions:

   i. The per capita demand for food is 30 units.

   ii. Population density is 40 people per square mile.

   iii. The land area of the region is 100 square miles.

   iv. The output of the typical food store is 6,000 units.

   a. How many food stores will there be in the region?

   b. How large is the market area of the typical food store?

3. Consider the market areas of hardware stores in two independent regions, Low and High. The average production-cost (APC) curves of the two regions reach their minimum points at the same level of output (1,000 units), but because Low has lower input costs, the minimum point of its APC curve has a lower average cost (the average cost of 1,000 units is $1 instead of $2). Will the market area in Low be larger, smaller, or the same as the market area in High? If you don't have enough information to answer the question, indicate what additional information you need and how you would use it.

4. Consider a regional economy with two cities. The two cities have the same population, but the average household income in city H exceeds that in city L. The residents of H and L consume Y. The characteristics of Y are as follows:

   i. The average production-cost (APC) curve is U-shaped.

   ii. The APC curve is the same at all locations.

   iii. Y is a standardized product, with no close substitutes or complements.

   iv. All households have the same tastes for Y.

   v. Y is inferior (negative income elasticity).

   a. How will the size of the average market area of Y in city H compare to the size of the average market area in city L?

   b. How would your response to (a) differ if the APC curve were a horizontal line?

5. Suppose that you intend to purchase the franchise rights for a pizza parlor. The franchiser has divided your region into two areas of equal size: H is a high-income area, and L is a low-income area. Suppose that the income elasticity of demand for pizza is zero: the consumption of pizza is independent of income. The income elasticity of demand for land is 1.0. Your objective is to maximize the quantity of pizzas sold.

   a. Which of the two franchises will you choose?

   b. How would your response to (a) change if the income elasticity of demand for pizza is 1.5?

6. In the example based on the data in Table 5–3, the implicit assumption is that travel costs were the same in the two cities. Suppose that the opportunity

cost of travel is higher in the wealthy city. How might this change the market areas in the wealthy city?

7. Consider the city of Vidville, where initially all video consumers travel to video outlets to rent videos. Suppose that when the video outlets offer home delivery, all video consumers switch to home delivery.

   a. Under what circumstances is the switch to home delivery rational?

   b. In what type of cities would you expect home delivery to be efficient?

8. In 1930, most rural children walked to school. By 1980, most of them rode school buses. Would you expect the average "market area" of rural schools to increase or decrease as a result of the school bus?

9. The introduction of parcel post decreased transportation costs and increased the market area of the typical firm. Can you think of any good for which a decrease in transportation costs is likely to decrease the market area?

10. In the city of Metro, retail firms locate either in the central area of the city or in one of the suburban subcenters. There are two retail goods sold in the city, A and B. The per capita demands for the two goods are equal. The scale economies associated with the production and sale of A are large relative to the scale economies associated with B. Where in the city will the firms selling A and B locate?

11. Consider a city with a uniform distribution of population where every household consumes the same number of video rentals. The city is two miles long and two miles wide. The mayor recently stated her policy for the location of video rental outlets: "A video outlet reaches the minimum point of its average production-cost curve at an output of 1,000 units. Since the total demand for video rentals is 4,000 units, we should have four video outlets. Since the distribution of population is uniform, the video outlets should be distributed uniformly throughout the city, with every outlet at the center of a one-square-mile market area." Comment on the mayor's policy. Will it lead to an efficient distribution of video outlets?

12. In the city of Zone, the actual number of grocery stores is less than the number that would occur in the absence of zoning. A recent survey of grocery prices suggests that Zone consumers pay less for groceries than people in a similar city without zoning. For example, the prices of Spam and Velveeta are 5 percent less in Zone.

    a. Is there any reason to doubt the validity of the survey?

    b. Suppose that the survey is valid. Does the zoning policy make the residents of Zone better or worse off?

13. A developer has requested a permit to build a drugstore in a rapidly growing part of your city. Your mission is to figure out whether the new drugstore is appropriate. What information do you need, and how would you use it?

14. Explain why poor areas of cities typically are served by small grocery stores, not by large grocery-store chains.

15. Consider a region in which all firms are market-oriented (all employment is in retail outlets). There are no shopping externalities, and all retail activities

are subject to the same degree of internal scale economies. In the last 10 years, the region's rank-size curve (with city rank on the horizontal axis and city size on the vertical axis) has become flatter.

a. What changes in market areas are lurking behind the flattening of the rank-size curve?

b. Provide an explanation for the changes in the market areas lurking behind the flattening of the rank-size curve.

16. Mr. Wizard, a regional planner, recently made the following statement: "If my assumptions are correct, all cities in this region will eventually be identical. They will be the same size and will sell the same set of goods."

a. Assuming that Mr. Wizard's reasoning is correct, what are his assumptions?

b. Are Mr. Wizard's assumptions realistic?

17. In the example based on the data in Table 5–5, the city had three fire station options (1, 4, or 10 fire stations). Suppose that two additional options appear. If the city builds six stations, the total operating cost will be $28,000, and the response time will be three minutes. If the city builds three stations, the total operating cost will be $15,000 and the response time will be six minutes. Given these two additional options, how many fire stations should the city build?

18. Consider the region of Readland, where every person makes one trip per month to the nearest public library. City H has a higher per capita income than city L. The two cities have the same total population and land area. Which city would you expect to have more public libraries?

19. Consider two cities with the same total population and land area. City H has higher per capita income than city L. Land, housing, and household possessions (things in the dwelling) are all normal goods: all three goods have positive income elasticities of demand.

a. Is the assumption of equal population density realistic? If land is a normal good, is it possible to have higher per capita income and the same population density?

b. Which city will have more fire stations?

20. Consider a city that must decide how many libraries to provide. The city assumes the travel cost is 10 cents per library trip per mile. The table below lists the average production costs (APC) and average distances to library patrons (AD) for different numbers of libraries.

Number of Libraries	APC	AD
1	$0.30	20
3	$0.40	10
5	$0.50	7
9	$0.90	4
11	$1.20	2

   a. If the city's objective is to minimize the average total cost of a library
       trip, and the city must choose from the options listed in the table, how
       many libraries should it provide?
   b. If the unit travel cost doubles, how many libraries should the city provide?

21. In Figure 5–12, the optimum number of facilities is 15 and the average
    total cost of public services is C^*. Use graphs to explain the effects of the
    following events on the optimum number of facilities and the average cost
    of public services.
    a. Transportation costs are cut in half.
    b. The city discovers a way to avoid the duplication of some equipment.
        The slope of the average production-cost curve decreases.

22. Some people claim that state capitals (e.g., Sacramento, California; Salem,
    Oregon; Olympia, Washington) are boring cities. Specifically, it is claimed
    that these cities have fewer goods than one finds in other cities of equal
    size. After checking a map to see where each of these capital cities is
    located, use central place theory to explain why they might be considered
    boring.

References and Additional Readings

General Discussions of Central Place Theory

Beckmann, M. J. "City Hierarchies and the Distribution of City Size." *Economic
    Development and Cultural Change* 7 (1958), pp. 243–48.
Christaller, Walter. *Central Places in Southern Germany,* trans. C. W. Baskin. Engle-
    wood, N.J.: Prentice Hall, 1966. The classic piece on central place theory.
Hamilton, Bruce W. "Market Failure in the Land of Losch." *Journal of Urban
    Economics* 12 (1989), pp. 143–55. Discusses the efficiency properties of spatial
    competition.
Hoover, Edgar M. *An Introduction to Regional Economics.* New York: Alfred A. Knopf,
    1975. Chapter 6, "The Location of Urban Places."
———. "Transport Costs and the Spacing of Central Places." *Papers of the Regional
    Science Association* 25 (1970), pp. 255–74. Discusses the effects of changes in
    transport costs on the size of the market area.
King, Leslie J. *Central Place Theory.* Beverly Hills, Calif.: Sage, 1984. A thorough dis-
    cussion of central place theory and its implications. Includes a careful discussion of
    the origins of central place theory.
Losch, August. *The Economics of Location.* New Haven, Conn.: Yale University Press,
    1954. A refinement of central place theory.
Mills, Edwin S., and Michael R. Lav. "A Model of Market Areas with Free Entry."
    Journal of Political Economy 72 (1964), pp. 278–88. Discusses the shapes of
    market areas.
"The Nature of Economic Regions." In *Regional Development and Planning: A Reader,*
    ed. John Friedman and William Alonso. Cambridge, Mass.: MIT Press, 1964. Dis-
    cusses the roles of scale economies and transport costs in determining the market
    area of the firm.

Noyelle, Thierry, and Thomas Stanback. *The Economic Transformation of American Cities.* Totawa, N.J.: Rowman and Allanheld, 1984. Discusses exceptions to the central place framework.

Parr, J. B. "Growth Poles, Regional Development, and Central Place Theory." *Papers of the Regional Science Association* 3 (1973(a)), pp. 173–212.

———. "Structure and Size in the Urban System of Losch." *Economic Geography* 49 (1973b), pp. 185–212.

Parr, J. B., and K. G. Denike. "Theoretical Problems in Central Place Analysis." *Economic Geography* 46 (1970), pp. 568–80.

Philbrick, Allen. "Areal Functional Organization in Regional Geography." *Papers of the Regional Science Association* 3 (1957), pp. 87–98. Describes the hierarchy of urban places.

Empirical Tests of Central Place Theory

Berry, Brian J. L. *Geography of Market Centers and Retail Distribution.* Englewood, N.J.: Prentice Hall, 1967. Discusses central place theory, including a review of empirical tests of the theory.

Berry, Brian J. L., and William L. Garrison. "The Functional Bases of the Central Place Hierarchy." *Economic Geography* 34 (1958), pp. 145–54. An empirical analysis of central place theory.

Lloyd, Peter E., and Peter Dicken. *Location in Space: A Theoretical Approach to Economic Geography.* New York: Harper & Row, 1977. Reviews empirical work on central place theory.

Preston, Richard E. "The Structure of Central Place Systems." In *Systems of Cities,* ed. L. S. Bourne and J. W. Simmons. New York: Oxford University Press, 1978, pp. 185–206. Empirical analysis of central place theory in the Pacific Northwest.

Rosen, Kenneth T., and Mitchell Resnick. "The Size Distribution of Cities: An Examination of the Pareto Law and Primacy." *Journal of Urban Economics* 8 (1980), pp. 165–86. Estimates the rank-size relationship and concludes that the rank-size rule is a poor approximation to the true size distribution.

Central Place Theory and Intraurban Distribution of Activity

Carol, H. "The Hierarchy of Central Functions within the City." *Annals of the Association of American Geographers* 50 (1960), pp. 419–38. Applies central place theory to the location of activities within cities.

Proudfoot, M. J. "The Outlying Business Centers of Chicago." *Journal of Land and Public Utility Economics* 13 (1937), pp. 57–70. Applies central place theory to the location of activities within cities.

Weiss, Leonard. "The Geographic Size of Markets in Manufacturing." *Review of Economics and Statistics* 54 (1972), p. 245.

Technology and the Urban Hierarchy

Berry, Brian J. L. "Hierarchical Diffusion: The Basis of Developmental Filtering and Spread in a System of Growth Centers." In *Growth Centers in Regional Economic Development,* ed. N. M. Hansen. New York: Free Press, 1972. Discusses how innovations are first utilized in large cities and then spread to urban areas lower on the urban hierarchy.

Huang, J. C., and P. Gould. "Diffusion in an Urban Hierarchy: The Case of Rotary Clubs." *Economic Geography* 50 (1974), pp. 333–40. Discusses how new organizations are first established in large cities and then spread to urban areas lower on the urban hierarchy.

Public Facilities

Dear, Michael. "Planning for Mental Health Care: A Reconsideration of Public Facility Location." *International Regional Science Review* 3 (1978), pp. 93–111.

Getz, Malcolm. *The Economics of the Urban Fire Department.* Baltimore: Johns Hopkins, 1979. Estimates the relationship between the density of stations and losses from fires. The elasticity of losses with respect to the number of stations per square mile is −0.70.

CHAPTER

6 Urban Economic Growth

An economic forecaster is like a cross-eyed javelin thrower: he doesn't win many accuracy contests, but he keeps the crowd's attention.
Anonymous

Earlier chapters have shown why cities exist and where they develop. This chapter takes a closer look at the economy of a particular city, exploring the market forces that determine the size of the economy. The first part of the chapter uses a simple model of the urban labor market to describe the economic growth process. If *economic growth* is defined as an increase in total employment, growth results from an increase in the demand for labor (caused by an increase in the demand for the goods produced in the city) or an increase in labor supply (caused by migration to the city).

The second part of the chapter explores the effects of various public policies on urban economic growth. The public sector can influence both sides of the urban labor market. For example, the provision of local public services such as schools, parks, and public safety increases the relative attractiveness of the city, causing in-migration that increases the supply of labor. On the demand side, the provision of industrial infrastructure such as roads and sewer systems decreases production costs and attracts firms. A city's tax policy also affects the supply and demand for labor: an increase in residential taxes decreases labor supply, and an increase in business taxes decreases labor demand.

The third part of the chapter describes two techniques used to forecast urban economic growth. Both forecasting techniques (the economic base study and input-output analysis) suffer from a number of conceptual problems that limit their applicability and accuracy. Nonetheless, they are the most frequently used—and abused—forecasting techniques, and a clear understanding of their strengths and limitations is useful for both policymakers and firms. Local governments use these techniques to generate economic forecasts that are then used to project the demands for local public services, and firms use the same type of economic forecasts to project the demands for their products.

125

The fourth part of the chapter explores the effects of employment growth on other measures of economic welfare, including the city's unemployment rate, its labor-force participation rate, and per capita income. This part of the chapter addresses two questions. First, when a city grows, what fraction of the new jobs are filled by newcomers, and what fraction are filled by original residents who would otherwise not be employed? Second, how does employment growth affect real income per capita?

The fifth part of the chapter presents facts concerning the composition of changes in total employment. The net change in total employment in a particular city can be divided into four components: jobs gained from the opening of new plants, jobs gained from the expansion of existing plants, jobs lost from plant closings, and jobs lost from the contraction of existing plants. This part of the chapter addresses the following question: do cities that grow rapidly have relatively large employment gains (from openings and expansions) or relatively small losses (from closures and contractions)? The discussion of the composition of changes in employment sets the stage for the final part of the chapter, which discusses plant-closure legislation.

The Urban Labor Market and Economic Growth

This part of the chapter describes a model of the urban labor market for a city that is part of a larger regional economy. The model is a long-run model in the sense that it assumes that households and firms can move freely between cities in the region. In the long run, each household lives in the city that maximizes its utility, and each firm locates in the city that maximizes its economic profit. As explained later in the chapter, the long-run mobility of households has important implications for the effects of employment growth on the welfare of the original residents of the city.

Suppose that the size of an urban economy is defined in terms of total employment. Figure 6–1 shows the supply and demand curves for the city's labor market. The equilibrium wage is $1,000 per month and equilibrium employment is 50,000 laborers. Economic growth, defined here as an increase in total employment, results from either an increase in demand (a rightward shift of the demand curve) or an increase in supply (a rightward shift of the supply curve).

The Demand for Labor

Labor demand comes from two types of activities. The **export** or **basic sector** sells its products to consumers outside the city. Examples of export firms are steel producers and computer manufacturers. In contrast, the **local** or **nonbasic sector** sells its products to consumers within the city. Examples of local producers are bakeries, bookstores, and local schools. Before discussing the city's labor-demand curve, it will be useful to explain the relationship between these two employment sectors.

The Multiplier Process.   Because export workers spend part of their income on local goods, an increase in export sales increases local sales. Table 6–1 shows the **multiplier effects** of a $100,000 increase in export sales. In round 1, the increase in

FIGURE 6–1   The Urban Labor Market

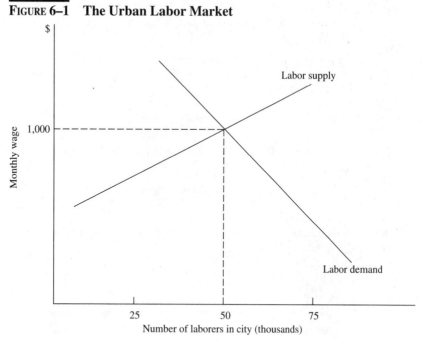

The labor market is in equilibrium if supply equals demand. The equilibrium wage is $1,000 per month, and the equilibrium number of laborers is 50,000.

export sales is paid out to workers, capitalists, and landowners in the form of wages, interest, and land rent, so local income increases by $100,000. If 60 percent of the increased income is spent on local goods, local consumption increases by $60,000. The first-round increase in local consumption is the second-round increase in local income: local producers pay the $60,000 to their workers, capitalists, and landowners. Because 60 percent of the increased income is spent on local goods, the second round increase in local consumption is $36,000. The spending and respending of income continues forever, but every spending round is smaller than the previous one because 40 percent of income is spent on imports.

The increase in the city's total income exceeds the original increase in export income. The marginal propensity to consume locally (*m*) is the fraction of income

TABLE 6–1   Increases in Local Spending from Increased Export Sales

Increase in	Round 1	Round 2	Round 3		Total
Local income	$100,000	$60,000	$36,000	...	$250,000
Local consumption	60,000	36,000	21,600	...	150,000
Imports	40,000	24,000	14,400	...	100,000

spent locally (0.60 in Table 6–1). If the original change in export sales is ΔX, the increase in total income is the sum of the income changes from a series of spending rounds:

$$\Delta \text{Total income} = \Delta X + m \cdot \Delta X + m^2 \cdot \Delta X + m^3 \cdot \Delta X + m^4 \cdot \Delta X + \ldots \quad (6\text{–}1)$$

The change in total income is the sum of an infinite series, and can be rewritten as

$$\Delta \text{Total income} = \Delta X \cdot \frac{1}{1 - m} \quad (6\text{–}2)$$

The **income multiplier** is defined as the change in total income per unit change in export sales:

$$\frac{\Delta \text{Total income}}{\Delta X} = \frac{1}{1 - m} \quad (6\text{–}3)$$

For example, if the marginal propensity to consume locally (m) is 0.60, the multiplier is

$$\frac{\Delta \text{Total income}}{\Delta X} = \frac{1}{1 - 0.60} = 2.5 \quad (6\text{–}4)$$

For every additional dollar of export sales, total income increases by 2.5 dollars. In Table 6–1, export sales increase by $100,000, so local production increases by $150,000 and total income increases by $250,000.

The multiplier process also affects employment. The **employment multiplier** is the change in total employment per unit change in export employment. If there is one job per $1,000 of sales, an increase of $100,000 in export sales will increase export employment by 100 jobs. Similarly, the additional $150,000 in local sales will increase local employment by 150 jobs. Total employment in the city will increase by 250, meaning that the employment multiplier is 2.5.

The employment multiplier is the same as the income multiplier because the sales volume is assumed to be the same in both sectors. If sales volume per local jobs is less than sales volume per export jobs, the employment multiplier exceeds the income multiplier because more local jobs will be supported by a given amount of sales. For example, if sales volume per local jobs is $500 instead of $1,000, local employment would increase by 300 instead of 150, and the employment multiplier would be 4.0 instead of 2.5. Conversely, if sales volume per local job exceeds $1,000, the employment multiplier would be less than the income multiplier.

A second method for computing the employment multiplier uses data on the composition of the work force. If B is the number of jobs in export industries and L is the number of jobs in local industries, total employment in the city is $B + L$, or T. The ratio (L/B) indicates how many local jobs are "supported" by each export job. For example, if $B = 20,000$ and $L = 30,000$, an economic "base" of 20,000 jobs supports 30,000 local jobs. Each export job supports 1.5 local jobs. The employment multiplier, defined as the change in total employment per additional export job, is

$$\frac{\Delta T}{\Delta B} = \frac{T}{B} = 2.5 \quad (6\text{–}5)$$

Every additional export job increases total employment by 2.5 jobs: in addition to the export job, there are 1.5 new "support" jobs in local industry.

The Labor-Demand Curve.   The city's labor-demand curve is negatively sloped for two reasons. First, as the city's wage increases, both exporters and local producers substitute capital for the relatively expensive labor. This is the **substitution effect**: an increase in the wage causes factor substitution that decreases the quantity of labor demanded. In other words, an increase in the wage causes firms to substitute nonlabor inputs (capital, land, raw materials) for labor. Second, as the city's wage increases, production costs increase, increasing the prices charged by the city's firms. As the prices of exports increase, the quantity of exports demanded decreases, so exporters need fewer workers. As the prices of local goods increase, city residents substitute imports for the relatively expensive local goods, so local firms need fewer laborers. This is the **output effect**: an increase in the city's wage increases prices and decreases output, decreasing the quantity of labor demanded. The demand curve is negatively sloped because an increase in wages generates both a substitution effect and an output effect.

What determines the slope of the demand curve? In other words, how rapidly does labor demand fall as the wage increases? The larger the substitution effect and the output effect, the greater the responsiveness of labor demand to changes in the wage, so the flatter the demand curve. If both the substitution effect and the output effect are relatively large, a given change in the wage will cause a relatively large decrease in the quantity of labor demanded, meaning that the demand curve will be relatively flat. The substitution effect will be relatively large if firms can easily substitute nonlabor inputs for labor. The output effect could be relatively large for two reasons. First, if labor costs are responsible for a relatively large share of total costs, the output price will be sensitive to changes in the wage: a small increase in the wage will cause a relatively large increase in the output price and thus a relatively large decrease in total production. Second, if the price elasticity of demand for the output is relatively large, a given increase in the output price will cause a relatively large decrease in total production. To summarize, the demand curve will be relatively flat if (1) labor and nonlabor inputs are good substitutes, (2) labor costs are a relatively large fraction of total costs, and (3) the demand for the city's output is relatively elastic.

What causes the demand curve to shift to the right or the left? The following factors determine the position of the curve:

1. **Demand for exports**. An increase in the demand for the city's exports increases export production and shifts the demand curve to the right: at every wage, more workers will be demanded.
2. **Labor productivity**. An increase in labor productivity decreases production costs, allowing export firms to cut prices and increase output. Although firms need fewer workers to produce a given amount of output, the decrease in price means that firms produce more output. If the increase in output is relatively large (if the price elasticity of demand for the city's output is relatively large), the demand for export workers

increases: the demand curve shifts to the right. Similarly, an increase in labor productivity allows local producers to underprice imports, increasing the demand for local workers. One way to increase productivity is to improve the quality of local public education.

3. **Business taxes**. An increase in business taxes (without a corresponding change in public services) increases production costs and decreases output, so the demand curve shifts to the left. The demand for labor decreases as export firms lose customers to exporters in other cities and local firms lose customers to importers. As discussed in Chapter 3, there is solid evidence that an increase in business taxes decreases business activity and thus decreases the demand for labor.

4. **Industrial public services**. An increase in the quality of industrial public services (without a corresponding increase in taxes) decreases production costs and increases output, so the demand curve shifts to the right. The demand for labor increases as export firms gain customers from exporters in other cities and local firms gain customers from importers. As discussed in Chapter 3, there is solid evidence that improvements in local infrastructure increase business activity and thus increase the demand for labor.

5. **Land-use policies**. Industrial firms require production sites that (*a*) are accessible to the intracity and intercity transportation networks and (*b*) have a full set of public services (water, sewerage, electricity). By coordinating its land-use and infrastructure policies to ensure an adequate supply of industrial land, a city can accommodate (*a*) existing firms that want to expand their operations and (*b*) new firms that want to locate in the city.

Figure 6–2 shows the multiplier effect of an increase in export sales. Suppose that an increase in the demand for exports increases the demand for export workers by 10,000. The city's demand curve will shift to the right from D_1 to D_2: at a wage of $1,000 per month, an additional 10,000 export workers will be demanded. This is the **direct effect** of an increase in export demand. If the employment multiplier is 2.5, every export job supports 1.5 local jobs, so the demand curve shifts to the right by an additional 15,000 workers (from D_2 to D_3). This is the **multiplier effect** of an increase in export demand. Total labor demand increases by 25,000 (2.5 times the increase in the demand for export laborers).

The Supply Curve

Consider next the supply side of the urban labor market. The supply curve is positively sloped because of the **migration effect**: an increase in the wage increases the relative attractiveness of the city, causing the migration of workers from other cities in the region. One of the assumptions underlying the supply curve is that the number of work hours per laborer is fixed: changes in the wage do not affect the number of work hours per laborer. This assumption is consistent with empirical evidence concerning the elasticity of work hours with respect to the wage: in aggregate, this

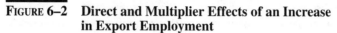

**FIGURE 6–2   Direct and Multiplier Effects of an Increase
in Export Employment**

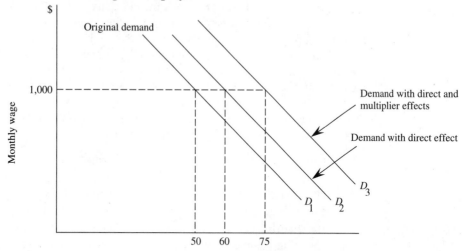

Number of laborers in city (thousands)

If export employment increases by 10,000 jobs, the demand curve shifts to the right in two steps. The shift from D_1 to D_2 is the direct effect of the increase in export employment. At a fixed wage, total employment rises from 50,000 to 60,000. The shift from D_2 to D_3 reflects the multiplier effect of the increase in export employment. If the employment multiplier is 2.5, local employment increases by 1.5 times the increase in export employment, increasing labor demand by an additional 15,000 jobs.

elasticity is close to zero. Another assumption underlying the supply curve is that the labor-force participation rate is unaffected by changes in the wage. In other words, an increase in the wage does not increase the fraction of the city's population in the work force. Given these two assumptions, an increase in the wage increases the supply of labor because more workers move to the city, not because existing workers work more hours or because more of the city's current residents join the work force.

Why is the supply curve positively sloped, and what determines the slope of the curve? An increase in total employment (and population) increases the total demand for most goods, causing increases in the prices of land, housing, and other goods. A growing city must offer a higher wage to compensate its workers for its higher cost of living. The results of Hamilton and Schwab (1985) and Bartik (1991) suggest that the elasticity of housing prices with respect to total employment is about 0.35: a 10 percent increase in total employment increases housing prices by about 3.5 percent. According to Bartik (1991), the elasticity of the cost of living with respect to city size (including all price changes) is about 0.20: a 10 percent increase in total employment increases the cost of living by about 2 percent. This means that to keep real wages constant, the city's nominal wage must rise by about 2 percent for every 10 percent increase in employment.

A number of empirical studies have estimated the responsiveness of wages to total employment. The results of Treyz and Stevens (1985), Robak (1982), and Bartik (1991) suggest that the wage for a given occupation increases at about the same rate as the cost of living. In other words, the elasticity of the nominal wage with respect to total employment is about 0.20: a 10 percent increase in total employment increases the wage by 2 percent. Alternatively, the elasticity of labor supply with respect to the wage is about 5.0: a 2 percent increase in the wage causes a 10 percent increase in labor supply. It's important to note that this is the labor-supply elasticity for an individual city. The elasticity is relatively large because workers migrate to cities that offer relatively high wages. The national supply elasticity is much lower than the local supply elasticity because there is less migration between nations than between cities.

What causes the supply curve to shift to the right or the left? The position of the supply curve is determined by the following factors:

1. **Environmental quality**. An increase in the quality of the environment (better air or water quality) increases the relative attractiveness of the city, causing migration to the city. The supply curve shifts to the right: at every wage, more workers are willing to work in the city.

2. **Residential taxes**. An increase in residential taxes (without a corresponding change in public services) decreases the relative attractiveness of the city, causing out-migration that shifts the supply curve to the left.

3. **Residential public services**. An increase in the quality of residential public services (without a corresponding increase in taxes) increases the relative attractiveness of the city, causing in-migration that shifts the supply curve to the right. The results of Eberts and Stone (1992) suggest that labor supply is responsive to changes in local infrastructure.

Equilibrium Effects of Demand and Supply Shifts

Figure 6–3 shows the effects of an increase in export sales on the urban labor market. The labor-demand curve shifts to the right by 25,000 workers, reflecting both the direct effect and the multiplier effect of an increase in 10,000 export jobs. As the population of the city increases, the prices of housing and land increase, requiring an increase in the wage to compensate workers for the higher cost of living. In other words, the city moves up its supply curve. The equilibrium wage rises from $1,000 per month to $1,300, and the equilibrium number of laborers increases from 50,000 to 66,000.

Figure 6–3 suggests that predicting the effects of an increase in export employment is tricky. The simple approach is to use the employment multiplier to predict the change in total employment from a projected change in export employment. In the numerical example, the predicted change in total employment from this method would be 25,000 (2.5 times 10,000). This approach provides an estimate of the horizontal shift of the demand curve, not the change in equilibrium employment. To accurately predict the change in total employment, one must also know the slopes of the supply and demand curves. The slope of the supply curve indicates how rapidly the wage increases with city size, and the slope of the demand curve indicates how rapidly the quantity of labor demanded decreases as the wage increases.

**FIGURE 6–3   Equilibrium Effects of an Increase
in Export Employment**

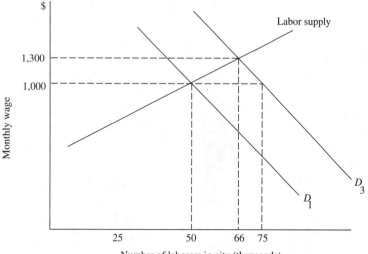

An increase in exports shifts the demand curve to the right by 25,000. As the city grows,
the prices of housing and land increase, requiring a higher wage to compensate workers for
the higher cost of living. The equilibrium wage increases from $1,000 to $1,300, and the
equilibrium number of laborers increases by only 16,000.

Figure 6–4 shows the effects of a rightward shift of the supply curve. Suppose that the city improves its residential public services. For example, the city could improve its public-safety programs or alter its transportation system to decrease commuting costs. In Figure 6–4, the labor-supply curve shifts to the right: at each wage, more people are willing to work in the city. The shift of the supply curve increases equilibrium employment and decreases the equilibrium wage. Figure 6–4 (next page), is consistent with the empirical evidence provided by Eberts and Stone (1992) concerning the effects of improvements in local infrastructure on wages and total employment. Workers accept lower wages because the city provides a superior mix of local public goods.

Public Policy and Economic Growth

Public policy affects the equilibrium number of workers by shifting the city's supply and demand curves. As explained earlier in the chapter, local government can shift the demand curve to the right by improving the local education system, public services, and business infrastructure, and cutting business taxes. Local government can shift the supply curve to the right by improving public services and residential infrastructure and cutting residential taxes. This part of the chapter explores the effects of two alternative policies: the subsidization of relocating firms and a tax on air pollution.

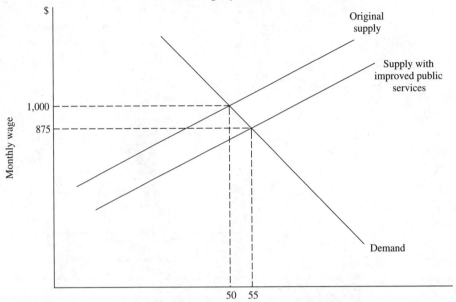

FIGURE 6–4   **Improvement in Public Services Shifts the Supply Curve and Increases Total Employment**

An improvement in local public goods increases the relative attractiveness of the city, shifting the supply curve to the right. The equilibrium number of laborers increases to 55,000, and the equilibrium wage falls to $875 per month. Workers accept a lower wage because the city provides a more efficient set of local public services.

Subsidy Programs

Many cities try to attract export firms by offering special subsidies for new firms. Levy (1985) describes several types of subsidy programs, including the following:

1. **Tax abatement**. In some cities, new firms are exempt from local property taxes for some period of time, often up to 10 years. Some cities offer tax abatements to all new developments, while others offer abatements only to firms that are assumed to be particularly sensitive to tax differentials.

2. **Industrial bonds**. Some cities issue tax-free industrial bonds to finance property development. The local government uses the revenue from the bonds to purchase the land, and leases the property to a private firm. Because the interest income from industrial bonds is not subject to federal taxes, the bond buyer accepts a relatively low interest rate (for example, 8 percent instead of 12 percent). Therefore, the lessee pays less than the market interest rate on the money borrowed to finance the project. The use of industrial bonds was sharply curtailed by the Tax Reform Act of 1986.

3. **Government loans and loan guarantees**. Some cities loan money to developers, and others guarantee loans from private lenders to developers. In both cases, developers borrow money at a relatively low interest rate: either the city charges an interest rate below the market rate, or the city decreases the risk associated with a private loan, allowing the developer to borrow private money at a relatively low interest rate.

4. **Site development**. Some cities subsidize the provision of land and public services for new development. The city purchases a site, clears the land, builds roads and sewers, and then sells the site to a developer at a fraction of the cost of acquiring and developing the site.

How do these subsidy programs affect the urban labor market? Any policy that decreases production costs will increase labor demand and increase equilibrium employment, everything else being equal. In the case of tax subsidies, not everything else is equal. Tax revenue supports local public services, so a community with low taxes is likely to also have inferior public services. The empirical evidence cited in Chapter 3 suggests that if a city cuts taxes and decreases its spending on public services (highways, education, public safety), it is unlikely to grow, and may in fact shrink. In contrast, if the city cuts taxes and decreases its spending on redistributional programs to the poor, the city is likely to grow. In other words, the effect of a tax cut depends on what type of services are cut along with taxes. If taxes are used to finance public services used by businesses, a tax cut is unlikely to stimulate economic growth.

What are the fiscal implications of these subsidy programs? Another objective of a subsidy program is to decrease the local tax burden. If a tax cut or a subsidy makes the city more attractive to firms, the city's tax base will increase, increasing total tax revenue. As the city grows, it will also spend more on local public services (roads, schools, police, fire protection). The subsidy program will be beneficial from the fiscal perspective if the increase in tax revenue exceeds the increase in the cost of public services.

Urban Growth and Environmental Quality

Is there a trade-off between environmental quality and economic growth? Suppose that a city adopts a pollution-abatement program. Will the abatement program increase or decrease the city's total employment?

Consider a city with two industries, a polluting steel industry and a relatively "clean" assembly plant. If the city imposes a pollution tax of $100, steel producers pay $100 for every ton of pollution they generate. The pollution tax affects both sides of the urban labor market.

1. **Shift of demand curve**. The tax increases the production costs of steel producers. In addition to paying for labor, capital, and land, a firm pays $100 for every ton of pollution. The increase in production costs increases the price of steel, decreasing steel production and decreasing the demand for labor. In Figure 6–5, the demand curve shifts to the left: at every wage, less labor is demanded.

FIGURE 6–5   **Pollution Tax Increases Total Employment**

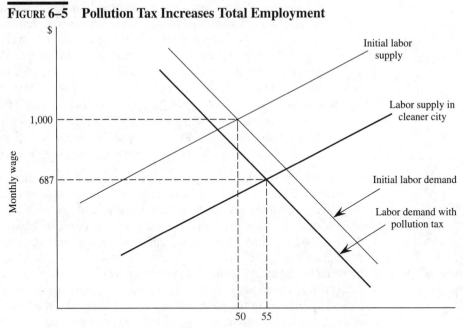

A pollution tax increases production costs, decreasing the demand for labor. It also improves environmental quality, increasing the supply of labor and decreasing the wage. The outward shift of the supply curve is large relative to the inward shift of the demand curve (people are relatively sensitive to air pollution), so total employment
increases. The increase in employment in the clean industry more than offsets the decrease in employment in the
polluting industry.

2. **Decrease in pollution**. The tax decreases air pollution for two reasons.
   First, steel producers will install pollution-control equipment as a means
   of decreasing their pollution taxes, so the amount of pollution generated
   per ton of steel will decrease. Second, the increase in the price of steel
   decreases total steel production.

3. **Shift of supply curve**. The improvement of the city's air quality
   increases the relative attractiveness of the city. People sensitive to air
   quality will move to the city, shifting the supply curve to the right.

Figure 6–5 shows one possible outcome of the abatement program. Since supply
increases and demand decreases, the program decreases the equilibrium wage. Since
the rightward shift of the supply curve is large relative to the leftward shift of the
demand curve, equilibrium employment increases. The supply shift will be relatively
large if households are relatively responsive to changes in environmental quality,
meaning that a large number of households migrate to the city as air quality improves.

How does the abatement program affect the distribution of employment between
the polluting industry and the clean industry? As the wage falls, the production costs
of both industries decrease. For the steel industry, the decrease in the wage partly
offsets the increase in pollution taxes. The abatement program is likely to generate

a net increase in production costs, so the polluting industry is likely to decrease its total work force. In contrast, the clean industry will simply pay lower wages, so its production costs will decrease and its total employment will increase. In Figure 6–5, the increase in employment in the clean industry more than offsets the decrease in employment in the steel industry, so total employment increases. This occurs because households are relatively sensitive to pollution, so that migration to the cleaner city causes a large decrease in the wage.

Figure 6–6 shows another possible outcome of the abatement program. In this case, households are less responsive to changes in environmental quality, so the increase in supply is small relative to the decrease in demand, and the equilibrium number of laborers decreases. Because the supply curve shifts by a relatively small amount, the wage decreases by a small amount. Therefore, the increase in employment in the clean industry is not large enough to offset the decrease in employment in the steel industry.

The lesson from Figure 6–5 and Figure 6–6 is that an abatement program may either increase or decrease total employment. Total employment will increase if the supply response (migration that decreases wages) is large relative to the demand response (the decrease in labor demand from the polluting industry). Total employment will decrease if the demand response is relatively large.

FIGURE 6–6   Pollution Tax Decreases Total Employment

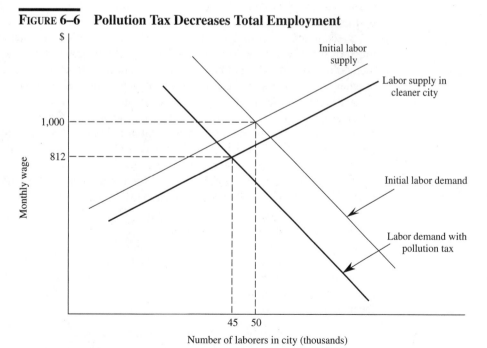

A pollution tax decreases the demand for labor and increases the supply of labor. The outward shift of the supply curve is small relative to the inward shift of the demand curve (people are relatively insensitive to air pollution), so total employment decreases.

Predicting Economic Growth

This section discusses two techniques that are used to predict future growth patterns. The economic base study is a simple, low-cost method for projecting employment growth. The input-output study provides a more sophisticated approach to economic forecasting. Both techniques are designed to estimate the increase in labor demand from an increase in export sales.

The Economic Base Study

According to economic base theory, the export industries form the **economic base** of the urban economy. Like a household, a city earns its livelihood by producing goods for others. Exports bring money into the local economy, increasing local income and employment through the multiplier process. The ultimate purpose of an economic base study is to estimate the increase in total employment generated by an increase in export employment. In algebraic terms,

$$\Delta T = \text{Multiplier} \cdot \Delta B = \frac{T}{B} \cdot \Delta B \qquad (6\text{--}6)$$

In other words, the predicted change in total employment (ΔT) equals the employment multiplier (T/B) times the change in export employment (ΔB). To predict the change in total employment, the economic forecaster needs (1) an estimate of the multiplier and (2) a projection of the change in export employment.

To compute the employment multiplier, the economic forecaster estimates how much of the city's work force is involved in export production. The most precise method of estimating B is to collect information on the actual shipments of goods to other cities. This approach is costly, and most cities use less expensive and less precise methods to estimate export employment.

The simplest method is to classify each industry as either an export industry or a local industry. For example, if the mitten industry is assumed to be an export industry, all the employees of mitten producers would be counted as export workers. If restaurant meals are assumed to be local goods, all the employees of restaurants would be counted as local workers. The problem with this crude method is that some mittens may be consumed locally and some meals may be eaten by nonresidents. In other words, since few industries are exclusively exporters or local producers, it is inappropriate to classify them as such.

Location-Quotient Approach.   The location-quotient approach recognizes that each industry produces partly for export and partly for local consumption. The trick is to estimate what portion of each industry's output is exported. An industry's true **location quotient** is

$$L_1 = \frac{\text{Mitten production in the city}}{\text{Mitten consumption in the city}} \qquad (6\text{--}7)$$

A quotient of 1.0 (the city's mitten production equals its mitten consumption) would indicate that all of the city's production is consumed within the city, so none of the mitten workers produce for export. If $L_1 = 5.0$, mitten production is five times local consumption, so only one fifth of mitten workers produce for the local market, and four fifths produce for export.

Data limitations prevent the direct estimation of the true location quotient. Instead, a proxy for the true location quotient is

$$L_2 = \frac{\dfrac{\text{City's mitten employment}}{\text{City's total employment}}}{\dfrac{\text{Nation's mitten employment}}{\text{Nation's total employment}}} \qquad (6\text{--}8)$$

The denominator (the share of national employment in mitten production) provides a measure of how much local production is needed to satisfy the local demand for mittens. For example, if 1 percent of national employment is in mitten production (the denominator is 0.01), the city is assumed to need 1 percent of its work force to satisfy its local mitten demand. If the city actually employs 6 percent of its workers in mitten production (if the numerator is 0.06), one sixth of the workers are assumed to produce for local consumption, and five sixths are assumed to produce for export.

There are three problems with the location-quotient approach. The first two are related to the choice of the national economy as the reference point.

1. **Uniform consumption patterns**. The approach assumes that every city in the nation has the same per capita demand for mittens. Of course, mitten consumption depends on weather, fashion, and the tastes for outdoor winter sports (skiing, ice fishing, snow shoveling). If a city's residents consume a relatively large amount of mittens, the location quotient L_2 will overestimate the number of export workers. Conversely, if city residents consume a relatively small amount of mittens, L_2 will underestimate the number of export workers.

2. **National self-sufficiency**. Another assumption of the location-quotient approach is that the nation neither imports nor exports mittens, so the share of national employment in mitten production is the share required for local self-sufficiency. If the nation exports mittens, the share of national employment in mitten production will overstate the share required for self-sufficiency, so the location quotient will underestimate the number of export workers. Conversely, if mittens are imported, the location quotient will overestimate the number of export workers.

3. **Industry grouping**. The location quotient is typically computed for a set of consumer goods, not for a particular product. For example, a city might compute a location quotient for the apparel industry, which includes mittens, pants, dresses, and children's clothes. Suppose that all the city's apparel workers produce mittens for export: no other apparel products are produced in the city. Suppose that the mitten industry is large enough that the city's location quotient for apparel is 1.0: the city uses the same share of its work force in mitten production as the nation uses in apparel production. The city's location quotient suggests that the city does not export apparel products, when in fact it exports

mittens and imports other apparel. Grouping goods into broad categories causes the location quotient to underestimate export employment.

The results of Tiebout (1962) suggest that location quotients systematically underestimate export employment. He compared estimates of export employment derived from location quotients to the estimates generated by direct surveys of manufacturers. Figure 6–7 shows his results for the city of Indianapolis. For example, the location quotient for the food industry suggests that 24 percent of food workers produce for export, while the direct survey suggests that 63 percent of food workers produce for export. For primary metals, the location quotient suggests that none of the workers in the industry produce for export, while the direct survey suggests that 99 percent of the workers produce for export. In general, Tiebout's results suggest that location quotients perform poorly in estimating export employment.

Estimating the Multiplier.   The second step in an economic base study is to compute the city's employment multiplier. For each industry, the location quotient generates an estimate of export employment. If T_i is total employment in industry i and L_i is the industry's location quotient, export employment in the industry is

$$B_i = \frac{L_i - 1}{L_i} \cdot T_i \qquad (6\text{--}9)$$

For example, if L_i is 4.0 and T_i is 800, B_i is 600; three fourths of the industry's workers produce for export. The city's total export employment is estimated by summing the export employment across individual industries. The employment multiplier is total employment divided by export employment.

FIGURE 6–7   Estimates of Export Employment from Surveys and Location Quotients

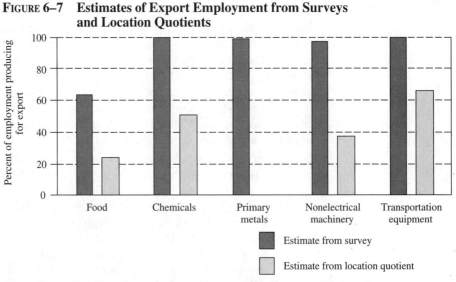

SOURCE: Charles M. Tiebout, *The Community Economic Base Study* (New York: Committee for Economic Development, 1962).

Projecting Growth in Export Industries.   The third step in an economic base study is to project the growth of the basic industry, that is, to estimate ΔB in equation (6–6). Given the uncertainties associated with predicting future events, export projection is more of an art than a science. One approach is to (1) estimate the national trend in the demand for a particular good and (2) assess the city's relative attractiveness to the firms producing that good. The city's economic forecaster could estimate the national demand for mittens for the next decade, looking at the trends in weather, winter sports, and fashion. If the city's relative attractiveness is not expected to change, the city's mitten production should increase at the same rate as national mitten consumption: a doubling of mitten consumption should double the city's mitten production and employment. If the city's relative attractiveness increases over time, its mitten production and employment should increase at a relatively fast rate.

Using the Economic Base Study.   Economic base studies are used to project population growth and the demand for public services. Suppose that a city projects that its mitten industry will grow by 1,000 jobs. If the employment multiplier is 2.5, the economic base approach suggests that total employment will increase by 2,500 jobs. If there are three residents per job, the population of the city will increase by 7,500 people, increasing the demand for all public services. For example, if there is one school-age child for every five residents, total enrollment in schools will increase by 1,500 students.

Local firms use the employment projections from the economic base study to predict the demands for their products. Suppose that the city's economic base study projects an increase in population of 7,500 people. If it takes 3,750 people to support a barber, there will be room for two more barbers in the city. If the city grows by 7,500 people per year and it takes 30,000 people to support a shopping center, there will be enough demand to support a new shopping center in four years.

Local governments also use economic base studies to guide their growth-management policies. If a local government can affect the sales and employment of its basic industry, it can control the city's population. Suppose that the city has a growth target of 15,000 additional people: it wants to increase its population by 15,000 people in the next 20 years. If there are three residents per job, the city will meet its population target if it allows an additional 5,000 jobs. If the employment multiplier is 2.5, the city will meet its employment and population targets if it allows 2,000 additional export jobs.

Input-Output Analysis

An alternative to an economic base study is an **input-output** study. Unlike the economic base study, the input-output study generates a complete accounting of the transactions between firms and households in the economy. This approach has two advantages over the economic base study. First, instead of assuming that every industry has the same multiplier, it derives a multiplier for each export industry. Second, instead of using the location-quotient approach to guess the volume of exports, it measures exports directly.

TABLE 6–2   **Transactions Table from Input-Output Study**

| | Producers | | | | | |
Inputs	Computer Firms	Wire Producers	Local Merchants	Households	Exports	Total
Computers	0	$ 300	$ 150	$ 180	$1,370	$2,000
Wire	$ 400	0	0	0	600	1,000
Local	0	0	0	2,500	—	2,500
Labor	1,000	600	2,000	0	0	3,600
Imports	600	100	350	920	—	2,170
Total	$2,000	$1,000	$2,500	$3,600	$1,970	

To explain the workings of an input-output study, consider a city that produces and consumes three goods: computers, electrical wire, and local consumer goods. Computers and wire products are produced for both export and local consumption. By definition, local merchants (restaurants, dry cleaners, grocery stores) produce goods for local consumption.

Transactions Table and Input Coefficients.   Table 6–2 shows the transactions in the city's economy. The first column of numbers shows the input usage of firms in the computer industry. To produce computers, they buy $400 of electrical wire, $1,000 of labor from city residents, and $600 of imported inputs (raw materials and intermediate inputs). The sum of these input costs equals the total output of the computer industry ($2,000). The next column shows the input usage of wire producers, who use computers, labor, and imported inputs to produce $1,000 of wire. The third column shows the input usage of local merchants, who use computers, labor, and imports to produce $2,500 of output. The household column shows how households divide their total income ($3,600) between computers ($180), local goods ($2,500), and imports ($920). The export column shows the exports of computers ($1,370) and wire ($600). The total column shows the sum of the items in each row. Note that the figures in the total column match the figures in the total row.

Table 6–3, which is derived from Table 6–2, provides a summary of the interactions between firms and households. The first column of numbers shows the **input coefficients** for the computer industry: for every dollar worth of computer production, the computer industry uses 20 cents worth of input from the wire industry, 50 cents worth of labor, and 30 cents worth of imported materials (e.g., silicon chips and plastic). The second and third columns show the input coefficients for wire producers and local merchants. The fourth column shows that households spend 5 percent of their income on home computers, 69 percent on local goods, and 26 percent on imports.

The Multiplier Process.   The information in Table 6–3 can be used to estimate the multiplier effects of an increase in computer exports. Suppose that computer exports

TABLE 6–3   Input Coefficients Table

| | Producers | | | |
Inputs	Computer Firms	Wire Producers	Local Merchants	Households
Computers	0.00	0.30	0.06	0.05
Wire	0.20	0.00	0.00	0.00
Local	0.00	0.00	0.00	0.69
Labor	0.50	0.60	0.80	0.00
Imports	0.30	0.10	0.14	0.26
Total	1.00	1.00	1.00	1.00

increase by $100. The increase in computer sales will increase local spending, precipitating a series of spending rounds. The first three spending rounds are shown in Figure 6–8.

Round 1   The increase in computer sales increases wire production by $20 (0.20 times $100) and wages by $50 (0.50 times $100).

Round 2   The $20 increase in wire production increases computer sales by an additional $6 (0.30 times $20) and wages by an additional $12 (0.60 times $20).
The first-round increase in wages ($50) increases home computer sales by $2.50 (0.05 times $50) and local consumption by $34.50 (0.69 times $50).

FIGURE 6–8   Multiplier Effects of a $100 Increase in Computer Exports

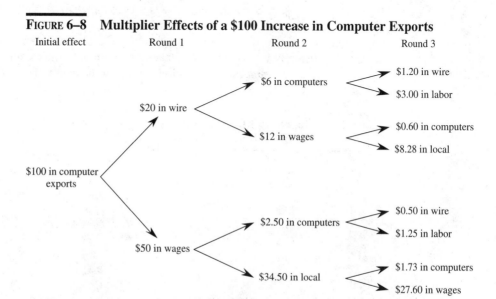

Round 3   The increases in computer sales, wages, and local sales cause additional increases in wire sales, wages, computer sales, and local consumption.

Because of the multiplier process, an increase in computer exports increases spending on all three goods.

The spending and respending of income continues forever, but every spending round is smaller than the previous one. The multiplier process eventually peters out because both producers and consumers spend some of their budgets on imports. As shown in the fifth row in Table 6–3 (Imports), there is a leakage of 30 percent in computer production, 10 percent in wire production, 14 percent in local goods production, and 26 percent from consumers. These leakages weaken the multiplier process, causing each spending round to be smaller than the previous round.

The input coefficients from Table 6–3 can be used to compute spending multipliers for the two export industries. For a description of the techniques used to derive the spending multipliers, see the references at the end of the chapter. In Table 6–4, the first column shows the multiplier effects of a $1 increase in computer exports. Total computer sales increase by $1.23; wire production increases by $0.25; and local sales increase by $1.17. The total multiplier effect is the sum of the effects on the three industries: a $1 increase in computer sales increases total sales by $2.65. Because the wire industry has a smaller import leakage (10 percent compared to 30 percent for the computer industry), it has a larger multiplier (3.04 versus 2.65).

Limitations of Economic Base and Input-Output Studies

This section discusses five defects that limit the applicability of the economic base and input-output approaches. There are two technical problems with the two approaches. First, the income and employment multipliers are assumed to be constant, regardless of city size. Second, the city's wage is assumed to be constant, regardless of city size. In addition, these approaches are misleading for three reasons. First, they suggest that the only way for a city to grow is by increasing its exports. Second, they suggest that the only way to increase total employment is by increasing the demand for labor. Third, they suggest that the city's fate is in the hands of outsiders.

TABLE 6–4   **Spending Multipliers from Input-Output Examples**

	Added Sales per Dollar of Additional Export Sales of	
	Computers	*Wire*
Computers	1.23	0.52
Wire	0.25	1.10
Local	1.17	1.42
Total	2.65	3.04

Constant Multipliers.   The multipliers derived from both the input-output and economic base approaches are assumed to be constant. In fact, a city's multipliers can change for three reasons.

1. **City size and consumer products**. Multipliers increase with city size, reflecting the ability of a larger city to support a wider variety of firms. As explained in Chapter 5, a larger city has enough demand to support activities with scale economies that are large relative to per capita demand. For example, if a city grows to the point at which it can support its own Mexican restaurant, city residents will patronize the local restaurant instead of traveling to another city. A larger fraction of increases in income will be spent locally, so the income and employment multipliers will increase.

2. **City size and intermediate inputs**. As the city grows, the demand for intermediate inputs grows, and more of these inputs will be provided locally instead of being imported. For example, if the computer industry grows to the point at which the city can support its own silicon chip maker, computer firms will spend less on imported inputs and more on locally produced inputs. Therefore, a given increase in computer exports will generate a larger increase in total income.

3. **Changes in input prices**. Changes in input prices cause factor substitution that changes the interactions among the economic sectors. Suppose that the city's wage increases, causing computer firms to substitute imported capital equipment for laborers. If the input coefficient for labor decreases from 0.50 to 0.40, only $40 of a $100 increase in computer exports will be paid to laborers. Because a smaller fraction of export income will be spent locally, the multiplier effect of an increase in exports will decrease.

Constant Wage.   The economic base and the input-output approaches assume that the city's wage is fixed, regardless of city size. In other words, they estimate the horizontal shift of the city's labor-demand curve, not the equilibrium change in employment. Suppose that an economic base study computes a multiplier of 2.5 and projects an increase in export employment of 10,000 jobs. Based on these numbers, the economic base approach would predict that total employment in the city would increase by 25,000 jobs. This is incorrect because the city's labor-supply curve is positively sloped, so an increase in labor demand increases the city's wage. In Figure 6–3, total employment increases by only 16,000 jobs, not 25,000 jobs. Because the economic base and the input-output approaches assume a fixed wage, they overestimate the stimulative effect of increases in exports.

Focus on Exports as Source of Economic Growth.   The economic base and input-output approaches suggest that the only way for a city to grow is by increasing its exports. The notion that economic growth requires an increase in exports is incorrect. Growth may also occur as a result of (1) a decrease in imports, (2) an increase in labor productivity, or (3) an increase in trade within the metropolitan area.

A decrease in imports has the same stimulative effect as an increase in exports. While an increase in exports increases the flow of money into the urban economy, a decrease in imports decreases the flow of money out of the economy. The economy can be stimulated by either increasing the inflow (exports) or decreasing the outflow (imports). To explain the notion of **import substitution**, suppose that a city initially spends $10 million per year on imported chairs. If consumers switch to locally produced chairs, the $10 million that previously left the region will now be paid to local producers and will be spent and respent in the local economy. The spending and respending of the $10 million has the same effect as a $10 million increase in export sales. If the spending multiplier is 2.5, the change in total income resulting from import substitution is $25 million. The possibility of import substitution suggests that economic development policies should consider decreasing imports as well as increasing exports.

The most compelling counterexample to the export-oriented theories of urban economic growth is the earth economy. The earth's economy has grown, despite the absence of exports to other worlds. Economic growth has occurred for two reasons. First, technological advances have increased output per person, increasing real income per capita. Second, changes in production and transportation technologies have increased trade between regions. Trade increases real income because it allows each region to specialize in the production of goods for which it has a comparative advantage. The same phenomena occur at the urban level: increases in labor productivity or trade within a metropolitan area increase per capita income, so the city's economy can grow without increasing exports.

The Demand Side of the Urban Labor Market.   Both the economic base and the input-output approaches focus attention on the demand side of the urban labor market. The idea is that growth occurs when the demand for the city's labor increases. As explained earlier in the chapter, an increase in labor supply also increases equilibrium employment, so growth can occur as a result of increases in either demand or supply. There are a number of public policies that shift the supply curve and increase equilibrium employment, including environmental policy (see Figure 6–5) and infrastructure policy (see Figure 6–4).

Do Outsiders Determine the City's Economic Fate?   The economic base and input-output approaches incorrectly suggest that the city's economic fate is in the hands of outsiders. In fact, there are several local public policies that can be used to increase the city's equilibrium employment. On the demand side, the city can shift the demand curve to the right by (1) cutting its business taxes, (2) improving its industrial infrastructure, or (3) increasing labor productivity by improving its educational system. On the supply side, the city can shift the supply curve to the right by (1) cutting its residential taxes, (2) improving its residential infrastructure, (3) improving its residential services such as schools, recreation, and public safety, or (4) improving the local environment.

It's important to note that public policy need not focus exclusively on increasing the city's exports. As explained earlier, among the alternative strategies are import substitution and increased trade within the metropolitan area. To the extent that public policy encourages import substitution or intracity trade, it can increase employment and income without increasing the city's exports.

Benefits and Costs of Employment Growth

This section of the chapter explores the trade-offs associated with increases in city size, addressing two questions about the effects of employment growth on the welfare of a city's residents. First, how many of the new jobs generated by economic growth are filled by newcomers, and how many are filled by original residents of the city who would otherwise not be employed? Second, how does an increase in total employment affect real income per capita? As explained earlier in the chapter, changes in nominal wages and prices usually offset one another, so the real wage for a given occupation is usually unaffected by an increase in total employment. This section discusses three other factors that affect real income: the unemployment rate, the labor-force participation rate, and occupational rank.

Who Gets the New Jobs?

Bartik (1991) studied the effects of employment growth on unemployment rates, labor-force participation rates, and migration rates in 89 metropolitan areas. Table 6–5 uses his results to show the effects of employment growth on the characteristics of a hypothetical metropolitan area.

The first column of numbers shows the characteristics of the city's labor market in the initial equilibrium. In the sample of cities examined by Bartik, the average unemployment rate (the percentage of people who were unsuccessful in their

TABLE 6–5   Long-Run Effects of Employment Growth on Employment Rate

	Initial Equilibrium	*Long-Run Equilibrium*	*Change*
Unemployment rate (u)	5.40%	5.33%	−0.07%
Participation rate (p)	87.50%	87.64%	0.14%
Employment rate ($e = (i - u) \cdot p$)	82.78%	82.97%	0.19%
Potential work force	120,809	121,737	928
Participating	105,708	106,687	
Unemployed	5,708	5,687	
Working	100,000	101,000	1,000
Not working	20,809	20,737	
New jobs filled by newcomers		770	
New jobs filled by original residents		230	
Filled by unemployed		70	
Filled by nonparticipants		160	

SOURCE: Calculations based on Table 4.5 in Timothy J. Bartik, *Who Benefits from State and Local Economic Development Policies?* (Kalamazoo, Mich.: Upjohn Institute, 1991).

search for work) was 5.40 percent, and the average labor-force participation rate (the percentage of working-age people who were actively involved in the labor market, either working or looking for work) was 87.50 percent. Suppose that the *employment rate* is defined as the percentage of working-age people who are employed. The employment rate is computed by multiplying the participation rate by 1 minus the unemployment rate. In Bartik's study, the average employment rate was 82.78 percent. The hypothetical city has a potential work force of 120,809 people; given the participation rate (87.50 percent), 105,708 participate in the labor market; given the unemployment rate of 5.40 percent, 5,708 of the participants are unemployed, leaving 100,000 people who are employed.

The second column of numbers in Table 6–5 shows the predicted long-run effects of a 1 percent increase in total employment (1,000 jobs). According to Bartik, the long run is about six years: it takes about six years for all the markets to fully adjust to the change in employment. Six years after the increase in total employment, the unemployment rate is 5.33 percent, the participation rate is 87.64 percent, and the employment rate is 82.97 percent. Migration to the city increases the city's potential work force by 928 people.

How many of the new jobs are filled by newcomers, and how many are filled by original residents who would otherwise not be employed? Since there are 1,000 new jobs and only 928 new potential workers, there are at least 72 new jobs for the original residents. If all the newcomers are employed (newcomers have a 100 percent participation rate and a zero unemployment rate), there will be only 72 new jobs for the original residents. If the newcomers have the same employment rate as the original residents, however, only 770 of the newcomers will be employed (82.97 percent of 928), so there will be 230 jobs left for the original residents. About a third of the 230 jobs will be filled by original residents who were previously unemployed, and the remaining two thirds will be filled by original residents who previously did not participate in the labor market. Figure 6–9 summarizes the results from Table 6–5: 77 percent of the new jobs are filled by newcomers, leaving 7 percent for original residents who were unemployed and 16 percent for original residents who did not participate in the labor market.

The simple lesson from Table 6–5 and Figure 6–9 is that employment growth causes in-migration and population growth. There are three implications from this lesson. First, if the city's work force is just as qualified for the new jobs as workers in other cities who have the option of migrating to the city, the original residents will get about a quarter of the new jobs. Second, if the city's workers are, on average, less qualified for the new jobs than workers in other cities, more of the jobs will be filled by workers migrating to the city. Third, employment growth increases population and thus increases the demands for housing, land, and public services. This suggests that local governments should coordinate their economic development policies with their policies concerning land use, transportation, and infrastructure investment.

Employment Growth and Real Income per Capita

How does employment growth affect a city's real income per capita? An increase in total employment could, in principle, increase per capita income in several ways:

**FIGURE 6–9   Distribution of 1,000 New Jobs between Original
Residents and Newcomers**

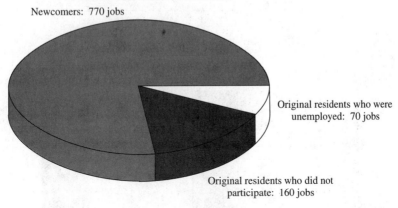

Newcomers: 770 jobs

Original residents who were
unemployed: 70 jobs

Original residents who did not
participate: 160 jobs

1. **Increase in the real wage for each occupation.** As explained earlier
   in the chapter, employment growth causes offsetting changes in nominal wages and living costs, so the real wage for a given occupation is
   unaffected by employment growth.

2. **Promotions.** Bartik (1991) shows that employment growth hastens workers'
   movement upward in the job hierarchy. It appears that an increase in the
   demand for labor causes firms to promote workers to higher-paying jobs
   more rapidly. Figure 6–10 shows, for different types of workers, the average
   percentage movement up the job hierarchy (and up the pay scale) from a 1
   percent increase in total employment. The average worker is promoted to
   a job with a wage that is 0.16 percent higher than the wage for the old job.
   A less-educated worker (3 years less education than average) is promoted
   to a job that pays 0.196 percent more; a young worker (12 years younger
   than average) is promoted to a job that pays 0.188 more; a black worker is
   promoted to a job that pays 0.215 percent more.

3. **Increase in employment rate.** As explained earlier, employment growth
   decreases the unemployment rate and increases the participation rate, so
   it increases the fraction of the working-age population that is employed.
   In Table 6–5, the 1 percent increase in employment increases the employment rate from 82.78 percent to 82.97 percent.

Figure 6–11 shows the combined effects of changes in real wages, occupational
rank, unemployment rates, and participation rates on real income per capita. For the
average household, a 1 percent increase in employment increases real income per
capita by 0.40 percent. In other words, the elasticity of real earnings with respect to
total employment is 0.40. The most important factors in the increase in income are
the increases in wages from being promoted to higher-paying jobs and the increases
in labor-force participation. The elasticities are larger for households that are less
educated, young, or black, because workers in these groups experience relatively
large benefits from promotion to higher-paying jobs.

FIGURE 6–10   **Effect of Employment Growth on Occupational Rank for Different Groups**

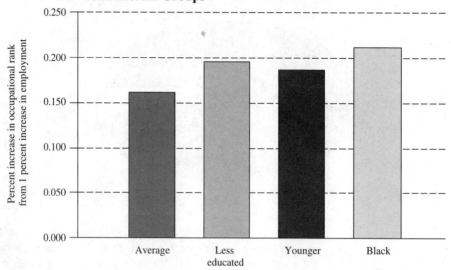

SOURCE: Timothy J. Bartik, *Who Benefits from State and Local Economic Development Policies?* (Kalamazoo, Mich.: Upjohn Institute, 1991).

FIGURE 6–11   **Effect of Employment Growth on Real Earnings per Capita for Different Groups**

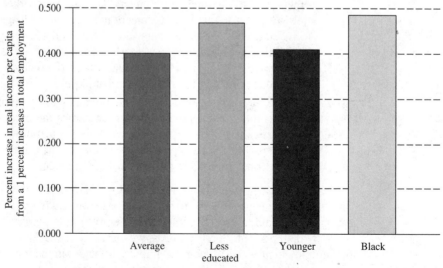

SOURCE: Timothy J. Bartik, *Who Benefits from State and Local Economic Development Policies?* (Kalamazoo, Mich.: Upjohn Institute, 1991).

Other Benefits and Costs of Employment Growth

There are a number of other benefits and costs from employment growth. On the benefit side, a larger city is able to exploit scale economies in the production of consumer goods and some public services. As explained in Chapter 5, a large city can support activities that have relatively large scale economies, so a larger city has a wider variety of goods and services. In addition, there are scale economies in the provision of some local public goods, so an increase in population decreases the average costs of some public goods. On the cost side, a large city also has relatively high commuting costs: as the land area of the city increases, the average commuting distance increases, increasing the average commuting cost. In addition, larger cities often have greater problems with pollution and traffic congestion. Finally, large cities typically have higher crime rates.

It's important to note that the problems of congestion, pollution, and crime are not caused by city size per se. They are caused by market failures that become worse as the city grows. As explained later in the book, there are a number of policies that address these problems directly. Therefore, the problems can be solved (or decreased to their optimum levels) without decreasing city size.

Composition of Changes in Employment

This section of the chapter examines the composition of changes in total employment. A city experiences an increase in total employment when the number of jobs gained from the opening of new plants and the expansion of existing plants exceeds the number of jobs lost from the closure and contraction of old plants. The question is whether cities that experience rapid employment growth have relatively large gains from plant openings and expansions or relatively small losses from plant closures and contractions. Conversely, do cities that grow slowly or shrink have relatively small gains from plant openings and expansions or relatively large losses from plant closures and contractions?

Eberts and Stone (1992) studied the composition of employment changes for 34 large metropolitan areas. In Table 6–6, the first column shows, for each city, the net change in employment as a percent of total employment. For example, Pittsburgh lost 8.19 percent of its total employment over this period. The second and third columns show the gains from plant openings and expansions, and the sixth column shows the total gross gain (the sum of gains from openings and expansions). For example, Pittsburgh experienced an 11.46 percent gain from openings and a 5.82 percent gain from expansions, for a total gross gain of 17.28 percent. The fourth, fifth, and seventh columns show the losses from plant closures and contractions. For example, Pittsburgh experienced a 13.76 percent loss from closures and an 11.71 percent loss from contractions, for a total gross loss of 25.47 percent.

Three conclusions can be drawn from the data in Table 6–6. First, there is a large range of changes in net employment, from −8.19 percent for Pittsburgh to +19.36 percent for San Diego. Second, the gross changes in employment (gains and losses) are large relative to the net changes. The average change from openings and

TABLE 6–6   Employment Changes from Plant Openings, Expansions, Closings, and Contractions, 1984–1986

Metropolitan Area	Net Employment Change (percent)	Percentage Employment Change Originating from				Percent from Open + Expand	Percent from Close + Contract
		Openings	Expansions	Closings	Contractions		
Pittsburgh	−8.19	11.46	5.82	−13.76	−11.71	17.28	−25.47
Houston	−5.41	16.75	7.54	−20.91	−8.80	24.29	−29.71
Akron	0.46	16.20	6.43	−13.99	−8.18	22.63	−22.17
New York	0.61	12.64	8.33	−15.38	−4.98	20.97	−20.36
Cleveland	0.64	13.31	8.48	−15.17	−5.98	21.79	−21.15
New Orleans	0.86	15.41	6.03	−13.94	−6.65	21.44	−20.59
Detroit	0.97	13.20	8.96	−15.40	−5.80	22.16	−21.20
Miami	2.18	15.48	8.72	−16.39	−5.63	24.20	−22.02
San Francisco	2.26	13.48	8.81	−14.27	−5.76	22.29	−20.03
Buffalo	2.57	15.36	7.26	−14.63	−5.42	22.62	−20.05
Cincinnati	3.16	13.27	8.25	−13.54	−4.82	21.52	−18.36
Los Angeles	3.95	16.78	9.78	−17.10	−5.52	26.56	−22.62
Kansas City	4.28	16.26	8.24	−14.76	−5.46	24.50	−20.22
Milwaukee	4.36	13.57	7.96	−11.71	−5.45	21.53	−17.16
Portland	5.43	20.12	8.14	−13.15	−9.68	28.26	−22.83
Chicago	5.54	16.31	8.83	−13.67	−5.92	25.14	−19.59
Dallas	5.68	20.03	10.44	−16.68	−8.10	30.47	−24.78
Denver	6.16	20.18	8.87	−15.16	−7.72	29.05	−22.88
Philadelphia	6.16	15.54	10.01	−13.87	−5.52	25.55	−19.39
Anaheim	6.88	19.44	11.42	−18.26	−5.72	30.86	−23.98
Newark	7.18	16.36	8.88	−12.61	−5.45	25.24	−18.06
San Jose	7.50	19.19	10.74	−16.21	−6.21	29.93	−22.42
St. Louis	8.19	16.48	8.62	−11.72	−5.20	25.10	−16.92
Tampa	8.68	20.73	9.89	−17.25	−4.70	30.62	−21.95
Indianapolis	8.70	17.64	10.09	−11.05	−7.98	27.73	−19.03
Birmingham	8.73	21.12	10.25	−15.51	−7.13	21.37	−22.64
Baltimore	8.93	19.00	10.82	−15.62	−5.27	29.82	−20.89
Seattle	11.08	21.58	10.02	−13.87	−6.65	31.60	−20.52
Greensboro	13.24	17.21	9.34	−8.73	−4.57	26.55	−13.30
Minneapolis	15.29	19.42	11.22	−9.82	−5.53	30.64	−15.35
Atlanta	15.58	22.18	12.61	−14.65	−4.55	34.79	−19.20
Columbus	15.90	20.47	9.74	−9.56	−4.75	30.21	−14.31
Rochester	19.33	29.66	7.13	−12.12	−5.35	36.79	−17.47
San Diego	19.36	27.32	12.93	−15.63	−5.26	40.25	−20.89
Average	6.36	17.74	9.14	−14.30	−6.22	26.88	−20.52

SOURCE: Table 2.3 in Randall W. Eberts and Joe A. Stone, *Wage and Adjustment in Local Labor Markets* (Kalamazoo, Mich.: Upjohn Institute, 1992).

expansions is over 26 percent, and the average change from closures and contractions is over 20 percent, compared to an average net change of about 6 percent. The fact that a city has a relatively small net change in employment does not mean that its economy is stagnant, but simply that the employment gains are close to the losses. For example, the five cities that had positive net changes less than 1 percent (Akron,

New York, Cleveland, New Orleans, and Detroit) had gross gains and losses between 20 and 23 percent.

The third conclusion from Table 6–6 is that rapidly growing cities have relatively large employment gains (from openings and expansions), not relatively small losses (from closures and contractions). Figure 6–12 shows the gross gains and gross losses for every third city in Table 6–6, arranged in ascending order of net employment changes. There is very little variation in the gross loss rates across cities. Except for Pittsburgh, all the cities have gross losses between 19 percent and 22.4 percent. In contrast, the gross gains vary considerably across cities, from about 17 percent to about 40 percent. The keys to rapid growth are openings and expansions: the three most rapidly growing cities (San Diego, Atlanta, and Seattle) have about the same gross losses as some of the slowest-growing cities (Pittsburgh, New York, Detroit, and Buffalo), but much larger gross gains.

FIGURE 6–12   Gross Gains and Losses in Employment in Selected Cities, 1984–1986

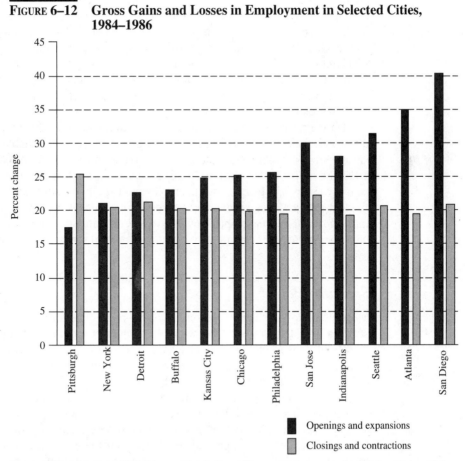

SOURCE: Table 2.3 in Randall W. Eberts and Joe A. Stone, *Wage and Adjustment in Local Labor Markets* (Kalamazoo, Mich.: Upjohn Institute, 1992).

Plant-Closure Legislation

In recent years, a total of 24 states have considered various types of laws that would impose penalties on firms that close their plants. These proposed plant-closing laws share two features: notification requirements and severance pay for workers.

Notification Requirement

Under the notification requirement, the firm would be required to give advance notification of a plant closing. The notification requirement may be as short as 30 days or as long as two years. Many of the proposed laws specify a notification period in excess of the federally mandated 60-day period (passed in 1988).

The notification requirement may increase the number of plant closures. To explain, suppose that your firm is in trouble: there is a 40 percent chance that your plant will close in the next year. Will you explain your troubles to your customers, creditors, and workers? If you do, your troubles may get worse instead of better. Your customers may look for more reliable suppliers. Your creditors, realizing the risk of lending money to a troubled firm, may be reluctant to lend you money. Your best workers may look for other jobs. Although you stand a 60 percent chance of survival if you retain your customers, creditors, and best employees, you may have only a 30 percent chance of survival if you lose them. The notification requirement forces the marginal firm to disclose its troubles to everyone, increasing the likelihood that the plant will close.

On the positive side, the notification requirement gives workers a head start in the search for new jobs. Suppose that the plant closing is inevitable: the plant will close even if advance notification is not given, and advance notification does not affect the timing of the closure. In this case, advance notice promotes efficiency because workers will face shorter unemployment spells because they can plan ahead. A plant closure idles productive workers, imposing a substantial opportunity cost in the form of decreased production. Advance notification decreases this opportunity cost. If the plant closing is unavoidable, more information is clearly better than less.

Severance Pay

Most plant-closure legislation contains some provisions for severance pay. In some states, a firm that closes a plant would be required to provide a lump-sum payment to each of its workers, the size of which depends on the worker's wage and length of employment. In other states, firms would be required to continue paying a former employee until the worker found another job.

The requirement for severance pay will decrease wages. In equilibrium, a worker's total compensation (wages plus fringe benefits) is determined by the worker's productivity. If workers are granted severance pay (one type of fringe benefit), firms decrease wages to compensate for the increase in fringe benefits. In the long run, a plant-closure law does not increase total compensation, but simply increases severance pay at the expense of wages.

Will a closure law impose an undesirable compensation package on workers? Before the closure law was passed, workers in unionized firms had the opportunity to negotiate a compensation package with low wages and high severance pay. The fact that they chose wages over severance pay suggests that they may be worse off under the closure law. Most workers are not in unions, however, so negotiations over severance pay and wages are often difficult and costly. For such workers, a plant-closure law places the government in the role of a labor negotiator, generating a compensation package with more severance pay and lower wages. One problem with this approach is that the mandated package is the same for all workers, regardless of their preferences for wages and severance pay.

Effects on the Labor Market and the Tax Base

Does plant-closing legislation promote efficiency in the labor market? Proponents argue that the closure of a plant generates externalities because it idles productive workers and decreases production, imposing a substantial opportunity cost on society. According to this line of reasoning, plant-closure legislation internalizes these external costs by forcing the firm to pay its idle workers until they find new jobs.

This reasoning ignores the fact that a plant closure sometimes increases employment elsewhere. Some firms close a plant in one city to open or expand a plant in another city. In fact, most closure legislation is motivated by the perception that firms are moving their operations from the Rustbelt to the Sunbelt. Even if a firm does not relocate its plant, the plant closure frees up resources that can be used elsewhere. Therefore, a plant closure may generate external benefits (an increase in Sunbelt employment) as well as external costs (a decrease in Rustbelt employment). To defend plant-closure laws on efficiency grounds, one must show that the external costs of a plant closure exceed its external benefits.

How will a closure law affect the city's tax base? The good news is that the law may delay the closure of some plants. The bad news is that the law may increase the number of marginal plants that eventually shut down. In addition, the closure law may discourage the development of new plants. In weighing alternative plant sites, a firm includes in its calculations the expected costs of eventually closing the plant. A city that requires severance pay and severance taxes will have relatively high plant costs, so firms are less likely to locate there. The short-run gains from keeping marginal plants on the tax rolls may be offset by long-term losses in employment and capital investment.

Alternative Policies

What are the policy options for a city facing plant closures? First, if the city wants to save a troubled industry, it could develop policies that decrease the industry's production costs. The city can decrease production costs by providing more efficient public services such as schools, roads, transit, and utilities. Second, the city could let marginal plants close, and then encourage the development of new industries. In a dynamic economy, changes in product demand and production technology are inevitable. If these changes make an industry obsolete, rescue attempts will be futile.

On the positive side, the death of one industry frees up resources (capital, labor, land) that can be used to produce other goods. One option for local government is to focus its economic development efforts on facilitating the transition from old industries to new ones. A third policy option is to attack the unemployment problem directly. Subsidized education and training will prepare workers for new employment opportunities. Subsidized job information and relocation assistance will encourage the unemployed to move to areas with better job opportunities.

Summary

1. Urban economic growth is represented by changes in the urban labor market.
   a. The demand for labor comes from exporters and local producers. An increase in export sales increases local sales through the multiplier process. The employment multiplier is the change in total employment per unit change in export employment.
   b. An increase in demand increases total employment and the city's wage. The demand curve shifts as a result of changes in the cost of producing exports and local goods.
   c. The supply of labor comes from city residents. The supply curve is positively sloped because an increase in city size increases housing and land prices, forcing firms to pay higher wages to compensate for the increased living costs. An increase in supply (caused by improvements in environmental quality or public services) increases total employment and decreases the wage.
2. Economic growth generates benefits and costs. The larger city can exploit scale economies in production, retailing, and public goods. On the cost side, the larger city has higher housing prices, longer commuting distances, and more pollution, congestion, and crime.
3. Public policy can stimulate economic growth by decreasing the production costs of exporters and local producers. Direct policies include public education and training programs (which increase labor productivity) and the efficient provision of public services and infrastructure. Indirect policies improve the quality of life of the city, attracting workers and decreasing wages.
4. Some cities try to attract firms by offering subsidies (tax abatement, industrial bonds, government loans, and subsidized site development).
   a. Because taxes support local public services, a tax cut may decrease spending on public services, making the city less attractive to firms.
   b. Subsidy programs that attract new firms often generate relatively small benefits for local workers because many of the new jobs are filled by newcomers.
   c. Subsidy programs often promote the growth of one city at the expense of another, causing inefficient location choices.

5. A pollution-abatement program may increase total employment. The abatement program decreases labor demand and increases labor supply. If people are relatively sensitive to pollution, the increase in supply will be large relative to the decrease in demand, and the city will grow.

6. An economic base study predicts trends in urban income and employment. It is based on the notion that a city must earn its livelihood by exporting. An economic base study has three steps:
   a. Estimate the amount of export employment. Location quotients provide inaccurate estimates of export employment.
   b. Compute the multiplier, equal to the ratio of total employment to export employment.
   c. Project growth in export sales or employment.

7. Economic base studies are used by local governments to predict the demands for local public goods (schools, sewerage, fire protection) and by firms to predict the demands for private goods (groceries, shoes).

8. An input-output study is more sophisticated than the economic base study. It is based on a complete accounting of the economy's transactions, so it more accurately measures export and local activities. Input coefficients summarize the interactions between different sectors and are used to derive income multipliers for each industry.

9. The economic base study and the input-output study share a number of defects that limit their applicability.
   a. The multipliers are assumed to be constant. The actual multiplier is likely to increase as the city grows and is likely to change with factor prices.
   b. The two approaches assume that the city's wage is fixed. They estimate the horizontal shift of the city's demand curve, not the change in equilibrium employment.
   c. Both approaches focus attention on the demand side of the economy, suggesting that the city's economic fate is determined by outsiders. In fact, local governments can stimulate growth through their provision of public services.

10. Employment growth increases real income per capita by (a) hastening the move up the job hierarchy and (b) increasing the labor-force participation rate. The elasticity of real earnings with respect to total employment is 0.40. The elasticity is larger for households that are less educated, young, or black, because such households experience relatively large benefits from being promoted to higher-paying jobs.

11. Rapidly growing cities have relatively large employment gains (from openings and expansions), not relatively small employment losses (from closures and contractions).

12. Plant-closure laws include provisions for advance notification of closure and severance pay for workers.
    a. The notification requirement may increase the likelihood that a marginal plant will close. On the benefit side, advance notice gives workers an

opportunity to look for alternative employment, so it shortens unemployment spells.

 b. The requirement for severance pay (an additional fringe benefit) will decrease wages. Some workers will be forced to accept an undesirable compensation package.

 c. Because a plant closure sometimes increases employment elsewhere, closure generates external benefits as well as external costs.

 d. A city with a declining industry could focus its development efforts on facilitating the transition from old industries to new ones.

Exercises and Discussion Questions

1. Suppose that a consulting firm has generated the following information about the economy of Growville:

 i. The current employment in export industries is 50,000.

 ii. The current total employment in the city is 150,000.

 iii. Export employment is expected to grow by 10,000 jobs.

 a. Is there enough information to accurately predict the effect of the increase in export employment on total employment?

 b. If you have enough information, predict the employment effect and illustrate your answer with a graph.

 c. If there is insufficient information, proceed with the analysis as far as you can and list the additional information you need to complete the analysis. Illustrate your answer with a graph.

2. Consider a self-contained city, that is, a city in which all workers live in the city. The initial equilibrium wage is $W°$, and the initial equilibrium employment is $N°$.

 a. Suppose that the demand for the city's exports increases. Use the conventional supply-demand graph to show the effects of the increase in export demand on the city's labor market. Label everything: the axes, the curves, the new equilibrium wage (W'), and the new equilibrium total employment (N').

 b. Suppose that the city institutes a growth-control program that holds the total housing stock (total square footage) at its initial level (before the increase in export demand). Use the same supply-demand graph to show the effects of the increase in export demand under the growth-control program. Label the equilibrium wage under the growth-control program $W*$ and the equilibrium total employment $N*$.

 c. Explain the differences between the market equilibrium (*a*) and the growth-control equilibrium (*b*).

3. Consider a city that uses a business tax to finance the provision of industrial services (roads, water, sewers). If the city does not provide these services, the individual firms must supply their own roads, water, and sewers. Suppose that the city decides to cut business taxes and expenditures on

industrial services by the same amount. Evaluate the effects of the new tax-expenditure policy on the city's labor market. Will total employment in the city increase or decrease?

4. Consider two cities, Flexville and Rigid City, that have the same equilibrium wage and the same equilibrium total employment. The export industries in the two cities produce the same good. In Flexville, export firms produce with variable factor proportions: the amount of labor per unit of output depends on the relative price of labor. In Rigid City, export firms produce with fixed factor proportions: the amount of labor per unit of output is fixed. Suppose that both cities find a way to increase the quality of residential public services (for example, public schools, parks, libraries) without increasing taxes. Use two graphs, one for each city, to show the effects of the improvements in public services on (*a*) equilibrium employment and (*b*) the equilibrium wage.

5. One of the assumptions lurking behind the city's labor-supply curve is that an increase in the wage does not increase the fraction of the city's population in the work force. Draw two supply curves, one under the assumption of a fixed participation rate and another under the assumption that the participation rate increases with the wage. Explain any differences between the two supply curves.

6. The section on environmental quality suggests that a pollution tax may increase total employment. Suppose that instead of using a pollution tax to reduce citywide industrial pollution by a total of 25 percent, the city requires that *each* polluting firm decrease its pollution by 25 percent.
   a. Is the uniform-reduction policy more or less efficient than the pollution-tax program? In other words, will the total cost of abatement be larger or smaller under the uniform-reduction policy?
   b. Is the city more or less likely to grow under the uniform-reduction policy? Demonstrate, using a graph.

7. Consider a city with the following characteristics:
   i. The price elasticity of demand for the city's output is -3.0.
   ii. The elasticity of labor supply with respect to environmental quality is 0.10.
   iii. Polluting firms produce with fixed factor proportions: labor per unit output is fixed.
   iv. Polluting firms initially employ 25 percent of the city's export workers.

Suppose that the city adopts a new environmental policy that increases its environmental quality by 10 percent and increases the price of the polluting industry by 2 percent.
   a. Assume that the city's wage is fixed. Predict the percentage decreases in the demand for workers in (*i*) the polluting industry and (*ii*) the export industry.
   b. By what percentage will the supply of labor increase?

    c. Under what conditions (what values of the relevant elasticities) will the equilibrium number of workers increase? Illustrate your answer with a graph.

8. Consider a city that has decided to impose a pollution tax on its polluting firms. Fill in the blanks to make the following statements correct, and then briefly explain your responses. The city is more likely to grow as a result of the pollution tax if

    a. The elasticity of the supply of labor with respect to environmental quality is relatively _____ (the labor-supply curve shifts by a relatively _____ amount when environmental quality improves).

    b. The elasticity of demand for labor (with respect to the wage) by the city's nonpolluting industries is relatively _____.

    c. The elasticity of the supply of labor with respect to the wage is relatively _____ (the labor-supply curve is relatively _____).

9. In a report issued in September 1989, a consulting firm estimated the economic impacts of moving the Los Angeles Raiders (a professional football team) to Sacramento. The economic base study was based on the following assumptions:

    i. Total attendance at the Raider games will be 700,000 people per year.

    ii. The average ticket price will be $30.

    iii. The average fan will spend $10 on food, merchandise, and parking.

    iv. Based on *ii* and *iii*, the average fan will spend a total of $40.

    v. Total "direct" spending will be $28 million per year ($40 · 700k).

Using a spending multiplier of 2.2, the consulting firm estimated the total economic impact of the Raiders to be $61.6 million per year. Critically appraise the methods used to compute the total economic impact of the Raiders.

10. There are two ways to increase total employment: increased exports and import substitution. In what way are increased exports and import substitution similar? In what way are they dissimilar?

11. Consider the trade-offs associated with choosing a reference region for defining a city's location quotient. The traditional approach [see equation (6–8)] is to compare the city economy to the national economy. What if the denominator of the location quotient was defined as the percentage of state employment in mitten production? Would the measured location quotient be closer to or farther from the city's true location quotient?

12. In Figure 6–2, the shift of the demand curve from D_2 to D_3, which reflects the multiplier process, is parallel. The implicit assumption is that the employment multiplier is constant. Draw the demand curves under the assumption that the multiplier increases with city size.

13. Suppose that you have been given the following data on the transactions within a city's economy:

| Inputs | Producers | | | Households | Exports | Total Output |
	Computer Firms	Wire Producers	Local Merchants			
Computers	$ 0	$' 350	$	$ 300	$	$2,000
Wire	500	0	0	0	500	1,000
Local goods	0	0	0	2,500	0	
Labor	1,000	600	2,000	0	0	3,600
Imports			300			1,650
Total	$2,000	$	$	$3,600	$	$

a. Fill in the transactions table.

b. Will this city have a larger or a smaller export multiplier than the city with the transactions listed in Table 6–2? Explain.

14. Suppose that wire production in the city with the input coefficients shown in Table 6–3 increases by $100.

   a. Compute the first, second, and third rounds of spending resultant from the increase in wire sales, using the format of Figure 6–8 to report your results.

   b. By how much does spending on wire, computers, and local goods eventually increase?

   c. What is the ultimate increase in total sales?

15. Consider a city that estimates its export multipliers from the input coefficients from a 1965 input-output study.

   a. Will the city overestimate or underestimate the stimulative effects of exports?

   b. If your answer to (a) is "It depends on . . . ," make a list of questions that you would ask Ms. Information, the most knowledgeable person in the city. Note: She does not know the current input coefficients.

References and Additional Readings

The Urban Labor Market

Bartik, Timothy J. *Who Benefits from State and Local Economic Development Policies?* Kalamazoo, Mich.: Upjohn Institute, 1991. Chapters 5 and 6 explore the effects of employment growth on housing prices and real wages.

Eberts, Randall W., and Joe A. Stone. *Wage and Adjustment in Local Labor Markets.* Kalamazoo, Mich.: Upjohn Institute, 1992. Discusses how local labor markets adjust to shifts in supply and demand.

Hamilton, Bruce, and Robert Schwab. "Expected Appreciation in Urban Housing Markets." *Journal of Urban Economics* 18 (1985), pp. 103–18. Estimates the relationship between city size and housing prices.

Henderson, J. V. *Urban Development: Theory, Fact, and Illusion.* New York: Oxford University Press, 1988. Chapter 6 estimates the relationship between wages and city size, environmental quality, weather, and crime rates.

Robak, Jennifer. "Wages, Rents, and the Quality of Life." *Journal of Political Economy* 90 (1982), pp. 1257–78. Estimates the relationship between wages and city size.

Rosen, Sherwin. "Wage-Based Indexes of Urban Quality of Life." In *Current Issues in Urban Economics,* ed. Peter Mieszkowski and Mahlon Straszheim. Baltimore: Johns Hopkins, 1979. Estimates the relationship between wages and city size, environmental quality, weather, and crime.

Treyz, George, and Benjamin Stevens. "The TFS Regional Modelling Methodology." *Regional Studies* 19 (1985), pp. 547–62. Estimates the relationship between wages and city size.

Public Policy and Economic Growth

Bartik, Timothy J. *Who Benefits from State and Local Economic Development Policies?* Kalamazoo, Mich.: Upjohn Institute, 1991. Chapter 2 discusses the effects of various public policies on economic development.

Harrison, Bennett, and Sandra Kanter. "The Political Economy of Job-Creation Business Incentives." *Journal of the American Institute of Planners* 44 (October 1978), pp. 424–35.

Levy, John M. *Economic Development Programs for Cities, Counties, and Towns.* New York: Praeger Publishers, 1985. Detailed discussion of economic development policies.

Peltz, Michael, and Marc Weiss. "State and Local Government Initiative for Economic Development through Technological Development." *Journal of the American Planning Association* 50 (1984), pp. 270–279.

Rasmussen, David W.; Marc Bendick; and Larry Ledebur. "Evaluating State Economic Development Incentives from a Firm's Perspective." *Business Economics* 10 (1982), pp. 23–29.

Schmenner, Roger W. *Making Business Location Decisions.* Englewood, N.J.: Prentice Hall, 1982. Discusses how firms make location decisions.

Senia, Al, and George Weimer. "The War Between the States for High Technology." *Iron Age,* September 5, 1983. Discusses competition among states for high-technology industries.

City Size and Environmental Policy

Henderson, J. Vernon. "Effect of Taxation of Externalities on City Size." In *Urban Growth Policy in a Market Economy,* ed. George S. Tolley, Philip E. Graves, and John L. Gardner. New York: Academic Press, 1979, pp. 91–97.

Izraeli, Oded. "Externalities and Intercity Wage and Price Differentials." In *Urban Growth Policy in a Market Economy,* ed. George S. Tolley, Philip E. Graves, and John L. Gardner. New York: Academic Press, 1979, pp. 159–94.

Infrastructure and Economic Growth

Aschauer, David A. "Rx for Productivity: Build Infrastructure." *Federal Reserve Bank of Chicago Letter* 13 (September 1988). Suggests that underinvestment in public infrastructure during the 1970s and 1980s caused productivity to grow at a relatively slow rate.

Blinder, Alan. "Are Crumbling Highways Giving Productivity a Flat?" *Business Week,* August 1988. Discusses Aschauer's study of the connection between productivity growth and investment in public infrastructure.

Eberts, Randall W., and Joe A. Stone. *Wage and Adjustment in Local Labor Markets.* Kalamazoo, Mich.: Upjohn Institute, 1992. Chapter 5 estimates the effect of changes in public infrastructure on the urban labor market.

Economic Base Theory and Input-Output Analysis

DiPasquale, Denise, and Karen Polenske. "Output, Income, and Employment Input-Output Multipliers." In *Economic Impact Analysis: Methodology and Applications,* ed. Saul Pleeter. Boston: Martinus Nijhoff, 1980, pp. 85–113.

Hoover, Edgar M., and Frank Giarratani. *An Introduction to Regional Economics.* New York: Alfred A. Knopf, 1985, Chapter 11. A discussion of economic forecasting techniques (economic base analysis and input-output analysis).

Isserman, Andrew M. "Estimating Export Activity in a Regional Economy: A Theoretical and Empirical Analysis of Alternative Methods." *International Regional Science Review* 5 (1980), pp. 155–84. Discusses location quotients and other methods for measuring export employment.

Miernyk, William H. *The Elements of Input-Output Analysis.* New York: Random House, 1965. Describes the nuts and bolts of input-output analysis.

Pleeter, Saul. "Methodologies of Economic Impact Analysis: An Overview." In *Economic Impact Analysis: Methodology and Applications,* ed. Saul Pleeter. Boston: Martinus Nijhoff, 1980, pp. 7–31.

Richardson, Harry W. *Input-Output Analysis and Regional Economics.* New York: John Wiley & Sons, 1972, pp. 1–52.

Tiebout, Charles M. *The Community Economic Base Study.* New York: Committee for Economic Development, 1962.

Critique of Economic Base and Input-Output Approaches

Chinitz, Benjamin. "Contrasts in Agglomeration: New York and Pittsburgh." In *Readings in Urban Economics,* ed. Matthew Edel and Jerome Rothenberg. New York: Macmillan, 1972. A discussion of the supply side of the urban economy.

North, Douglass C. "Location Theory and Regional Economic Growth." In *Regional Policy: Readings in Theory and Application,* ed. John Friedmann and William Alonso. Cambridge, Mass.: MIT Press, 1975. States the case for the export-driven model of regional growth.

Tiebout, Charles M. "Exports and Regional Economic Growth." In *Regional Policy: Readings in Theory and Application,* ed. John Friedmann and William Alonso. Cambridge, Mass.: MIT Press, 1975. Critiques the standard export-driven growth model.

Costs and Benefits of Employment Growth

Bartik, Timothy J. *Who Benefits from State and Local Economic Development Policies?* Kalamazoo, Mich.: Upjohn Institute, 1991. Chapters 4 and 7 discuss the effects of employment growth on employment rates and real income per capita.

Mishan, E. J. *The Costs of Economic Growth*. London: Staples Press, 1967. Discusses the costs and benefits of regional growth.

Summers, Gene. *The Invasion of Non-Metropolitan America by Industry: A Quarter Century of Experience*. New York: Praeger Publishers, 1976. Describes the effects of new plants on small towns.

Composition of Changes in Employment

Armington, Catherine, and Marjorie Odle. "Small Business—How Many Jobs?" *Brookings Review*, Winter 1982, pp. 14–17. A critique of Birch's work.

Birch, David. "Who Creates Jobs?" *The Public Interest,* Fall 1981. Discusses the role of small business in economic development.

Eberts, Randall W., and Joe A. Stone. *Wage and Adjustment in Local Labor Markets*. Kalamazoo, Mich.: Upjohn Institute, 1992. Chapter 2 presents facts on employment changes from plant openings, expansions, closures, and contractions.

U.S. Small Business Administration. *The State of Small Business: 1984*. Washington, D.C.: Government Printing Office, 1984. Chapters 1, 2, and 4 discuss the debate over David Birch's work.

Plant-Closure Legislation

Edel, Matthew. "People versus Place in Urban Impact Analysis." In *The Urban Impacts of Federal Policy,* ed. Norman J. Glickman. Baltimore: Johns Hopkins, 1980, pp. 175–91. Discusses the issue of whether policy should be directed toward people or places.

Hekman, John S., and John S. Strong. "Is There a Case for Plant Closing Laws?" *New England Economic Review,* July/August 1980, pp. 34–51. Discusses the pros and cons of closing laws and describes Sweden's policies for plant closures. Explores some of the evidence concerning the effects of plant closures in the Frostbelt.

McKenzie, Richard. *Plant Closings: Public or Private Choices*. Washington, D.C.: Cato, 1982. A discussion of plant-closure laws.

Winnick, Louis. "Place Prosperity vs. People Prosperity." In *Essays in Urban Land Economics*, ed. James Gillies. Los Angeles: University of California Press, 1966.

PART II

Land Rent and Urban Land-Use Patterns

The first part of this book explains why cities exist and where they develop, but not how activities are arranged within cities. This second part examines the spatial structure of cities, taking a close look at land use within cities. It explores the market forces and government policies that determine the equilibrium land-use pattern.

This part is divided into five chapters. Chapter 7 develops the basic concepts of land rent and land use: it explains the factors that determine the equilibrium price of land and shows how land is allocated among alternative land uses. Chapter 8 discusses land rent and land use in the monocentric city, explaining why commercial and industrial activity was concentrated in the central core area. It also explains why the poor tend to locate in central cities. Chapter 9 uses general-equilibrium analysis to explore the interactions between the residential land market, the business land market, and the urban labor market. Chapter 10 describes land use in the modern cities, explaining why the traditional monocentric city was replaced by the modern multicentric city. Chapter 11 discusses the role of local government in the urban land market, exploring the market effects of zoning and other land-use controls.

CHAPTER 7 Introduction to Land Rent and Land Use

The trouble with land is that they're not making it anymore.
Will Rogers

This chapter introduces some basic concepts of land rent and land use, setting the stage for the discussion of urban land use in Chapters 8 through 11. This chapter addresses three questions about the land market. First, what determines the price of land? Second, who benefits from public policies that increase the fertility or accessibility of land? Third, does the land market allocate land efficiently?

It will be useful to define two terms, *land rent* and *market value*. Like other assets, land yields a stream of marketable services and thus a stream of income. For example, agricultural land yields a stream of agricultural output (bushels of corn), generating a stream of income for the farmer. Similarly, a parking lot in the city yields a stream of parking services, generating a stream of income for the parking firm. When a landowner grants the rights to use his land to another individual or a firm, he charges **land rent.** If a farmer is granted the right to grow corn on a plot of land, the rent might be $1,000 per acre per year. If a firm is granted the right to operate a parking lot on a plot of land, the rent might be $5,000 per acre per year.

What determines the market value of land? The **market value** of land equals the **present value** of the stream of rental income generated by the land. To explain the concept of present value, consider an asset that generates R of income each year and is expected to generate this income for n years. If the market interest rate is i, the present value of the stream of earnings from the asset is

$$PV = \sum_{t=0}^{n} \frac{R}{(1 + i)^t} \qquad (7\text{--}1)$$

167

For example, if an asset is expected to generate $20 of net income per year, starting today and lasting for a total of five years, and the interest rate is 10%, the present value of the asset is

$$PV = 20 + \frac{20}{1.10} + \frac{20}{1.21} + \frac{20}{1.33} + \frac{20}{1.46} \tag{7-2}$$

$$PV = 20 + 18.18 + 16.53 + 15.04 + 13.70 = \$83.45 \tag{7-3}$$

If the stream of earnings lasts forever, the equation for present value simplifies to

$$PV = \frac{R}{i} = \frac{20}{0.10} = 200 \tag{7-4}$$

For example, if the $20 annual income lasts forever, the present value of the asset is $200.

The present value is the maximum amount that an investor is willing to pay for an asset, given an alternative investment that yields i percent per year. Suppose that the alternative is a savings account that yields 10 percent per year. The investor can either invest in an asset that yields $20 per year forever or invest in a savings account that yields 10 percent per year. At a purchase price of $200, the investor is indifferent between spending $200 on the asset and investing the same amount in a savings account: in both cases, the annual income is $20. At a purchase price less than $200, the investor prefers the asset to the savings account. For example, if the price is $100, the investor can make $20 per year by investing $100 in the asset, compared to $10 per year by investing the same amount in a savings account. Similarly, for a purchase price exceeding $200, the savings account is more lucrative than the asset.

The market value of land is the present value of the annual rental payments from the land. Land used for residential, commercial, and industrial activities can, in principle, yield a constant stream of rental income. In contrast with agricultural land, which can deteriorate with use, developed land does not deteriorate. Therefore, the market value equals the annual rent divided by the interest rate. For example, if the annual rent on a plot of land is $5,000 per acre and the market interest rate is 10 percent, the market value of land is $50,000 per acre. The market value of land equals the present value because the present value makes an investor indifferent between buying the land (spending $50,000 to earn $5,000 per year in land rent forever) and putting the $50,000 in a bank account with a 10 percent interest rate (earnings of $5,000 per year).

This book uses land rent—not market value—as the **price of land**. Most of the other relevant economic variables are defined as streams of revenue or costs. For example, a household earns an annual income, and a firm computes its annual profits as its annual revenue less its annual cost. To be consistent, the *price of land* is defined as the annual payment in exchange for the right to use the land: the *price of land* is synonymous with *land rent*. Given the simple relationship between rent and value, it's easy to make the translation from land rent to market value: just divide the annual rent by the market interest rate.

Land Rent and Fertility

David Ricardo (1821) is credited with the idea that the price of agricultural land is determined by its fertility. The more productive the land, the more a tenant farmer is willing to pay to use the land. Fertility analysis demonstrates some of the most important concepts of land rent in a simple and compelling way.

Consider an agricultural county where tenant farmers use land of varying fertility to grow corn. The characteristics of the local economy are as follows:

1. **Fixed prices.** The prices of the output (corn) and inputs (labor, seed, fertilizer, capital) are determined in national markets, so local farmers take the prices as given. The prices are the same at all locations in the county.

2. **Zero economic profit.** There is free entry into farming, so all farmers make zero economic profits (normal accounting profits).

3. **Fertility of land.** There are three types of land: *h* (high fertility), *m* (medium fertility), and *l* (low fertility).

4. **Land to highest bidder.** Landowners rent their land to the highest bidder.

5. **Zero transport costs.** Transport costs are assumed to be so small that they can be ignored. Later in the chapter, this assumption will be relaxed.

Figure 7–1 shows the conventional cost curves for one-acre plots of the three types of land. The marginal-cost curves (MC) are positively sloped, and pass through the U-shaped average total-cost curves (ATC) at the minimum points of average cost curves. The cost curves include all the nonland costs of production, including the costs of raw materials (seeds and fertilizer), capital (tractors), and labor. They also include the opportunity cost of being a farmer, for example, the money the farmer gives up by being a farmer instead of a steelworker.

The positions of the cost curves depend on the fertility of the land. A farmer on relatively fertile land can produce the same amount of corn with smaller quantities of the nonland inputs. Because the farmer spends less money on seeds, fertilizer, tractors, and labor, his average cost curves are lower. In general, the higher the fertility, the lower the cost curves.

How much are farmers willing to pay for the three types of land? In Figure 7–1, the national corn market generates an equilibrium price of $10: supply intersects demand at a price of $10. Farmers are price takers and maximize profit where price equals marginal cost. The profit-maximizing output on the high-fertility land is 220 bushels per acre, generating profit equal to the shaded area. In this example, profit equals $1,320 per acre per year (total revenue of $2,200 less a total cost of $880). A farmer would be willing to pay up to $1,320 per year to use one acre of the high-fertility land. Similarly, a farmer would be willing to pay up to $320 per year for the medium-fertility land. For the low-fertility land, production costs are so high that corn production is not profitable at a price of $10, so a corn farmer would not be willing to pay anything for the low-fertility land.

FIGURE 7–1 Fertility and Land Rent

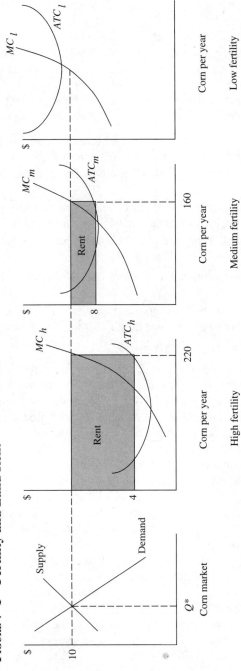

The equilibrium price of corn is $10 per bushel. Competition for land forces farmers to pay their surplus (total revenue less total nonland cost) to landowners. The high-fertility land has lower production costs and higher pre-rent profit, so farmers are willing to pay more rent. The medium-fertility land earns less rent because it has higher production costs. The low-fertility land generates no profits, so its rent is zero.

Competition and Land Rent

Competition among prospective farmers bids up the price of land to the point at which economic profit is zero (accounting profit is normal). Farmers are willing to pay up to $1,320 for the high-fertility land, and are forced by competition to do so: at any rent less than $1,320 per acre, the landowner will be able to find another farmer willing to pay slightly more to use the land. Similarly, the equilibrium rent on the medium-fertility land is $320. Because the equilibrium land rents make economic profits equal to zero, farmers are indifferent between different plots of land. Although the high-fertility land has lower production costs, the savings in production costs are offset by higher land costs.

In equilibrium, land rent equals the excess of total revenue over nonland costs. This is the **leftover principle**: because of competition among farmers for land, the landowner gets the leftovers. This principle assumes that individual plots of land have unique characteristics, but farmers are all the same. Competition among a large number of farmers, each of whom has the same cost curves, bids up the price of high-fertility land to the point at which economic profit is zero. If the farmer on the high-fertility land pays less than the excess of total revenue over nonland cost, the farmer would be evicted and replaced with another farmer willing to pay the leftovers (total revenue less nonland cost) for the opportunity to earn normal accounting profits.

The leftover principle does not hold if there are restrictions on entry and competition. One restriction on entry comes from patents. If farmer Tom holds the patent for a particular farming technique, he has lower production costs than all other farmers. For example, suppose that Tom can produce an acre's worth of corn for a pre-rent profit of $2,000, and other farmers, using inferior techniques, generate a pre-rent profit of only $500. The landlord is unable to charge Tom a rent of $2,000 because the threat of eviction is a hollow one: there are no other farmers with the same production costs, so there are no farmers willing to pay $2,000 per acre. Instead, Tom pays only $500, allowing him to make an economic profit of $1,500. The landowner does not get the leftovers because the patent restricts competition. Once the patent expires and all farmers have access to the same technology, the landowner can increase land rent and convert the economic profit into increased land rent.

Land Rent and Public Policy

Fertility analysis can be used to predict the effects of public policy on land rent. Suppose that an agricultural county builds an aqueduct and provides free irrigation to farmers. Who benefits from the irrigation project?

Consider first the possibility that the irrigation project does not affect the equilibrium price of corn. The irrigation project decreases farmers' production costs, shifting the cost curves downward, as shown in Figure 7–2. For all three types of land, pre-rent profits increase: high-fertility land and medium-fertility land become more profitable, and low-fertility land now generates a positive profit. As profit increases, competition among farmers bids up land rent to the point at which economic profit is zero. The savings in production costs are paid to landowners in the form of higher rent, so the benefits of the irrigation project go to landowners.

FIGURE 7–2 Effects of Irrigation Project on Land Rent and Corn Price

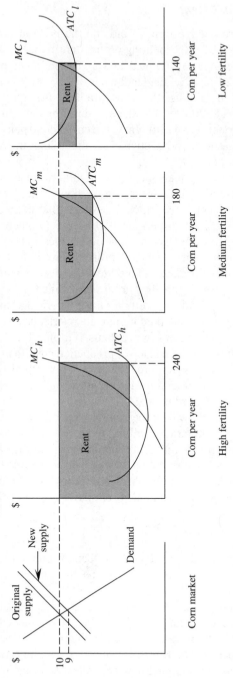

An irrigation project decreases production costs for all three types of land. If the price of corn stays at $10, the shaded areas show the land rent on the three types of land. The supply of corn will increase because land is used more intensively (output increases on the high-fertility and medium-fertility land) and marginal (low-fertility) land is brought into production. The increase in supply decreases the equilibrium price of corn, so the rent on each plot of land is actually less than the shaded area.

Will the price of corn be affected by the irrigation project? The project increases the supply of corn for two reasons. First, the project shifts the marginal-cost curves downward, increasing the profit-maximizing outputs of the high-fertility and medium-fertility farms. Second, marginal land (low-fertility land) is brought into production. For these two reasons, the supply curve shifts to the right, decreasing the equilibrium price of corn. Therefore, corn consumers benefit from the irrigation project. As the price of corn decreases, the pre-rent profits of farmers decrease, decreasing land rent. In other words, consumers gain at the expense of landowners.

What determines the distribution of benefits between landowners and corn consumers? The general rule is that the smaller the geographical area covered by the irrigation program, the larger the share of the benefits that go to landowners. Consider first an irrigation project that decreases the production costs of a single 50-acre plot of land. The project causes a trivial increase in supply and virtually no change in the price of corn. Therefore, all the benefits go to the landowner. Consider next a national irrigation project that decreases the production costs of all corn farmers. The project causes a large increase in supply (existing land is cultivated more intensively and more land is brought under production), so it decreases corn prices significantly. In this case, a large share of the benefits goes to consumers.

The benefits of the irrigation project are **capitalized** into the market value of land. Since the project increases the annual rent, it increases the present value of the stream of earnings from land, increasing its market value. For example, suppose that the annual rent on high-fertility land increases from $1,320 per acre per year to $1,500. If the market interest rate is 10 percent, equation (7–4) suggests that the market value of land rises from $13,200 per acre to $15,000 per acre.

Land Rent and Accessibility

This section uses a model developed by Von Thunen (in 1826) to explain why land rent increases with the accessibility of land. In the Von Thunen model, accessibility replaces fertility as the determinant of land rent. The Von Thunen approach will be used in Chapter 8 (Land Use in the Monocentric City) to discuss urban land rent and land use.

Consider a county where all land is used to grow carrots. The characteristics of the economy are as follows:

1. **Fixed prices.** The prices of the output (carrots) and inputs (labor, seed, fertilizer, capital) are determined in national markets, so farmers take the prices as given. The prices are the same at all locations.
2. **Marketplace.** All carrots are transported from farms to a central marketplace at a cost of t per ton per mile.
3. **Competitive markets.** There is free entry into carrot farming. In equilibrium, all farmers make zero economic profits (normal accounting profits).
4. **Fertility of land.** All land is equally fertile, so production costs are the same at all locations.

Linear Land-Rent Function

Suppose that carrots are produced with fixed factor proportions. In other words, farmers do not engage in factor substitution as the relative prices of inputs change. The typical farmer occupies one acre of land and produces Q tons of carrots, which are sold at a price of P per ton. If the unit transport cost is t per ton per mile, total transport cost for a farm located u miles from the marketplace is

$$TC = t \cdot Q \cdot u \tag{7–5}$$

For example, if unit transport cost (t) is \$4 per ton per mile and the farmer produces 20 tons per acre, transport cost is \$80 for a farm one mile from the market, \$160 for a farm two miles from the market, and so on. If the farmer spends C on nonland production costs (labor, raw materials, and the opportunity cost of farming time) and land rent is R, the profit per acre is

$$\pi = P \cdot Q - C - t \cdot Q \cdot u - R \tag{7–6}$$

For zero economic profit, the bid rent for land is

$$R = P \cdot Q - C - t \cdot Q \cdot u \tag{7–7}$$

Because land near the marketplace (u) has relatively low transport costs, the farmer is willing to pay more for this land.

Figure 7–3 shows the **bid-rent function** of the typical farmer. The numerical assumptions are listed below the graph. Total revenue per acre (shown by the horizontal line) is the same at all locations because price and quantity do not vary across space. Total cost is the sum of nonland cost per acre and transport costs. The total-cost curve is positively sloped because transport costs increase with distance to the market; the slope of the cost curve is ($t \cdot Q$). The farmer's bid rent for a particular location is total revenue less total cost, so the bid-rent function is negatively sloped. The bid rent is \$250 at the marketplace and falls by \$80 per mile.

The **land-rent function** shows the equilibrium land rent for different locations. Farmers compete for land, bidding up land rent to the point at which economic profit is zero at every location. If all farmers are identical (they all have the same production costs and transport costs), the land-rent function is the same as the bid-rent function of the typical farmer. The land-rent function makes farmers indifferent among all land in the county: as the farmer approaches the market, the savings in transport costs are exactly offset by increases in land rent.

Factor Substitution: Convex Land-Rent Function

The bid-rent function in Figure 7–3 is linear because the farmer is assumed to be inflexible. The farmer produces 20 tons of carrots with one acre of land and \$50 worth of nonland inputs, regardless of the relative price of land. This section shows that if farmers engage in factor substitution, the bid-rent function is convex instead of linear.

Consider a flexible farmer, defined as one who changes input proportions as the relative price of land changes. If the farmer moves to relatively expensive land, she

FIGURE 7–3   Revenue, Cost, and Bid Rent for the Carrot Farmer

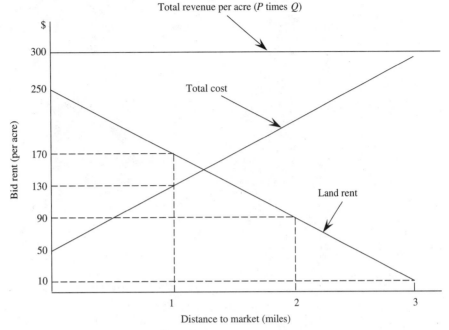

Land rent equals total revenue less nonland costs and transport costs. The farmer's total revenue is $300 and nonland cost is $50. Transport cost increases by $80 for every mile from the marketplace, so the slope of the bid-rent function is $80.

substitutes nonland inputs (capital, labor, raw materials) for land, so she can produce 20 tons of carrots on a smaller plot of land. The farmer's production isoquant, mapped in Figure 7–4, shows the different input combinations that produce 20 tons of carrots: the possibilities include points B (0.80 acres of land and $60 of nonland inputs) and C (0.60 acres and $80 of nonland inputs).

Table 7–1 shows how to compute the farmer's bid-rent function. If the farmer uses T acres of land, the new expression for profit is

$$\pi = P \cdot Q - C - t \cdot Q \cdot u - R \cdot T \tag{7–8}$$

Economic profit is zero if the total payment for land is

$$R \cdot T = P \cdot Q - C - t \cdot Q \cdot u \tag{7–9}$$

Dividing each side by T gives the bid rent per acre:

$$R = \frac{P \cdot Q - C - t \cdot Q \cdot u}{T} \tag{7–10}$$

At a location three miles from the market, the flexible farmer uses the same input combinations as the inflexible farmer (one acre of land and $50 worth of nonland inputs), and is willing to pay the same amount in land rent ($10). As the farmer moves toward the marketplace, the price of land increases, causing movement up

FIGURE 7–4   Isoquant for 20 Tons of Carrots

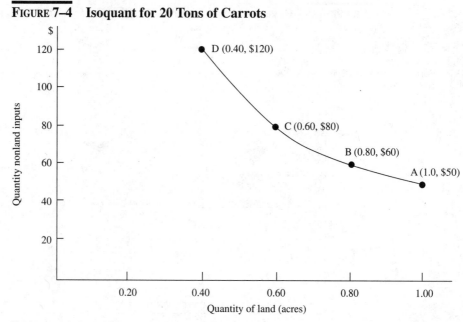

The isoquant shows the different combinations of land and nonland inputs needed to produce 20 tons of carrots. As the farmer moves toward the market, the price of land increases, so the farmer moves up the isoquant, substituting nonland inputs for land.

the isoquant, from point B (two miles), to C (one mile), to D. For each location, the pre-rent profit is total revenue less nonland costs and transport costs [the right-hand side of equation (7–9)]. The bid rent per acre equals the pre-rent profit divided by the size of the farm (in acres). For a farm two miles from the market, pre-rent profit is $80 on 0.80 acres of land, so the farmer is willing to pay $100 per acre ($80/0.80).

TABLE 7–1   Costs and Land Rent for the Flexible Farmer

Distance to Market (miles)	Farm Size (acres)	Total Revenue	Nonland Costs	Transport Costs	Pre-Rent Profit	Rent per Acre
0	0.4	$300	$120	$ 0	$180	$450
1	0.6	300	80	80	140	233
2	0.8	300	60	160	80	100
3	1.0	300	50	240	10	10

Assumptions
Output = 20 tons
Price = $15
Transport cost = $4 per ton per mile
Pre-rent profit = Total revenue − Nonland costs − Transport cost
$$\text{Rent} = \frac{\text{Pre-rent profit}}{\text{Farm size}}$$

FIGURE 7–5   **Bid-Rent Functions of Inflexible and Flexible Farmers**

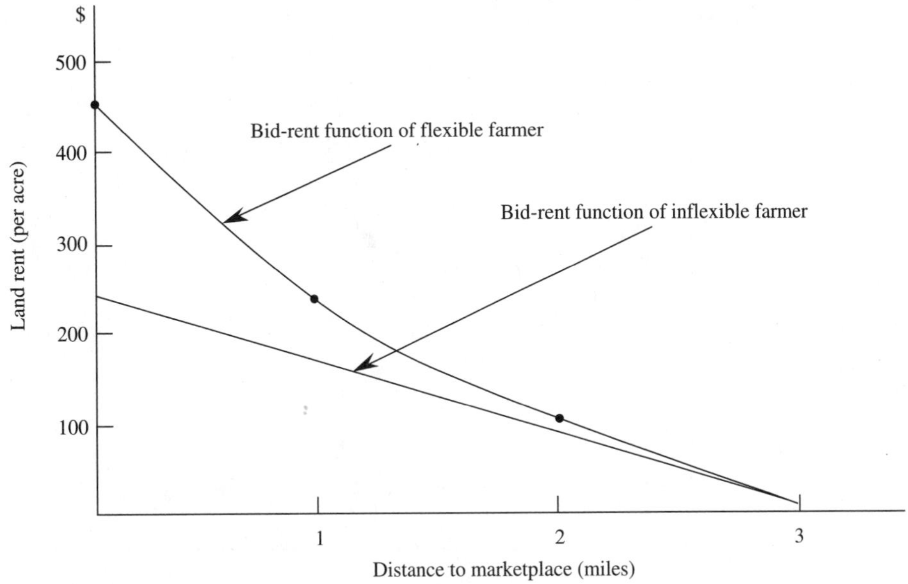

The bid-rent function of the inflexible farmer is linear because carrots are produced with fixed factor proportions. In contrast, the flexible farmer is more efficient, so the farmer has lower production costs and can pay more rent.

The bid rent increases as the farmer approaches the market, rising to $450 for a farm close to the marketplace.

Figure 7–5 shows the bid-rent functions of the flexible and inflexible farmers. The flexible bid-rent function lies above the inflexible one for all locations except $u = 3$, that is, the flexible farmer outbids the inflexible one for all land except at $u = 3$. To explain the ability of the flexible farmer to outbid the inflexible one, suppose that both farmers start at $u = 3$. At $u = 3$, both farmers have the same bid rent ($10) because they use the same input combination (1 acre of land and $50 of nonland inputs). Suppose that each farmer considers a one-mile move toward the marketplace, which would decrease transport costs by $80. Since the inflexible farmer does not change his input combinations, his bid rent would increase by $80. In contrast, the flexible farmer would substitute nonland inputs for the relatively expensive land (moving up the isoquant from point A to B in Figure 7–4). Given the higher price of land at $u = 2$, point B is more efficient than point A, so the flexible farmer has lower production costs. The decrease in production costs from factor substitution increases the bid rent for land, so the flexible farmer can outbid the inflexible farmer.

Figure 7–6 shows the general shape of the bid-rent functions of flexible and inflexible farmers. Because the inflexible farmer uses the same input combination at all locations, the bid-rent function simply reflects differences in transport costs: the bid-rent function is linear, with a slope equal to transport cost per mile. In contrast, the flexible farmer engages in factor substitution, generating savings in both transportation costs and production costs as the farmer moves toward the marketplace. As a result, the flexible bid-rent function is convex, as shown by R_f. The two bid-rent

FIGURE 7–6   Flexible versus Inflexible Bid-Rent Functions

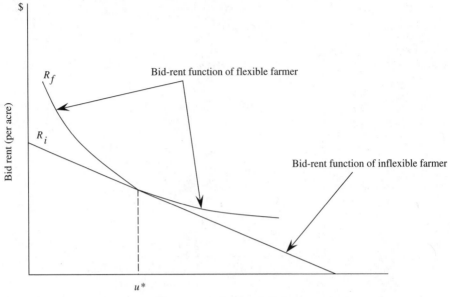

The flexible farmer is more efficient than the inflexible one, and is therefore able to pay more for land. The rent functions are tangent at the point at which the inflexible farmer is lucky enough to choose the efficient input combination.

functions are tangent at the point at which the two farmers choose the same input combination (u^*).

Will landowners rent land to inflexible farmers? For most plots of land, flexible farmers outbid inflexible farmers. The inflexible farmer will get land only if the farmer is lucky enough to choose the efficient input combination. In general, inflexibility means inefficiency, so the competition for land eliminates inefficient farmers.

Decrease in Transport Costs and Land Rent

How does a decrease in transport costs affect the bid-rent function? In Figure 7–7, the original bid-rent function is R_0 and the radius of the carrot farming district is u_0 miles. For land beyond u_0, transport costs are so high that carrot farmers are not willing to pay anything for land. Suppose that a new highway is built, decreasing the cost of transporting carrots to the market. The decrease in transport costs per mile decreases the slope of the bid-rent function. If the price of carrots is fixed, the bid-rent function shifts from R_0 to R_1, so the radius of the carrot district increases from u_0 miles to u_1 miles. In this case, the benefits of decreased transport costs go to landowners: land within the original farm district commands a higher rent, and marginal land (between u_0 and u_1) now commands a positive rent.

The decrease in transport costs increases the supply of carrots for two reasons. First, land in the original carrot district is used more intensively. As land rent rises,

FIGURE 7–7   Effect of Decreased Transport Cost on Bid-Rent Function

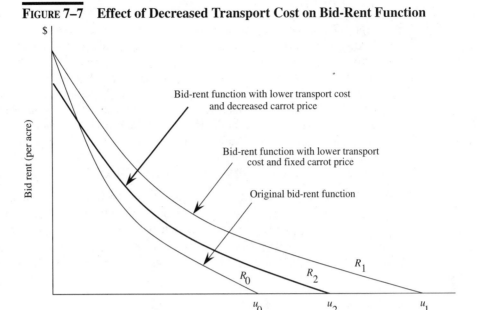

A decrease in transport costs decreases the slope of the bid-rent function. If the price of carrots is fixed, the function shifts from R_0 to R_1. If the supply of carrots increases and the market price drops, the bid-rent function shifts downward from R_1 to R_2.

farmers economize on land by substituting nonland factors for land. As farmers move up their isoquants, output per acre increases. Second, marginal land (between u_0 and u_1) is brought into production, increasing the total acreage of carrot production.

What are the implications of the increased carrot supply for the bid-rent function? If the increase in supply is large enough to decrease the equilibrium price of carrots, total revenue per acre decreases, decreasing the amount farmers are willing to pay for land. As shown in Figure 7–7, the decrease in the price of carrots shifts the bid-rent function downward from R_1 to R_2. The downward shift of the bid-rent function decreases the radius of the carrot district from u_1 to u_2.

The benefits of the highway are shared by landowners and consumers. Landowners can charge a higher rent because their land is more accessible, and carrot consumers face lower prices because there is a greater supply of carrots. As explained earlier for the irrigation project, the distribution of benefits between landowners and consumers depends on the geographical extent of the public works program. If a single county improves its road to increase the accessibility of its carrot-growing land, the supply of carrots will increase by a trivial amount and the price will decrease by a trivial amount. Therefore, most of the benefits of the highway go to landowners. In contrast, a national highway program is likely to increase supply and decrease price by relatively large amounts. Therefore, some of the benefits of new highways go to consumers.

Two Land Uses

Figure 7–8 shows how land is allocated between two competing users. Because land is allocated to the highest bidder, land within u' miles of the market is occupied by activity E, and land beyond u' is occupied by C. The equilibrium land-rent function (the thick line in Figure 7–8) shows the market rent for different locations. For u less than u', E outbids C, so the land-rent function is the same as E's bid-rent function. For u greater than u', the land-rent function is the same as C's bid-rent function.

Activity E occupies the land closest to the market because it has a relatively steep bid-rent function. The bid-rent function is negatively sloped because of transport costs, so the higher the transport costs, the steeper the bid-rent function. Transport costs are relatively high if the output is relatively heavy or costly to ship.

1. **More output per acre: eggplant and cotton.** Because eggplant farmers produce more tons per acre than cotton farmers, they have higher transport costs and a steeper bid-rent function (everything else being equal).

2. **Higher unit transport costs: eggs and carrots.** Although carrots can be thrown in the back of a truck, eggs must be placed in egg cartons. A ton

FIGURE 7–8   The Activity with the Steeper Bid-Rent Function Locates Near the Market

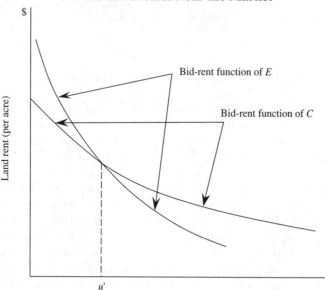

Because activity E's bid-rent function is steeper than C's, E occupies land closer to the marketplace. E has a relatively steep bid-rent function because it has relatively high transport costs, a result of either higher unit transport costs (eggs versus carrots) or more tons per acre (eggplant versus cotton). The equilibrium land-rent function is the thick line (the E bid-rent function for $u < u'$, and the C bid-rent function for $u > u'$). Land is allocated to its "highest and best use."

of eggs takes up more space than a ton of carrots, so eggs have a higher unit transport cost. Egg producers have higher total transport costs and thus a steeper bid-rent function (everything else being equal).

In general, the activity with higher transport costs (higher transport rate or greater weight) occupies the central land.

Does the land market allocate land efficiently? The market allocates central land to the activity with the highest transport costs, that is, the activity with the most to gain from proximity to the market. To explain, suppose that an eggplant farmer starts at a location one mile from the market and then swaps locations with a cotton farmer three miles from the market. Since the eggplant farmer has higher transport costs per acre of production, the land swap increases eggplant transportation costs by more than it decreases cotton transport costs, so total transport costs increase. In general, because the market allocates central land to the activity with relatively large transport costs, it minimizes total transportation costs. In the terms used by land developers, land is allocated to its "highest and best use."

The conclusion that the land market allocates land efficiently rests on the assumption that there are no externalities in land use. If there are externalities, the market allocation is inefficient, and government intervention can be justified on efficiency grounds. The issue of land-use externalities will be examined in detail in later chapters.

Market Interactions

The demand for land is derived from the demand for outputs (corn, carrots, housing, retail goods, manufactured goods). This section examines the interactions between the land market and the output market. The discussion addresses a sort of chicken-and-egg question about the land market: is the price of land high because the price of output is high, or is the price of output high because the price of land is high?

The Corn Laws Debate

The British Corn Laws of the 1800s restricted grain imports to Britain. The decrease in the supply of imported grain increased the demand for domestically produced corn. Figure 7–9 shows the effects of the Corn Laws on the corn market and the land market.

1. **Corn market.** The Corn Laws shifted the demand curve from d_1 to d_2. The price of domestic corn increased from P_1 to P_2, and the quantity of corn produced increased from C_1 to C_2.

2. **Land market.** As domestic corn production increased, the demand for land increased. In Figure 7–9, the increase in corn production shifted the demand curve for land from D_1 to D_2. Because the supply curve is perfectly inelastic (they aren't making land any more), the increase in demand increased the price of land from R_1 to R_2.

FIGURE 7–9   **The Corn Laws Debate**

(A)

Corn market

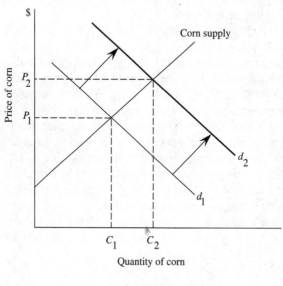

(B)

Land market

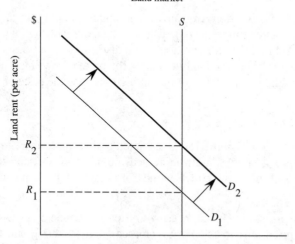

The Corn Laws restricted grain imports, increasing the demand for domestic corn and its price. Corn production increased from C_1 to C_2, increasing the demand for land from D_1 to D_2. The price of land increased from R_1 to R_2. The price of land is high because the price of corn (and the production of corn) is high.

To summarize, the price of land is high because the price of corn is high. The Corn Laws increased the price of corn, which stimulated the production of corn and the demand for corn-growing land. Landowners responded by increasing the price of land to allocate the fixed resource among competing land uses. The lesson is that high land prices are the result of high corn prices, not the reason for high corn prices.

Housing Prices and Land Prices

The lesson from the Corn Laws debate is applicable to the urban housing market. Consider the following statement: "Greedy landowners in the San Francisco Bay Area have increased the price of land, increasing the price of housing." In fact, the price of land is high because the demand for housing (and the demand for land on which to build housing) is high. As the demand for housing increases, the price of housing increases, causing builders to buy more land to build more houses. The increase in the demand for land increases the price of land. Or consider the following: "The price of land in Boston is so high that few people can afford to live there." In fact, the price of land in Boston is high because so many people *can* afford to live there. The large demand for housing generates a large demand for land, which causes a relatively high price of land. The high price of land is the result—not the cause—of high housing prices.

The Single Tax

In 1880, Henry George proposed a 100 percent tax on rental income. The proposed tax was dubbed the "single tax" because it would have generated enough revenue to support all levels of government at the time. The spirit of the single tax is best expressed by George himself. The following is from an interview with David Dudley Field (in the *North American Review* in 1885):

> *Field:* Then suppose A to be the proprietor of a thousand acres on the Hudson, chiefly farming land, but at the same time having on it houses, barns, cattle, horses, carriages, furniture; how is he to be dealt with under your theory?
>
> *George:* He would be taxed on the value of his land, and not on the value of his improvements and stock. . . . The effect of our present system, which taxes a man for values created by his labor and capital, is to put a fine upon industry, and repress improvement. The more houses, the more crops, the more buildings in the country, the better for us all, and we are doing ourselves an injury by imposing taxes upon the production of such things.
>
> *Field:* Then you would tax the farmer whose farm is worth $1,000 as heavily as you would tax the adjoining proprietor, who, with the same quantity of land, has added improvements worth $100,000; is that your idea?
>
> *George:* It is. The improvements made by the capitalist would do no harm to the farmer, and would benefit the whole community, and I would do nothing to discourage them.

Field: A large landlord in New York owns a hundred houses, each worth, say, $25,000 (scattered in different parts of the city); at what rate of valuation would you tax him?

George: On his houses, nothing. I would tax him on the value of the lots.

Field: As vacant lots?

George: As if each particular lot were vacant, surrounding improvements remaining the same.

Field: Well, what do you contemplate as the ending of such a scheme?

George: The taking of the full annual value of land for the benefit of the whole people. I hold that land belongs equally to all, that land values arise from the presence of all, and should be shared among all.

George proposed the single tax for both equity and efficiency reasons. On the equity issue, George argued that land rent is determined by nature and society, not by the efforts of landowners. As discussed earlier in the chapter, agricultural land rent is determined by the fertility of the soil and its accessibility to markets. Similarly, the urban land rent is determined by its accessibility to other activities. In George's time, cities were growing rapidly, causing rapid increases in land rent and value. George argued that landowners did nothing to deserve the increases in property value, so that any windfall gains from urban growth should be taxed away.

On the efficiency issue, George argued that the land tax would eliminate the need for taxes on improvements. The elimination of improvement taxes would stimulate investment in houses, crops, and buildings. The land tax would not affect the supply of land because the supply of land is fixed. The replacement of the improvement tax with the land tax would increase the total wealth of society.

The single tax has been criticized for three reasons. First, the single tax would decrease the net return to the landowner (net land rent) to zero, making the market value of land zero. In other words, the government would essentially confiscate the land. This strikes many people as inequitable. Second, if the net return on land is zero, landowners will abandon their land, leaving government bureaucrats to decide who uses the land. Unlike the private owner, who receives more income if the land is used efficiently, the bureaucrat has nothing to gain from the efficient use of land. Therefore, the government land market is less likely to allocate land to its highest and best use. The third criticism is that it is difficult to measure land rent (and the appropriate tax). Most land has structures or other improvements, and it is difficult to separate the value generated by the raw land from the value generated by the improvements.

An alternative to the single tax is a **partial land tax**. Under a partial tax, land is taxed at less than 100 percent of its value. A partial land tax would be less confiscatory than the single tax: like conventional taxes on labor and capital, the partial tax would confiscate only a portion of the taxpayer's resources. In addition, because a partial tax leaves landowners with a positive net return, the land market will continue to be run by those who have a private interest in allocating land to its highest bidder.

Another alternative to a pure land tax is the **two-rate tax,** or the **split tax**. Under the conventional property tax, land and improvements are taxed at the same rate.

A 3 percent property tax is actually a 3 percent tax on land and a 3 percent tax on improvements. Under a split tax, the tax rate on land may be 9 percent, while the tax rate on improvements may be 1 percent. The split tax is widely used in Australia and New Zealand. It is also used in some cities in Pennsylvania: Pittsburgh implemented a split tax in 1913, and six other cities, including Scranton and Harrisburg, have adopted the split tax in recent years.

The replacement of the conventional property tax with the split tax would stimulate capital investment. The switch to the split tax would decrease the tax rate on capital, encouraging capital improvements. Suppose, for example, that Rhonda would like to add a recreation room to her house. The new room would increase the assessed value of her house by $20,000. Under a conventional 3 percent property tax, her tax liabilities would increase by $600 per year. Under a split tax with a 1 percent rate on improvements, her tax liabilities would increase by only $200 per year. The tax penalty from the home improvement would be lower under the split tax, so Rhonda would be more likely to improve her house.

The same argument applies to investment in commercial and industrial property. Under the split tax, the tax liability of the property owner is only 1 percent of market value, so investments that increase the market value of the property have smaller tax penalties. The owner of an apartment building is more likely to install a new roof if the roof (and the associated increase in assessed value) increases his tax liability by a relatively small amount.

Summary

1. According to the leftover principle, the bid rent for land equals the difference between total revenue and total cost. Competition for land ensures that the landowner gets the excess of total revenue over total cost.

2. Land that is relatively fertile has relatively low production costs, so it commands a higher rent.

3. A policy that increases fertility (e.g., an irrigation project) generates benefits for both landowners and consumers.
   a. The project decreases production costs, increasing land rent.
   b. If the supply of the agricultural good increases, the price decreases, generating benefits for consumers.
   c. The distribution of benefits between landowners and consumers depends on the geographical extent of the program: the smaller the geographical area affected by the project, the smaller the price decrease and the larger the rent increase.

4. The benefits of an irrigation project are capitalized into the market value of land: the increase in rent increases the present value of rental income, increasing the market value of land.

5. The bid-rent function shows how much a firm is willing to pay for land at different distances from the market. The function is negatively sloped:

transportation costs are lower near the market, so rent is higher. The rent function is convex—not linear—if firms substitute nonland inputs for land as the price of land increases.

6. A decrease in transport costs decreases the slope of the bid-rent function. If the resulting increase in supply of agricultural goods decreases agricultural prices, the bid-rent function shifts downward. The benefits of increased accessibility are shared by consumers and landowners.

7. If there are two land uses, the activity with the higher transport costs has a relatively steep bid-rent function and occupies the land closest to the market.
   a. The bid-rent function is relatively steep if (1) output per acre is relatively large or (2) unit transport costs are relatively high.
   b. The market allocates central land to the activity with the most to gain from proximity.

8. The demand for land is derived from the demand for output (e.g., corn, housing). The price of land is high because the demand for output is high. Expensive land is the result—not the cause—of expensive output.

9. Henry George proposed the single tax, a 100 percent tax on rental income.

Exercises and Discussion Questions

1. In the state of California, rice growers burn their field stubble to sanitize their fields. The field burning causes serious air pollution. The alternative sanitizing method costs $150 per acre. Consider a county where rice farmers are currently willing to pay $500 per acre for land, and corn farmers (who do not sanitize their fields) are willing to pay $300 per acre. The total output of the county is small enough that the prices of rice and corn are unaffected by events in the county. Suppose that field burning is outlawed in the county, forcing rice farmers to switch to the alternative sanitizing method.
   a. How does the field-burning law affect rice consumers, corn consumers, farmers, and landowners? In other words, who bears the cost of the pollution-control program?
   b. How would your answer to (*a*) change if the cost of the alternative method is $250 per acre?
   c. How would your answer to (*b*) change if field burning is outlawed in the entire state of California?

2. Critically appraise the following statement:

   I would like to clear the air with some facts about rice straw burning. Burning is the only economical way to prevent stem rot in rice. This disease would drastically reduce the yield of rice grown on the same land the next year. The California Department of Agriculture estimates the cheapest alternative to rice straw burning, which involves baling and hauling it elsewhere, would cost about $150 per acre. The opponents of straw burning suggest the savings ($150 per acre) go straight into the pockets of growers. Actually, straw burning decreases the prices of Rice Krispies and other rice products, so the savings go to consumers.

3. Consider an agricultural economy with the following characteristics:

   i. All the land in the region is initially used by tenant farmers to grow indigo.

   ii. The price of indigo is determined in international markets.

   iii. The tenant initially pays the landowner 30 percent of the indigo harvest as rent.

   iv. Output per acre is 1,000 units per year and the price of indigo is $2 per unit.

   v. The interest rate is 10 percent per year.

   a. Compute (1) nonland cost per acre per year and (2) the market value of land.

   b. Suppose that the price of indigo drops to $1.90. Assuming that the tenant continues to grow indigo on the land, compute the equilibrium rent (1) in dollars, (2) in units of indigo, and (3) as a percent of the indigo harvest.

   c. By how much does the market value of land drop as a result of the decrease in the price of indigo (assuming the tenant grows indigo)?

   d. How would your answer to (c) change if there is an alternative crop with the same nonland costs and output per acre?

4. Suppose that Mr. Greengenes, a farmer and genetic engineer, develops a new method for growing corn that decreases the cost of growing corn by $300 per acre. Greengenes's landlord rejoices, saying, "According to the leftover principle, you will pay me $300 more in rent." Is the landlord correct? If not, is he applying the leftover principle incorrectly, or is the principle wrong?

5. Consider a county where farmers produce with fixed factor proportions and truck their output to a central marketplace. Draw the land-rent function under the following circumstances:

   a. Unit transport cost is a constant t per ton per mile.

   b. Unit transport cost increases as the farmer approaches the marketplace (a result of traffic congestion).

   c. Unit transport cost decreases as the farmer approaches the marketplace, a result of better roads closer to the market.

6. Using the information in Table 7–1, recompute the land-rent function for the following events. Assume that the farm size at each location is fixed (0.4 acres at $u = 0$, 0.6 acres at $u = 1$, and so on).

   a. A herd of rabbits invades the county, stealing $50 worth of carrots per acre.

   b. The unit cost of transport increases from $4 to $5.

   c. The price of carrots increases from $15 to $40.

   d. Is the assumption of a fixed farm size at each location realistic? If not, how would your answer to (c) change if farm sizes could change?

7. Consider a flexible carrot farmer. Complete the following table, assuming that (1) the farmer produces 10 tons of carrots, (2) the price of carrots is $40 per ton, and (3) transport cost per ton per mile is $5.

Distance to Market (miles)	Farm Size (acres)	Total Revenue	Nonland Costs	Transport Costs	Pre-Rent Profit	Rent per Acre
0	0.70		$66			
1	0.80		52			
2	0.90		40			
3	1.00		30			

8. Consider the input combinations listed in Table 7–1. As the price of land increases, the farmer substitutes nonland inputs for land. As the farmer uses less and less land, the trade-off between land and nonland inputs becomes less favorable.
   a. In what sense does the trade-off become less favorable?
   b. Why does the trade-off become less favorable?

9. Suppose that two activities, F and R, compete for land. Activity R produces a good that requires fixed factors of proportion. Factor substitution is impossible. Activity F engages in factor substitution: as the relative price of land increases, the firm substitutes nonland inputs for land.
   a. Draw a pair of bid-rent functions showing F occupying the land closest to the market. In what sense is it efficient for F to occupy central land?
   b. Draw another pair of bid-rent functions showing F occupying land close to the market and far from the market, and R occupying the intermediate land. In what sense is it efficient for F to occupy land close to and far from the market?

10. Pick the word in parentheses that makes the following statement correct: "As a firm's isoquant gradually changes in shape from a straight line to an L-shaped curve, the firm's bid-rent function becomes (*less, more*) curved." Note: *Less curved* means closer to a straight line.

11. Consider Euphoric County, where a large share of the arable land is used to grow M. The production of M is illegal: there are severe penalties imposed on M growers, but no penalties imposed on M consumers. Suppose that M is a competitive industry, with equilibrium profits equal to zero: total revenue equals total costs. Included in the costs are the costs associated with engaging in illegal activities (the opportunity cost of time spent in jail, legal costs, concealment costs). Suppose that Euphoric County legalizes the production of M.
    a. Depict graphically the effects of legalization on the equilibrium price and quantity of M. Explain your graph.

  b. Depict graphically the effects of legalization on the price of land in Euphoric County. Explain your graph.

12. The residents of mobile home parks own their dwellings, and rent land from absentee landowners. Consider a city in which all land is currently occupied by mobile home parks. Suppose the city imposes a 50 percent tax on land, to be paid (in legal terms) by the person who occupies the land (the tenant, either a mobile home owner or some other user). Who actually pays the tax?

13. What would be the effect of a partial land tax ($100 per acre) on land rent, land values, and corn prices?

14. As the flexible farmer approaches the marketplace, the farmer substitutes nonland inputs for land. As a result, the land-rent function of the flexible farmer is steeper than the land-rent function of the inflexible farmer. What happens as the flexible farmer moves *away* from the marketplace? Is the flexible land-rent function steeper or flatter than the inflexible function? Explain.

References and Additional Reading

Alonso, William. *Location and Land Use.* Cambridge, Mass.: Harvard University Press, 1964.

———. "A Theory of the Urban Land Market." In *Readings in Urban Economics,* ed. Matthew Edel and Jerome Rothenberg. New York: Macmillan, 1972. Extends the standard model of agricultural land rent to the urban land market.

George, Henry. *Progress and Poverty.* New York: Schalkenbach Foundation, 1954. Discusses George's theory of land rent and explains the single-tax proposal.

Mills, Edwin S. "The Value of Urban Land." In *The Quality of the Urban Environment,* ed. H. Perloff. Washington, D.C.: Resources for the Future, 1969. Traces the theory of land rent from Ricardo's fertility analysis to the modern theory of urban land rent.

Ricardo, David. *Principles of Political Economy and Taxation.* 1821. Reprint. London: John Murray, 1886. Explains fertility analysis and Ricardo's views on other matters.

CHAPTER 8

Land Use in the Monocentric City

The outcome of the city will depend on the race between the automobile and the elevator, and anyone who bets on the elevator is crazy.
Frank Lloyd Wright

This chapter uses the concepts developed in Chapter 7 to discuss land rent and land use in the monocentric or core-dominated city. The monocentric city was the dominant urban form until the early part of the 20th century. In the monocentric city, commercial and industrial activity is concentrated in the central core area. During the last 70 or 80 years, most large metropolitan areas have become multicentric, with suburban subcenters that complement and compete with the central core area. This chapter explains the market forces behind the development of the monocentric city, and Chapter 10 discusses the market forces behind the transformation of monocentric cities to multicentric ones.

Why study the monocentric city? Although few of today's large cities are monocentric, the analysis of the monocentric city is important for four reasons. First, the monocentric city was the dominant urban form until the early part of the 20th century, so urban history is largely a history of the monocentric city. Second, many of today's small- and medium-sized cities are still monocentric. Third, to understand the transition from the traditional monocentric city to the modern multicentric city, one must understand the forces behind the development of the monocentric city in the first place. Fourth, many of the lessons from the monocentric model can be extended to the modern multicentric city.

The discussion of the various land users in the monocentric city proceeds from the city center outward. The first section derives the bid-rent functions of three business sectors (manufacturers, office firms, retailers), and uses the bid-rent functions to discuss land-use patterns in the central business district. The second section examines the location choices of households, deriving the bid-rent function for residential land. The third explains why employment is concentrated in the city center, that is, why the city is monocentric. The fourth section derives the residential bid-rent

191

function under a more realistic set of assumptions than those of the simple mono-centric model. The final two sections deal with empirical issues, addressing three questions. First, why do poor households tend to locate in the central city, while wealthy households tend to locate in the suburbs? Second, how rapidly does land rent fall as distance to the city center increases? Third, what is the relationship between population density and distance to the city center?

The traditional monocentric city has the transportation technology of the 19th century. The monocentric model has four key assumptions:

1. **Central export node.** All manufacturing output is exported from the city through a railroad terminal at the city center (a central export node).
2. **Horse-drawn wagons.** Manufacturers transport their freight from their factories to the export node by horse-drawn wagons.
3. **Hub-and-spoke streetcar system.** Commuters and shoppers travel by streetcar from the residential areas to the central business district (CBD). The streetcar lines are laid in a radial pattern: the lines form spokes that lead into the CBD (the hub).
4. **Agglomerative economies.** The office industry is dependent on face-to-face contact: employees from different office firms meet in the city center to transact business.

Under these assumptions, the city center is the focal point of the entire metropolitan area: manufacturers are oriented toward the export node; office firms are oriented toward the central market area; retailers are oriented to the hub of the streetcar system; and households are oriented toward employment and shopping opportunities in the central core area.

Commercial and Industrial Land Use

This section discusses land rent and land use in the central business district (CBD) of the monocentric city. Three activities occupy the central core area: manufacturers, office firms, and retailers.

The Bid-Rent Function of Manufacturers

Suppose that manufacturers in the monocentric city produce baseballs. The firms in the baseball industry have the following characteristics:

1. **Production.** Firms produce baseballs with land, labor, capital, and raw materials. Every firm produces B tons of baseballs per month.
2. **Fixed prices.** The prices of baseballs and nonland inputs (labor, capital, and raw materials) are determined in national markets, so firms take these prices as given. The prices are the same at all locations in the city.
3. **Competitive markets.** There is free entry into the industry. In equilibrium, each firm makes zero economic profits (normal accounting profits).

4. **Baseball freight cost.** Baseballs are shipped by horse-drawn wagon from the factory to the central railroad terminal, where they are exported to other cities.

5. **Raw material freight cost.** Raw materials are imported to the city by rail. The intracity freight cost of raw materials is small enough to ignore.

6. **Factor substitution.** Baseball makers engage in factor substitution: as the price of land increases, firms substitute nonland inputs for land.

For the purposes of choosing a location within the city, baseball firms are market-oriented. The intracity freight cost of raw materials is assumed to be negligible, and the costs of other inputs (capital and labor) are assumed to be the same at all locations within the city. Because input costs are the same throughout the city, a firm's location decision is based on access to its market. Once a firm decides to locate somewhere in the city, the relevant market is the destination of baseballs *within* the city, that is, the central railroad terminal.

The firm's profit equals total revenue less the cost of inputs, intracity freight, and land. Total revenue is the price of baseballs (P_b) times the quantity produced (B). C is the cost of all nonland inputs (capital, labor, raw materials). If freight cost is t per ton per mile, total freight cost for a location u miles from the export node is t times B times u. If R is land rent per acre and T is the acreage of the factory site, the profit at a location u miles from the export node is

$$\pi = P_b \cdot B - C - t \cdot B \cdot u - R \cdot T \qquad (8\text{--}1)$$

All markets are perfectly competitive, so the firm's economic profit is zero. According to the leftover principle, the firm is willing to pay its landowner the excess of total revenue over the cost of nonland inputs and freight cost. As shown in Chapter 7, the expression for the bid rent is derived by setting $\pi = 0$, adding $R \cdot T$ to both sides of the profit equation, and dividing by T. The firm's bid rent *per acre* is the pre-rent profit divided by land consumption:

$$R = \frac{P_b \cdot B - C - t \cdot B \cdot u}{T} \qquad (8\text{--}2)$$

The **bid-rent function** indicates how much the typical firm is willing to pay *per acre* for different production sites in the city. Table 8–1 shows how to compute the bid rent for different distances from the city center, given values for P_b, B, C, t, T, and u. The bid-rent function, shown in Figure 8–1, is negatively sloped because freight cost increases as the firm moves away from the city center.

The bid-rent function is convex because firms engage in factor substitution. As the firm approaches the city center with its higher land cost, the firm substitutes nonland inputs (capital and labor) for land, producing the same tonnage of baseballs with less land and more of the other inputs. From Table 8–1, the firm uses one acre of land and $1,400 worth of other inputs for a location three miles from the city center, and 0.40 acres and $2,600 worth of nonland inputs for a location near the city center. The bid-rent function of the typical baseball firm will be used to represent the bid-rent function of the entire manufacturing sector.

TABLE 8–1   The Bid-Rent Function of Baseball Manufacturers

Miles from Export Node	Size of Site (acres)	Total Revenue	Nonland Costs	Freight Costs	Pre-Rent Profit	Rent per Acre
0	0.4	$6,000	$2,600	$ 0	$3,400	$8,500
1	0.6	6,000	2,000	900	3,100	5,167
2	0.8	6,000	1,600	1,800	2,600	3,250
3	1.0	6,000	1,400	2,700	1,900	1,900

Assumptions:
1. Output = 6 tons of baseballs
2. Price = $1,000 per ton
3. Transport cost = $900 per mile
4. Pre-rent profit = Total revenue − Nonland cost − Freight cost
5. Rent = $\dfrac{\text{Pre-rent profit}}{\text{Size of factory site}}$

FIGURE 8–1   Bid-Rent Function of Baseball Firms

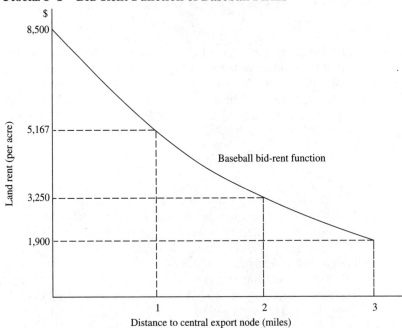

The bid-rent function of baseball firms is negatively sloped because freight costs increase as the distance to the city's central export node increases. It is convex (not linear) because firms substitute nonland inputs for land as the price of land increases.

The Bid-Rent Function of Office Firms

Although firms in the office sector provide a wide variety of goods and services, office firms share two important characteristics. First, they gather, process, and distribute information. Because information becomes obsolete quickly, office firms must be able to collect and distribute it rapidly. Second, office firms rely on face-to-face contact in the collection, processing, and distribution of information. For example, accountants explain and interpret the information in accounting reports. The loan officers of banks meet with prospective borrowers to appraise their credit-worthiness. The investment advisors of finance firms meet with clients to assess their attitudes toward risk and their investment inclinations. In general, office firms rely on speedy face-to-face contact in collecting and distributing information. In contrast to baseball makers, who throw their baseballs into the back of a horse-drawn wagon, office firms transmit their output in the minds and briefcases of their employees.

Suppose that office firms in the monocentric city provide financial services. The finance industry has the following characteristics.

1. **The office.** Every finance firm is based in an office. The nonland cost of the office (capital and labor cost) is C per month. The "output" of the firm is investment consultations, and each firm produces A consultations per month.

2. **Travel to city center.** The manager of each firm travels from the office to the city center (the hub of the streetcar system) to consult with clients. Every consultation requires one trip to the city center.

3. **Fixed prices.** The prices of financial advice and nonland inputs are determined in national markets, so finance firms take the prices as given. The prices are the same at all locations in the city.

4. **Competitive markets.** There is free entry into the industry. In equilibrium, all firms make zero economic profits (normal accounting profits).

5. **Factor substitution.** Finance firms engage in factor substitution: as the price of land increases, they substitute nonland inputs for land.

The travel cost of an office firm equals the opportunity cost of the manager's travel between the office and the clients in the city center. Suppose that the manager takes t minutes to walk one block, and the wage is W per minute. If the office is u blocks from the city center, the travel cost per consultation is

$$TC = t \cdot W \cdot u \qquad (8\text{--}3)$$

For example, if $t = 3$ minutes per block and $W = \$4$ per minute, travel cost per consultation per block is $12, so a firm located 10 blocks from the city center incurs a travel cost of $120 per consultation. If the firm provides A consultations per month, the monthly travel cost for a location u blocks from the city center is

$$TC = t \cdot W \cdot A \cdot u \qquad (8\text{--}4)$$

If $A = 200$ consultations per month, the monthly travel cost is $2,400 for a location one block from the city center, $4,800 for a location two blocks from the city center, and so on.

The firm's total profit is total revenue less the cost of nonland inputs, land, and travel. If the price of a consultation is P_a, rent per acre is R, and the firm occupies T acres of land, profit is

$$\pi = P_a \cdot A - C - R \cdot T - t \cdot W \cdot A \cdot u \qquad (8\text{--}5)$$

Since markets are perfectly competitive, economic profit is zero in equilibrium. According to the leftover principle, the firm is willing to pay the landlord the excess of total revenue over nonland cost. The bid rent *per acre* of land is the pre-rent profit divided by the amount of land consumed:

$$R = \frac{P_a \cdot A - C - t \cdot W \cdot A \cdot u}{T} \qquad (8\text{--}6)$$

The bid-rent function indicates how much the office firm is willing to pay for different office sites. Table 8–2 shows how to compute the bid rent for different distances from the city center, given values for $P_a, A, C, t, W, T,$ and u. The bid-rent function, shown in Figure 8–2, is negatively sloped because travel cost increases as the firm moves away from the city center.

The bid-rent function is convex because office firms engage in factor substitution. As the firm approaches the city center, it substitutes nonland inputs (capital and labor) for the relatively expensive land, producing the same number of consultations with less land and more of its nonland inputs. In other words, office firms near the city center occupy taller buildings. The bid-rent function of the typical office firm will be used to represent the bid-rent function of the entire office sector.

Land Use in the Central Business District

In the monocentric city, manufacturers and office firms are oriented toward the central business district. Manufacturers are attracted by the central export node, and office firms cluster around the city center to facilitate face-to-face contact. How is CBD land allocated between the two activities?

Figure 8–3 shows the bid-rent functions of manufacturers (R_m) and office firms (R_o). Figure 8–3 also shows the bid-rent function of city residents (R_h), which is derived later in the chapter. Because land is allocated to the highest bidder, office firms outbid manufacturers for land within u_o miles of the city center, generating an office district with a radius of u_o miles. Manufacturers outbid office firms and residents for land between u_o and u_m miles of the city center, generating a manufacturing district with a width of $(u_m - u_o)$ miles. The central area of the city is occupied by the office industry because the office bid-rent function is steeper than the manufacturing bid-rent function.

The office bid-rent function is relatively steep because the office industry has relatively high transportation costs. Office firms rely on frequent face-to-face contact, using high-priced financial consultants to transport their output to clients in the city center. In contrast, the manufacturing industry ships its output by horse-drawn wagon, so its transport costs are relatively low. In the numerical examples shown in Tables 8–1 and 8–2, the baseball manufacturer has monthly freight costs of $900 per mile, while the office firm has monthly travel costs of $2,400 *per block*. The

---

TABLE 8–2   The Bid-Rent Function of Office Firms

Blocks from City Center	Size of Site (acres)	Total Revenue	Nonland Cost	Freight Cost	Pre-Rent Profit	Rent per Acre
0	0.4	$9,600	$3,600	$ 0	$6,000	$15,000
1	0.6	9,600	2,400	2,400	4,800	8,000
2	0.8	9,600	1,800	4,800	3,000	3,750
3	1.0	9,600	1,500	7,200	900	900

Assumptions:
1. Output (A) = 200 consultations
2. Price = $48 per consultation
3. Travel time (t) = 3 minutes per block
4. Opportunity cost (W) = $4 per minute
5. Travel cost = $t \cdot A \cdot W$ = $2,400 per block
6. Pre-rent profit = Total revenue − Nonland cost − Travel cost
7. Rent = $\dfrac{\text{Pre-rent profit}}{\text{Size of office site}}$

FIGURE 8–2   The Bid-Rent Function of Office Firms

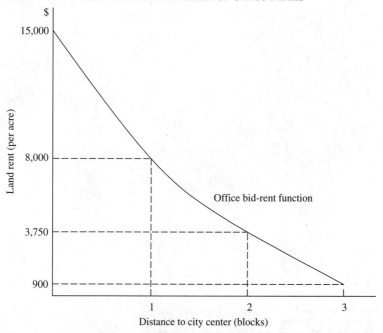

The office bid-rent function is negatively sloped because travel costs increase as distance to the central marketplace increases. It is convex because firms substitute nonland inputs for land as the price of land increases.

FIGURE 8–3   Bid-Rent Functions and Land Use in the Central Business District

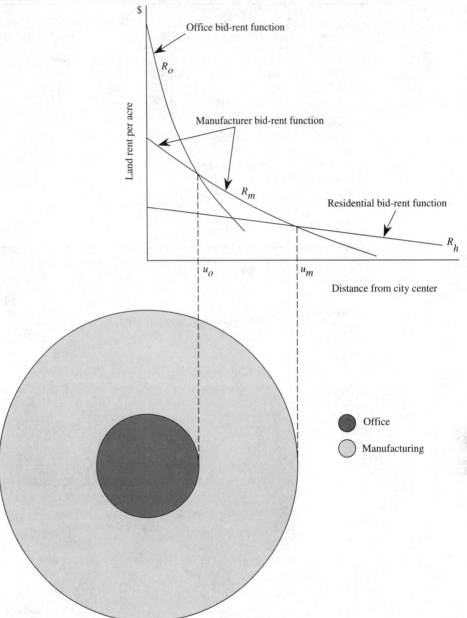

The office industry has a relatively steep bid-rent function because the travel cost of people exceeds the travel cost of freight. The office industry outbids manufacturers for land near the city center. Central land is occupied by the activity with the most to gain from proximity (decreased transportation costs).

bid-rent functions are negatively sloped because of transportation cost, so the larger the transportation cost, the larger the slope.

Does the land market allocate land efficiently? In the terms used by land developers, is land allocated to its "highest and best use"? The office industry, with its higher transportation costs, occupies the land closest to the city center. This allocation is efficient because the office industry has the most to gain from proximity to the city center. To explain, suppose that a finance firm one block from the city center swaps locations with a manufacturer three blocks (one-fifth of a mile) from the city center. The land swap increases the finance firm's travel costs by $7,200 (three blocks times $2,400 per block), but decreases the baseball firm's freight costs by only $180 (one-fifth mile times $900 per mile). Office travel costs increase by more than freight costs decrease, so total transportation costs increase. The market allocation, which gives central land to the office industry, minimizes total transportation costs.

Location of Retailers

Where in the monocentric city do retailers locate? Central place theory, which is used in Chapter 5 to explain the regional distribution of retailers, is also applicable to the intracity distribution of retailers. Retailers carve up the city into market areas, with the size of the market areas determined by scale economies, per capita demand, and transportation costs.

Large Scale Economies—Glove Sellers.   Consider first an activity for which scale economies are large relative to per capita demand, for example, a glove store. The glove market has the following characteristics:

1. **Single glove store.** The scale economies of glove selling are exhausted only at outputs that are large *relative* to the total demand for gloves, so there is a single glove store in the city. The efficient size for the glove seller is 5,000 pairs of gloves per month, and total demand for gloves is 5,000 per month.
2. **Glove consumers.** Consumers are distributed uniformly throughout the city.
3. **Perfect competition.** Although there is a single glove seller, entry into the glove market is not very costly. Given the threat of entry, economic profit is zero.

The retailer's profit at a particular location is the excess of total revenue over total cost. Suppose that the profit margin (price less average cost) is constant. If P_g is the price of gloves, G is the quantity sold, and AC_g is the average cost, pre-rent profit is

$$\pi = G \cdot (P_g - AC_g) \qquad\qquad (8\text{--}7)$$

For example, if P_g is $9 and AC_g is $5, the profit margin is $4. If G is 5,000, total profit would be $20,000.

At what location will the glove store earn the most profit? If the profit margin is constant, the firm maximizes total profit by maximizing sales volume (G). As shown in Chapter 5, sales volume is maximized at the center of the market area (the median location) for the simple reason that the central location is accessible to the most consumers. Since the glove store sells to people throughout the city, profit is maximized at the city center. The benefit of the central location is reinforced by the hub-and-spoke streetcar system of the monocentric city, which delivers suburban commuters and shoppers to the city center.

Because there is free entry into the glove-selling business, the glove store makes zero economic profit. Competition for the best glove-selling site bids up the price of land to the point at which economic profit is zero. If the glove store refuses to pay its economic profits to the landowner, the landowner will rent the site to another glove seller.

Moderate Scale Economies—Hat Sellers.   Consider next an activity for which scale economies are moderate relative to per capita demand, for example, hat stores. The hat industry has the following characteristics:

1. **Five hat stores.** The scale economies of hat selling are moderate *relative to* the total demand for hats, so there are five hat stores in the urban area. The efficient sales volume for each hat store is 4,000 hats per month, and the total demand is 20,000 hats per month.

2. **Hat consumers.** Consumers are distributed uniformly throughout the monocentric city.

3. **Perfect competition.** Entry into the hat market is not very costly. Given the threat of entry, economic profit is zero.

The pre-rent profit of an individual store is total revenue less total cost. If H is the number of hats sold, P_h is the price of hats, and AC_h is the average cost, total profit is

$$\pi = H \cdot (P_h - AC_h) \tag{8–8}$$

For example, if P_h is $8 and AC_h is $5, the profit margin is $3. If H is 4,000, total profit would be $12,000.

According to the simple version of central place theory, hat sellers divide the city into five equal market areas, and each hat seller locates at the center of a market area. This result can also be expressed in terms of bid-rent functions. The bid-rent function of a particular hat store depends on where the other stores locate. Locations close to other hat stores have lower sales volume, so the hat seller is willing to pay less in rent. The bid-rent function of the hat industry has five peaks, one at the center of each market area.

Will hat sellers adopt the location pattern predicted by the simple version of central place theory? The simple version of the theory assumes that unit travel cost (the cost per mile) is the same in all directions. In the monocentric streetcar city, this assumption is violated: the hub-and-spoke streetcar system collects people along the suburban spokes and delivers them to the central "hub." Travel along the spokes into the city is cheaper than travel between the spokes, so a trip from a house in the suburbs to a downtown hatter may be easier than a trip to a suburban hatter. If so, most—if not all—of the hat sellers locate in the downtown core area.

The tendency for hat sellers to cluster in the core area is reinforced by **shopping externalities** (explained in Chapters 2 and 5). If hats from different stores are **imperfect substitutes**, hat consumers travel to several stores to compare hats, and shopping cost is lower if the stores are clustered. Since the core area (the hub of the streetcar system) is accessible to the entire urban area, hatters are likely to cluster near the city center. If hats and gloves are **complementary goods,** consumers save on shopping costs if hat stores are near the glove store in the city center. In terms of central place theory, hat sellers compromise on their central place locations to exploit two types of shopping externalities: the externalities from comparison shopping and the externalities from one-stop shopping. Given the hub-and-spoke streetcar system, the retail clusters are likely to be in the downtown core area.

Residential Land Use

This section uses a simple model of the residential sector to explore residential land use in the monocentric city. According to the leftover principle, the bid rent for residential land equals the excess of total revenue over total cost. The first step in the analysis of residential land rent examines the revenue side of housing production. The housing-price function shows the relationship between housing prices and distance to the city center.

The simple model of the residential sector has a number of simplifying assumptions. Later in the chapter, each of these assumptions will be dropped.

1. One member of each household commutes to a job in the central business district (CBD).
2. Noncommuting travel is insignificant.
3. Public services and taxes are the same at all locations.
4. Air quality is the same at all locations.
5. All households have the same income and tastes for housing.
6. The opportunity cost of commuting time is zero.

The first four assumptions make the CBD the focal point of city residents. All jobs are in the CBD, while all the other things that people care about (public services, taxes, air quality) are distributed uniformly throughout the city. Given the fifth assumption, the choices of the "typical" household can be used to represent the choices of all households in the city. The sixth assumption means that the simple model ignores the time costs of commuting.

The Housing-Price Function

As explained in Chapter 14 (Why Is Housing Different?), the price of housing is usually defined as the price per unit of housing service. For the purposes of this chapter, the *price of housing* is defined as the price *per square foot* of housing per month. If a household rents a 1,000-square-foot house for $250 per month, the price of housing is 25 cents per square foot ($250 divided by 1,000 square feet). The **housing-price function** indicates how much a household is willing to pay for dwellings at different locations in the city. There are two types of housing-price functions, linear and convex.

Linear Housing-Price Function: No Consumer Substitution.   Figure 8–4 shows the housing-price function for a simple case described by the following set of assumptions.

1. **Identical dwellings.** Every dwelling in the city has 1,000 square feet of living space.
2. **Fixed budget.** The typical household has a fixed budget of $300 per month to spend on commuting and housing costs.
3. **Commuting cost.** The monthly costs of commuting are $20 per mile per month: the household pays $20 per month in commuting costs for a residence one mile from the city center, $40 per month for a residence two miles from the city center, and so on.

How much is the household willing to pay for dwellings at different locations in the city? At the city center, commuting costs are zero, so the household can spend its entire $300 budget on housing. For a 1,000-square-foot house, the price is 30 cents per square foot. At a distance of six miles from the center, commuting costs

FIGURE 8–4   Housing-Price Function for a City with Identical (1,000-square-foot) Dwellings

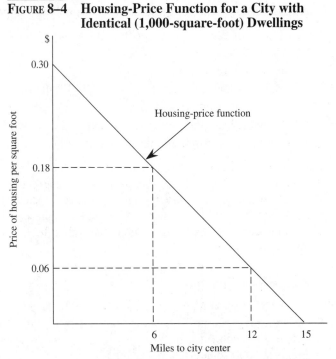

The price of housing drops from 30 cents per square foot at the city center to 6 cents per square foot 12 miles from the city center. The price increases as commuting cost decreases (as distance to the center decreases), making households indifferent among all locations within the city.

are $120, so the household has $180 left to spend on housing (18 cents per square foot). In Figure 8–4, the slope of the function is two cents per mile.

The negatively sloped housing-price function is necessary for **locational equilibrium**. Locational equilibrium occurs when all households are satisfied with their location choices, that is, no household wants to change its location.

To explain why the equilibrium housing-price function is negatively sloped, suppose that the function starts out as a horizontal line. If the price of housing is 15 cents per square foot throughout the city, the household can get a 1,000-square-foot dwelling anywhere in the city for $150 per month. Suppose that a household starts out in a dwelling 10 miles from the city center. Because a move toward the city center decreases commuting costs without affecting rent, the household will move closer to the city center. Other households have the same incentive to move closer to the center. As the demand for housing near the city center increases, the price of housing near the center increases; as the demand for suburban housing decreases, the price of suburban housing decreases. In other words, the movement of households toward the city center transforms a horizontal housing-price function into a negatively sloped function.

The equilibrium housing-price function makes residents indifferent among all locations because differences in commuting costs are offset by differences in housing costs. The good news from a one-mile move toward the city center is that commuting costs decrease by t (commuting cost per mile). The bad news is that housing costs increase by ΔP (the change in the price per square foot) times H (housing consumption in square footage). The household will be indifferent between the two locations if the decrease in commuting costs equals the increase in housing costs:

$$t = -\Delta P \cdot H \qquad (8\text{–}9)$$

If $t = 20 and $H = 1,000$ square feet, the household will be indifferent between the two locations if the price of housing increases by two cents per square foot. In Figure 8–4, the price of housing increases by two cents per mile as the household moves toward the city center.

Convex Function: Consumer Substitution.   The housing-price function in Figure 8–4 is linear because the city's dwellings are identical: everyone lives in a 1,000-square-foot house, regardless of the price of housing. A more realistic assumption is that housing consumption depends on the price of housing. In other words, households obey the law of demand, decreasing the quantity demanded as the price increases. As a household moves toward the city center, it pays a higher price for housing, so it occupies a smaller dwelling. As the relative price of housing increases, the household substitutes nonhousing goods (pizza, hot dogs, stereo equipment) for housing.

Figure 8–5 shows the effects of consumer substitution on the housing-price function. The assumed pattern of housing consumption is shown below the graph. Suppose that a household moves from a distance of 12 miles (where the price of housing is 6 cents per square foot) to 9 miles. If housing consumption is fixed at 1,000 square feet, the household would be willing to pay an additional $60 for housing (the decrease in commuting cost), or 6 cents more per square foot. Because its housing consumption drops from 1,000 square feet to 750 square feet, the household is

FIGURE 8–5   **Housing-Price Function with and without Consumer Substitution**

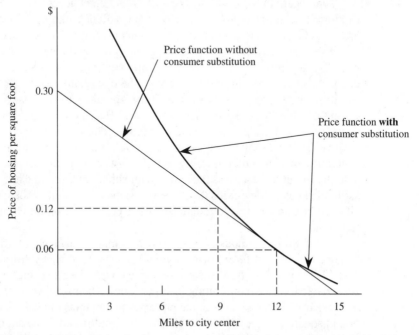

As the household approaches the city center, the price of housing increases. If the household substitutes other goods for housing, the housing-price function is convex, not linear.

Assumed Consumption Pattern:

Distance to city center (miles)	3	6	9	12
Housing consumption (square feet)	400	600	750	1,000

willing to pay more than an additional 6 cents per square foot to offset the decrease in commuting costs. In general, as a household moves toward the high-priced city center, it occupies smaller dwellings, requiring progressively larger increases in the price *per square foot* of housing to offset the fixed $20 per mile decrease in commuting costs. The lesson from Figure 8–5 is that if consumers obey the law of demand, the housing-price function is convex, not linear.

The slope of the housing-price function can be expressed in simple algebraic terms. Since both the price of housing (P) and housing consumption (H) vary with distance to the city center (u), the trade-off between commuting and housing costs can be rewritten as

$$\Delta u \cdot t = -\Delta P(u) \cdot H(u) \qquad (8–10)$$

At a given location (u), the change in commuting cost (the change in u times the transport cost per mile) equals the change in the housing price times housing consumption. The equation can be rearranged to show the slope of the housing-price function:

$$\frac{\Delta P(u)}{\Delta u} = -\frac{t}{H(u)} \qquad (8–11)$$

In the numerical example, t is $20 and $H(9)$ is 750, so the slope of the housing-price function at $u = 9$ is $0.0267 (20/750), compared to a slope of $0.02 under the assumption of fixed housing consumption. Since $H(6)$ is 60, the slope at $u = 6$ is $0.033 (20/600). As the household moves toward the city center, housing consumption decreases, increasing the slope of the housing-price function.

How rapidly does the price of housing decrease as distance to the city center increases? The *housing-price gradient* is defined as the percentage change in the price of housing per mile. Dividing both sides of (8–11) by P,

$$\frac{\Delta P/P}{\Delta u} = -\frac{t}{H(u) \cdot P(u)} \tag{8–12}$$

In words, the housing-price gradient equals transport cost per mile divided by housing expenditures. If the full cost of commuting (including monetary and time costs) is $1 per round-trip mile, the monthly commuting cost (for 20 workdays per month) is $20 per round-trip mile. If the household spends $500 per month on housing, the rent gradient is 4 percent per mile (20/500).

The Residential Bid-Rent Function

The **residential bid-rent function** indicates how much housing producers are willing to pay for land at different locations in the city. According to the leftover principle, housing producers are willing to pay land rent equal to the excess of total revenue over total cost. There are two types of bid-rent functions, one that occurs if housing is produced with fixed factor proportions, and one that occurs if housing firms engage in factor substitution.

The Bid-Rent Function with Fixed Factor Proportions.   Consider first the possibility that housing is produced with fixed factor proportions. The characteristics of firms in the housing industry are as follows:

1. **Production.** Each firm produces Q square feet of housing, using land and other inputs. Once the firm erects a building, it can be used as a single dwelling (with Q square feet of space), or divided into x units, each of which has (Q/x) square feet of living space.
2. **Nonland cost.** Firms use K worth of nonland inputs for each building.
3. **Fixed factor proportions.** Each firm produces its Q square feet of housing with T acres of land and K worth of other inputs, regardless of the price of land.
4. **Housing prices.** The housing-price function is negatively sloped and convex.
5. **Perfect competition.** The markets are perfectly competitive, so the firm makes zero economic profits.

According to the leftover principle, the bid rent for land equals the excess of total revenue over total nonland cost. Total revenue equals the price of housing (P) times Q, and total cost is nonland cost (K) plus land cost (R times T). Since P varies with the distance to the city center (u), the bid rent for land is

$$R(u) = \frac{P(u) \cdot Q - K}{T} \qquad (8\text{--}13)$$

If the price of housing decreases as u increases, the residential bid-rent function is negatively sloped.

Figure 8–6 maps the residential bid-rent function. The horizontal line is nonland cost per acre, assumed to be the same at all locations. Since the bid rent equals total revenue less nonland cost, the bid-rent function lies below the revenue function, with the distance between the two equal to the cost of nonland inputs. At u^*, total revenue equals nonland cost, so the bid rent for land is zero. The bid-rent function is convex because the housing-price function is convex.

The Bid-Rent Function with Factor Substitution.   The bid-rent function shown in Figure 8–6 is based on the assumption that housing is produced with fixed factor proportions. Housing firms use the same input combination at all locations, regardless of the price of land. What happens if firms substitute other inputs for land as the price of land increases?

FIGURE 8–6   **Housing-Price and Bid-Rent Function**

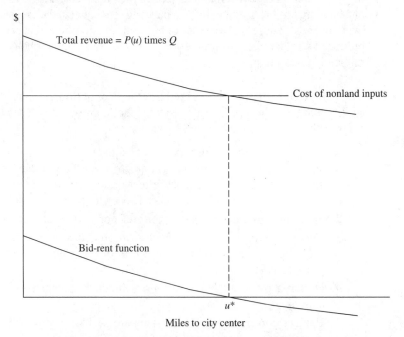

The bid rent of the housing firms equals total revenue per acre less the cost of nonland inputs. Total revenue (the price of housing times square footage produced) decreases as the distance to the city center increases because the housing-price function is negatively sloped. The cost of nonland inputs is the same at all locations. The bid-rent function is convex because the housing-price function (and the revenue function) is convex. At u^*, the cost of nonland inputs equals total revenue, so the bid rent equals zero.

FIGURE 8–7   **The Residential Bid-Rent Function with Factor Substitution**

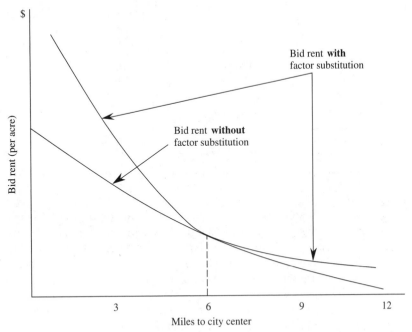

Factor substitution (substituting nonland inputs for land as the price of land increases) increases the convexity of the bid-rent function.

Figure 8–7 shows the bid-rent functions for inflexible and flexible housing producers. The inflexible firm uses the same input combination throughout the city. In contrast, the flexible firm substitutes nonland inputs for land as the price of land increases, building progressively taller buildings as it approaches the city center. The flexible rent function lies above the inflexible rent function at every location except $u = 6$. At this location, the input combination of the inflexible firm is, by chance, the efficient combination, so the two builders use the same input combination. While the inflexible firm's input ratio is efficient for $u = 6$, it is inefficient for other locations (too low for locations closer to the city center and too high for locations farther from the city center). For all locations except $u = 6$, the flexible firm produces housing for a lower cost and thus outbids the inflexible firm.

Summary: The Convex Bid-Rent Function.   There are two lessons from the analysis of residential land rent. First, the bid-rent function is negatively sloped because the housing-price function is negatively sloped. Second, the bid-rent function is convex because of both consumer substitution (which makes the housing-price function convex) and factor substitution (which increases the convexity of the rent function).

How rapidly does the price of residential land decrease as distance to the city center increases? The **rent gradient** is defined as the percentage change in land rent (or market value) per mile. The gradient depends on (1) the housing-price gradient

---

TABLE 8–3   Land-Rent Gradient

	Location	
	A	*B*
Distance to city center (miles)	4	5
Market value of housing ($)	150,000	144,000
Land value ($)	30,000	24,000
Capital value ($)	120,000	120,000

Assumptions:
1. At location A, land value is 20 percent of the market value of housing.
2. Housing-price gradient is 4 percent per mile.

---

and (2) the relative importance of land in the production of housing. In Table 8–3, the housing-price gradient is 4 percent (a one-mile move away from the city center decreases the market value of housing by 4 percent, from $150,000 to $144,000) and the value of land is assumed to be 20 percent of the total property value at location A. Because the price of capital is the same at all locations, land absorbs the entire $6,000 decrease in market value, dropping from $30,000 to $24,000, a 20 percent decrease. Since the market value is simply the present value of the annual rental income (annual rent divided by the interest rate), the rent gradient (percentage change in land rent per mile) is 20 percent, or five times the housing-price gradient.

The relationship between the housing-price gradient and the rent gradient can be stated algebraically as

$$\text{Rent gradient} = \frac{1}{\text{Land's share of house value}} \cdot \text{Housing-price gradient} \quad (8\text{–}14)$$

The smaller the land's share of house value, the larger the percentage decrease in land rent needed to absorb a given decrease in the price of housing. For example, if land's share of house value is 10 percent, the rent gradient is 10 times the housing-price gradient.

Residential Density

How does population density vary within the monocentric city? Table 8–4 shows how to compute population density at different locations in the city. The first step is to compute the lot size (the amount of land occupied per household). Lot size increases with distance to the city center for two reasons:

1. **Consumer substitution.** The price of housing decreases as the distance to the city center increases, and households respond to lower housing prices by consuming more housing. In Table 8–4, housing consumption rises from 1,404 square feet for a household 0.20 miles from the city center (location A) to 3,000 square feet for a household four miles from the center (location B).

TABLE 8–4   **Population Density at Different Locations**

	Location	
	A	B
Distance to city center (miles)	0.2	4.0
Housing consumption (square feet)	1,404	3,000
Land per square foot of housing (square feet)	0.33	2.2
Lot size (square feet)	468	6,600

2. **Factor substitution.** The price of land decreases as the distance to the city center increases, and housing firms respond to lower land prices by using more land per unit of housing. In Table 8–4, at a distance of 0.20 miles from the city center, every square foot of living space comes with 0.33 square feet of land. In other words, people live in three-story apartment buildings. At a distance of four miles from the center, the amount of land per square foot of housing is 2.20: households live in one-story houses with lot sizes 2.2 times the "footprint" of the house.

Lot size equals housing consumption (in square feet of living space) times the amount of land per unit of housing. Because of consumer substitution and factor substitution, the lot size increases as distance increases: a household located 0.20 miles from the center uses only 468 square feet of land (sharing the 1,404 square feet under the three-story apartment building with two other households), while a household located 4 miles from the center uses 6,600 square feet of land. In this example, residential density at a location 0.20 miles from the city center is about 14 times the density 4 miles from the center.

Land Use in the Monocentric City

Figure 8–8 shows the land-use pattern of the monocentric city. The office bid-rent function intersects the manufacturing function at a distance of u_o miles from the city center, so the office district is a circle with radius u_o miles. The manufacturing bid-rent function intersects the residential function at a distance of u_m miles from the city center, so the manufacturing district is a ring of width $(u_m - u_o)$ miles. The residential bid-rent intersects the agricultural bid-rent function at a distance of u_h miles, so the residential district is a ring of width $(u_h - u_m)$ miles. The retail bid-rent function is omitted from this diagram in the interests of simplicity. As explained earlier, most retailers congregate at the center of the monocentric city.

Activities are arranged according to their transportation costs: the higher the transportation cost, the closer to the city center. As explained in Chapter 7, the activity with relatively high transport costs has a relatively steep bid-rent function, and thus locates closer to the marketplace. In the monocentric city, the market is the city center, where office workers meet with clients and manufacturers load their output

FIGURE 8–8   **Bid-Rent Functions and Land Use in the Monocentric City**

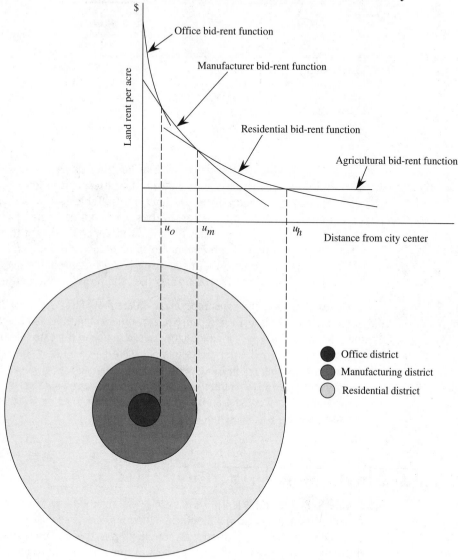

onto ships or trains. The office sector, with the highest transport costs and thus the steepest bid-rent function, occupies land closest to the center. Manufacturing, with the next highest transport costs and thus the next steepest bid-rent function, occupies the next ring of land. The residential sector, with relatively low transport costs and thus a relatively flat bid-rent function, occupies the land farthest from the city center.

This spatial arrangement has two interesting features. First, office firms occupy the central area of the CBD. As explained earlier in the chapter, office firms have relatively high transport costs and thus a relatively steep bid-rent function because office output is transmitted by office workers, while manufacturing output is transported by horse-drawn wagon.

The second feature of the monocentric city is that employment is concentrated in the CBD, not distributed throughout the city. Why do all the manufacturers and office firms locate in the CBD? To explain this monocentric location pattern, consider a baseball firm that is considering a move from the CBD to a suburban location. What are the trade-offs associated with a move to the suburbs?

1. **Higher freight costs.** The firm will be farther from the central export node, so it will pay higher freight costs.
2. **Lower wages.** The firm will be closer to its work force, so workers will commute shorter distances. The wage compensates workers for commuting costs: the longer the commuting distance, the higher the wage. When the firm moves closer to its work force, it decreases its workers' commuting costs, so the firm can pay a lower wage.

The firm's location decision is determined by the outcome of a tug-of-war. On one side is the central export node, which pulls the firm toward the CBD. On the other side is its suburban work force, which pulls the firm toward the low-wage suburbs.

In the monocentric city, the tug-of-war was won by the CBD because the cost of moving freight was large relative to the cost of moving workers. Freight traveled by horse-drawn wagon, a relatively slow and expensive travel mode. In contrast, workers traveled by streetcar, a relatively fast and inexpensive travel mode. Although wages were lower in the suburbs, the wage differential was relatively small because commuting by streetcar was fast and efficient: workers demanded a relatively small premium to commute to CBD jobs. If a firm moved to the suburbs, the small savings in wages would be more than offset by an increase in the cost of shipping freight to the central export node. In the monocentric city, it was cheaper to bring the workers from the suburbs to the central-city factory than to bring the output from a suburban factory to the central export node.

The same analysis applies to office firms. Although a move from the CBD to the suburbs would decrease wages, it would also increase the costs of travel between the office and the central market area: managers would spend more time traveling between the office and clients in the city center. Given the frequency of travel to clients in the central market area, the increase in travel costs would dominate the savings in wages. In the monocentric city, it was cheaper to bring the workers from the suburbs to a central-city office than to bring the output (in the minds and briefcases of managers) from a suburban office to clients in the city center.

Relaxing the Assumptions

The simple monocentric model has a number of unrealistic assumptions about residential land use. This section derives the residential bid-rent function under more realistic sets of assumptions. The assumption that the city is monocentric is maintained: all employment is assumed to be in the CBD.

Changes in Commuting Assumptions

The simple model is based on a number of simplifying assumptions about commuting. What happens if these assumptions are dropped?

1. **Time cost of commuting.** The simple model assumes that the only cost of commuting is a monetary cost, that is, money spent on cars (for gasoline and maintenance) or public transit (bus tickets). In fact, commuting time comes at the expense of work or leisure, so there is an opportunity cost associated with commuting. The unit cost of commuting (t) is actually the monetary *and* time costs per mile of travel. Studies of commuting behavior suggest that most people value commuting time at between one third and one half the wage rate. For a worker with a wage of $10, the time cost of commuting is between $3.33 and $5.00 per hour. Commuting costs are discussed in greater detail in chapters 19 (Autos and Highways) and 20 (Mass Transit).

2. **Noncommuting travel: uniform distribution of destinations.** The simple model assumes that noncommuting travel is insignificant. This assumption is unrealistic because households travel to different destinations within the city for shopping and entertainment. Suppose that shopping and entertainment destinations are distributed uniformly throughout the urban area. For example, the household commutes northward to a job in the city center and also travels north to a museum, south to a grocery store, west to a disco, and east to the shore. If the frequency and distance of travel to the four sites are about the same, any change in residence causes a relatively small change in total noncommuting travel time. If the household moves south, the cost of museum travel increases, but the cost of the grocery travel decreases. If the household travels in all directions for shopping and entertainment, noncommuting costs usually offset one another, and it is appropriate to focus on commuting as the primary factor in the location decision.

3. **Noncommuting travel: concentrated destinations.** Consider next the possibility that shopping and entertainment sites are concentrated rather than dispersed. Suppose that members of a household travel to the city center for work, shopping, and entertainment. As the household moves closer to the city center, it saves on travel costs for commuting, shopping, and entertainment, so the savings in travel cost are relatively large and the housing-price function is relatively steep. In general, the more frequent the travel to the city center, the steeper the housing-price function and the residential bid-rent function.

4. **Two-earner households.** The simple model assumes that a single person from each household commutes to the city center. Suppose that all the households in a city are suddenly transformed into two-earner households. What happens to the housing-price function? If two members of each household commute to the CBD and have the same commuting cost per mile, a household that moves closer to the city center experiences

double the savings in commuting costs. In equilibrium, the housing-price function and the bid-rent function will be steeper in the two-earner city, reflecting the greater savings associated with living closer to central-city jobs.

Variation in Tastes for Housing

The simple model assumes that every household has the same tastes for housing. The housing-price function of the "typical" resident is used to represent the housing-price function of the entire city. Suppose that there are two types of households in the city, large and small, and that all households have the same income. The "tastes" for housing are dictated by the number of children: the small household lives in a small dwelling, and the large household lives in a large dwelling.

Where in the city will the two types of households live? Since land is rented to the highest bidder, the division of residential land between the two household types is determined by the bid-rent functions of the two groups. As shown in Chapter 7, the land user with the steeper bid-rent function occupies land closer to the city center. Since the residential bid-rent function is determined by the housing-price function, the user with the steeper housing-price function has a steeper bid-rent function.

Which household has the steeper housing-price function? The expression for the housing-price function is

$$\frac{\Delta P(u)}{\Delta u} = \frac{-t}{H(u)} \tag{8-15}$$

If the two households have the same commuting cost per mile (t), the small household has a steeper housing-price function because it consumes less housing (smaller H). Because the small household consumes a smaller amount of housing (in square feet), it takes a larger change in the price of housing per square foot to compensate for an increase in commuting cost.

Figure 8–9 shows the bid-rent functions for the two households. The bid-rent function of the small household is steeper because its housing-price function is steeper. The two functions intersect at a distance of four miles from the city center, so small households occupy dwellings within four miles of the city center, and large households occupy dwellings outside the four-mile radius. Large households occupy low-price suburban housing because they live in large houses and thus have more to gain from inexpensive suburban housing.

Spatial Variation in Public Goods and Pollution

The simple model has a number of assumptions that make the city center the focal point of the city. Except for jobs in the CBD, all the things that people care about (public services, taxes, pollution, amenities) are distributed uniformly throughout the city. What happens if these things are not distributed uniformly?

Public Goods and Taxes.   Taxes and public services vary within a metropolitan area. Suppose that the quality of public schools varies within the city, but the cost

FIGURE 8–9   Bid-Rent Function and Family Size

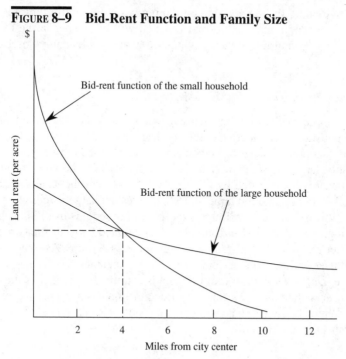

The slope of the bid-rent function decreases as housing consumption increases, so large households, who live in large houses, have relatively flat bid-rent functions. Large families have the most to gain from low suburban housing prices, so they outbid small households for suburban housing.

of schools (tuition and taxes) is the same throughout the city. In equilibrium, the price of housing is higher in the communities with better schools. Parents pay for better public schools indirectly: instead of paying higher taxes, they pay more for housing and residential land. Similarly, the prices of housing and land are higher in communities with lower crime rates. The same argument applies to variation in taxes. If two communities have the same level of public services but one community has higher taxes, the price of housing is higher in the low-tax community.

Pollution and Amenities.   The simple model assumes that environmental quality is the same at all locations in the city. To explain the effects of pollution on housing and land prices, suppose a polluting factory moves into the center of a previously clean city. If the smoke and smell from the factory are heaviest in the central area of the city, the factory decreases the relative attractiveness of dwellings near the city center, decreasing the price of housing. In addition, the factory increases the relative attractiveness of more remote dwellings, increasing the price of suburban housing.

Figure 8–10 shows the effects of the polluting factory on the housing-price function. P_c is the price function in the absence of pollution (the clean city), and P_s is the price function with a small amount of pollution. The pollution from the central-city factory decreases the slope of the housing-price function. As a household moves toward the city center there are costs (more pollution) as well as benefits (lower

FIGURE 8–10   **Pollution in the Central City and Housing Prices**

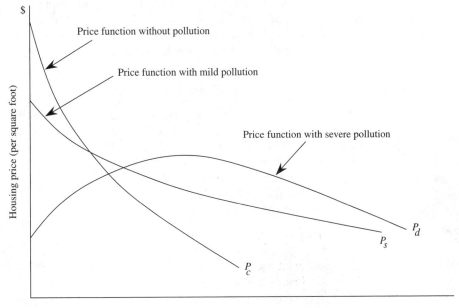

Air pollution from a central-city factory decreases housing prices near the city center and increases housing prices far from the city center. The more severe the pollution, the greater the change in housing prices.

commuting costs), so in the polluted city, the price of housing increases less rapidly as one approaches the city center. If the city has a high level of pollution, the housing-price function may be positively sloped, as shown by P_d. In this case, central-city pollution is so obnoxious that the advantages of a central-city dwelling (lower commuting costs) are dominated by its disadvantages (greater exposure to pollution). As a result, people are willing to live near the city center only if they are compensated in the form of lower housing prices.

Changes in the housing-price function cause similar changes in the residential bid-rent function. A relatively flat housing-price function (P_s) generates a relatively flat bid-rent function. Similarly, a positively sloped housing-price function (P_d) generates a positively sloped residential bid-rent function.

The same arguments apply to locations that have positive locational attributes (amenities) such as scenic views or access to parks. If people get utility from scenic views or park access, they are willing to pay more for dwellings that provide such amenities.

Income and Location

In U.S. cities, the wealthy tend to locate in the suburbs, and the poor tend to locate near the city center. In other words, average household income increases as one moves away from the city center. Because the most expensive land is near the city center, this location pattern is puzzling: why should the poor occupy the most expensive housing and land? There are several theories of this observed pattern of income segregation. The first is based on the simple monocentric model, and the others are based on extensions of the monocentric model.

Trade-off between Land and Commuting Costs

According to the simple monocentric model, a household chooses the location that provides the best trade-off between land costs and commuting costs. One theory of income segregation, developed by Alonso (1964) and Muth (1969), suggests that central locations provide the best trade-off for the poor, while suburban locations provide the best trade-off for the wealthy.

Table 8–5 shows the trade-offs between land costs and commuting costs for a household with the following characteristics:

1. The household takes the residential land-rent function as given. The second column of the table shows the land rent (per month per acre) for different locations, and the third column shows the changes in land rent for one-mile moves away from the city center.
2. Land consumption by the household is 0.20 acres, regardless of location (the fourth column in the table).
3. Commuting cost is $40 per round-trip mile per month.

The marginal benefit of distance, defined as the decrease in the household's land cost from a one-mile move outward, equals the decrease in land rent times land consumption. For example, a one-mile move away from the city center decreases land rent per acre by $700 and decreases land cost by $140 (0.20 times $700). The marginal benefit decreases as we move down the table because land rent falls at a decreasing rate: the land-rent function is convex. The marginal cost of a one-mile move outward, defined as the increase in commuting cost, equals the commuting cost

---

**TABLE 8–5   Trade-Offs between Land Cost
and Commuting Cost**

Distance to City Center (miles)	Land Rent per Acre	Decrease in Land Rent	Land (acres)	Marginal Benefit	Marginal Cost
0	$3,800				
1	3,100	$700	0.2	$140	$40
2	2,500	600	0.2	120	40
3	2,000	500	0.2	100	40
4	1,600	400	0.2	80	40
5	1,300	300	0.2	60	40
6	1,100	200	0.2	40	40
7	1,000	100	0.2	20	40

per mile per month ($40). Suppose that the household tentatively decides to live in the city center. Given the numbers in the table, a one-mile move outward would decrease land cost by more than it would increase commuting cost ($140 versus $40), so a central-city location is clearly inferior to a location one mile from the city center.

The optimum location is where the marginal benefit from a one-mile move outward (the savings in land cost) equals the marginal cost (the increase in commuting cost). In Table 8–5, the optimum location is six miles from the city center. At any location closer to the center, the marginal benefit exceeds the marginal cost, so the household will be better off at a more distant location. At six miles, the marginal benefit equals the marginal cost.

Figure 8–11 shows the benefit and cost curves from Table 8–5. The optimum location is where the marginal-benefit curve intersects the marginal-cost curve. The position of the marginal-benefit curve is affected by the household's land consumption: the larger the lot, the larger the benefit associated with lower land rent at more remote locations. In Figure 8–11, an increase in land consumption shifts the benefit curve upward, increasing the optimum distance. The position of the cost curve is determined by commuting costs: an increase in commuting costs shifts the cost curve upward and decreases the optimum distance.

FIGURE 8–11   Trade-Offs between Land Cost and Commuting Cost

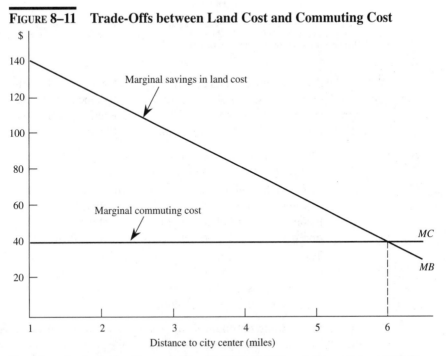

The optimum location is where the marginal benefit of distance (*MB*) equals the marginal cost (*MC*). The marginal benefit equals the decrease in land rent times land consumption. The marginal-benefit curve is negatively sloped because the land-rent function is convex. The marginal cost equals the increase in commuting cost per mile.

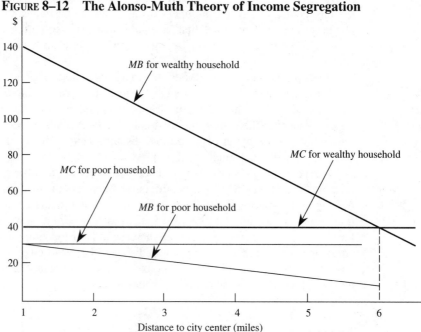

FIGURE 8–12   The Alonso-Muth Theory of Income Segregation

If the income elasticity of demand for land is large relative to the income elasticity of commuting cost, the gap between the marginal-benefit curves will be larger than the gap between the marginal-cost curves. Therefore, the poor live near the central city, and the wealthy live in the suburbs.

Under what circumstances will the poor locate near the central city, while the wealthy locate in the suburbs? Figure 8–12 shows the benefit and cost curves underlying the Alonso-Muth theory of income segregation. Consider the location choice of a poor household with the following characteristics:

1. The household has one fifth the income of the wealthy household whose characteristics are shown in Table 8–5.
2. The poor household consumes one fifth as much land as the wealthy household (0.04 acres). In other words, land is a normal good, with an income elasticity of demand (the percentage difference in land consumption divided by the percentage difference in income) equal to 1.0.
3. The commuting cost of the poor household is 70 percent the commuting cost of the wealthy household ($28 per month per mile). The poor household has a lower commuting cost because it has a lower wage and thus a lower opportunity cost of commuting.

In Figure 8–12, the optimum location for the wealthy household is six miles from the city center, and the optimum location for the poor household is one mile from the center.

What are the assumptions underlying this theory of income segregation? The benefit and cost curves in Figure 8–12 are drawn under the assumption that the income elasticity of demand for land is large relative to the income elasticity of commuting cost (the percentage difference in commuting cost divided by the percentage difference in income). Although both land consumption and commuting cost increase with income, the increase in land consumption is relatively large. Therefore, the gap between the two marginal-benefit curves is larger than the gap between the marginal-cost curves, so the poor occupy central-city housing.

Wheaton (1977) provides empirical evidence that questions the validity of the Alonso-Muth model of income segregation. His results suggest that the income elasticity of demand for land equals the income elasticity of commuting cost. Therefore, an increase in income shifts the benefit and cost curves upward by about the same amount (in percentage terms). In Figure 8–13, the poor household (with one fifth the income of the wealthy household) has half the land consumption and half the commuting cost of the wealthy household. There is a 50 percent gap between the benefit curves of the two households, and the same gap between the cost curves, so the optimum location for both households is six miles from the city center. This result suggests the observed locational pattern (poor central-city residents and wealthy suburbanites) cannot be explained by the trade-off between commuting cost and land cost. Wheaton's results suggest that one must look beyond the simple monocentric model to explain the observed pattern of income segregation.

FIGURE 8–13   Location Choices Using Wheaton's Results

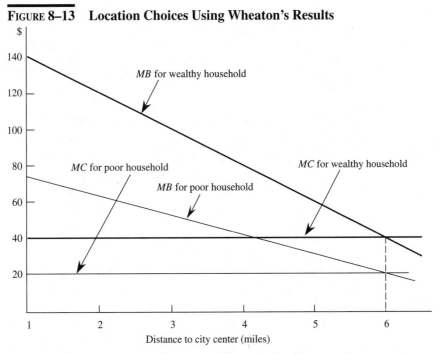

If the income elasticity of demand for land equals the income elasticity of commuting cost, the gap between the marginal-benefit curves equals the gap between the marginal-cost curves (in percentage terms). Therefore, the simple monocentric model predicts that location choices are unaffected by income: both households in the example pick a location six miles from the city center.

Other Explanations

Some alternative explanations of income segregation are based on factors excluded from the simple monocentric model.

1. **New suburban housing.** Suppose that the utility generated from a particular dwelling decreases over time as the dwelling deteriorates and becomes obsolete. In other words, people get less utility out of an older house because it is less fashionable, has higher maintenance costs, and is equipped with fewer modern gadgets. The wealthy, who demand high-quality housing, occupy new housing instead of used housing. As an urban area grows, it expands outward, and developers build new housing for high-income households in the peripheral areas. The poor are left with old houses in the central city.

2. **Fleeing central-city problems.** As explained later in the book, poverty contributes to three urban problems. First, crime rates are higher among the poor, in part because the poor face a relatively low opportunity cost of committing crime. Second, fiscal problems are more likely in a jurisdiction with a large fraction of low-income citizens. Third, students from poor families have relatively low achievement levels and pull down the achievement levels of other students. To escape these problems, wealthy households flee to the suburbs, leaving large concentrations of poor households behind.

3. **Suburban zoning.** As explained in Chapter 11 (Land-Use Controls and Zoning), suburban governments use zoning to exclude low-income households. Therefore, only the wealthy have the opportunity to escape the problems of the central city.

Income and the Residential Bid-Rent Function

The issue of income segregation can also be explained with the housing-price function and the residential bid-rent function. As explained earlier in the chapter, the activity with the steeper bid-rent function occupies land closer to the city center. Since the residential bid-rent function is determined by the housing-price function, the poor occupy central land if they have a steeper housing-price function. Figure 8–14 shows two residential bid-rent functions, one for low-income housing and one for high-income housing. The low-income function is steeper because the poor have a steeper housing-price function.

Why do the poor have a steeper housing-price function? In the simple monocentric model, the expression for the slope of the housing-price function is

$$\frac{\Delta P}{\Delta u} = -\frac{t}{H(u)} \tag{8–16}$$

An increase in income increases both t (the opportunity cost of commuting) and H (housing consumption), so rising income has an ambiguous effect on the slope of the

FIGURE 8–14   Bid-Rent Function and Income

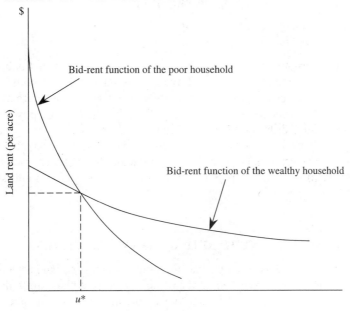

The wealthy have a flatter bid-rent function, so the poor occupy central land (land less than u^* miles from the city center). The wealthy have a flatter bid-rent function because they are sensitive to crime, pollution, and the quality of schools, and the central cities have more crime and pollution, and inferior schools.

housing-price function. If the increase in H exceeds the increase in t (if the income elasticity of demand for housing exceeds the income elasticity of commuting cost), the wealthy have a flatter housing-price function and a flatter residential bid-rent function. This is the Alonso-Muth theory of income segregation.

Wheaton's results suggest that the slope of the housing-price function is independent of income. If H and t increase at the same rate as income increases, the two housing-price functions have the same slope, so the two residential bid-rent functions have the same slope. Therefore, if the poor have a relatively steep bid-rent function, it is not because of the trade-off between commuting costs and housing costs.

The alternative explanations of income segregation suggest that the slope of the residential bid-rent function is affected by other factors. Specifically, if central cities have higher taxes, inferior schools, and more pollution and crime, households are willing to pay more for housing and land in the suburbs. In other words, the problems of the central city decrease the slope of the bid-rent function. If the income elasticities of demand for safety, clean air, and education are relatively large, the bid-rent function of wealthy households will be flatter than the bid-rent function of poor households. In other words, if the wealthy are willing to pay much more than the poor for safety, clean air, and superior education, wealthy households will outbid poor households for land in areas that are relatively safe and clean and provide high-quality education. Wasylenko (1984) summarizes the empirical evidence supporting these alternative explanations of income segregation.

Policy Implications

These alternative theories of income segregation suggest that public policy can affect the location choices of wealthy and poor households. A housing policy that encourages the renovation of central-city housing stock may cause some high-income households to return to the central city. Policies that decrease poverty decrease crime rates, reduce fiscal problems, and improve central-city schools, encouraging high-income households to live in the central city. Similarly, policies that address the crime and education problems directly increase the relative attractiveness of central-city locations. Finally, policies that control exclusionary zoning allow the poor to move to the suburbs.

Empirical Estimates of Rent and Density Functions

This section discusses empirical studies of land rent and land use in the monocentric city. The studies are based on data from the early 20th century, during the heyday of the monocentric city. Chapter 10 (Suburbanization and Modern Cities) discusses land-use patterns in modern cities. One of the key questions in Chapter 10 is: how "monocentric" are modern cities? In other words, are the patterns of land rent and land use in modern cities roughly consistent with the patterns predicted by the monocentric model?

Estimates of the Land-Rent Function

A number of researchers have estimated the relationship between land rent and distance to the city center. Mills (1969) used data collected by Homer Hoyt to estimate the relationship between land *value* and distance. As explained in Chapter 7, land value is the present value of land rent, so it's easy to make the translation from value to rent. Mills assumes the following relationship between value and distance:

$$V(u) = B \cdot e^{-c \cdot u} \qquad (8\text{--}17)$$

where

$V(u)$ = Value of land u miles from the city center
B = parameter to be estimated from the data
e = Base of the natural logarithm
c = parameter to be estimated from the data

Figure 8–15 shows the estimated relationship for Chicago in 1928, when the city was monocentric. The value of land drops from about $140,000 per acre at the city center to about $114,000 at 1 mile from the center, to about $17,000 at 10 miles from the city center. The value of land falls by 21 percent per mile, that is, the **rent gradient** is 21 percent.

FIGURE 8–15   Value of Land in Chicago in 1928

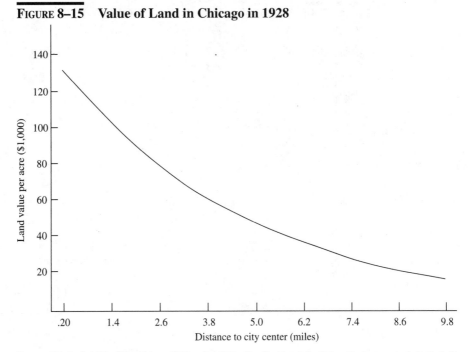

SOURCE: Edwin S. Mills, "The Value of Urban Land," in *The Quality of the Urban Environment,* ed. H. Perloff (Washington, D.C.: Resources for the Future, 1969).

Estimates of the Population-Density Function

How does population density vary within the monocentric city? The density function describes the relationship between population density and distance to the city center. Mills (1972) has estimated the density functions for 18 metropolitan areas for different years. The assumed relationship between density and distance is

$$D(u) = A \cdot e^{-g \cdot u} \qquad (8\text{–}18)$$

where

$D(u)$ = Population density u miles from the city center (people per square mile)

A = Parameter to be estimated from the data

e = Base of the natural logarithm

g = Parameter to be estimated from the data

Figure 8–16 shows the estimated relationship for Baltimore in 1920, when the city was monocentric. Population density drops from about 60,000 people per square mile at a distance of 0.20 miles from the city center, to about 34,000 at a distance of 1 mile, to about 4,200 at a distance of 4 miles. The density gradient, defined as the percentage change in population density per mile, is about 70 percent.

FIGURE 8–16   **Population Density in Baltimore in 1920**

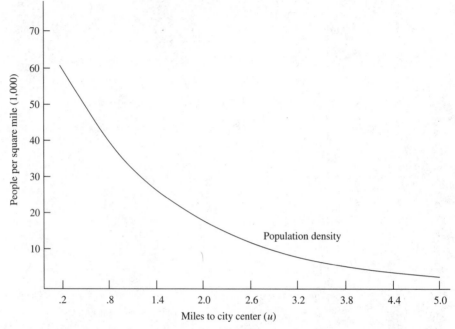

The density function is negatively sloped because (1) housing consumption increases with u (a result of declining housing prices) and (2) land per unit of housing increases with u (a result of declining land prices).
SOURCE: Edwin S. Mills, *Studies in the Structure of the Urban Economy* (Baltimore: Johns Hopkins, 1972).

Summary

1. The monocentric city has the following characteristics:
   a. All manufacturers export their output through a central export node.
   b. Manufactured goods are transported within the city by horse-drawn wagon.
   c. Office workers travel by foot from offices to a central market area to exchange information.
   d. Commuters and shoppers travel on a hub-and-spoke streetcar system.
2. The manufacturing bid-rent function is negatively sloped because transport cost is lower near the export node. It is convex because of factor substitution.
3. The office bid-rent function is negatively sloped because travel costs are lower near the central market area. It is convex because of factor substitution.
4. Transport costs in the monocentric city are relatively high for office firms, so the office bid-rent function is relatively steep and office firms occupy the central area of the city.

5. The location choices of retailers depend on scale economies, per capita demand, and shopping externalities. In the monocentric city, the hub-and-spoke streetcar system makes central locations accessible to the entire urban area, causing most retailers to locate there.

6. In the simple monocentric model, all employment is in the CBD, and other things that residents care about (e.g., public services, taxes, pollution) are the same at all locations within the city.

7. The housing-price function shows the price of housing (per square foot of living space) for different locations in the city. The function is negatively sloped because commuting costs increase with the distance to the city center. It is convex because of consumer substitution: as the price of housing rises, consumers substitute other goods for housing.

8. The residential bid-rent function shows the amount housing producers are willing to pay for residential land at different locations in the city. It is negatively sloped because the housing-price function is negatively sloped. It is convex because of consumer substitution (which makes the housing-price function convex) and factor substitution.

9. The density function shows the number of people per acre for different locations in the city. It is negatively sloped for two reasons.
    a. Housing prices are higher near the city center, so housing consumption is lower (fewer square feet of living space per household).
    b. Land prices are higher near the city center, so the amount of land per square foot of housing is lower.

10. Activities in the monocentric city are arranged according to their transportation cost: the higher the transportation cost, the closer to the city center.
    a. The city center is occupied by the office sector rather than the manufacturing sector because office output is transmitted by high-cost office workers, while manufacturing output is transported by horse-drawn wagon.
    b. Employment is concentrated in the CBD because the cost of commuting (from the suburbs to the CBD factories and offices) is low relative to the cost of moving output (from the suburbs to the city center). Freight travels by horse-drawn wagon, a relatively slow and expensive travel mode. In contrast, workers travel by streetcar, a relatively fast and inexpensive travel mode.

11. If the assumptions of the simple monocentric model are dropped, the housing-price function and the residential bid-rent change.
    a. The opportunity cost of commuting is the value of forgone work or leisure time. The typical commuter values commuting time at between one third and one half of his or her wages. The unit cost of commuting is the sum of time and monetary costs.
    b. Noncommuting travel to the CBD increases the slopes of the housing-price and bid-rent functions because total travel costs increase more rapidly as the household moves away from the CBD.

  c. The two-earner household has a relatively steep housing-price function if both earners commute to the CBD.

  d. The prices of housing and land are higher in communities with superior local public goods and low taxes.

  e. The prices of housing and land are higher in communities with clean air, scenic views, and access to parks.

12. The slopes of the housing-price and land-rent functions depend on housing consumption. A household that occupies a relatively large house has a relatively flat housing-price function and a relatively flat bid-rent function, so the household lives relatively far from the city center. Such a household has more to gain from inexpensive suburban housing.

13. In U.S. cities, the wealthy tend to locate in the suburbs, and the poor tend to locate near the city center. One theory of income segregation suggests that the location choices of wealthy and poor households are based on different trade-offs between commuting and land costs. This theory has been refuted by empirical evidence, suggesting that the observed pattern of segregation is caused by other factors, such as the demand for new suburban housing, the desire to escape central-city problems, and exclusionary zoning in the suburbs.

Exercises and Discussion Questions

1. In the city of Trekburg, manufacturers have two options for intracity freight. They can use a conventional transportation system (the truck) or a matter transmitter, which instantly transports the output from the factory to the central export node ("Beam it over, Scotty"). A transmitter can be rented for C per year, and running the machine is costless. The transmitter can transport output up to a distance of two miles. All manufacturing output goes through the export node.

  a. Draw the bid-rent function for a firm that uses the matter transmitter, and label it M.

  b. On the same graph, draw the bid-rent function for a firm that uses the truck, and label it T.

  c. Will every manufacturer use the matter transmitter? If not, where will the firms using the truck be located?

2. Consider a traditional 19th-century monocentric city with a CBD radius of one mile. In 1869, buildings at the edge of the CBD are four stories tall. In 1870, all the buildings in the CBD are destroyed by an earthquake, and the mayor of the city announces that the maximum building height in the rebuilt city will be four stories. In addition, business development will be confined to a circle with a one-mile radius, that is, the size of the CBD is fixed. Suppose that the city is small enough that events in the city do not affect the equilibrium prices of its export goods (office or manufacturing goods).

    a. Draw the business bid-rent function before the earthquake and label it R°. Draw the business bid-rent function after the earthquake (with the height restrictions) and label it R^*.

    b. Explain any differences between the two bid-rent functions.

    c. Suppose that the city is large enough that events in the city affect the price of its exports. Will the height restrictions increase or decrease the price of the goods? What are the implications of the change in the price of goods on the business bid-rent function?

3. Complete the following table, given the following assumptions:

    i. The office firm produces 100 consultations per month.

    ii. The consultation fee is $75.

    iii. Travel time is five minutes per block.

    iv. The opportunity cost of travel time is $3 per minute.

    v. Every consultation requires one trip to the city center.

Distance to City Center (miles)	Size of Site (acres)	Total Revenue	Nonland Cost	Travel Cost	Pre-Rent Profit	Rent per Acre
0	0.40		$3,600			
1	0.70		2,000			
2	0.90		1,200			
3	1.00		900			

4. Consider an office firm with the following characteristics: the wage of executives is $120 per hour, and the executive takes four minutes to walk one block (eight minutes to make a round trip); the price of output is $150, and the firm produces 50 consultations (requiring 50 trips to the city center); at a location four blocks from the city center, the firm occupies a one-acre site and spends $1,000 on nonland inputs.

    a. What is the travel cost per block?

    b. How much is the firm willing to pay for land four blocks from the city center?

    c. Given the available information, is it possible to compute how much the firm is willing to pay for land one block from the city center? If not, what additional information do you need?

5. Consider two monocentric cities: Rigid City, where office firms produce with fixed factor proportions, and Flexville, where office firms produce with variable factor proportions. In each city, the CBD is a circular area with a radius of one mile, and all land in the CBD is used for office space. At the edge of the CBD there is 5,000 square feet of office space per acre, and the bid rent for office land is $20,000 per year. Suppose that each city imposes an annual tax of $1 per square foot of office space. Assume that the cities are small enough that the equilibrium price of office services is unaffected by events

in the cities. For each city, draw the office bid-rent function before and after the new office tax. Provide numbers for the bid rents (pre-tax and post-tax) at the CBD edges. Explain any differences in the effects of the tax in the two cities.

6. Depict graphically the effects of the following changes on the division of CBD land between office firms and manufacturers:
   a. The unit freight cost decreases.
   b. The price of office output increases.
   c. The opportunity cost of executive travel decreases.

7. Consider an industry that makes table tennis balls and competes with the baseball makers for land near the central export node. Each table tennis ball firm produces the same amount of output as a baseball firm (five tons of balls), sells for the same price ($160 per ton), and has the same production isoquants. Which activity will locate closer to the export node?

8. Consider a monocentric city in which the unit cost of commuting is $10 per mile per month. A household located eight miles from the city center occupies a dwelling with 1,200 square feet at a monthly rent of $600. Nonland cost per dwelling is $200, and there are four houses per acre.
   a. What is the price (per square foot) of housing at $u = 8$? What is the bid rent at $u = 8$?
   b. Assume that the demand for housing is perfectly inelastic. What is the price of housing at $u = 5$?
   c. Assume that housing firms do not engage in factor substitution. What is the bid rent at $u = 5$?
   d. How would your answers to (b) and (c) change if the demand for housing is price-elastic and firms engage in factor substitution? Would the prices of housing and land be larger or smaller?

9. Choose one word in each set of parentheses to make the following statements correct, and then explain your choice of words.
   a. "The flatter the demand curve for housing, the (*more, less*) curvature in the housing-price function. In other words, the flatter the housing demand curve, the (*more, less*) convex the housing-price function."
   b. "The flatter the demand curve for housing, the (*more, less*) curvature in the residential bid-rent function."

10. Consider a region with two cities: Lawland (L) and Violateville (V). The two cities differ in their demand curves for housing: consumers in Lawland have negatively sloped demand curves; consumers in Violateville have positively sloped demand curves (consumers in Violateville actually consume more housing as the price of housing increases). Draw the housing-price functions for the two cities (labeled *PL* for Lawland and *PV* for Violateville) under the assumption that *PL* = *PV* at a distance of five miles from the city center. Briefly explain any differences between the two housing-price functions.

11. Depict graphically the effects of the following changes on the equilibrium housing-price function:

 a. The workweek is shortened from five days per week to four days per week.

 b. The workers in two-earner households start riding to work together.

12. Suppose that a city restricts the heights of residential structures. The maximum height is four stories, the height that would normally occur at a distance of five miles from the city center. Draw two residential bid-rent functions, one for the city in the absence of height restrictions and one with height restrictions.

13. Between 1940 and 1965, the average household size increased dramatically. Draw two housing-price functions (one for 1940 and one for 1965) and explain the differences between the two functions. Could the increase in household size explain part of the suburbanization that occurred between 1940 and 1965?

14. Consider the example of the trade-offs associated with location choices in Table 8–5. Suppose the poor household (with one fifth of the income of the wealthy household) consumes 0.15 acres of land and has a monthly commuting cost of $15 per mile.

 a. What are the implied income elasticities of land consumption and commuting cost?

 b. What is the optimum distance for the poor household?

 c. What are the implications for income segregation?

15. Suppose that the income elasticity of demand for land is +0.75. The unit commuting cost (cost per mile) is the sum of monetary cost (30 cents per mile) and time cost (opportunity cost). Suppose that the typical commuter earns a wage of $12 and takes 30 minutes to commute 10 miles to work. Every worker values commuting time at half of his or her wage. Can the observed pattern of income segregation be explained by the trade-offs between commuting cost and land cost? If there's not enough information to answer the question, what additional information do you need, and how would you use it?

16. Suppose that the demand for housing (H = square feet of housing space per capita) and the demand for land (T = square feet of land per square foot of housing space) are described by the following equations (P = price of housing, and R = land rent per square foot):

$$H = 1,500 - 500 \cdot P$$

$$T = \frac{1}{10,000} \cdot (15,000 - R)$$

 Compute land consumption per capita for the following locations:

 a. Location A: $P = 1.5$ and $R = 12,000$

 b. Location B: $P = 1.0$ and $R = 10,000$

 c. Location C: $P = 0.3$ and $R = 3,000$

17. In Figure 8–5, the introduction of consumer substitution increases the price of housing at all locations. Comment on the following: "Something is wrong

here. As we move from a world without substitution to a world with substitution, overall demand for housing decreases. Yet Figure 8–5 shows an increase in the price of housing. How can price rise when demand falls?"

References and Additional Readings

Location of Office Firms

Clapp, J. M. "Endogenous Centers: A Simple Departure from the NUE Model." *Papers of the Regional Science Association* 54 (1984), pp. 13–24. Describes the process by which contacts between firms cause the development of a CBD and subcenters.

David, Philip. *Urban Land Development.* Homewood, Ill.: Richard D. Irwin, 1970. Discusses the rent function of commercial firms.

O'Hara, D. J. "Location of Firms within a Square Central Business District." *Journal of Political Economy* 85 (1977), pp. 1189–207. Discusses how interfirm contacts cause the development of a central business district.

Tauchen, H., and Anne Witte. "An Equilibrium Model of Office Location and Contact Patterns." *Environment and Planning A* 15 (1983), pp. 1311–26. Discusses how interfirm contacts cause the development of a central business district.

———. "Socially Optimal and Equilibrium Distributions of Office Activity: Models with Exogenous and Endogenous Contacts." *Journal of Urban Economics* 15 (1984), pp. 66–86. Discusses two sources of market failure in the location decisions of office firms: agglomeration economies and transaction externalities.

Transportation, Land Rent, and Land Use

Alcaly, Roger E. "Transportation and Urban Land Values: A Review of the Theoretical Literature." *Land Economics* 52 (1976), pp. 42–53. Discusses the effects of changes in transport cost on land rent.

Meyer, J.; John Kain; and M. Wohl. *The Urban Transportation Problem.* Cambridge, Mass.: Harvard University Press, 1965. Discusses the effects of the trend toward two-earner households and noncommuting travel on the residential rent function.

Housing-Price Function

Jackson, Jerry. "Intraurban Variation in the Price of Housing." *Journal of Urban Economics* 6 (1979), pp. 465–79. Estimates the housing-price function, finding that housing prices fall by about 2 percent per mile.

Kain, John F., and John M. Quigley. "Measuring the Value of Housing Quality." *Journal of the American Statistical Association* 65 (1970), pp. 532–38. Estimates the relationship between various housing characteristics (including location) and the price of housing.

King, Thomas. "The Demand for Housing: Integrating the Roles of Journey to Work, Neighborhood Quality, and Prices." In *Household Production and Consumption,* ed. Nester Terleckyj. New York: National Bureau of Economic Research, 1975. Estimates the relationship between various housing characteristics (including location) and the price of housing.

Quigley, John M. "Housing Demand in the Short Run: An Analysis of Polytomous Choice." *Explorations in Economic Research* 3 (1976), pp. 76–102. Estimates the effects of location on the implicit prices of different components of housing.

Straszheim, Mahlon. *An Economic Analysis of the Urban Housing Market.* New York: National Bureau of Economic Research, 1975. Estimates the effects of location on the implicit prices of different components of housing.

Empirical Studies of Population Density and Land Rent

Mills, Edwin S. *Studies in the Structure of the Urban Economy.* Baltimore: Johns Hopkins, 1972. Chapter 3 estimates population and employment density functions for U.S. cities.

———. "The Value of Urban Land." In *The Quality of the Urban Environment,* ed. H. Perloff. Washington, D.C.: Resources for the Future, 1969. Estimates the land-rent function in Chicago for 1836 to 1959.

Muth, Richard. *Cities and Housing.* Chicago: University of Chicago Press, 1969. A classic study of residential location decisions in Chicago. Chapter 7 estimates the density function for several U.S. cities.

Income and Location

Alonso, William. *Location and Land Use.* Cambridge, Mass.: Harvard University Press, 1964. Expands the Von Thunen model to the location decisions of households.

Downs, Anthony. *Urban Problems and Prospects.* Chicago: Markham, 1970. Suggests that the building of new housing on the periphery of the metropolitan area contributes to the suburbanization of high-income households.

LeRoy, Stephen, and Jon Sonstelie. "Paradise Lost and Regained: Transportation Innovation, Income, and Residential Segregation." *Journal of Urban Economics* 13 (1983), pp. 67–89. Discusses the effects of different transport modes on the location patterns of different income groups.

Muth, Richard. *Cities and Housing.* Chicago: University of Chicago Press, 1969. A classic study of residential location decisions in Chicago. Chapter 2 models the location decision, and Chapter 10 provides empirical evidence that suggests that the tendency for higher-income households to locate farther from the city center is caused by differences in the trade-offs between housing and commuting costs.

Wasylenko, Michael J. "Disamenities, Local Taxation, and the Intrametropolitan Location of Households and Firms." In *Research in Urban Economics,* vol. 4, ed. Robert Ebel. Greenwich, Conn.: JAI Press, 1984. Reviews the empirical evidence concerning the effects of income on location. Also reviews the evidence concerning the intrametropolitan location choices of firms.

Wheaton, William. "Income and Urban Residence: An Analysis of Consumer Demand for Location." *American Economic Review* 67 (1977), pp. 620–31. Suggests that the income elasticity of demand for land is close to the income elasticity of time cost, meaning that the tendency for the poor to locate near the city center cannot be explained by the simple monocentric model.

Miscellaneous

Clawson, Marion. "Urban Sprawl and Speculation in Suburban Land." In *Urban Economic Issues,* ed. Stephen Mehay and Geoffrey Nunn. Glenview, Ill.: Scott, Foresman,

1984, pp. 47–52. Analyzes the market for undeveloped land and suggests that urban sprawl is efficient.

Eberts, Randall. "An Empirical Investigation of Intraurban Wage Gradients." *Journal of Urban Economics* 10 (1981), pp. 50–60. Estimates the variation in wages within a metropolitan area.

Modeling the Monocentric City

Mills, Edwin S. "Planning and Market Processes in Urban Models." In *Public and Urban Economics,* ed. Ronald Grieson. Lexington, Mass.: Lexington Books, 1976. A model of urban land use that uses linear and nonlinear programming to allocate land to alternative activities.

———. *Studies in the Structure of the Urban Economy.* Baltimore: Johns Hopkins, 1972. Chapter 5 derives the conditions under which the monocentric city is more efficient than a city with dispersed employment.

Wheaton, William. "Monocentric Models of Urban Land Use: Contributions and Criticisms." In *Current Issues in Urban Economics,* ed. Peter Mieszkowski and Mahlon Straszheim. Baltimore: Johns Hopkins, 1979. Discusses several renditions of the traditional monocentric model.

CHAPTER 9

General-Equilibrium Land Use

Everything should be explained as simply as possible, but not more so.
Albert Einstein

This chapter uses general-equilibrium analysis to explore the interactions between different parts of the urban economy. In contrast with partial-equilibrium analysis, which examines a single market in isolation, general-equilibrium analysis recognizes that markets are interdependent and explores the effects of changes in one market on related markets.

Urban general-equilibrium analysis explores the interactions between the residential land market, the business land market, and the urban labor market. It is used to predict the effects of changes in one part of the urban economy on land use throughout the urban area. This chapter uses general-equilibrium analysis to explore the effects of three changes in the monocentric city: an increase in export sales, the introduction of a streetcar system, and an increase in the residential property tax. Later in the book, general-equilibrium analysis is used to explore the land-use effects of changes in technology and public policy. Chapter 10 (Suburbanization and Modern Cities) explores the land-use effects of the truck and the automobile. Chapter 11 (Land-Use Controls and Zoning) examines the general-equilibrium effects of various land-use controls. Chapter 19 (Autos and Highways) explores the effects of highway congestion on land-use patterns.

General-Equilibrium Conditions

Figure 9–1 shows the equilibrium land-use pattern of a monocentric city. The bid-rent function of the business sector (office firms and manufacturers) is negatively sloped, reflecting the benefits of locating near the central market area and the central export node. The bid-rent function of residents is negatively sloped, reflecting the benefits of locating near jobs in office and manufacturing firms. The central business

FIGURE 9–1   **Equilibrium Land-Use Pattern in a Monocentric City**

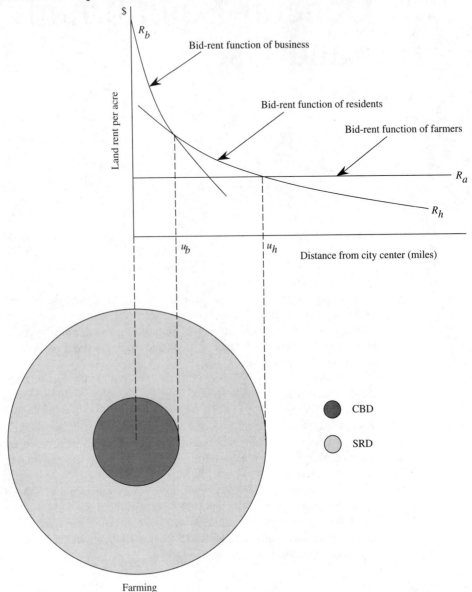

Business firms outbid residents for central land, generating a CBD with radius u_b. The SRD is the area over which residents outbid firms and farmers, that is, a ring with width $(u_h - u_b)$.

district (CBD) is the area over which firms (office firms and manufacturers) outbid residents, so the radius of the CBD is u_b miles. The suburban residential district (SRD) is the area over which residents outbid firms and farmers, so the SRD is a ring of width $(u_h - u_b)$ miles. For land beyond u_h, farmers outbid residents, so the radius of the city is u_h miles.

The monocentric city is assumed to be one of hundreds of cities in a regional economy. The city is "open" in the sense that households and firms can costlessly enter or leave the city. The city is "small" in the sense that it is a trivial part of the regional economy, so that changes in the city do not affect the common utility level of the region's residents. Any change that increases the utility level of the city's residents causes in-migration from the rest of the region. This migration bids up the prices of housing and land (increasing the cost of living), decreasing the utility level of the city's residents. Migration continues until the original utility level is restored.

The urban economy achieves general equilibrium when four conditions are satisfied simultaneously:

1. **Locational equilibrium for firms.** If all firms make zero profits at all locations, there is no incentive to change locations. This condition is guaranteed by the business bid-rent function, R_b: competition for land bids up the price of land at locations with relatively low transportation costs, so firms are indifferent among all locations in the city.

2. **Locational equilibrium for households.** If all households achieve the same utility level at all locations in the city, there is no incentive to change locations. This condition is guaranteed by the residential bid-rent function, R_h: competition for land bids up the price of land at locations with relatively low commuting costs, so households are indifferent among all locations in the city.

3. **Competitive bidding.** Land is allocated to the highest bidder. This condition is satisfied if landowners, like other people in a competitive economy, seek the highest return on their assets.

4. **Labor-market equilibrium.** The total demand for labor (from office firms and manufacturers in the CBD) equals the total supply of labor (from residents in the SRD).

To summarize, general equilibrium occurs when both the land market and the labor market are in equilibrium at the same time.

Numerical Examples of General-Equilibrium Analysis

This section uses two numerical examples to explain the principles of general-equilibrium analysis. An increase in export sales has a direct effect on the CBD land market, and the introduction of a streetcar system has a direct effect on the SRD land market.

Initial Equilibrium

Table 9–1 shows the numbers associated with the monocentric city depicted in Figure 9–1. In initial equilibrium, the CBD radius is two miles, and the city radius is six miles. The land area of the CBD is computed with the formula for the area of a circle:

$$\text{CBD land area} = \pi \cdot (u_b)^2 \qquad (9\text{–}1)$$

TABLE 9–1   **General-Equilibrium Effects of an Increase in Export Price and Export Sales**

	Initial Equilibrium	Partial Equilibrium	General Equilibrium
Radius of CBD in miles (u_b)	2.0	2.5	2.2
Area of CBD (square miles)	12.56	19.63	15.20
Width of SRD in miles ($u_h - u_b$)	4.0	3.5	4.3
Area of SRD (square miles)	100.48	74.58	117.47
Radius of city in miles (u_h)	6.0	6.0	6.5
Area of city (square miles)	113.04	113.04	132.67
Wage ($ per hour)	10.0	10.0	13.0
Average labor density (workers per square mile)	20,000	22,000	21,000
Total labor demand (workers)	251,200	431,750	319,150
Average household density (households per square mile)	2,500	2,500	2,717
Total labor supply (workers)	251,200	186,438	319,150

Because u_b is 2 miles, the CBD land area is 12.56 square miles. The land area of the city is

$$\text{City land area} = \pi \cdot (u_h)^2 \tag{9–2}$$

Because u_h is 6 miles, the land area of the city is 113.04 square miles. The land area of the residential district is the difference between the land areas of the city and the CBD, or 100.48 square miles.

The city is in general equilibrium because total labor supply equals total labor demand. Total labor demand equals the land area of the CBD times the average number of workers per square mile:

$$\text{Total demand} = \text{CBD land area} \cdot \text{Average employment density} \tag{9–3}$$

In Table 9–1, the average employment density is 20,000 workers per square mile, so total labor demand is 251,200. Total labor supply equals the land area of the SRD times average household density (assuming that there is one worker per household):

$$\text{Total supply} = \text{SRD land area} \cdot \text{Average household density} \tag{9–4}$$

In Table 9–1, the average household density is 2,500 per square mile, so total labor supply is 251,200. Labor supply equals labor demand, so the land-use allocation shown in Figure 9–1 is an equilibrium allocation.

Increase in Export Sales

Suppose that the price of baseballs (the city's export good) increases. What are the effects of the price increase on the city's land and labor markets?

Consider first the effect of the price increase on the CBD land market. In the short run, the increase in price increases the profits of baseball firms. The demand for CBD land increases as (1) existing baseball firms increase their output and (2)

FIGURE 9–2   Partial-Equilibrium Effects of an Increase in Export Price and Export Sales

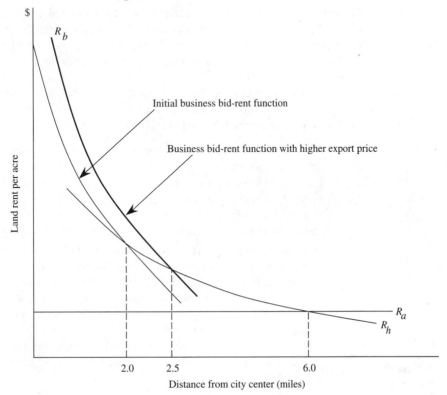

An increase in the price of exports shifts the business bid-rent function upward. The CBD expands (the radius increases from 2.0 miles to 2.5 miles) at the expense of the SRD (the width decreases from 4.0 miles to 3.5 miles).

new firms enter the baseball industry. The increase in the demand for land shifts the bid-rent function for business land upward, as shown in Figure 9–2. The upward shift of R_b is consistent with the leftover principle: at the higher baseball price, firms have a greater excess of revenue over nonland cost, so they are willing to pay more for land. As the business bid-rent function shifts upward, the CBD expands at the expense of the residential area: the radius of the business district increases from 2.0 miles to 2.5 miles, and the SRD shrinks from a width of 4.0 miles to 3.5 miles.

How does the upward shift of the business bid-rent function affect the urban labor market? Total labor demand increases for two reasons:

1. **CBD territory effect.** As shown in the second column of Table 9–1, the land area of the CBD increases from 12.56 square miles to 19.63 square miles.

2. **Employment density effect.** The increase in the relative price of land causes baseball firms to substitute nonland inputs (capital and labor) for land, increasing labor density (workers per square mile). In the second

column of Table 9–1, labor density has increased from 20,000 workers per square mile to 22,000.

In combination, these two effects increase total labor demand from 251,200 to 431,750. The upward shift of the business bid-rent function also decreases total labor supply: the CBD encroaches on SRD land, decreasing total supply from 251,200 to 186,438. Because labor demand increases and labor supply decreases, there is excess demand for labor.

The increase in price increases labor demand while it decreases labor supply, and the excess demand for labor increases the city's wage. The increase in the wage increases the quantity of labor supplied for two reasons:

1. **SRD territory effect.** An increase in the wage increases the relative attractiveness of the city. Laborers from the rest of the region move to the city, bidding up the prices of housing and residential land. R_h shifts upward, increasing the size of the SRD as residents outbid farmers (for land near the city border) and firms (for land near the CBD border). As the residential district expands, total labor supply increases.

2. **Household density effect.** As the price of housing increases, households substitute nonhousing goods for housing, so housing consumption per household decreases. In addition, as the price of residential land increases, housing producers substitute capital for land, so the amount of land per unit of housing decreases. In combination, these two changes decrease land consumption per household, that is, every household occupies a smaller lot. The decrease in land consumption increases household density (the number of households and laborers per square mile), increasing total labor supply.

To summarize, the increase in the wage increases the quantity of labor supplied because both the size and the density of the residential district increase.

How does the increase in the wage affect the demand side of the labor market? The increase in the wage decreases the quantity of labor demanded for two reasons:

1. **CBD territory effect.** An increase in the wage increases production costs. Some firms decrease their output, and other firms shut down. The decrease in production activity decreases the demand for land, so the business bid-rent function drops. As the CBD loses territory to the residential district, total labor demand decreases.

2. **Employment density effect.** The increase in the wage decreases land rent. As the relative price of labor increases, firms substitute land for the relatively expensive labor. Labor density (the number of workers per square mile) decreases.

To summarize, the increase in the wage decreases the quantity of labor demanded because both the size and the density of the business district decrease.

These two changes in the labor market narrow the gap between labor supply and labor demand. The wage continues to rise until general equilibrium is restored. Figure 9–3 shows the new equilibrium allocation of land, and the third column of

---

FIGURE 9–3   General-Equilibrium Effects of an Increase in Export Price and Export Sales

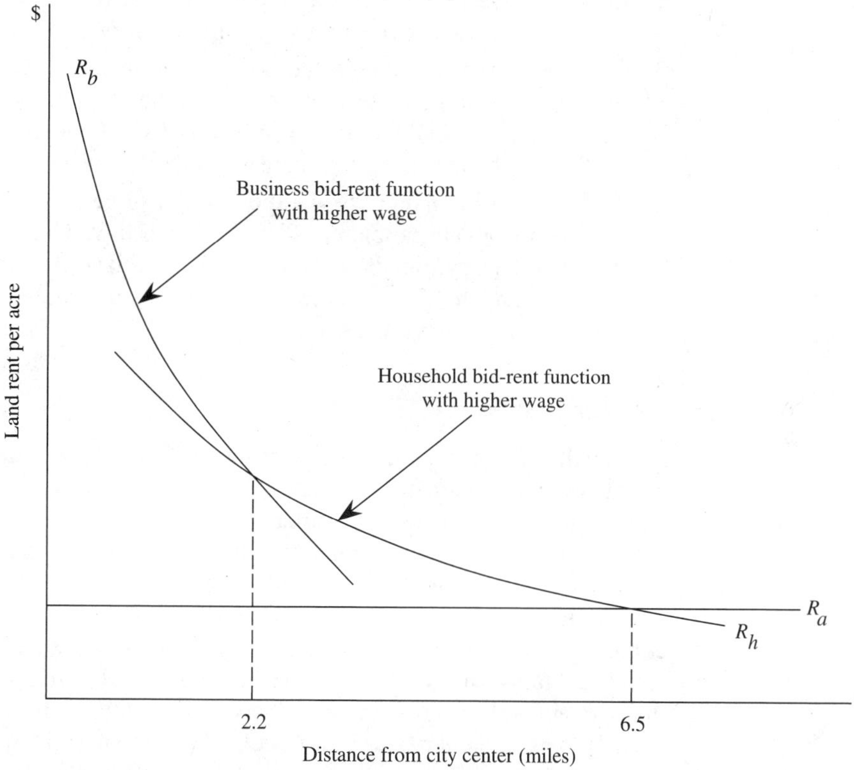

The increase in the export price causes excess demand for labor, increasing the city's wage. The increase in the wage shifts the business bid-rent function downward and shifts the residential bid-rent function upward. The net effect is a larger CBD (the radius increases from 2.0 miles to 2.2 miles) and a larger SRD (the width increases from 4.0 miles to 4.3 miles).

Table 9–1 shows numbers behind the new allocation. The new equilibrium wage is $13 per hour (up from $10). The CBD radius is 2.2 miles, and labor density is 21,000 workers per square mile, so total labor demand is 319,150. The SRD is 4.3 miles wide and household density is 2,717 per square mile, so total labor supply is the same as total demand. In other words, general equilibrium is restored with a wage of $13. For a lower wage, labor demand would exceed supply; for a higher wage, supply would exceed demand.

There are four lessons from the general-equilibrium analysis of the increases in the export price:

1. **Market interactions.** Changes in the CBD (the business land market) affect the city's labor market and its residential land market. The upward shift of the business bid-rent function increases the size and the density of the CBD, causing excess demand for labor. The resulting increase in the wage shifts the bid-rent function of residents upward, increasing the size and density of the SRD.

2. **Shifts in bid-rent functions.** The increase in the export price causes an upward shift of the business bid-rent function (a partial-equilibrium effect). The resulting increase in the wage causes a downward shift of the business bid-rent function (a general-equilibrium effect).

3. **Land rent.** The increase in the export price increases land rent throughout the city. The increase in export production increases the demand for land in both the CBD and the residential district, so landowners throughout the city benefit from the increase in export sales.

4. **Welfare effects of increased export sales.** In general equilibrium, the city's residents are no better off in the larger city. The increase in the wage is offset by higher costs of housing and land, leaving the utility level unchanged. The increase in export sales increases the number of residents, not their utility.

A Streetcar System

As a second illustration of general-equilibrium analysis, suppose that the city installs a streetcar system. The streetcar decreases the time and monetary cost of commuting, causing a number of changes in the urban economy.

How does the streetcar system affect the residential bid-rent function? As explained in Chapter 8 (Land Use in the Monocentric City), the slope of the bid-rent function is determined by commuting costs: the lower the unit cost of commuting, the flatter the bid-rent function. In Figure 9–4, the streetcar system decreases the slope of the bid-rent function and increases the width of the SRD from 4 to 6.2 miles. The streetcar system makes peripheral areas accessible to CBD jobs, allowing residents to outbid farmers for land near the city's edge. In addition, residents outbid firms for the land near the CBD border. This is the partial-equilibrium effect of the streetcar system.

The upward tilt of the residential bid-rent function increases total labor supply for two reasons:

1. **SRD territory effect.** The expansion of the residential district increases labor supply. Table 9–2 shows an increase in the land area of the residential district from 100.48 square miles in column one to 190.88 square miles in column two.

2. **Household density effect.** The increases in the prices of housing and land cause consumer substitution (consumers substitute nonhousing goods for housing) and factor substitution (housing producers substitute nonland inputs for land). The lot size per household decreases, increasing population density. Table 9–2 shows an increase in household density from 2,500 in column one to 2,700 in column two.

To summarize, the streetcar system increases the quantity of labor supplied because it increases both the size and the density of the residential district. The streetcar system increases the relative attractiveness of the city, causing in-migration that bids up the price of land. People migrate from other cities because workers in the streetcar city

FIGURE 9–4   The Partial-Equilibrium Effect of the Streetcar System

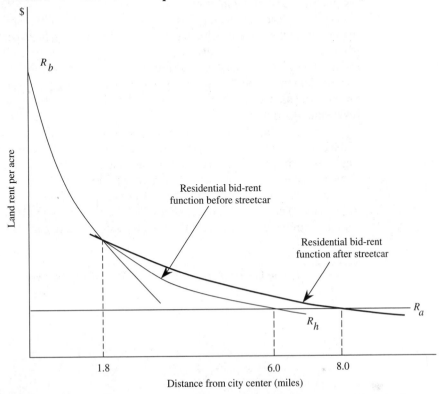

The streetcar system decreases commuting cost, decreasing the slope of the residential bid-rent function. The width of the SRD increases from four miles to six miles, and the city radius increases from six miles to eight miles.

TABLE 9–2   General-Equilibrium Effects of a Streetcar System

	Initial Equilibrium	Partial Equilibrium	General Equilibrium
Radius of CBD in miles (u_b)	2.0	1.8	2.3
Area of CBD (square miles)	12.56	10.18	16.61
Width of SRD in miles ($u_h - u_b$)	4.0	6.2	4.8
Area of SRD (square miles)	100.48	190.88	141.68
Radius of city in miles (u_h)	6.0	8.0	7.1
Area of city (square miles)	113.04	201.06	158.29
Wage ($ per hour)	10.0	10.0	6.0
Average labor density (workers per square mile)	20,000	20,000	22,000
Total labor demand (workers)	251,200	203,575	365,433
Average household density (households per square mile)	2,500	2,700	2,579
Total labor supply (workers)	251,200	515,380	365,433

have shorter commuting times, so they have higher net income (gross labor income less the time cost of commuting).

The streetcar causes an excess supply of labor. The CBD shrinks, so labor demand falls at the same time that labor supply increases. The excess supply of labor decreases the city's wage, causing changes on both sides of the labor market. On the demand side, the business bid-rent function shifts upward, increasing both the territory and the employment density of the CBD. On the supply side, the residential bid-rent function shifts downward, decreasing both the territory and density of the residential district.

These two changes in the labor market narrow the gap between labor supply and labor demand. The wage continues to drop until general equilibrium is restored. Figure 9–5 shows the new equilibrium allocation of land, and the third column of Table 9–2 shows numbers behind the new equilibrium. The new equilibrium wage is $6 per hour (down from $10). The CBD radius is 2.3 miles, and the SRD is 4.8 miles wide. The equilibrium number of laborers is 365,433. There are three basic lessons from the general-equilibrium analysis of the streetcar:

FIGURE 9–5   The General-Equilibrium Effect of the Streetcar

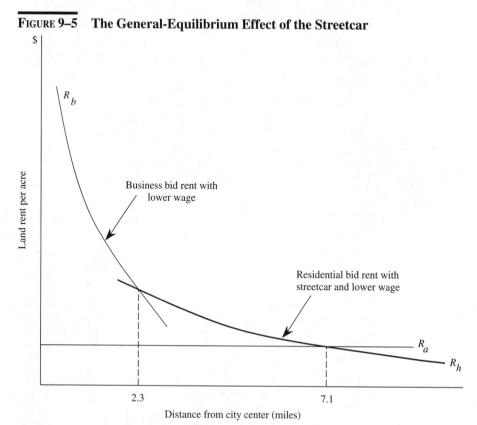

The streetcar causes excess supply of labor, decreasing the city's wage. The business bidrent function shifts upward, and the residential bid rent shifts downward. The CBD grows, and the SRD shrinks. General equilibrium is restored with a larger SRD (the width increases from 4.0 miles to 4.8 miles) and a larger city (the radius increases from 6.0 miles to 7.1 miles).

1. **Tilt and shift of the residential bid-rent function.** The streetcar affects the residential bid-rent function in two ways. The upward tilt (or flattening) of the function is the partial-equilibrium effect, which occurs because the streetcar decreases commuting cost. The downward shift is the general-equilibrium effect, which occurs because the streetcar causes an excess supply of labor, decreasing the city's wage.

2. **Land rent.** The streetcar increases land rent in both the SRD and the CBD. The streetcar increases the accessibility of residential land, so residents are willing to pay more for land. The streetcar also decreases wages and production costs, so firms are willing to pay more for land in the CBD. Landowners throughout the city benefit from the streetcar.

3. **Welfare effects of the streetcar.** In general equilibrium, the city's residents are no better off with the streetcar. Because the city is "open," the streetcar causes in-migration from the rest of the region that decreases wages and increases the prices of housing and land. The benefits of the streetcar (faster and cheaper commuting) are offset by lower wages and a higher cost of living.

The General-Equilibrium Effects of the Property Tax

Consider a city that initially finances all of its public services with a land tax. If all the land in the city is owned by people living outside the city, the city's public services are initially financed by a tax on absentee landowners. Suppose that the city replaces its land tax with a tax on residential capital (improvements such as houses and apartments), and the capital tax is paid by the city's residents. Under the new tax policy, city residents pay more taxes but do not receive more public services.

How does the property tax affect the city's economy? There are two ways to answer this question. First, a graph can be used to show the partial-equilibrium effects of the tax. Second, a computer can be used to show the general-equilibrium effects of the tax.

Figure 9–6 shows the partial-equilibrium effects of the residential property tax. The property tax is a tax on both land and capital (improvements), so the tax liability increases with the amount of improvements. As explained in Chapter 8 (Land Use in the Monocentric City), the capital-land ratio increases as one approaches the city center because housing producers substitute capital for relatively expensive land. Because the amount of improvements per acre is larger closer to the city center, the tax liability per acre increases as one approaches the city center. For example, an apartment building on a one-acre site two miles from the city center faces a higher tax liability than a single-family home on a one-acre site five miles from the city center. Therefore, the closer the site to the city center, the larger the downward shift of the bid-rent function. This is shown in Figure 9–6: the gap between the pre-tax and post-tax bid-rent functions increases as one approaches the city center.

What are the general-equilibrium effects of the residential property tax? In other words, how does the tax affect the urban labor market? The downward shift of the residential bid-rent function decreases the territory and the density of the

FIGURE 9–6   **Partial-Equilibrium Effects of the Residential Property Tax**

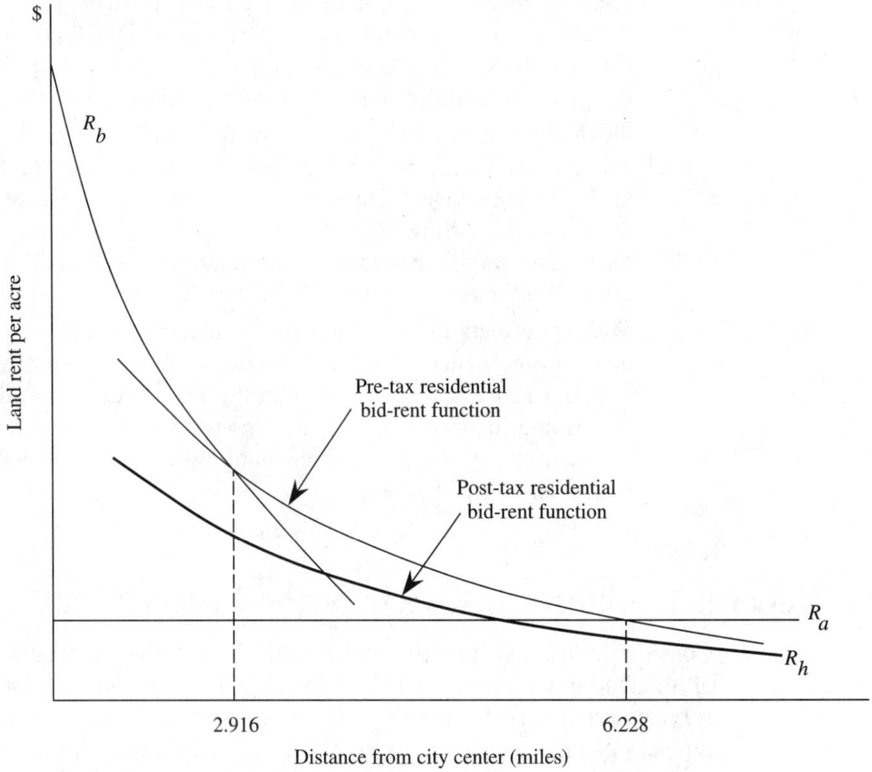

The residential property tax is partly a tax on improvements, so it generates a larger tax burden on locations with large capital-land ratios. Therefore, the gap between the pre-tax and the post-tax residential bid-rent functions increases as one approaches the city center.

residential district, causing an excess demand for labor. The city's wage increases, causing changes in the CBD and SRD that narrow the gap between supply and demand. In the CBD, the increase in the wage increases production costs and decreases the bid rent for business land. The resulting decrease in the size and the density of the CBD decreases the quantity of labor demanded. In the SRD, the increase in the wage shifts the residential bid-rent function upward. The resulting increases in the size and the density of the residential district increase the quantity of labor supplied. The wage continues to fall until general equilibrium is restored.

What will the city look like after general equilibrium is restored? One way to answer this question is to use a computer to generate two pictures of the urban economy, one before the property tax is imposed and one after the economy has adjusted to the new tax. An urban general-equilibrium computer model allocates different plots of land in a hypothetical city to firms (labor demanders) and households (labor suppliers). If a particular allocation does not satisfy the conditions for general equilibrium, the computer tries a different allocation. This groping process continues until an equilibrium allocation is found. The computer model can be designed to compute a pre-tax equilibrium and a post-tax equilibrium. By comparing the "before" and

TABLE 9–3   **General-Equilibrium Effects of the Residential Property Tax**

	Initial Equilibrium	*General Equilibrium*
Number of households	250,038	255,853
Territories		
Radius of CBD (miles)	2.916	2.85
Width of SRD (miles)	3.582	3.378
Radius of city (miles)	6.498	6.228
Input Prices		
Wage ($ per hour)	10.00	10.02
Median CBD land rent ($ per acre per year)	28,999	26,016
Median SRD land rent ($ per acre per year)	2,886	2,761
Density		
Average labor density (workers per square mile)	9,360	8,851
Average household density (households per square mile)	2,359	2,344
Land Rent		
CBD land rent ($ per week)	7,053,134	6,258,973
SRD land rent ($ per week)	3,580,168	3,163,577
Total land rent ($ per week)	10,633,302	9,422,550

SOURCE: Arthur M. Sullivan, "The General Equilibrium Effects of the Residential Property Tax: Incidence and Excess Burden," *Journal of Urban Economics* 18 (1985), pp. 235–50.

"after" snapshots of the urban economy, one can identify the general-equilibrium effects of the property tax.

Sullivan (1985) used a computer model to simulate the effects of a 1.7 percent residential property tax. The results of the study are listed in Table 9–3. The hypothetical city has an initial work force of about 250,000 and a population of about 500,000. The property tax decreases the city's land area, population, employment density, and population density. Although the tax applies only to residential property, it ultimately affects land rent and land use throughout the city. Land rent at the median CBD location decreases 11 percent (to $26,016 per acre per year), and land rent at the median SRD location decreases 4 percent (to $2,761 per acre per year). Employment density decreases 5.7 percent, and household density decreases 1 percent. The decrease in total land rent is about 160 percent of the total revenue from the property tax. The computer model provides a comprehensive view of the general-equilibrium effects of the property tax.

Summary

1. In the small, open city, the utility level of residents is fixed: any change that increases the relative attractiveness of the city causes in-migration that increases housing and land prices, decreasing utility to its original level.

2. The urban economy achieves general equilibrium when four conditions are met.
   a. Firms make zero economic profit at all locations (guaranteed by the bid-rent functions).
   b. Households achieve the same utility level at all locations (guaranteed by the bid-rent functions).
   c. Land is rented to the highest bidder.
   d. Total demand for labor (from firms in the business district) equals total supply (from residents in the residential district).
3. An increase in the export price shifts the business bid-rent function upward, increasing labor demand as the size and the density of the CBD increase.
   a. The excess demand for labor increases the wage.
   b. The increase in the wage shifts the residential bid-rent function upward, increasing the quantity of labor supplied as the size and the density of the SRD increase.
   c. The increase in the wage also shifts the business bid-rent function downward, decreasing the quantity of labor demanded as the size and the density of the CBD decrease.
   d. The wage continues to rise until labor supply equals labor demand.
4. The streetcar system decreases the slope of the residential bid-rent function, tilting it upward. The size and the density of the residential district increase, increasing total labor supply.
   a. The excess supply for labor decreases the wage.
   b. The decrease in the wage shifts the business bid-rent function upward, increasing the quantity of labor demanded as the size and the density of the CBD increase.
   c. The decrease in the wage shifts the residential bid-rent function downward, increasing the quantity of labor supplied as the size and the density of the SRD decrease.
   d. The wage continues to drop until labor supply equals labor demand.
5. In general equilibrium, city residents are no better off with the streetcar. Migration to the open city decreases wages and increases the prices of housing and land, offsetting the benefits of the streetcar.
6. The property tax decreases the slope of the residential bid-rent function, decreasing the supply of labor as the residential district decreases in size and density. In general equilibrium, the property tax decreases the city's size, density, and total land rent.

Exercises and Discussion Questions

1. Suppose that the intracity truck is introduced into the traditional monocentric city, decreasing the cost of intracity freight. Depict graphically the partial-equilibrium and general-equilibrium effects of the truck.
2. Consider the city of Swampville, a city that recently drained a swamp near its city center and thus increased the supply of developable CBD land by

10 percent. Predict the effects of the draining of the swamp on (*a*) land rent in the CBD, (*b*) land rent in the residential district, (*c*) employment density, (*d*) residential density, (*e*) the equilibrium wage, and (*f*) total employment.

3. Consider a traditional 19th-century monocentric city with a CBD radius of one mile. In 1869, buildings at the edge of the CBD are four stories tall. In 1870, all the buildings in the CBD are destroyed by an earthquake. The mayor of the city announces that in the rebuilt city (*i*) the maximum building height will be four stories and (*ii*) business development will be confined to a circle with a one-mile radius: the radius of the CBD is fixed at one mile. Discuss the effects of the height restriction on (*a*) the demand for labor, (*b*) the supply of labor, (*c*) the equilibrium wage, (*d*) residential density, and (*e*) the city radius.

4. Suppose a city restricts the heights of its residential structures. The maximum building height is four stories, the height that would normally occur at a distance of five miles from the city center.
   a. Draw two residential bid-rent functions, one for the city in the absence of height restrictions and one with height restrictions.
   b. Discuss the effects of the height restrictions on wages, total employment, and land rent in the CBD.

5. Suppose a city imposes a gas tax of $1 per gallon and uses the increase in tax revenue to decrease other taxes. The tax liability of the typical resident is unchanged by the change in tax policy.
   a. Draw two residential bid-rent functions, one before the gas tax and one after the tax is imposed.
   b. Discuss the effects of the gas tax on wages, total employment, and land rent in the CBD.

6. Suppose that the government subsidizes the construction of radial highways. How will such a policy affect land rent, land use, and wages in cities?

7. Suppose that the government subsidizes the production of agricultural products. How will such a policy affect land rent, land use, and wages in cities?

8. Suppose a city builds a streetcar system and passes a law that prevents any outsiders from moving to the city. In other words, the city keeps its population at its pre-streetcar level, so it is a "closed" city instead of an open one. Depict graphically the partial-equilibrium and general-equilibrium effects of the streetcar in the closed city.

9. Chapter 6 (Urban Economic Growth) uses a supply-demand model to depict the urban growth process.
   a. Use the supply-demand model to depict the general-equilibrium effects of the streetcar shown in Table 9–2. Be sure that your picture matches the numbers in the table.
   b. Compute the elasticity of labor demand with respect to the wage.

10. Use a graph to show the partial-equilibrium effects of a tax on business property. Outline the general-equilibrium effects of the business property tax. How do these general-equilibrium effects of the business property tax differ from the effects of the residential property tax?

11. Consider a rectangular city with the following characteristics:
    i. The city is two miles wide.
    ii. The CBD is on a harbor, and the SRD stretches to the east of the CBD.
    iii. Manufacturers transport their output from factories to the CBD docks by horse-drawn wagon.
    iv. Labor demand is a fixed 2,000 workers per square mile (no factor substitution).
    v. Labor supply is a fixed 500 workers per square mile (no consumer or factor substitution).
    vi. In the initial equilibrium, the wage is $10, the CBD is one mile long, and the SRD is four miles long.

    a. Draw the bid-rent functions consistent with the assumptions above.
    b. Show that the city is in equilibrium with a one-mile CBD and a four-mile SRD.

Suppose that the intracity truck replaces the horse-drawn wagon. The partial-equilibrium effect of the truck is to increase the CBD's length by 0.50 miles.

    c. Depict graphically the partial-equilibrium effect.
    d. What is the partial-equilibrium effect on the labor market: by how much does labor demand exceed labor supply?
    e. Will the wage increase or decrease?
    f. The table below lists the length of the CBD and the length of the city for different wages. What is the new equilibrium wage for the city?

Wage ($ per hour)	CBD Length (miles)	SRD Length (miles)	City Length (miles)
10.0	1.50	4.0	5.50
11.0	1.42	4.3	5.75
12.0	1.33	4.7	6.00
13.0	1.25	5.0	6.25
14.0	1.17	5.3	6.50

References and Additional Readings

Theoretical General-Equilibrium Models

Brueckner, Jan K. "Labor Mobility and the Incidence of the Residential Property Tax." *Journal of Urban Economics* 10 (1982), pp. 173–82. Uses a theoretical general-equilibrium model to explore the effects of the residential property tax on the urban labor market.

Mills, Edwin S. "An Aggregative Model of Resource Allocation in a Metropolitan Area." *American Economic Review, Papers and Proceedings,* May 1967, pp. 197–210.

Reprinted in *Readings in Urban Economics,* ed. Matthew Edel and Jerome Rothenberg. New York: Macmillan, 1972. The first general-equilibrium model of the urban economy.

Polinski, A. M., and D. L. Rubinfeld. "The Long-Run Effects of a Residential Property Tax and Local Public Services." *Journal of Urban Economics* 5 (1978), pp. 241–62. A theoretical model that explores the interactions between a city's land markets and its labor market. Discusses the general-equilibrium effects of the property tax on a number of city characteristics.

Wheaton, William. "Monocentric Models of Urban Land Use: Contributions and Criticisms." In *Current Issues in Urban Economics,* ed. Peter Mieszkowski and Mahlon Straszheim. Baltimore: Johns Hopkins, 1979. Discusses several renditions of the traditional monocentric model.

Computer Models of Urban Land Use

Birch, David; Reilly Atkinson; Sven Sundstrom; and Linda Stack. *Patterns of Urban Change.* Lexington, Mass.: Lexington Books, 1974. A simulation model that predicts the location patterns of housing and employment.

Mills, Edwin S. "Planning and Market Processes in Urban Models." In *Public and Urban Economics,* ed. Ronald Grieson. Lexington, Mass.: Lexington Books, 1976. A model that uses linear and nonlinear programs to allocate land to different activities.

Sullivan, Arthur M. "The General Equilibrium Effects of the Residential Property Tax: Incidence and Excess Burden." *Journal of Urban Economics* 18 (1985), pp. 235–50. Uses a computational model of a monocentric city to simulate the general-equilibrium effects of the residential property tax.

Computer Models of Residential Land Use

Arnott, R. J., and J. G. MacKinnon. "The Effects of the Property Tax: A General Equilibrium Simulation." *Journal of Urban Economics* 4 (1977), pp. 389–407. Uses a general-equilibrium model of the residential sector to compute the effects of the property tax on residential land rent and land use.

Carlton, D. W. "The Spatial Effects of a Tax on Housing and Land." *Regional Science and Urban Economics* 11 (1981), pp. 509–27.

Grieson, Ronald. "The Economics of Property Taxes and Land Values: The Elasticity of Supply of Structures." *Journal of Urban Economics* 1 (1974), pp. 367–81.

Leroy, S. F. "Urban Land Rent and the Incidence of Property Taxes." *Journal of Urban Economics* 3 (1976), pp. 167–79.

Mills, Edwin S. *Studies in the Structure of the Urban Economy.* Baltimore: Johns Hopkins, 1972. A general-equilibrium model is used to simulate the effects of transportation congestion on residential land rent and land use. The demand side of the urban labor market is not included in the model.

Solow, Robert M. "Congestion Costs and the Use of Land for Streets." *Bell Journal of Economics and Management Science* 4 (1973), pp. 602–18. Uses a general-equilibrium model of the residential sector to simulate the effects of congestion externalities on residential land use and the use of land for streets.

———. "Congestion, Density, and the Use of Land in Transportation." *Swedish Journal of Economics* 74 (1972), pp. 161–73. Uses a general-equilibrium model of the residential sector to simulate the effects of congestion externalities on residential land use and the use of land for streets.

Suburbanization and Modern Cities

A suburb is a place where a developer cuts down all the trees to build houses, and then names the streets after the trees.
Bill Vaughn

This chapter explains the decline of the traditional monocentric city and the rise of the modern multicentric city. In the traditional monocentric city, most economic activity was concentrated in the central core area. The entire metropolitan area was oriented toward the employment and shopping opportunities in the central city. In the modern multicentric city, a large fraction of employment is in suburban areas, with much of the suburban employment in subcenters. People who live in metropolitan areas are now less dependent on the central city for employment and shopping.

This chapter has seven parts. The first part discusses the facts on suburbanization, focusing on the changes in the spatial distributions of population and employment in the last several decades. The second through the fifth parts discuss the reasons for the suburbanization of manufacturers, population, retailers, and office firms. The sixth part discusses the development of suburban subcenters in Chicago, Los Angeles, and Houston. The final part of the chapter focuses on land-use patterns in the modern multicentric city.

Suburbanization Facts

What are the facts on the suburbanization of employment and population? Figure 10–1 shows the distribution of population and employment between central cities and suburbs in 1948 and 1980. The percentage of the metropolitan population in central cities dropped from 64 percent in 1948 to 43 percent in 1980, and the percentage of manufacturing employment dropped from 67 percent to 46 percent. The losses in trade and service employment were even larger: the percentage of wholesaling employment in central cities dropped from 92 percent to 56 percent.

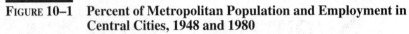

FIGURE 10–1   **Percent of Metropolitan Population and Employment in Central Cities, 1948 and 1980**

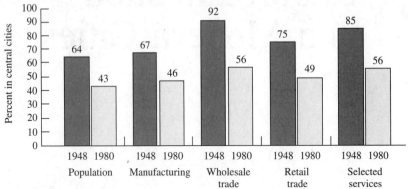

SOURCES: 1948 data from John F. Kain,"The Distribution and Movement of Jobs and Industry," in *The Metropolitan Enigma*, ed. James Q. Wilson (Cambridge, Mass.: Harvard University Press, 1968); 1980 data from U.S. Bureau of the Census, *Journey to Work*, PC 80-2-6D (Washington, D.C.: U.S. Government Printing Office), 1984.

The percentage of retail employment dropped from 75 percent to 49 percent; the percentage of service employment dropped from 85 percent to 56 percent.

It's important to note that part of the measured increase in the share of activity in the suburbs results from urban growth with fixed central-city boundaries. As an urban area grows, most growth occurs on the periphery. As the metropolitan area expands outward, an increasing share of its population lives outside the fixed boundaries of the central city. If the suburban population is assumed to be the population outside the central-city border, growth causes suburbanization.

Table 10–1 provides a closer look at the distribution of employment between central cities and suburbs in 1980. The employment sectors are listed in declining order of importance. Three sectors had more than three fifths of metropolitan employment in central cities: public administration (62 percent), transportation, communications, and utilities (61 percent), and finance, insurance, and real estate (63 percent). The three service sectors (professional and related services, business and repair services, and personal services) had between 53 percent and 57 percent of their employment in central cities. The other sector that had a majority of employment in the central city is wholesale trade (56 percent).

What happened to the distribution of employment between central cities and suburbs during the 1980s? Unfortunately, the relevant data from the 1990 census was not available at the time this book was printed. Figure 10–2 shows the spatial distributions of population and employment of the 60 largest metropolitan areas in 1986. The figure shows the percentages of population and employment in central cities (the political city), central business districts (the core area of the central city), the rest of the central cities, and outside central cities. Employment is more centralized than population: central cities contain 51 percent of metropolitan employment but only 41 percent of metropolitan population; CBDs contain 17 percent of metropolitan employment but only 2 percent of metropolitan population. Manufacturing is the

TABLE 10–1   Distribution of Employment between Central Cities and Suburbs by Type of Employment, 1980

	Employment in SMSAs (1,000)	*Employment in Central Cities (1,000)*	*Percent in Central Cities*	*Percent in Suburbs*
Total	67,728	35,698	53	47
Manufacturing	15,190	7,060	46	54
Professional and related services	14,067	7,966	57	43
Retail trade	10,905	5,330	49	51
Transportation, communication, utilities	5,083	3,095	61	39
Finance, insurance, real estate	4,634	2,926	63	37
Public administration	3,780	2,343	62	38
Construction	3,673	1,716	47	53
Business and repair services	3,124	1,700	54	46
Wholesale trade	3,069	1,706	56	44
Other industries	2,173	779	36	64
Personal services	2,031	1,077	53	47

SOURCE: U.S. Bureau of the Census, *Journey to Work,* PC 80-2-6D (Washington, D.C.: U.S. Government Printing Office, 1984), Table 1.

most suburbanized of the three types of employment: 58 percent of manufacturing jobs are located outside central cities. The jobs grouped under F.I.R.E. (finance, insurance, and real estate) and services are the most centralized: 58 percent of these jobs are in central cities (24 percent in CBDs and another 34 percent in other parts of central cities), leaving 42 percent for suburban areas.

FIGURE 10–2   Distribution of Population and Employment for 60 Largest Metropolitan Areas, 1986

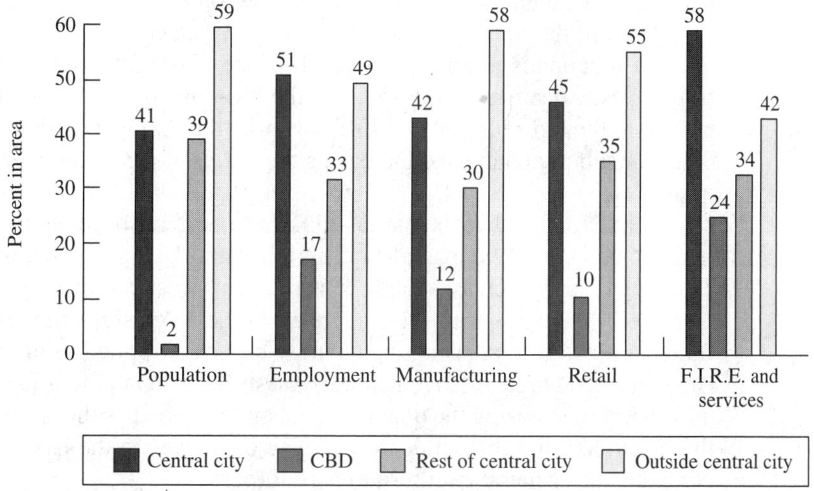

SOURCE: Author's calculations based on data from the Wharton Urban Decentralization Project.

Suburbanization of Manufacturing

The share of metropolitan manufacturing employment in central cities decreased from about two thirds in 1948 to less than half in 1986. Mills (1972) provides evidence that the suburbanization of manufacturing started long before 1948. What caused the suburbanization of manufacturing employment?

The Intracity Truck

Moses and Williamson (1972) explain how the intracity truck encouraged the suburbanization of manufacturing. In the monocentric city of the 19th and early 20th centuries, freight was shipped within cities by horse-drawn wagons. Starting about 1910, manufacturers switched from the horse wagon to the truck. The truck was both faster and cheaper: around 1920, the truck was half as costly ($0.15 per ton per mile versus $0.33), and at least twice as fast. Once the intracity truck was introduced, its use spread rapidly: for example, the number of trucks in the city of Chicago increased from 800 in 1910 to 23,000 in 1920.

As explained in Chapter 8 (Land Use in the Monocentric City), the location decision of a manufacturing firm is determined by the outcome of a tug-of-war. On one side is the central export node, which pulls the firm toward the city center because freight costs are lower for firms near the export node. On the other side is the suburb, which pulls the firm toward low-wage suburban locations. In the era of the horse-drawn wagon and the streetcar, the cost of moving freight was large relative to the cost of moving people, so manufacturers located in the city center. It was cheaper to ship the workers from the suburbs to the central-city factory than to ship the output from a suburban factory to the export node. The intracity truck decreased freight cost, weakening the pull toward the central export node, so the tug-of-war was more frequently won by the suburb. Although a suburban location was inefficient with the horse-drawn wagon, it was efficient with the truck.

How did the intracity truck affect the bid-rent function of manufacturers? The bid-rent function is negatively sloped because of freight costs. The truck decreased freight costs, decreasing the slope of the bid-rent function. This is shown in Figure 10–3: the bid-rent function tilts upward, allowing manufacturers to outbid residents for suburban land and increasing the radius of the manufacturing district from u' to u''.

Figure 10–3 shows the partial-equilibrium effects of the intracity truck. As explained in Chapter 9 (General-Equilibrium Land Use), the expansion of the manufacturing district increases labor demand, causing excess demand for labor and an increase in the city's wage. The increase in the wage shifts the residential bid-rent function upward (increasing the quantity of labor supplied as the size and the density of the residential district increase) and shifts the manufacturing bid-rent function downward (decreasing the quantity of labor demanded as the size and the density of the manufacturing district decrease). These changes in the labor and land markets continue until general equilibrium is restored.

FIGURE 10–3   **The Partial-Equilibrium Effects of the Intracity Truck**

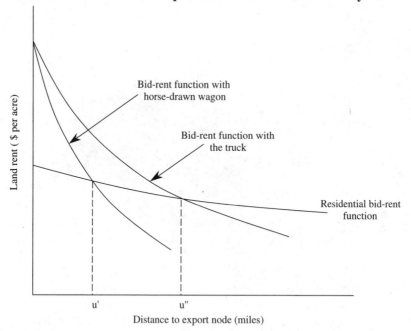

The replacement of the horse-drawn wagon with the truck decreased freight costs, decreasing the slope of manufacturing bid-rent function. The radius of the manufacturing district increased from *u'* to *u''*.

The Intercity Truck

Two decades after the truck was first introduced, manufacturers started using the truck for intercity transport. Improvements in the truck made long-distance travel feasible, and the expansion of the intercity highway system facilitated intercity truck traffic. Eventually, the truck became competitive with the train and the ship for intercity freight. As manufacturers switched from trains and ships to trucks, they were freed from their dependence on the railheads and ports in city centers, and moved to sites accessible to the intercity highways. The freight costs associated with suburban sites decreased, allowing manufacturers to move closer to their suburban workers.

In 1956, the interstate highway system was authorized by Congress, and the bulk of the system was in place by the late 1970s. The highway system decreased the relative cost of shipping by truck, causing more manufacturers to switch their freight operations from ships and trains to trucks. More recently, cities have built circumferential highways (beltways) that are connected to the interstate highway system. Manufacturers locate close to the suburban beltways because they provide easy access to the interstate system.

Figure 10–4 shows the bid rent for manufacturing land at different locations in a beltway city. The figure is drawn under the assumption that the beltway circles the city at a distance of 2.5 miles. In the beltway city, manufacturers can transport

FIGURE 10–4   Manufacturing Bid Rent in Beltway City

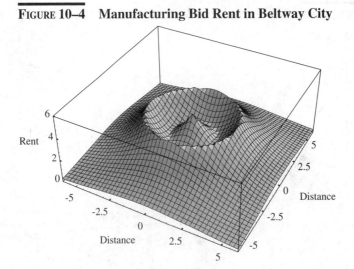

their output to the beltway or to a central export node (a railhead or a port at the city center). The bid-rent function forms a peak at the central export node (as in the monocentric city) and a circular ridge centered on the beltway. Manufacturers are likely to outbid other land users for land near the suburban beltway.

The Automobile

The automobile contributed to the suburbanization of manufacturers. To explain the effects of the automobile, consider a firm with a highly skilled work force: only one in 1,000 people has the skills required to work for the firm. Suppose that the firm employs 100 people, and the firm's workers are distributed uniformly throughout a streetcar city of 100,000 people. Where in the city will the firm locate? Because the firm draws laborers from the entire metropolitan area, it locates at a point that is accessible to the entire urban area. In the hub-and-spoke streetcar city, the city center (the hub) is the most accessible location.

Where will the firm locate in a modern automobile city? In the auto city, employees can drive their cars from their homes to any location in the urban area. While the firm might still locate in the city center, it could also locate along an urban highway or a suburban beltway because such sites are accessible to residents throughout the metropolitan area. In general, the automobile loosened the ties to the streetcar nodes in the core area, allowing the suburbanization of firms with specialized labor forces.

Single-Story Plants

Another factor in the suburbanization of manufacturing was the switch from the traditional multistory plants of the 19th century to single-story plants. To exploit new production technologies (assembly-line production and materials-handling techniques such as the forklift truck), manufacturers built single-level facilities. As land consumption increased, the forces pulling the firms toward the suburbs (low-cost land and low wages) dominated the forces pulling the firms toward the central city (lower freight costs), and many manufacturers moved to the suburbs.

Suburban Airports

The increased importance of air freight is another reason for the suburbanization of manufacturing. A firm that transports a relatively large fraction of its output by air experiences a relatively strong pull toward an airport. For some types of firms, the suburban airport has replaced the old central export node (railhead or port facility) as the point of orientation. As explained later in the chapter, many modern cities have clusters of employment near suburban airports.

The Suburbanization of Population

The share of metropolitan population living in central cities dropped from about two thirds in 1948 to just over two fifths in the 1980s. Mills (1972) provides evidence of suburbanization as far back as 1880. As explained in Chapter 8, the **density function** describes the relationship between population density and distance to the city center. Mills estimated the density functions for four metropolitan areas (Baltimore, Milwaukee, Philadelphia, and Rochester) between 1880 and 1963. The assumed relationship between density and distance is

$$D(u) = A \cdot e^{-g \cdot u} \tag{10–1}$$

where

$D(u)$ = Population density u miles from the city center (people per square mile)

A = Parameter estimated from the data

e = The base of the natural logarithm

g = Parameter to be estimated from the data

Table 10–2 shows the average density gradient (defined as the percentage change in population density per mile) for the four cities between 1880 and 1963. The gradient decreases over time, indicating that the population density function flattened out over time. The third column of the table uses the estimated density gradients to compute the percentage of the metropolitan population living within three miles of the city center. Between 1880 and 1963, the percentage dropped from 88 percent to 24 percent.

This section discusses five possible reasons for the suburbanization of population:

1. Increase in real income.
2. Decrease in commuting cost.
3. Central-city problems: race, crime, taxes, education.

TABLE 10–2   **Average Density Gradients for Four Metropolitan Areas, 1880–1963***

Year	Average Gradient	Percent of Population within Three Miles of City Center
1880	1.22	88%
1890	1.06	83
1900	0.96	78
1910	0.80	69
1920	0.69	61
1930	0.63	56
1940	0.59	53
1948	0.50	44
1954	0.40	34
1958	0.35	28
1963	0.31	24

*The metropolitan areas are Baltimore, Milwaukee, Philadelphia, and Rochester.
SOURCE: Edwin S. Mills, *Studies in the Structure of the Urban Economy* (Baltimore: Johns Hopkins, 1972).

4. Following the firms to the suburbs.
5. Public policy.

Increase in Real Income

Did income growth contribute to the suburbanization of population? As explained in Chapter 8, an increase in income has an ambiguous effect on the relative attractiveness of the suburbs because it has two conflicting effects on the relative cost of a suburban location.

1. **Increase in commuting cost.** An increase in real income increases the amount of income sacrificed per minute of travel time: it increases the opportunity cost of commuting. Therefore, an increase in income increases the relative attractiveness of dwellings close to the workplace. For someone who works in the CBD, an increase in income increases the relative attractiveness of central-city housing. This is the **opportunity-cost effect:** an increase in income increases the opportunity cost of commuting, pulling households toward the central city.

2. **Increase in land consumption.** Because land is a normal good, an increase in income increases land consumption (lot size). Income growth increases the relative attractiveness of locations with low-priced land (the suburbs). A household that occupies a large lot is willing to commute long distances to occupy low-cost suburban land. This is the **consumption effect:** an increase in income increases lot size, pulling households toward inexpensive suburban land.

Given these conflicting effects, it is not possible to predict, on theoretical grounds, whether income growth contributes to suburbanization. Income growth causes suburbanization if the consumption effect dominates the opportunity-cost effect. This will occur if the income elasticity of demand for land exceeds the income elasticity of commuting costs. As explained in Chapter 8, the land elasticity is close to the commuting-cost elasticity, so the two effects almost cancel each other out. Therefore, it does not appear that income growth contributed very much to the suburbanization of population.

Decrease in Commuting Cost

Over the last 140 years, technological innovations have decreased the monetary and time costs of commuting. In the 1800s, the development of new transit systems decreased the cost of commuting from the suburbs to the central core. The most important innovations were the horse-drawn streetcar (developed in the 1850s) and the conventional streetcar (developed in the 1890s). In the last 60 years, improvements in the automobile and the intracity highway network have decreased the cost of personal commuting. The automobile increased travel speeds, decreasing the time cost of commuting.

Chapter 9 explains the partial- and general-equilibrium effects of the streetcar. The same analysis applies to other changes that decrease commuting costs, such as the introduction of the automobile. The sequence of changes in the urban economy is as follows:

1. The slope of the residential bid-rent function decreases (the function tilts upward), increasing the size and density of the residential district.
2. The increase in the supply of labor decreases the city's wage.
3. The decrease in the wage shifts the business bid-rent function upward, increasing the quantity of labor demanded as the size and the density of the CBD increase.
4. The decrease in the wage shifts the residential bid-rent function downward, decreasing the quantity of labor supplied as the size and the density of the residential district decrease.
5. The wage continues to drop until labor supply equals labor demand.

In equilibrium, the streetcar (or automobile) increases the population and land area of the monocentric city. The increase in the relative accessibility of suburban locations increases the share of population in the suburbs.

Figure 10–5 shows the initial bid-rent functions and the bid-rent functions after the metropolitan area has fully adjusted to the lower commuting costs. Suppose that the central city is a circular area with a radius of three miles: locations beyond three miles from the city center are considered suburban. Before the streetcar (or automobile), the CBD radius is one mile, the metropolitan radius is four miles, and a relatively small fraction of the population lives in the suburban area. The decrease in commuting costs shifts the bid-rent functions outward, increasing the radius of the metropolitan area. The fraction of the population living outside the central-city

FIGURE 10–5   Suburbanization Caused by a Decrease in Commuting Cost

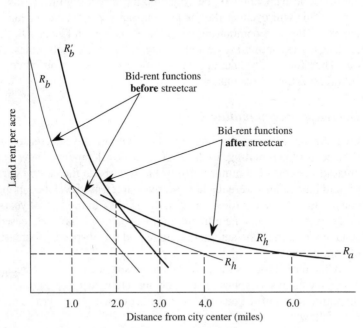

A change in technology that decreases the unit cost of commuting (streetcar or automobile) causes suburbanization: a larger fraction of the population lives beyond the central-city border (three miles from the city center).

border increases for two reasons. First, the suburban area grows: the width of the suburban ring increases from three miles to four miles. Second, the price of suburban land increases, increasing population density within the suburban area.

In the late 1800s and early 1900s, many landowners profited from the introduction of streetcars. In a number of cities, speculators bought large tracts of undeveloped land just outside the city's borders, and patiently awaited the extension of streetcar service to their land. Other investors took a more active role. In Cleveland, the Von Sweringen brothers bought a large parcel of undeveloped land from the local society of Shakers. When the Cleveland State Railways refused to extend their streetcar service to the undeveloped area, the Von Sweringen brothers built their own streetcar line to the area, which became known as Shaker Heights. The brothers' land, which was appraised at $240,000 in 1900, increased in value to $80 million by 1930.

Central-City Problems

Other theories of suburbanization focus on the negative locational attributes (disamenities) of central cities. The following factors encourage households to move from the central city to the suburbs:

1. **Old housing.** The deterioration of the central-city housing stock encourages households to move to the suburbs, where newer housing is readily available.

2. **Race and income.** Some households move to the suburbs to escape racial conflict; others move to avoid living near low-income households.

3. **Central-city fiscal problems.** Many central cities have relatively high taxes, encouraging households to move to low-tax suburbs. The causality goes both ways: fiscal problems cause suburbanization, and suburbanization contributes to central-city fiscal problems.

4. **Crime.** Most central cities have relatively high crime rates, encouraging households to move to the suburbs. The reasons for the relatively high central-city crime rates will be discussed in Chapter 22 (Crime and Punishment).

5. **Education.** Suburban schools are typically superior to central-city schools, encouraging households to relocate in suburban school districts. The reasons for the inferiority of central-city schools will be explained in Chapter 21 (Education).

Empirical studies of the suburbanization process provide support for the theory that central-city problems encourage suburbanization. The empirical literature is reviewed by Wasylenko (1984). Bradbury, Downs, and Small (1982) tested various theories of suburbanization, using a sample of 121 SMSAs for the period 1970–1975. They found that a metropolitan area experienced relatively rapid suburbanization if its central city had (1) a relatively old housing stock, (2) relatively high taxes, and (3) a relatively large black population. Another factor in suburbanization was the number of suburban local governments: the larger the number of suburban governments to choose from, the more rapid the suburbanization. Frey (1979) found that metropolitan areas with high taxes, high crime rates, and low educational expenditures experienced relatively rapid suburbanization.

Following Firms to the Suburbs

As explained earlier in the chapter, manufacturing employment shifted from the central city to the suburbs for a number of reasons, including the development of the truck, the adoption of assembly-line production techniques, and the building of circumferential highways. As explained later in the chapter, retailers and office firms have also moved to the suburbs, forming suburban subcenters. The suburbanization of employment contributed to the suburbanization of population because some workers followed their employers to the suburbs.

In the multicentric city, workers commute to jobs along suburban beltways and in suburban subcenters. Table 10–3 shows commuting patterns within metropolitan areas in 1980. In the United States, about 40 percent of workers commute within suburban areas, about twice the percentage who commute from the suburbs to the central city. In the Northeast, the number of workers commuting within the suburbs is over three times the number commuting from the suburbs to the central city.

TABLE 10–3   **Commuting Patterns within Metropolitan Areas for Different Regions, 1980**

| Region | Percentage of Total Work Trips within Metropolitan Areas | | | |
	Central City to Central City	Central City to Suburb	Suburb to Central City	Suburb to Suburb
Total United States	33.1	6.7	20.1	40.1
Northeast	32.2	4.7	15.3	47.8
North central	30.7	7.0	20.3	42.0
South	36.1	6.1	23.7	34.1
West	32.4	9.3	19.9	38.4

SOURCE: U.S. Bureau of the Census, *Journey to Work, Metropolitan Commuting Flows* (Washington, D.C.: U.S. Government Printing Office, 1984).

How does the suburbanization of employment affect the residential bid-rent function? Workers are willing to pay more for housing and land near beltways and suburban subcenters because such locations have a relatively low commuting cost. In the modern multicentric city, the residential bid-rent function has several peaks, one at the city center and one for each concentration of employment. McDonald and McMillen (1990) show that land rent increases as one approaches the employment subcenters in the Chicago metropolitan area. Specifically, a one-mile move toward the O'Hare Airport subcenter increases the price of land by 4.5 percent.

Public Policy and Suburbanization

A number of public policies affect the intraurban location choices of households, encouraging households to live in the suburbs. Among the public policies to be discussed later in the book are the following:

1. **Subsidies for homeownership.** The federal tax code allows the deduction of interest paid on home loans, providing an implicit subsidy for homeownership. Federal mortgage programs (FHA guaranteed mortgages) also decrease the cost of ownership. These housing subsidies encourage suburbanization because they increase housing consumption and increase the relative attractiveness of the suburbs, where housing is relatively inexpensive.

2. **Commuting externalities.** Because commuting generates congestion externalities and pollution externalities, the marginal private cost of commuting is less than the marginal social cost. As explained in Chapter 19 (Autos and Highways), the internalization of these externalities would increase the relative cost of suburban living, encouraging commuters to live closer to their workplaces.

3. **Fragmented system of local government.** Some households move to the suburbs to flee central-city fiscal problems. The fragmented system

of local government encourages suburbanization because it provides alternatives to the central-city government. Chapter 16 (Overview of Local Government) explores the role of metropolitan consolidation (a switch to a metropolitan government) on the location decisions of households. The issue is whether consolidation would discourage suburbanization.

4. **Highway construction.** The building of the highway system decreased commuting costs, increasing the relative attractiveness of the suburbs.

Gentrification: Return to the City?

In the 1970s and 1980s, the popular press publicized the renovation of central-city housing by wealthy households. To many people, the efforts of these households signaled a change in residential location patterns. It appeared that many high-income households were abandoning the suburban lifestyle to embrace an urban one. The process is labeled *gentrification* because poor households are replaced by relatively wealthy ones.

The most important fact about renovation and gentrification is that the number of renovations is relatively small. In the late 1970s, renovation and gentrification in the 30 largest cities were concentrated in about 100 neighborhoods and involved less than one half of 1 percent of the housing stock in these cities (Frieden and Sagalyn, 1991). In most cities, the number of dwellings renovated each year is a small fraction of the number of dwellings that are abandoned. Kern (1984) describes the characteristics of renovators. The typical renovator is wealthy, young, highly educated, and either single or married with less than two children. Such households are attracted to central-city locations because they (1) patronize cultural establishments in the central city, (2) have a relatively high commuting cost, and (3) have relatively low demands for housing and land. Most of the renovators moved from one part of the central city to the area being renovated, not from the suburbs back to the central city. These facts suggest that gentrification involves a relatively small number of households and does not signal a fundamental change in residential location patterns.

Suburbanization of Retailers

The share of metropolitan retail employment in central cities decreased from about two thirds in 1948 to less than half in the 1980s. There are three principal reasons for the suburbanization of retailing.

Following the Consumers

The suburbanization of population caused some retail activity to move to the suburbs. According to the simple version of central place theory discussed in Chapter 5 (How Many Cities?), a retail firm locates at the center of its market area. If scale economies are small relative to demand density (per capita demand times population density), market areas are relatively small. A retail firm with a relatively small market area is likely to follow its consumers to the suburbs. In contrast, a retail firm with relatively large scale economies would not necessarily follow its customers to the suburbs: if there is a single store for the entire metropolitan area, the most accessible location might still be in the city center.

The more sophisticated version of central place theory considers the effect of shopping externalities on retailers' location choices. If there are benefits from one-stop shopping and comparison shopping, retailers may compromise on their ideal (central place) locations to exploit the externalities associated with comparison shopping and one-stop shopping. The more sophisticated theory predicts that some retailers with moderate scale economies (relative to demand density) will not follow their consumers to the suburbs, but will stay in the city center to exploit shopping externalities. It also suggests that retailers will form clusters (shopping centers and malls) in the suburbs.

The Automobile

The automobile, which replaced the hub-and-spoke streetcar system, loosened the ties to the city center. Before the development of the automobile, a retailer with relatively large scale economies was tied to the CBD because that's where the streetcar delivered all the consumers. If shoppers use the auto instead of the streetcar, they can easily travel from their homes to any point in the metropolitan area, so even a suburban store can draw consumers from the entire metropolitan area. Retailers no longer had to be in the city center to be accessible to consumers throughout the metropolitan area, and many moved to the suburbs.

What about a retailer with moderate scale economies? In the hub-and-spoke streetcar city, travel from the suburb to the city center (along the spokes) was fast and inexpensive, while travel within the residential areas (between the spokes) was costly. A suburban store could not survive because intrasuburban travel costs were high: if it located at the geographical center of its suburban market area, few consumers would show up. If shoppers use the auto instead of the streetcar, travel costs within the residential area decrease, allowing the store to locate at the center of its suburban market area.

Population Growth

The third reason for retail suburbanization is population growth. As the population of a metropolitan area increases, the total demand for retail goods increases. As total demand increases, the equilibrium number of retail stores increases. Some of the new stores locate in the suburban areas.

To explain this idea, consider the demand for wigs. Suppose that scale economies in wig retailing are exhausted with an output of 500 wigs per store per month, and the per capita demand for wigs is 0.01 wigs per person per month. A city with a population of 50,000 has a total demand of 500 wigs per month, and can support a single wig store in the city center. If the city grows to 500,000, and the demand for wigs per capita remains constant, the city supports 10 wig stores. If wig shopping is not subject to shopping externalities (comparison shopping and one-stop shopping), the wig stores divide the metropolitan area into 10 market areas, and each wig store locates in the center of a market area. Because some of the market areas are centered in the suburbs, some wig stores locate in the suburbs. If there are shopping externalities, wig stores may compromise on their ideal (central place) locations, but some wig stores are still likely to locate in the suburbs.

Suburbanization of Office Employment

Before the early 1970s, most office firms were still located in the city center because they were dependent on face-to-face contact with other firms, and the CBD provided a central meeting place for workers from different firms. Although some office activities had moved to the suburbs by the early 1970s, these were typically the "back-office" operations of insurance firms and banks, operations involving paper processing rather than face-to-face contact. For such activities, a CBD location was unnecessary. For most office activities, the advantages of the CBD (opportunities for timely contact with other firms) outweighed the disadvantages (high wages and rents).

During the 1970s and 1980s, suburban office space grew at a rapid rate. Nationwide, suburban office employment grew over seven times faster than central-city office employment during the 1970s (116 percent versus 15 percent). According to Cervero (1986), the most rapid growth in suburban office employment occurred in medium-sized metropolitan areas (with populations between 250,000 and 1 million). The suburban office boom continued into the 1980s. For example, suburban office space in the Chicago metropolitan area more than doubled between 1980 and 1987, increasing the suburban share of total office space from 29 percent to 38 percent.

Suburbanization and Clustering of Offices

Pivo (1990) discusses the suburbanization of office space in six metropolitan areas: Denver, Houston, Los Angeles, San Francisco, Seattle, and Toronto. Some of his results are shown in Table 10–4. The second column shows, for each metropolitan area, the percentage of office space contained in the central business district. In five of the six metropolitan areas, the CBD contained less than half of the total office space; in four of six, the CBD contained less than a third of the total office space. At the national level, central business districts contained about 47 percent of metropolitan office space.

The third column in Table 10–4 shows the number of suburban office clusters. Pivo defines a *cluster* as two or more office buildings within a quarter-mile area. Under this relatively permissive definition of a cluster, about 88 percent of the suburban office space in the six metropolitan areas is clustered. The number of clusters varies across metropolitan areas, reflecting differences in total suburban office space: the larger the total office space in a metropolitan area, the larger the number of suburban clusters. The size distribution of clusters was consistent across metropolitan areas: the largest 10 percent of clusters contained about half of the total office space;

TABLE 10–4   **Characteristics of Suburban Office Clusters**

Metropolitan Area	Percent of Space in CBD	Number of Clusters	Percent of Suburban Cluster Space Close to		
			Freeway	Interchange	Rail Transit
Denver	27	63	73	36	
Houston	20	160	70	29	
Los Angeles	12	270	66	30	
San Francisco	31	102	93	52	10
Seattle	45	30	93	69	
Toronto	54	52	79	27	25

SOURCE: Gary Pivo, "The Net of Mixed Bead: Suburban Office Development in Six Metropolitan Regions," *Journal of the American Planning Association,* Autumn 1990, pp. 457–69.

the largest 25 percent contained about two thirds of the total space; the largest 50 percent of clusters contained about nine tenths of the total space.

The fourth, fifth, and sixth columns of Table 10–4 demonstrate the importance of access in the location of the clusters. The fourth column shows the percentage of suburban (clustered) office space within a half mile of a freeway: the percentages range from 66 percent (Los Angeles) to 93 percent (San Francisco and Seattle). The fifth column shows the percentage of office space within a mile of a freeway interchange: the percentages range from 29 percent (Houston) to 69 percent (Seattle). The sixth column shows, for the two cities with rail transit systems, the percentage of office space within walking distance of a rail transit station (a quarter mile): 10 percent for San Francisco and 25 percent for Toronto.

Communications Technology and Office Suburbanization

One factor in the suburbanization of office employment is the advances in communications technology (satellites, fiber optics, and solid-state electronics) that have decreased the cost of transmitting data, voices, and pictures. The new technology has generated two new methods of communication: electronic mail and teleconferencing. These new communication methods have made some types of office activities less dependent on face-to-face contact. As an activity becomes less dependent on face-to-face contact, the relative attractiveness of a CBD location decreases.

Electronic Mail.   Office firms use electronic mail to send messages, documents, and data over computer lines. Electronic mail decreases the need for face-to-face contact because information can be sent over computer lines instead of being delivered by employees. Electronic mail allows the suburbanization of firms involved in the rapid turnaround of documents and reports.

To explain the effects of electronic mail, consider Abby, who runs an accounting firm. Abby gets 50 pages of data from her client (another firm) and condenses the information into an income statement. The client demands that the income statement be ready within 24 hours. In the absence of electronic mail, Abby would locate near her

CBD customers to ensure the timely pickup of her client's data and the timely delivery of her income statement. The development of electronic mail allows Abby to move to the suburbs. Her inputs (the client data) and her output (the income statement) can be sent over telephone lines, so she can do her accounting in the suburbs, far from her CBD clients. Because Abby is not dependent on face-to-face contact, but on report-to-face contact, electronic mail allows her to escape the high wages and high rents of the CBD.

Electronic mail has caused the **decoupling** of some CBD firms. Many firms split their operations into suburban activities and CBD activities. Suppose that a firm has a large number of accountants, whose only task is to condense information into reports, that is, they compute bottom lines. The accountants do not interact with people outside the firm, but simply provide condensed information to the firm's executives, who then use the information in their interactions with other firms.

In the absence of electronic mail, the firm's accountants and executives must be in the same location to facilitate the rapid turnaround of information. Given the need for face-to-face interactions among the executives of different firms, the firm locates in the CBD. If the accounting information can be transmitted electronically, however, the accounting division can move to the suburbs, and the firm can send information between the suburban accountants and the CBD executives over telephone lines. Because electronic mail facilitates intrafirm communication, it allows the firm to decouple its operations, moving its support staff to the suburbs while keeping its executives in the CBD.

Teleconferencing.   The second new communications method, the teleconference, is essentially a video meeting. The teleconference is superior to the telephone conference because it allows both visual and verbal communication. The teleconference decreases the need for face-to-face contact within and between firms: instead of sending employees across town to another office, the firm can send them down the hall to the video room.

Because the video camera does not transmit as much information as a face-to-face encounter, the teleconference is not a perfect substitute for face-to-face contact. While the video camera focuses on one or two people in a meeting, a person who is physically present can watch everyone in the room, picking up verbal and nonverbal cues from a large number of people. In addition, the video camera cannot transmit tactile information. The tactile information provided by face-to-face encounters is sometimes useful: a firm, enthusiastic handshake sends a message that cannot be easily conveyed through a video camera.

Because the teleconference is not a perfect substitute for face-to-face contact, it is unlikely to cause substantial suburbanization of office firms. Most of the face-to-face contact that occurs in the CBD is between employees of different firms. The subtle interactions between firms often require face-to-face contact. When people from different firms meet, one of the purposes of the meeting is to establish trust. Because it is easier to establish trust in a face-to-face encounter, a video meeting is inappropriate for some types of interactions.

The teleconference approach is inefficient for firms whose interactions are infrequent and unpredictable. If two firms contact each other only once or twice a year, it may be inefficient for each of them to incur the fixed costs of establishing a video link. If a firm has a small number of encounters with a large number of firms, it may be more efficient to locate near the other firms in the CBD and rely on face-to-face contact.

In most urban areas, office employment occurs in both the CBD and suburban areas. The CBD contains activities for which face-to-face contact is still important (negotiation, design, marketing, and research). In contrast, suburban areas contain activities for which electronic communication is a perfectly good substitute for face-to-face contact.

Suburban Subcenters and Modern Cities

Many of the firms that moved to the suburbs located close to other firms. The clustering of firms in a few suburban locations caused the development of suburban subcenters. This part of the chapter discusses the rationale for suburban subcenters and presents some facts on subcenters in three metropolitan areas: Chicago, Los Angeles, and Houston.

The clustering of firms in suburban subcenters results from agglomerative economies in production. In a cluster of manufacturers or office firms, the total demand for some intermediate inputs is large enough to support external suppliers, who can exploit scale economies and thus produce the intermediate inputs at a lower cost. For example, manufacturers in a cluster may save money by purchasing business services (repair, maintenance, accounting) from a common supplier. Alternatively, if there are scale economies in printing glossy brochures and reports, a large cluster of office firms can support a printing firm, allowing each firm to save on printing costs. The same principle applies to restaurants and hotels: one rule of thumb is that a cluster of office firms with total office space of 2.5 million square feet can support a 250-room hotel.

Subcenters in Chicago

McDonald and McMillen (1990) show that there were four employment subcenters in the Chicago metropolitan area in 1970. They define a *subcenter* as an area with a relatively high employment density (workers per acre) and a relatively large employment ratio (total employment divided by the number of residents). In other words, a subcenter has more workers per acre and more jobs per resident than the area surrounding the subcenter. The authors identified three manufacturing subcenters which together contained 13.9 percent of the metropolitan area's manufacturing employment. The rest of the area's manufacturing employment was divided between the CBD (15.2 percent) and locations outside the CBD and subcenters (70.9 percent). Together, the four subcenters contained 14.4 percent of the metropolitan area's total employment. The rest of the area's employment was divided between the CBD (23 percent) and locations outside the CBD and subcenters (62.6 percent).

McDonald and McMillen note four changes in Chicago's subcenters since 1970. First, O'Hare Airport has emerged as a major employment subcenter. Second, the older manufacturing subcenters have declined in importance, a result of a shift in the metropolitan economy away from its heavy reliance on manufacturing. Third, Du-Page County has developed a subcenter that is based on research and development, communications, corporate headquarters, and light manufacturing. Fourth, like other cities, Chicago has experienced rapid growth in suburban offices, and some of the new offices are located in subcenters. Between 1980 and 1987, the amount of office space in the suburbs more than doubled, increasing the percentage of the metropolitan area's office space outside the CBD from 29 percent to 38 percent.

Subcenters in Los Angeles

Giuliano and Small (1991) use data on the spatial distribution of activity in the Los Angeles metropolitan area to show that there were 28 subcenters in Los Angeles County and Orange County in 1980. They define a subcenter as a zone where the employment density is at least 10 workers per acre and total employment is at least 10,000 workers. In contrast, employment density in the CBD (downtown Los Angeles) is 36 workers per acre and total employment is 469,000. Figure 10–6 shows the shares of employment and population in the CBD (downtown L.A.), the subcenters, and other locations. Total employment in the subcenters was about twice the employment in the CBD (23 percent versus 11 percent). Two thirds of the metropolitan area's employment was outside the center and the subcenters. In terms of population, 1 in 10 people lived in either the CBD or a subcenter.

FIGURE 10–6   **Distribution of Employment and Population between CBD, Subcenters, and Other Areas: Los Angeles in 1980**

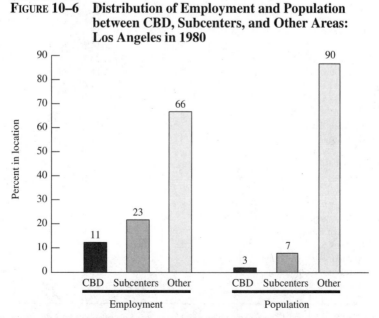

SOURCE: Genevieve Giuliano and Kenneth Small, "Subcenters in the Los Angeles Region," *Regional Science and Urban Economics* 21 (1991).

Table 10–5 shows the characteristics of the CBD and the 28 subcenters. The subcenters are listed after the CBD in descending order with respect to total employment. The subcenters vary in employment density (workers per acre). The average employment density of the subcenters is 17.7 workers per acre, compared to 36.0 in the CBD. Giuliano and Small examined the relationship between employment density and distance to the CBD and found a negative relationship between density and distance. This result is consistent with the predictions of the model of the monocentric city. In the case of Los Angeles, there is a negative relationship despite the fact that a relatively small fraction of total employment is in the CBD.

The subcenters vary with respect to employment ratios (jobs per resident). The average employment ratio of the subcenters is 1.58 jobs per resident, compared

TABLE 10–5   Characteristics of the CBD and Subcenters in the Los Angeles Metropolitan Area

Rank	Location	Employment (1,000)	Workers per Acre	Jobs per Resident	Distance to CBD (miles)
1	Downtown Los Angeles (CBD)	469	36.0	1.47	0.1
2	Los Angeles West	176	25.5	1.37	15.8
3	Santa Monica	65	16.9	1.11	16.7
4	Hollywood	64	21.4	0.73	7.3
5	Los Angeles Airport	59	16.7	4.32	18.8
6	Orange County Airport	48	16.1	1,589.87	40.7
7	Glendale	43	15.5	1.07	12.3
8	Commerce	42	17.0	4.05	9.8
9	Vernon/Huntington Park	39	33.2	2.42	4.9
10	San Pedro	38	15.7	2.74	23.3
11	Santa Ana	38	17.3	1.51	32.9
12	Inglewood	37	14.6	1.24	14.7
13	Pasadena	36	25.3	1.73	12.1
14	Long Beach Airport	33	15.5	3,684.78	23.3
15	Marina Del Ray	32	11.4	1.28	14.0
16	Long Beach	30	18.0	0.84	25.3
17	Van Nuys Airport	28	12.6	2.04	22.1
18	Burbank Airport	26	28.4	10.86	16.5
19	Hawthorne	18	12.4	0.74	13.5
20	Canoga Park/Warner Center	17	11.2	1.21	27.4
21	Lawndale	17	17.1	1.36	20.5
22	L.A. East	16	37.3	2.30	6.8
23	Fullerton	16	11.4	4.97	27.3
24	Downey	15	17.3	2.38	14.8
25	Santa Ana South	14	12.2	1.76	37.4
26	Sherman Oaks	13	11.9	1.04	18.6
27	Burbank S.W.	13	18.0	1.92	14.1
28	Anaheim/Orange/Garden Grove	11	11.3	1.06	30.2
29	Garden Grove/Stanton	10	12.9	5.60	26.6
	All subcenters	994 (total)	17.7 (average)	1.58 (average)	

SOURCE: Genevieve Giuliano and Kenneth Small, "Subcenters in the Los Angeles Region," *Regional Science and Urban Economics* 21 (1991).

to 1.47 in the CBD and 0.43 for the entire metropolitan area. Except for the airport subcenters, which have few residents and thus large employment ratios, the employment ratios of the subcenters are relatively small. This suggests that the subcenters are not isolated employment centers, but instead provide a mixture of jobs and dwellings.

Giuliano and Small suggest that the subcenters can be divided into five types: mixed industrial, mixed service, specialized entertainment, specialized manufacturing, and specialized service. Most of the mixed-industrial subcenters started out as low-density manufacturing areas near transport nodes (airport, port, or marina) and grew as they attracted other activities. Most of the mixed-service subcenters are like traditional downtowns: they provide a wide range of services. Many of these subcenters functioned as independent centers before they were absorbed into the metropolitan economy. The specialized-manufacturing subcenters include areas near airports that produce aerospace equipment and older manufacturing areas. In the service-oriented subcenters, 90 percent of employment is in service activities such as medical care, entertainment, and education.

There are four basic conclusions from this study of the Los Angeles area. First, the subcenters differ in the mixes of goods and services they provide, suggesting that the subcenters play diverse roles within the metropolitan economy. Second, many of the subcenters are highly specialized, suggesting that there are large localization economies (clustering of firms in the same industry to share input suppliers, save on labor costs, and share information). Third, employment in the metropolitan area is relatively dispersed: two thirds of total employment is outside the CBD and the subcenters. Fourth, employment density decreases as distance from the center increases, despite the fact that the center contains a relatively small fraction of total employment.

Subcenters in Houston

Mieszkowski and Smith (1991) explore the land-use patterns in the Houston metropolitan area and identify 10 subcenters. In 1985, total employment in the individual subcenters was between 16,000 and 86,000, compared to total employment in the CBD of 156,000. In 1985, the CBD contained about 10 percent of the metropolitan area's total employment, leaving 23 percent for the subcenters and 67 percent for areas outside the CBD and subcenters. The corresponding figures for 1970 were 14 percent for the CBD, 11 percent for the subcenters, and 75 percent for areas outside the CBD and subcenters.

Like many other cities, Houston experienced rapid growth in its office space. Between 1969 and 1989, total office space increased more than seven-fold, from 25 million square feet to 182 million square feet. The most rapid increases occurred in the suburbs, both inside and outside subcenters, so the suburban share of office space increased. Figure 10–7 shows the shares of office space in the CBD, the subcenters, and other areas for 1969 and 1989. By 1989, over three fourths of office space was outside the CBD, and over half of the office space was in suburban subcenters.

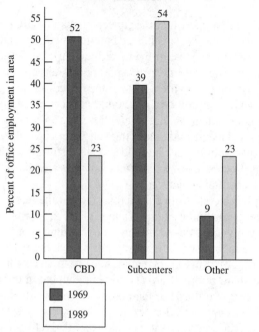

FIGURE 10–7   Percentages of Houston's Office Employment in the CBD, Subcenters, and Other Areas, 1969 and 1989

SOURCE: Peter Mieszkowski and Barton Smith, "Urban Decentralization in the Sunbelt: The Case of Houston," *Regional Science and Urban Economics* 21 (1991).

Land Use in the Modern City: Urban Villages?

The monocentric, core-dominated city has been gradually replaced with the multicentric, suburbanized city. Figure 10–8 shows land rent at different locations in a metropolitan area that has a beltway (located 2.5 miles from the city center) and two employment subcenters along the beltway. The land-rent surface has local peaks at the city center and the subcenters, and forms a circular ridge centered on the beltway. Because the key factor in determining employment density and population density is the price of land, Figure 10–8 could also be used to show density at different locations in the metropolitan area.

The modern city, with its suburban subcenters, has been called a system of **urban villages.** In many metropolitan areas, suburban subcenters contain mid-rise office buildings, hotels, shopping malls, and entertainment facilities. Therefore, people in the area surrounding an employment subcenter have the option of traveling to the subcenter for work, shopping, and play. In other words, the subcenter is the core of an urban village. The urban-village idea was recently incorporated into the planning

FIGURE 10–8   Land Bid Rent in Beltway City

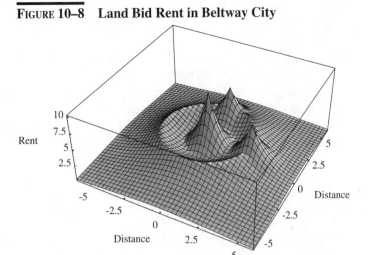

process in Phoenix: for planning purposes, there are nine urban villages, with an average population of 100,000. By the year 2000, planners expect to have a total of 12 urban villages, with an average population of 125,000.

Most cities in the United States are experiencing the urban-village phenomenon. Subcenters are developing in the rapidly growing Sunbelt cities (Atlanta, Phoenix, Dallas, Houston, and San Francisco) as well as in cities with less rapid growth (St. Louis, Detroit, and Kansas City). Subcenters are also developing in the nation's oldest and most traditional cities (New York, Boston, Chicago, Baltimore). In most urban areas, the fraction of office and retail employment in suburban subcenters is increasing.

The development of urban villages results from the suburbanization and clustering of retailers and office firms. Retailers moved to the suburbs to be closer to their suburban customers, and many retailers clustered in malls and subcenters to exploit shopping externalities. Office firms moved to the suburbs to get better access to their suburban work forces and clustered in subcenters to exploit agglomerative economies in the provision of business services, restaurants, and hotels.

Summary

1. The truck contributed to the suburbanization of manufacturing employment for two reasons.

    a. The intracity truck replaced the horse-drawn wagon, decreasing freight costs relative to commuting costs, pulling firms toward the low-wage suburbs.

    b. The intercity truck replaced the boat and train for intercity freight, freeing manufacturers from central export nodes. Firms moved closer to their suburban workers.

2. The growing importance of air freight has caused some manufacturers to locate close to suburban airports.

3. The automobile replaced the streetcar as the principal means of commuting, making locations throughout the urban area accessible to workers. Firms with specialized labor forces were able to move to the suburbs.

4. Because the income elasticity of demand for housing is close to the income elasticity of commuting costs, it appears that income growth had a relatively small effect on suburbanization.

5. The suburbanization of population occurred for five reasons.
    a. Decreases in commuting costs (from the streetcar and the auto) increased the accessibility of suburban locations.
    b. Central-city problems (racial tensions, deteriorating housing, high taxes, high crime rates, inferior schools) encouraged some households to flee to the suburbs.
    c. The suburbanization of employment opportunities contributed to the suburbanization of population as households followed the firms to the suburbs.
    d. The underpricing of commuting (commuting and pollution externalities) decreases the relative cost of suburban locations.
    e. The fragmented system of local government allows households to escape central-city housing problems.

6. In the modern multicentric city, workers commute to jobs in both the CBD and suburban subcenters. Workers are willing to pay more for housing and land near employment centers (everything else being equal), so the land-rent function has several peaks, one near the CBD and one near each subcenter.

7. Retailers moved to the suburbs for three reasons:
    a. Some retailers followed consumers to the suburbs.
    b. The replacement of the streetcar with the automobile increased the accessibility of noncentral locations.
    c. Population growth increased the equilibrium number of retailers. Some of the new retailers located in the suburban areas.

8. During the 1970s and 1980s, suburban office space grew at a rapid rate. Nationwide, suburban office employment grew over seven times faster than central-city office employment during the 1970s (116 percent versus 15 percent).

9. Advances in communication technology decreased the need for face-to-face contact among office workers, allowing some firms to move to the low-wage suburbs and allowing others to decouple their operations into CBD activities and suburban activities.

10. The clustering of firms in suburban subcenters results from agglomerative economies in production. Firms in the subcenters share input suppliers, a labor force, and information.

11. The 28 subcenters in the Los Angeles metropolitan area contain about 23 percent of the area's employment and 9 percent of its population. The subcenters are specialized: they differ in the mixes of goods and services they provide.

12. The monocentric, core-dominated city has been gradually replaced with the multicentric, suburbanized city. The land-rent surface has local peaks at the city center and the subcenters, and forms a ridge centered on the beltway.

13. The development of suburban subcenters (urban villages) is explained by the suburbanization and clustering of retailers and office firms. Retailers moved to the suburbs to be closer to their customers and clustered in subcenters to exploit shopping externalities. Manufacturing and office firms moved to the suburbs to be closer to their work forces and clustered to exploit agglomerative economies in production.

Exercises and Discussion Questions

1. Consider a manufacturing firm that exports some of its output by train (through a central export node) and the rest by truck (the truck exits the metropolitan area using a suburban beltway). Suppose that production costs (including labor costs) are the same at all locations. The unit cost of transporting output inward (toward the central export node) is t_i, and the unit cost of transporting output outward (toward the beltway) is t_o. The volume of output going to the central export node is w_i, and the volume going to the beltway is w_o.

   a. Under what conditions will the firm's bid-rent function be positively sloped?

   b. How would your answer to (a) change if wages were lower in the suburbs?

2. Consider a metropolitan area with a 10-mile radius. Two members of the Dink household work: Mr. Dink commutes to the city center ($u = 0$), and Ms. Dink commutes to a suburban subcenter four miles due east of the city center. Depict the household's housing-price functions for three cases:

   a. Travel time per mile is the same in both directions (toward the city center and away from the city center), and Mr. and Ms. Dink have the same opportunity cost of travel time.

   b. Because the bulk of workers commute to the city center, the travel time per mile of inward commuting (toward the city center in the morning rush hour and away from the center in the evening rush hour) exceeds the travel time of outward commuting (away from the city center during the morning rush hour and toward the center during the evening rush hour). Mr. and Ms. Dink have the same opportunity cost of travel time.

   c. Travel time per mile is the same in both directions, but Ms. Dink has a higher opportunity cost of travel time.

3. Consider a city where a single firm sells pet rocks, a good with a large income elasticity of demand. The firm is located in the central shopping area of the city. Suppose that households in the city experience an increase in income.
    a. Assume that the number of pet rock firms is fixed at one. What is the effect of the increase in income on the firm's bid rent for land at the city center?
    b. Is it realistic to assume that the number of pet rock firms will remain constant?
    c. If the number of firms is allowed to vary, what is the effect of the increase in income on the retail bid-rent function?
4. Comment on the following statement: "Instead of investing money in traditional radial mass-transit systems (hub-and-spoke systems), we should be investing in circumferential transit systems. We should build a circular transit system along the urban beltways."
5. The traditional core-dominated city was a segregated city in the sense that all employment was in one area (the core) and all residents lived in another area (the satellite). The modern city is less segregated in the sense that employment is dispersed throughout the city, in subcenters and along suburban beltways. Mr. Wizard recently made the following statement: "If my assumptions are correct, land use in the typical American city will soon be completely integrated. I predict that each manufacturer and each office firm will be surrounded by its work force: the metropolitan area will have dozens of 'company villages.' A firm will be at the center of each village, and the firm's workers will occupy the land surrounding the factory or office. Every worker will be employed in the firm at the center of the village. That's integration."
    a. Assume that Mr. Wizard's reasoning is correct. What are his assumptions? In other words, under what set of assumptions will a system of company villages develop?
    b. Are Mr. Wizard's assumptions realistic?
6. The development of the internal-combustion engine caused fundamental changes in urban land-use patterns. The transformation from the core-dominated city to the modern suburbanized city took only about 50 years. Given the rapid pace of technological change, it seems likely that some future innovation will cause another transformation of cities. Given your knowledge of science fiction and fact, describe an innovation that would cause fundamental changes in the spatial structure of cities.
7. Table 10–5 shows the rank and total employment for the CBD and the 28 subcenters in the Los Angeles metropolitan area. Is the size distribution of the employment centers consistent with a hierarchical system of centers? How closely does the size distribution of employment centers fit the rank-size rule (see Chapter 5)?
8. *Telecommuting* refers to a system under which employees work at home for one or more days per week and use personal computers and telephone

lines to interact with people in the office. Consider an office firm that must decide whether to locate in the CBD or along a suburban beltway (to be closer to its suburban work force). Discuss the effects of telecommuting on the relative attractiveness of the CBD.

9. Consider the following statement: "The large traditional monocentric city of the 19th century was a fluke, a result of a particular sequence of technological transportation innovations over the 19th and 20th centuries. If the sequence of innovations had been slightly different, the large monocentric city would have never developed. Instead, we would have gone from the small cities of the 18th century directly to the large multicentric, suburbanized city that we see today."

   a. List the innovations that caused the development of the large monocentric city in the 19th century and the development of the multicentric, suburbanized city of the 20th century.

   b. Explain how a reordering of the sequence of innovations would have caused the development of large multicentric, suburbanized cities instead of large monocentric cities.

10. Consider a modern city in which office employment has been steadily shifting from the city center to suburban locations along beltways. Suppose that the city improves its mass-transit system, decreasing the monetary and time costs of radial travel. Assume that the improvement in the transit system does not affect the spatial distribution of residents. Will the improvement in the transit system speed up or slow down the movement of office firms to the suburbs?

11. Consider a modern city where firms are located in the central business district or along a circumferential highway. Congestion is not a problem: everyone travels at the legal speed limit. Suppose that in an attempt to internalize the pollution externalities from auto use, the city imposes a $2 per gallon tax on gasoline. Assume that (*i*) everyone continues to drive himself or herself to work and (*ii*) the tax does not affect the spatial distribution of residences. Will the gas tax increase, decrease, or not affect the fraction of employment in the central business district?

12. Consider two metropolitan areas, Anville and Diamondburg. The names indicate the type of industry in each metropolitan area: export workers in Anville produce anvils; export workers in Diamondburg cut diamonds. Suppose that all output is exported through an export node at the center of the city. Would you expect the two cities to have the same spatial distributions of employment? If not, what differences would you expect?

13. One of the major conundrums of urban spatial analysis is the occurrence of tall residential facilities for the elderly (RFE) in areas of the city where other residents occupy low-density housing (single-family homes or low-rise apartment buildings). The RFEs defy the conventional logic that building heights depend on the price of land. Provide an explanation for the occurrence of relatively tall RFEs.

14. Consider a city that is expected to grow in the following fashion: between 1990 and 1995, relatively wealthy households will move to the city; between 1995 and 2000, relatively poor households will move to the city. A developer has asked the city planning department to allow "leapfrog" development. Specifically, the developer wants to develop a site eight miles from the city center at a time when there is plenty of vacant land within an eight-mile radius of the city center.

    a. Why does the developer want to engage in leapfrog development?

    b. Is leapfrog development efficient?

15. Some retailers locate along major streets, forming commercial strips. Why don't these retailers locate in the city center or in a suburban mall?

References and Additional Readings

General Suburbanization

Chinitz, Benjamin. *City and Suburb*. Englewood, N.J.: Prentice Hall, 1965. A collection of essays on the causes and effects of suburbanization.

Frieden, Bernard J., and Lynne B. Sagalyn. *Downtown, Inc.: How America Rebuilds Cities*. Cambridge, Mass.: MIT Press, 1991. Discusses efforts to rebuild downtown areas.

Greenwood, Michael. "Metropolitan Growth and the Intrametropolitan Location of Employment, Housing, and Labor Force." *The Review of Economics and Statistics* 62 (1980), pp. 491–501.

Harrison, B. *Employment and Economic Development*. Washington, D.C.: Urban Institute, 1974. Discusses the interdependence of households and firm location decisions, showing that the suburbanization of residences contributed to the suburbanization of retailers and service establishments.

Mills, Edwin S. *Studies in the Structure of the Urban Economy*. Baltimore: Johns Hopkins, 1972. Documents the suburbanization of employment and population between 1880 and 1963.

Stanback, Thomas, and Richard Knight. *Suburbanization and the City*. Montclair, N.J.: Allanheld, Osmun and Company, 1976. Documents suburbanization trends and the implications for the metropolitan economy.

Central-City Problems and the Suburbanization of Population

Bradbury, Katharine L.; Anthony Downs; and Kenneth A. Small. *Urban Decline and the Future of American Cities*. Washington, D.C.: Brookings Institution, 1982. Discusses the reasons behind the decline of central cities.

Frey, W. H. "Central City White Flight: Racial and Non-Racial Causes." *American Sociological Review* 44 (1979), pp. 425–88. Tests various theories of suburbanization, focusing on the effects of central-city problems on suburbanization.

Grubb, W. N. "The Flight to the Suburbs of Population and Employment, 1960–1970." *Journal of Urban Economics* 11 (1982), pp. 348–67. Examines the role of taxes, education, and crime rates on suburbanization.

Kern, Clifford R. "Upper Income Residential Revival in the City." In *Research in Urban Economics,* vol. 4, ed. Robert Ebel. Greenwich, Conn.: JAI Press, 1984. Discusses the facts on gentrification, including the characteristics of renovators.

Laska, Shirley, and Daphne Spain. *Back to the City: Issues in Neighborhood Renovation.* New York: Pergamon Press, 1980. Case studies of gentrification.

Reschovsky, A. "Residential Choice and the Local Public Sector: An Alternative Test of the Tiebout Hypothesis." *Journal of Urban Economics* 6 (1979), pp. 501–20. Examines the role of taxes, local expenditures, and school quality on suburbanization.

Wasylenko, Michael J. "Disamenities, Local Taxation, and the Intrametropolitan Location of Households and Firms." In *Research in Urban Economics,* vol. 4, ed. Robert Ebel. Greenwich, Conn.: JAI Press, 1984. Reviews the empirical evidence concerning the effects of income on location.

Suburbanization of Manufacturers

Erickson, R., and M. Wasylenko. "Firm Location and Site Selection in Suburban Municipalities." *Journal of Urban Economics* 8 (1980), pp. 69–85. Examines the influences of labor markets, land prices, transportation facilities, fiscal variables, and agglomeration economies on the intrametropolitan location decisions of firms.

Hoover, Edgar M., and Raymond Vernon. *Anatomy of a Metropolis.* Cambridge, Mass.: Harvard University Press, 1959. Discusses the suburbanization of manufacturers in the New York area.

Kitigawa, Evylyn M., and Donald Bogue. *Suburbanization of Manufacturing Activity within Standard Statistical Metropolitan Areas.* Oxford, Ohio: Scripps Foundation, 1955. Discusses the suburbanization of manufacturing before World War II.

Moses, Leon, and Harold Williamson. "The Location of Economic Activity in Cities." In *Readings in Urban Economics,* ed. Matthew Edel and Jerome Rothenberg. New York: Macmillan, 1972. Discusses the role of the intraurban and interurban truck on the suburbanization of manufacturing.

Struyk, Raymond. "Evidence on the Locational Activity of Manufacturing Industries in Metropolitan Areas." *Land Economics* 48 (1972), pp. 377–82.

Wasylenko, Michael J. "Disamenities, Local Taxation, and the Intrametropolitan Location of Households and Firms." In *Research in Urban Economics,* vol. 4, ed. Robert Ebel. Greenwich, Conn.: JAI Press, 1984. Reviews the evidence concerning the intrametropolitan location choices of firms.

Suburbanization of Office Firms and Services

Cervero, Robert. *Suburban Gridlock.* New Brunswick, N.J.: Center for Urban Policy Research, 1986. Discusses the recent growth in office employment and its implications for transportation planning.

Clapp, J. M. "Endogenous Centers: A Simple Departure from the NUE Model." *Papers of the Regional Science Association* 54 (1984), pp. 13–24. Describes the process through which contacts between firms cause the development of a CBD and subcenters.

Hughes, James W., and George Sternlieb. "The Suburban Growth Corridor." In *America's New Market Geography,* ed. George Sternlieb and James W. Hughes. New Brunswick, N.J.: Center for Urban Policy Research, 1988. Discusses the market forces behind the recent office construction boom in suburbs.

Mills, Edwin S. "Service Sector Suburbanization." In *America's New Market Geography,* ed. George Sternlieb and James W. Hughes. New Brunswick, N.J.: Center for Urban Policy Research, 1988. Discusses the recent trends in the suburbanization of services and compares the spatial distributions of workplaces and residences.

Pivo, Gary. "The Net of Mixed Bead: Suburban Office Development in Six Metropolitan Regions." *Journal of the American Planning Association,* Autumn 1990, pp. 457–69. Discusses the suburbanization and clustering of office space between 1960 and the late 1980s.

Effects of Beltways

Bone, A. J., and Martin Wohl. *Economic Impact Study: Massachusetts' Route 128.* Cambridge, Mass.: MIT Transportation Engineering Division, 1958.

Bureau of Population and Economic Research. *The Socio-Economic Impact of the Capital Beltway on Northern Virginia.* Charlottesville, Va.: Bureau of Population and Economic Research, University of Virginia, 1968. Discusses the effect of the beltway in the Washington, D.C., metropolitan area.

Levitan, Don. "Massachusetts' Route 128: A Nonemulative Enigma." *Transportation Research Record,* no. 583 (1976), pp. 45–54. Discusses the effects of Boston's beltway.

Mills, Florence. "Effects of Beltways on the Location of Residences and Selected Workplaces." *Transportation Research Record,* no. 812 (1981), pp. 26–33. Compares changes in population and employment in metropolitan areas with and without beltways. Concludes that beltways did not have a significant effect on central-city employment.

Payne-Maxie Consultants. *The Land Use and Urban Development Impacts of Beltways: Case Studies.* Washington, D.C.: U.S. Department of Transportation and U.S. Department of Housing and Urban Development, 1980. Discusses the effects of beltways in eight different metropolitan areas.

Telecommunications and Land Use

Chinitz, Benjamin. "The Influence of Communication and Data Processing Technology on Urban Form." In *Research in Urban Economics,* vol. 4, ed. Robert Ebel. Greenwich, Conn.: JAI Press, 1984, pp. 67–77. Discusses the effects of new communication technologies on the location decisions of office firms.

Moss, Mitchell. "Telecommunications: Shaping the Future." In *America's New Market Geography,* ed. George Sternlieb and James W. Hughes. New Brunswick, N.J.: Center for Urban Policy Research, 1988. Discusses the effects of new communication technologies on location patterns.

Salomon, I. "Telecommunications and Travel Relationships: A Review." *Transportation Research, A* 20A (1986), pp. 223–38. Discusses the effects of telecommunication technologies on location patterns.

Suburban Subcenters and Modern Cities

Giuliano, Genevieve, and Kenneth Small. "Subcenters in the Los Angeles Region." *Regional Science and Urban Economics* 21 (1991). Discusses the characteristics of the CBD and 28 subcenters in the Los Angeles metropolitan area.

Helsley, Robert, and Arthur Sullivan. "Urban Subcenter Formation." *Regional Science and Urban Economics* 21 (1991), pp. 255–75. Explores the economic forces behind the development of subcenters.

McDonald, John F., and Daniel McMillen. "Employment Subcenters and Land Values in a Polycentric Urban Area: The Case of Chicago." *Environment and Planning, A* 22 (1990), pp. 1561–74. Identifies four employment subcenters in the Chicago metropolitan area and discusses the effects of subcenters on residential land values.

Mieszkowski, Peter, and Barton Smith. "Urban Decentralization in the Sunbelt: The Case of Houston." *Regional Science and Urban Economics* 21 (1991). Discusses the characteristics of the CBD and 10 subcenters in the Houston metropolitan area.

Future Location Patterns

Anas, Alex, and Leon Moses. "Transportation and Land Use in the Mature Metropolis." In *The Mature Metropolis,* ed. Charles L. Leven. Lexington, Mass.: Heath, Lexington, 1978.

Macrae, Norman. "Tomorrow's Agglomeration Economies." In *The Mature Metropolis,* ed. Charles L. Leven. Lexington, Mass.: Heath, Lexington, 1978. Predicts future development patterns based on predictions about agglomeration economies.

Land-Use Controls and Zoning

This chapter discusses the government role in the urban land market. The discussions in Chapters 7 through 10 assume that land is allocated to the highest bidder, that is, the government is not involved in the urban land market. In fact, local governments use a number of policies to control land use. Most cities have zoning plans that limit the location choices of most activities. Some cities use zoning and other land-use controls to limit population growth. This chapter addresses three basic questions related to various types of land-use controls. First, why do cities control land use? Second, what are the market effects of land-use controls? Third, what are the legal foundations for zoning and other land-use controls?

Controlling Population Growth

Some local governments use land-use policies to limit population growth. The purpose of a growth-control policy is to control the undesirable side effects of growth (pollution, congestion, crime, the loss of a small-town atmosphere). This section discusses two growth-control policies: urban service boundaries and limits on the number of building permits issued.

Urban Service Boundary

One way to control population growth is to limit the land area of the city. If a city refuses to extend urban services (e.g., sewers, roads, schools, parks) beyond an **urban service boundary,** it limits growth to the area within the boundary.

Figure 11–1 shows the equilibrium land-use pattern in a monocentric city. The residential bid-rent function intersects the agricultural bid-rent function at a distance of eight miles from the city center, so the city radius is eight miles. An implicit assumption of this model is that the city government provides urban services out to a distance of eight miles from the city center. The business bid-rent function intersects

FIGURE 11–1 **Partial-Equilibrium Effect of an Urban Service Boundary**

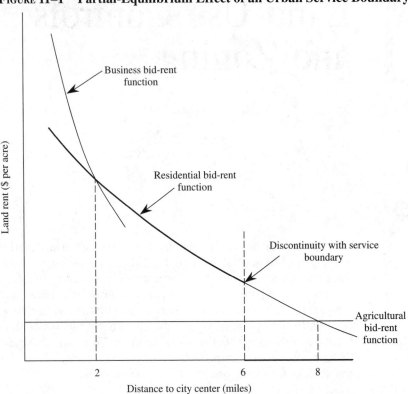

In the market equilibrium, the CBD radius is two miles and the city radius is eight miles. An urban service boundary prevents residential development beyond six miles, so the residential bid rent drops to zero between six and eight miles from the city center. This is the partial-equilibrium effect of the service boundary.

the residential bid-rent function at a distance of two miles from the city center, so the equilibrium CBD radius is two miles.

Suppose that the city refuses to extend urban services beyond six miles from the city center. Unless residents can provide their own roads, sewage systems, and schools, residential development outside the boundary is impossible. Therefore, the residential bid rent drops to zero at a distance of six miles from the city center. This is shown in Figure 11–1 as a discontinuity in the residential bid-rent function at a distance of six miles. This is the partial-equilibrium effect of the urban service boundary: land beyond $u = 6$ is rendered uninhabitable, so the market rent on land outside the boundary drops to the agricultural bid rent.

What are the general-equilibrium effects of the urban service boundary? The service boundary decreases the size of the residential district, decreasing the city's total labor supply and thus increasing the city's wage. The increase in the wage increases the relative attractiveness of the city, causing migration that bids up the prices of housing and land. The quantity of labor supplied increases for two reasons:

1. **Increased population density.** The increases in housing and land prices decrease lot sizes: households occupy smaller dwellings, and housing producers use less land per unit of housing. The number of households (and workers) per acre increases.

2. **Increased residential territory.** The upward shift of the residential bid-rent function allows households to outbid businesses for land near the CBD border. Therefore, the residential district expands inward toward the city center.

The increase in the wage also affects the market for business land. Production costs increase, decreasing the relative attractiveness of the city as a production site. The demand for CBD land decreases, causing a downward shift of the business bid-rent function. The quantity of labor demanded decreases for two reasons:

1. **Decreased employment density.** The increase in the relative price of labor decreases the city's employment density (the number of laborers per acre).

2. **Decreased business territory.** The CBD shrinks as businesses lose land to the residential district.

The city's wage continues to rise until general equilibrium (labor supply equals labor demand) is restored.

Figure 11–2 shows the new equilibrium allocation of land. The CBD radius is 1.5 miles (down from 2 miles), and the city radius is 6 miles (the radius dictated by the urban service boundary). The service boundary has different effects in the city's two land markets. In the residential district, the service boundary increases the prices of housing and land, thus increasing population density. In contrast, the service boundary decreases both land rent and employment density in the CBD.

Who gains and who loses from the service boundary? People who own land outside the service boundary lose: for land between $u = 6$ and $u = 8$, the market rent drops to the agricultural bid rent, decreasing the market value of land. People who own residential land within the service boundary win: the increased demand for residential land (caused by the increase in the wage) bids up the price of land within the boundary. People who own land within the CBD lose: the decrease in the demand for CBD land (caused by the increase in the wage) decreases the price of business land.

Building Permits

Some cities control residential growth by limiting the number of building permits issued. By limiting the number of new dwellings built per year, a city can control its growth rate.

Consider a city that initially has no limit on the number of building permits issued. Figure 11–3 shows the city's market for new housing: the supply curve *AG* intersects the demand curve at point *F,* generating an equilibrium quantity of 100 houses per year and an equilibrium price of $50,000 per house. The city issues 100 free permits per year, which are used to build houses with a market value of $50,000.

FIGURE 11–2   **General-Equilibrium Effect of an Urban Service Boundary**

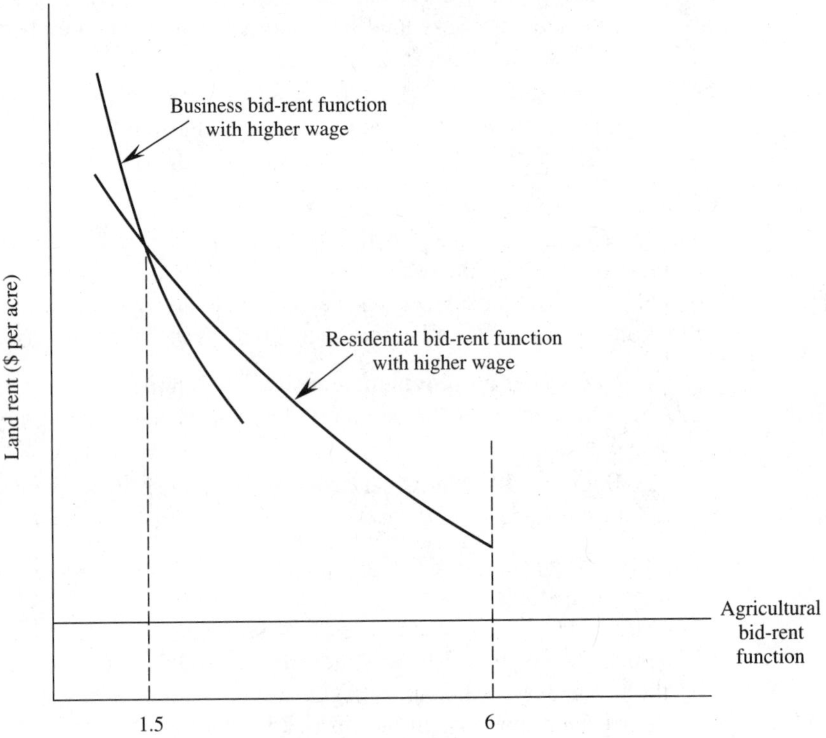

The urban service boundary decreases the supply of labor, increasing the city's wage. The increase in the wage shifts the residential bid-rent function upward (increasing the quantity of labor supplied) and shifts the business bid-rent function downward (decreasing the quantity of labor demanded). General equilibrium is restored with a smaller, less dense CBD and a more dense residential district.

Developers make zero economic profits (normal accounting profits), meaning that the cost of producing each house (the sum of land, labor, and capital cost) is $50,000.

Suppose that the city limits the number of building permits to 60 per year. The new supply curve for housing is *ACE:* the maximum number of new houses is 60, so the supply curve becomes vertical at 60 dwellings. The new supply curve intersects the demand curve at an equilibrium price of $70,000. In other words, the permit policy increases the equilibrium price of housing by $20,000.

The permit policy also decreases the cost of producing housing. The permit policy decreases the number of houses built, so it decreases the demand for land. For example, if houses are built on quarter-acre lots, the permit policy decreases the demand for land from 25 acres per year (100 times 0.25) to 15 acres per year. The decrease in the demand for land decreases the market price of land, decreasing the cost of producing housing. This is shown by the housing supply curve: if 100 houses are built, the production cost is $50,000 per house; if only 60 houses are built, the

FIGURE 11–3   Market Effects of Building Permits

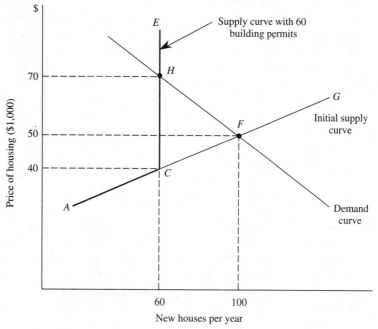

If the city decreases the supply of building permits from 100 to 60, the supply curve for housing shifts from *AG* to *ACE*. The new equilibrium is point *H* (price of housing = $70,000). Point *C* shows the cost of producing 60 houses ($40,000). The difference between the price and the cost is the equilibrium price of the building permit ($30,000).

cost drops to $40,000 per house. Because the permit policy decreases the number of houses built, it decreases the price of land, allowing developers to build houses at a lower cost.

The city must decide how to allocate the 60 building permits among its developers. One option is to auction the permits to the highest bidders. What is the monetary value of a building permit? A person with a building permit can make a profit equal to the difference between the market price of a house ($70,000) and the cost of producing the house ($40,000), so the monetary value of a permit is $30,000. If the city auctions the permits, the market price would be $30,000.

Some cities allocate their building permits to development projects that promote their development objectives. If the city is interested in high-density housing, it could allocate the permits to a high-density housing project. Alternatively, the city could allocate the permits to a project in an area targeted for development. Many cities use sophisticated point systems to rate and rank alternative development proposals. Among the criteria for which points are assigned are various design features (the exterior appearance of the dwellings, the amount of open space within the project), density, and the proximity of the project to existing public infrastructure (roads, schools, sewer lines).

Land-Use Zoning: Types and Market Effects

A zoning plan designates a set of admissible land uses for each plot of land in a city. In theory, the purpose of zoning is to promote public health, safety, and welfare. The principal means of promoting health, safety, and welfare is the separation of incompatible land uses.

The first zoning ordinances were used by the wealthy to exclude the poor. In the 1880s, the city of San Francisco passed laws to segregate its Chinese population. When explicit segregation was declared unconstitutional, the city passed a zoning law that banned laundries from certain neighborhoods. The zoning law did not violate the Constitution because it promoted public welfare by keeping an undesirable land use (laundries) out of some residential areas. Because the Chinese operated most of the city's laundries, the zoning law provided a legal means of segregation. In New York City in 1916, the rapid growth of employment in offices and garment factories increased the number of low-wage women on the streets of midtown Manhattan. The owners of exclusive Fifth Avenue stores feared that the increased traffic of poor women would be bad for business, and proposed zoning laws that limited building sizes and building heights. The law limited the growth of office buildings and garment factories, decreasing the number of clerical and garment workers walking along Fifth Avenue. The zoning law was declared constitutional because it promoted public welfare by controlling the nuisances created by tall buildings (shadows, blocked light, disruption of views).

There are many types of zoning, each of which has at least one purpose. This section divides zoning into three types. The purpose of **nuisance zoning** is to separate incompatible land uses. Cities use **fiscal zoning** to exclude households that would not pay their share of the costs of local government. **Design zoning** is a sort of macroarchitecture: planners arrange activities within the city to promote the efficient use of the city's infrastructure.

Nuisance Zoning

Nuisance zoning (or externality zoning) is the practice of separating land uses that are considered incompatible. The classic example is the glue factory: one way of dealing with the air pollution generated by the glue factory is to move the factory into an industrial zone, far from residential areas. Similarly, the externalities generated by retailers (traffic congestion and noise) can be controlled by establishing a retail zone. There are also externalities generated by high-density housing: apartment buildings cause traffic and parking problems, and also block views and light. These externalities can be controlled by establishing a zone for high-density housing.

Industrial Nuisances.   Industrial firms generate all types of externalities, including noise, glare, dust, odor, vibration, and smoke. Zoning separates residential and industrial land uses, reducing the exposure to air and noise pollution. Zoning is appealing as an environmental policy because of its simplicity: the easiest way to limit exposure to pollution is to separate polluters from their potential victims. The problem with zoning as an environmental policy is that zoning does not reduce the total amount of pollution, it just moves it around. If one municipality's industrial zone is far from its own residents but close to the residents of a nearby municipality, industrial zoning may actually increase the total exposure to pollution. Because zoning does not provide firms with the incentive to decrease pollution, it is less effective than other environmental policies.

Alternative to Industrial Zoning: Spatial Effluent Fees.   When economists hear the word *pollution,* their knee-jerk response is "effluent fees." An effluent fee is a tax on pollution. For efficiency purposes, the fee should be set equal to the marginal external cost of pollution, that is, the cost to society of an additional unit of pollution. For example, if one ton of sulfur dioxide generates a social cost of $2, the effluent fee should be $2 per ton. The effluent fee "internalizes" the pollution externality, forcing polluters to pay for pollution in the same way that they pay for labor, capital, and raw materials. The firm has an incentive to decrease pollution because abatement decreases the firm's effluent bill. If the effluent fee equals the marginal external cost of pollution, firms generate the optimum level of pollution.

In theory, a system of effluent fees would generate both the optimum level of pollution and the optimum spatial distribution of pollution. If the effluent fee varies across space, a firm would pay a higher effluent fee for pollution generated near sensitive areas (e.g., residential areas). For example, the effluent fee might be $2 per ton of pollution if the firm is 10 miles from the residential area and $5 per ton if the firm is 4 miles from the residential area. Under a system of spatial effluent fees, the firm would base both its production decisions and its location decision on effluent fees. If the effluent fees are set equal to the marginal external cost of pollution, the firm would choose both the optimum location and the optimum level of pollution.

To explain the differences between zoning and effluent fees, consider a rectangular city with the following characteristics:

1. Residents live in the western part of the city and commute eastward to a polluting steel mill.
2. The longer the distance between the residential area and the mill, the higher the wage: workers are compensated for commuting cost in the form of higher wages. The firm's total labor cost equals the wage (dollars per worker) times the total quantity of labor.
3. The longer the distance between the mill and the residential area, the lower the effluent fee. The firm's total pollution cost equals the effluent fee (dollars per ton) times the amount of pollution.
4. The city starts with an industrial zoning policy under which the steel mill is located 10 miles from the residential area.

Figure 11–4 shows the total cost of producing steel at different locations. The positively sloped curve shows labor cost, which increases from $20 for a location adjacent to the residential district to $63 in the industrial zone (10 miles from the residential area). The negatively sloped curve shows pollution cost, which decreases from $60 at a location adjacent to the residential district to $5 in the industrial zone. The variation in the pollution cost reflects the variation in the effluent fee. The U-shaped curve shows total cost, the sum of labor cost and pollution cost, which

FIGURE 11-4   **Spatial Effluent Fees and Optimum Location**

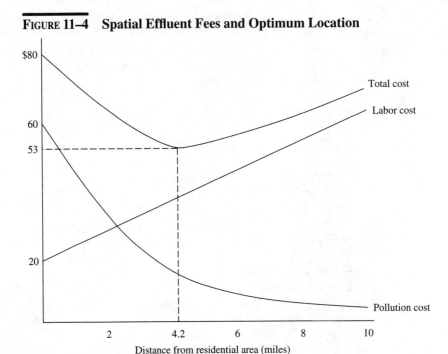

Total cost is the sum of labor cost and pollution cost. As the polluting firm moves toward the residential district, pollution cost increases (more residents are affected by pollution, so the effluent fee increases), but labor cost decreases (commuting distances decrease, so the wage decreases). Total cost is minimized at a distance of 4.2 miles from the residential area.

decreases from $80 for a location adjacent to the residential district to $53 for a location 4.2 miles from the residential area, then increases to $70 in the industrial zone.

Suppose the firm starts in the industrial zone. As the firm moves toward the residential district, there are benefits and costs. On the benefit side, labor cost decreases as the firm moves closer to its work force. On the cost side, the effluent fee increases because the firm's pollution affects more people, so pollution cost increases. Given the shapes of the labor-cost and pollution-cost curves, total cost is minimized at a location 4.2 miles from the residential district. If the city switches from a zoning policy to an effluent-fee policy, the steel producer would move from the industrial zone to a location 4.2 miles from the residential district, decreasing its total cost from $70 to $53.

The effluent-fee policy is more efficient than the zoning policy for two reasons. First, the effluent policy allows the firm to choose the location that minimizes production cost. From the social perspective, the new location is more efficient because the savings in commuting cost (as indicated by the labor-cost curve) exceed the increase in pollution cost (as indicated by the pollution-cost curve). Second, the effluent-fee policy forces the firm to pay for pollution, so pollution decreases to its optimum level.

Will all the polluting firms leave the industrial zone when the city switches from industrial zoning to effluent fees? A firm will stay in the industrial zone if the pollution-cost curve is steeper than the labor-cost curve. In this case, a move toward the residential district increases pollution cost by more than it decreases labor cost, so total production cost increases. Nonetheless, the effluent-fee policy is still more efficient than industrial zoning because the effluent-fee policy decreases pollution to its optimum level.

Why do cities use zoning instead of effluent fees to control industrial pollution? There are two principal reasons. First, industrial zoning is simple compared to a system of spatial effluent fees. To set the effluent fees, the city would have to estimate the marginal external cost of pollution for different locations in the city, and to collect the fees, the city would have to monitor the polluting firms. It would certainly be easier to put all the polluters in an industrial zone. Second, a switch from zoning to effluent fees may increase pollution in some neighborhoods. Although the factory produces less pollution under the effluent-fee policy, it may locate closer to the residential district. Therefore, some neighborhoods may become more polluted. The fact that pollution is at its optimum level is small consolation to those who breathe the dirty air. The switch to effluent fees would improve efficiency and generate a net gain for society, so it would be possible, in principle, to compensate those who breathe dirtier air. In fact, compensation is rarely attempted, so local opposition to effluent fees remains.

Performance Zoning.   Traditional zoning is based on a zoning map and a land-use list. The zoning map shows the zoning classification for each plot of land in the city, and the list shows the admissible land uses for each zoning classification. If an activity is designated *heavy industry,* every firm involved in this activity must locate in the heavy-industry zone, regardless of how much noise, odor, or smoke the individual firms actually generate. The alternative to traditional zoning is **performance zoning**, under which the city sets performance standards for each zone. For industrial uses, performance standards typically set upper limits for the amount of noise, glare, odor, vibration, gas, and smoke emitted by the firms. Performance zoning is a sort of compromise between traditional zoning and effluent fees: although performance zoning does not force firms to pay for pollution, it does encourage abatement because it gives cleaner firms more location options.

Retail Nuisances.   Retailers generate a number of externalities that affect nearby residents. The traffic generated by retailers causes congestion, noise, and parking problems. A traditional zoning plan establishes retail zones to decrease the exposure to these externalities. For example, zoning prevents the invasion of quiet residential neighborhoods by shoppers and delivery trucks.

Under performance zoning, the city allows retailers in a particular zone as long as they satisfy performance standards for parking, traffic, and noise. For each area, the city may specify a minimum number of parking places, a minimum speed for traffic, and a maximum noise level. These performance standards force commercial developments to provide off-street parking to control parking problems, signalization and street improvements to control traffic problems, and berms and landscaping to control noise problems. Performance zoning allows the mixing of commercial and residential land uses because retailers take steps that shield residents from the undesirable effects of commercial development.

Residential Nuisances. Most residential externalities are generated by high-density housing. Suppose that a developer builds a four-story apartment complex in a neighborhood with single-family homes. The apartment complex increases traffic volume, increasing congestion and noise, and increases the demand for on-street parking, causing a shortage of parking spaces. In addition, the tall apartment building is likely to deprive neighbors of scenic views and sunlight.

Under conventional zoning, the apartment building would be excluded from the low-density neighborhood. Conventional zoning shields the residents of single-family homes from externalities by excluding high-density housing.

The alternative to conventional zoning is performance zoning. Under a performance-based zoning policy, the apartment complex would be allowed if the developer took the following steps:

1. **Off-street parking.** The developer provides enough off-street parking to prevent parking problems.

2. **Street improvements.** The developer pays for street improvements that prevent congestion problems.

3. **Building design.** The building is designed to prevent loss of views and sunlight. The developer uses landscaping to establish a buffer between the apartment building and the single-family homes.

The idea behind performance zoning is that the apartment building should be judged on the basis of its actual effects on the neighborhood, not on the simple fact that it is high-density housing. If a high-density project does not generate externalities, it would be allowed in the neighborhood.

Income-Related Residential Externalities. There are three types of residential externalities that encourage wealthy households to exclude poor ones.

1. **Education.** As explained in Chapter 21 (Education), the students from poor families have low achievement levels and pull down the achievement levels of other students. By excluding poor households, wealthy households may improve the quality of neighborhood schools.

2. **Crime.** As explained in Chapter 22 (Crime and Punishment), crime is more prevalent among the poor because they have a lower opportunity cost of crime (fewer legal opportunities) and punishment (lower opportunity cost of prison time). By excluding poor households, wealthy households may decrease the neighborhood crime rate.

3. **Housing externalities.** Housing is a normal good, so the poor consume less housing. In addition to consuming fewer square feet of living space, they also spend less on upkeep and the external appearance of their houses and lots. Because the market value of a particular house depends in part on the external appearance of neighboring houses, property values are typically lower in neighborhoods with a large number of poor households. By excluding poor households, wealthy households may keep their property values high.

Fiscal Zoning

The second type of zoning occurs because local governments finance public services with the property tax. Under **fiscal zoning,** a city excludes households that would impose fiscal burdens on local government. Suppose that a household consumes $3,000 worth of local services but pays only $2,000 in local property taxes. Such a household generates a fiscal burden because its tax contribution is less than the cost of its local public services. Fiscal burdens may be generated by (1) households living in high-density housing, (2) households living in the fringe areas of the city, and (3) new commercial and industrial development.

High-Density Housing.   As explained in Chapter 18 (Local Taxes and Intergovernmental Grants), the most important source of local revenue is the property tax. Because a household's tax liability increases with its housing consumption, a household in a small house or apartment pays a relatively small amount in taxes, and is therefore more likely to impose a fiscal burden on local government. Local governments exclude households by zoning for low-density (high-value) housing.

Large-lot zoning establishes a minimum lot size for residential development. Land and housing are complementary goods, so the city can use restrictions on lot size to indirectly establish a minimum house value. Suppose that a city breaks even on a house worth $125,000: the tax liability of such a house equals the cost of supplying public services to the household living in the house. According to one rule of thumb, the market value of land is about 20 percent of the total property value (the value of the structure and the land). If the price of land is $50,000 per acre, a half-acre lot ($25,000 worth of land) produces a house worth $125,000 (five times $25,000). A minimum lot size of one half an acre ensures that the government breaks even on all new houses.

To explain the effects of large-lot zoning on the urban land market, consider an unzoned city with 120 acres of undeveloped land. As shown in Figure 11–5, the equilibrium price of land is $20,000 per acre. At this price, the total demand for land equals the fixed supply, and land is divided equally between single-family homes (SFHs) and apartments (60 acres in each).

Suppose that the city passes a zoning ordinance that limits apartment buildings to a total of 40 acres of land. What happens to the equilibrium price of land? In Figure 11–5, the city moves up the demand curve for apartment land from point *B* to point *E:* since only 40 acres are available for apartments, developers are willing to pay $40,000 per acre for apartment land. At the same time, the city moves down the other demand curve from point *A* to point *C:* there are now 80 acres available for single-family homes, and the surplus of land decreases the price per acre from $20,000 to $15,000.

This example shows the effects of large-lot zoning on landowners and housing consumers. Zoning makes land for apartments a relatively scarce commodity, so the owners of apartment land gain from large-lot zoning. In contrast, zoning makes land for single-family homes a more plentiful commodity, so the owners of land destined for single-family homes lose. What about housing consumers? The increase in the cost of apartment land increases the costs of apartments, so apartment dwellers lose. In contrast, the land cost of single-family homes decreases, so home buyers gain.

FIGURE 11–5   **Large-Lot Zoning and the Price of Land**

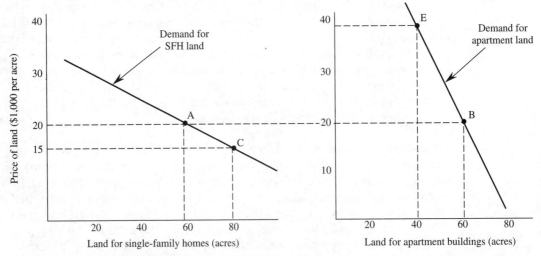

A fixed amount of land (120 acres) is divided between single-family homes and apartments. In the absence of large-lot zoning, the price of land is $20,000 per acre, and land is divided equally between apartments and homes (60 acres for each type of housing; points *A* and *B*). If apartment acreage is limited to 40 acres (point *E*), 80 acres are left for single-family homes (point *C*). The price of apartment land rises to $40,000, and the price of land for single-family homes drops to $15,000.

Exclusionary and Inclusionary Zoning.   Large-lot zoning is often labeled **exclusionary zoning** because it excludes low-income households. The exclusion is both direct and indirect. In the example above, large-lot zoning prevented the construction of 20 acres of apartments. Because low-income households are more likely to occupy apartments, the decrease in the number of apartment buildings decreases the number of low-income residents. In addition, the zoning policy increases the price of apartments, indirectly excluding low-income households: the apartments that are built are too expensive for many poor households.

In response to the exclusion problem, many cities have developed **inclusionary zoning** policies. Under an inclusionary housing program, the local government forces local developers to build dwellings for low-income households. The dwellings are typically sold to low-income households for less than the cost of construction. By providing subsidized dwellings for low-income residents, the local community partly offsets the exclusionary effects of fiscal zoning. Most dwellings built for inclusionary purposes are not typical low-income dwellings, but are medium-income dwellings provided to the poor at the price of low-income dwellings.

Who pays for inclusionary zoning? The requirement of subsidized housing has the same effect as a development tax. Suppose that a developer builds five inclusionary units and loses $10,000 per unit, generating a total loss of $50,000. If the developer is allowed to build 50 houses for the open market, the effective tax per market dwelling is $1,000 ($50,000 divided by 50). The developer makes zero economic profit (normal accounting profit) with or without inclusionary zoning, so the implicit tax is passed on to consumers (housing prices increase) and landowners (the price of vacant land decreases). In other words, housing consumers and landowners pay for inclusionary zoning.

Fringe Land Use. New housing is usually built on the fringe of the metropolitan area. If the costs of supplying public services are higher in fringe areas, the tax contribution of new housing may be less than the cost of public services. Therefore, new housing may impose a fiscal burden on the city.

To explain the fiscal burden of fringe housing, consider a city with the following characteristics:

1. The current average cost of public services is $500 per household per year.
2. The typical household owns a house worth $50,000 and pays a property tax of $500 per year (1 percent of market value).
3. A developer has proposed a new residential development on fringe land. The market value of the new houses is the same as existing houses ($50,000).
4. The new development would require the expansion of the city's public services (widening of streets, expansion of the sewage system, extension of bus routes). The full cost of serving the new houses would be $600 per house per year.

Given these assumptions, every new house generates a fiscal burden of $100 per year ($600 − $500). A simple way to prevent the new development and the associated fiscal burden is to zone the vacant land for agricultural use. If the city sets a minimum lot size of 20 acres, no additional houses will be built on the land, so the expansion of city services is unnecessary.

An alternative to low-density zoning is a tax surcharge for new development. Suppose that the city imposes an annual surcharge of $100 per new house. The annual tax liability of new housing would be $600 ($500 in property tax plus the $100 surcharge), and the occupants of new housing would pay the full cost of the new public services. The surcharge would eliminate the fiscal burden of new housing, so the city would be more likely to approve the development project.

An alternative to an annual tax surcharge is a one-time **impact fee** or **development tax**. By paying an impact fee, the developer compensates the local government for the fiscal burden of new housing. If the city collects a $1,000 impact fee from the developer and invests the money in the bank at a 10 percent interest rate, it can use the annual interest earnings ($100) to cover the difference between the tax contribution and the public-service cost of new housing. Who pays the impact fee? In a competitive market, the developer makes zero economic profits, so the fee is passed on to consumers (housing prices increase) and landowners (land prices decrease).

Lillydahl et al. (1988) describe impact-fee policies in four states: California, Florida, Oregon, and Colorado. In California, local communities are allowed to impose fees for transportation facilities (bridges, major thoroughfares, and freeways), drainage facilities, sewers, parks, and schools. In 1985, the average impact charge was $3,527 per dwelling in the San Francisco Bay area and $9,500 in San Diego. In Florida, the most common impact fees are for water and sewers; in 1985, the average impact fee was about $3,000 per dwelling. In Oregon, impact fees are called *systems development charges,* and are typically used to support water, sewer, street, and park facilities. During the 1980s, impact fees averaged about $2,500 per dwelling in the Portland metropolitan area. In Colorado, cities along the Front Range (from Colorado Springs to Fort Collins and including the Denver area) impose impact fees most frequently for water, sewers, parks and recreation, drainage, and street facilities.

Commercial and Industrial Development.   In some cities, commercial and industrial development generates fiscal burdens. If the city cannot pass on the cost of new infrastructure to new firms and employees, it may restrict development by (1) limiting the supply of commercial and industrial land and (2) restricting building heights.

The city of San Francisco recently adopted a zoning plan that restricts building heights in its downtown area. The objective of the policy is to limit the number of people working downtown. By limiting the number of downtown workers, city officials hope to control the volume of traffic on the bridges into the city, all of which are already congested. An alternative to the zoning policy would be to increase the carrying capacity of the bridges, with the cost of the capacity expansion imposed on new employers. Since this is impractical, the city has decided to use its zoning policy to limit total employment.

Some cities impose impact fees on commercial and industrial developers, using the revenue from the fees to expand local transportation networks. For example, in the Westchester area of western Los Angeles, developers pay a one-time fee of $2,010 for each additional rush-hour trip generated by new office buildings. The revenue from the impact fee is used to widen the roads used by the employees of the new office buildings. Impact fees can reduce the fiscal burden of new development, decreasing the opposition to development.

Design Zoning

The third type of zoning is a form of macroarchitecture. Just as an architect designs an individual house, the planner designs a city, arranging activities to promote the efficient use of the city's infrastructure (streets, sewage systems, water systems). Residential and employment growth is directed to areas where infrastructure can be efficiently provided. Design zoning is also used to preserve open space.

Directed Development.   Some cities use zoning to direct residential development to particular areas. To explain the effect of such zoning, consider a metropolitan area with the following characteristics:

1. There are 50 acres of vacant land: 25 acres to the north of the city and 25 acres to the south.
2. The city wants to accommodate 500 new households on its vacant land.
3. Under the initial zoning ordinance, both areas are zoned for 10 dwellings per acre: 250 households would live in the north and 250 would live in the south.

Suppose that the city changes its zoning policy. It decides to preserve the north area and accommodate all 500 households in the south area. It could do so by zoning the north area for low-density use and the south area for 20 dwellings per acre. What are the effects of the rezoning on land prices? The rezoning decreases the market price of northern land because the landowner has fewer land-use options. In contrast, the southern landowner has more options, so the price of southern land increases. The change in zoning policy is clearly inequitable: southern landowners gain at the expense of northern landowners.

An alternative to rezoning is a system of **transferable development rights (TDRs).** Under a TDR policy, the city establishes a **preservation zone** (the north area) and a **development zone** (the south area). The south area is zoned for 10 dwellings per acre, giving Mr. South (the southern landowner) the right to build a total of 250 dwellings. Ms. North (the northern landowner) is not allowed to develop her land, but is instead issued 250 development coupons. These development coupons can be used to override zoning restrictions in the development zone. If South wants to build 20 dwellings on one acre of land, he must purchase 10 development coupons from North. The TDR policy gives each landowner development rights (the right to build 250 houses) and allows the owners of preserved land to transfer their development rights to other areas of the city. When the northern landowner sells her coupons, she is at least partially compensated for the losses in property value caused by the rezoning of her land.

Figure 11–6 shows the effects of zoning and TDRs on the prices of southern and northern land. In the initial equilibrium (both areas zoned for 10 dwellings per acre), land sells for $50,000 per acre. Suppose that northern land is zoned for preservation, but southern land is still zoned for 10 dwellings per acre. The rezoning of northern land decreases its price to $30,000 because the landowner has fewer development options. When northern land is taken off the residential market, the resulting shortage of residential land increases the price of southern land to $60,000. Under a TDR policy, northern landowners receive development coupons that can be used to override the density limits (10 dwellings per acre) in the development zone. The relaxation of density limits gives southern landowners more development options, increasing the market value of their land from $60,000 to $75,000. Southern landowners are willing to pay up to $15,000 for an acre's worth of development coupons, so the market value of an acre's worth of transferable development rights is $15,000.

The TDRs diminish the inequities caused by preservation zoning. In the absence of the transferable rights, the owner of the preserved land suffers a loss of $20,000 per acre ($50,000 − $30,000). In contrast, if the allowable density is 20 dwellings per acre, the southern landowner receives a gain of $25,000 per acre. Under the TDR policy, the owner of the preserved land sells her development rights to the landowners in the development zone for $15,000 per acre, so her net loss from the zoning policy is only $5,000. In contrast, the landowner in the development zone pays $15,000 per acre for the rights to build more than 10 dwellings per acre, so his net gain from the zoning policy is only $10,000 per acre.

What determines the market value of the development coupons? The coupons have a positive price because they allow landowners in the development zone to exceed the normal density restrictions. The market price depends on the power of the

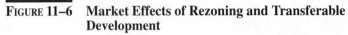

FIGURE 11–6   **Market Effects of Rezoning and Transferable Development**

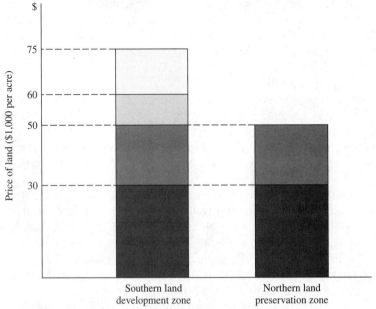

In the initial equilibrium, the price of land is $50,000 per acre. If the north area is rezoned for preservation, the demand for southern land will increase (increasing its price to $60,000), and the demand for northern land will decrease (decreasing its price to $30,000). Under a TDR policy, northern landowners receive development coupons that can be used to override density limits in the development zone. The relaxation of density limits increases the market value of southern land from $60,000 to $75,000, so southern landowners are willing to pay up to $15,000 for an acre's worth of development coupons.

coupons to override density restrictions: if the coupons allow a 100 percent increase in density, they are obviously more valuable than they would be under a 15 percent density bonus. The market price also depends on the underlying demand for high-density housing in the development zone. If households in the development demand low-density housing, a developer won't need the development coupons, and the market price of the coupons will be relatively low. In contrast, if there is a strong demand for high-density housing in the development zone, the market price of the coupons will be relatively high.

Open-Space Zoning.   Some cities zone parcels of land as "open space," "green belts," or "agricultural preserves." This type of zoning provides city dwellers with open space by denying landowners the full use of their land.

     Is open-space zoning efficient? The alternative to zoning is the outright purchase of land for open space. If the city were to purchase land instead of zoning it for open space, the city would preserve land only if the marginal benefit of open space exceeds

FIGURE 11–7   **Inefficiency of Open-Space Zoning**

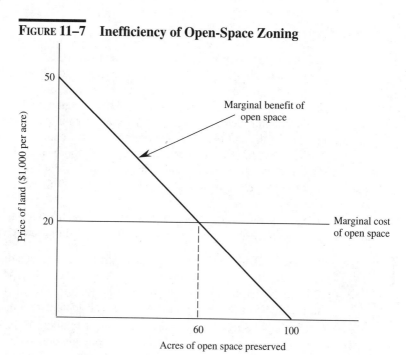

The opportunity cost of open space is the value of land in an alternative use (housing). The optimum amount of open space is 60 acres (where the marginal-benefit curve intersects the marginal-cost curve). If the government does not compensate landowners for open-space zoning, it will preserve 100 acres (the point at which the marginal benefit of open space is zero).

the marginal cost. If the city faces the full cost of open space, it chooses the optimum amount of open space. In contrast, if the city simply zones the land for open space, it is likely to consume too much open space.

Figure 11–7 shows the costs and benefits of open space. The marginal-benefit curve is negatively sloped, reflecting the diminishing marginal utility of open space. The marginal cost of open space is the opportunity cost of using the land for open space instead of residential development. For example, if housing developers are willing to pay $20,000 for undeveloped land, the marginal cost of open space is $20,000 per acre. If the city purchases land for open space, it will outbid developers for 60 acres of land. This is an efficient allocation of land: for the first 60 acres of open space, the value of land as open space exceeds the value of land in housing. For the 61st through the 100th acres, the value of land in housing exceeds the value as open space, so 40 acres are developed.

Suppose that the city simply zones land for open space. From the perspective of city officials, the marginal cost of open space is zero. The city preserves all land for which the marginal benefit (from the demand curve) is positive, so it zones for 100 acres of open space instead of 60. This is inefficient because the 61st through the 100th acres are more valuable as housing land.

A City without Zoning?

What would an unzoned city look like? Would glue factories and pizza parlors invade quiet residential neighborhoods? Would land use be disorderly and ugly?

Some tentative answers to these questions come from Siegan's (1972) analysis of Houston, the only metropolitan area in the United States without zoning. Land use in the city is controlled by restrictive covenants, voluntary agreements among landowners that limit land uses and structures. The covenants governing residential subdivisions (over 7,000 in number) are typically more strict than conventional zoning. They have detailed restrictions on architectural design, external appearance, and lot maintenance. The covenants for industrial parks limit the activities that can locate in the park.

How does Houston compare to zoned cities? Although a rigorous comparison of land-use patterns may be impossible, some tentative observations can be made:

1. **Dispersion of industry.** The spatial distribution of Houston's industrial firms is similar to that of zoned cities. As in other cities, Houston's industrial firms locate close to the transportation network (near railroads and highways) and tend to cluster to exploit localization economies.

2. **Retailers.** Like retailers in most cities, most retailers in Houston locate along major thoroughfares in strip developments and shopping centers. Few retailers locate in quiet residential neighborhoods. This is the same pattern observed in zoned cities. Retailers locate along major thoroughfares because such locations provide large volumes of foot and auto traffic. Many retailers are subject to shopping externalities (from the benefits of one-stop shopping and comparison shopping), so they cluster in shopping centers, malls, and downtown areas.

3. **Strip development.** Houston appears to have more strip development (retail and commercial establishments along arterial routes) than do zoned cities.

4. **Apartments.** Low-income housing is more plentiful and relatively inexpensive. There is a wide range of densities in apartment projects: the projects occupied by the wealthy have more open space and lower density, while the projects occupied by the poor have higher density.

5. **Single-family homes.** In some areas, Houston homes have relatively small backyards; in other areas, lot sizes are similar to those in zoned cities.

There are two lessons from Houston's experience without zoning. First, in the absence of zoning, landowners have the incentive to negotiate restrictions on land use. It seems that neighborhood externalities are large enough to justify the cost of developing and enforcing restrictive covenants. This is the **Coase solution** to externalities (named after R. H. Coase): the parties affected by externalities negotiate a contract to solve the externality problem. Second, in the absence of zoning, most industrial firms cluster in locations accessible to the transportation network, and most retailers cluster in shopping centers and retail strips. If a city were to drop its zoning plan, it is unlikely that glue factories and pizza parlors would invade quiet residential neighborhoods.

The Legal Environment of Land-Use Controls

Local governments, which are creatures of state governments, derive their power to control land use from the states. In most states, enabling legislation for zoning is patterned after the Standard State Zoning Enabling Act, which was developed by the U.S. Department of Commerce in 1926. Section 1 of the Enabling Act states:

> Grant of Power. For the purpose of promoting health, safety, morals, or the general welfare of the community, the legislative body of cities and incorporated villages is hereby empowered to regulate and restrict the height, number of stories, and size of buildings and other structures, the percentage of the lot that may be occupied, the size of yards, courts, and other open spaces, the density of population, and the location and use of buildings, structures, and land for trade, industry, residence, or other purposes.

The model legislation grants local governments broad powers in the regulation of land use. Zoning is considered a legitimate exercise of the **police power** of local government if it promotes the public health, safety, and welfare.

Current zoning laws are the result of over 60 years of legal decisions. In the last six decades, individuals affected by specific zoning laws have sued local governments, forcing state and federal courts to rule on the constitutionality of zoning ordinances. If a particular type of zoning is declared unconstitutional, all cities get the message from the courts, and rewrite their zoning ordinances to drop the illegal practices. On the other hand, if a zoning practice is upheld as constitutional, the practice spreads to other local governments. In other words, zoning law is evolutionary. Early court decisions established three criteria for the constitutionality of zoning: substantive due process, equal protection, and just compensation.

Substantive Due Process

The case of *Euclid* v. *Ambler* (1924) established the standards for **substantive due process**. According to the due-process criterion, zoning must be executed for a legitimate public purpose using reasonable means. In the early 1920s, the city of Euclid, Ohio, enacted a zoning ordinance that restricted the location, size, and height of various types of buildings. Ambler Realty had purchased some property between the railroad tracks and a major thoroughfare, and expected to sell the land to an industrial developer. When the city zoned its land for residential use, Ambler sued, claiming that the separation of industrial and residential land uses did not serve a legitimate public purpose. The Supreme Court ruled against Ambler, concluding that the zoning ordinance satisfied the standards for substantive due process because it had some "reasonable relation" to the promotion of "health, safety, morals, and general welfare." In other words, nuisance zoning (separating different land uses) is a legitimate use of the city's police power because it promotes public health and safety.

One interpretation of the *Euclid* decision is that a zoning ordinance is constitutional as long as it generates some benefit for the local community. The court did not say that the benefits of zoning must exceed its costs, but that the benefits of zoning must be positive. Fischel (1985) calls this *benefit* analysis, as opposed to *benefit-cost* analysis. The court defined the possible social benefits from zoning in broad terms, to include monetary, physical, spiritual, and aesthetic benefits.

Equal Protection

The second criterion for the constitutionality of zoning is **equal protection.** The equal-protection clause of the Fourteenth Amendment requires that all laws be applied in an impersonal (nondiscriminatory) fashion.

Recent court cases have tested whether fiscal zoning violates the principle of equal protection. Fiscal zoning excludes households who do not pay their share of the cost of local public services. Local governments have been sued by people outside the city, who claim that fiscal zoning systematically excludes some types of people from the city. The plaintiffs argue that zoning laws are not applied in an impersonal manner, but instead treat some people differently than others: rich and poor are treated differently, as are whites and blacks.

The federal courts have upheld the constitutionality of exclusionary zoning. In the *Euclid* decision, the Supreme Court suggested that although a zoning ordinance must generate some benefit for insiders (citizens of the community), the effects of zoning on outsiders are unimportant. In *Warth* v. *Selden* (1975), the court dismissed the claims of outsiders because they did not prove that the zoning ordinance caused specific personal damage. In *Village of Arlington Heights* v. *Metropolitan Housing Corporation* (1977), the court dismissed the claims of outsiders because they did not prove discriminatory intent on the part of zoning officials. In *Ybarra* v. *Town of Los Altos Hills,* the court ruled that although zoning laws that discriminate on the basis of race are unconstitutional, zoning laws that discriminate on the basis of income are legal. In general, the federal courts have adopted a noninterventionist approach to exclusionary zoning.

Some state courts have adopted a more activist role. In *Southern Burlington County NAACP* v. *Mount Laurel* (1975), the New Jersey Supreme Court ruled that Mount Laurel's exclusionary zoning harmed low-income outsiders. The court directed the city to develop a new zoning plan under which the city would accommodate its "fair share" of low-income residents. The implication from *Associated Home Builders Inc.* v. *City of Livermore* (California Supreme Court, 1976) is that the courts will judge zoning on the basis of its effects on both insiders and outsiders. If a zoning ordinance does not represent a reasonable accommodation of the competing interests of insiders and outsiders, it may be declared unconstitutional. In Oregon, state law requires municipalities to plan and zone land for a diversity of housing types and income levels. According to Fischel (1985), few state courts have followed the lead of the New Jersey court, so the *Mount Laurel* decision has not affected exclusionary zoning practices in many states. Given the decisions from federal courts, exclusionary zoning is still considered legal.

Just Compensation

The third criterion for the constitutionality of zoning is **just compensation**. The Fifth Amendment states "... nor shall private property be taken for public use, without just compensation." This is the **taking clause**: if the government converts land from private to public use, the landlord must be compensated.

How is the taking clause applied to zoning? Most zoning ordinances do not actually convert land to public use, but merely restrict private use. For example, nuisance zoning prevents a landowner from building a factory in a residential area, and large-lot zoning prevents a landowner from building high-density housing. By restricting the use of private land, zoning decreases the market value of the property. The policy issue is whether landowners should be compensated for the loss of property value caused by zoning. For example, if large-lot zoning decreases a landowner's property value by $5,000, should the local government pay $5,000 in compensation?

According to Fischel (1985), the courts have provided mixed and confusing signals to local zoning authorities. The courts routinely uphold zoning laws that cause large losses in property values, suggesting that as long as the landowner is left with some profitable use of his land, compensation is not required. The courts have developed four rules to determine whether compensation is required.

1. **Physical invasion.** Compensation is required if the government physically occupies the land. The invasion rule is applicable only when the government actually occupies the land. It does not apply to most zoning actions, in which the government merely restricts private land use.

2. **Diminution of value and reasonable beneficial use.** The origin of this rule is *Pennsylvania Coal* v. *Mahon* (1922), in which Justice Holmes states, "... while property may be regulated to a certain extent, if regulation goes too far it will be recognized as a taking." In other words, compensation is required if zoning decreases the property value by a sufficiently large amount. Unfortunately, the courts have not indicated how far zoning must go before compensation is required. A related rule is **reasonable beneficial use:** if zoning leaves the landowner with options that provide a reasonable rate of return, no compensation is required.

3. **Balancing means (benefit-cost).** According to this rule, compensation is required if the cost of a zoning ordinance (the loss in property value) exceeds the benefit to the local community. Because this rule requires compensation for inefficient zoning ordinances, it discourages inefficient zoning practices. For example, suppose that a zoning ordinance decreases property values by $50 and generates a $30 benefit to the community. According to the balancing-means rule, compensation must be paid. Taxpayers will oppose the ordinance because the cost of compensating landowners exceeds the benefit generated by the ordinance. If the balancing-means rule were used, voters would approve only efficient zoning ordinances.

4. **Harm prevention.** According to this rule, compensation is not required if the zoning ordinance prevents a harmful use of the land. In other words, zoning is not a taking if it prevents the landowner from using land in ways that are detrimental to the general public. The harm-prevention rule suggests that a landowner, like a car owner, has limited property rights. The car owner has the right to drive her car, but she must stop at red lights. Should the driver be compensated for the opportunity cost of time spent waiting for the light to turn green? Since the traffic lights prevent a harmful use of the car, compensation is not required. Similarly, landowners have limited property rights: if zoning prevents the landlord from building a polluting factory in a residential district, compensation is unnecessary because nuisance zoning prevents a harmful use of the land. Most zoning ordinances are judged by a broad interpretation of the harm-prevention rule: if an ordinance promotes public health, safety, or welfare, compensation is usually not required.

Summary

1. Some cities use land-use regulations to control population growth.
   a. An urban service boundary controls population growth by decreasing the supply of land available for development. Land prices within the boundary increase, and prices outside the boundary decrease.
   b. A limit on building permits decreases the number of houses that can be built, increasing housing prices and decreasing land prices.
2. A zoning plan designates a set of admissible land uses for each plot of land in the city. There are three types of zoning: nuisance zoning, fiscal zoning, and design zoning.
3. Nuisance zoning decreases the exposure to pollution, noise, and congestion externalities.
   a. An alternative to industrial zoning is a system of spatial effluent fees.
   b. An alternative to industrial and commercial zoning is performance zoning, under which the city develops performance standards for noise, glare, odor, smoke, parking, and traffic.
   c. High-density housing produces congestion, noise, and parking problems, and sometimes blocks light and views. Performance zoning can be used to shield low-density housing from these effects, allowing high-density housing to locate near single-family homes.
   d. In the absence of conventional residential nuisances (traffic, blocked views and light) and fiscal problems, the wealthy still have the incentive to exclude the poor. By doing so, they may increase school achievement, decrease crime rates, and protect property values.

4. Fiscal zoning excludes households who impose a fiscal burden on the city. Fiscal burdens may be generated by high-density housing, fringe housing, and new commercial and industrial development.

5. Local governments use large-lot zoning to exclude high-density (low-income) housing.
   a. Zoning decreases the supply of high-density housing, excluding the poor in two ways: there are fewer low-income dwellings and the available dwellings are more expensive.
   b. The price of land zoned for high-density housing increases, and the price of land zoned for low-density housing decreases.

6. Under an inclusionary zoning policy, developers provide subsidized new dwellings to low-income residents. The cost of inclusionary housing is borne by housing consumers (higher housing prices) and landowners (lower land prices).

7. Fringe development often imposes a fiscal burden on the city: the taxes from new development fall short of the cost of extending public services to the urban fringe.
   a. Cities prevent fringe development by zoning vacant land for low-density use (e.g., agriculture).
   b. The alternative to fiscal zoning is a system of impact fees or development taxes.

8. Commercial development sometimes generates fiscal burdens. If the city cannot pass the cost of new infrastructure on to new firms and employees, it may limit the supply of land and restrict building heights. Some cities use impact fees to pay for new infrastructure.

9. Design zoning is a form of macroarchitecture: zoning promotes the efficient use of infrastructure and provides open space.
   a. Some cities use zoning to direct development to particular areas and use transferable development rights to prevent horizontal inequities.
   b. In the absence of compensation, open-space zoning produces an inefficient amount of open space.

10. The market value of a development coupon is determined by (*a*) the power of the coupon to override density restrictions and (*b*) the underlying demand for high-density housing in the development zone.

11. The zoning authority of local governments comes from state governments. There are three criteria for the constitutionality of zoning: due process, equal protection, and just compensation.
    a. Zoning satisfies the due-process criterion if it promotes public health, safety, and welfare.
    b. Federal courts have rejected the claims that fiscal (exclusionary) zoning violates the equal-protection clause of the U.S. Constitution. In contrast, some state courts have declared fiscal zoning unconstitutional.
    c. Zoning is one of the police powers of local government, so compensation is generally not required.

Exercises and Discussion Questions

1. In Figure 11–3, the equilibrium price of building permits is $30,000. Suppose that the demand curve shifts down and intersects the supply curve at a quantity of 50 dwellings per year. What is the equilibrium price of permits?

2. In the analysis of the building-permit policy (Figure 11–3), the decrease in the number of building permits (from 100 to 60) increased the equilibrium price of housing but decreased the price of land. Critically appraise the following statement from a landowner who recently read Chapter 7 of *Urban Economics:* "According to the leftover principle, the landowner gets the leftover (the excess of total revenue over total cost), so an increase in the price of housing should increase—not decrease—the price of land. Either the leftover principle is wrong or the analysis of the permit policy is wrong."

3. Consider the building-permit policy depicted in Figure 11–3, with an equilibrium price of permits equal to $30,000. Suppose that the city announces on January 1 that 300 days later (October 28) it will give the 60 permits to the first 60 licensed building contractors through the planning office door. Because the police department expects a line to form outside the planning office, the police chief announces that the following queuing rules will be enforced:

   i. No cuts: when a person joins the queue, he or she goes to the end of the queue.

   ii. No substitutions: no one can reserve a place in line for anyone else.

   To receive a permit, a licensed contractor must be one of the first 60 people in line and must remain in the line until October 28. Therefore, instead of an equilibrium price for the permits, there is an equilibrium waiting time (time spent in line). Suppose that 25 of the city's 100 licensed contractors have an opportunity cost of $150 per day; 25 have an opportunity cost of $300 per day; 25 have an opportunity cost of $600 per day; and 25 have an opportunity cost of $1,000 per day.

   a. What is the equilibrium waiting time?

   b. Suppose that the city eliminates the no-substitution rule. Would you expect the equilibrium waiting time to increase, decrease, or not change?

4. Use Figure 11–4 to show the effects of the following changes on the optimum location of the polluting factory. Do the changes cause the optimum location to move closer to or farther from the residential area?

   a. The unit commuting cost (cost per mile) increases.

   b. Residents become more sensitive to pollution.

   c. The polluting firm discovers a new method of pollution abatement that cuts abatement cost in half.

5. Consider a city where a polluting industry is separated from the residential area by a 5-mile buffer. The following table lists the wages and effluent fees for different locations within the buffer zone: the closer the firm to the residential district, the lower the wage and the higher the effluent fee. Sup-

pose that the firm uses 450 hours of labor per week and generates 20 units of pollution per week.

Commute Distance (miles)	Effluent Fee ($ per ton)	Wage ($ per hour)
5	1.0	10.0
4	2.5	9.9
3	4.5	9.8
2	7.0	9.7
1	10.0	9.6

    a. Assume that the quantities of output and input are constant. What is the optimum location for the firm?

    b. What is the social cost of the segregation zoning policy? In other words, if the city prevents the firm from locating at its optimum location, what is the cost to society?

6. Suppose that a city eliminates all zoning. What types of retailers would you expect to move from the retail zones to the residential zones?

7. Suppose that all local taxes are eliminated and all funding for local public services comes from state governments. Would you expect any changes in local zoning practices?

8. Suppose that you are a member of the zoning board in a growing city. A residential developer appears before the board with a proposal to develop a parcel of land at the city's edge. The proposed development would increase the population of the city by 5 percent. The developer makes the following statements:

    i. Because the development will increase the population of the city by 5 percent, it will increase tax revenue by 5 percent.

    ii. Because the development will increase the population of the city by 5 percent, it will increase the total cost of public services by 5 percent.

    iii. Given (*i*) and (*ii*), the development will not create a fiscal burden on the city, and therefore should be approved.

    a. How would you respond to statements (*i*) and (*ii*)? Are the developer's calculations correct?

    b. What additional information would you need to evaluate the fiscal effects of the proposed development?

9. In a certain city, all new housing is built on the city's edge (10 miles from the city center). The city institutes the following policy: every new house will be subject to a $1,000 impact fee or development tax. The fee is paid by the firm that builds the house.

    a. Who will actually pay the development tax?

    b. Will the development tax affect the radius of the city? Explain, using a graph.

    c. Would you expect the implementation of the development tax to change the city's zoning practices?

10. In Figure 11–5, large-lot zoning increases the price of apartment land and decreases the price of land for single-family homes. Under what circumstances (what values of the relevant elasticities) will the zoning policy increase the total value of land in the city?

11. Consider a large metropolitan area in which there is a large number of suburban municipalities, each of which has some vacant land. In each municipality except municipality Z, high-density housing (apartments) is explicitly outlawed. Suppose that Z starts out with no controls on residential land use, and its vacant land is expected to be divided equally between high-density housing (apartments) and single-family homes (SFHs). The price of land for apartments equals the price of land for SFHs. Suppose that Z institutes a large-lot zoning policy that limits high-density housing to one quarter of its available land.
    a. Depict graphically the effects of Z's zoning policy on the prices of apartment land and SFH land within the municipality.
    b. Will the zoning policy increase or decrease the total value of land within municipality Z?

12. Suppose that a city has recently proposed the rezoning of a 10-acre parcel of land, from low-density use (1 dwelling per acre) to high-density use (20 dwellings per acre).
    a. Who will support the zoning change? Who will oppose the rezoning?
    b. Describe a policy under which all parties will agree to the rezoning if in fact the rezoning is efficient.

13. Ollie recently bought the Notel Hotel in downtown Portland and intends to demolish the hotel and replace it with an office building with 100,000 square feet of office space. When the city planner hears about Ollie's plans, he quickly rezones the hotel site as a historical preserve, preventing the demolition of the hotel.
    a. You have been asked to estimate Ollie's loss from the rezoning of his land. What information would you collect, and how would you use it?
    b. The city offers Ollie development coupons (TDRs) that permit the development of 100,000 square feet of office space somewhere else in the city. What determines the market value of the coupons?
    c. Under what circumstances will Ollie be worse off as a result of the zoning and TDR policy?

14. Consider the North/South TDR example in the section on design zoning. Suppose that instead of issuing 10 development coupons per acre (250 in total), the government issues 5 per acre (125 total).
    a. Will the new policy increase or decrease the equilibrium price of TDRs?
    b. Under what conditions (what values of the relevant elasticities) will the typical TDR recipient be better off with 5 coupons instead of 10?

15. Suppose that city U establishes an urban service boundary five miles from the city center. People who own land outside the boundary object to it and demand compensation. Design a practical scheme under which those who are harmed by the service boundary will be compensated for their losses. Be

specific. How will the money for compensation be raised? Who will actually pay for the compensation package? How will you determine the amount of compensation per landowner?

16. Using Figure 11–7, compute the total welfare loss caused by a switch from the optimum policy (purchase of land for open space) to open-space zoning.

17. Suppose that a city provides open space by purchasing land from landowners, not by zoning land for open space. If someone suggests that the city buy another plot of land for open space, the mayor appears on local television and solicits contributions to the city's open-space fund. The city will purchase the land for open space if the total contributions exceed the market price of the land. If the contributions do not cover the cost of the land, the city will not buy the land and will return the contributions to the individual donors. Will the city provide the optimum amount of open space?

18. Consider the following quote: "Depending on the variable one controls, a zoning policy may either increase or decrease the price of undeveloped land within and around the zoned city." Explain this statement, using examples of the variables that are controlled by the various zoning policies.

19. Consider two of the compensation rules developed by the courts: the *diminution-of-value* rule and the *balancing-means* rule. Will these rules promote horizontal equity (the equal treatment of equals)?

20. Comment on the following statement: "The courts should not be involved in overseeing local zoning practice. Such matters are the responsibility of the legislative branch of government. Let democracy work."

References and Additional Readings

General Readings on Land-Use Controls and Zoning

Bosselman, Fred; David Callies; and John Banta. *The Taking Issue*. Washington, D.C.: Council on Environmental Quality, 1973. A history of zoning that focuses on the issue of compensation.

Delafons, John. *Land-Use Controls in the United States*. Cambridge, Mass.: MIT Press, 1969. A history of zoning and other land-use controls.

Fagin, Henry. "Regulating the Timing of Urban Development." *Management and Control of Growth*, vol. 1. Washington, D.C.: The Urban Land Institute, 1975. Discusses the reasons for design zoning.

Fischel, William. *The Economics of Zoning Laws*. Baltimore: Johns Hopkins, 1985. A comprehensive economic analysis of land-use zoning, including discussions of the legal foundations of zoning and the effects of zoning on housing prices and location patterns.

Lillydahl, Jane H.; Arthur C. Nelson; Timothy V. Ramis; Antero Rivasplata; and Steven R. Schell. "The Need for a Standard State Impact Fee Enabling Act." *Journal of the American Planning Association* 54 (Winter 1988), pp. 7–17. Describes impact-fee policies in four states (California, Florida, Oregon, and Colorado) and argues for a national standard for impact fees.

Mills, Edwin. "Economic Analysis of Urban Land-Use Controls." In *Current Issues in Urban Economics*, ed. Peter Mieszkowski and Mahlon Straszheim. Baltimore: Johns Hopkins, 1979. A discussion of the use of zoning as a means of controlling externalities. Includes a historical sketch of land-use controls.

Patterson, T. *Land Use Planning: Techniques of Implementation*. New York: Van Nostrand Reinhold, 1977. Chapter 2 describes the basic features of zoning policies.

Siegan, Bernard. *Land Use without Zoning*. Lexington, Mass.: D. C. Heath, 1972. A discussion of land use in Houston, a city without zoning.

Growth Controls

Alonso, William. "Urban Zero Population Growth." In *The Urban Economy*, ed. Harold M. Hochman. New York: W. W. Norton, 1976.

Cooley, Thomas F., and C. J. LaCivita. "A Theory of Growth Controls." *Journal of Urban Economics* 12 (1982), pp. 129–45. Explores the factors that lead communities to control population growth, including rising costs of public services and limitations on the property tax.

White, Michelle. "Self-Interest in the Suburbs: The Trend toward No-Growth Zoning." *Policy Analysis* 4 (1978), pp. 185–204. Discusses the reasons for no-growth zoning and suggests public policies that might reverse the no-growth trend.

Nuisance Zoning and Performance Zoning

Kendig, Lane. *New Standards for Nonresidential Uses*. Report 405. Chicago: American Society of Planning Officials, 1987. Shows how performance zoning can be used to control externalities from nonresidential land uses.

———. *Performance Zoning*. Chicago: American Planning Association, 1980. Discusses performance zoning as a means of controlling residential nuisances.

Meshenberg, Michael J. *The Administration of Flexible Zoning Techniques*. Report 318. Chicago: American Society of Planning Officials, 1976. Discusses various types of flexible zoning, including planned unit development, special permits, floating zones, overlay zoning, contract zoning, and transfer of development rights.

Moore, Terry. "Why Allow Planners to Do What They Do?" *American Institute of Planners Journal* 44 (1978), pp. 387–98. Describes the reasons for planning and zoning in terms of market failure.

Porter, Douglas R.; Patrick L. Phillips; and Terry J. Lassar. *Flexible Zoning: How It Works*. Washington, D.C.: Urban Land Institute, 1988. Contrasts traditional zoning with more flexible approaches developed in recent years. Discusses the effects of flexible zoning in seven communities.

Fiscal Zoning and Inclusionary Zoning

Brooks, Mary E. "Housing Trust Funds: Lessons from Inclusionary Zoning." In *Inclusionary Zoning Moves Downtown*, ed. Dwight Merriman, David J. Brower, and Philip D. Tegeler. Chicago: American Planning Association, 1985, pp. 7–22. Describes housing trust funds, which use money collected from office and commercial developers to subsidize new housing.

Davidoff, P., and L. Davidoff. "Opening the Suburbs: Toward Inclusionary Controls." *Management and Control of Growth* 1 (1975), pp. 540–50.

Dowall, David E. "The Effects of Tax and Expenditure Limitations on Local Land Use Policies." *Perspectives on Local Public Finance and Public Policy* 1 (1983), pp. 69–87. Suggests that fiscal limitations (e.g., Proposition 13) will make fiscal zoning more prevalent. Discusses the implications of fiscal zoning for housing costs and the imbalance between jobs and residents.

Franklin, H. M.; D. Falk; and A. Levin, *In-Zoning: A Guide for Policy Makers on Inclusionary Land Use Programs.* Washington, D.C.: Potomac Institute, 1974. Part I discusses the legal reasons for inclusionary zoning.

Schwartz, Seymour I., and Robert A. Johnston. "Inclusionary Housing Programs." *American Planning Association Journal* 49 (1983), pp. 3–21. Describes inclusionary programs in several California cities.

Transferable Development Rights

Roddewig, Richard J., and Cheryl A. Inghram. *Transferable Development Rights Programs: TDRs and the Real Estate Marketplace.* Report 401. Chicago: American Society of Planning Officials, 1987. Case studies of TDR programs in four cities (New York City, Denver, Seattle, San Francisco) and two counties. Also explores the legal foundations of TDRs.

Schnidman, F. "TDR: A Tool for More Equitable Land Management?" *Management and Control of Growth* 4 (1978), pp. 52–57.

The Administration of Zoning

Babcock, Richard R. *The Zoning Game.* Madison: University of Wisconsin Press, 1966. Discusses the political and legal aspects of zoning.

Babcock, Richard R., and Charles Siemon. *The Zoning Game Revisited.* Boston: Oelgeschlager, Gunn, and Hain, 1985. Accounts of 11 zoning conflicts.

Hinds, D.; N. Carn; and O. Ordway. *Winning at Zoning.* New York: McGraw-Hill, 1979. Gives practical tips for dealing with zoning authorities.

Market Effects of Zoning

Babcock, Richard. "The Spatial Impact of Land-Use and Environmental Controls." In *The Prospective City*, ed. Arthur Solomon. Cambridge, Mass.: MIT Press, 1980.

Courant, Paul N. "On the Effect of Fiscal Zoning on Land and Housing Values." *Journal of Urban Economics* 3 (1976), pp. 84–94. Explores the effect of fiscal zoning on total land value, reaching conclusions different from Ohls, Weisberg, and White.

Dowall, David E. "Reducing the Cost Effects of Local Land Use Controls." *Journal of the American Planning Association* 47 (1981), pp. 145–53. Discusses the effects of land-use controls on the prices of housing and land. Proposes a monitoring system to control the inflationary effects of land-use controls.

———. "The Suburban Squeeze: Land-Use Policies in the San Francisco Bay Area." *Cato Journal* 2 (1982), pp. 709–33. Discusses local land-use policies and their effects on the regional economy.

Grieson, Ronald E., and James R. White. "The Effects of Zoning on Structures and Land Markets." *Journal of Urban Economics* 10 (1981), pp. 271–85. Explores the effects of three types of zoning (restrictions on density, lot size, and allowable uses) on the prices of housing and land.

Lustig, Morton, and Janet Rothenberg Pack. "A Standard for Residential Zoning Based Upon the Location of Jobs." *Journal of the American Institute of Planners* 40 (1974), pp. 333–45. Proposes that residential zoning be used to match labor supply (residential land use) with labor demand (commercial and industrial land use).

Ohls, James C.; Richard C. Weisberg; and Michelle J. White. "The Effect of Zoning on Land Value." *Journal of Urban Economics* 1 (1974), pp. 428–44. Discusses the effect of fiscal zoning on (1) the value of land zoned for different uses and (2) total land value. Also discusses the trade-offs associated with nuisance zoning.

———. "Welfare Effects of Alternative Models of Zoning." *Journal of Urban Economics* 3 (1976), pp. 95–96. Discusses the reasons for the different conclusions of Courant.

White, Michelle J. "The Effect of Zoning on the Size of Metropolitan Areas." *Journal of Urban Economics* 2 (1975), pp. 279–90. Explores the effect of large-lot zoning on the land area and total land value of a metropolitan area, showing that the effects of zoning on both variables are ambiguous.

PART III

The Federal Response to Urban Problems

This section discusses two urban problems that are addressed by the federal government: poverty and housing. The federal government uses a number of policies to combat poverty, including cash assistance, education and training programs, and payments in kind (food stamps, medical care, housing assistance). The problem of inadequate housing is related to the poverty problem in the sense that an increase in income would allow an ill-housed family to move to a better dwelling. Most housing policies, like antipoverty policies, are redistributional in nature.

The federal government is responsible for income redistribution because local redistributional efforts will be weakened by the mobility of taxpayers and transfer recipients. Suppose that a city imposes a tax on its wealthy citizens to finance transfer payments to the poor. Some wealthy households would leave the city to escape the tax, and some poor households would enter the city to get the transfer payment. In combination, the flight of the wealthy and the migration of the poor would weaken the city's redistribution program: there would be less money to transfer to more poor households. A national redistribution program will be more successful because there is less mobility between nations than between cities.

There are four chapters in this section. Chapter 12 discusses the various causes of poverty, including slow economic growth, residential segregation, inadequate education, labor-market discrimination, and increases in female-headed households. Chapter 13 explores the effects of various types of antipoverty proposals to reform the current welfare system. Chapter 14 explains why housing is different from other goods. Chapter 15 takes a detailed look at several types of housing policies, including public housing, housing vouchers, and community-development programs.

What Causes Poverty?

Now, too much of nothing
Can make a man ill at ease.
One man's temper might rise
While another man's temper might freeze.
Bob Dylan

Although there are poor people in every segment of society, the incidence of poverty is greatest among women, children, racial minorities, and central-city residents. This chapter explores the various causes of poverty, including slow macroeconomic growth, racial segregation and discrimination, inferior education, and increases in the number of female-headed households. In the passionate debates over poverty, the facts on poverty are often overlooked, misunderstood, or manipulated to support a particular position. In the words of Mark Twain, some people "use the facts like a drunk uses a lamp post—for support, not illumination." An informed discussion of poverty and its policy implications must be preceded by a careful discussion of the facts. The first section of the chapter discusses the facts on poverty, many of which are in conflict with the popular images of poverty and the assumptions used in public debates.

Poverty Facts

What is poverty? The U.S. government defines a poor household as one whose total income is less than the amount required to satisfy the "minimum needs" of the household. The government estimates a minimum food budget for each type of household and multiplies the food budget by three to get the official **poverty budget.** A household with income less than the official poverty budget is considered poor. In 1989, the poverty budget was $6,250 for a single person, $12,560 for a four-person household, and $21,100 for an eight-person household.

Who and Where Are the Poor?

Table 12–1 shows the composition of the poor population in 1990. For each type of household, the poverty rate equals the percentage of households with incomes less than the official poverty budget. The table reveals several facts.

1. **Race.** The number of poor whites is over twice the number of poor blacks, and about four times the number of poor Hispanics. Nonetheless, the poverty rates for blacks and Hispanics are about three times that of whites. Figure 12–1 shows the poverty rates for different races. Among Hispanics, poverty rates vary for groups of different cultural backgrounds: poverty rates are highest among those of Puerto Rican and Mexican heritage (38 percent and 26 percent, respectively) and lowest among those of Cuban heritage (14 percent). The poverty rate among

---

TABLE 12–1   **The Poverty Population in 1990**

Group	Persons in Poverty (1,000)	Poverty Rate (percent)
All persons	33,585	13.50
Race		
White	22,326	10.70
Black	9,837	31.90
Hispanic	6,006	28.10
Location		
In metropolitan areas	24,510	12.70
In central cities	14,254	19.00
Outside central cities	10,255	8.70
Outside metropolitan areas	9,075	16.30
Household Head		
Married-couple families	2,981	5.70
Male householder	349	12.00
Female householder	3,768	33.40
Age		
Aged persons (over 65)	3,658	12.20
Children (under 15 years)	11,802	21.40
Education of Household Head		
Did not complete high school	8,092	23.60
Completed high school, no college	5,457	8.90
Some college education	1,679	5.80
Completed college	961	2.80

SOURCES: U.S. Bureau of the Census, *Poverty in the United States: 1990* (Washington, D.C.: U.S. Government Printing Office, 1991); U.S. Bureau of the Census, *Current Population Reports,* Series P-60, no. 175 (Washington, D.C.: U.S. Government Printing Office, 1991), Tables 1, 11.

FIGURE 12–1   Poverty Rates by Race and Location

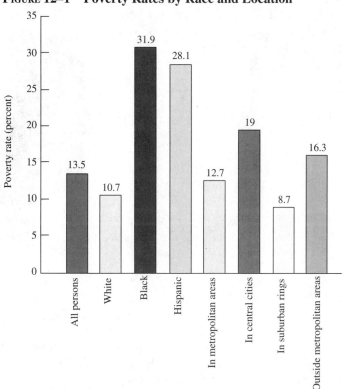

SOURCES: U.S. Bureau of the Census, *Poverty in the United States: 1990* (Washington, D.C.: U.S. Government Printing Office, 1991); U.S. Bureau of the Census, *Current Population Reports,* Series P-60, no. 175 (Washington, D.C.: U.S. Government Printing Office, 1991), Tables 1, 11.

Asians and Pacific Islanders is about 14 percent, close to the national average.

2. **Location.** The poverty rate of central cities is more than twice the suburban rate. The poverty rate outside metropolitan areas is about one third higher than the metropolitan rate. Figure 12–1 shows the poverty rates for different locations.

3. **Male versus female.** The poverty rate for female-headed households is almost six times the rate for households headed by a married couple. The table does not show the poverty rate for households headed by a black female, which is over 50 percent.

4. **The aged.** One of the successes in the war on poverty has been the decrease in poverty among the aged: their poverty rate dropped from 35 percent in 1959 to 12.2 percent in 1990, largely as a result of increased social security benefits.

FIGURE 12–2   Years of Pretransfer Poverty from Birth to Age 10 for White and Black Children

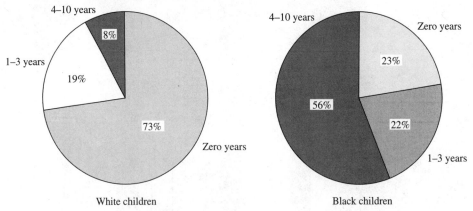

White children
Black children

SOURCE: David T. Ellwood, *Poor Support* (New York: Basic Books, 1988), Figure 6.2, p. 201.

5. **Children.** Over one fifth of children lived in poverty in 1990. Figure 12–2 provides a closer look at poverty among black and white children. Over half of black children spend more than 4 of their first 10 years in poverty, compared to only 8 percent of white children. Only about a quarter of black children escape poverty altogether, compared to about three quarters of white children.

6. **Education.** Poverty rates are negatively related to the level of education. The poverty rate of high school dropouts is over twice the rate of high school graduates, and about four times the rate of those who attend at least one year of college.

Where Do the Poor Get Their Money?

Table 12–2 shows the distribution of work effort of poor household heads in 1987. Over half of the poor household heads worked at least part-time for part of the year, and over 1 million worked full-time for the entire year. Because the typical poor household has four members, this means that over 4 million poor people were in households with a full-time worker. If one assumes that part-time workers averaged 20 hours per week, over two million household heads worked at least the equivalent of 20 full-time weeks (800 hours for the year). In other words, about a quarter of the poor (8 million of 32 million) were in households where the household head worked the equivalent of 20 weeks per year. The implication is clear: half-time employment is not enough to escape poverty.

The working poor receive relatively low wages. Among poor household heads who work full-time, the typical wage is between $3.50 and $4.00. The annual income from a $4 wage is $8,320, which falls short of the poverty level for a three-person

TABLE 12–2   Work Effort of Poor Nonaged Household Heads, 1987

Weeks Worked	Full-Time Workers (1,000)	Part-Time Workers (1,000)	Total Workers (1,000)
50–52	1,024	309	1,333
40–49	254	110	364
27–39	236	128	391
14–26	361	212	573
1–13	371	278	649
Total 1–52	2,273	1,037	3,310
Did not work	—	—	2,961
Total			6,271

SOURCE: Bradley Schiller, *The Economics of Poverty and Discrimination*, 5th ed. (Englewood Cliffs, N.J.: Prentice Hall, 1989).

household by $1,480. For the poor who work part-time, the gap between market income and the poverty level is even larger.

Table 12–3 provides a closer look at the income sources of poor households. Male-headed households receive a large share of their income from earnings (63 percent), and a small share from welfare programs (23 percent). For female-headed households, the percentages are reversed (26 percent from earnings and 60 percent from welfare). The differences are explained in large part by the greater child-care responsibilities of women, which limit their working time.

TABLE 12–3   Income Sources for Poor Households

	Male-Headed Household		Female-Headed Household	
	Amount ($)	Percent of Total	Amount ($)	Percent of Total
Earnings	5,136	62.63	1,722	25.70
Welfare programs	1,909	23.28	4,049	60.43
Cash benefits	1,110	13.54	2,398	35.79
Food stamps	666	8.12	1,106	16.51
Housing assistance	133	1.62	545	8.13
Social security	562	6.85	414	6.18
Unemployment	340	4.15	91	1.36
Other	253	3.09	424	6.33
Total	8,200	100.00	6,700	100.00

SOURCE: Bradley Schiller, *The Economics of Poverty and Discrimination,* 5th ed. (Englewood Cliffs, N.J.: Prentice Hall, 1989).

Tables 12–2 and 12–3 suggest two principal reasons for poverty. The first is the lack of employment: a large fraction of poor households lack a full-time worker. The second is low wages: a full-time job at the minimum wage of $4.25 per hour does not generate enough income to lift a household out of poverty. To escape poverty, the household head must earn more than the minimum wage. The remainder of the chapter explores the reasons why some types of workers have low employment rates and low wages.

Economic Growth and Stagnation

Perhaps the most important reason for poverty is slow macroeconomic growth. Stated another way, the most powerful means of decreasing poverty is through economic growth. According to the queuing theory of unemployment, prospective workers form an employment line (a queue) outside the factory or office building. A worker's position in the line is determined by his or her productivity: the lower his productivity, the further down the line he is positioned. Because employers draw workers from the front of the line, the lowest-productivity workers are the last to be hired. They are more likely to be hired when economic growth increases the demand for labor: firms hire workers further down the employment queue, employing low-productivity workers who would normally be unemployed. Because economic growth generates jobs for marginal (low-productivity) workers, it decreases poverty. In contrast, a recession decreases the demand for labor, and the least productive workers are the first to be fired.

There is conclusive evidence that economic growth decreases poverty. Ellwood (1987) predicts poverty rates for different years using two macroeconomic variables (the unemployment rate and median earnings), and compares the predicted rates with the actual poverty rates. His results for male-headed households are shown in Figure 12–3. The predicted rates are very close to the actual poverty rates for male-headed households, suggesting that the state of the economy has a strong influence on the poverty rates of male-headed households: an increase in the unemployment rate increases the poverty rate, and vice versa. In contrast, economic growth plays a less important role in the poverty of female-headed households. Because fewer female household heads work for pay, they are less affected by changes in the demand for labor.

A number of studies have estimated the effects of recessions on poor households. Gramlich and Laren (1984) estimated the effects of changes in unemployment rates on the earnings of different types of households. The earnings of both poor and middle-income households decreased as the unemployment rate rose, but the relative loss of poor households was about three times the loss of middle-income households. In terms of racial differences, a one-point increase in the unemployment rate decreased the income of white males by 1.2 percent, but decreased the earnings of nonwhite males by 2.0 percent. The implications are clear: since recessions impose relatively large costs on the poor, policies that promote macroeconomic growth reduce poverty.

FIGURE 12–3   **Expected versus Actual Poverty**

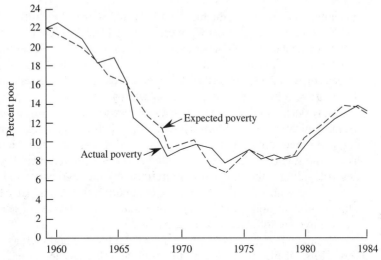

Expected poverty is based solely on the median earnings of full-year, full-time male workers and the unemployment rate.
SOURCE: David T. Ellwood, *Divide and Conquer* (New York: Ford Foundation, 1987), p. 16.

Blank and Blinder (1986) examine the effects of changes in unemployment and inflation on poverty rates. They conclude that rising unemployment between 1973 and 1983 added over five percentage points to the poverty rate: if the 1983 unemployment rate had been equal to the 1973 rate, the 1983 poverty rate would have been 10.1 percent instead of 15.2 percent. Stated another way, a one-point increase in the prime-age male unemployment rate increases the poverty rate by 0.70 percentage points. Although the poverty rate also increases with the inflation rate, the relationship is weak relative to the relationship between poverty and unemployment. In other words, the poor are harmed more by unemployment than by inflation.

The results of Bartik's (1991) study of urban employment growth (see Chapter 6) are consistent with the notion that poor households experience relatively large benefits from economic growth. When a city's economy grows by 1,000 jobs, 770 of the new jobs are filled by newcomers, leaving 230 jobs for the original residents of the city. About a third of the 230 jobs are filled by original residents who were previously unemployed, and the remaining two thirds are filled by original residents who previously did not participate in the labor market. The increase in employment increases real income per capita because it increases the labor-force participation rate and speeds up the promotion of city residents to higher-paying jobs. Bartik predicts that a 1 percent increase in total employment increases real per capita income by 0.40 percent for the population as a whole, 0.43 percent for less-educated workers, and 0.44 percent for black workers.

Residential Segregation

As shown in Table 12–1, the black poverty rate is over three times the white poverty rate. One reason for the greater poverty among black households is residential segregation. In most metropolitan areas, blacks are concentrated in central cities: in 1980, about 74 percent of metropolitan blacks lived in central cities, compared to only 35 percent of whites (Kain, 1985). In other words, only 26 percent of blacks lived in the suburbs, compared to 65 percent of whites.

How does racial segregation affect poverty rates? As discussed in Chapter 10 (Suburbanization and Modern Cities), almost half the jobs in manufacturing, retailing, and offices are now in suburban areas. Because only about a quarter of blacks live in the suburbs, blacks have limited access to suburban employment opportunities. According to the **spatial mismatch theory,** the segregation of blacks in the central city, far from suburban employment opportunities, contributes to black poverty. The suburbanization of employment in recent decades has increased poverty because blacks have not followed jobs to the suburbs.

Residential segregation can decrease real income and increase poverty in three ways. First, if blacks are forced to commute relatively long distances to suburban jobs, they have a lower net hourly wage (the gross wage less commuting cost) and less time for work or leisure. Therefore, central-city blacks who work in the suburbs have lower net incomes. Second, to the extent that a higher commuting cost discourages work effort, segregation decreases employment rates. Third, much of the information about job opportunities comes through informal channels: workers find out about job openings from neighbors and friends. The segregation of blacks in the central city decreases their access to this informal information network, increases search costs, and thus decreases employment rates.

Why don't central-city blacks commute to suburban jobs? Commuting is costly for central-city residents because (1) most transit systems are designed to deliver suburban residents to the city center and are ill-suited for bringing central-city residents to suburban jobs and (2) relatively few central-city households own cars. Even if commuting were feasible, finding a suburban job would be difficult because blacks in the central city have limited access to the informal job-information network.

Why Segregation?

Why are blacks concentrated in central cities? Kain (1985) discusses several possible reasons for segregation:

1. **Voluntary segregation.** Perhaps blacks prefer to live in segregated neighborhoods. The evidence from attitudinal surveys suggests the opposite: most blacks would in fact prefer to live in integrated neighborhoods (Kain, 1985). To a black household, an "integrated" neighborhood is one that is equally divided between whites and blacks (Clark, 1991).

2. **Lower incomes.** Perhaps blacks cannot afford suburban housing and are forced to live in low-cost housing in the central city. A recent study by Gabriel and Rosenthal (1989) suggests that a black household with

the same income and other characteristics as the average white suburban household is much less likely to live in the suburbs. Kain (1985)
poses the following question: if location decisions were based strictly
on nonracial factors (income, family type, age of household head), how
many black households would live in the suburbs? His answer is that
3.6 million black households would live in the suburbs, about twice the
actual number of black suburban households. The results of Gabriel and
Rosenthal and Kain suggest that the low rate of black suburbanization is
caused by factors other than income.

3. **Racial prejudice.** It appears that many whites prefer to live in segregated neighborhoods. Among whites who prefer integrated neighborhoods, an *integrated* neighborhood is one in which 80 percent of the residents are white and only 20 percent are black (Clark, 1991). In contrast,
   blacks prefer neighborhoods that are split equally between whites and
   blacks.

4. **Discrimination by real estate agents.** The actions of real estate agents
   promote racial segregation. A 1979 study by the Department of Housing and Urban Development estimated that 27 percent of rental agents
   and 15 percent of house sellers discriminated against blacks. Discrimination was defined as "failing to provide important, necessary information to rent or purchase a home" to a person of a particular race. Black
   home buyers who inquired about four different advertised homes had a
   48 percent chance of encountering discriminatory treatment for at least
   one home, and renters had an 85 percent chance of encountering discriminatory treatment for at least one of four rental properties.

5. **Exclusionary zoning.** As explained in Chapter 11, suburban governments use zoning to exclude low-income households from their jurisdictions. Exclusionary zoning is motivated in part by fiscal concerns: if
   low-income households do not pay their "fair share" of the costs of local
   public services, they are excluded by suburban governments. Since the
   average income of blacks is lower than that of whites, exclusionary zoning has a larger effect on black households. Exclusionary zoning is also
   motivated by concerns over crime and education: the wealthy exclude the
   poor to keep crime rates low and educational achievement high.

There is some evidence that racial segregation decreased during the 1970s. According to Kain (1985), the fraction of black households living outside central cities
increased from 18.1 percent in 1970 to 25.8 percent in 1980. Most of the increase
in the number of black suburbanites was caused by (1) the expansion of central-city
ghettos across central-city lines and (2) the growth of suburban concentrations of
blacks. There was, however, a small movement of blacks into previously white suburban neighborhoods. In the San Francisco Bay area, the number of suburban communities with between 50 and 1,000 black households increased from 22 in 1970 to
40 in 1980. In Chicago, the number of such neighborhoods increased from 11 to 39.
Although these changes are relatively small, they may suggest that the forces that
inhibit black suburbanization are weakening.

Evidence on the Spatial Mismatch Theory

The spatial mismatch theory suggests that racial segregation in central cities increases black poverty. The first evidence in support of this theory is from Kain (1968), who estimates that racial segregation in Chicago decreased employment opportunities for blacks by over 20,000 jobs. Two recent studies of the spatial mismatch hypothesis have generated conflicting results.

Using data from Chicago, Ellwood (1986) suggests that spatial mismatch is a relatively small factor in black youth unemployment. Although jobs are moving to the suburbs faster than black teenagers, most teenagers (both black and white) do not work in their own neighborhoods anyway, so the location of jobs is relatively unimportant. The unemployment rates of blacks seem to be unrelated to their proximity to jobs. For example, the West Side of Chicago, where jobs are plentiful, has about the same black teenage unemployment rate as the South Side, where jobs are scarce. Ellwood concludes that the high unemployment rates and low participation rates of black teenagers are caused by racial factors, not by a spatial mismatch between residence and workplaces. As pointed out by Leonard (1986) and Ihlanfeldt and Sjoquist (1990), there are a number of problems with the data used by Ellwood, so his results must be interpreted with caution.

Using data from the Philadelphia metropolitan area, Ihlanfeldt and Sjoquist (1990) suggest that the spatial mismatch is an important factor in black youth unemployment. For all youths, black and white, the likelihood of being employed drops as commuting distance (the distance between the residence and employment opportunities) increases. One reason for the lower employment rate for black youths (27 percent versus 49 percent for white youths) is that the average commute time for blacks is 26 minutes, compared to 18.5 minutes for whites. The authors conclude that between a third and a half of the gap in employment rates is explained by the fact that black youths live further from jobs.

In another study, Ihlanfeldt (1991) tests for the mismatch hypothesis in 50 metropolitan areas. His principal conclusions are as follows:

1. Overall, inferior access to employment opportunities explains between 24 percent and 27 percent of the gap between black and white employment rates and between 29 percent and 34 percent of the the gap between Hispanic and white employment rates.
2. The spatial mismatch is more important in larger metropolitan areas. In small cities, only 3 percent of the gap between black and white employment rates is explained by inferior access; in medium-sized cities, inferior access is responsible for 14 percent of the gap; in large cities, inferior access is responsible for about a quarter of the gap.

What conclusions can be drawn from the conflicting evidence concerning the spatial mismatch theory? The three recent studies suggest that there is still some uncertainty about the relative importance of the spatial mismatch effect. Nonetheless, there is a consensus that even if the mismatch theory is correct, the other factors in black poverty are probably more important. A reasonable conclusion from the studies by Ihlanfeldt and Sjoquist is that the mismatch is responsible for about a quarter of the gap between black and white employment rates, leaving three quarters to be explained by labor-market discrimination, differences in education, and other factors.

The Policy Response

The government can promote the suburbanization of blacks in three ways. First, if the federal government enforces its fair-housing laws, it could reduce the discriminatory treatment of blacks in the suburban housing market. Second, local governments could change their zoning laws to allow the suburbanization of blacks and other minorities. Third, if state governments provided more support for local-government services, the incentives for exclusionary zoning would decrease.

Education and Poverty

As shown in Table 12–1, the poverty rate depends on the education level of the household head: the lower the education level, the greater the poverty rate. Table 12–4 provides a closer look at the effects of education on employment and earnings, showing the relationship between education and unemployment rates, labor-force participation rates, work time, and average earnings. The unemployment rate of high school dropouts is over six times the rate for college graduates, and almost twice the rate for high school graduates. The lower labor-force participation rate among less-educated people is evidence of "discouraged workers": because these people have a more difficult time finding jobs, they are less likely to continue looking.

How does education affect employment and earnings? The theory of human capital stresses the effects of increased education on worker productivity. The idea is that schools teach skills that (1) can be directly applied to tasks on the job and (2) allow workers to learn more quickly on the job. Education is also a signaling device: a diploma shows a prospective employer that the person is sufficiently smart and dedicated to survive a rigorous educational program, and is thus likely to be a good worker.

TABLE 12–4   Education and Success in the Labor Market

	High School Dropouts	High School Graduates	College Graduates
Unemployment rate	15.4%	8.6%	2.5%
Labor-force participation rate	61%	81%	88%
Full-time workers	57%	76%	84%
Average earnings	$15,266	$18,370	$28,519

SOURCE: Bradley Schiller, *The Economics of Poverty and Discrimination*, 5th ed. (Englewood Cliffs, N.J.: Prentice Hall, 1989).

Education and Changes in Central-City Employment

The employment problems of central-city blacks have been exacerbated by changes in the structure of the central-city economy. Table 12–5 shows the changes in central-city employment between 1953 and 1985 for five cities (New York, Philadelphia, Boston, Baltimore, and St. Louis). Total employment in jobs requiring relatively low skills and education has decreased: in 1985, manufacturing employment was 40 percent of its 1953 level, and retail and wholesale employment was 70 percent of its 1953 level. In contrast, employment in jobs requiring higher skills and education has increased: total employment in white-collar services more than tripled between 1953 and 1985.

Kasarda (1988) provides further evidence of the increased educational require-ments of central-city employment. Figure 12–4 shows employment changes between 1970 and 1985 in two groups of cities. In the five northern and eastern cities, the number of jobs requiring less than a high school education dropped by over 900,000, while the number of jobs requiring some college education increased by 428,000. In the four growing southern and western cities, employment growth was more rapid in jobs requiring some college education.

Because the average education level of blacks is relatively low, they are unable to take full advantage of the new employment opportunities in white-collar indus-

---

TABLE 12–5   **Employment in Five Central Cities by Sector, 1953–1985**

	1953		1985	
Employment Sector	*Number (1,000)*	*Percent of Total*	*Number (1,000)*	*Percent of Total*
Total employment	4,940	100	4,662	100
Manufacturing	1,867	38	743	16
Retail and wholesale	1,335	27	954	20
White-collar services	925	19	2,218	48
Blue-collar services	577	12	561	12
Other	236	5	186	4

Central cities: New York, Philadelphia, Boston, Baltimore, and St. Louis.
Definitions
  1. Total employment: total classified employment excluding government employment and sole proprietors.
  2. White-collar services: service industries (excluding government, retail, wholesale) in which more than half of employees hold executive, managerial, professional, or clerical positions.
  3. Blue-collar services: service industries (excluding government, retail, wholesale) in which less than half of employees hold executive, managerial, professional, or clerical positions.
SOURCE: Computed from Table 9 in John Kasarda, "Jobs, Migration, and Emerging Urban Mismatches," in *Urban Change and Poverty,* ed. Michael McGeary and Laurence Lynn (Washington, D.C.: National Academy Press, 1988), pp. 170–171.

FIGURE 12–4   **Change in Number of Jobs with Different Education Requirements, 1970–1985**

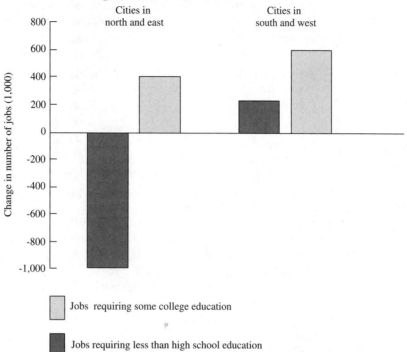

Cities in north and east: New York, Philadelphia, Boston, Baltimore, and St. Louis.
Cities in south and west: Atlanta, Houston, Denver, and San Francisco.
SOURCE: John Kasarda, "Jobs, Migration, and Emerging Urban Mismatches," in *Urban Change and Poverty*, ed. Michael McGeary and Laurence Lynn (Washington, D.C.: National Academy Press, 1988), page 177.

tries. Most of the new white-collar service jobs in central cities require at least some college education. Nationwide, the high school completion rates for blacks and Hispanics are much lower than the completion rate for whites. In the high school class of 1982, 22 percent of the black students and 28 percent of the Hispanic students failed to graduate with their class, compared to 15 percent of whites and 8 percent of Asians (O'Hare et al.,1991). Only about 27 percent of central-city blacks complete one year of college, compared to 40 percent of central-city whites (Kasarda, 1988).

Evidence of the Effects of Education on Poverty

The National Bureau of Economic Research (NBER) completed a comprehensive study of black youths in the inner-city areas of Boston, Chicago, and Philadelphia (Freeman and Holzer, 1986). The study explored the various factors that contribute to the inner-city unemployment problem, including inadequate education. Some of the conclusions of the study are as follows:

1. Graduation from high school increased earnings in two ways: it increased wages by 15 percent and increased hours worked by 6 percent.
2. An increase in the number of years in school increased wages, decreased participation in crime, and decreased the amount of time spent in non-productive activities (activities other than schooling and employment, including hanging out, watching TV, and getting high).
3. An increase in school performance (measured by grades) increased wages, decreased the likelihood of dropping out, and improved work habits.

The general conclusion of the study is that education has a strong effect on the employment prospects of inner-city youths.

The Title I programs of the federal government are special programs for disadvantaged youths. In 1984, the federal government spent $3.4 billion on Title I programs. A total of 5 million children were served by the programs, with an average cost per child of about $700 (Glazer, 1986). What are the effects of these programs?

A recent study of the Perry Preschool Programs in Ypsilanti, Michigan, suggests that the program is a resounding success (Berrueta-Clement et al., 1984). The study compares teenagers who participated in the preschool program to those who did not. Compared to the control group, program participants had higher high school completion rates (67 percent versus 49 percent), lower arrest rates (by a margin of 40 percent), and half the teenage pregnancy rate. The estimated benefit-cost ratio of the program was 7.0. This study shows that preschool programs may generate substantial long-term benefits.

Glazer (1986) summarizes the results of several other studies of Title I programs. One comprehensive study suggests that Title I programs have increased achievement in mathematics and reading, with the largest gains in the early grades. Other studies by the National Assessment of Educational Progress (NAEP) show that Title I programs have narrowed the achievement gaps between black and white students, with the largest relative gains at the elementary level (NAEP, 1981; National Center for Education Statistics, 1982).

Labor-Market Discrimination

Discrimination in the labor market takes two forms, employment discrimination and wage discrimination. *Employment discrimination* refers to the practice of systematically hiring one racial group over another, despite the fact that both groups are equally productive and are paid the same wage. *Wage discrimination* is defined as paying different wages to equally productive workers. Both types of discrimination have the potential to increase poverty among racial minorities because minority workers are either not hired or hired at a lower wage.

Differences in Earnings

Table 12–6 shows the median earnings for white, black, and Hispanic men. For all workers, the gap between white and black earnings is $7,776, and the gap between

TABLE 12–6   **Median Annual Earnings by Race and Education, Men Aged 16 and Over, 1986**

	White Workers	Black Workers	Hispanic Workers
All workers	$25,890	$18,114	$16,711
Education Level			
High school dropout	18,547	14,681	13,816
High school graduate	23,524	16,629	17,984
Some college time	26,206	21,182	22,254
College graduate	32,789	27,245	28,332

SOURCE: Bradley Schiller, *The Economics of Poverty and Discrimination,* 5th ed. (Englewood Cliffs, N.J.: Prentice Hall, 1989).

white and Hispanic earnings is $9,179. Part of this gap is caused by differences in education. The gaps for workers of particular educational levels are slightly smaller: the black-white gap for high school graduates is $6,895, and the gap for college graduates is $5,544. Because blacks typically receive inferior education, a simple comparison based on years of schooling is deceptive. According to Schiller (1989), the typical black high school graduate has the same educational preparation as the typical white high school dropout, so the gap between a black high school graduate and a white person with the same educational preparation is $1,918. Schiller concludes that a black worker earns about 90 percent of the earnings of a white worker with an equivalent educational background.

The earnings gap is decreased further if one controls for other factors such as age, labor skills, and location. Research on race differences in earnings suggests that about three fourths of the earnings gap can be explained by differences in education, age, skills, and location, leaving one quarter of the gap unexplained. The unexplained portion is caused by racial discrimination.

Theories of Discrimination

There are two theories of labor-market discrimination. The first theory, developed by Becker (1957), explains the competitive forces that limit discrimination. The second theory, developed by Phelps (1972) and Arrow (1973), explains why discrimination may persist.

Becker's theory suggests that market forces limit the extent of wage discrimination. Consider a city with two types of workers, black and white. Suppose that they have the same **value of marginal product (VMP)**, defined as the marginal physical product of labor times the market price of the product produced. Suppose that white workers are paid their VMP ($6) but blacks are paid only $5. If you were a profit-maximizing firm, what would you do? If you hire black workers, you will have lower production costs than your all-white competitors, so your sales and profits will increase. What's good for you is good for other capitalists, so other firms will hire the undervalued black workers. As the demand for blacks increases and the demand for whites decreases, the gap between black and white wages decreases. In equilibrium, whites and blacks have the same wage.

Under what conditions does wage discrimination persist? If a white firm can keep other firms from entering its industry, it can protect itself from the competition of color-blind firms. Bigotry is not costless, however. The white monopolist pays relatively high wages to its white workers, and its higher production costs force its consumers to pay a relatively high price. In addition, profits are lower, so stockholders pay for bigotry in the form of lower dividends and stock prices. Job discrimination may persist if (1) bigoted firms are protected from competition and (2) consumers and stockholders are willing to pay for their bigotry.

The same arguments apply to sex discrimination. If the female wage is less than the male wage and men and women are equally productive, profit-seeking firms will hire women and fire men, narrowing the wage gap. In equilibrium, one would expect equally productive men and women to earn the same wage. Job discrimination may persist if (1) sexist firms are protected from competition and (2) consumers and stockholders are willing to pay for their sexism.

As explained earlier, the empirical evidence does not support this simple theory of discrimination. After controlling for all nondiscriminatory factors, there is still a large gap between the wages of whites and blacks. Obviously, there is something wrong with the simple model.

The theory of **statistical discrimination** shows that the black-white wage differential persists if there is imperfect information about worker productivity. Suppose that an employer must hire one of two workers, a black or a white. If the firm knew which worker had the higher VMP, it would obviously hire the more productive worker. Such information is not available, however, so the employer must guess which worker has the higher VMP. Suppose that because of differences in education and work experience, the average black is less productive than the average white, although some blacks are more productive than some whites. If the employer has no other information on the productivities of the applicants, the best choice, in a statistical sense, is the white worker. White workers are chosen over equally productive (or more productive) black workers because black workers are less productive *on average*. In this case, discrimination occurs because of imperfect information, not bigotry.

Demographic Change: Female-Headed Households

As shown in Table 12–1, the poverty rate of female-headed households is almost three times the poverty rate of male-headed households. Female-headed households are more likely to be poor for three reasons. First, most of these households are single-parent households, so the woman must juggle employment and child-care responsibilities. For many women, especially those with preschool children, full-time work is not feasible. Second, women earn lower wages than men, so a given amount of work generates less income. Third, only one third of female-headed households receive child-support payments from absent fathers.

Facts on Family Structure

The number of female-headed households has increased rapidly in the last few decades. Between 1970 and 1985, the percentage of white households headed by a female increased from 9.6 percent to 13.4 percent (U.S. Bureau of the Census, 1986). For blacks, the percentage of households headed by a female increased from 31.8 percent to 43.9 percent. According to Sawhill (1988), the increase in the number of female-headed households between 1967 and 1985 added between one and two percentage points to the overall poverty rate.

An increase in the number of female-headed households means that fewer children are raised in two-parent households. Figure 12–5 shows, for both white and black households, the percentage of children living with married couples. Between 1960 and 1988, the percentage of black children living in two-parent households dropped from 67 percent to 39 percent. For whites over the same period, the percentage of children in two-parent households dropped from 91 percent to 79 percent.

Another part of the increase in the number of female-headed households is the increase in the number of births to single mothers. Figure 12–5 shows, for both white and black households, the percentages of births to unmarried women. By 1988, well over half of black births were to single mothers, compared to a figure of 23 percent in 1960. Between 1960 and 1988, the share of white births to single women increased almost sevenfold, from 2.3 percent to 15.7 percent.

Family Structure and Welfare Payments

What caused the changes in family structure shown in Figure 12–5? What changes over the last few decades caused the increases in (1) the number of female-headed households, (2) the percentage of children in single-parent households, and (3) the percentage of births to single mothers?

FIGURE 12–5   Living Arrangements of White and Black Children

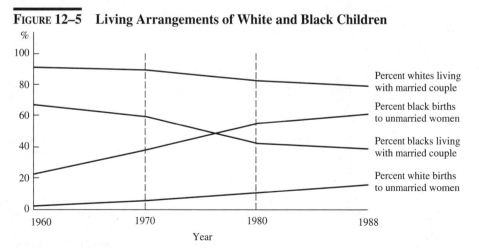

SOURCE: David T. Ellwood and Jonathan Crane, "Family Change among Black Americans: What Do We Know?" *Journal of Economic Perspectives* 4 (Fall 1990), pp. 65–84.

One theory of the changing family structure, popularized by Murray (1984), is that the welfare system is responsible for the increases in female-headed households. Murray argues that generous welfare payments make it possible for women to raise children outside of marriage: because single women can rely on the welfare system for support, they have less need for a husband. According to this theory, the growth in female-headed households (and the associated increases in the percentage of children in single-parent households) results from increases in the real value of welfare payments.

This theory is easily refuted by looking at the facts on welfare payments and single-parent households. Figure 12–6 shows the time trends of welfare payments per household (Aid to Families with Dependent Children (AFDC) and food stamps, in 1988 dollars) and the percentage of black children living in single-parent households. Although there is a positive relationship between welfare payments and the percentage of black children in single-parent households during the 1960s, the relationship is negative since 1970. Between 1970 and 1988, the real value of welfare payments per household decreased by about 22 percent, while the percentage of black children in single-parent households increased from 42 percent to 61 percent.

Figure 12–6 also shows the time trend in the percentage of black children residing in households receiving AFDC. If AFDC were responsible for the increases in the

FIGURE 12–6   Welfare Benefits and Living Arrangements of Black Children

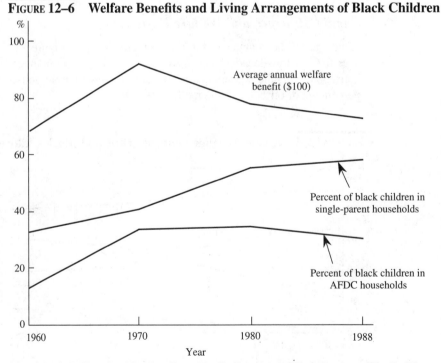

SOURCE: David T. Ellwood and Jonathan Crane, "Family Change among Black Americans: What Do We Know?" *Journal of Economic Perspectives* 4 (Fall 1990), pp. 65–84.

number of black children in single-parent households, we would expect the percentage of children in AFDC households to increase more rapidly than the percentage in single-parent households. In fact, between 1970 and 1988, while the percentage of black children in single-parent households increased, the percentage of children in AFDC households decreased.

There have been a number of rigorous statistical studies of the effects of welfare payments on family structure. On a theoretical level, the idea that an increase in support for single mothers increases the number of single mothers is a sensible one: if we decrease the cost of single parenthood, we expect that, at the margin, some women will choose single motherhood over the alternatives. The issue is really an empirical one: by how much does AFDC increase the number of single parents?

Wilson and Neckerman (1986) review the literature on the connection between welfare payments and family structure. They come to the following conclusions:

1. There is no evidence that welfare payments affect the number of out-of-wedlock births. States with relatively generous welfare programs did not have higher birth rates among unmarried women.

2. There is some evidence that welfare encourages divorce and separation. States with relatively generous welfare programs have higher rates of marital dissolution. Ellwood and Bane (1985) estimate that a $100 increase in monthly AFDC benefits would cause a 10 percent increase in the number of divorced or separated mothers.

In general, it appears that AFDC encourages women to set up independent households, but does not encourage them to bear more children. Garfinkel and McLanahan (1986) suggest that the rising AFDC benefits between 1960 and 1975 increased the number of female-headed households by between 9 percent and 14 percent. Because the actual number of female-headed households increased by over 100 percent, it is clear that AFDC played a small role in the growth of female-headed households.

Family Structure and the Status of Black Men

Wilson and Neckerman (1986) propose an alternative theory for the increase in female-headed households. They compute a "marriageability index" for black men, which is defined as the number of employed black men per 100 black women. The idea behind this theory is that a decrease in the employment rate of black men discourages marriage and the formation of two-parent households.

Figure 12–7 shows the time trends in the marriageability index and marriage rates for young black men (20 to 24 years old). Between 1960 and 1980, the index dropped from 68 (68 employed men per 100 women) to 55, while the marriage rate dropped from 35 percent to 11 percent. Between 1960 and 1980, the two curves move in the same direction, providing some support for the theory. Between 1980 and 1988, however, the marriageability index rose while the marriage rate fell. Over this period, employed black men became more plentiful, but their marriage rates dropped. In fact, marriage rates among employed black men have been dropping since 1970, suggesting that eligibility is not the primary factor in declining marriage rates.

FIGURE 12–7   **Black Male Marriageability Index and Percent Married, 1960–1988**

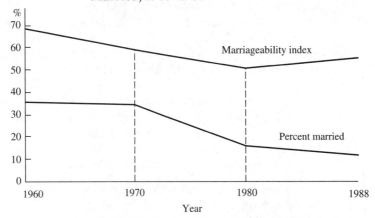

SOURCE: David T. Ellwood and Jonathan Crane, "Family Change among Black Americans: What Do We Know?" *Journal of Economic Perspectives* 4 (Fall 1990), pp. 65–84.

There have been a number of rigorous studies of the relationship between employment rates and marriage rates. According to Ellwood and Crane (1990), these studies suggest that although there is a positive relationship between employment and marriage rates, the relationship is weak. In other words, there is evidence that changes in black male employment rates have a relatively small effect on marriage rates and family structure.

Summary: What Causes Changes in Family Structure?

The reasons for the recent changes in family structure are still unknown, at least to economists. Ellwood and Crane (1990) suggest that changes in family structure result from complex interactions of social, cultural, legal, and economic factors, and that it will be difficult to disentangle these factors to determine which factors are the most important and thus worthy of attention by the public sector. Since poverty rates are the greatest among single-parent households, our ignorance about the reasons for changes in family structure is troublesome.

Poverty in the Central City

One of the most difficult problems in the urban economy is the concentration of poverty in the central city. Particularly disturbing is the continued concentration of poor blacks in certain areas of central cities. In 1983, less than half of the inner-city blacks in Boston, Philadelphia, and Chicago were employed (Freeman and Holzer, 1986). In contrast, 61 percent of U.S. blacks and 76 percent of U.S. whites were employed. Along with low employment rates, central cities have high crime rates and widespread drug abuse.

The reasons for central-city poverty are discussed earlier in the chapter. Although the majority of jobs are now in the suburbs, the vast majority of blacks continue to live in central cities. Moreover, an increasing share of central-city jobs require a college education, so most blacks are unable to take advantage of new job opportunities in the central city. Racial discrimination contributes to the black poverty problem: segregation inhibits the movement of blacks to the suburbs, and job discrimination limits their employment options. Education problems also contribute to poverty: central cities have inferior schools, so the average black teenager emerges from the education system with lower skills than her white counterpart.

The National Bureau of Economic Research (NBER) completed a comprehensive study of the black youth unemployment problem. Freeman and Holzer (1986) summarize the findings of the study. Some of their conclusions are as follows:

1. **Local labor market.** Cities with relatively strong labor markets had relatively low black teenage unemployment rates. For example, the employment rate in Boston (a city with a relatively healthy economy) was 10 percentage points above the employment rates in Chicago and Philadelphia. This finding is consistent with the notion that the most effective way to reduce poverty is through macroeconomic growth.

2. **Spatial mismatch.** Blacks who lived relatively close to jobs did not have lower unemployment rates, that is, physical proximity to jobs did not decrease unemployment rates. This conclusion is based on Ellwood's (1986) study of Chicago (discussed earlier in the chapter). Blacks on the West Side, where jobs are plentiful, did not have lower unemployment rates than blacks on the South Side, where jobs are scarce. In addition, whites hold most of the jobs in the border areas between white and black neighborhoods.

3. **Competition with women.** Cities with the highest proportion of adult females in the labor market had the worst labor market for black teenagers (the lowest wages and participation rates). It seems that increases in female participation rates have decreased employment opportunities for young blacks.

4. **Discrimination.** Prospective employers treated black applicants differently than white ones. In general, employers were less courteous to black applicants.

5. **Family experience.** Black youths were more likely to be employed if other members of the family were employed. This suggests that adult joblessness increases youth unemployment, that is, employment problems are passed from generation to generation.

6. **Reservation wage.** Black and white youths had comparable reservation wages (defined as the lowest acceptable wage). Because employers regarded blacks as less productive, the relatively high black reservation wage increased black unemployment.

7. **Illegal opportunities.** Crime rates were higher in cities with fewer legal opportunities. Crime rates were also affected by the perceived risks and returns of crime: teenagers who perceived that the risks were low and returns were high were more likely to commit crime.

8. **Welfare involvement.** Teenagers from welfare families had more trouble in the labor market, even after controlling for differences in income and family structure. Youths living in public housing did worse than their peers who lived in private housing.

9. **Education.** Employment and wages were affected by the amount of schooling and school performance. Youths with more years of schooling and higher grades had higher wages, more work hours, and lower crime rates.

The NBER study suggests that the problems of black inner-city teenagers are caused by many factors, including weak labor markets, competition with women, discrimination, opportunities for crime, and inadequate education. It suggests that a comprehensive approach is required to decrease youth unemployment.

Summary

1. A poor household is defined as one whose total income is less than three times the minimum food budget. Poverty rates are greatest among racial minorities, women, and central-city residents.

2. Economic growth decreases poverty because the poor are the last hired and the first fired.

3. One theory of black poverty is that blacks have been confined to the central city while employment has shifted to the suburbs. There is conflicting evidence about the effects of residential segregation (and limited access to jobs) on black poverty rates.

4. The poverty rate depends on the education level of the household head: the unemployment rate of high school dropouts is over six times the rate of college graduates and about twice the rate of high school graduates. A study of inner-city youth suggests that increased education increases wages and earnings and decreases crime rates.

5. Studies of education programs suggest that some of them increase achievement.
   a. The Perry Preschool Programs increased high school completion rates and decreased arrest rates.
   b. Studies of Title I programs suggest that they have increased achievement, with the largest gains at the elementary level.

6. Job discrimination contributes to poverty: in some circumstances, blacks are paid less than whites, and women are paid less than men. Although market forces limit the extent of job discrimination, wage differences persist because of statistical discrimination.

7. Economic growth is a necessary—but not sufficient—condition for reducing poverty: because the poor are the last hired, it is a necessary condition; because the poor must have the skills for the new jobs and must live near the new jobs, it is not a sufficient condition.

8. The number of female-headed households has increased rapidly in the last few decades, increasing poverty rates.
   a. It appears that AFDC has increased the number of female-headed households by a small amount.
   b. The increase in male joblessness played a minor role in the increase in female-headed households.

9. One of the most difficult problems in the urban economy is the concentration of poverty among blacks in the central city. A study of the black youth unemployment problem suggests that low employment rates are caused by weak labor markets, competition with adult females, discrimination, opportunities for crime, and inadequate education, among other factors.

Exercises and Discussion Questions

1. The section on job discrimination suggests that the market penalizes racist and sexist firms because such firms are underpriced by color-blind and sex-blind firms. As a result, there are limits on the extent of wage discrimination.
   a. What if all firms (capitalists and managers) are color-blind, but white laborers refuse to work with black laborers? Will wage discrimination (lower wages for blacks) persist?
   b. What if firms and employees are color-blind, but white consumers refuse to purchase goods produced by blacks? Who bears the cost of bigotry? Will wage discrimination persist?

2. Suppose that a comparable-worth law is enacted, requiring a 20 percent increase in the wages of workers in female-dominated occupations. Who will bear the costs of this policy? How will the policy affect nonworking women and women who work in male-dominated occupations?

3. Consider a city with 10,000 jobs in the central city and 20,000 jobs in a suburban jurisdiction. Suppose that black workers are confined to the central city, but whites can live in either jurisdiction. Suppose further that travel costs are so high that workers live and work in the same jurisdiction.
   a. Under what circumstances will racial segregation not affect the wages of white and black workers?
   b. Suppose that the circumstances you identify in (a) occurred in 1950. Would you still expect them to occur in 1993?

4. Comment on the following: "Black central-city residents are poor because they do not have access to suburban employment opportunities. I propose that we supply each central-city household with a car. Such a plan will reduce poverty at a relatively low cost."

5. Consider a segregated city in which all blacks live in the central city. In the suburb (eight miles from the central city), manufacturing firms in industry X employ black workers.

   a. Use the numbers shown below to compute the black suburban wage.

      i. The unit cost of commuting (including monetary and time costs) is 40 cents per mile.

     ii. The wage for blacks in the central city is $10 per hour, and blacks work eight hours per day.

   b. Use the numbers shown below to predict the effects of racial segregation on black suburban employment. In other words, predict the percentage increase in total black employment that would result from a decrease in the black commute distance from eight miles to zero.

    iii. The price elasticity of demand for X's product is −2.0.

    iv. Labor is responsible for 80 percent of production costs.

     v. Firms produce X's product with fixed factor proportions.

6. The proportion of households headed by females increased rapidly during the 1960s and 1970s. Comment on the following statement: "The most important factor in the increase in female-headed households was increases in AFDC (Aid to Families with Dependent Children) payments."

References and Additional Readings

Poverty Facts

O'Hare, William P.; Kelvin M. Pollard; Taynia L. Mann; and Mary M. Kent. "African Americans in the 1990s." *Population Bulletin* 46 (July 1991).

U.S. Bureau of the Census. *Current Population Reports*, Series P-60. Washington, D.C.: U.S. Government Printing Office, 1991. Estimates poverty rates by status of household head and place of residence. Reports unemployment rates for different races and education levels.

U.S. Office of Management and Budget. *Budget of the United States Government, Fiscal Year 1987*. Washington, D.C.: U.S. Government Printing Office, 1986. Projects spending on anti-poverty programs.

General References

Ellwood, David T. *Poor Support*. New York: Basic Books, 1988. A detailed description and analysis of poverty among two-parent families, single-parent families, and residents of inner-city neighborhoods.

Sawhill, Isabel V. "Poverty in the U.S.: Why Is It So Persistent?" *Journal of Economic Literature* 26 (1988), pp. 1073–119. Explores the reasons for the persistence of poverty between the middle 1960s and 1988. Examines the influence of five factors: demographic changes (increased number of female-headed households), sluggish macroeconomic growth, inadequate investment in human capital, work disincentives of the welfare system, and the growing underclass. Concludes that the most important factors were demographic changes and rising unemployment.

Schiller, Bradley. *The Economics of Poverty and Discrimination.* 5th ed. Englewood Cliffs, N.J.: Prentice Hall, 1989.

Poverty and Economic Growth

Blank, Rebecca M., and Alan S. Blinder. "Macroeconomics, Income Distribution, and Poverty." In *Fighting Poverty: What Works and What Doesn't,* ed. Sheldon H. Danziger and Daniel H. Weinberg. Cambridge, Mass.: Harvard University Press, 1986. Explores the relationship between macroeconomic conditions (unemployment and inflation) and poverty. Concludes that the poor suffer more from unemployment than inflation.

Danziger, Sheldon H., and Peter Gottschalk. "Do Rising Tides Lift All Boats? The Impact of Secular and Cyclical Changes on Poverty." *American Economic Review* 76 (1986), pp. 405–10.

Ellwood, David T. *Divide and Conquer.* New York: Ford Foundation, 1987.

Gottschalk, Peter, and Sheldon H. Danziger. "Macroeconomic Conditions, Income Transfers, and the Trend in Poverty." In *The Social Contract Revisited,* ed. D. Lee Bauden. Washington, D.C.: Urban Institute, 1984.

Gramlich, Edward, and Deborah Laren. "How Widespread Are Income Losses in a Recession?" In *The Social Contract Revisited,* ed. D. Lee Bauden. Washington, D.C.: Urban Institute, 1984. Estimates the distributional effects of recessions.

Segregation and Poverty: The Spatial Mismatch Theory

Clark, William A. "Residential Preferences and Neighborhood Racial Segregation: A Test of the Schelling Segregation Model." *Demography* 28 (1991), pp. 1–19. Describes the differences in preferences for integrated neighborhoods between whites and blacks.

Ellwood, David T. "The Spatial Mismatch Hypothesis: Are There Teenage Jobs Missing in the Ghetto?" In *The Black Youth Employment Crisis,* ed. Richard B. Freeman and Harry J. Holzer. University of Chicago Press, 1986, pp. 147–85. Provides evidence from Chicago that questions the validity of the spatial mismatch hypothesis.

Freeman, Richard B., and Harry J. Holzer. "The Black Youth Employment Crisis: Summary of Findings." In *The Black Youth Employment Crisis,* ed. Richard B. Freeman and Harry J. Holzer. University of Chicago Press, 1986. Summarizes the results of a series of studies that explore the reasons for the high unemployment among black youths.

Gabriel, Stuart A., and Stuart S. Rosenthal. "Household Location and Race: Estimates of a Multinomial Logit Model." *Review of Economics and Statistics,* 1989, pp. 240–49. Shows that the location choices of black households are relatively insensitive to changes in income and other socioeconomic characteristics.

Ihlanfeldt, Keith R. "Intra-Urban Job Accessibility and Youth Employment Rates." Policy Research Center Paper No. 18. Atlanta: Georgia State University, 1991. Provides evidence from 50 metropolitan areas that relatively low employment rates for black and Hispanic youths are caused, in part, by inferior access to employment opportunities.

Ihlanfeldt, Keith R., and David L. Sjoquist. "Job Accessibility and Racial Differences in Youth Employment Rates." *American Economic Review* 8 (1990), pp. 267–76. Provides evidence from Philadelphia that inferior access is responsible for between a third and a half of the gap between black and white employment rates.

Kain, John T. "Black Suburbanization in the Eighties: A New Beginning or a False Hope?" In *American Domestic Priorities,* ed. John Quigley and Daniel Rubinfeld. Berkeley and Los Angeles: University of California, 1985. Describes recent trends in the suburbanization of blacks.

——. "Housing Segregation, Negro Employment, and Metropolitan Decentralization." *Quarterly Journal of Economics* 82 (1968), pp. 175–97.

——. "Housing Segregation, Negro Employment, and Metropolitan Decentralization: A Retrospective View." In *Patterns of Racial Discrimination.* Vol.1, *Housing,* ed. George Von Furstenburg, Bennett Harrison, and Ann R. Horowitz. Lexington, Mass.: D. C. Heath, 1974. Kain's response to Mooney.

Kasarda, John. "Urban Change and Minority Opportunities." In *The New Urban Reality,* ed. Paul Peterson. Washington, D.C.: Brookings Institution, 1985. Discusses the effects of changes in the spatial distribution of employment on central-city blacks. Also discusses the mismatch between central-city employment opportunities and the labor skills of central-city residents.

Leonard, Jonathan. "Comment." In *The Black Youth Employment Crisis,* ed. Richard B. Freeman and Harry J. Holzer. University of Chicago Press, 1986, pp. 185–90. Critiques the Ellwood paper.

Mills, Edwin S., and Richard Price. "Race and Residence in Earnings Determination." *Journal of Urban Economics* 17 (1985), pp. 1–7. Estimates the wage differentials caused by racial segregation and discrimination.

Mooney, Joseph D. "Housing Segregation, Negro Employment: An Alternative Perspective." *Quarterly Journal of Economics* 84 (1969), pp. 299–311. Critique of Kain's results.

Orr, Larry L. *Income, Employment, and Residential Location.* New York: Academic Press, 1975. A study of the spatial mismatch theory.

Pettigrew, Thomas. "Racial Change and the Intrametropolitan Distribution of Black Americans." In *The Prospective City,* ed. Arthur P. Solomon. Cambridge, Mass.: MIT Press, 1980.

Straszheim, Mahlon R. "Discrimination and the Spatial Characteristics of the Urban Labor Market for Black Workers." *Journal of Urban Economics* 7 (1980), pp. 119–40. Shows that black wages are higher in the suburbs than in the central city, reflecting the segregation of blacks in central cities.

U.S. Bureau of the Census. *Poverty in the United States: 1990.* Washington, D.C.: U.S. Government Printing Office, 1991.

U.S. Department of Housing and Urban Development. *Measuring Racial Discrimination in American Housing Markets.* Washington, D.C.: U.S. Government Printing Office, 1979.

——. *Recent Evidence on Discrimination.* Washington, D.C.: U.S. Government Printing Office, 1984.

Yinger, John. "Prejudice and Discrimination in the Urban Housing Market." In *Current Issues in Urban Economics,* ed. Peter Mieszkowski and Mahlon Straszheim. Baltimore: Johns Hopkins, 1979.

Education and the Evaluation of Title I Programs

Aaron, Henry J. *Politics and the Professors—The Great Society in Perspective.* Washington, D.C.: Brookings Institution, 1978. Discusses the uncertainty about the relationship between education and poverty.

Berrueta-Clement, John R., et al. *Changed Lives: The Effects of the Perry Preschool Programs on Youths through Age 19.* Ypsilanti, Mich.: High-Scope Press, 1984. Reports the results of a successful preschool program.

Glazer, Nathan. "Education and Training Programs and Poverty." In *Fighting Poverty: What Works and What Doesn't,* ed. Sheldon H. Danziger and Daniel H. Weinberg. Cambridge, Mass.: Harvard University Press, 1986. Discusses the effects of compensatory education on poverty, suggesting that preschool and elementary-school programs are most effective.

Jenks, Christopher. "Comment." In *Fighting Poverty: What Works and What Doesn't,* ed. Sheldon H. Danziger and Daniel H. Weinberg. Cambridge, Mass.: Harvard University Press, 1986. Discusses the effects of compensatory education on poverty, concluding that our understanding of the relationship between education and poverty is limited.

Kasarda, John. "Jobs, Migration, and Emerging Urban Mismatches." In *Urban Change and Poverty,* ed. Michael McGeary and Laurence Lynn. Washington, D.C.: National Academy Press, 1988.

National Assessment of Educational Progress. *Has Title I Improved Education for Disadvantaged Students? Evidence from Three National Assessments on Reading.* Washington, D.C.: U.S. Department of Education, 1981. Reports the results of NAEP tests showing increasing relative scores for minority students participating in Title I programs.

National Center for Education Statistics. *The Condition of Education: A Statistical Report.* Washington, D.C.: U.S. Department of Education, 1982. Reports the results of NAEP tests.

Labor-Market Discrimination

Arrow, Kenneth. "The Theory of Discrimination." In *Discrimination in Labor Markets,* ed. Orley Ashenfelter and Albert Rees. Princeton: Princeton University Press, 1973. Describes the phenomenon of statistical discrimination, which explains the persistence of wage differentials.

Becker, Gary S. *The Economics of Discrimination.* University of Chicago Press, 1957. Describes the market theory of discrimination, which suggests that competition limits the extent of wage discrimination.

Phelps, Edmund. "The Statistical Theory of Racism and Sexism." *American Economic Review* 62 (1972), pp. 659–61. Explains the theory of statistical discrimination.

Smith, James P., and Finis Welch. "Race Differences in Earnings: A Survey and New Evidence." In *Current Issues in Urban Economics,* ed. Peter Mieszkowski and Mahlon Straszheim. Baltimore: Johns Hopkins, 1979. Summarizes the evidence on wage discrimination.

Thurow, Lester C. *Poverty and Discrimination.* Washington, D.C.: Brookings Institution, 1969. Discusses the link between poverty and racial discrimination (unequal pay for equal work, denial of access to high-paying jobs).

U.S. Commission on Civil Rights. *Unemployment and Underemployment among Blacks, Hispanics, and Women.* Washington, D.C.: U.S. Government Printing Office, 1982. Discusses labor-market discrimination against minority groups.

Increase in Female-Headed Households: Reasons and Effects on Poverty

Bane, Mary Jo. "Household Composition and Poverty." In *Fighting Poverty: What Works and What Doesn't*, ed. Sheldon H. Danziger and Daniel H. Weinberg. Cambridge, Mass.: Harvard University Press, 1986. Discusses the effects of changes in family structure on poverty rates, suggesting that such changes between 1959 and 1979 increased the 1979 poverty rate by two percentage points.

Ellwood, David T., and Mary Jo Bane. "The Impact of AFDC on Family Structure and Living Arrangements." *Research in Labor Economics* 7 (1985), pp. 137–208. Explores the relationship between welfare benefit levels and family structure.

Ellwood, David T., and Jonathan Crane. "Family Change among Black Americans: What Do We Know?" *Journal of Economic Perspectives* 4 (Fall 1990), pp. 65–84.

Ellwood, David T., and Lawrence H. Summers. "Poverty in America: Is Welfare the Answer or the Problem?" In *Fighting Poverty: What Works and What Doesn't*, ed. Sheldon H. Danziger and Daniel H. Weinberg. Cambridge, Mass.: Harvard University Press, 1986. Discusses the effects of AFDC on family structure, addressing the issue of whether AFDC causes the breakup of families.

Garfinkel, Irwin, and Sara S. McLanahan, *Single Mothers and Their Children: A New American Dilemma*. Washington, D.C.: Urban Institute, 1986.

Moffit, Robert. "Work Incentives in the AFDC System: An Analysis of the 1981 Reforms." *American Economic Review* 76 (1986), pp. 219–23.

Murray, Charles. *Losing Ground: American Social Policy, 1950–1980*. New York: Basic Books, 1984. Argues that welfare policy was a large factor in the growth of female-headed households.

Wilson, William Julius, and Kathryn Neckerman. "Poverty and Family Structure: The Widening Gap between Evidence and Public Policy Issues." In *Fighting Poverty: What Works and What Doesn't*, ed. Sheldon H. Danziger and Daniel H. Weinberg. Cambridge, Mass.: Harvard University Press, 1986. Examines changes in fertility rates and family structure and the effects of welfare policy on the number of female-headed households. Concludes that male joblessness is the most important factor in the increase in female-headed households.

Urban Underclass

Auletta, Ken. *The Underclass*. New York: Random House, 1982.

Lemann, Nicholas. "The Origins of the Underclass." *Atlantic Monthly* (June and July 1986). Discusses the development of a black underclass in central cities.

Ricketts, Erol R., and Isabel V. Sawhill. "Defining and Measuring the Underclass." *Journal of Policy Analysis and Management* 7 (1988), pp. 316–25.

Wilson, William Julius. "The Urban Underclass in Advanced Industrial Society." In *The New Urban Reality*, ed. Paul Peterson. Washington, D.C.: Brookings Institution, 1985. Discusses the special problems of the urban underclass.

CHAPTER 13 Poverty and Public Policy

This chapter discusses several programs designed to reduce poverty, including education and training programs, cash assistance, and in-kind transfers (food stamps and medical care). The principal question of this chapter is: how effective are these policies in decreasing poverty and welfare dependence? The chapter also evaluates various welfare-reform proposals, including the negative income tax, workfare, and a recent proposal that would combine child support from absent fathers with tax credits for poor working mothers. Finally, this chapter addresses the special problems of the central city: what can be done to increase the incomes and decrease the welfare dependence of central-city residents?

Employment and Job-Training Programs

As explained in the previous chapter, the federal government can use macroeconomic policies to stimulate economic growth and decrease poverty. Since the early 1960s, the federal government has supplemented its macroeconomic policies with employment and job-training programs. Employment programs operate on the demand side of the market, providing direct employment for the poor. These programs are sometimes used when the government fears that the stimulation of the national economy will increase the inflation rate. Job-training programs operate on the supply side of the labor market: they increase the labor skills of the poor, making them more attractive to private industry. Spending on employment and training programs increased during the 1960s and 1970s, and then fell during the 1980s: real spending per capita (in 1972 dollars) rose from 2.9 cents in 1965 to 29 cents in 1979, and then fell to 6.4 cents in 1984 (Bassi and Ashenfelter, 1986).

Since the early 1960s, there have been dozens of employment and training programs. Bassi and Ashenfelter (1986) and Schiller (1989) outline the history of the various programs and summarize the results of many of the benefit-cost studies of the programs. Some of the most important programs are the following:

1. **Manpower Development and Training Act (1962).** Although the original purpose of this program was to provide training to experienced workers displaced by changes in the labor market (typically male heads of households), it evolved into a program to assist the hard-core unemployed. The program increased the earnings of male participants by about $200 per year and increased the earnings of women by about $500 per year.

2. **Job Corps (1965).** The Job Corps program is an intensive training and counseling program for disadvantaged youths (low-income and minority youths between the ages of 6 and 12). In 1980, the cost per participant was $13,000. The program increases employment rates and earnings, and decreases welfare dependence, out-of-wedlock births, and criminal activity. The estimated benefit-cost ratio of the program is about 1.45.

3. **Work Incentive Program (WIN) (1965).** The purpose of WIN was to encourage AFDC recipients to get jobs. The program provided day care, transportation, counseling, and job-placement services to welfare mothers. Funding for this program decreased sharply during the 1980s, and the program was eventually dropped in 1987.

4. **Public Employment Program (PEP) (1971).** Under PEP, the federal government subsidized employment in state and local governments. A small amount of money was also provided for training. After they left the program, women and minorities earned significantly more than they did before the program. In contrast, the program did not increase the earnings of white men.

5. **Comprehensive Employment and Training Act (CETA) (1974).** The CETA program was a mixture of employment and training programs. The federal government gave money to local "prime sponsors" to run employment and training programs. Between 1974 and 1982, CETA served a total of 30 million people, with most of the participants coming from low-income and minority households: in 1983, about 95 percent of the participants came from disadvantaged households. Researchers have examined the effects of CETA on the earnings of participants after they leave the program. There are four basic results:
   a. The earnings of women increased, but the earnings of men did not. Three years after participation, women were earning between $600 and $1,200 more as a result of the program, a substantial increase relative to their preprogram earnings ($2,700).
   b. The earnings of women increased as a result of increases in hours worked, not increases in wages.
   c. The largest gains were experienced by the most disadvantaged workers.
   d. The most effective components of CETA were classroom training, on-the-job training, and public-service employment. The least effective component was a program that acclimated participants to the work environment without much training or actual work.

6. **National Supported Work Demonstration (NSWD) (1975).** This experimental program enrolled several "problem" groups (long-term AFDC recipients, reformed drug addicts, reformed offenders, and high school dropouts) in a highly structured program with counseling and work experience. For AFDC recipients, the program increased both wages and the hours worked. For ex-addicts, the program generated a large decrease in crime rates but only a small increase in earnings. The estimated benefit-cost ratio was over 2.0 for AFDC recipients and about 1.9 for ex-addicts. The program had relatively small effects on youths and reformed offenders, so the benefit-cost ratios for these groups were less than 1.0.

7. **Youth Employment Demonstration Projects Act (YEDPA) (1977).** This program was similar to the Job Corps program, and it generated similar results. The most effective parts of the YEDPA program were remedial education, job training, and training in job-search skills.

8. **Job Training Partnership Act (JTPA) (1982).** JTPA replaced CETA, bringing two basic changes in employment and training policies. First, JTPA does not provide any public employment, but instead focuses on job training. Second, JTPA enrolls disadvantaged people *and* dislocated workers (people who have lost jobs because of plant closures and permanent layoffs). In 1988, about 1 million people participated in JTPA job-training and job-search programs (Schiller, 1989).

There are four general conclusions from the benefit-cost studies of employment and job-training programs. First, programs that focus on youths (e.g., Job Corps and YEDPA) are successful. Second, programs that stress classroom teaching and on-the-job training often increase the earnings of women, particularly those with little prior work experience. Third, the successful job-training programs increase earnings by increasing the number of hours worked, not by increasing wages. Fourth, training programs have relatively small effects on the earnings of adult men.

Direct Income Transfers: AFDC and SSI

Table 13–1 shows federal spending on various antipoverty programs in 1987. Total spending was over $100 billion. About one quarter of this sum was spent on direct income transfers: Aid to Families with Dependent Children (AFDC), Supplemental Security Income (SSI), and General Assistance. The bulk of AFDC money went to female-headed households. SSI is a special program for the aged, the blind, and the permanently disabled. General Assistance is a program for the poor who do not qualify for AFDC or SSI.

Total spending on AFDC was $16 billion in 1987. AFDC payments went to a total of 11 million people, with an average payment of $123 per recipient per month. The federal government provides about half the funds for AFDC, with state and local governments contributing the other half. State governments set the eligibility requirements and the benefit levels. In most states, eligibility for AFDC is limited

---

TABLE 13–1   Spending on Transfer Programs in 1987

Program	Number of Recipients (millions)	Average Monthly Benefit ($)	Annual Cost ($ billion)
Income Transfers			
Aid to Families with Dependent Children (AFDC)	11	123	16.3
Supplemental Security Income (SSI)	4	252	9.9
General Assistance (GA)	1	144	1.4
In-Kind Transfers			
Medicaid	23	179	49.3
Food stamps	21	46	12.5
Housing assistance	4	57	11.2
School lunch program	24	11	3.2
Total			103.8

SOURCE: Bradley Schiller, *The Economics of Poverty and Discrimination,* 5th ed. (Englewood Cliffs, N.J.: Prentice Hall, 1989).

---

to families in which one parent is either absent or disabled. In 1987, the average monthly payment for a three-person household ranged from $114 in Alabama to $553 in California. Nationwide, the average monthly payment for a three-person household was $359.

AFDC and SSI are "means-tested" programs in the sense that the payment to a household depends on its earnings (market income). Under AFDC, the first $30 of monthly market income does not affect the AFDC payment, but every additional dollar decreases the AFDC payment by one dollar. Under SSI, the recipient can earn $65 of market income per month without affecting the SSI grant, and every additional dollar decreases the SSI payment by 50 cents.

AFDC and Work Incentives: Theory

How does AFDC affect the labor supply of recipients? Figure 13–1 shows the trade-offs between income and leisure time for Judy, a potential AFDC recipient. The horizontal axis measures the number of leisure (nonworking) hours per week, and the vertical axis measures her weekly income. Suppose that Judy's wage is $4 per hour, and she has 100 hours per week to allocate between work and other activities. One option is point *A* (zero income and 100 hours of free time). As her work time increases, Judy moves up her budget line (*AB*), increasing her income by $4 per hour of work. In other words, the opportunity cost of leisure time is $4 per hour.

Judy's negatively sloped indifference curves reflect her preferences for income and nonworking time. For example, she is indifferent between points *C* and *F*: point *F* has less income but more leisure time, and the lower income is offset by more nonworking time. Given her budget line and the shapes of her indifference curves, she maximizes utility at point *C*: she chooses 80 hours of leisure time, 20 hours of work (100 minus 80), and $80 of income ($4 times 20).

FIGURE 13–1   AFDC Decreases Hours Worked from 20 to 0

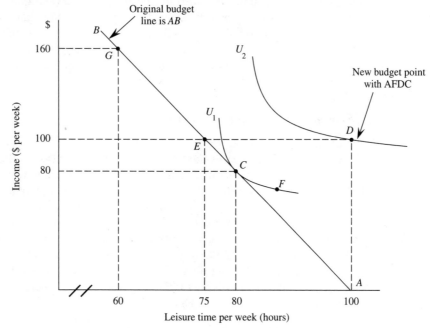

Given her original budget line, Judy maximizes utility at point *C* (20 hours of labor and $80 income).
AFDC (payment of $100) adds point *D* to the budget set. Utility is higher at point *D* because Judy gets
more leisure time and more income. Therefore, AFDC decreases work effort from 20 hours to zero.

Suppose that Judy is offered an AFDC payment of $100 per week. The cash
payment adds point *D* to her budget set: she can have 100 hours of leisure time
(zero hours of work) and an income of $100. If her AFDC payment is reduced by
one dollar for every dollar of market income, her new budget line is *ADEB:* starting
from point *D,* a one-hour reduction in leisure time (a one-hour increase in labor time)
increases her labor income by $4, but also decreases her AFDC payment by the
same amount. This dollar-for-dollar trade-off continues until she exhausts her AFDC
payment. Therefore, for up to 25 hours of work (75 hours of leisure), her net wage
is zero.

Given the shapes of Judy's indifference curves, utility is maximized at point
D, so she accepts the AFDC payment. Under the AFDC program, she can have both
more income and more leisure time, so her choice is an easy one. The AFDC program
decreases Judy's labor supply from 20 hours per week to zero.

For some workers, the choice between working and AFDC is not so straightforward. Suppose that before the offer of AFDC, Judy worked full-time (40 hours per
week). In Figure 13–1, she starts at point *G,* with an income of $160 per week. Will
she enroll in an AFDC program offering $100 per week? If she joins the AFDC pro-
gram, she would sacrifice $60 of income (the difference between her market income
and the AFDC payment) to get 40 hours of extra nonworking time. She will accept
AFDC if the value of the extra time is large relative to the income sacrifice.

AFDC is attractive to single mothers with low wages or small children. If the wage is low, the income sacrificed by accepting AFDC (and quitting a job) is relatively small. For many poor households, wages are so low that the acceptance of AFDC increases household income. The presence of preschool children encourages use of AFDC because (1) many mothers want to participate in their child's development and (2) the cost of child care decreases the net wage. If, say, Judy pays $1 per hour for someone to take care of her children, her net wage is $3, not $4.

AFDC and Work Incentives: Evidence

What are the actual effects of AFDC on labor supply? A number of studies have shown that AFDC decreases the labor supply of recipients (see Blank, 1985). The reasons are rather simple. First, recipients have relatively low wages, so their market incomes either exceed the AFDC payment by a small amount or are less than the AFDC payment. AFDC is a good deal because it (1) increases the opportunities for nonwork activities and (2) either increases total income or decreases it by a small amount. Second, for incomes above $30 per month, the net wage of an AFDC recipient is zero (AFDC falls by $1 for every dollar of market income), so there is little incentive to work more than a few hours per week. Given the combination of low market earnings, child-care responsibilities, and a 100 percent tax rate, it is not surprising that few AFDC recipients work.

The Negative Income Tax

The alternative to the conventional welfare program is a negative income tax. Figure 13–2 shows labor-income trade-offs under a negative income tax. The wage of the household's worker is $4 per hour. The negative income tax has a basic grant of $100 and a marginal tax rate of 50 percent. A household with zero market income receives the basic grant ($100). For every additional dollar of market income (every quarter hour of work), the grant decreases by 50 cents. For example, if the household works 10 hours per week and earns $40, the grant decreases by $20, from $100 to $80, so the household's total income would be $120. The grant is exhausted at a market income of $200 (50 hours of work).

The Response of Recipients

Figure 13–3 shows the effect of the negative income tax on Mary, an AFDC recipient with a wage of $4. In the absence of income assistance, she works 30 hours per week and earns $120 (point *F*). Under AFDC, utility is maximized at point *D*, so Mary quits her job and collects $100 in AFDC. Under a negative income tax with a basic grant of $100 and a tax rate of 50 percent, her budget line is *ADB:* the grant is $100 for zero market income, and decreases by 50 cents for every dollar of market income. The grant runs out when her market income reaches $200 (labor time equals 50 hours). Under the negative income tax, Mary maximizes her utility at point *K,* with 80 hours of leisure, 20 hours of labor (100 minus 80), $80 of market income

FIGURE 13–2   **Labor-Income Choice under a Negative Income Tax**

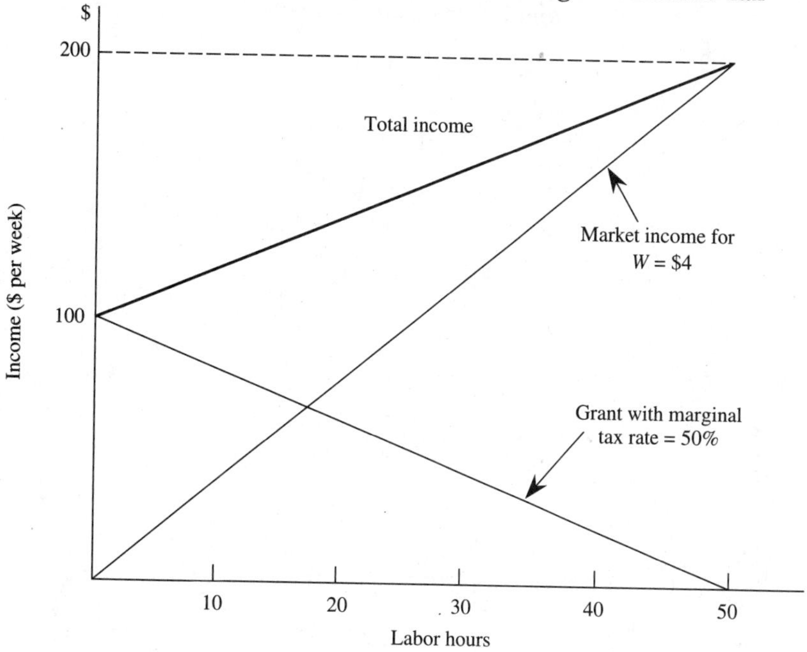

The wage is $4 per hour, the basic grant under the negative income tax is $100, and the marginal tax rate is 50 percent. The grant is exhausted when labor equals 50 hours per week (market income is $200). Total income is the sum of market income and the grant.

($4 times 20), a grant of $60 ($100 minus half of $80), and total income of $140 ($80 plus $60).

The switch from AFDC to the negative income tax decreases Mary's grant but increases her total income. Because her net wage increases from zero to $2, she increases her hours worked from zero to 20, and keeps half of her market income. As a result, her total income increases from $100 (the AFDC grant) to $140 (market income plus the $60 grant). The switch in welfare policy saves taxpayers money because every $1 of market income decreases Mary's grant by 50 cents: Mary earns $80 in market income, saving taxpayers $40.

The Negative Income Tax and Work Effort

The negative income tax has been proposed as an unconditional grant. In other words, it would be available to all households, not just those currently eligible for AFDC. How would it affect the work effort of different types of households? Three types of households would be eligible for support under a negative income tax:

1. **Current AFDC recipients.** As shown in Figure 13–3, the switch from AFDC to the negative income tax increases Mary's work effort from zero hours to 20 hours.

FIGURE 13–3   **Negative Income Tax Increases Recipient Income and Decreases the Transfer**

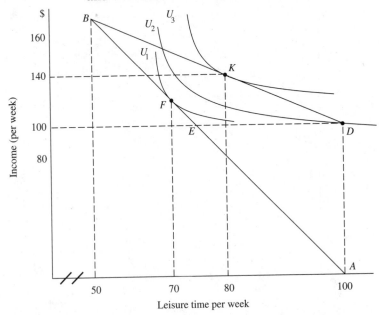

Given her original budget line, Mary maximizes utility at point F (30 hours of labor and $120 income). AFDC (payment of $100) adds point D to the budget set, and Mary maximizes utility at point D. Under a negative income tax with a grant of $100 and a 50 percent marginal tax rate, the budget line is ADB. Utility is maximized at point K, with 80 hours of leisure time, 20 hours of work, $80 of market income, and $60 of grant income. The switch from AFDC increases Mary's income by $40 and saves taxpayers $40.

2. **Poor households ineligible for AFDC, with persons capable of working.** This type of household may start at point F in Figure 13–3. Under the negative income tax, the household moves from point F to point K, decreasing work effort from 30 hours to 20 hours.

3. **Households without persons capable of working** (the elderly, the disabled, and households with very young children). This type of household is eligible for some type of support (AFDC or SSI), so it picks point D before and after the negative income tax. Since working is not an option for this type of household, the negative income tax has no effect on work effort.

To summarize, the negative income tax is likely to increase work effort among current AFDC recipients and decrease work effort among households that are currently ineligible for AFDC.

What are the facts on the labor-supply effects of the negative income tax? The federal government ran a series of experiments in the 1960s and 1970s to test the effects of a negative income tax. Poor households were divided into two groups: one group was eligible for a negative-income tax program, and the other group continued to receive conventional welfare payments. The negative-income tax program was more generous than existing programs, with basic grants between 95 percent and 140 percent of the official poverty level. The marginal tax rates were all above 50 percent. The negative income tax decreased the labor supply of men, women, and youth: the average reduction in hours worked was 10 percent for men, 14 percent for female household heads, and 24 percent for youths. These supply responses were large enough to disturb most policymakers. As a result, the negative income tax dropped off the welfare-reform agenda.

The basic problem with the negative income tax is that it enrolls two different types of households in a single program. For a household in which no one is capable of working, the basic grant should be high enough to provide adequate support. In contrast, for a household with people capable of working, the marginal tax rate should be low enough to encourage work effort. The government is unlikely to adopt a program with both a large basic grant and a low marginal tax rate because such a program would be extremely expensive. If the government chooses a large basic grant and a high marginal tax rate, it would provide adequate support for worker-less households, but would also discourage work effort. If it chooses a small basic grant and a low tax rate, work effort would be encouraged, but workerless households would receive inadequate support. One response to this problem is to have one redistributional program for workerless households and another program for households with people capable of working.

In-Kind Transfers

As shown in Table 13–1, federal spending on in-kind programs exceeded $76 billion in 1987, about three times the total spending on direct transfers. The three largest in-kind programs are medicaid ($49.3 billion), food stamps ($12.5 billion), and housing ($11.2 billion). This section discusses medicaid and food stamps. Housing programs are discussed in Chapter 15 (Housing Policies).

Medicaid provides free medical care to the recipients of AFDC and SSI. It is essentially a free medical insurance policy: the government agrees to cover all the recipient's medical expenses, just as a private insurer would. The difference is that medicaid is free. In 1987, two thirds of medicaid funds went to aged and disabled households (SSI recipients). In a comprehensive evaluation of the medicaid program, Starr (1986) suggests that the program was responsible for increases in life expectancy and decreases in infant mortality among the poor.

Under the food-stamp program, poor households are given coupons that can be exchanged for food. The food-stamp allotment depends on household income. Every additional dollar of market income decreases the food-stamp allotment by 30 cents, so the effective marginal tax rate is 30 percent.

Figure 13–4 shows the effects of a $100 food-stamp allotment on the recipient. The food-stamp program shifts the budget line from AB to AGD. Ann starts at point R (spending $50 on food), and moves to point G under the food-stamp program. In contrast, Bill moves from point P ($300 on food) to Q. For Bill, the food-stamp program is equivalent to a cash transfer of $100 because he uses the food stamps to

FIGURE 13–4   The Equivalence of Food Stamps and Cash

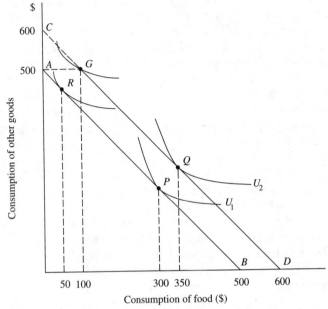

With an original budget line of *AB*, Bill chooses point *P* ($300 on food and $200 on other goods). The budget line with $100 worth of food stamps is *AGD* and Bill moves to point *Q*. Food stamps are equivalent to a $100 cash transfer (budget line *CD*) because Bill uses the stamps to decrease his own food expenditures, freeing up $100 to spend on either food or other goods. If Ann starts at point *R*, she spends less than $100 on food, so she cannot use the food stamps to replace her own food expenditures. Therefore, she would prefer $100 in cash to $100 worth of food stamps.

free up $100 of his own $300 food budget. In contrast, Ann initially spends only $50 on food, so she can use food stamps to replace only $50 worth of food spending. For Ann, the food-stamp program is equivalent to a cash transfer of less than $100.

Most food-stamp recipients are like Bill: their desired spending on food exceeds the food-stamp allotment. Therefore, the value of food stamps to recipients is close to the market value of the stamps. According to Smeeding (1982), one dollar of food stamps is worth about 97 cents to the typical recipient. Evidence from welfare experiments supports the idea that food stamps are equivalent to cash transfers. In one experiment, the replacement of food stamps with cash payments did not affect the food consumption of recipients (Blanchard et al., 1982).

Effects of Cash and In-Kind Transfers on Poverty

This section addresses two questions about the effects of government transfer programs. First, how do the transfer programs affect the typical poor household? Second, to what extent do the programs decrease poverty?

TABLE 13–2   Earnings, Benefits, and Income for Single Mother with Two Children

Level of Work and Wages	Earnings	Day Care	Taxes + EIC*	AFDC + Food Stamps	Disposable Income	Medicaid
No work	0	0	0	$6,284	$6,284	Yes
Full-time at $4.00 per hour	8,000	−3,000	171	1,624	6,795	Yes
Full-time at $5.00 per hour	10,000	−3,000	−172	970	7,798	No
Full-time at $6.00 per hour	12,000	−3,000	−515	538	9,023	No

*Taxes + EIC include
1. Social security tax of 7.15 percent.
2. EIC: refundable credit of 14 percent of earned income to a maximum of $868.

Source: David T. Ellwood, *Poor Support* (New York: Basic Books, 1988), p. 139.

Effects of Transfers on the Typical Poor Household

Table 13–2 shows an example of the options faced by the typical poor household, a female-headed household with two children. It shows annual disposable income for different amounts of work and wages, taking into account the effects of market income on income transfers and in-kind transfers. If the household head does not work, her disposable income equals the sum of AFDC and food stamps ($6,284). As her income increases, her benefits from transfer programs decrease.

If the woman accepts a job paying $4 per hour, there is bad news and good news. The bad news is that she spends money on day care and receives less from AFDC and food stamps. The good news is that she earns income and also gets an earned income tax credit. Poor households receive a 14 percent tax credit on earned income, with a maximum credit of $868. The net result of these changes in day-care costs, welfare payments, wages, and tax credits is an increase in disposable income of $511.

Working is slightly more lucrative at higher wages. Although a higher wage generates more earnings, it also increases taxes (the earned income tax credit is eventually dominated by income and payroll taxes) and decreases the AFDC payment and the food-stamp allotment. Even if the woman worked a full-time job at a wage of $6, her disposable income would still be below the poverty line ($9,800). An added problem is that she eventually loses her medicaid coverage. For a low-wage single mother, the benefits of working are relatively small.

Effects of Transfer Programs on Poverty

Table 13–3 shows the effects of various transfer programs on poverty rates. In the absence of transfer payments, the overall poverty rate would have been over 20 percent, and the poverty rate for aged persons would have been over 55 percent. Social security and other nonwelfare transfers cut the poverty rate for the aged to 15 percent and decreased the poverty rate for families by about 2 percentage points. Cash transfers decreased the poverty rates of nonaged households by an additional percentage

TABLE 13–3   Effects of Transfer Programs on Poverty, 1988

	Percent of Group in Poverty			
	Before Transfers	*After Social Security and Nonwelfare Transfers*	*After Cash Welfare Transfers*	*After Cash, Food Stamps, and Housing*
All persons	20.8	14.5	13.6	12.2
Families with children	19.5	17.4	16.5	14.6
Aged persons	55.8	15.3	13.9	11.8

SOURCE: U.S. Congress, Committee on Ways and Means, *Background Material and Data on Programs within the Jurisdiction of the Committee on Ways and Means* (Washington, D.C.: U.S. Government Printing Office, 1988).

point. Finally, food stamps and housing programs cut poverty rates of aged persons and families by an additional two percentage points.

Welfare Reform

The Family Support Act of 1988 is the most recent attempt to reform the U.S. welfare system. The legislation is designed to move people off the welfare rolls into productive employment. States are directed to enroll their welfare recipients in programs offering remedial education, job training, work experience, and assistance with job searches. By 1995, 20 percent of welfare recipients are supposed to be enrolled in these self-help programs. Parents with small children (less than three years old) are not required to participate in the training and search programs. The legislation also directed the states to require 16 hours of community service per month from two-parent welfare households.

Workfare

Workfare is defined as a program under which welfare recipients are forced to participate in various employment and training programs. Wiseman (1987) describes workfare as a process, a series of steps that a potential welfare recipient must go through to qualify for support. Figure 13–5 shows Wiseman's version of the workfare process.

1. **Preliminary assessment.** A social worker gathers information about the applicant's skills and employment record and finds out what kind of assistance will be needed (e.g., child care, transportation) to get the person back to work.
2. **Job search.** After developing a job-search strategy, the applicant searches for a job under the close supervision of a search supervisor. If the applicant finds a job, she drops out of the workfare process; if the job pays enough, she also drops out of the welfare system.

FIGURE 13–5   **The Workfare Process**

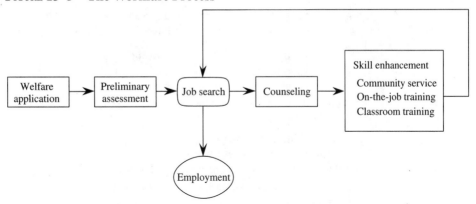

SOURCE: Michael Wiseman, "How Workfare Really Works," *Public Interest* 89 (Fall 1987), p. 39.

3. **Counseling.** If the applicant does not find a job after several weeks, she moves into a counseling program. The counselor determines the reasons for the unsuccessful job search and designs a program to enhance the applicant's employability.

4. **Skill enhancement.** Some of the enhancement options are unpaid work experience (community service), on-the-job training (public or private), or classroom training for specific skills.

5. **Job search.** When the enhancement program is completed, the applicant searches again, and ideally finds a job and drops out of the workfare process. If not, she is sent back to counseling.

This model of workfare differs from the popular vision of workfare in one important respect. The "work" in workfare is often assumed to be mandatory community service for no pay. In fact, community service is but one of the options under the skill-enhancement step of the program. Participants can also "work" in the classroom or earn money while acquiring on-the-job training.

What happens if the applicant refuses to go through the workfare process? A mild form of punishment is to remove some of the applicant's discretion in spending his welfare check. For example, the agency might pay his landlord and deduct the rent from his welfare check. A more severe punishment is to cut the welfare payment.

The experiments with workfare suggest that it can move a small number of people off the welfare rolls. In a widely cited experimental program in San Diego, 47.3 percent of workfare participants were receiving public assistance nine months after enrolling in the program, compared to 53 percent of a control group that did not go through the workfare process. In other words, workfare decreased the welfare caseload by a relatively small amount.

Reform Proposal: Child Support and Earned Income Credit

Garfinkel and Uhr (1984) and Ellwood (1988) have proposed several changes in welfare policy. Their reform proposals have four features:

1. **Child-support requirements.** Absent fathers would be required to pay child support. For example, an absent father of two children would be required to pay one quarter of his income for child support. Under the current system, only about one third of female-headed households receive child support.

2. **Minimum child support.** The federal government would guarantee a minimum level of child support, for example $1,750 per child per year. The federal government would make up the difference between the father's contribution and the minimum support level. The minimum child-support program would replace AFDC.

3. **Increased earned income tax credit.** The current EIC, which is 14 percent of earned income with a maximum credit of $868, would be increased to 25 percent of earned income with a maximum credit of $2,000.

4. **Child-care tax credit.** Poor families would receive a 30 percent tax credit for child care.

Table 13–4 shows the effects of such a scheme on the typical poor female-headed household. The figures are based on the assumption that the mother receives only the minimum level of child support. Many poor female-headed households would in fact receive greater child-support payments from the absent father though others would receive less. The proposed scheme allows a single working mother to keep more of her earned income because (1) the earned income tax credit is more generous, (2) the cost of day care is reduced by the child-care credit, and (3) the child-support payment does not decrease as her income increases.

TABLE 13–4   **Earnings, Benefits, and Income for Single Mother with Two Children under Higher Earned Income Tax Credit and Guaranteed Child Support**

Level of Work and Wages	Earnings	Day Care	Taxes + EIC*	Child Support	Disposable Income
No work	0	0	0	$3,500	$ 3,500
Full-time at $5.00 per hour	10,000	−3,000	+1,185	3,500	11,685
Full-time at $6.00 per hour	12,000	−3,000	+642	3,500	13,142

*Taxes and EIC include
  1. 30 percent child-care tax credit.
  2. Social security tax of 7.15 percent.
  3. EIC of 25 percent up to $8,000; reduced by 20 cents per dollar above $8,000.
SOURCE: David T. Ellwood, *Poor Support* (New York: Basic Books, 1988), p. 167.

The proposal has several desirable features. First, if the absent father earns enough income, the 25 percent support payment will lift many female-headed house-holds out of poverty. For example, if the father's income is $22,000, the child-support payment would be $5,500, not just 3,500. Second, because the working woman keeps more of her earnings, it encourages work effort. Finally, it may actually save money. According to Garfinkel, if the collection rate from absent fathers is 80 percent and the minimum child-support benefit is $2,000 per child, the program would cost less than the current welfare system. The program is sufficiently attractive that it is being tried in the state of Wisconsin.

The Problems of the Central-City Economy

One of the most difficult problems in the urban economy is the concentration of poverty in the central city. Among the reasons for central-city poverty (discussed in the previous chapter) are (1) the segregation of blacks in central cities, far from suburban employment opportunities (the spatial mismatch problem), (2) increases in the education and skill requirements of central-city jobs, (3) labor-market discrimi-nation, and (4) inadequate education. The NBER study of black teenage unemploy-ment suggests that some causes of the problems of black inner-city teenagers are weak labor markets, competition with adult females, discrimination, opportunities for crime, and inadequate education.

One approach to solving the inner-city poverty problem is based on the spatial mismatch theory. The idea is that poverty is caused by spatial considerations and can be solved by one of two spatial policies: dispersal of the central-city population or economic development of the inner-city economy.

Dispersal Policies

Under a dispersal policy, central-city blacks would be moved to suburban communi-ties. The idea behind dispersal is that blacks should live near suburban employment centers. As discussed in Chapter 12, the government could promote black subur-banization with fair-housing laws, less restrictive zoning, and state support of local governments.

The critics of the dispersal option raise four questions:

1. **Integration.** Will dispersal cause real integration, or the development of smaller, more numerous concentrations of racial minorities (mini-ghettos)?
2. **Black underclass.** Will dispersal allow the most mobile and wealthy blacks to move to the suburbs, leaving immobile and poor blacks in the central city? When middle-income blacks (e.g., clerical workers and midlevel managers) leave the central city, it becomes a less at-tractive location for employers, so employment opportunities for poor blacks (e.g., janitors) decrease. In addition, the departure of middle-income blacks decreases the demand for retail goods, decreasing the

employment opportunities for low-skilled retail workers. Some people fear that the departure of middle-income blacks will cause more poor blacks to slip into the underclass, a group of people dependent on crime, drugs, and welfare.

3. **Cultural disruption.** Will the dispersal of blacks disrupt black culture and society?

4. **Spatial mismatch.** What if the spatial mismatch theory is incorrect and geographical access to jobs is not the source of the black unemployment problem? If so, simply moving blacks to the suburbs will not solve the problem. If poverty is caused by job discrimination, inferior education, and low skills, these other sources of poverty must be addressed.

The Development Option

The alternative to dispersal is the development of the central-city economy. In contrast to the dispersal policy, which brings workers to suburban jobs, the development policy bring jobs to central-city residents.

There are three approaches to development policy. First, under the **black capitalism** approach, the government encourages the development of black businesses. The experiences with black capitalism have not been encouraging (see Bates and Bradford, 1979). Second, **community development corporations (CDCs)** assist black businesses, oversee large development projects, and run various community projects (housing assistance, job training). Third, the government can establish **enterprise zones**, areas of the city where firms (1) pay lower taxes, (2) receive subsidies for worker training, and (3) are exempted from many local regulations. Given the limited experience with enterprise zones, it is too early to say whether they will be effective.

The critics of the development option raise five questions:

1. **Viable location.** Is the central city a viable location for firms? The suburbanization of jobs was caused by fundamental changes in the economy (e.g., the development of the auto and the truck, innovations in information technology). Given the advantages of a suburban location, a firm in the central city may be unable to compete with its suburban counterpart.

2. **Zero-sum employment changes.** Will the gain in central-city employment come at the expense of employment elsewhere in the city?

3. **Low skills.** Do central-city residents have the education and skills to work in new stores, factories, and offices?

4. **Migration.** How many new central-city jobs are filled by current residents of the central city? How many are filled by newcomers? As explained in Chapter 6, at the metropolitan level, about three fourths of new jobs are filled by newcomers. Since intracity mobility is greater than

intercity mobility, an even larger fraction of new central-city jobs are likely to be filled by newcomers.

5. **Spatial mismatch.** What if the spatial mismatch theory is incorrect and geographical access to jobs is not the source of the black unemployment problem? If this theory is incorrect, bringing jobs to the central city will not solve the problem. Other sources of poverty (job discrimination, inferior education, and low skills) must be addressed.

The debate over dispersal versus development has continued for decades. The issues are complex, and the questions raised by each side are not easily answered. In recent years, several states have experimented with enterprise zones. The information from these experiments will be valuable in the debate over the merits of the development option.

Conclusion—What Can Be Done about Poverty?

There is no single policy that will eliminate poverty. Nonetheless, there are many policies that could be used to whittle the problem down to a more manageable size. Title I education programs have increased the achievement levels of disadvantaged students, increasing their earning potential. Job-training programs have increased the earnings of the most disadvantaged workers. The reform of child-support laws would increase support from absent fathers, decreasing poverty among female-headed households. An increase in the earned income tax credit would decrease poverty and increase the incentives for welfare recipients to work. Finally, workfare may increase the employment opportunities of welfare recipients. Each of these policies may have a small effect on the poverty problem, but together they could decrease poverty significantly.

Summary

1. Some government job-training programs have been successful for some participants.
   a. Youth programs (Job Corps and YEPTA) increased earnings and decreased crime rates.
   b. Programs that stress classroom teaching and on-the-job training increased the earnings of women, particularly those with little prior work experience.
2. Because AFDC recipients have low wages, AFDC increases the opportunities for nonwork activities (e.g., child care), and either increases income or decreases it by a small amount. AFDC discourages work effort because the marginal tax rate is close to 100 percent.
3. An alternative to AFDC is a negative income tax, under which recipients would keep a large fraction of their market income. The problem with such

a program is that some households (those not eligible for AFDC) would decrease their labor supply.

4. The two largest in-kind transfer programs are medicaid and food stamps.
   a. Medicaid is equivalent to a private medical insurance policy. Medicaid
      has improved the health of the poor.
   b. Food-stamp allotments typically fall short of the food consumption of re-
      cipients, so food stamps are equivalent to cash payments.

5. Federal transfer programs decreased the overall poverty rate from 20.8 percent to 12.2 percent.

6. Under workfare, welfare recipients participate in various employment and
   training programs. The Family Support Act of 1988 has a workfare component that is designed to move people off the welfare rolls into productive
   employment.

7. One reform proposal combines required child-support payments from absent
   fathers, a minimum child-support payment from the government, a tax credit
   for day care, and an increase in the earned income tax credit. Such a program would eliminate the need for AFDC and would encourage work effort.

8. Under a dispersal policy, blacks would be moved closer to suburban employment centers. The critics of the dispersal approach suggest that the suburbanization of employable blacks will contribute to the development of a permanent underclass in the central city.

9. Under a development policy, jobs would be moved closer to central-city
   blacks. Development strategies include black capitalism, community development corporations, and enterprise zones. The critics of the development approach suggest that the central city is not a viable location for most firms and
   that any central-city employment gains come at the expense of other areas of
   the city. If central-city residents do not have the skills for the new jobs, the
   new jobs will be filled by newcomers.

Exercises and Discussion Questions

1. Figure 13–1 shows the budget line for AFDC as if every dollar of market
   income decreases the AFDC payment by one dollar. Under current policy, the
   first $30 of market earnings do not affect the AFDC payment. Draw a budget
   line consistent with the current AFDC policy.

2. The city of Berkeley recently started a program under which citizens can
   purchase vouchers that can be redeemed for food at local restaurants. The
   idea is that the citizens can give the vouchers—instead of cash—to people
   asking for handouts. Suppose that the program causes all donors to switch
   from cash to food vouchers. Under what conditions will the voucher program
   make the typical recipient better off? Illustrate your answer with a graph.

3. Explain why the food-stamp program can have the same effect on the consumption pattern and well-being of recipients as an outright cash transfer of
   the same amount.

4. Until 1979, food stamps were sold to recipients at a fraction of their market value. Consider a household with a monthly income of $500. Suppose that the government charges $1 for a food stamp with a market value of $2, with a maximum of 100 food stamps per household per month.
   a. Draw the household's budget line with and without the food-stamp program.
   b. Under what circumstances will the food-stamp program be equivalent to a $100 cash payment?

5. Suppose that the government replaces AFDC with a refundable earned income tax credit of 50 percent. The government pays every current AFDC recipient 50 cents for every dollar of wage income. Consider the effects of the wage subsidy on the welfare recipient whose choices are shown in Figure 13–1.
   a. Draw the budget line for AFDC and the refundable tax credit.
   b. How does the policy change affect the hours of labor? Is she more or less likely to continue working?
   c. Suppose that the recipient's elasticity of supply of labor is 0.80: a 10 percent increase in the wage increases the number of hours worked by 8 percent. By how much will labor supply increase?
   d. How does the policy change affect the government's welfare budget?

References and Additional Readings

General References

Ellwood, David T. *Poor Support*. New York: Basic Books, 1988. A detailed description and analysis of poverty among two-parent families, single-parent families, and residents of inner-city neighborhoods.

U.S. Office of Management and Budget. *Budget of the United States Government, Fiscal Year 1987*. Washington, D.C.: U.S. Government Printing Office, 1986. Projects spending on antipoverty programs.

Evaluation of Employment and Job-Training Programs

Bailey, Thomas R. "Market Forces and Private Sector Processes in Government Policy: The Job Training Partnership Act." *Journal of Policy Analysis and Management* 7 (1988), pp. 300–315.

Bassi, Laurie, and Orley Ashenfelter. "The Effect of Direct Job Creation and Training Programs on Low-Skilled Workers." In *Fighting Poverty: What Works and What Doesn't*, ed. Sheldon H. Danziger and Daniel H. Weinberg. Cambridge, Mass.: Harvard University Press, 1986. Discusses the history of employment and job-training programs and summarizes the conclusions from several studies of these programs.

Bloom, Howard S., and Maureen A. McLaughlin. *CETA Training Programs: Do They Work for Adults?* Washington, D.C.: Congressional Budget Office, 1982. Analysis of the costs and benefits of the CETA program.

Haveman, Robert. *A Decade of Federal Anti-Poverty Programs: Achievements, Failures and Lessons*. New York: Academic Press, 1977. Discusses the programs initiated under the Economic Opportunity Act of 1964 (the "war on poverty").

Manpower Demonstration Research Corporation. *Summary and Findings of the National Supported Work Demonstration.* Cambridge, Mass.: Ballinger, 1980. Estimates benefit-cost ratios for participants in work-experience programs.

Schiller, Bradley. *The Economics of Poverty and Discrimination.* 5th ed. Englewood Cliffs, N.J.: Prentice Hall, 1989. Chapter 12 provides a historical sketch of employment and training programs.

The Negative Income Tax

Aaron, Henry J. "Six Welfare Questions Still Searching for Answers." *Brookings Review,* Fall 1984. Summarizes the results of the negative income tax experiment.

Robins, Philip K.; Robert G. Spiegleman; and Samuel Weiner. *A Guaranteed Annual Income: Evidence from a Social Experiment.* New York: Academic Press, 1980.

Rossi, Peter, and Katherine Lyall. *Reforming Public Welfare: A Critique of the Negative Income Tax Experiment.* New York: Sage Publications, 1976.

In-Kind Transfers: Food Stamps and Medicaid

Aaron, Henry J. "Six Welfare Questions Still Searching for Answers." *Brookings Review*, Fall 1984. Discusses the political feasibility of converting from in-kind to cash programs.

Blanchard, Lois; J. S. Butler; T. Doyle; R. Jackson; J. Ohls; and Barbara Posner. *Final Report, Food Stamp SSI/Elderly Cash-Out Demonstration Evaluation.* Princeton, N.J.: Mathematica Policy Research, 1982. When food-stamp recipients were given cash instead of food stamps, expenditures on food did not change. This suggests that food stamps are equivalent to cash payments.

Smeeding, Timothy M. "Alternative Methods for Evaluating Selected In-Kind Transfer Benefits and Measuring Their Effect on Poverty." U.S. Bureau of the Census, Technical Paper No. 50. Washington, D.C.: U.S. Government Printing Office, 1982. Estimates the value of in-kind transfers to the recipients. Estimates that $1 of food stamps is worth 97 cents to the typical recipient, $1 of medicaid is worth 44 cents, and $1 of public housing is worth 80 cents.

Starr, Paul. "Health Care for the Poor: The Past 20 Years." In *Fighting Poverty: What Works and What Doesn't,* ed. Sheldon H. Danziger and Daniel H. Weinberg. Cambridge, Mass.: Harvard University Press, 1986. Discusses the effects of medicaid on the health of the poor.

Effects of Government Transfer Programs on Poverty

Danziger, Sheldon H.; Robert H. Haveman; and Robert D. Plotnick. "Anti-Poverty Policy: Effects on the Poor and the Non-Poor." In *Fighting Poverty: What Works and What Doesn't*, ed. Sheldon H. Danziger and Daniel H. Weinberg. Cambridge, Mass.: Harvard University Press, 1986. Estimates the combined effects of cash and in-kind transfers on poverty. Concludes that these programs decreased the number of people in poverty by about 46 percent.

Paglin, Morton. "Poverty in the United States: A Reevaluation." *Policy Review* 8 (1979), pp. 7–24. Discusses the effects of in-kind transfers on poverty rates.

U.S. Congress, Committee on Ways and Means. *Background Material and Data on Programs within the Jurisdiction of the Committee on Ways and Means.* Washington,

D.C.: U.S. Government Printing Office, 1988. Estimates the effects of different transfer programs on poverty rates.

Reform Proposal: Child-Care Support

Ellwood, David T. *Poor Support.* New York: Basic Books, 1988. Chapter 5 discusses poverty among female-headed households and describes a reform proposal centered on requirements for child support by absent fathers.

Garfinkel, Irwin. "Child Support Assurance: A New Tool for Achieving Social Security." University of Wisconsin, 1985. Unpublished paper.

Garfinkel, Irwin, and Elizabeth Uhr. "A New Approach to Child Support." *Public Interest*, Spring 1984. Proposes a scheme under which absent parents would pay a child-support tax.

Reform Proposal: Workfare

Frielander, Daniel; Barbara Goldman; Judith Gueron; and David Wong. "Initial Findings from the Demonstration of State Work-Welfare Initiatives." *American Economic Review, Papers and Proceedings* 76, no. 2 (1986), pp. 224–29. Discusses the effects of a program under which AFDC recipients receive work experience and job training. Concludes that workfare may decrease the number of welfare recipients.

Gideonse, Sarah K., and William R. Meyers. "Why Workfare Fails." *Challenge* 31 (January–February 1988). Argues that the poor will not escape poverty unless they receive basic education and job skills. Discusses some of the reasons for the failure of the Work Incentives Program (WIN) and the implications for workfare.

Gueron, Judith M. "Work and Welfare: Lessons from Employment Programs." *Journal of Economic Perspectives* 4 (1990), pp. 79–98. Discusses the design of work/welfare programs and their effects on employment, earnings, and the costs of the welfare system.

Long, David A. "The Budgetary Implications of Welfare Reform: Lessons from Four State Initiatives." *Journal of Policy Analysis and Management* 7 (1988), pp. 289–99.

Mead, Lawrence M. "The Potential for Work Enforcement: A Study of WIN." *Journal of Policy Analysis and Management* 7 (1988), pp. 264–88.

Wiseman, Michael. "How Workfare Really Works." *Public Interest* 89 (Fall 1987), pp. 36–47. Describes the features of the typical workfare system and discusses the key questions to be asked in the evaluation of a workfare program.

Transfer Policy

Bane, Mary Jo, and David T. Ellwood. "Slipping into and out of Poverty: The Dynamics of Spells." *Journal of Human Resources* 21 (1986). Discusses the fact that many families stay on welfare for long periods of time.

Blank, Rebecca M. "The Impact of State Economic Differentials on Household Welfare and Labor Force Behavior." *Journal of Public Economics* 28 (1985), pp. 20–30.

Danziger, Sheldon H., and Daniel Fester. "Income Transfers and Poverty in the 1980s." In *American Domestic Priorities*, ed. John Quigley and Daniel Rubinfeld. Berkeley and Los Angeles: University of California, 1985. Reviews the recent history of income-transfer programs.

Smolensky, Eugene. "Is a Golden Age in Poverty Policy Right Around the Corner?" *Focus*, Spring 1985. Discusses means of preventing the development of a permanent underclass of welfare dependents.

Development versus Dispersal

Banfield, Edward C. "Why Government Cannot Solve the Urban Problem." In *The Urban Economy*, ed. Harold M. Hochman. New York: W. W. Norton, 1976, pp. 257–72.

Bateman, Worth, and Harold M. Hochman. "Social Problems and the Urban Crisis: Can Public Policy Make a Difference?" In *The Urban Economy*, ed. Harold M. Hochman. New York: W. W. Norton, 1976, pp. 283–93.

Bates, Timothy, and William Bradford. *Financing Black Economic Development*. New York: Academic Press, 1979. Describes experiences with subsidized loans for black capitalism.

Brimmer, Andrew F., and Henry S. Terrell. "The Economic Potential of Black Capitalism." In *The Urban Economy*, ed. Harold M. Hochman. New York: W. W. Norton, 1976, pp. 239–56. Discusses the problems confronting the black capitalism approach. Concludes that the approach is unlikely to substantially improve the economic position of blacks.

Butler, Stuart M. "Free Zones in the Inner City." In *Urban Economic Development*. Vol. 27 of *Urban Affairs Annual Reviews*, ed. Richard D. Bingham and John P. Blair. Beverly Hills, Calif.: Sage Publications, 1984.

Edel, Matthew. "Development versus Dispersal: Approaches to Ghetto Poverty." In *Readings in Urban Economics*, ed. Matthew Edel and Jerome Rothenberg. New York: Macmillan, 1972, pp. 307–25.

Garn, Harvey A.; Nancy L. Tevis; and Carl E. Snead. *Evaluating Community Development Corporations: A Summary Report*. Washington, D.C.: Urban Institute, 1976. Describes experiences with CDCs.

Harrison, Bennett. "Ghetto Economic Development." *Journal of Economic Literature* 12 (1974), pp. 1–37.

Kain, John F., and Joseph J. Persky. "Alternatives to the Guilded Ghetto." *Public Interest*, Winter 1969, pp. 74–87. Reprinted in *The Urban Economy*, ed. Harold M. Hochman. New York: W. W. Norton, 1976, pp. 211–25.

Orfield, Gary. "Ghettoization and Its Alternatives." In *The New Urban Reality*, ed. Paul Peterson. Washington, D.C.: Brookings Institution, 1985.

CHAPTER 14 Why Is Housing Different?

This is the first of two chapters on urban housing. It explains why housing is a unique commodity, focusing on six features that make housing different from other goods. First, the stock of housing is heterogeneous: dwellings differ in size, location, age, floor plan, interior features, and utilities. Second, housing is immobile: it is impractical to move dwellings from one location to another. Third, housing is durable: if properly maintained, a dwelling can be used for many decades. Fourth, housing is expensive: to purchase a dwelling, the typical household must borrow a large sum of money. Fifth, moving costs are relatively high: in addition to the substantial monetary cost of moving, there are also costs associated with leaving the old neighborhood—with its schools, stores, and friends—behind. Finally, some people care about the racial and ethnic background of their neighbors, leading to racial discrimination and segregation.

The remainder of the chapter explains how these six characteristics affect the housing market. The first section shows that because housing is heterogeneous and immobile, the housing market is split into a set of distinct but related housing submarkets. The second and third sections explore some of the implications of durability. The second section discusses the landlord's decisions concerning maintenance and repair and explains some of the market forces behind the abandonment of older housing in central cities. The third section describes the filtering model of housing, a model that explains the process through which used housing is passed from one type of household to another. The fourth section discusses the household's decision about whether to rent or own and explores the effects of public policy on the choice between renting and owning. The fifth section discusses the effects of moving costs on housing consumption. The sixth section discusses the income and price elasticities of demand for housing. The final section explores the effects of racial prejudice and discrimination on housing prices and the racial composition of neighborhoods.

Heterogeneity and Immobility

The housing stock is heterogeneous in the sense that each dwelling offers a different set of features or a different bundle of housing services. There are two types of housing features: dwelling characteristics and site characteristics.

Consider first the features of the dwelling itself. Dwellings differ in size (square footage of living space) and layout (the arrangement of rooms within the dwelling). They also differ in the quality and efficiency of kitchen equipment and utility systems (heating, air conditioning, plumbing, electrical). Other differences occur in the interior design (type of flooring, windows, cabinets) and structural integrity (the durability of the foundation and the roof). To summarize, each dwelling offers a different combination of size, layout, utilities, interior design, and structural integrity.

Because housing is immobile, one component of the housing bundle is the residential location. A house buyer purchases both a dwelling and a set of site characteristics. One site characteristic is accessibility: sites differ in their access to jobs, shopping, and entertainment. Another characteristic is the provision of local public services: metropolitan areas have dozens of local governments, each of which provides a different combination of taxes and public services (schools, fire protection, police services). A third characteristic is environmental quality: sites differ in air quality and noise levels (from cars, trucks, airplanes, and factories). A final site characteristic is the appearance of the neighborhood (the exterior features of neighboring houses and lots). To summarize, housing is consumed along with a residential site, so the housing bundle includes several site attributes, including access to different facilities, tax liabilities, public services, environmental quality, and neighborhood characteristics.

The Price of Housing: The Hedonic Approach

What determines the equilibrium price of a dwelling? The hedonic approach is based on the notion that a dwelling is composed of a bundle of individual components, each of which has an implicit price. The market price of a dwelling is the sum of the prices of the individual components.

To explain the hedonic approach, consider a housing market in which dwellings differ in only five ways. The dwellings differ in access to jobs in the city center, the number of bedrooms, the age of the roof, air pollution, and the quality of local schools. A hedonic study of the market might generate the following information:

1. **Base price.** The average house has three bedrooms, is five miles from the city center, and has a roof six years old. The price of the average house is $70,000.
2. **Access price.** The price of housing drops by $1,000 for every additional mile from the city center; more accessible dwellings have higher prices.
3. **Bedroom price.** The price of housing increases by $10,000 for every additional bedroom; larger dwellings have higher prices.
4. **Roof price.** The price of housing decreases by $100 for every additional year of roof age; an older roof means that the roof must be replaced sooner, so the market price of the dwelling is lower.
5. **Air quality price.** The price of housing decreases by $500 for every additional unit of air pollution; dwellings in areas with relatively clean air have higher prices.

6. **School price.** The price of housing increases by $600 for every one-unit increase in the quality of the local elementary school (measured by the average test score); dwellings in areas with better schools have higher prices.

To predict the price of a particular dwelling, one needs information on location, the number of bedrooms, the age of the roof, air quality, and the quality of the elementary school. For example, consider a four-bedroom house located three miles from the city center that has a two-year-old roof. The pollution level is three units below the average and the average test score is two points above the average. Such a house sells for $85,100, the base price of $70,000 plus $10,000 for the extra bedroom, $2,000 for the shorter commute, $400 for the four extra years of roof life, $1,500 for the relatively low pollution level, and $1,200 for the relatively high average test score.

Kain and Quigley (1975) use data from the St. Louis housing market in the 1960s to estimate the dollar values of different housing attributes. Table 14–1 shows some of their results. There are three types of housing characteristics: the quality of the dwelling itself, the size of the dwelling, and site characteristics. The numbers in the table show the increases in monthly rent (for rental housing) and market value (for owner-occupied housing) resulting from one-unit increases in the various housing attributes. For example, a one-unit increase in interior quality (a measure of the quality of floors, windows, walls, ceilings, stairways) increases monthly rent by $1.31 (about 2.1 percent of the average monthly rent of $61.34), and increases market value

TABLE 14–1   Change in Housing Prices from One-Unit Increases in Housing Attributes: A Hedonic Study of the St. Louis Housing Market

Attribute	Rental Market: Increase in Monthly Rent ($)	Owner-Occupied Market: Increase in Market Value ($)
Dwelling Quality		
Interior	1.31	818
Central heating	4.44	—
Age	−0.29	−100
Size of Dwelling		
Number of rooms	22.63	1,453
Number of baths	9.07	769
Site Characteristics		
Exterior quality of adjacent dwellings	1.86	777
Exterior quality of dwellings on block	3.71	419
Miles from CBD	−0.30	−354
Average monthly rent = $61.34		
Average market value = $14,596		

SOURCE: John F. Kain and John M. Quigley, *Housing Markets and Racial Discrimination: A Microeconomic Analysis* (New York: National Bureau of Economic Research, 1975), Table 8.3.

by $818 (about 5.6 percent of the average market value of $14,596). Rental units with central heating rent for $4.44 more per month, and older dwellings have lower rents and market values. The price of housing is also affected by dwelling size: a second bathroom adds $9.07 to monthly rent and $769 to market value. The exterior quality of nearby dwellings was measured on a scale of 1 (bad) to 5 (excellent). A one-unit increase in the quality of adjacent dwellings increased rent by $1.86 and market value by $777, while a one-unit increase in the quality of dwellings on the block increased rent by $3.71 and market value by $419. The final variable is distance to the central business district: a one-mile increase in distance to the employment center decreased rent by $0.30 and value by $354.

Choosing a Dwelling

How does a household choose among alternative dwellings, each of which provides a different bundle of characteristics? The household must find the dwelling with the best combination of features at the best price. Most consumers do not have access to a hedonic study of their housing market. As they shop, they gather their own information about the implicit prices of location, size, and design features. Eventually, the household chooses a bundle that maximizes the household's utility subject to its budget constraints.

The household chooses the dwelling that provides the best affordable combination of features. Consider a housing market in which dwellings differ in only two respects: size (square feet of living space) and quality (of floors, walls, roof). Figure 14–1 shows the housing choices for three different households.

The budget lines in Figure 14–1 show the combinations of size and quality that exhaust a household's housing budget. *AB* is the budget line for middle-income households *S* and *L,* and *CD* is the line for *H,* a high-income household. The position of the budget line is determined by the household's housing budget: the larger the budget, the larger the set of affordable combinations of size and quality. The slope of the budget line is determined by the implicit prices of size and quality: the larger the price of quality relative to the price of size, the flatter the budget line.

The indifference curves in Figure 14–1 show the different combinations of quality and size that generate the same utility level for a given household. Three indifference curves are shown, one each for households *S, H,* and *L.* The indifference curves are negatively sloped, reflecting the household's subjective trade-off between quality and size: as quality decreases, the household needs a larger dwelling to achieve the same utility level.

Housing choices reflect the households' preferences and income. Given the shape of its indifference curves, household *L* (a middle-income household) chooses a large, low-quality dwelling. Although household *S* has the same income and housing budget as *L, S* chooses a smaller, higher-quality dwelling. Its choice is rational because *S* has relatively strong preferences for quality, as shown by the shape of its indifference curve. Household *H* has a higher income and a larger housing budget, so it chooses a large, high-quality dwelling. The high-income household faces the same monetary trade-off between size and quality (the same opportunity cost) but it has more money to spend on both size and quality.

FIGURE 14–1   Households with Different Income and Preferences Choose Dwellings of Different Size and Quality

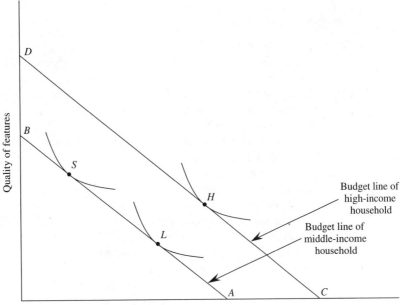

The household's choice of size and quality reflects its subjective trade-off (as represented in its indifference curves), the market trade-off (as shown in the slope of the budget line), and household income (which determines the position of the budget line). Households S and L have different tastes for housing: L chooses a large, low-quality dwelling, while S chooses a small, high-quality dwelling. The high-income household (H) chooses a large, high-quality dwelling.

Segmented but Related Markets

The heterogeneity of the housing stock means that a city's housing market is composed of a number of submarkets. The housing market is segmented with respect to size, location, and quality. For example, some households look for small dwellings, while others look for large ones. Therefore, there is one market for small dwellings and another market for large ones. Similarly, some households look for houses accessible to central-city jobs, while others look for houses in high-quality school districts. Finally, some households look for new houses, full of modern conveniences, while others look for older houses with old-world charm.

Although the housing market is segmented into submarkets, the submarkets are related because consumers have some flexibility in their housing choices. As the relative price of three-bedroom houses increases, some households switch from the three-bedroom market to the two-bedroom market. Similarly, as the price of older houses increases relative to the price of new ones, some households switch to the new-housing market. In other words, dwellings from different submarkets are imperfect substitutes, so households move between the submarkets in response to changes in the relative prices of different types of housing. The implications of housing submarkets are discussed later in the chapter.

Neighborhood Effects

The quantity of housing services produced by a particular dwelling depends not only on the characteristics of the dwelling, but also on the characteristics of its neighborhood. When one homeowner improves the appearance of his house by painting it or repairing its broken windows, the neighborhood becomes a more desirable place to live, so the market values of surrounding houses increase. This is the **neighborhood effect**: positive changes in the exterior appearance of one house causes spillover benefits (increases in market value) for surrounding houses. Although there is no doubt that neighborhood effects exist, there is some question as to their magnitude and geographical extent.

Economists use the hedonic approach to estimate the magnitude of neighborhood effects (see Crecine, Davis, and Jackson, 1967; and Kain and Quigley, 1975). In Table 14–1, a one-unit increase in the quality of adjacent dwellings increased monthly rent by $1.86 and increased market value by $777. Similarly, improvements to other dwellings on the block increased rent and market value. The evidence from hedonic studies suggests that neighborhood effects are highly localized: the spillover benefits from positive changes in the exterior appearance of one house are confined to dwellings within a few hundred feet of the house.

Durability of Housing

Housing is more durable than most goods. If a dwelling is maintained properly, it can last 100 years or more. Although dwellings deteriorate over time, they do so at a relatively slow rate. The durability of housing has three implications for the housing market. First, the landlord can control the rate of physical deterioration by spending money on repair and maintenance. Second, there is a large supply of used housing on the market every year. The general rule of thumb is that new construction in a given year is between 2 percent and 3 percent of the total housing stock. Over the course of a decade, new dwellings provide about 20 percent to 30 percent of the housing stock, so between 70 percent and 80 percent of households live in dwellings that are at least 10 years old. The final implication is that the supply of housing is relatively inelastic: the market is dominated by the stock of used housing, so changes in price cause relatively small changes in the quantity supplied.

Deterioration and Maintenance

A property owner can control the rate of physical deterioration by spending time and money on repair and maintenance. The landlord has the incentive to maintain and repair her property because these activities increase the quantity of housing services (Q) generated by the dwelling. Consumers are willing to pay more for a dwelling that generates a larger quantity of housing services, so an increase in maintenance increases rent and market value. The question for the landlord is: how much should I spend on maintenance?

Figure 14–2 shows the benefits and costs of maintenance. The horizontal axis measures the quantity of housing services generated by the dwelling (Q), which the landlord can affect by repairing broken windows and leaky roofs, maintaining the heating and plumbing systems, and painting the house. The total-cost curve shows the sum of fixed costs (independent of Q) and variable costs. The fixed costs include the cost of managing the property (collecting rent, advertising for tenants) and taxes. The variable costs include repair and maintenance costs. The cost curve is positively sloped because variable costs increase with Q: it costs more to maintain a dwelling at a higher Q. The cost curve is convex from below, a result of diminishing returns to maintenance: as Q increases, it becomes progressively more costly to maintain the property at the given Q. The straight line in Figure 14–2 shows the relationship between total revenue (rent per month) and Q. The implicit assumption is that the price per unit of Q is constant: a dwelling with twice the quantity of housing services commands twice the rent.

FIGURE 14–2   Optimum Quantity of Housing Services

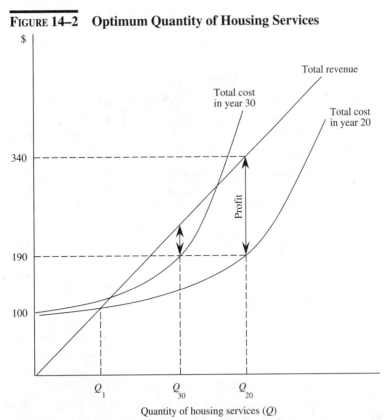

The optimum quantity of housing services is the Q at which profit (total revenue less total cost) is maximized. In year 20, profit is maximized at Q_{20}. The aging of the dwelling increases maintenance cost, shifting the cost curve upward and decreasing the optimum Q.

Profit equals the difference between total revenue and total cost. In year 20 (20 years after the dwelling was built), the landlord has the lower of the two cost curves. Profit is positive above Q_1, and reaches its maximum level at Q_{20}. At this Q, the slope of the revenue curve equals the slope of the cost curve: the marginal benefit (change in total revenue per unit change in Q) equals marginal cost (the change in total cost per unit change in Q). Therefore, the profit-maximizing landlord chooses an output of Q_{20} units of housing services.

The optimum quantity changes over time, a result of changes in variable costs or changes in demand.

1. **Changes in variable costs.** As the dwelling ages, it becomes progressively more costly to maintain at a given quality level. In Figure 14–2, between years 20 and 30, the fixed cost does not change, but maintenance cost increases, causing an upward tilt of the total-cost curve. By year 30, the optimum quantity drops from Q_{20} to Q_{30}, and the landlord's profit falls.

2. **Changes in demand.** Suppose that the demand for housing in a particular area decreases, decreasing the equilibrium price of rental housing. In Figure 14–2, the total-revenue function would tilt downward (pivoting from the origin), decreasing the profit associated with every Q. As the revenue function tilts downward, the optimum Q decreases.

The Retirement Decision

What happens when the profit from rental housing is negative? Suppose that because of changes in costs or demand, the total-cost curve lies above the total-revenue curve for all values of Q. Rental housing is clearly unprofitable, leaving the landlord with three options: conversion, boarding up, and abandonment.

1. **Conversion.** A dwelling can be converted to nonresidential use, such as an office, a store, or a parking lot. Conversion is profitable if the alternative activity generates enough profit to offset the cost of conversion to the nonresidential use. If conversion would require the demolition of the dwelling and the construction of a new building, conversion cost is relatively high, and conversion is unlikely.

2. **Boarding up.** A dwelling can be boarded up and taken off the market temporarily. The board-up option is profitable if two conditions are met. First, if the landlord expects the market rent to increase sometime in the future, the expected future profit is positive. Second, if the landlord's carrying cost (the opportunity cost of keeping his money in housing instead of a bank account) is relatively low, the cost associated with waiting for the market rent to increase is relatively low. This type of temporary retirement was common during the Great Depression.

3. **Abandonment.** The owner can disown the dwelling, walking away from the property. Abandonment is profitable if the alternative uses (retail, commercial, industrial) do not generate enough profit to cover the cost of

converting the property from residential to nonresidential use. If conversion cost is high, the market value of the property is zero, so there is no reason to keep title to the land.

Retirement results from three types of changes that decrease the profitability of rental housing. On the demand side of the market, a decrease in average income or a decrease in population decreases the demand for housing in certain areas. As the market rent falls, the total-revenue curve tilts downward, decreasing profit. On the supply side, an increase in the supply of rental housing decreases market rents and profits. Finally, as the dwelling ages, increases in maintenance cost decrease profits for a given total-revenue curve, increasing the likelihood of conversion or abandonment.

Abandonment and Public Policy

How does tax policy affect abandonment? White (1986) shows that the property tax increases the frequency of abandonment. Because old, low-quality dwellings have relatively high tax liabilities, landlords have less incentive to keep title to their properties. By abandoning them, they can avoid taxes.

Figure 14–3 shows the effects of the property tax on the landlord's revenue and cost. Given the initial total-revenue curve, the optimum quantity of housing services is Q_0; total revenue is $340, total cost is $190, and profit is $150 per month. Suppose that the assessed value of the rental property is $24,000 and the tax rate is 3 percent of assessed value per year, or $720 per year ($60 per month). If so, the post-tax profit is $90 ($150 − $60).

Suppose that the demand for housing decreases, tilting the total-revenue curve downward. The profit-maximizing Q drops to Q_2, and pre-tax profit drops to $48 ($210 − $162). The decrease in profit decreases the market value of the property: an investor is willing to pay less for the property because it yields less profit. In a perfect tax world, the government would decrease the assessed value of the property to reflect its lower market value, thus decreasing the landlord's tax liability. If the tax stays at $60, however, the post-tax profit is negative ($48 − $60 = −$12), so the landlord is likely to abandon the property. To prevent abandonment, the government would have to cut the tax liability to less than $48.

White (1986) explores the effects of various factors on abandonment in New York City and concludes that the property tax is by far the most important factor. She estimates that the elasticity of abandonment with respect to the property tax is 1.65: a 10 percent increase in the property tax increases the frequency of abandonment by 16.5 percent. For example, if the average assessed value of properties in the Brownsville section of Brooklyn were cut by $1,000 (a 6 percent reduction) the resulting decreases in property taxes would cut the abandonment rate from 17 percent per year to 14.8 percent. Given this large elasticity, a tax cut would generate a fiscal surplus for the city: although the tax liability per property would decrease, the direct revenue loss would be offset by (1) an increase in the number of properties on the tax rolls and (2) a decrease in the number of properties that the city must either take over or demolish.

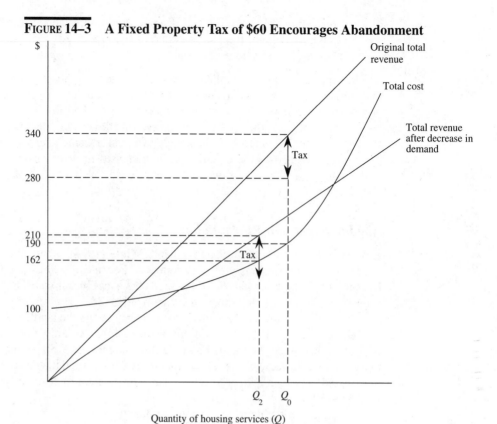

FIGURE 14–3   **A Fixed Property Tax of $60 Encourages Abandonment**

If the property tax is fixed at $60 per month, post-tax profit is $90 instead of $150. A decrease in demand tilts the revenue curve downward, decreasing the optimum service level to Q_2. Pre-tax profit is $48, but post-tax profit is −$12. A fixed property tax causes abandonment despite a positive pre-tax profit. A reassessment of the property would decrease the tax liability and make abandonment less likely.

Because abandonment is the ultimate neighborhood externality, it contributes to the problems of central-city neighborhoods. Abandoned buildings provide targets for vandals and graffiti artists, and quickly become eyesores. Even worse, they often become the temporary homes and retail outlets for transients and drug dealers, so they contribute to crime. For these reasons, abandonment decreases the relative attractiveness of the neighborhood, decreasing the rent that other landlords can charge for their properties. Abandonment feeds on itself, transforming livable neighborhoods into unlivable ones.

Durability and Supply Elasticity

The durability of housing also has important implications for the market supply curve. Consider the response to an increase in the demand for housing. In the short run, the supply of housing is fixed, so the increase in demand increases the equilibrium price. In the long run, suppliers respond to the increase in market price by increasing the quantity of housing supplied. The questions are: by how much will supply increase, and how soon will it increase?

There are three types of supply responses to an increase in price:

1. **Build new dwellings.** As the price rises, new housing becomes more profitable, so more dwellings are built. Most of the new dwellings are built on vacant land in the suburbs.

2. **Slow deterioration of used dwellings.** As the price of housing increases, the benefit of maintaining dwellings increases. Landlords spend more on maintenance and repair, slowing the deterioration rate and decreasing the number of dwellings retired from the housing stock.

3. **Remodel used dwellings.** Some landlords upgrade their dwellings, increasing the quantity of housing services generated.

Because the bulk of housing is used housing, the supply response will be relatively large only if the second and third responses (the used-housing responses) are relatively large.

How elastic is the supply of used housing? Because dwellings deteriorate slowly over time, a decrease in the deterioration rate has only a small effect on the housing market. Although an increase in price slows down the deterioration process, the process is slow in the first place. In addition, remodeling is extremely expensive, so it takes a very large price hike to make modifications worthwhile. For these two reasons, housing supply is inelastic for relatively long periods of time. In other words, the supply side of the housing market is sluggish: it takes suppliers a long time to respond to an increase in the demand for housing. In the meantime, the price of housing remains relatively high.

The same argument applies to a decrease in housing demand and the resulting decrease in the market price. A decrease in price decreases the incentives for maintenance, so dwellings deteriorate at a faster rate and more dwellings are retired. Even the fastest deterioration rate is relatively slow, so the decrease in the quantity supplied is relatively small for relatively long periods of time. Although dwellings can be converted to other uses, the high cost of conversion inhibits this response. Because a decrease in price causes relatively small changes in a large part of the market, supply is relatively inelastic for a long period of time. Therefore, the price of housing will be relatively low for a long period of time.

What is the price elasticity of the supply of housing? Unfortunately, economists have been unable to answer this question. It is difficult to estimate the supply elasticity because it is difficult to measure the quantity of housing services. The existing studies of housing supply suffer from a number of statistical problems (see Olsen, 1987; and Quigley, 1979), so their results must be interpreted with caution. Ozanne and Struyk (1978) estimate that the supply elasticity of used housing is between 0.20 and 0.30. In other words, a 10 percent increase in the market price increases the quantity of used housing on the market by between 2 percent and 3 percent. Over a 10-year period, new construction provides only about 30 percent of the housing stock, so their estimate applies to 70 percent of the housing stock for a 10-year period. De Leeuw and Ekanem (1971) estimate that the long-run supply elasticity for rental housing is between 0.30 to 0.70. In other words, the available evidence suggests that the supply of housing is relatively inelastic over relatively long periods of time.

The Filtering Model of the Housing Market

The filtering model captures some of the essential features of the market for used housing. It describes the interactions between different housing submarkets and the process through which a dwelling passes from one use to another. The filtering process has two basic features:

1. **Decrease in housing services.** The quantity of housing services produced by a particular dwelling decreases over time. The decrease in Q results from physical deterioration, technological obsolescence, and changes in housing fashion.
2. **Decrease in occupant income.** The dwelling is occupied by households with progressively lower incomes. As Q decreases, the dwelling is occupied by households that demand progressively lower quantities of housing services, typically households with lower incomes.

The filtering model can be used to address two questions. First, why do the poor occupy used housing instead of new housing? Second, do the poor benefit from subsidy policies that encourage the building of new housing for the wealthy?

Why Do the Poor Occupy Used Housing?

Most poor households occupy used housing. To explain why the poor occupy leftover housing, consider a city with the following characteristics:

1. **Three income groups.** There are three income groups: wealthy, middle-income, and poor.
2. **Rising income.** Real income is increasing over time, increasing the desired quantities of housing services for all three income groups.
3. **Costly upgrading.** It is relatively costly to upgrade dwellings: increases in quality and size are relatively expensive.
4. **Deterioration.** Houses are built every decade, and deteriorate by five units of housing services per decade.

Figure 14–4 shows the city's housing market in 1980. The wealthy demand 160 units of housing service and occupy new houses (point *f*). The middle-income households demand 135 units of service (point *d*), occupying houses built in 1970 (which produced 140 units of service when they were new and 135 units one decade later). The middle-income households occupy smaller and lower-quality dwellings than the wealthy. The poor households demand 110 units of service and live in houses built in 1960 (point *b*).

FIGURE 14–4   **Filtering: The Allocation of Housing in 1980 and 1990**

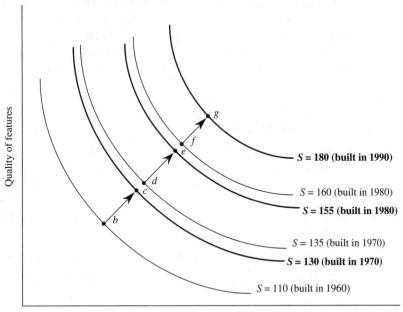

In 1980, the poor are at point b, the middle-income households are at point d, and the wealthy are at point f. Rising income increases the housing consumption of the rich, and they move into new housing in 1990 (point g). The middle-income households move into the 1980 housing vacated by the wealthy (from point d to e), and the poor move into the 1970 housing vacated by the middle-income households (point b to c).

Suppose that the real incomes of all three groups increase between 1980 and 1990. The desired quantities of housing service increase to 180 for the rich, 155 for the middle-income households, and 130 for the poor. Figure 14–4 shows one possible arrangement of the 1990 housing market. New dwellings with 180 units of service are built for the wealthy, so they move from point f to point g. The middle-income households occupy the dwellings vacated by the rich, moving from point d to e (the dwellings built in 1980 generate 155 units of housing service one decade later). The poor occupy the dwellings vacated by the middle-income households, moving from point b to c.

Why should the wealthy live in new houses? If the wealthy did not occupy new housing, they could be accommodated by upgrading the 1980 houses. Since a 1980 house would normally produce only 155 units of housing service in 1990, substantial modifications would be required to increase its service level to 180 units. Rooms would be added, the roof and plumbing would be upgraded, and the house would be remodeled to accommodate changes in housing tastes. Since these modifications would be costly, it is usually more efficient to build new housing for the wealthy.

If new housing is built for the wealthy, there is a plentiful supply of used housing for middle-income households. When the wealthy vacate the 1980 dwellings, the market values of the leftover houses decrease. Because the market value of a used 155-unit dwelling is less than the cost of building a new 155-unit dwelling, the middle-income households live in leftover houses. As the middle-income households vacate the 1970 dwellings, their prices fall, making the used 130-unit dwellings a bargain for the poor. Since there is a plentiful supply of used housing (with unfashionable design and old pipes), a used, low-quality dwelling is less expensive than a new one.

Construction Subsidies

Consider next the issue of who benefits from subsidies for new housing. Suppose that the government subsidizes the construction of new housing for middle-income (as opposed to low-income) households. How does the subsidy program affect low-income households?

To explain the effects of construction subsidies on low-income households, consider a city with the following characteristics:

1. **Fixed number of households.** There are 120 households in the city.
2. **Housing submarkets.** There are two submarkets: the market for medium-quality housing and the market for low-quality housing.
3. **Quality level.** Landlords respond to changes in relative prices by moving their dwellings between the two submarkets: dwellings can be upgraded to the medium-quality submarket or downgraded to the low-quality submarket.
4. **Imperfect substitutes.** The two types of housing are imperfect substitutes: consumers move between the two markets in response to changes in market prices.

Figure 14–5 shows the initial equilibrium in the housing market. In the medium-quality submarket, there are 40 dwellings at a price of $30 per square foot. In the low-quality submarket, there are 80 dwellings at a price of $20 per square foot.

Suppose that the city subsidizes the construction of new medium-quality housing. In Figure 14–5, the subsidy shifts the supply curve to the right from S_1 to S_2, increasing the quantity supplied at every price: at the original price of $30, there would be 80 dwellings instead of 40. Since the quantity supplied exceeds the quantity demanded, the price of medium-quality housing decreases. As the price of medium-quality housing decreases, two things happen.

1. **Demand effect.** The decrease in the relative price of medium-quality housing increases the quantity demanded: some households move from low-quality dwellings into medium-quality dwellings, causing movement downward along the demand curve D_1.
2. **Supply effect.** As the price of medium-quality dwellings decreases, the quantity supplied decreases as some landlords downgrade their dwellings to the more lucrative low-quality submarket: the market moves down-

FIGURE 14–5   **Effects of Subsidy for Medium-Quality Housing on Medium-Quality and Low-Quality Submarkets**

A: Medium-quality submarket

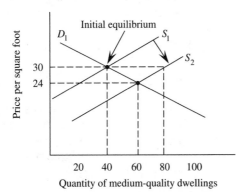

B: Low-quality submarket

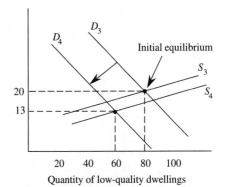

Construction subsidies shift the supply curve for medium-quality (new) dwellings outward. In equilibrium, the price drops from $30 to $24 and the quantity increases from 40 to 60.

The decrease in the price of medium-quality dwellings increases the supply of low-quality dwellings: dwellings filter downward and decrease the demand for low-quality dwellings as consumers switch from the low-quality market to the medium-quality market. The price decreases from $20 to $13 and the quantity decreases from 80 to 60.

ward along the supply curve S_2, decreasing the quantity of medium-quality housing supplied.

In equilibrium, the subsidy increases the quantity of medium-quality housing and decreases its price. In Figure 14–5, the number of medium-quality dwellings increases from 40 to 60, and the price decreases from $30 to $24.

The changes in the medium-quality submarket cause two types of changes in the low-quality submarket.

1. **Substitution effect.** As consumers of low-quality dwellings move into medium-quality dwellings, the demand curve for low-quality dwellings shifts to the left. This is shown in Figure 14–5 as a shift from D_3 to D_4. Because the two types of housing are substitutes, a decrease in the price of medium-quality housing decreases the demand for low-quality housing.

2. **Filtering effect.** The downgrading of dwellings from the medium-quality submarket to the low-quality submarket shifts the supply curve of low-quality housing to the right. This is shown in Figure 14–5 as a shift from S_3 to S_4.

The new equilibrium occurs where the new demand curve (D_4) intersects the new supply curve (S_4). The subsidy program for medium-quality housing decreases the price of low-quality housing from $20 to $13 and decreases the quantity of low-quality dwellings from 80 to 60.

The construction subsidies also cause the retirement of 40 dwellings. Since the population is fixed at 120 households, every new house causes one retirement. The number of households in the medium-quality submarket increases by only 20 (from 40 to 60), leaving 20 of the 40 new houses to filter down to the low-quality market. The number of households in the low-quality submarket decreases by 20 (from 80 to 60), so there are 40 extra houses in the low-quality submarket. Therefore, the 40 lowest-quality houses are retired from the housing stock.

Summary: Filtering and Public Policy

The benefits of housing subsidies are not confined to the households who occupy the subsidized dwellings. The households who initially occupy low-quality dwellings benefit for two reasons. First, the subsidies decrease the price of medium-quality houses, allowing some of the households to move into medium-quality dwellings. Second, houses filter down from the medium-quality submarket to the low-quality submarket, decreasing the price of low-quality housing.

What about the submarket for high-quality housing? Consider a model with three submarkets: high-quality, medium-quality, and low-quality. The subsidy increases the supply and decreases the price of medium-quality housing, so it slows the downward filtering of dwellings from the high-quality submarket to the medium-quality submarket. The increase in the supply of high-quality dwellings decreases the price of high-quality housing. Therefore, the occupants of high-quality housing also benefit from subsidies for medium-quality housing.

The same analysis applies to policies that decrease the supply of medium-quality dwellings. Suppose that growth controls or zoning policies decrease the supply of new medium-quality houses. The decrease in supply increases the price of medium-quality housing, increasing the benefits of maintaining dwellings for the medium-quality market. Landlords spend more on maintenance and repair, slowing the filtering process and decreasing the supply of low-quality housing. At the same time, some consumers are unwilling to pay the higher prices in the medium-quality submarket, so they flee to the low-quality submarket. Growth controls on new medium-quality housing increase the price of low-quality housing because they decrease the supply *and* increase the demand for these dwellings. Consequently, some of the costs of growth control and zoning are borne by low-income households.

The High Cost of Housing

When a household buys a home, it typically spends between two and four times its annual income on the house. The large cost of housing has two implications for the housing market. First, given the large investment required for homeownership, a large fraction of households rent instead of owning. In the United States, about one third of households are renters. Second, most middle-income households use homeownership to accumulate wealth. In other words, a large fraction of middle-income savings is tied up in dwellings. This section explores the household's choice between renting and owning and the effects of public policy on this choice.

The Cost of Renting

The cost of renting a dwelling is simply the rent paid to the landlord. In a competitive market, landlords make zero economic profit (normal accounting profit), so the annual rent equals the landlord's annual cost. In the absence of taxes, the landlord has three types of costs:

1. **Capital cost.** If the landlord borrows money to purchase the dwelling, the capital cost is the annual interest cost, equal to the market interest rate (i) times the purchase price, or value, of the dwelling (V). If she uses her own money to purchase the dwelling, the capital cost is the opportunity cost of investing her money in housing instead of a bank account earning an interest rate of i percent.

2. **Depreciation.** If the market value of the house decreases by d percent per year, the annual depreciation cost is d times V.

3. **Maintenance cost.** If the annual cost of routine maintenance is m percent of the market value of the dwelling, the annual maintenance cost is m times V. The maintenance cost includes the opportunity cost of the landlord's time.

The expression for the annual cost of a rental dwelling is

$$C_r = V \cdot (i_r + d_r + m_r) \qquad (14\text{–}1)$$

where i_r is the interest rate paid by the landlord, d_r is the depreciation rate for rental housing, and m_r is the maintenance cost. Suppose that $V = \$50,000$, $i_r = 10$ percent, $d_r = 1$ percent, and $m_r = 4$ percent. If so, the annual cost is \$7,500, the sum of \$5,000 in capital cost, \$500 in depreciation cost, and \$2,000 in maintenance cost. In a taxless world, the landlord charges an annual rent of \$7,500, thus covering her costs and making zero economic profit.

What happens if the market value of the dwelling increases over time? If the dwelling appreciates over time instead of depreciating, d_r is a negative number. For example, if the market value increases by 8 percent per year, d_r is -0.08 instead of $+0.01$, and the landlord earns \$4,000 per year in appreciation. What is the new equilibrium rent? Economic profit is zero if total cost (for capital and maintenance) equals the sum of rent and appreciation. Since total cost is \$7,000, the equilibrium rent is \$3,000 (\$7,000 = \$4,000 in appreciation plus \$3,000 in rent). The equilibrium rent is lower because the landlord earns money by owning the property, and therefore needs less rental income to generate zero economic profit.

The Cost of Homeownership

Consider next the cost of owning a home. In the absence of taxes, the homeowner incurs the same types of costs as the landlord (capital, depreciation, and maintenance). If the homeowner borrows money to buy his home, the capital cost is the annual mortgage-interest payment. If he pays cash for the house, the capital cost is the opportunity cost of investing his money in a house rather than a bank account. In either case, the capital cost is the market interest rate (i) times the value of the house (V). The homeowner also incurs depreciation cost (d times V) and maintenance cost (m times V). The maintenance cost includes the opportunity cost of time spent fixing faucets, painting walls, and keeping the books. The annual cost of ownership is

$$C_o = V \cdot (i_o + d_o + m_o) \tag{14-2}$$

where i_o is the interest rate paid by the homeowner, d_o is the depreciation rate for owner-occupied housing, and m_o is the maintenance cost for owner-occupied housing. If the dwelling appreciates over time, d_o is a negative number, and the net cost of ownership is lower.

Indifference between Renting and Owning?

Under what circumstances is a household indifferent between owning and renting? The household is indifferent between owning and renting if $C_r = C_o$. If landlords face the same interest rate and depreciation rate and incur the same maintenance cost, the annual cost of renting equals the annual cost of homeownership. The cost of renting is often higher for three reasons.

The **renter externality** causes the depreciation rate on rental property to be relatively high. Because the renter has no long-term stake in the dwelling, he has little incentive to participate in everyday maintenance. As long as the tenant is not inconvenienced by small problems (e.g., a leaky pipe), he is unlikely to report the problem to the landlord. Although the landlord would benefit from finding out about the problem (she could prevent the small problem from becoming a big one), the tenant does not have the proper incentive to inform the landowner. The externality occurs because the tenant does not directly benefit from better care of the property. In contrast, the homeowner receives all the benefits from everyday maintenance, so he is more likely to fix the leaky pipe immediately to prevent long-term damage to the dwelling. If tenants do not keep their landlords fully informed about the condition of the house, rental property has a higher maintenance cost and a higher depreciation rate. In other words, the renter externality increases the market rent on residential property.

The cost of renting is relatively high for two other reasons. First, rental property is a riskier investment (it has a higher default rate), so lenders charge higher interest rates on loans for rental property. Second, some homeowners use work on the house (maintenance, repair, and yard work) as a hobby, so they have a lower maintenance cost than a landlord. Homeowners often use work on the house as a means of accumulating wealth in their spare time. For these reasons, the annual cost of homeownership is often less than the annual rent on an equivalent rental dwelling, even without considering the tax advantages of homeownership.

What type of household rents instead of owning? Three factors tend to push some households toward renting. The first is low income: to qualify for a home loan, the household must have enough income to pay the mortgage. The second is mobility: given the substantial transactions cost of executing a home loan, frequent movers tend to rent rather than own. The third is a distaste for work on the home and yard:

if a person is unwilling to do everyday maintenance and small repairs, renting is relatively attractive.

Taxes and Housing

The federal government provides a number of tax breaks for both rental and owner-occupied property. The tax breaks for rental property decrease the landlord's costs, and these savings are passed on to consumers in the form of lower rent. The tax breaks for homeowners are more explicit: homeowners deduct interest costs from their gross income, so they pay lower taxes. What are the net effects of these tax breaks? Do they encourage or discourage homeownership?

Rental Tax Break: Rapid Depreciation.   The tax code allows the landlord to deduct the full value of his property before the property actually wears out. In other words, the tax code allows the **rapid depreciation** of property (also called *accelerated depreciation*). Suppose that the landlord builds a dwelling at a cost of $60,000. If the dwelling has a useful life of 60 years and deteriorates at a constant rate, the economic cost of depreciation is $1,000 per year. Under a system of rapid depreciation, the dwelling may have a "tax life" of only 15 years, meaning that the deduction for depreciation is $4,000 per year for the first quarter of the dwelling's life, and zero for the rest of its life.

Rapid depreciation does not change the total deductions for depreciation, but simply allows landlords to deduct depreciation cost sooner, and thus pay taxes later. If rapid depreciation defers a $100 tax bill for eight years, the landlord can place the $100 in a bank and earn interest for eight years. When the tax comes due, the landlord pays the tax bill with the $100 principal and keeps the interest. The deferral of taxes decreases the net tax liability because the landlord can earn interest on the deferred taxes. In other words, rapid depreciation decreases the **present value** of the landlord's tax liability. In a competitive environment, all landlords make zero economic profits, so the decrease in taxes is passed on to renters in the form of lower rent.

Ownership Tax Break: Mortgage Deduction.   The federal tax code also decreases the cost of homeownership. Taxpayers can deduct mortgage-interest payments from their gross income, so every dollar of mortgage interest decreases the federal tax liability by the taxpayer's marginal tax rate. For example, if the taxpayer's marginal tax rate is 28 percent, every dollar spent on mortgage interest decreases the tax liability by 28 cents. Table 14–2 shows the tax benefits of homeownership for three households. The poorest household does not have enough deductions to justify itemizing its deductions, so it receives no benefit from the mortgage deduction. Household B, an itemizer with a marginal tax rate of 15 percent, receives a 15-cent subsidy, and household C, with a marginal tax rate of 28 percent, receives a subsidy of 28 cents.

The tax benefit increases with household income for two reasons. First, under a progressive tax system, the marginal tax rate increases with income, so the tax benefit

TABLE 14–2   Tax Benefits of Homeownership and Income

Household	Income	Marginal Tax Rate	Mortgage Interest	Tax Benefit	Benefit as Percent of Income
A	$20,000	Nonitemizer	$ 5,000	0	0
B	30,000	15%	7,000	$1,050	3.50
C	50,000	28%	11,000	3,080	6.16

per dollar of mortgage payment increases with income. Second, because the demand for housing increases with income, wealthier households have larger mortgage payments and thus larger deductions. In 1985, the mortgage deduction decreased federal tax revenue by about $34 billion (U.S. Census Bureau, 1985).

The mortgage deduction increases housing consumption because it decreases the net cost of housing. Figure 14–6 shows the effect of the subsidy on the housing consumption of a household with a 28 percent marginal tax rate. The demand curve shows the marginal benefit of housing consumption (the willingness to pay for housing). The horizontal line at $1 shows the marginal social cost or opportunity cost of

FIGURE 14–6   Mortgage Subsidy Increases Housing Consumption

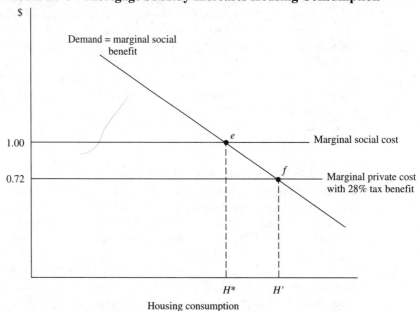

The optimum housing consumption occurs at point *e*, where the marginal social benefit (shown by the demand curve) equals the marginal social cost. If the marginal tax rate is 28 percent, the mortgage subsidy decreases the marginal private cost of housing from $1 to 72 cents, increasing housing consumption from H^* to H'. Consumers pay less than the marginal social cost of housing, so they consume too much housing and divert investment from other uses.

housing: by spending $1 on housing, society forgoes $1 worth of investment in other capital goods (e.g., factories, machines, schools). The optimum housing consumption is H^*, the amount such that the marginal social benefit equals the opportunity cost. For consumption above H^*, the marginal benefit is less than the opportunity cost: the money would be more efficiently spent on factories, machines, or schools.

The mortgage deduction causes inefficiency because it creates a gap between the marginal private cost and the marginal social cost of housing. In the absence of the subsidy, the household pays $1 per unit of housing, and chooses the point where the demand curve intersects the marginal social-cost curve (point e). When the private cost drops from $1 to 72 cents, the household increases its housing consumption from H^* to H'. This is inefficient because the household's benefit from increased housing consumption (from the demand curve) is less than the opportunity cost of spending on housing (from the marginal social-cost curve). By spending more on housing, society has less to spend on factories, machines, and schools. The household makes an inefficient choice because the government pays 28 percent of its housing bill.

Struyk, Mayer, and Tuccillo (1983) suggest that the mortgage deduction has contributed to recent declines in U.S. productivity. The idea is that the deduction encourages the investment in housing at the expense of industrial investment, so there is less capital equipment (factories and machines) per worker. Rosen (1979) estimated the effect of the mortgage deduction on housing consumption in the 1970s, before the 1981 and 1986 tax changes. He estimated that the deduction increased housing consumption by about 14 percent, suggesting that a substantial amount of capital is diverted to residential uses.

Mortgage Deduction and Imputed Rental Income.   Under the federal tax code, both landowners and homeowners can deduct their interest cost in computing their taxable incomes. Does this mean that the mortgage deduction for homeowners is neutral with respect to the consumer's choice between owning and renting?

To explain the bias toward ownership created by the mortgage deduction, consider Fred the homeowner and Barney the landlord. All dwellings in city B are identical rock hovels that sell for $2,000. Fred has two housing options. First, he can borrow $2,000 from the bank to purchase a home. If the interest rate is 10 percent, the mortgage-interest payment for a perpetual loan is $200 per year, so the cost of ownership in the absence of tax benefits is $200. Second, he can rent an identical dwelling from Barney. Since the houses are made of stone, there are no maintenance or repair costs, so Barney's only expense is the capital cost of $200 per year. The market rent ($200) is the same as the cost of ownership, so Fred is indifferent between owning and renting.

The mortgage deduction creates a bias toward homeownership because it allows Fred the homeowner to deduct expenses that do not generate taxable income. Contrast the mortgage deduction for Fred (homeowner) with the mortgage deduction for Barney (landlord). Barney's deduction is sensible because Barney declares his rental income as taxable income. He declares $200 of rental income per house, and deducts $200 in mortgage cost. His taxable income from his property is zero because his deduction equals his rental income. In contrast, Fred does not declare any rental income from his property, but still deducts his mortgage cost. Fred's mortgage deduction does not offset rental income, but simply subsidizes the cost of homeownership.

The government could eliminate the tax bias toward homeownership in one of two ways. The simple and obvious one is to eliminate the interest deduction for homeowners. An alternative is to force Fred to declare his **imputed rental income** as taxable income. The imputed rental income is the income earned from owning a dwelling and renting it to yourself. Alternatively, it is the money you could earn if you rented your dwelling to someone else. Fred's imputed rental income is $200 per year. If he were to declare $200 of imputed rental income and then deduct his $200 mortgage cost, the two items would cancel one another, and the ownership bias would disappear. His taxable income would be the same whether he rents or owns, so he would be indifferent between renting and owning.

Rationale for the Favorable Treatment of Homeownership.   Because the mortgage deduction favors ownership over renting, it increases homeownership rates. In 1980, 66 percent of U.S. households were owner-occupants, up from 48 percent in 1945. According to Hendershott and Shilling (1982), about one quarter of the increase in ownership rate was caused by the favorable tax treatment of homeownership.

The principal rationale for the tax breaks for homeownership is the renter externality. If renters do not have the proper incentive to participate in everyday maintenance, a subsidy for homeownership may be justified on efficiency grounds: the subsidy discourages renting, decreasing the inefficiencies resulting from the renter externality. This rationale raises two questions. First, how large is the renter externality, and how large must the ownership subsidy be to counteract the externality? Second, what is the appropriate form for the ownership subsidy? Does the present system, under which the wealthiest households receive the largest subsidies, internalize the externality in the most efficient manner?

There have been a number of proposals to modify the mortgage deduction. One option is to replace the deduction with a tax credit equal to a fixed percentage of the household's mortgage cost. For example, if the tax credit is 15 percent, every household would receive a tax cut equal to 15 percent of its mortgage cost. Under a tax credit, all taxpayers would receive the same percentage subsidy for homeownership. A second option is to place a ceiling on the amount of mortgage interest that can be deducted. This would decrease the subsidy to the wealthiest households.

The Net Effects of the Tax Code: Renting versus Owning.   What is the net effect of the federal tax code on the choice between renting and owning? For renters, rapid depreciation decreases the cost of supplying rental housing, decreasing market rents. For owner-occupants, the mortgage deduction decreases the cost of ownership. Does the tax code decrease the cost of renting by more than it decreases the cost of ownership?

The net effect of the tax code depends on a number of factors. One of the factors is the generosity of depreciation allowances: the more rapidly rental property can be depreciated, the larger the tax benefits and the lower the market rent on rental property. Two studies in the early 1980s suggested that the tax code decreased the relative cost of renting, causing a bias toward rental housing (King and Fullerton, 1984; Gordon, Hines, and Summers, 1986). Since 1986, however, depreciation rules have become less generous. For example, the tax life of rental property increased from 15 years to 27.5 years; the allowable depreciation rate dropped from an average of 6.7 percent per year to about 3.6 percent. As a result, the tax liabilities of rental property have increased, increasing market rents and decreasing the bias toward rental housing.

Inflation and Homeownership.

How does inflation affect the costs and benefits of homeownership on a household that has a fixed-rate mortgage? Consider first the effect of unanticipated inflation. Suppose that the inflation rate increases from 4 percent to 10 percent. The increase in inflation increases the appreciation rate of the property from 4 percent to 10 percent, so the benefits of homeownership increase. For a household holding a fixed-rate mortgage, the increase in the inflation rate does not affect the monthly mortgage payment, so it does not affect the costs of ownership. Consider next the effects of anticipated inflation. If inflation is anticipated, mortgage lenders build the expected inflation rate into the mortgage interest rate. For example, if the expected inflation rate increases from 4 percent to 10 percent, the interest rate might increase from 8 percent to 14 percent. In this case, the home purchaser pays a higher mortgage interest rate to get the higher appreciation rate.

An alternative to a fixed-rate mortgage is one where the mortgage interest rate is adjusted periodically to reflect changes in market interest rates. Under an adjustable-rate mortgage an increase in the inflation rate increases the monthly mortgage payment because the increase in inflation increases the mortgage interest rate. As a result, unanticipated inflation increases both the benefits and costs of ownership.

Large Moving Cost

For most households, a change in housing consumption requires a move to a different dwelling. Moving cost is substantial: in addition to the large cost of moving furniture, clothes, and kitchen equipment, there is also a large cost associated with leaving behind the old neighborhood—with its people, schools, and stores. In other words, a move to a new neighborhood disrupts social and consumption patterns, imposing a substantial cost on the household. A household changes its housing consumption only if the benefits of moving (the opportunity to live in a dwelling with a better combination of housing services and cost) exceeds the cost of moving.

Figure 14–7 shows the choices faced by a household that experiences an increase in income. The household starts with income I_1 and chooses point b (the point at which its indifference curve is tangent to its initial budget line). An increase in income to I_2 shifts the budget line upward, giving the household two choices.

FIGURE 14–7   **Moving Cost and Responses to Increases in Income**

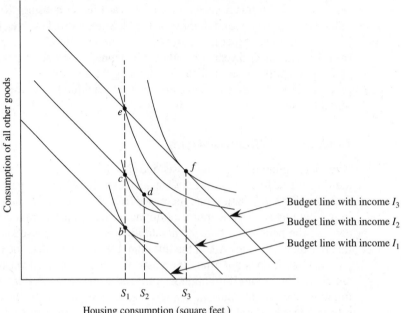

An increase in income shifts the budget line upward. In the absence of moving cost, the household would move from point *b* to point *d*, moving to a larger house (S_2 square feet of living space). If moving is costly, the household stays in its present house, choosing *c* instead of *d*. If income increases again and the household does not move, it chooses point *e*. The household moves to a larger dwelling (point *f*) if the resulting increase in utility is large enough to offset moving cost.

One option is to stay in its original house and spend all the extra income on non-housing goods (point *c*). Alternatively, the household could move to a larger house (S_2 square feet instead of S_1 square feet), choosing point *d*. In the absence of moving cost, utility would be higher at point *d* (point *d* lies on a higher indifference curve), but the question is whether the increase in utility is large enough to justify the cost of moving. If the moving cost is relatively high, the household stays in its original house and chooses point *c*. If income increases to I_3, the budget line shifts upward again, and the household faces the same choice: stay put (point *e*), or pay the moving cost and move to a larger house (point *f*). Because the gap between the initial housing consumption (S_1) and the desired housing consumption (S_3) is relatively large, the household is more likely to move than it was when the gap was relatively small ($S_2 - S_1$).

There are two lessons from Figure 14–7. First, a small change in income (or price) is unlikely to change housing consumption. Most households tolerate some dissatisfaction with their housing circumstances because moving is costly. A household moves to a different dwelling only if the change in income or price is large relative to moving cost. Second, when a household changes houses, it is likely to make a large change in its housing consumption. A household moves when its dissatisfaction with its current dwelling is large enough to justify the cost of moving.

Income and Price Elasticities

The demand for housing depends on household income and the price of housing. A number of studies have estimated the responsiveness of housing demand to changes in income and price.

Permanent Income and Income Elasticity

Because of large moving cost, households base their consumption choices on permanent, or long-run, income. Given the cost of moving, the household makes a long-term commitment to living in a particular dwelling. The commitment is based on the household's expected income over several years. Therefore, to estimate the income elasticity of demand for housing (the percentage change in housing consumption divided by the percentage change in income), one must use a measure of the permanent (long-run) income of the household, not its income in any particular year.

To explain the proper estimation of income elasticity, suppose that Lucky has a steady wage income of $20,000. In 1991, she wins $10,000 at a bingo game. As a result of her windfall, she increases her housing consumption by 5 percent, moving to a slightly larger rental apartment. If her income elasticity is computed using her income in 1990 and 1991, the elasticity would be computed as 0.10 (a 5 percent increase in housing consumption divided by a 50 percent increase in income). To correctly estimate the income elasticity, one must use a measure of her permanent income, defined as her average income over some period of time. One approach is to translate the windfall into an equivalent annual income. If Lucky invests her $10,000 prize in a bank account yielding 10 percent interest, her annual income from the prize would be $1,000, meaning that the bingo prize increases her permanent income by 5 percent. The income elasticity would then be computed as 1.0 (the 5 percent increase in housing consumption divided by the 5 percent increase in permanent income).

What is the income elasticity of demand for housing? There have been dozens of studies of housing demand, and there is a consensus on three points. First, the overall income elasticity is about 0.75 (Ellwood and Polinski, 1979): a 10 percent increase in income increases housing consumption by about 7.5 percent. Second, the income elasticity for renters is less than the income elasticity for owner-occupants. Third, the income elasticity increases with income. According to Ihlanfeldt (1982), the elasticity for low-income households is between 0.14 and 0.62, and the elasticity for high-income households is between 0.72 and 1.10.

The results of hedonic studies can be used to estimate the income elasticities of demand for individual components of the housing bundle. Follain and Jiminez (1985) summarize the results from several hedonic studies and come to three conclusions:

1. The demand for living space is inelastic with respect to income: in seven of nine cases, the elasticity is below 0.46.
2. The demand for structural quality is highly elastic with respect to income: in four of five cases, the elasticity exceeds 1.64.

3. The demand for neighborhood amenities such as public safety is highly elastic with respect to income.

The hedonic studies suggest that, compared to the demand for housing in general, the demand for living space is less income-elastic and the demands for structural quality and neighborhood amenities are more income-elastic.

Price Elasticities

What is the price elasticity of demand for housing? Most estimates of the price elasticity fall between -0.75 and -1.20 (Ellwood and Polinski, 1979). The consensus is that demand is slightly price-inelastic (an elasticity slightly less than 1.0 in absolute value). This means that an increase in price increases total expenditures on housing by a small amount: an increase in price decreases the quantity demanded by a slightly smaller percentage amount, so total expenditure (price times quantity) increases by a small amount.

Racial Discrimination and Segregation

This section explores the issue of racial prejudice and discrimination in the urban housing market. After reviewing facts on discrimination and segregation, the section discusses the effects of discrimination on (1) housing prices paid by blacks and whites and (2) the transformation of white neighborhoods into mixed or black neighborhoods.

Yinger (1979) provides a useful set of definitions of prejudice, discrimination, and segregation. **Prejudice** is defined as a negative *attitude* toward members of a particular racial group. For the purposes of this chapter, prejudice is reflected in an aversion to living near members of another race. **Racial discrimination** is defined as *behavior* that results in differential treatment based on race: members of a group subject to racial discrimination are denied rights or opportunities because of their race, not because they lack the formal qualifications for those rights or opportunities. The degree of **residential segregation** indicates the racial mixture of a city's neighborhoods. A city is completely segregated when racial groups are divided into homogeneous neighborhoods, so that no neighborhood contains members of more than one racial group. A city is completely integrated when each neighborhood is heterogeneous, with proportional representation of each racial group in each neighborhood.

Segregation Facts

The most popular measure of the segregation of two racial groups is the **index of dissimilarity**. The index shows the percentage of either racial group that would have to relocate to achieve complete integration. A value of zero implies that the city is completely integrated: each neighborhood has the same racial mixture as the metropolitan area, so there is no need to relocate people to achieve proportional representation.

In contrast, a value of 100 implies that the city is completely segregated, so that all the members of one race would have to relocate to achieve complete integration.

Figure 14–8 shows the index of dissimilarity for eight central cities and their suburbs (in 1980). Among the central cities, the most segregated is Chicago: to achieve complete integration, 92 percent of minority households would have to relocate. The least segregated of the central cities is Denver, with a value of 70. The suburbs are less segregated than the central cities: the average index for the suburbs is 57, compared to 82 for the central cities. Between 1970 and 1980, the index dropped in seven of the eight central cities and in three of the eight suburban areas. During this period, the average central-city index dropped from 86 to 82 and the average suburban index dropped from 57 to 56.

FIGURE 14–8   Index of Dissimilarity for Selected Central Cities and Their Suburbs, 1980

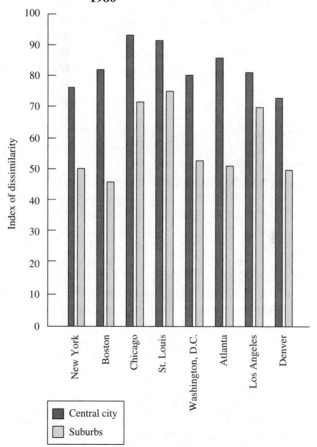

SOURCE: Thomas A. Clark, "The Suburbanization Process and Residential Segregation," in *Divided Neighborhoods,* ed. Gary A. Tobin (Beverly Hills, Calif.: Sage Publications, 1987).

Blacks are the most segregated of all the racial minorities. Using data from Chicago, Woolbright and Hartmann (1987) show that the black-white index of dissimilarity is 24 points higher than the Hispanic-white index and 40 points higher than the Asian-white index. Using data from Kansas City, Darden (1987) shows that blacks are highly segregated regardless of education, income, and occupational status. Although segregation is less severe among more educated households, even college graduates are highly segregated: the index for college graduates is 74, compared to 82 for high school graduates and 83 for those who have not attended high school. The index varies slightly with household income without an obvious pattern: the index is 83 for households with an income of $5,000, 84 for an income of $10,000, 83 for an income of $20,000, 82 for an income of $30,000, and 88 for an income of $50,000.

What Causes Segregation?

Racial segregation is caused, in part, by segregation with respect to income. To explain, consider a city in which neighborhoods are homogeneous with respect to income: there is a poor neighborhood and a wealthy neighborhood. If blacks are poorer than whites, income segregation contributes to racial segregation. As an extreme example, suppose that all the poor are black, and all the blacks are poor. In this case, the city is completely segregated even if there is no racial prejudice: the poor neighborhood is 100 percent black and the wealthy neighborhood is 100 percent white. As a more realistic example, suppose that black households have a lower average income, but there are some wealthy black households. In this case, income segregation causes partial racial segregation: the poor neighborhood has a relatively large number of black households.

How important is income segregation in explaining racial segregation? There is conclusive evidence that differences in income play a relatively small role in racial segregation. According to Farley (1983), differences in income and other socioeconomic characteristics are responsible for about 25 percent of segregation in central cities and about 15 percent of segregation in suburban areas. The studies by Gabriel and Rosenthal (1989) and Kain (1985) discussed in Chapter 12 suggest that the low rate of black suburbanization is caused by factors other than income.

A common misconception is that all racial groups (whites, blacks, and Hispanics) prefer segregated neighborhoods. If this were true, it would suggest that racial segregation is voluntary. The evidence from household surveys suggests that blacks and Hispanics prefer integrated neighborhoods, not segregated ones. Figure 14–9 shows the neighborhood preferences of black, Hispanic, and white households. About a sixth of white households prefer to live in mixed neighborhoods (50 percent white), compared to 57 percent of blacks and 46 percent of Hispanics. In contrast, about three fourths of white households prefer highly segregated neighborhoods (few or no households of other races), compared to 23 percent of blacks and 18 percent of Hispanics. These results suggest that there is a basic conflict between whites, who generally prefer segregation, and blacks and Hispanics, who generally prefer integration.

FIGURE 14–9   Preferences for Mixed and Segregated Neighborhoods: Blacks, Hispanics, and Whites

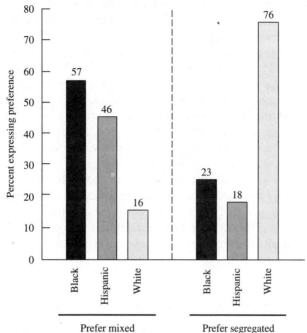

SOURCE: U.S. Department of Housing and Urban Development, *The 1978 HUD Survey of the Quality of Community Life: A Data Book* (Washington, D.C.: U.S. Government Printing Office, 1979).

Housing Prices with Fixed Populations

This section explores the effects of racial prejudice and discrimination on housing prices. The principal question is: how does the price of housing vary within a segregated city? The conclusion is that in a city with a fixed black population, blacks pay less than whites for identical dwellings.

To explain the effects of prejudice and discrimination on the price of housing, consider a mixed-race city with the following characteristics:

1. There is a fixed number of households of each race.
2. All households have the same income.
3. All dwellings in the city are identical.
4. All dwellings are equally accessible to employment opportunities.
5. Blacks have a moderate preference for living near white households.
6. Whites have a strong aversion to living near black households.

Suppose that the city starts with a segregated housing market: blacks live close to the city center and whites live in a suburban ring. The question is, what housing-price function is consistent with racial segregation? In other words, what set of housing prices will sustain the segregated housing pattern?

Figure 14–10 shows a housing-price function that is consistent with racial segregation. The border between the black area and the white area is u^*. The solid line shows the price function under which households have no incentive to relocate. In the black area ($u < u^*$), the price function is positively sloped, reflecting blacks' preferences for proximity to whites. Black households are willing to pay $48,000 for a dwelling in the city center, compared to $60,000 for a dwelling at the border between the two areas. In the white area ($u > u^*$), the positively sloped price function reflects whites' aversion to living close to blacks. White households are willing to pay $60,000 for a dwelling at the border, compared to $84,000 for a dwelling at the location most distant from the black area. The black price function is flatter than the white price function because blacks have relatively weak preferences for living near whites.

Figure 14–10 suggests that blacks pay less than whites for identical dwellings. All dwellings are assumed to be identical in terms of their physical characteristics and accessibility, yet the equilibrium price increases with the distance from the city center. The average black household (located in the center of the black area) pays $54,000, compared to $72,000 for the average white household (located in the center

FIGURE 14–10   Equilibrium Housing-Price Function in Segregated City

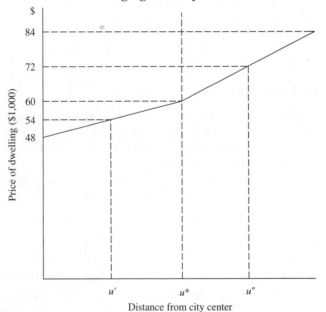

In a segregated city where both blacks and whites prefer to live near whites, the housing-price function is positively sloped. Blacks living at $u < u^*$ are willing to pay more for dwellings closer to the white area, and whites living beyond u^* are willing to pay less for dwellings close to the black area.

of the white area). In this case, whites pay for their aversion to living near blacks in the form of higher housing prices.

As pointed out by Yinger (1979), there are two key assumptions underlying the result that blacks and whites are completely segregated. First, the preference of blacks for white neighbors is weaker than the preference of whites for white neighbors. This means that whites outbid blacks for all dwellings beyond u^*. In contrast, if some blacks had relatively strong preferences for white neighbors, they could outbid whites for dwellings beyond u^* and thus disrupt the segregated pattern. In this case, complete segregation is not a market equilibrium. The second key assumption is that all households have the same income. In combination with the assumption that blacks have relatively weak preferences for living close to whites, the assumption of equal incomes means that whites outbid blacks for all dwellings beyond u^*. If this assumption were dropped, wealthy black households could outbid whites for some dwellings beyond u^*, so complete segregation would not be a market equilibrium.

Population Growth and Broker Discrimination

Figure 14–10 predicts that blacks pay less than whites for identical dwellings. This prediction is inconsistent with empirical studies from the 1970s, which suggest that blacks paid more—not less—than whites. The apparent inconsistency can be explained by the rapid growth of urban black populations during the 1960s and 1970s. In other words, the first assumption of the model underlying Figure 14–10 (a fixed number of households), was not satisfied during this period.

Consider a city that experiences rapid growth in its black population. In the absence of restrictions on the size of the black area, we would expect the black area to expand outward to accommodate the larger black population. As the black population increases, competition for housing increases the amount blacks are willing to pay for housing near the old border (u^*). If black households are allowed to compete with whites for housing near u^*, blacks will outbid white households, causing the black area to expand outward.

If whites are averse to living near blacks, they have an incentive to prevent the expansion of the black area. White households can turn their prejudicial attitudes into discriminatory behavior by refusing to deal with real estate brokers who sell dwellings to blacks. A broker who sells to blacks will have fewer white customers and may make less money. If the penalty for selling to blacks (fewer white customers) is large enough, brokers will engage in discriminatory behavior that promotes segregation and prevents the expansion of the black area.

Brokers use a number of techniques to discourage black buyers. The first technique is called *racial steering:* the broker directs individual buyers to neighborhoods full of households of the same race. In other words, black buyers are not given information about dwellings in predominantly white neighborhoods. Second, brokers provide inferior service to black households by (1) misrepresenting the housing market, (2) delaying transactions, and (3) giving less help in arranging financing.

A **fair-housing audit** provides information on the extent of racial discrimination. The auditor sends two individuals who are identical except for race (they have the same income, education, household size) to real estate brokers to inquire about housing. According to Yinger (1986), there is conclusive evidence that blacks are treated differently from otherwise identical whites: blacks are shown fewer dwellings, steered into certain neighborhoods, and given less advice and assistance on financing options.

Figure 14–11 shows the effects of black population growth when the border between the black area and the white area is fixed. Population growth shifts the black portion of the housing-price function upward. If racial discrimination on the part of brokers prevents the expansion of the black area, the typical black household (at the midpoint u') pays \$78,000 for a dwelling, compared to \$72,000 for the typical white (at u''). These figures are roughly consistent with empirical results from the 1970s that showed blacks paying higher housing prices. Unfortunately, there have been no careful studies of the black-white price differential since the late 1970s, so it's unclear whether blacks continue to pay more for housing.

Neighborhood Transition

Consider a neighborhood that is changing from a segregated white neighborhood to a mixed-race neighborhood. This section discusses the factors that determine how rapidly the neighborhood changes.

FIGURE 14–11   Black and White Housing Prices with Black Population Growth

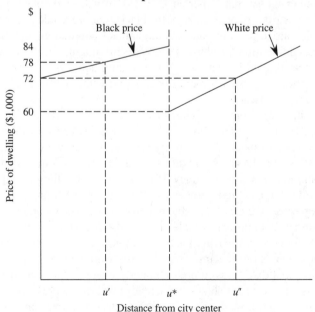

In a city with a growing black population and a fixed black area, the typical black (at u') pays more than the typical white (at u'') for housing.

An important factor in the speed of neighborhood transition is the attitude toward integration. A white household who prefers a segregated neighborhood is likely to leave the neighborhood as its minority population grows. According to household surveys, the number of departing whites increases with the minority's share of the neighborhood population. According to one survey, the percentage of whites who say that they will leave increases from 7 percent in a neighborhood with 7 percent minorities, to 24 percent in a neighborhood with 20 percent minorities, to 41 percent in a neighborhood with 33 percent minorities, to 64 percent in a neighborhood with 60 percent minorities. These numbers explain why many neighborhoods change rapidly from highly segregated white neighborhoods to highly segregated minority neighborhoods. An increase in the share of minority households decreases the attractiveness of the neighborhood to many white households, causing white flight and further increases in the minority share.

Galster (1990) studied the racial transformation of neighborhoods in the Cleveland metropolitan area during the 1970s. He explored the factors that determine the rate at which the black share of a neighborhood's population increases over time. The most important factors are (1) the initial black share of population, (2) white attitudes toward segregation, and (3) the proximity of the neighborhood to other neighborhoods where blacks are in the majority.

Figure 14–12 shows Galster's results for three types of neighborhoods. The curves show the gains in the black share of population (in percentage points) over the 1970–80 decade for different initial black shares. Curve A shows this relationship for a neighborhood that (1) is not adjacent to a black-majority neighborhood and (2) has "average" white preferences for segregation. For example, a neighborhood that starts the decade as 10 percent black gains 5.5 percentage points over the decade, so the neighborhood is 15.5 percent black at the end of the decade. Along the positively sloped portion of the curve, the gain in the black share increases with the initial black share. For example, if the initial share is 20 percent, the gain is 9.5 percentage points, so the 1980 share is 29.5 percent. For the type of neighborhood shown by curve A, there is a black majority by the end of the decade if the initial black share exceeds about 37 percent (point X).

Curve C in Figure 14–12 shows the changes in the black share of population for a neighborhood that (1) is adjacent to a black-majority neighborhood and (2) has relatively strong white preferences for segregation. For a given initial share, this neighborhood experiences more white flight than the average neighborhood, so the gain in the black share is relatively large. For example, for an initial share of 10 percent, the gain is 20 percentage points, so the black share at the end of the decade is 30 percent. This type of neighborhood is more likely to have a black majority by the end of the decade than the average neighborhood: for any initial share greater than 22 percent (point Z), the black gain is large enough to generate a black majority.

During the 1970s, two municipalities in the Cleveland area (Shaker Heights and Cleveland Heights) used public policy to encourage racially balanced neighborhoods. The idea was to encourage blacks to move into white neighborhoods, but to prevent the development of black-majority neighborhoods. There were a number of features of this "affirmative marketing" policy, including (1) information and

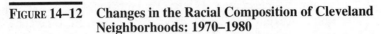

FIGURE 14–12   **Changes in the Racial Composition of Cleveland Neighborhoods: 1970–1980**

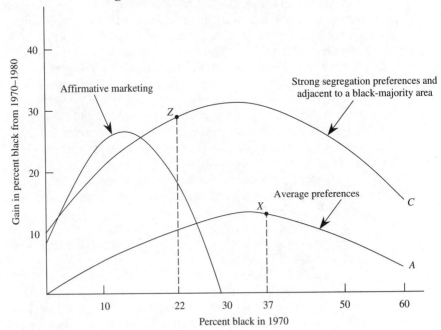

SOURCE: George C. Galster, "Neighborhood Racial Change, Segregationist Sentiments, and Affirmative Marketing Policies," *Journal of Urban Economics* 27 (1990), pp. 344–61.

persuasion campaigns to attract blacks, (2) policies to maintain the quality of housing and public services (especially education) to discourage the departure of households who place a high value on the quality of housing and public services, and (3) special broker services for members of the "underrepresented" racial group, typically whites. To prevent the white flight that might drop the number of white households below 50 percent, the municipalities catered to white households.

The third curve in Figure 14–12 shows the gain in the black share for a neighborhood that (1) engaged in affirmative marketing and (2) is not adjacent to a black-majority neighborhood. For a neighborhood with a small initial black share, the black gain in this type of neighborhood exceeds the gain experienced by the average neighborhood (shown by curve *A*). For example, for an initial share of 10 percent, the black gain in the affirmative-marketing neighborhood is 24.5 percentage points, compared to 5.5 points in the average neighborhood. In contrast, for a large initial black share, the affirmative-marketing neighborhood experiences a relatively small gain. For example, for an initial share of 28 percent, the black gain is 3 percentage points, compared to 12 points in the average neighborhood. In the neighborhood with affirmative marketing, the black share of the population is stable if the initial share is about 30 percent.

The success of affirmative marketing depends on whether or not the neighborhood is adjacent to a black-majority neighborhood. If it is not, the black share of

FIGURE 14–13   **Threshold Black Shares for Different Types of Neighborhoods**

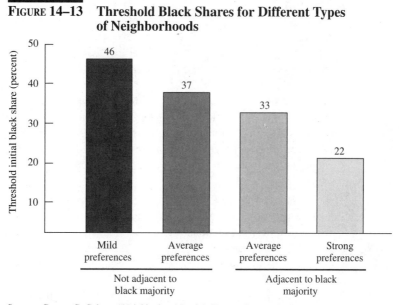

SOURCE: George C. Galster, "Neighborhood Racial Change, Segregationist Sentiments, and Affirmative Marketing Policies," *Journal of Urban Economics* 27 (1990), pp. 344–61.

population by the end of the decade never exceeds 30 percent, so the policy achieves its objective of a racially balanced neighborhood. In contrast, the policy is ineffective in neighborhoods that are adjacent to black-majority neighborhoods: if such a neighborhood starts the decade with a black share of at least 12 percent, it will have a black majority by the end of the decade.

Figure 14–13 summarizes Galster's results for neighborhoods that did not adopt affirmative-marketing policies. For each type of neighborhood, the figure shows the minimum initial black share that generates a black majority by the end of the decade. The threshold share is larger for neighborhoods that are distant from black-majority neighborhoods and have relatively weak white preferences for segregation. The smallest threshold (22 percent) is for a neighborhood that is adjacent to a black-majority area and has strong white preferences for segregation.

Summary

1. Housing is different from other commodities because it is heterogeneous, immobile, and durable. Housing is costly in two senses: it is a large part of the household budget and changes in housing consumption are costly.

2. Housing is heterogeneous in the sense that every dwelling provides a different bundle of features. Dwellings differ in size, layout, the quality of utility systems, and interior design. Sites differ in access, tax liabilities, local public goods, environmental quality, and neighborhood appearance.

    a. The hedonic approach is based on the notion that a dwelling is composed of a bundle of individual components, each of which has an implicit price.

    b. Housing consumers choose the dwelling that provides the best combination of features at the best price, trading off quality, size, location, and other attributes.

    c. The heterogeneity of the housing stock means that a city's housing market is segmented with respect to size, location, and quality: the market is composed of a number of submarkets.

    d. Positive changes in the exterior appearance of one house cause spillover benefits (increases in market value) for surrounding houses (the neighborhood effect).

3. Housing is durable, and the landlord can control the rate of physical deterioration by spending money on repair and maintenance.

    a. Spending on maintenance and repair determines the quantity of housing services generated by the dwelling. At the optimum quantity, the marginal benefit (the change in total revenue) equals marginal cost (the change in total cost).

    b. When the profits from housing are negative, dwellings are retired from the housing stock. There are three types of retirement: conversion to another use, boarding up, and abandonment.

    c. Retirement results from decreases in market price (from a decrease in demand or an increase in supply) or an increase in maintenance cost.

    d. A recent study suggests that the property tax encourages abandonment.

4. The supply of housing is relatively inelastic for relatively long periods of time because the bulk of the housing stock is used housing. There are no reliable estimates of the price elasticity of supply.

5. According to the filtering model, the quantity of housing services generated by a dwelling decreases over time, so the dwelling is occupied by households with progressively lower incomes. The filtering model explains why the poor occupy used housing and shows that the poor benefit from the subsidization of new housing for the middle-income households.

6. The costs of rental housing and owner-occupied housing are determined by the cost of capital (the opportunity cost of money invested in housing), depreciation, and maintenance cost. Three factors push many households toward homeownership: the renter externality (tenants have little incentive to inform landlords of maintenance problems), higher interest rates for rental property loans, and the hobby aspect of repair and maintenance.

7. The federal tax code has special tax breaks for rental and owner-occupied housing.

    a. Rapid depreciation of rental property defers taxes, increasing the profitability of rental property and decreasing monthly rent.

    b. The deductibility of mortgage interest decreases the cost of homeownership, increasing ownership rates and increasing housing consumption.

c. The net effect of the tax code on homeownership depends on marginal tax rates and the generosity of depreciation allowances, both of which have changed over time.

8. The cost of moving is relatively large, so households change their housing consumption infrequently and make large changes when they move.

9. The income elasticity of demand for housing is about 0.75, and the price elasticity is between −0.75 and −1.20.

10. The index of dissimilarity shows the percentage of one racial group that would have to relocate to achieve complete integration.

   a. In eight selected metropolitan areas between 1970 and 1980, the average central-city index dropped from 86 to 82 and the average suburban index dropped from 57 to 56.

   b. Blacks are the most segregated of all racial minorities and are highly segregated regardless of education, income, and occupational status.

   c. Differences in income and other socioeconomic characteristics are responsible for about 25 percent of segregation in central cities and about 15 percent of segregation in suburban areas.

   d. About a sixth of white households prefer to live in mixed neighborhoods, compared to 57 percent of blacks and 46 percent of Hispanics.

11. Racial prejudice and discrimination affect the housing prices paid by blacks and whites.

   a. In a city with a fixed black population, blacks pay less than whites for identical dwellings.

   b. If discrimination prevents the expansion of the black area when the black population grows, blacks pay more—not less—than whites for identical dwellings. A number of empirical results from the 1970s showed that blacks paid higher housing prices.

12. A study of the racial transformation of neighborhoods in the Cleveland metropolitan area during the 1970s suggests that the most rapid transformation occurs in neighborhoods that (a) start with a relatively large black share of population, (b) have white households with strong preferences for living with other whites, and (c) are close to neighborhoods where blacks are in the majority.

13. An affirmative-marketing program is more likely to result in a racially balanced neighborhood if the neighborhood is not close to a black-majority neighborhood.

Exercises and Discussion Questions

1. Consider an apartment building that does not generate enough rental revenue to cover the landlord's costs.

   a. Use a graph to show this situation (see Figure 14–2).

 b. Suppose that the government provides a 50 percent subsidy for operating, maintenance, and repair costs. Show the effects of the subsidy program on your graph. What happens to the optimum Q and the likelihood of retirement?

2. Suppose that you own an apartment building that does not generate enough rental revenue to cover your costs. You have two options: first, you could demolish the building and set up a parking lot; second, you could abandon the building. Suppose that the cost of demolition is $20,000 and the annual profit from the parking lot would be $1,500. Should you demolish or abandon? If you don't have enough information to answer this question, list the information you need and explain how you would use it.

3. Dwellings are eventually retired from the housing stock as a result of either decreases in market rent (a downward tilt of the total-revenue curve in Figure 14–2) or rising maintenance cost (an upward tilt of the total-cost curve).

 a. Use a graph like Figure 14–2 to prove or disprove the following statement: "A dwelling that leaves the market as a result of decreases in market rent leaves the market at a higher quantity of housing services (a larger Q) than one that leaves as a result of increases in maintenance cost."

 b. Explain why this statement is true or false.

4. In city E, all households have the same income and real income is constant over time. Will there be filtering in the city?

5. Consider city B, which has a fixed population. In an attempt to decrease total residential energy consumption, the city has adopted policy E: all new housing in the city must be equipped with an energy-saving device that decreases the dwelling's energy consumption by 10 percent.

 a. Evaluate the effects of policy E on the city's new and used housing markets. What happens to the prices of new and used housing?

 b. What happens to the quantities of new and used housing?

 c. Under what circumstances will total energy consumption in the city increase?

 d. Describe and analyze a more effective conservation policy.

6. The real estate brokers in city F are baffled. Although dwellings are subject to the normal physical and fashion deterioration over time, there is little filtering. In contrast to most cities, in which the typical house changes hands every 7 years (usually going to a household with a lower income than the previous owner), the typical house in the city changes hands every 50 years. Explain this phenomenon.

7. Fill in the blanks to make the following statement correct and then explain your choice of words. The benefits of a subsidy for medium-quality housing are transmitted up the housing-quality hierarchy because it _____ the filtering process and down the housing-quality hierarchy because it _____ the filtering process.

8. Compute the annual cost of renting and homeownership under the following set of assumptions:
   - *i.* The market interest rate is 12 percent for rental property and 10 percent for owner-occupied property.
   - *ii.* The market value of the typical house is $100,000.
   - *iii.* Maintenance cost is 5 percent per year on rental property and 2 percent per year on owner-occupied property.
   - *iv.* The marginal tax rate of the typical household is 28 percent.
   - *v.* Both types of properties are appreciating by 4 percent per year.
   - *vi.* Rapid depreciation decreases the annual cost of rental property by 25 percent.

9. Comment on the following statement: "Property values in this city are increasing rapidly, rising at an annual rate of about 20 percent. This will cause many households to switch from renting to owning."

10. The owners of rental property can deduct routine maintenance cost from their gross income; homeowners cannot. Does the deductibility of maintenance cost decrease the relative cost of renting, thus creating a bias toward renting?

11. Consider a city where the demand for housing for the typical household is

$$Q = 1,000 - 1,000 \cdot P$$

   where Q is the square footage of housing demanded and P is the price per square foot. The original price of housing is 50 cents per square foot.
   - *a.* Draw the demand curve for housing.
   - *b.* How many square feet of housing does the typical household demand?
   - *c.* What is the consumer surplus associated with a price of 50 cents? Suppose that the price of housing decreases to 40 cents.
   - *d.* What is the consumer surplus at the new price, assuming that the household does not move to a new residence?
   - *e.* What is the consumer surplus at the new price, assuming that the household moves to a new residence?
   - *f.* If the cost of moving is $25, will the typical household move to a new residence?

12. In city D, landlords charge a security deposit of $900 and do not refund the money when the tenant leaves. Suppose that a new deposit law is passed. The law requires that all landlords refund 100 percent of the security deposit unless the landlord can prove that the tenant damaged or dirtied the dwelling. Comment on the following statement: "The new law will save the typical tenant $900."

13. Comment on the following statement: "I live in an apartment complex built in a year when interest rates were relatively low. My rent is lower than the rent on other apartments because the cost of financing the complex is relatively low."

14. In Figure 14–10, the housing-price function for blacks is flatter than the housing-price function for whites. Why?

15. One of the assumptions lurking behind Figure 14–10 is that all dwellings are equally accessible to employment opportunities. Draw a new housing-price function under the assumption that all workers commute to the city center, so commuting cost increases with u (distance to the center).

References and Additional Readings

Overview

Arnott, Richard. "Economic Theory and Housing." In *Handbook of Regional and Urban Economics*, vol. 2, ed. Edwin S. Mills. New York: Elsevier-North Holland Publishing, 1987. Reviews various models of the urban housing market and suggests directions for future research.

Olsen, Edgar O. "A Competitive Theory of the Housing Market." *American Economic Review* 59 (1969), pp. 612–22.

———. "The Demand and Supply of Housing Service: A Critical Survey of the Empirical Literature." In *Handbook of Regional and Urban Economics*, vol. 2, ed. Edwin S. Mills. New York: Elsevier-North Holland Publishing, 1987. Reviews empirical studies of housing supply and demand.

Quigley, John M. "What Have We Learned about Housing Markets?" In *Current Issues in Urban Economics*, ed. Peter Mieszkowski and Mahlon Straszheim. Baltimore: Johns Hopkins University Press, 1979. A review of theoretical and empirical research in housing.

U.S. Bureau of the Census. *Statistical Abstract of the United States: 1986*. Washington, D.C.: U.S. Government Printing Office, 1985.

Supply of New Housing

Follain, James R. "The Price Elasticity of the Long-Run Supply of New Housing Construction." *Land Economics* 55 (1979), pp. 190–99.

Muth, Richard. "The Demand for Non-Farm Housing." In *The Demand for Durable Goods*, ed. Arnold C. Harberger. University of Chicago Press, 1960. Estimates the elasticity of supply of new housing.

Supply of Used Housing

Farb, Warren E. "An Estimate of the Relative Supply and Demand for Substandard Rental Housing in Major U.S. Cities." Ph.D. dissertation, Washington University, St. Louis, 1971. Suggests that the supply of low-quality housing is highly elastic.

Ingram, Gregory K., and Yitzhak Oron. "The Behavior of Housing Producers." In *Residential Location and Urban Housing Markets*, ed. Gregory K. Ingram. New York: National Bureau of Economic Research, 1977. Discusses a landlord's choice of quality level, based on costs and benefits (rent) of different quality levels.

Kain, John, and William Apgar. "Simulation of Housing Market Dynamics." *Journal of the American Real Estate and Urban Economics Association* 7 (1979), pp. 505–38. A simulation model in which landlords choose a quality level consistent with profit maximization.

Abandonment

Muth, Richard F. "The Demand for Non-Farm Housing." In *The Demand for Durable Goods*, ed. Arnold Harberger. University of Chicago Press, 1960, pp. 29–96.

Peterson, George. "The Effect of Federal Taxes on Urban Form." In *The Prospective City*, ed. Arthur Solomon. Cambridge, Mass.: MIT Press, 1979. Discusses the effects of federal taxes on abandonment.

Sterlieb, George, and Robert Burchell. *Residential Abandonment: The Tenement Landlord Revisited.* New Brunswick, N.J.: Rutgers University Press, 1973.

White, Michelle. "Property Taxes and Urban Housing Abandonment." *Journal of Urban Economics* 20 (1986), pp. 312–30. Explores the effects of inflexible property taxation on the frequency of abandonment and concludes that the property tax encourages abandonment.

Supply Elasticities

De Leeuw, Frank, and Nkanta Ekanem. "The Supply of Rental Housing." *American Economic Review* 61 (1971), pp. 806–17.

Grieson, Ronald E. "The Supply of Rental Housing: Comment." *American Economic Review* 63 (1973), pp. 433–36.

Mason, John M. "The Supply Curve for Housing." *Journal of the American Real Estate and Urban Economics Association* 7 (1979), pp. 362–77.

Ozanne, L., and Raymond Struyk. "The Price Elasticity of Supply of Housing Services." In *Urban Housing Markets: Recent Directions in Research and Policy*, ed. L. S. Bourne and J. R. Hitchcock. University of Toronto Press, 1978. Estimates the supply elasticity of used housing.

Smith, Barton A. "The Supply of Urban Housing." *Quarterly Journal of Economics* 90 (1976), pp. 389–406.

The Hedonic Approach

Brown, H. James. "Micro Neighborhood Externalities and Hedonic Housing Prices." *Land Economics* 56 (1980), pp. 125–41.

Crecine, John; Otto Davis; and John Jackson. "Urban Property Markets: Some Empirical Results and Their Implications for Municipal Zoning." *Journal of Law and Economics* 10 (1967), pp. 79–100.

De Salvo, Joseph S. "Benefits and Costs of New York City's Middle-Income Housing Program." *Journal of Political Economy* 83 (1975), pp. 791–805. Found that housing projects for middle-income housing increased the values of nearby properties by about 5 percent. Also estimated the welfare losses from using public housing instead of cash transfers as 45 percent of the program cost.

Follain, James R., and Emmanuel Jiminez. "Estimating the Demand for Housing Characteristics." *Regional Science and Urban Economics* 15 (1985), pp. 77–107. A survey and critique of hedonic studies of the housing market.

Freeman, A. Myrick III. "The Hedonic Approach to Measuring Demand for Neighborhood Characteristics." In *The Economics of Neighborhood*, ed. David Segal. New York: Academic Press, 1979.

Kain, John F., and John M. Quigley. *Housing Markets and Racial Discrimination: A Microeconomic Analysis*. New York: National Bureau of Economic Research, 1975. A hedonic study of the St. Louis housing market.

———. "Measuring the Value of Housing Quality." *Journal of the American Statistical Association* 65 (1970), pp. 532–38.

King, Thomas. "The Demand for Housing: Integrating the Roles of Journey to Work, Neighborhood Quality, and Prices." In *Household Production and Consumption*, ed. Nester Terlecky. New York: National Bureau of Economic Research, 1975. A hedonic study of housing.

———. "The Demand for Housing: A Lancastrian Approach." *Southern Economics Journal* 43 (1976), pp. 1077–87. A hedonic study of housing prices.

Mills, Edwin S. "Housing Policy as a Means to Achieve National Growth Policy." In *Housing in the Seventies: Working Papers*, vol. 1. Washington, D.C.: U.S. Government Printing Office, 1976. Suggests that neighborhood effects are real but are relatively small, between 5 and 15 percent of the amount invested in a dwelling.

Straszheim, Mahlon. "Estimation of the Demand for Urban Housing Services from Household Interview Data." *Review of Economics and Statistics* 55 (1973), pp. 1–8. A hedonic study of housing prices.

———. *An Economic Analysis of the Urban Housing Market*. New York: National Bureau of Economic Research, 1975. A hedonic study of housing prices.

Demand Elasticities

Ellwood, David, and Mitchell Polinski. "An Empirical Reconciliation of Micro and Grouped Estimates of the Demand for Housing." *Review of Economics and Statistics* 61 (1979), pp. 199–205.

Ihlanfeldt, Keith R. "Property Tax Incidence on Owner-Occupied Housing: Evidence from the Annual Housing Survey." *National Tax Journal* 35 (1982).

Mayo, Stephen K. "Theory and Estimation in the Economics of Housing Demand." *Journal of Urban Economics* 10 (1981), pp. 95–116.

Polinski, Mitchell. "The Demand for Housing: A Study in Specification and Grouping." *Econometrica* 45 (1977), pp. 447–62.

Filtering

Brueggeman, William B. "An Analysis of the Filtering Process with Special Reference to Housing Subsidies." In *Housing in the Seventies: Working Papers*, vol. 2. Washington, D.C.: U.S. Government Printing Office, 1976, pp. 842–56. Discusses the process through which subsidies for high-quality housing generate benefits for the occupants of low-quality housing.

Grisby, William. *Housing Markets and Public Policy*. Philadelphia: University of Pennsylvania Press, 1963. Discusses the filtering process.

Kain, John F., and William C. Apgar. "Simulation of Housing Market Dynamics." *Journal of the American Real Estate and Urban Economics Association* 3 (1975), pp. 508–38.

Lowry, Ira S. "Filtering and Housing Standards: A Conceptual Analysis." *Land Economics* 36 (1960), pp. 362–70.

Ohls, James C. "Public Policy toward Low Income Housing and Filtering in Housing Markets." *Journal of Urban Economics* 2 (1975), pp. 144–71.

Sweeney, James L. "A Commodity Hierarchy Model of the Rental Housing Market." *Journal of Urban Economics* 1 (1975), pp. 288–323.

Neighborhood Dynamics

Downs, Anthony. "Key Relationships between Urban Development and Neighborhood Change." *Journal of the American Planning Association* 45 (1979), pp. 462–72.

Grisby, William; Morton Baratz; and Duncan Maclennan. *The Dynamics of Neighborhood Change and Decline*. Philadelphia: University of Pennsylvania, 1984. Discusses the theories of neighborhood decline.

Heilbrun, James. "On the Theory and Policy of Neighborhood Consolidation." *Journal of the American Planning Association* 45 (1979), pp. 417–27. Advocates a resettlement program for central cities, under which households would be moved to certain neighborhoods. The remaining neighborhoods would be cleared for new development.

Stegman, Michael A. "The Neighborhood Effects of Filtering." *Journal of the American Real Estate and Urban Economics Association* 5 (1977), pp. 227–41. Discusses the effects of new construction on the demand for central-city housing. Advocates the reorientation of federal programs away from policies that encourage the production of new suburban housing.

Stegman, Michael, and David Rasmussen. "Neighborhood Stability in Changing Cities." *American Economic Review* 70 (1980), pp. 415–19.

Taxes and Homeownership

Gordon, Roger H.; James R. Hines; and Lawrence Summers. "Notes on the Tax Treatment of Structures." Working Paper no. 1896, National Bureau of Economic Research, Cambridge, Mass., 1986.

Hendershott, Patric H., and James Shilling. "The Economics of Tenure Choice, 1955–79." In *Research in Real Estate*, ed. C. Sirmans. Greenwich, Conn.: JAI Press, 1982, pp. 105–33.

King, Mervyn A., and Don Fullerton, eds. *The Taxation of Income from Capital: A Comparative Study of the United States, the United Kingdom, Sweden, and West Germany*. University of Chicago Press, 1984. Estimates that rental housing is subsidized more heavily than owner-occupied housing.

Rosen, Harvey S. "Housing Decisions and the U.S. Income Tax: An Econometric Analysis." *Journal of Public Economics* 67 (1979), pp. 1–23.

Struyk, Raymond. *Urban Homeownership*. Lexington, Mass: D. C. Heath, 1976. Explores the effects of mortgage subsidy on homeownership. Suggests that households are responsive to changes in the relative cost of ownership.

Struyk, Raymond J., Neil Mayer, and John A. Tuccillo. *Federal Housing Policy at President Reagan's Midterm*. Washington, D.C.: Urban Institute, 1983.

White, Larry J., and Michelle J. White. "The Tax Subsidy to Owner-Occupied Housing: Who Benefits?" *Journal of Public Economics* 7 (1977), pp. 111–26.

Discrimination and Segregation

Bailey, Martin J. "A Note on the Economics of Residential Zoning and Urban Renewal." *Land Economics* 35 (1959), pp. 288–92.

Berry, Brian. "Ghetto Expansion and Racial Residential Segregation in an Urban Model." *Journal of Urban Economics* 3 (1976), pp. 397–423.

Clark, Thomas A. "The Suburbanization Process and Residential Segregation." In *Divided Neighborhoods,* ed. Gary A. Tobin. Beverly Hills, Calif.: Sage Publications, 1987.

Courant, Paul. "Racial Prejudice in a Search Model of the Urban Housing Market." *Journal of Urban Economics* 5 (1978), pp. 329–45.

Courant, Paul, and John Yinger. "On Models of Racial Prejudice and Urban Residential Structure." *Journal of Urban Economics* 4 (1977), pp. 272–91.

Darden, Joe T. "Choosing Neighbors and Neighborhoods: The Role of Race in Housing Preference." In *Divided Neighborhoods*, ed. Gary A. Tobin. Beverly Hills, Calif.: Sage Publications, 1987. Shows that racial segregation is caused largely by racial discrimination, not by income segregation or voluntary segregation.

Farley, John E. *Segregated City, Segregated Suburbs: Are They Products of Black-White Socioeconomic Differentials?* Edwardsville: Southern Illinois University, 1983. Concludes that differences in income and other socioeconomic characteristics play a small role in racial segregation.

Galster, George C. "Neighborhood Racial Change, Segregationist Sentiments, and Affirmative Marketing Policies." *Journal of Urban Economics* 27 (1990), pp. 344–61. Explores the factors that determine the rate at which the racial composition of a neighborhood changes.

King, Thomas, and Peter Mieszkowski. "Racial Discrimination, Segregation, and the Price of Housing." *Journal of Political Economy* 8 (1973), pp. 590–601. Provides evidence that blacks pay more than whites for housing.

Smith, Barton. "Racial Composition as a Neighborhood Amenity." In *The Economics of Urban Amenities*, ed. Douglas B. Diamond and George S. Tolley. New York: Academic Press, 1982. Reviews theoretical models of racial discrimination and segregation and provides evidence that blacks paid less than whites for housing in Houston.

U.S. Department of Housing and Urban Development. *The 1978 HUD Survey of the Quality of Community Life: A Data Book.* Washington, D.C.: U.S. Government Printing Office, 1979.

Woolbright, Louie Albert, and David J. Hartmann. "The New Segregation: Asians and Hispanics." In *Divided Neighborhoods*, ed. Gary A. Tobin. Beverly Hills, Calif.: Sage Publications, 1987.

Yinger, John. "Caught in the Act: Measuring Racial Discrimination with Fair Housing Audits." *American Economic Review* 76 (1986), pp. 881–93. Relates the results of housing audits to various theories of discrimination and prejudice.

———. "Prejudice and Discrimination in the Urban Housing Market." In *Current Issues in Urban Economics*, ed. P. Mieszkowski and M. Straszheim. Baltimore: Johns Hopkins, 1979, pp. 430–68. Discusses the causes and consequences of racial prejudice and discrimination. Summarizes the empirical evidence that blacks paid more than whites for housing.

———. "The Racial Dimension of Urban Housing Markets in the 1980s." In *Divided Neighborhoods*, ed. Gary A. Tobin. Beverly Hills, Calif.: Sage Publications, 1987. Discusses recent evidence of discriminatory treatment of black house buyers and policy implications.

15 Housing Policies

This is the second of two chapters on the urban housing market. It discusses three types of housing policies. The first is housing assistance: the federal government uses various policies to improve the housing conditions and decrease the housing cost of poor households. Second, the federal government uses a number of community development programs to support local efforts to improve housing conditions and revitalize neighborhoods. Third, under a rent-control policy, the local government sets a maximum price for rental housing.

There are two distinct types of housing-assistance programs. The first type operates on the supply side of the housing market: the government either builds new housing for the poor (public housing) or subsidizes private developers to build and manage low-income housing. The second type of assistance policy operates on the demand side of the market: the government hands out coupons that can be used to rent existing housing.

Since 1980, the focus of federal housing policies has shifted back and forth between supply-side and demand-side policies. In 1980, about 188,000 households were added to housing-assistance programs, with about 130,000 households placed in new dwellings and 58,000 given housing coupons. In 1986, 99,000 households were added, with only 13,000 housed in new dwellings. The National Housing Affordability Act of 1992 represents a shift back to supply-side policies. The legislation provides funds to build an additional 360,000 low-income housing units over a two-year period.

Conditions of Housing and Neighborhoods

The original goal of federal housing policy was to provide "a decent home and a suitable environment for every U.S. family." Have these objectives been met? Are most citizens living in decent houses in suitable neighborhoods?

Housing Conditions and Rent Burdens

Table 15–1 shows the percentage of households that experienced housing problems in 1990. The definitions of housing problems come from the U.S. Department of Housing and Urban Development (HUD). A dwelling is considered "inadequate" if it has incomplete plumbing or kitchen facilities, structural problems (e.g., cracked walls, leaking roof, broken plaster), deficiencies in common areas (stairwells, hallways), or unsafe heating or electrical systems. A dwelling is "crowded" if there is more than one person per room. A household is "cost-burdened" if it spends more than 30 percent of its gross income on housing.

There are three conclusions we can draw from Table 15–1. First, overcrowding is a relatively small problem: only 2.7 percent of all households live in overcrowded housing, and only 7.5 percent of poor households (income less than half the median area income) are overcrowded. Second, the most prevalent problem is affordability. The number of cost-burdened households is almost four times the number of house-

TABLE 15–1   **The Condition of the Housing Stock and Housing Cost Burdens, 1991**

	Percent of Households
All Households	
Inadequate	7.9
Crowded	2.7
Cost-burdened	28.0
Total with problems	38.7
Poor Households	
Inadequate	17.4
Crowded	7.5
Cost-burdened	62.1
Total with problems	87.0
Metropolitan Residents	
Inadequate	7.3
Crowded	2.9
Cost-burdened	29.6
Total with problems	39.8
Black Households	
Inadequate	17.4
Crowded	5.2
Cost-burdened	38.0
Total with problems	60.6

SOURCE: U.S. Department of Commerce, *Annual Housing Survey for the United States,* 1991.

holds in inadequate housing. The affordability problem is most extensive among black and poor households: 4 in 10 black households and 6 in 10 poor households are cost-burdened. Third, the most severe problems are experienced by poor households and black households. Most (87 percent) poor households have some sort of housing problem, and 6 in 10 are cost-burdened. Almost two thirds of black households experience problems: about 1 in 4 black households lives in inadequate or overcrowded housing, and an additional 4 in 10 are cost-burdened.

In the last several decades, there has been considerable progress in improving the condition of the housing stock. The percentage of households in overcrowded housing dropped from 13.5 percent in 1950 to 2.9 percent in 1991. The percentage of urban households living in "substandard" housing (defined differently from inadequate housing) was 21.9 percent in 1950, but the percentage in inadequate housing was only 7.3 percent in 1991.

Neighborhood Conditions

Table 15–2 provides evidence concerning the level of neighborhood dissatisfaction for various types of households. The first column of numbers shows the percentage of households of each type that gave their neighborhood a score of 3 or less on a 10-point scale. The greatest dissatisfaction is among households living in multifamily dwellings in central cities. For example, 16.8 percent of low-income black households living in multifamily housing in the central city said that their neighborhood was of "poor" quality and 36.1 percent of these households said that the neighborhood was so bad that they wanted to move. Among similar households living in single-family housing in the suburbs, only 3.3 percent considered their neighborhood to be of poor quality and only 13.6 percent said that they wanted to move. The figures for low-income white households are 11.2 percent (poor quality) and 22.3 percent (want to move) for multifamily housing in the central city and 3.4 percent (poor quality) and 10.0 percent (want to move) for single-family housing in the suburbs. Neighborhood dissatisfaction varies with race and income: blacks are generally more dissatisfied than whites, and low-income households are more dissatisfied than high-income households.

Boehm and Ihlanfeldt (1991) explore the effects of various neighborhood characteristics on the perceived quality of the neighborhood. Their results suggest that dissatisfaction is most prevalent in neighborhoods with high crime rates, high noise levels, run-down and abandoned buildings, and large quantities of trash, litter, and junk.

One of the implications from Table 15–2 is that the incidence of neighborhood dissatisfaction is higher among black households. Boehm and Ihlanfeldt show that the most important factors in explaining the difference in satisfaction are differences in (1) crime rates, (2) the amount of litter, trash, and junk, (3) the quality of buildings, and (4) the number of abandoned buildings.

Figure 15–1 shows the results of the following thought experiment. Suppose that the crime rate in the typical black neighborhood changes to the crime rate that prevails in the typical white neighborhood. By how much would the gap between black

TABLE 15–2   Opinion of Neighborhood by Race, Income, Structure Type, and Location

Household Type	Neighborhood Quality Is Poor (%)	Want to Move (%)
Black, low, multi, city	16.8	36.1
Black, high, multi, city	9.7	32.2
Black, high, multi, suburbs	6.3	25.7
Black, low, multi, suburbs	10.5	25.6
White, low, multi, city	11.2	22.3
White, high, multi, city	5.7	21.8
Black, low, single, city	10.3	19.7
Black, high, single, city	5.4	17.4
White, high, multi, suburbs	3.9	16.3
White, low, single, city	6.5	15.9
White, high, single, city	3.3	15.4
Black, high, single, city	3.3	14.9
White, low, multi, suburbs	5.2	14.1
Black, low, single, suburbs	3.3	13.6
White, high, single, suburbs	1.8	10.4
White, low, single, suburbs	3.4	10.0

Definitions
Poor quality: score 3 or less on a10-point quality scale.
Low: income in bottom third of income distribution.
High: income in top two thirds of income distribution.
Multi: live in multifamily housing.
Single: live in single-family dwelling.
City: live in central city.
Suburbs: live in suburban area.

SOURCE: Thomas P. Boehm and Keith R. Ihlanfeldt, "The Revelation of Neighborhood Preferences: An N-Chotomous Multivariate Probit Approach," *Journal of Housing Economics* 1 (1991), pp. 33–59.

and white dissatisfaction decrease? The answer is that the gap would decrease by 12 percent. Figure 15–1 shows the results of repeating this thought experiment for the other factors that contribute to neighborhood dissatisfaction: abandoned buildings are responsible for 14 percent of the gap, and litter, trash, and junk are responsible for another 17 percent.

Supply-Side Policy: Public Housing

In 1987, about 1.3 million households lived in public housing. The number of public housing units increased from 478,000 in 1960 to 1.2 million in 1980. Since then, the number of occupied units has increased slowly, reflecting the shift in funding toward

FIGURE 15–1 **Reasons for the Gap between White and Black Neighborhood Dissatisfaction**

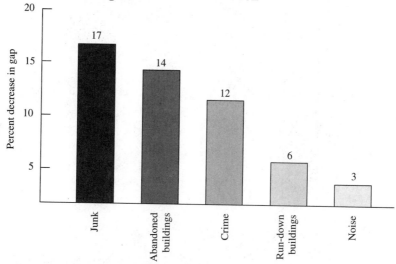

SOURCE: Thomas P. Boehm and Keith R. Ihlanfeldt, "The Revelation of Neighborhood Preferences: An N-Chotomous Multivariate Probit Approach," *Journal of Housing Economics* 1 (1991), pp. 33–59.

demand-side policies. Public housing is built and managed by local public housing authorities. The federal government is involved in four ways:

1. **Capital subsidies.** Public housing is built with tax-exempt bonds. After the federal government pays off the bonds, the project becomes the property of the local housing authority.

2. **Operating subsidies.** Originally, the public housing program was based on the notion that the local housing authority would charge enough rent to cover the project's operating costs. During the 1960s, operating costs rose rapidly while the average income level of tenants decreased. As a result, the rent-income ratios of public housing tenants increased to relatively high levels. The federal government intervened, setting a maximum rent-income ratio of 0.25. To cover the difference between the tenant contribution and the project's operating costs, the federal government provided operating subsidies. In 1981, the maximum rent-income ratio was raised to 0.30. By 1984, operating subsidies covered about 40 percent of operating cost and cost the federal government a total of $1.6 billion per year.

3. **Modernization subsidies.** The federal government also provides subsidies for the repair and renovation of old housing projects. In 1984, the total budget for modernization was $1.4 billion.

4. **Tenant selection.** The federal government places restrictions on what types of households qualify for public housing. One rule specifies that

FIGURE 15–2   **Public Housing Increases Housing Consumption**

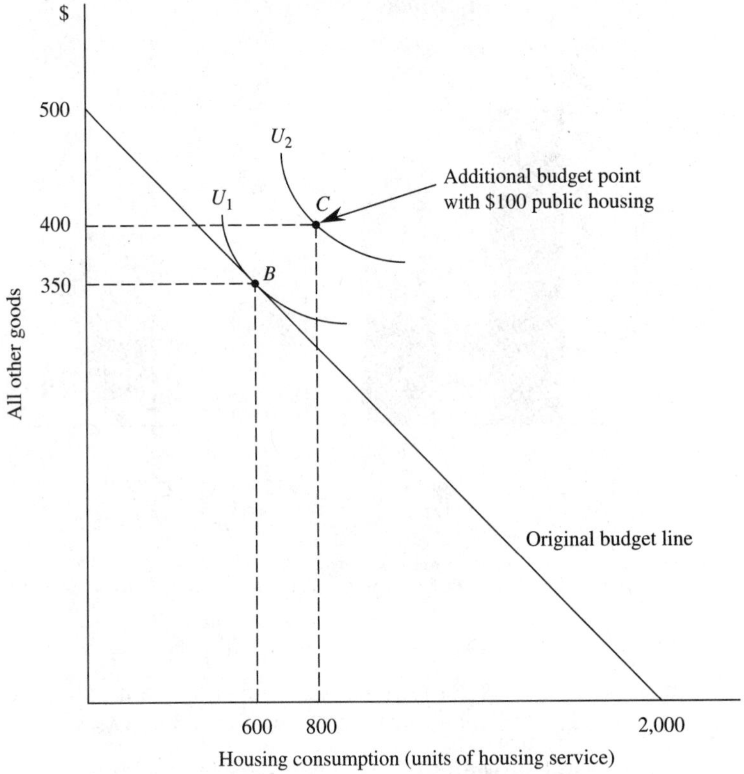

Income is $500 and the price of housing is 25 cents per unit of housing service. With the original budget line, the household chooses point *B*. Public housing (apartments generating 800 units of service at a cost of $100) adds point *C* to the budget set. Public housing allows the household to increase its consumption of both housing and other goods.

households are eligible for public housing only if their income is less than 80 percent of the median income of the area. In 1974, Congress directed local housing authorities to admit households from every income group within the eligible range. The idea was to integrate the projects with respect to income, thus preventing large concentrations of the poorest households. In 1981, Congress reversed itself, directing the housing authorities to allocate the bulk of units (75 percent of units built before 1981 and 95 percent of units built after 1981) to households with "very low" incomes (less than half the median area income).

Public Housing and Housing Consumption

Figure 15–2 shows the effects of public housing on the housing consumption of recipients. The horizontal axis measures housing consumption (measured as the quantity of housing services generated by the dwelling), and the vertical axis measures the

FIGURE 15–3   Public Housing Decreases Housing Consumption

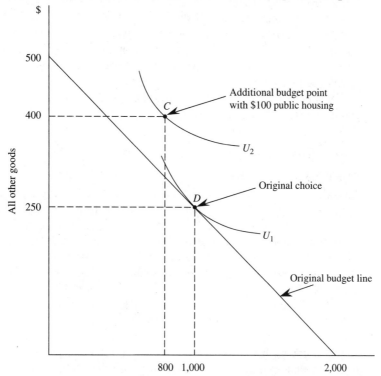

The household starts at point *D* (1,000 square feet of housing and $250 of other goods).
Public housing adds point *C* to the budget set. If the household occupies public housing, it
decreases its housing consumption from 1,000 to 800 and increases its consumption of other
goods from $250 to $400.

monthly consumption of all other goods (in dollars). The original budget line is drawn
under the assumptions that (1) monthly income is $500 and (2) the price of housing is
25 cents per unit of housing service per month. Given the household's preferences for
housing (as represented by the negatively sloped indifference curves), the household
chooses point *B*, spending $150 on housing (occupying a 600-unit dwelling) and
$350 on other goods.

Suppose that the typical public dwelling is an apartment that generates 800 units
of housing service and is provided to the poor for $100. Public housing adds point *C*
to the household's budget set: the household can consume an 800-unit apartment and
have $400 left to spend on other goods. Given the household's indifference curves,
utility is maximized at point *C*, so the household moves into public housing. The
public housing program increases housing consumption (from 600 to 800 units of
housing service) and decreases housing cost (from $150 to $100).

Will public housing always increase housing consumption? Figure 15–3 shows
the choices of a household with the same income as the household in Figure 15–2,

but different tastes for housing. In the absence of public housing, the household lives in a 1,000-unit apartment (point *D*). The household spends $250 on housing (1,000 units times 25 cents per unit), leaving $250 for other goods. If the household moves into public housing, it occupies a dwelling with fewer units of housing service (800 units) and has an additional $150 to spend on other goods. Public housing increases utility if the additional $150 worth of nonhousing goods is worth the sacrifice of 200 units of housing service. Given the indifference curves in Figure 15–3, utility is higher at point *C* than at point *D*, so the household accepts the offer of public housing and decreases its housing consumption.

Public Housing and Recipient Welfare

Would the household be better off with cash instead of subsidized public housing? Consider first the possibility that the cost of public housing is the same as the cost of private housing (25 cents per unit). It costs the government $200 to build and maintain the 800-unit apartment, so the subsidy per dwelling is $100 ($200 less the $100 rent charged to tenants), and the alternative to public housing is a $100 cash payment to the household. In Figure 15–4, a $100 cash payment shifts the recipient's budget line upward by $100. The household chooses point *E* instead of point *C* and achieves a higher utility level.

This conclusion is not a result of an arbitrary placement of the indifference curves, but of basic microeconomic principles. The household would prefer the cash because it provides more consumption options. The cash allows the household to choose point *E* (the public housing point) or any other point along the new budget line. The household would be better off with the cash if it chooses any point except *C* (i.e., if it does not spend exactly $200 on housing). If the objective of public policy is to increase the household's utility, a cash payment is superior to public housing.

How much is public housing worth to the tenant? The value of public housing can be measured by answering the following question: what cash payment would make the household indifferent between the cash and a $100 housing subsidy? In other words, what cash payment would move the household to indifference curve U_2? In Figure 15–5, a $75 payment shifts the budget line outward, and the household maximizes utility at point *F*. Since the household reaches the indifference curve U_2, it is indifferent between $75 in cash and the $100 housing subsidy. Studies by Kraft and Olsen (1977), Barton and Olsen (1976), and Murray (1975) suggest that tenants receive a benefit of about 75 cents per dollar spent on public housing. More recently, Smeeding (1982) estimated that the benefit per dollar is 80 cents.

How does the cost of new public housing compare to the cost of private housing? Public housing is more expensive for two reasons. First, the private sector can build *new* low-income housing more efficiently than the public sector: Weicher (1979) cites a number of studies showing that new public housing costs more than new private housing. Second, there is a plentiful supply of used low-quality housing, so even the least costly new housing costs more than used housing. According to the National Housing Review (1974), the cost of new public housing is about 33 percent higher than the cost of used private housing. If new public housing costs one third more than used private housing, the government spends $266 (not $200) to provide

FIGURE 15–4   **Public Housing versus Cash Payment**

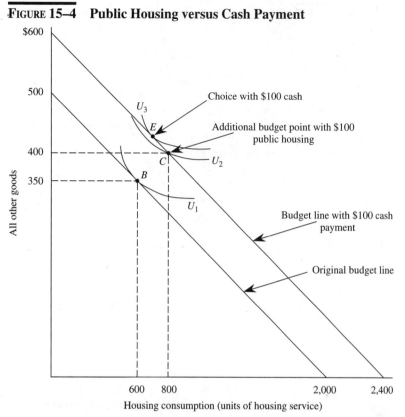

The alternative to public housing (800 units of housing service at a price of $100 instead of $200) is a $100 cash payment. Under public housing, the household chooses point C. The $100 cash payment shifts the budget line up by $100, and the household chooses point E. Utility is higher under the cash payment because the household can decide how to spend the money.

a new 800-unit apartment. Therefore, the government's cost of getting to point C in Figure 15–4 (the public housing option) is $166 ($266 less the $100 rent paid by tenants). In contrast, the cost of getting to point E (the cash option) is only $100, so the cash option generates a larger increase in utility for about three fifths of the cost.

   What is the bang per buck of public housing? In other words, what is the recipient benefit per dollar spent on public housing? As shown in Figure 15–5, recipients receive a benefit of $75 from public housing, so the bang from public housing is $75. If the government spends $266 to build the apartment and collects $100 in rent from the tenant, the government's cost is $166. Therefore, the bang per buck is 45 cents ($75 divided by $166).

Living Conditions in Public Housing

Public housing projects suffer from a number of problems, including high rates of drug abuse and crime. Figure 15–6 shows the incidence of violent crime in three

FIGURE 15–5   Monetary Value of Public Housing

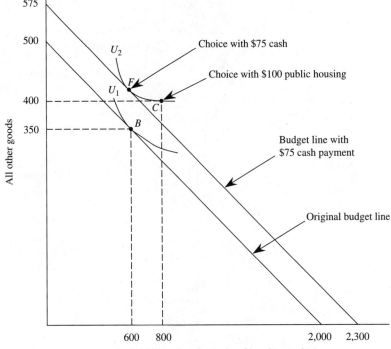

Public housing ($100 for an 800-unit apartment) is equivalent to a $75 cash payment. A $75 payment allows the household to choose point *F*, which is on the same indifference curve as point *C* (the point chosen with public housing). The household is indifferent between $100 public housing and a cash payment of $75.

public housing projects in the city of Chicago. The crime rates in the projects were between 1.86 and 3.81 times the crime rate for the central city as a whole.

The crime rates in housing projects are relatively high for three reasons. First, the residents of the projects are relatively poor (in Chicago, the median household income of project residents is $5,000, compared to $22,000 for the central city as a whole), and crime rates are higher among the poor. Second, many of the units in the projects have been abandoned by the city and have been taken over by drug abusers and gangs. Third, the physical layout of the typical project—a cluster of high-rise buildings—may contribute to crime. If crime rates are higher in high-density clusters of poor households, one option for decreasing crime is to replace the high-rise clusters with low-rise buildings dispersed throughout the metropolitan area.

The Market Effects of Public Housing

Figure 15–7 shows the short-run and long-run market effects of public housing. In the short run, the supply of housing from the private sector is perfectly inelastic:

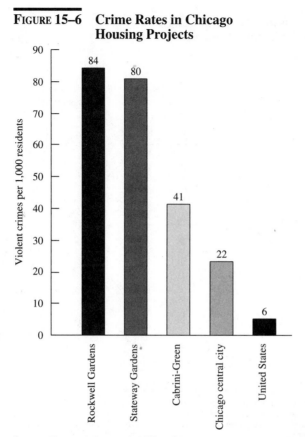

FIGURE 15–6 Crime Rates in Chicago Housing Projects

SOURCE: *Newsweek*, January 2, 1989, p. 25.

500 dwellings are provided, regardless of price. At the initial equilibrium (point *B*), the price is $250 per dwelling per month. If the local housing authority builds 200 new public housing dwellings, the demand curve for private housing shifts to the left by 200 dwellings: the 200 households in public housing leave the private housing market. As the poor move into public housing, they vacate private dwellings, causing excess supply that decreases the price of housing from $250 to $150 (point *C*). In the short run, all housing consumers gain from the public housing program: some households occupy subsidized public housing, and others pay lower prices for private housing.

What happens to the private market over time? In Figure 15–7, the intermediate-run supply curve (the supply curve over a five-year period) is positively sloped. The decrease in the price of housing caused by public housing decreases the profitability of private dwellings, so fewer low-quality dwellings are supplied. The supply response takes two forms:

1. **More retirement.** As explained in Chapter 14 (Why Is Housing Different?), a decrease in the price of low-quality dwellings makes economic profits negative for some dwellings, so more dwellings are retired from

FIGURE 15–7   **Short-Run and Long-Run Effects
of Public Housing**

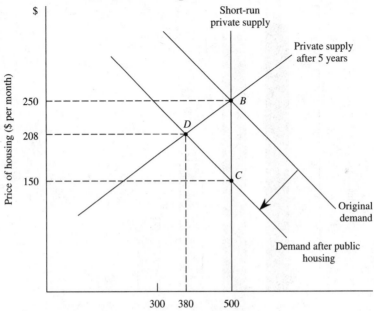

Public housing decreases the demand for private low-income housing by 200 dwellings. In
the short run, the supply of private housing is fixed, so the price of private dwellings drops
from $250 to $150. Over a five-year period, the decrease in the price of private housing
decreases the quantity of housing supplied from 500 to 380, so the price rises to $208. The
longer the period of time, the greater the displacement of private housing and the smaller the
net decrease in price.

the housing market. The retired dwellings are either converted to another
use or abandoned.

2. **Slower downward filtering.** As the price of low-quality housing decreases relative to the price of medium-quality housing, landlords hold
   their dwellings in the medium-quality submarket for a longer period of
   time.

In other words, more dwellings drop out of the low-quality submarket and fewer
dwellings filter down into the low-quality submarket. As the number of low-quality
dwellings decreases, the market price rises. The exit process continues until the price
is high enough to restore zero economic profits (normal accounting profits). In Figure
15–7, a total of 120 private dwellings are withdrawn from the market, and the price
rises from $150 to $208. Because public housing displaces private housing, there is
a net increase in supply of only 80 dwellings.

Ohls (1975) used a computer model of the housing market to explore the effects of public housing on the filtering process. He divided the housing stock into

60 quality levels, and allocated housing in each level to the city's households: the highest-quality dwellings were occupied by the wealthy; the lowest by the poor. Under a public housing policy, the bottom fifth of the population is removed from the private housing market, causing the following changes:

1. The amount of new private construction decreased: the decrease in the demand for used low-quality housing decreased the incentive to build new housing.
2. Fewer dwellings filtered down to the low-quality submarket: the low-quality market became less lucrative, so the filtering rate decreased.
3. The retirement rate increased: the decrease in the demand for low-quality dwellings decreased the incentive to keep low-quality dwellings on the market, so the retirement rate increased.

In general, the private market responded by building fewer dwellings, slowing the filtering process, and increasing the retirement rate.

Supply-Side Policy: Subsidies for Private Housing

An alternative to public housing is the subsidization of private housing. There are two subsidy programs for new low-income rental housing, Section 236 and Section 8. A third program, Section 235, provides interest subsidies to poor homeowners. Under both rental programs, the federal government subsidizes landlords who build new housing and rent to poor households. Both subsidy programs have the same market effects as public housing: they decrease the demand for low-quality private dwellings, decreasing the equilibrium price of private housing. The decrease in price decreases the quantity of private dwellings supplied.

Section 236

Under the Section 236 program (started in 1968), the government contracts with a private developer to build low-income housing. The government pays the landlord an annual subsidy to cover the difference between the rental payments of tenants and the cost of building and operating the property.

The tenant's monthly rent is determined by the household's income. The basic rent is defined as the rent that would have prevailed if the project had been financed with money borrowed at a 1 percent interest rate. The tenant's rent is either the basic rent or 30 percent of household income, whichever is greater: if the basic rent is more than 30 percent of income, the household pays the basic rent; if the basic rent is less than 30 percent of household income, the household pays 30 percent of household income. The government pays the landlord the difference between the tenant contribution and market rent, which is defined as the rent required to cover all the developer's costs.

To explain, suppose that the market rent is $300 and the basic rent is $200. For a household with a monthly income of $500, the basic rent is more than 30 percent of income ($150), so the household pays the basic rent. The federal government pays the difference between the market rent and basic rent, or $100. For a household with income of $800, the basic rent is less than 30 percent of income, so the household pays $240 (30 percent of its income) to the landlord, and the government pays the remaining $60.

Section 8–New Housing

Under the Section 8 program (started in 1974), private developers and local housing authorities submitted plans for low-income housing to the Department of Housing and Urban Development (HUD). If HUD approved a particular project, it signed a 20-year contract to provide annual payments to cover the difference between tenants' rental payments and the landlord's costs. The subsidy per eligible tenant equaled the difference between the fair market rent and the rent actually paid by low-income tenants. Under the contract, the developer was guaranteed the fair market rent on all units occupied by eligible households.

The household's rental payment depended on its income. To qualify for assistance, the household had to live in a new dwelling that satisfied minimum physical standards and rented for no more than the fair market rent, defined as the rent that would be charged for a standard dwelling. The eligible household paid 30 percent of its income toward housing. The subsidy to the landlord equaled the gap between the tenant's payment and the fair market rent:

$$\text{Fair market rent} = \text{Subsidy} + 0.30 \cdot \text{Income} \qquad (15\text{--}1)$$

For example, if the fair market rent was $400 and household income was $600, the household paid $180 in rent (30 percent of $600), and the subsidy was $220 ($400 − $180).

The Section 8–New Housing program was eliminated in 1983, in large part because it was so expensive: in 1982, the average annual subsidy for a new Section 8 unit was over $6,000.

Demand-Side Policy: Consumer Subsidies

Supply-side housing policies help the poor by building more low-income housing. An alternative approach is to give subsidies directly to the poor and let them choose their own housing. Under a demand-side policy, low-income households are given housing coupons that can be redeemed for housing. Like the food-stamp program, the housing-coupon program allows the poor to make their own consumption choices. Coupons have two advantages over public housing. First, under some circumstances, the coupons are equivalent to cash. As shown earlier in the chapter, a cash payment generates a larger increase in utility than an equal expenditure on public housing. Second, the coupons can be spent on used dwellings, which are typically less expensive than new dwellings. There are two types of housing coupon programs: rent certificates and housing vouchers.

Rent Certificates: Section 8–Existing Housing

Under the Section 8–Existing Housing program (started in 1975), poor households are issued rent certificates that can be used to rent existing housing. To qualify for Section 8 assistance, a household's income must be less than 80 percent of the area's median family income. Under legislation passed in 1981, the bulk of funds are allocated to households with "very low" income (less than half the median area income). In 1988, about 780,000 households received rent certificates.

There are two restrictions on the housing choices of recipients. First, the rental dwelling must meet minimum physical standards for size and quality. Second, the household cannot spend more than the fair market rent, defined by HUD as a reasonable rent for a standard low-income dwelling. The eligible household pays 30 percent of its income toward housing and receives a rent certificate to cover the difference between its contribution and the actual rent:

$$\text{Subsidy} = \text{Actual rent} - 0.30 \cdot \text{Income} \qquad (15\text{--}2)$$

For example, suppose that the fair market rent is $400 and the household's income is $600. The household's contribution is $180, and the subsidy equals the difference between the actual rent (up to a maximum of $400) and $180. If the actual rent is $350, the subsidy is $170.

Figure 15–8 shows the household's choice between housing and other goods under the rent-certificate program. Household income is $600 per month, and the fair market rent is $400. The original budget line *AB* shows the initial trade-off between spending on housing and other goods: every dollar of spending on housing decreases spending on other goods by one dollar. The certificate program adds the points between *C* and *D* to the budget set: the household receives a subsidy equal to the gap between its actual spending on housing (its monthly rent) and 30 percent of its income ($180). Therefore, it can consume $420 worth of nonhousing goods and between $180 and $400 worth of housing. If the household rents an apartment for $181, it receives a subsidy of $1; if it rents an apartment for $400, it receives a subsidy of $220. Because the government pays the difference between actual rent and $180, an increase in housing consumption does not decrease the consumption of other goods as long as rent is less than the fair market rent. If the household spends more than the fair market rent ($400), it is ineligible for the certificate program, so it is stuck with the original budget line.

How does the certificate program affect the household's budget choice? In the absence of moving cost, a move from *E* to *D* increases utility. It makes sense to go all the way to *D* because between points *C* and *D* the opportunity cost of more housing is zero: the tenant contribution to housing is fixed at $180 and the government pays any increase in rent. If moving cost is relatively large, however, the household moves straight up from *E* to *F*. In this case, the increase in utility is not large enough to offset the moving cost, so the household stays in its original residence and spends the entire subsidy on other goods.

One of the surprising results of the rent-certificate program was that relatively few households moved to dwellings that rented for the fair market rent. In Figure 15–8, most households moved from point *E* to *F*, not *E* to *D*. This occurred

FIGURE 15–8   **Effects of Section 8 Rent Certificate on Housing Consumption**

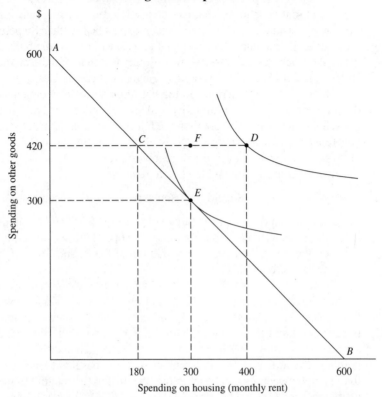

With the original budget line *AB*, the household spends $300 on rent and $300 on other goods (point *E*). The rent-certificate program with a fair market rent of $400 adds points between *C* and *D* to the budget set: the government pays the difference between actual rent and 30 percent of income ($180), so the opportunity cost of spending beyond $180 is zero. In the absence of moving cost, the household switches to point *D* because it lies on a higher indifference curve. If the moving cost is relatively large, the household chooses point *F*.

despite the fact that the entire increase in rent would have been covered by the subsidy. Most households stayed in their existing dwellings, and used the subsidy to cut their housing costs. This result suggests that the cost of moving is relatively large.

Housing Vouchers

The housing-voucher program was started on an experimental basis in 1983. The eligibility requirements for housing vouchers are similar to those for rent certificates: the bulk of payments go to the very poor. To qualify for a voucher, the household must occupy a dwelling that meets the minimum quality standards. A voucher differs from a rent certificate in one important respect: the recipient can use the voucher to rent any dwelling that meets minimum physical standards. In 1988, about 156,000 households received vouchers.

The face value of the voucher is based on household income and the fair market rent. The formula is

$$\text{Face value} = \text{Fair market rent} - 0.30 \cdot \text{Income} \qquad (15\text{--}3)$$

Figure 15–9 shows the household's choice between housing and other goods under the voucher program. Household income is $600 and the fair market rent is $400, so the face value of the voucher is $220 ($400 − $180). The voucher program shifts the budget line from *AB* to *AFG*. Point *F* is in the new budget set because the household could use the voucher to get $220 worth of housing and spend all of its own income ($600) on other goods. As spending on housing rises above $220, there is a dollar-for-dollar trade-off between housing and other goods. The voucher program gives the household more options than the rent-certificate program because the voucher is equivalent to a cash transfer. In the absence of moving cost, the household with the choices shown in Figure 15–9 increases spending on housing from $300 (point *E*) to about $345 (point *H*), leaving $175 of the subsidy to spend on other goods. If the cost of moving is relatively large, the household chooses point *J* and spends the entire subsidy on other goods.

The voucher household also has the option of spending more than the fair market rent. In other words, the household has access to points along the budget segment *DG*. In contrast to the rent-certificate program, the voucher program allows the household to spend as much as it wants on housing.

In 1988, the budgetary cost of housing vouchers exceeded the cost of rent certificates by about $23 per recipient (Mariano, 1989). The reason is simple: under the voucher program, the voucher covers the gap between the fair market rent and 30 percent of income, while the rent certificate covers the gap between the household's *actual rent* and 30 percent of income. As long as the actual rent is less than the fair market rent, the subsidy is larger under the voucher. In Figure 15–9, the two programs have the same budgetary costs only if all rent-certificate households choose point *D*. If a rent-certificate recipient pays less than the fair market rent, the savings go to the government, so the certificate program costs less than the voucher program.

Market Effects of Consumer Subsidies

What are the market effects of rent certificates and housing vouchers? To explain the market effects, consider a city with the following characteristics:

1. The city has poor families and middle-income families.
2. To qualify for a housing voucher, a poor household must occupy a moderate-quality dwelling (one that generates at least 800 units of housing service).
3. The poor households initially live in low-quality dwellings (which generate only 600 units of housing service).

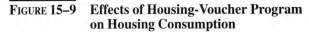

FIGURE 15–9   **Effects of Housing-Voucher Program on Housing Consumption**

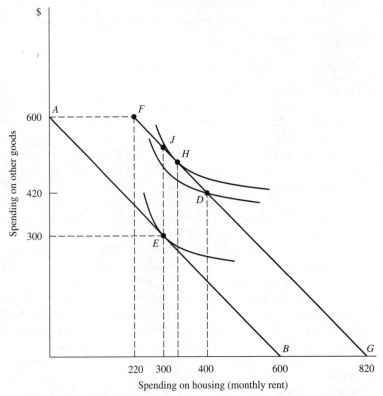

With the original budget line *AB*, the household spends $300 on rent and $300 on other goods (point *E*). The voucher program with a fair market rent of $400 shifts the budget line outward to AFG. The household receives a voucher worth $220 (the difference between the rent standard and 30 percent of income). In the absence of moving cost, the household chooses point *H*, and is better off than it would be under a rent-certificate program (point *D*). If the cost of moving is relatively large, the household chooses point *J*.

4. Middle-income households live in moderate-quality dwellings (800 units of housing service) and medium-quality dwellings (1,000 units of housing service).

Figure 15–10 shows the short-run effects of the coupon program on the moderate-quality submarket. The voucher program shifts the demand curve outward, increasing the market price from $250 (point *B*) to $350 (point *E*). Because the supply of moderate-quality housing is fixed in the short run, the vouchers simply bid up the price of housing. Who gains and who loses in the short run? Although voucher recipients pay more for housing, they also have more money to spend on housing. In contrast, nonrecipients (middle-income households) pay higher housing prices without the benefit of housing vouchers.

What happens to the moderate-quality market after five years? Figure 15–10 shows the intermediate-run supply curve (the supply curve over a five-year period).

FIGURE 15–10   Short-Run and Long-Run Effects of Housing Vouchers

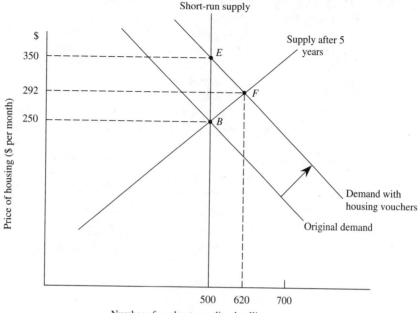

The housing-voucher program increases the demand for moderate-quality dwellings. In the short run, the supply of moderate-quality housing is fixed, so the price increases from $250 to $350. Over a five-year period, the increase in the price of housing increases the quantity supplied from 500 to 620, and the price drops to $292. The longer the period of time, the greater the increase in the quantity supplied and the smaller the net increase in price.

The increase in price increases the profitability of moderate-quality dwellings, increasing the quantity supplied, for three reasons:

1. **Downward filtering.** Dwellings filter down more rapidly from the medium-quality submarket to the more lucrative moderate-quality sub-market.

2. **Increased maintenance.** The owners of moderate-quality dwellings spend more on maintenance and repair to keep their dwellings in the market for a longer period of time: downward filtering is slowed.

3. **Upward filtering.** Dwellings from the low-quality submarket are up-graded to serve the more lucrative moderate-quality submarket.

For these reasons, the quantity of moderate-quality dwellings supplied increases as the price increases. In equilibrium (point *F*), the price of moderate-quality housing is $292 and the number of dwellings is 620.

How does the voucher program affect the medium-quality submarket? The increase in the price of moderate-quality dwellings increases the price of medium-quality dwellings for two reasons. First is the demand effect: the increase in the relative price of moderate-quality dwellings causes some consumers to switch to the medium-quality submarket. The demand for medium-quality dwellings increases, increasing the market price. Second is the supply effect: the increase in the relative price of moderate-quality dwellings hastens the filtering of medium-quality dwellings downward to the moderate-quality submarket. In combination, the increase in demand and decrease in supply increase the market price of medium-quality dwellings. Because of the interactions between the housing submarkets, the voucher program increases the prices of all types of housing.

Ohls (1975) used a computer model of the housing market to explore the effects of consumer subsidies on the filtering process. As explained earlier, his model divides the housing stock into 60 quality levels, with the wealthy occupying the highest-quality dwellings and the poor occupying the lowest-quality dwellings. Under his consumer subsidy program, the government provides a 50 percent housing subsidy for the poorest fifth of the population. The subsidy program causes the following changes in the market:

1. The poorest households upgrade to higher-quality housing, moving from quality level 5 to 8. The typical recipient moves from quality level 8 to 11.
2. The increase in the demand for moderate-quality housing stimulates new construction (at the high-quality level) because the market for used housing becomes more lucrative.
3. Filtering down to the moderate-quality range speeds up, and filtering down from the moderate-quality range slows down.

The Experimental Housing Allowance Program

An alternative to a housing voucher is a housing allowance. A housing allowance is a cash payment, the size of which equals the gap between a given fraction of household income (e.g., 30 percent) and the fair market rent. To qualify for a housing allowance, the household must occupy a dwelling that meets minimum quality standards. A housing allowance is equivalent to a housing voucher if (1) the two programs have the same quality standards, (2) the face value of the voucher equals the allowance payment, and (3) the household's rent exceeds the face value of the voucher. If the household spends more than the voucher value on housing, the household can substitute the voucher for its own spending on housing, freeing up an amount of cash equal to the face value of the voucher.

Under the Experimental Housing Allowance Program (EHAP), the federal government conducted a number of experiments with housing allowances. The **demand experiment** offered housing allowances to a small sample of poor renter households in two cities (Phoenix and Pittsburgh). The purpose of the experiment was to examine the effects of the program on eligible households. The most important policy issues concerned participation rates (how many would participate), the mobility of participants (how many would move to higher-quality dwellings), and housing consumption (how much housing consumption would increase). The **supply experiments** offered allowances to all poor households in two counties (Brown

County, Wisconsin, and St. Joseph County, Indiana). The purpose of the supply experiment was to examine the effects of housing allowances on the market price of housing. The principal question was whether a citywide assistance program would increase housing prices.

The experiments generated three conclusions about the responses of eligible households:

1. **Low participation rates.** Between 40 percent and 45 percent of the eligible households participated in the allowance programs. Participation rates were sensitive to the quality standards: the stricter the standards, the lower the participation rate.

2. **Small changes in housing consumption.** Between one quarter and one third of the allowance payment was used to increase housing consumption, and the remainder was spent on other goods. In other words, most of the allowance money was used to decrease rent burdens. The measured income elasticity of demand of allowance recipients was relatively low: between 0.20 and 0.44 for renters, and about 0.45 for owner-occupants.

3. **Mobility.** Relatively few households changed dwellings. In Pittsburgh, 40 percent of allowance recipients moved over a two-year period, compared to 35 percent of households in a control group. In Phoenix, 63 percent of recipients moved, compared to 53 percent of the control households. The allowance program did not encourage integration with respect to race or income.

The general conclusion is that the housing allowances caused relatively small changes in housing choices. Recipients spent most of the money on nonhousing goods, and few moved from their original dwellings.

The allowance program did not cause any measurable price increases in the two cities involved in the supply experiment. Because participation rates were relatively low and recipients spent a relatively small fraction of their allowances on housing, the rightward shift of the demand curve was relatively small. To the extent that the demand for housing increased, the supply of housing was sufficiently elastic to accommodate the increased demand without any measurable price effects.

What are the lessons from the supply experiment? As pointed out by Kain (1981), the supply experiment tested the effects of one type of allowance program, with minimal housing quality standards and relatively low participation rates. Because the allowance program increased the housing consumption of a small number of households by relatively small amounts, it is not surprising that housing prices did not rise. If a national housing allowance program had higher participation rates, larger allowance payments, and more stringent housing standards, it would shift the housing demand curve by a larger amount and would probably increase housing prices. Kain cites studies by the National Bureau of Economic Research and the Urban Institute that suggest such an allowance program would increase prices in some housing submarkets.

Supply versus Demand Policies

What are the trade-offs associated with supply-side policies (public housing) and demand-side policies (housing vouchers)? From the perspective of the recipient, the voucher program has two advantages over subsidized public housing. First, the voucher is equivalent to an income transfer, so it generates a larger increase in utility per dollar spent on housing programs. Second, the voucher allows tenants to occupy relatively inexpensive used housing, so a fixed budget provides more housing per budget dollar.

The disadvantage of the voucher program is that it increases the price of housing. The recipient would be better off under the voucher program if the program causes a relatively small increase in the price of housing. This occurs if the elasticity of supply is relatively large. As explained in Chapter 14 (Why Is Housing Different?), little is known about the intermediate-run and long-run elasticities of supply of housing. Unless one knows something about the individual housing submarkets in a city, it is difficult to predict the effects of a voucher program on the price of housing.

What are taxpayers' and nonrecipients' perspectives toward public housing and housing vouchers? Two factors contribute to public support of public housing over housing vouchers. First, taxpayers seem to care about the housing consumption of recipients, not necessarily their utility levels. If public housing generates a larger increase in housing consumption, it is considered a superior policy. Second, nonrecipients pay a higher price of housing under a demand-side policy, and a lower price under a supply-side policy. For these two reasons, taxpayers and nonrecipients may prefer public housing over housing vouchers even if recipients are better off under the voucher program.

Community Development and Urban Renewal

There are dozens of programs and policies that fit under the term *community development.* The legislated mandate for federally supported community development calls for "Systematic and sustained action by the federal, state, and local governments to eliminate blight, to conserve and renew older areas, to improve the living environment of low- and moderate-income families, and to develop new centers of population growth and economic activity." The two principal purposes of community development policies are to (1) revitalize declining areas of the city and (2) improve the housing of poor households. Community development policies are neighborhood-oriented in the sense that they concentrate spending in relatively small geographical areas.

Urban Renewal

Urban Renewal, the first community development program in the United States, was established under the Housing Act of 1949 and eventually dropped in 1973. The national government provided local governments with the power and the money to demolish and rebuild parts of their cities. Local agencies acquired property under the right of eminent domain, cleared the site of "undesirable" uses (like low-income housing and small businesses), and then either built a public facility or sold the site to a private developer. The local agencies charged the developer less than the cost of acquiring and clearing the site, and the federal government covered two thirds of the local government losses. The private developer built housing (usually for middle-income and high-income households), government buildings, or commercial establishments.

According to the Congressional Research Service, Urban Renewal had the following effects:

1. **Demolition.** A total of 600,000 dwellings were demolished, displacing about 2 million people, most of whom were poor.
2. **New housing.** A total of 250,000 new dwellings were built, most of which were occupied by middle-income and high-income households.
3. **Public facilities.** The total floor space of new public facilities was 120 million square feet.
4. **Commercial facilities.** The total floor space of new commercial facilities was 224 million square feet.
5. **Property assessments.** The assessed value of property on renewed sites increased by 360 percent.

In sum, Urban Renewal generated both costs and benefits. It displaced poor households, but also provided housing for middle-income and rich households, allowed the construction of commercial and public facilities, and increased tax revenue.

Was Urban Renewal worthwhile? The critics of the program focus on its demolition aspects, pointing out that 2 million poor people were displaced. The defenders of the program focus on its rebuilding aspects, pointing out that the new commercial developments provided jobs for the poor residents of the central city.

Recent Community Development Programs

More recent federal community development programs have avoided many of the problems of the Urban Renewal program. The newer programs are executed on a smaller scale, so they displace fewer households, and they place a greater emphasis on providing housing for the poor.

Table 15–3 shows HUD's 1987 budget for community development. The total budget was over $3.5 billion, with about $2 billion used for Community Development Block Grants (CDBGs). The CDBG program is an entitlement program, with funds allocated to cities and states on the basis of population and other factors. The allocation formula gives relatively large grants to cities with relatively old and overcrowded housing, high poverty rates, and slow growth rates. The second largest program is the State and Small Cities Program, which gives money to states that is then distributed to small cities ineligible for CDBG funds. The third largest allocation goes to Urban Development Action Grants (UDAGs), which are used to

TABLE 15–3 **Community Development Budget of Department of Housing and Urban Development, 1987**

Program	Funding ($ million)
Community Development Block Grants	
Housing rehabilitation	876
Jobs programs	254
Public works	536
Public services	242
Assistance to homeless	46
Total	1,954
State and Small Cities Program	883
Urban Development Action Grants	325
Rental rehabilitation	200
Emergency shelter grants	60
Other	133
Total	3,555

SOURCE: U.S. Department of Housing and Urban Development, *1988 Community Development Programs: State Reports* (Washington, D.C.: U.S. Government Printing Office, 1989), pp. 1–4.

leverage private investments in community development. Under the UDAGs program, the federal government provides small subsidies to transform slightly unprofitable private development projects into profitable ones. The fourth largest allocation is for rental rehabilitation: these grants subsidize the renovation of low-income rental housing. The fifth largest allocation is for emergency shelter: these grants subsidize shelters for the homeless.

Cities can spend their community development grants on a wide variety of projects. Under the Carter administration, cities were required to spend a large fraction of the grants on projects that directly benefited poor households and low-income neighborhoods. Under the Reagan administration, many of these restrictions were dropped. The projects funded by the various funding programs can be divided into four types:

1. **Improved housing.** Some programs support local projects that renovate buildings, enforce building codes, and build new low-income housing.
   - The Boston Housing Partnership used $8.5 million in CDBG funds to acquire and rehabilitate 700 rental units.
   - The city of Cleveland joined with a nonprofit organization and a private developer to build a 183-unit rental housing project, using $4.4

million in federal funds ($1.7 million from CDBG and $2.7 million from UDAG) to leverage $9.9 million from private and other sources.

2. **Renewed infrastructure.** Some programs support projects that improve streets, roads, and water and sewage facilities.
   - In Fort Worth, Texas, the Main Street Project used $2.6 million in UDAG funds to improve the street's infrastructure (new curbs, gutters, sidewalks, and street lighting). As part of the renovation program, private developers agreed to build a $48 million hotel.
   - The city of Oshkosh, Wisconsin, used $600,000 of CDBG and UDAG funds to expand its airport to accommodate increased traffic.

3. **Job development.** Some programs support projects that encourage economic development and job creation.
   - In St. Louis, Union Station was renovated with $10.2 million in CDBG and UDAG money and $126 million in other public and private funds. The station was developed into a hotel-retail-entertainment complex that produced 2,000 new jobs, over 50 percent of which were filled by minorities. The project rejuvenated a part of the city that had been dormant for 15 years.
   - Salt Lake City is using a $1.1 million UDAG to support the construction of a downtown auto mall, using the grant to leverage $4.7 million in private financing.
   - Baltimore used $10 million in UDAG funds to support the revitalization of its Inner Harbor. Private investment in office space, retail space, and a hotel totaled $73.4 million and produced 1,600 jobs.

4. **Responsive public services.** Some programs support public services for the elderly, the homeless, and children.
   - Orange County, California, used $892,000 in CDBG funds to support the construction of a $7.5 million facility to provide emergency services for abused, abandoned, or neglected children.
   - Phoenix used $361,000 in CDBG funds to build a recreation center for the handicapped.
   - Fort Worth, Texas, used $106,000 in CDBG funds to start a neighborhood youth project designed to curtail gang activity.

These examples show that community development funds are spent on a wide variety of projects.

What are the effects of community development programs? The programs that support housing projects supplement federal housing programs (public housing, subsidized new construction, housing vouchers). The difference is that the city has more control over the spending of community development funds. Other community development programs support economic development projects and can be evaluated as alternative means of promoting local economic growth. The costs and benefits of economic development programs are discussed in Chapter 6 (Urban Economic Growth).

Rent Control

During World War II, the federal government instituted a national system of rent controls. Following the war, New York City was the only city to retain rent controls. During the 1970s, rent control returned to dozens of cities, including Boston, Cambridge, Los Angeles, Washington, D.C., Albany, Berkeley, and Santa Monica.

Market Effects of Rent Control

To explain the market effects of rent control, consider a city with the following characteristics:

1. All households live in identical apartments.
2. The equilibrium rent is $600 per month.
3. The equilibrium number of apartments is 90.
4. The apartments are made of stone and do not deteriorate over time.
5. The city sets a maximum rent of $400.

Figure 15–11 shows the short-run and long-run effects of rent control. The short run is defined as the period of time over which the supply of housing is fixed at 90 dwellings. In the short run, rent control does not affect the supply of housing, but simply transfers $200 per month from the landlord to the tenant.

In the long run, the supply of apartments depends on the price of rental housing. As rent decreases, some landlords convert their property to more lucrative uses: some apartment buildings are converted to condominiums, and other buildings are demolished to make way for commercial land uses. In Figure 15–11, rent control decreases the number of apartments from 90 to 50. As the price of rental housing decreases, the market moves downward along the long-run supply curve. The supply response to rent control depends on the long-run elasticity of supply. The more elastic the supply, the larger the decrease in the quantity of housing supplied.

Rent control causes a shortage of housing. At the controlled price of $400, the quantity of apartments demanded is 120, compared to a supply of only 50 apartments. There are too many tenants chasing too few apartments. In such a market, tenants spend relatively large amounts of time and money searching for apartments. For tenants, rent control brings good news and bad news: although rent control decreases the rent, it also increases search costs.

Rent control produces winners and losers. The city's population can be divided into four groups:

1. **Nonmovers.** Some households live in the city when rent control is implemented and occupy the same apartment for life. These households are winners in the rent-control game: they pay a lower price for the same apartment.

FIGURE 15–11   Short-Run and Long-Run Effects of Rent Control

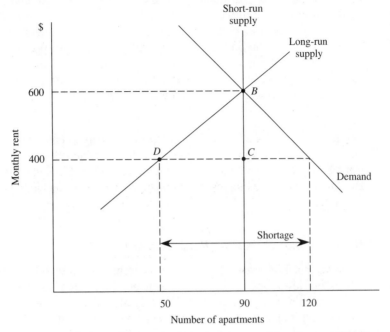

In the short run, the supply of apartments is fixed, so rent control (maximum rent $400) sim-
ply transfers income from landlords to tenants: the market moves from point *B* to *C*. In the
long run, the decrease in price decreases the quantity supplied: the market moves from point
C to point *D*. The shortage (the gap between demand and supply) is 70 apartments.

2. **Successful searchers.** Some people move to the city after rent control
   is implemented. They spend several months searching for an apartment
   and eventually find one. The full cost of a rent-controlled apartment is
   the sum of the rent ($400 per month) and the opportunity cost of search
   time. The full cost of a rent-controlled apartment may exceed the full
   cost of an uncontrolled apartment ($600 per month and small search
   cost). In general, if the search cost is relatively large, the benefit of rent
   control (decreased rent) is smaller than the cost (increased search cost),
   so successful searchers are losers in the rent-control game.

3. **Displaced households.** Some tenants are displaced when apartments are
   converted or demolished, and are unsuccessful in their search for a new
   apartment. In Figure 15–11, the number of dwellings decreases by 40
   (from 90 to 50), so 40 households are displaced. The displaced households are obviously losers.

4. **Landlords.** Rent control decreases the annual rental income per apartment from $7,200 ($600 times 12 months) to $4,800. Because the market
   value of an apartment building reflects its income-earning potential, the

announcement of the rent-control program decreases the market value of the city's apartment buildings. If Barney owns an apartment building when rent control is announced, he pays for rent control in the form of a decreased market value. He cannot escape the effects of rent control by selling the building to someone else: once prospective owners hear about rent control, they want to pay less for the building. According to Smith and Tomlinson (1981), Toronto's rent-control program decreased the market value of apartment buildings by about 40 percent over a five-year period (1975–80).

Olsen (1972) estimated the effects of New York City's rent-control program on tenants and landlords. Ignoring search cost, he estimated that the occupants of controlled units experienced a 3.4 percent increase in real income. On the other hand, landlords experienced losses in real income about twice as large as the total gain of tenants.

Distributional Effects of Rent Control

Gyourko and Linneman (1989) use data from 1968 to estimate the distributional effects of New York City's rent-control program. They estimate the decrease in rents experienced by different types of households. Their results provide insights into the distribution of benefits from rent control across income groups. The principal policy question is: do most of the benefits from rent control go to poor households?

Figure 15–12 shows the relationship between the benefit from rent control (the decrease in annual rental payments) and household income. All the figures are in 1984 dollars. The top line shows the benefit-income relationship for households that occupy controlled units. The average benefit among occupants of controlled dwellings was $2,440 per year, and the average savings as a percentage of income was 27 percent. The benefit per household increases slowly with income. At each income level, there is a wide variation in the benefits experienced by individual households. For example, the average gain for households with incomes of $20,000 was $2,440, but many households had much larger benefits and many had much smaller benefits.

The middle line in Figure 15–12 shows the benefit-income relationship for all renting households. The average benefit among renting households was about $1,311 per year. The average benefit among renting households is smaller than the average benefit among the occupants of controlled units because the benefits are spread over more households: only 57 percent of renting households occupy controlled units. The benefit per household decreases as income increases, reflecting the fact that the average income of households in controlled units is lower than the average income of renting households: poor households are overrepresented in controlled dwellings, so poor households, on average, experience larger benefits from rent control.

The lower line in Figure 15–12 shows the benefit-income relationship for all households, including both renters and homeowners. The average benefit among all

FIGURE 15–12   Benefits from Rent Control for Different Income Levels in New York City

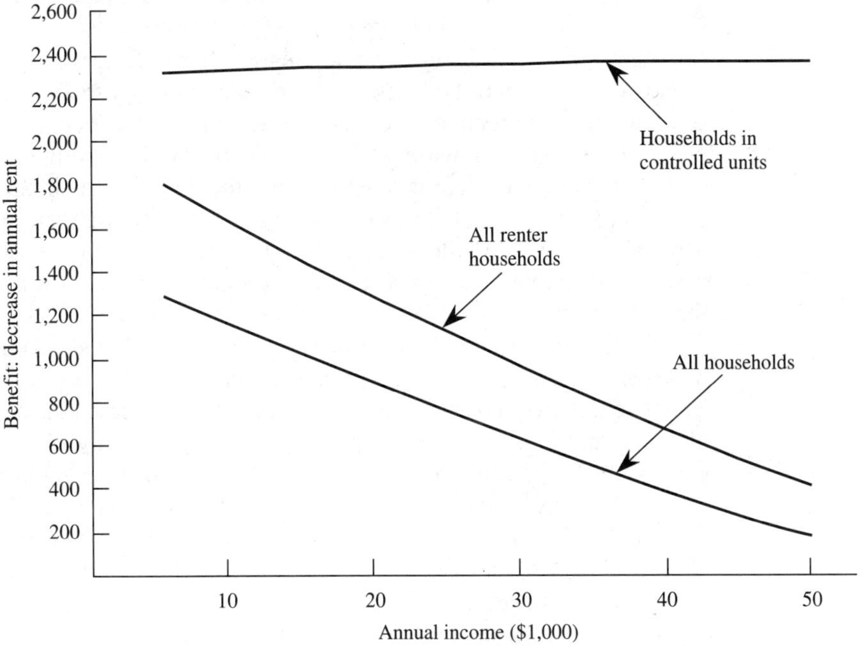

SOURCE: Joseph Gyourko and Peter Linneman, "Equity and Efficiency Aspects of Rent Control: An Empirical Study of New York City," *Journal of Urban Economics* 26 (1989), pp. 54–74.

households was about $856 per year. The average benefit among all households is relatively small because less than a third of the households occupy controlled units. The benefit decreases as income increases, reflecting the relatively low income of households in controlled units.

Figure 15–12 suggests that the benefits of rent control are mildly progressive in the sense that the average benefit per household decreases as income increases. It's important to note, however, that the benefits experienced by households within an income group vary widely across households. The variation in benefits across households within an income group occurs for two reasons. First, only some of the households of a given income level occupy controlled dwellings (and receive benefits from rent control). The other households (renters of uncontrolled units and homeowners) receive no benefits from rent control. Second, among households that occupy controlled dwellings, there is a large variation in the benefits from rent control. Given the large variation in the benefits within each income group, rent control is a very blunt tool for income redistribution.

Deterioration and Maintenance

One of the assumptions of the simple model of the rent-control city is that apartments are made of stone, so dwellings do not deteriorate over time. This is clearly unrealistic. Suppose that housing is subject to physical deterioration: to maintain a dwelling at a given service level, the landlord must spend money on routine maintenance and repair. Suppose that in the initial equilibrium, the typical $600 apartment generates 1,000 units of housing service ($Q = 1,000$).

Rent control discourages routine maintenance, so apartments deteriorate more rapidly. In an uncontrolled city, landlords spend money to keep their apartments at a service level high enough to justify a $600 rent. If the apartment deteriorates to $Q = 900$, tenants are unwilling to pay $600 rent for the dwelling. In the rent-control city, there is no incentive to keep the apartment at $Q = 1,000$ because the landlord cannot charge $600 for the dwelling. Landlords decrease their spending on repair and maintenance, thus allowing apartments to deteriorate to a service level consistent with the $400 rent. Under a rent-control program, tenants may eventually get what they pay for.

Studies of rent-control cities show that landlords do indeed cut back on maintenance and repair. The Rand Corporation studied the effects of rent controls in New York City (1970), and concluded that rent control decreased the quality and quantity of rental housing. Between 1960 and 1967, the inventory of "sound" housing increased by 2.4 percent, the inventory of "dilapidated" housing increased by 44 percent, and the inventory of "deteriorating" housing increased by 37 percent. Between 1965 and 1967, 114,000 dwellings were retired from the housing stock. A study of Cambridge, Massachusetts, found that maintenance cost per apartment decreased by $50 per year (Navarro, 1987).

Gyourko and Linneman (1990) examined the effects of rent controls on the quality of rental housing in New York City in 1968. They show that rent-controlled buildings are less likely than uncontrolled buildings to be in "sound" condition, meaning that rent-controlled buildings are more likely to be deteriorating or dilapidated. One measure of the effect of rent control is the decrease in the probability that a building is sound, given that the building is subject to rent control. For example, if the probability of being sound is 0.90 for uncontrolled buildings (90 percent of uncontrolled buildings are sound) but only 0.85 for controlled buildings, rent control decreases the probability of being sound by 0.05.

Figure 15–13 shows the decrease in the probability that a building is sound for several types of low-rise buildings (less than seven stories) in Manhattan, Brooklyn, and Queens. For buildings in Manhattan built before 1947, rent control decreases the probability by about 0.09 (from 0.63 to 0.54). Newer buildings, which are more likely to be sound, experience smaller decreases in the probability of being sound. For buildings in Manhattan built between 1947 and 1959, rent control decreases the probability of being sound by about 0.04 (from 0.89 to 0.85); for buildings built between 1960 and 1968, rent control decreases the probability of being sound by 0.01 (from 0.98 to 0.97). The effects of rent control are smaller in the two other boroughs of New York.

Housing Submarkets

One of the assumptions of the rent-control model is that all households live in identical apartments. If there are housing submarkets, the analysis changes in two ways.

FIGURE 15–13   **Rent Control and the Probability that a Building Is Sound**

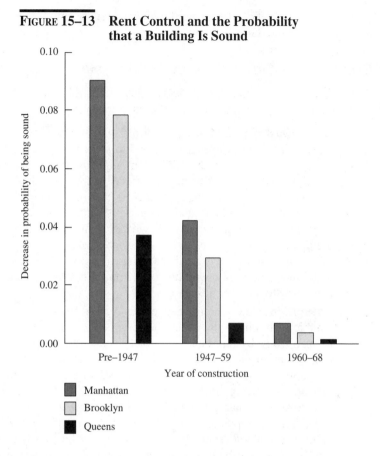

SOURCE: Joseph Gyourko and Peter Linneman, "Rent Controls and Rental Housing Quality: A Note on the Effects of New York City's Old Controls," *Journal of Urban Economics* 27 (1990), pp. 398–409.

Consider first the possibility that there are two controlled submarkets. There are large apartments (equilibrium rent of $600 and controlled rent of $400) and small apartments (equilibrium rent of $300 and controlled rent of $200). Rent control inhibits movement between the two markets because the search cost is large. Suppose that a household would like to move from a large apartment to a small one. In the rent-control city, there are two options. First, the household can stay in their large apartment, paying $400 per month. Second, they can spend time and money searching for a small apartment (which rents for $200). If the search cost is relatively high, they are better off staying in their original apartment.

Consider next the possibility that some of the dwellings in the city are not subject to rent control. Rent control decreases the supply of housing in the controlled sector. The displaced households move into the uncontrolled submarket, bidding up the price of housing. Therefore, part of the cost of rent control is borne by households living in uncontrolled dwellings.

Controlling the Supply Response to Rent Control

Rent control decreases the quantity and quality of rental housing. Cities have developed a number of policies to diminish this supply response.

1. **Rent adjustments.** Most rent-control laws allow periodic increases in rent, with the allowable increase tied to some price index, for example, the consumer price index (CPI). Rent adjustments weaken rent controls and diminish the negative supply effects of the controls. In most rent-control cities that use rent adjustments, controlled rents rise more slowly than the cost of building and maintaining rental housing. In New York City, controlled rents rose by 110 percent between 1943 and 1968, while the operating costs of rental housing increased by 285 percent (de Salvo, 1971). In Toronto, controlled rents increased by 39 percent between 1975 and 1980, while the operating cost of rental housing increased by 75 percent (Smith and Tomlinson, 1981).

2. **Exemption of new housing.** Most rent-control laws exempt new construction from controls. If new housing is exempt from controls, it may be unaffected by rent control. In fact, tenants displaced from the controlled market increase the demand for new rental housing, stimulating the supply of new rental housing. It is possible that new housing offsets the loss in housing stock caused by rent control. But there are two reasons to suspect that new housing will not offset the effects of rent control. First, new housing is typically a small part of the housing market, so it would take a relatively large increase in the supply of new housing to counteract the effects of rent control. Second, builders and owners are likely to be skeptical about the city's promise to never impose rent control on this year's new rental housing. If builders suspect that today's new housing will become tomorrow's rent-control housing, they may be reluctant to supply new housing.

3. **Restrictions on conversions.** Many cities restrict the conversion of rental housing to condominiums. If successful, these restrictions limit the conversion of rental housing to other uses, diminishing the supply effects of rent control.

4. **Subsidies for new construction.** Public policies encourage the building of new dwellings to replace the dwellings lost as a result of rent control. The city of Toronto offered low-interest construction loans to housing firms. In the United States, one of the purposes of public housing is to replace the dwellings lost because of rent control.

5. **Vacancy decontrol.** In some cities, rent is fixed during a tenancy, but can be changed when a new tenant moves into the dwelling. This provision increases the landlord's rental income, weakening rent control. It also increases the incentive for long-term occupancy.

Another way to decrease the supply effect of rent control is to cheat. Tenants and landlords often find ways to violate the spirit of rent-control laws. Landlords charge tenants "key money" (e.g., $5,000 for a key to the apartment) or nonrefundable security deposits. To the extent that landlords use indirect payments to increase the net price of housing, the negative supply response to rent control is reduced. Tenants also collect bribes for rent-controlled apartments: when a tenant vacates a controlled apartment, he can charge the new tenant a finder's fee. The fee is often implicit: in California, old tenants reportedly sold bean-bag chairs to new tenants, charging hundreds of dollars for chairs that sold for just a few dollars in thrift stores. Tenant bribery does not increase the supply of housing, but simply transfers income from the new tenant to the old one.

Alternatives to Rent Control

In many cities, rent control is viewed as an indirect form of income redistribution. The idea is to take money from wealthy landlords and give it to poor tenants. At best, rent control is a blunt instrument for redistribution. Rent control helps all of the occupants of controlled dwellings, rich and poor alike. Moreover, a poor person who occupies a controlled dwelling is worse off under rent control if the search cost is larger than the savings in rent.

Suppose that a city wants to redistribute income from the wealthy to the poor. What are the alternatives to rent control? The first option is to finance income redistribution with a land tax. Because the supply of land is perfectly inelastic, the land tax will not affect the supply of land or the supply of housing. Therefore, the land tax will not cause the same supply problems as rent control. The second approach is to leave income redistribution to the federal government. Local attempts at income redistribution are likely to be frustrated by the movement of households into and out of the city. If the city gives the proceeds of a land tax to its poor residents, poor people from other cities may migrate to the city, diluting the effects of the redistribution program. Because international mobility is less than intercity mobility, a national redistribution program does not suffer from this problem.

Summary

1. The condition of the U.S. housing stock has improved considerably over the last several decades. Nonetheless, about two thirds of poor households experience some sort of housing problem, usually inadequate housing or high housing costs. Over half of black households experience housing problems.

2. More than 1 million households live in public housing. Public housing is built and managed by local housing authorities. The federal government provides subsidies for capital cost, operating cost, and modernization, and specifies who is eligible for public housing.

    a. Public housing may increase or decrease housing consumption, depending on the recipient's willingness to trade off consumption of housing and other goods.

    b. Public housing produces a relatively small increase in recipient welfare per dollar because (*i*) the monetary value of public housing is about 75 percent of its market value and (*ii*) public housing costs more than used private housing.

    c. In the short run, the supply of private housing is fixed, so public housing decreases the market price of housing by a large amount.

    d. Over time, the decrease in the price of housing decreases the quantity of private dwellings supplied as more dwellings are retired and fewer dwellings filter down to the low-quality submarket. The more elastic the supply, the greater the displacement of private housing and the smaller the net decrease in market price.

3. Under the Section 236 program, the household pays 30 percent of its income or the basic rent, whichever is larger, and the government pays the landlord the difference between the tenant contribution and the market rent.

4. There are two types of consumer subsidies: Section 8 rent certificates and housing vouchers.

    a. The rent certificates cover the difference between the actual rent and 30 percent of household income, and can be used on dwellings that rent for less than the fair market rent.

    b. The face value of a housing voucher equals the gap between fair market rent and 30 percent of household income, and can be used on any dwelling satisfying minimum physical standards.

    c. Both subsidy programs shift the demand curve outward, increasing the market price in the short run. Over time, the quantity of housing increases as (*i*) fewer dwellings are retired and (*ii*) more dwellings filter down from higher-quality submarkets. The larger the supply elasticity, the smaller the net increase in price.

5. The Experimental Housing Allowance Program (EHAP) tested a program of housing allowances (cash payments to poor households). The demand for housing increased by a relatively small amount because (*i*) participation rates were relatively low, (*ii*) few households changed dwellings, and (*iii*) only a small fraction of the allowance payment was spent on housing. The small shift of the demand curve caused no measurable increases in housing prices.

6. There are dozens of policies and programs that fit under the term *community development*. The two principal purposes of such policies are to (*i*) revitalize declining areas of the city and (*ii*) improve the housing of poor households.

7. Under the Urban Renewal program, the federal government subsidized the replacement of low-income housing with middle-income and high-income housing, public facilities, and commercial establishments.

8. More recent community development programs support local projects that improve low-income housing and local infrastructure, stimulate economic development, and develop new public services for handicapped, elderly, and disadvantaged citizens.

9. Rent control has the following effects on the housing market.

   a. The supply of dwellings decreases, causing a housing shortage that increases search cost.

   b. Spending on maintenance and repair decreases, so individual dwellings produce lower quantities of housing services.

   c. Consumer mobility decreases, and consumers make inefficient housing choices.

10. Rent-control cities use a number of policies to control the decrease in supply caused by rent control, including rent adjustments, exemption of new housing, restrictions on conversion, subsidies for new construction, and vacancy decontrol.

Exercises and Discussion Questions

1. In Figure 15–3, the offer of $100 public housing decreased housing consumption. Suppose that the government increases the rent on an 800-unit dwelling from $100 to $150.

   a. Using a graph similar to Figure 15–3, show the budget point with (*i*) $100 public housing and (*ii*) $150 public housing.

   b. Assume that the household starts with housing consumption of 1,000 units. Draw a set of indifference curves such that the household accepts the offer of $100 public housing, but is indifferent between its original choice and $150 public housing.

2. Suppose that the household in Figure 15–3 starts with housing consumption of 1,200 units of housing service instead of 1,000. Is this household more or less likely to decrease its housing consumption to get public housing? Explain.

3. Figure 15–4 shows that the consumer prefers cash to free public housing. The figure was drawn under the assumption that a system of cash transfers would not increase the price of housing.

   a. Redraw the budget line under the assumption that the cash transfers increase the price of housing from 25 cents to 50 cents per unit.

   b. Draw a set of indifference curves such that the consumer prefers free public housing (with no change in price) to the cash transfer (with the associated increase in price).

   c. Under what conditions (what values of the relevant elasticities) will low-income households prefer new housing to the cash?

   d. Where are these conditions likely to be met? That is, for what group of individuals and what locations are these conditions likely to be met?

4. Comment on the following statement of Mr. Taxpayer: "I support public housing rather than cash transfers because I want to be sure that the recipients of public assistance increase their housing consumption. If we give them cash, they will spend the money on something else."

5. According to Mr. Wizard, a realtor in Modville, "If my assumptions are correct, the long-run market effects of public housing are nil. The building of 200 public housing dwellings will affect neither the equilibrium price of housing nor the quantity of housing."
   a. What are Mr. Wizard's assumptions?
   b. Use Mr. Wizard's assumptions to predict the long-run market effects of housing vouchers.

6. In the early days of Section 8 rent certificates, the recipient received 25 percent of the savings associated with renting a dwelling for less than the fair market rent. Draw Figure 15–8 and add the budget line under the early version of the rent-certificate program.

7. Explain the following quote from a housing official: "Our housing-assistance budget is $3 billion. If we use vouchers instead of rent certificates, we will serve 9,500 fewer households."

8. Suppose that you are interested in maximizing the welfare of the poor. You must choose between cash payments and free housing. What data do you need? Explain how you would use the data.

9. Suppose that the poor households of city H are enrolled in a federal housing-allowance program. You are a middle-income renter in the city.
   a. Will you be helped or harmed by the allowance program?
   b. If you will be harmed, what variables determine how much you will be harmed? In other words, what are the relevant elasticities, and how does the cost you incur vary with them?
   c. How would your answer to (*a*) change if you owned your home?

10. Contrast the effects of rent control in two cities. In city R, the elasticity of supply of housing is 5.0 (i.e., a 10 percent increase in the price of housing increases the quantity of housing by 50 percent). In city S, the supply of housing is less elastic: the supply elasticity is 0.40.

11. Cheating on rent control is common. If you were a prospective tenant in a rent-controlled city, would you encourage your prospective landlord to cheat?

12. Figure 15–13 suggests that the effects of rent control increase with the age of the building. Provide an explanation for this result.

13. Discuss the trade-offs associated with demolishing the high-rise clusters of public housing and replacing them with dispersed low-rise buildings.

References and Additional Readings

Description of Federal Housing Policies

Aaron, Henry J. "Rationale for a Housing Policy." In *Federal Housing Policies and Programs,* ed. J. Paul Mitchell. New Brunswick, N.J.: Center for Urban Policy Research, 1985. Discusses frequently cited justifications for federal housing policies.

Jacobs, Barry G.; Kenneth R. Harney; Charles L. Edson; and Bruce S. Lane. *Guide to Federal Housing Programs.* 2nd ed. Washington, D.C.: Bureau of National Affairs, 1986. A detailed description of federal housing policies (public housing, housing subsidies, consumer subsidies, and community development).

Mariano, Ann. "The Voucher Controversy Drags On." *Washington Post,* February 18, 1989. Discusses the budgetary costs of vouchers and rent certificates.

Mitchell, J. Paul. "The Historical Context for Housing Policy." In *Federal Housing Policies and Programs,* ed. J. Paul Mitchell. New Brunswick, N.J.: Center for Urban Policy Research, 1985. A historical sketch of federal housing policy.

Struyk, Raymond J.; Neil Mayer; and John Tuccillo. *Federal Housing Policy at President Reagan's Midterm.* Washington, D.C.: Urban Institute, 1983. Explains the changes in federal housing policies (assisted housing, community development, and housing finance) during the early 1980s.

Struyk, Raymond J.; Margery A. Turner; and Makiko Ueno. *Future U.S. Housing Policy: Meeting the Demographic Challenge.* Washington, D.C.: Urban Institute, 1983. Discusses the implications of demographic changes (changes in family structure and the aging of society) for federal housing policy.

U.S. Department of Commerce, *Annual Housing Survey for the United States,* 1991.

Weicher, John. "Urban Housing Policy." In *Current Issues in Urban Economics,* ed. Peter Mieszkowski and Mahlon Straszheim. Baltimore: Johns Hopkins University Press, 1979.

Condition of the Housing Stock and Neighborhood Dissatisfaction

Boehm, Thomas P., and Keith R. Ihlanfeldt. "The Revelation of Neighborhood Preferences: An N-Chotomous Multivariate Probit Approach." *Journal of Housing Economics* 1 (1991), pp. 33–59.

Irby, Iredia. "Attaining the Housing Goal." Washington, D.C.: U.S. Department of Housing and Urban Development, Division of Housing and Demographic Analysis, July 1986. Describes the condition of the housing stock in 1983.

Supply versus Demand Policies

Maisel, Sherman. "The Agenda for Metropolitan Housing Policies." In *American Domestic Priorities—An Economic Appraisal,* ed. John M. Quigley and Daniel L. Rubinfeld. Berkeley: University of California Press, 1985. Discusses housing policies in the middle 1980s.

Olsen, Edgar. "Housing Programs and the Forgotten Taxpayer." *The Public Interest* 66 (1982), pp. 97–109. Discusses alternative housing policies from the perspective of taxpayers.

Welfare Effects of Public Housing

Aaron, Henry, and George M. von Furstenberg. "The Inefficiency of Transfers in Kind: The Case of Housing Assistance." *Western Economic Journal* 9 (1971), pp. 184–91. Estimates a welfare loss from public housing of between 10 percent and 18 percent.

Barton, David M., and Edgar O. Olsen. "The Benefits and Costs of Public Housing in New York City." Institute for Research of Poverty Discussion Paper 373-76, University of Wisconsin, Madison, 1976. Estimates the welfare loss from public housing (relative to cash transfers) as 25 percent of program cost.

Kraft, John, and Edgar O. Olsen. "The Distribution of Benefits from Public Housing." In *The Distribution of Benefits from Public Housing.* Vol. 41 of *Studies in Income and Wealth,* ed. F. Thomas Juster. New York: National Bureau of Economic Research, 1977. Estimates the welfare losses from using public housing instead of cash transfers as 27 percent of the program cost.

Murray, Michael P. "The Distribution of Tenant Benefits in Public Housing." *Econometrica* 43 (1975), pp. 771–88. Estimates the welfare losses from using public housing instead of cash transfers as 16 percent to 20 percent of the program cost.

Muth, Richard F. *Public Housing: An Economic Evaluation.* Washington, D.C.: American Enterprise Institute, 1973. Estimates the welfare losses from using public housing instead of cash transfers as 45 percent of the program cost. Argues for the replacement of traditional housing programs with rent certificates, which would operate in the same way as food stamps.

National Housing Review. *Housing in the Seventies.* Washington, D.C.: U.S. Government Printing Office, 1974. Discusses the equity and efficiency effects of housing programs.

Smeeding, Timothy M. "Alternative Methods for Evaluating Selected In-Kind Transfer Benefits and Measuring Their Effect on Poverty." Technical Paper no. 50, U.S. Bureau of the Census, Washington, D.C., 1982. Estimates the value of in-kind transfers to the recipients. Estimates that $1 of public housing is worth 80 cents to the typical recipient.

Smolensky, Eugene. "Public Housing or Income Supplements: The Economics of Housing for the Poor." *Journal of the American Institute of Planners* 34 (1968), pp. 94–101.

Market Effects of Public Housing

Ohls, James C. "Public Policy toward Low-Income Housing and Filtering in Housing Markets." *Journal of Urban Economics* 2 (1975), pp. 144–71. Uses a computer model to simulate the effects of public housing on the filtering process.

Experimental Housing Allowance Program (EHAP)

Aaron, Henry J. "Policy Implications: A Policy Report." In *Do Housing Allowances Work?* ed. Katherine Bradbury and Anthony Downs. Washington, D.C.: Brookings Institution, 1981. Compares the effect of allowances to cash transfers and construction subsidies. Discusses the value of social experiments such as EHAP.

Allen, Garland E.; Jerry J. Fitts; and Evelyn S. Glatt. "The Experimental Housing Allowance Program." In *Do Housing Allowances Work?* ed. Katherine Bradbury and Anthony Downs. Washington, D.C.: Brookings Institution, 1981. A description of the housing allowance experiments.

Downs, Anthony, and Katherine Bradbury. "Conference Discussion." In *Do Housing Allowances Work?* ed. Katherine Bradbury and Anthony Downs. Washington, D.C.: Brookings Institution, 1981. A summary of the discussion of a conference on EHAP.

Frieden, Bernard J. "Housing Allowances: An Experiment that Worked." *The Public Interest* 59 (1980), pp. 15–35. A summary of the results of the allowance experiment.

Hanushek, Eric A., and John M. Quigley. "Consumption Aspects." In *Do Housing Allowances Work?* ed. Katherine Bradbury and Anthony Downs. Washington, D.C.: Brookings Institution, 1981. Discusses the responses of EHAP participants to housing allowances, focusing on the effects on housing consumption and the quality of housing.

Kain, John F. "A Universal Housing Allowance Program." In *Do Housing Allowances Work?* ed. Katherine Bradbury and Anthony Downs. Washington, D.C.: Brookings Institution, 1981. Discusses the implications of EHAP for a national housing-allowance program. Suggests that EHAP was not a true test of a national program because participation rates and housing-quality standards were relatively low.

Mills, Edwin S., and Arthur M. Sullivan. "Market Effects." In *Do Housing Allowances Work?* ed. Katherine Bradbury and Anthony Downs. Washington, D.C.: Brookings Institution, 1981. Discusses the market effects of the EHAP supply experiments.

Rossi, Peter H. "Residential Mobility." In *Do Housing Allowances Work?* ed. Katherine Bradbury and Anthony Downs. Washington, D.C.: Brookings Institution, 1981. Discusses the effects of EHAP on household mobility.

Straszheim, Mahlon R. "Participation." In *Do Housing Allowances Work?* ed. Katherine Bradbury and Anthony Downs. Washington, D.C.: Brookings Institution, 1981. Discusses the factors that explain the relatively low participation rates in EHAP.

Struyk, Raymond J., and Mac Bendick. *Housing Vouchers for the Poor.* Washington, D.C.: Urban Institute, 1981. A detailed description of the Experimental Housing Allowance Program.

Rent Controls

De Salvo, J. S. "Reforming Rent Controls in New York City." Regional Science Association Papers 2 (1971), pp. 195–227.

Gyourko, Joseph, and Peter Linneman. "Equity and Efficiency Aspects of Rent Control: An Empirical Study of New York City." *Journal of Urban Economics* 26 (1989), pp. 54–74.

———. "Rent Controls and Rental Housing Quality: A Note on the Effects of New York City's Old Controls." *Journal of Urban Economics* 27 (1990), pp. 398–409.

Lett, Monica. *Rent Control: Concepts, Realities and Mechanisms.* New Brunswick, N.J.: Rutgers University Press, 1976. A general description of rent-control policies.

Navarro, Peter. "Rent Control in Cambridge, Massachusetts." *Public Interest* 91 (1987), pp. 83–100.

Olsen, Edgar. "An Econometric Analysis of Rent Control." *Journal of Political Economy* 80 (1972), pp. 1081–100.

Rand Corporation. "The Effects of Rent Control on Housing in New York City." In
Rental Housing in New York City: Confronting the Crisis. Publication no. RM-6190-
NYC. New York, 1970.

Smith, Lawrence B., and Peter Tomlinson. "Rent Control in Ontario, Roofs or Ceilings."
American Real Estate and Urban Economics Journal 9 (1981), pp. 93–114.

Urban Renewal

Anderson, Martin. *The Federal Bulldozer.* Cambridge, Mass.: MIT Press, 1964. Argues
that urban renewal destroyed low-income housing, displacing poor households.

Davis, Otto, and Andrew B. Whinston. "The Economics of Urban Renewal." In *Urban
Renewal: The Record and the Controversy,* ed. James Q. Wilson. Cambridge, Mass.:
MIT Press, 1966, pp. 50–67.

Rothenberg, Jerome. *Economic Evaluation of Urban Renewal.* Washington, D.C.: Brookings Institution, 1967.

Weicher, John. *Urban Renewal: National Program for Local Problems.* Washington,
D.C.: American Enterprise Institute, 1973.

Weiss, Marc A. "The Origins and Legacy of Urban Renewal." In *Federal Housing Policies and Programs,* ed. J. Paul Mitchell. New Brunswick, N.J.: Center for Urban
Policy Research, 1985. Discusses the politics of urban renewal and housing policies.

Community Development

U.S. Department of Housing and Urban Development. *1988 Community Development
Programs: State Reports.* Washington, D.C.: Government Printing Office, 1989.
Shows HUD's community development budget and describes how cities and states
have used federal community development funds.

PART IV

Urban Problems and
Local Government

In contrast with the federal government, whose urban policies are primarily redistributional in nature, local governments are involved in resource allocation. Local governments build the streets, provide mass transit, run the public school system, and manage the criminal-justice system. Local spending programs are supported by taxes on property, income, and retail sales. This section discusses the efficiency and distributional effects of local spending and tax policies. Chapter 16 provides an overview of local government, explaining the basic reasons for local government. Chapter 17 discusses how local budget decisions are made, focusing on how citizens influence budget decisions through their voting and location choices. Chapter 18 deals with local revenue sources, examining the incidence of local taxes and the local responses to intergovernmental grants.

Chapters 19 through 22 examine individual spending programs of local governments. Chapters 19 and 20 discuss urban transportation. The first of these chapters explores three problems caused by automobiles: congestion, pollution, and highway accidents. The second chapter deals with mass transit, showing how commuters choose a travel mode and how planners choose a transit system. Chapter 21 considers some of the spatial aspects of education, showing how the fragmented system of local government causes inequalities in educational spending and achievement. It also discusses various policies to offset spending and achievement inequalities, including intergovernmental grants and desegregation. Chapter 22 presents the economic approach to crime and crime fighting, discussing the optimum amount of crime and alternative means of controlling crime.

CHAPTER
16

Overview of Local Government

A community is like a ship: everyone ought to be prepared to take the helm.
Henrik Ibsen

This chapter provides an overview of the taxing and spending policies of the local public sector. The first part of the chapter presents the facts on local government, including information on spending programs and revenue sources. The second and third parts discuss the economic rationale for local government, explaining why goods such as public schooling, public-safety services, parks, and transit systems are produced by local governments rather than private firms or higher levels of government. The fourth part explores the trade-offs associated with metropolitan consolidation. The fifth part discusses the reasons for—and responses to—the rising cost of local public services. The final part explores the reasons for the fiscal distress experienced by many central cities in the last few decades.

Local-Government Facts

Local governments are creatures of state governments in the sense that localities derive their taxing and spending powers from the states. There is considerable variation across states in the amount of power delegated to local governments. One measure of the relative importance of a local government in a particular state is the ratio of local spending to state spending: the larger the ratio, the greater the spending power of localities. In 1985, the average ratio was 0.75: local spending was about 75 percent of state spending (Advisory Commission on Intergovernmental Relations, 1987). Some of the states with relatively low spending ratios were Alaska (0.05), Hawaii (0.25), New Mexico (0.29), Delaware (0.37), Massachusetts (0.43), and Kentucky (0.43). Some of the states with relatively high spending ratios were New York (1.27), New Hampshire (1.12), Texas (1.04), and Colorado (1.04).

451

TABLE 16–1   Types of Local Government

Type of Government	Number of Units (1992)	Percent of Total Local Expenditure*
County	3,043	23
Municipality	19,296	33
Township	16,666	3
School district	14,556	30
Special district	33,131	10
Total	86,692	100

Definitions
  1. Municipality: a municipal corporation provides general local government for a specific concentration of population.
  2. Township: serves the inhabitants of an area defined without regard to population concentrations.
  3. Special district: independent, special-purpose governmental unit.

*Percents don't add to 100 due to rounding.

SOURCES: U.S. Bureau of the Census, *Statistical Abstract of the United States 1990* (Washington, D.C.: U.S. Government Printing Office, 1990); U.S. Bureau of the Census, *City Government Finances in 1986* (Washington, D.C.: U.S. Government Printing Office, 1987).

As shown in Table 16–1, there are over 86,000 local governments in the United States. In terms of total expenditures, the most important types of local governments are municipalities (33 percent of local-government expenditures) and school districts (30 percent of local expenditures).

Local-Government Spending

Table 16–2 shows the spending of local governments and municipalities on various goods and services. The largest spending category for local government is education, with $684 per capita, about 42 percent of total spending. The spending of municipalities is more evenly divided, with the largest expenditures on administration and finance ($122 per capita), police protection ($99), education ($89), highways ($68), sewerage ($61), and fire protection ($53).

In the postwar period, there have been two distinct trends in local spending. Between 1950 and 1976, local spending rose from about 5 percent to 9.2 percent of GDP. Three factors contributed to the steady growth in the postwar period. First, increases in real income increased the demand for many of the services provided by local governments. Second, the postwar baby boom increased the number of children attending local public schools. Third, for reasons described later in the chapter, the cost of providing local public services increased. The second trend in local spending is the decrease in the relative importance of local government in the last 15 years: between 1976 and 1986, local spending dropped from 9.2 percent to around 8 percent

TABLE 16–2   **Per Capita Expenditures of Local Government**

	Annual Spending per Capita, 1986–1987	
Expenditure Category	*All Local Governments*	*Municipalities*
Education Services		
Education	$684	$ 89
Libraries	12	11
Social Services		
Public welfare	79	43
Hospitals	92	37
Health	32	13
Transportation		
Highways	87	68
Other	27	31
Public Safety		
Police protection	88	99
Fire protection	43	53
Other	31	17
Environment and Housing		
Natural resources	11	1
Parks and recreation	38	40
Housing and community development	43	37
Sewage services	61	61
Solid waste management	27	30
Administration and Finance	186	122
General Expenditure	85	83

SOURCES: Figures for all local governments are from U.S. Bureau of the Census, *City Government Finances*, vol. 4 (Washington, D.C.: U.S. Government Printing Office, 1988) and U.S. Bureau of the Census, *Compendium of Government Finances*, no. 5 (Washington, D.C.: U.S. Government Printing Office, April 1990). Figures for municipalities are from U.S. Bureau of the Census, *City Government Finances*, vol. 4 (Washington, D.C.: U.S. Government Printing Office, 1988); and U.S. Bureau of the Census, *Finances of Municipal & Township Government*, no. 4 (Washington, D.C.: U.S. Government Printing Office, March 1990).

of GDP. Since the mid-1970s, real income has increased at a relatively slow rate and the number of school children has increased slowly. As a result, the relative size of the local sector has decreased.

Revenue Sources

Table 16–3 shows the distribution of revenue for different types of local governments. For local governments as a whole, 40 percent of total revenue comes from intergovernmental grants, 37 percent comes from local taxes, and the remaining 23 percent comes from charges and general revenue. School districts are heavily dependent on intergovernmental grants, receiving about 55 percent of their revenue

TABLE 16–3   **Revenue Sources of Local Governments, 1985–1986**

	Percent of General Revenue from			
Type of Government	*Intergovernmental Grants*	*Local Taxes*	*Charges and General Revenue*	*Total*
County	37%	37%	26%	100%
Municipality	30	42	28	100
Township	29	56	15	100
School district	55	37	8	100
Special district	29	15	57	100
All local governments	40	37	23	100

SOURCE: U.S. Bureau of the Census, *City Government Finances in 1986* (Washington, D.C.: U.S. Government Printing Office, 1987).

from the federal and state governments. For municipal governments, 30 percent of revenue comes from grants, 42 percent comes from local taxes, and 28 percent comes from user charges and general revenue. In contrast, special districts are heavily dependent on user charges, receiving about 57 percent of their revenue from charges and general revenue.

FIGURE 16–1   **Percent of Local Tax Revenue from Various Sources, 1984**

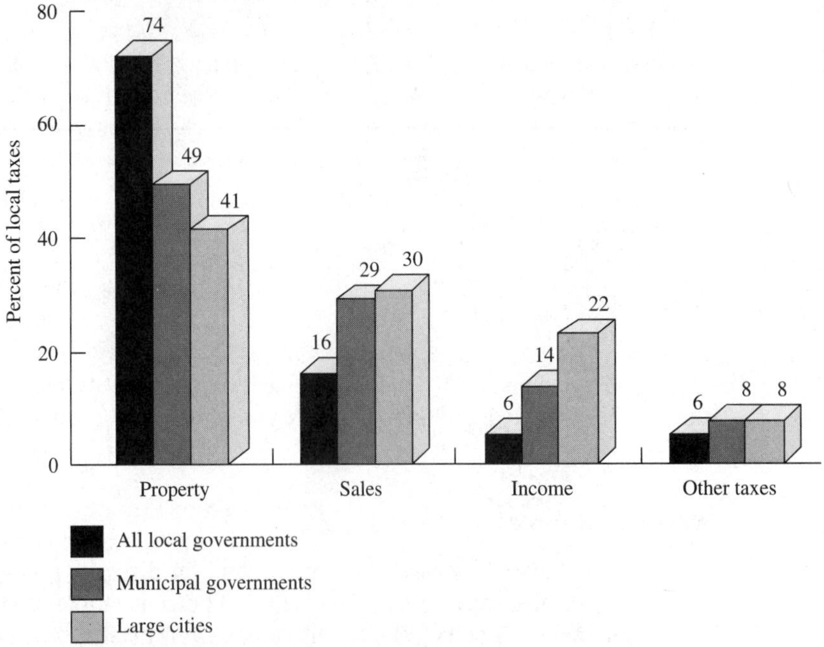

SOURCES: U.S. Bureau of the Census, *Census of Governments* and *City Government Finances in 1984–1985* (Washington, D.C.: U.S. Government Printing Office, 1986).

Figure 16–1 shows the distribution of tax revenue for municipalities and all local governments. In 1984, the property tax generated about three fourths of all local tax revenue. Municipalities are less dependent on the property tax: for municipalities as a whole, the property tax generated about half of tax revenue; for large municipalities (population greater than 300,000), the property tax generated only about 41 percent of tax revenue. The second largest revenue source is the sales tax: it generated 16 percent of total tax revenue and 29 percent of municipal tax revenue. The third largest source is the local income tax, which generated 6 percent of local taxes and 14 percent of municipal taxes.

Figure 16–2 shows the time trends for intergovernmental grants from the federal and state governments. The relative importance of state grants increased steadily between 1965 and 1975, reaching a peak of almost 40 percent of the amount generated by local governments. Since then the relative importance of state grants has fallen to about 24 percent of locally generated revenue. Federal grants have followed a similar path: their relative importance rose steadily between 1965 and 1978 and has fallen since then.

Intergovernmental grants support dozens of local programs. The programs receiving the largest number of grants are education (about 18 percent of all intergovernmental grants), public welfare (14 percent), housing and community development (10 percent), highways (8 percent), and health and hospitals (2 percent). The

FIGURE 16–2   Federal and State Grants to Cities as Percentages of Locally Generated Revenue, 1965–1988

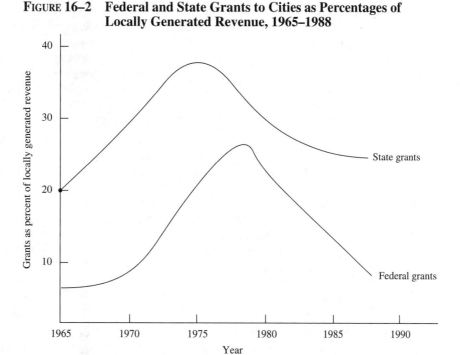

SOURCE: Helen Ladd and John Yinger, *America's Ailing Cities: Fiscal Health and the Design of Urban Policy* (Baltimore: Johns Hopkins University Press, 1989).

municipal spending programs that are most heavily dependent on intergovernmental grants are welfare (76 percent), housing and community development (62 percent), and education (52 percent) (U.S. Bureau of the Census, 1987).

The Role of Local Government

What is the role of local government in the market economy? This question can be answered by asking two separate questions. First, what is the role of government in the market economy? Second, how does local government fit into the general scheme of government involvement?

Musgrave and Musgrave (1980) distinguish between three types of government policies. The first is stabilization policy: the government uses monetary and fiscal policy to control unemployment and inflation. Under the second type of policy, income redistribution, the government uses taxes and transfers to alter the distributions of income and wealth. The third policy is resource allocation: the government makes decisions about what to produce and how to produce it. When the government actually produces a particular good or service, it makes these resource-allocation decisions directly. When the government subsidizes or taxes private activities, it influences the resource-allocation decisions of the private sector.

How do local governments fit into this three-part scheme of governmental activity? The responsibility for stabilization policy has been assumed by the national government for two reasons. First, although each local government could print its own money and execute its own monetary policy, such a system would be chaotic. Instead, the national government prints the money and manages a national monetary policy. Second, because a large fraction of local income is spent on goods produced outside the local area, local monetary and fiscal policies would be relatively weak and ineffective. Consider a city that wants to stimulate the local economy, and tries to do so by cutting its taxes without changing its spending on local public goods. This deficit-spending policy will be ineffective because a large fraction of the tax cut will be spent on imports, so the tax cut will have a relatively small local multiplier effect. Fiscal policy is more effective at the national level because a relatively small fraction of national income is spent on imports, so a national tax cut has a relatively large multiplier effect.

Consider next the distribution role of government. Local attempts to redistribute income will be frustrated by the mobility of taxpayers and transfer recipients. Suppose that a city imposes a tax on its wealthy citizens and uses the tax revenue to finance transfer payments to the poor. To escape the tax, some wealthy households will leave the city, causing a decrease in total tax revenue. At the same time, some poor households will migrate to the relatively generous city, causing a decrease in the transfer payment per recipient. In combination, the fleeing of the wealthy and the migration of the poor weakens the city's redistribution program: there is less money to transfer to more poor households. A national redistribution program is more effective because there is less mobility between nations than between cities.

The third role of government is resource allocation. As was shown in Table 16–2, local governments are responsible for the provision of several goods and services, including education, highways, police and fire protection, parks, and sewers. Under what conditions can government provision of these goods be justified on efficiency grounds? There are three possibilities. First, the good may be produced under conditions that generate a natural monopoly. Second, the good may generate positive externalities. Finally, the good may have the characteristics of a local public good.

Natural Monopoly

A natural monopoly occurs if the production of a particular good is subject to relatively large scale economies. In Figure 16–3, the long-run average total-cost curve for sewage services is negatively sloped over a wide range of output, reflecting the fact that (1) there is a substantial fixed cost associated with setting up a sewage system and (2) the marginal cost of adding another customer is relatively small. Because the average cost curve is negatively sloped, the marginal cost is less than average cost (the marginal cost pulls down the average cost as quantity increases). Sewage service is a natural monopoly in the sense that a single sewage authority (providing S^* units of service) could serve the city at a lower average cost than several sewage authorities (for example, five firms, each supplying S' units).

FIGURE 16–3   Natural Monopoly in Sewage Services

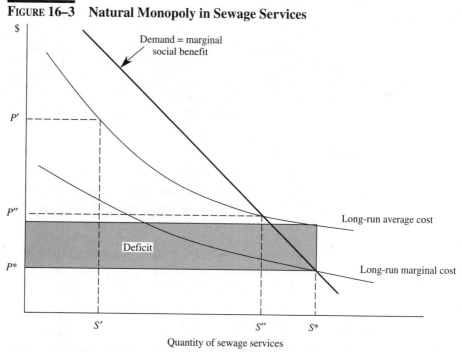

Sewage service is a natural monopoly: scale economies generate a negatively sloped long-run average cost curve. The optimum output is where the demand curve intersects the marginal-cost curve. Since the optimum price is less than the average total cost, the sewage system generates a deficit. The government could provide sewage service itself, covering the deficit with general tax revenue. Alternatively, the government could regulate a private sewage authority.

What is the optimum level of sewage service? The basic efficiency rule is that an activity should be increased to the point at which the marginal social benefit of the activity equals the marginal social cost. In Figure 16–3, the demand curve, which shows consumers' willingness to pay for different levels of sewage service, is also the marginal-social-benefit curve. The optimum output (S^*) is the output at which the demand curve intersects the marginal-cost curve. One problem with an output of S^* is that a firm producing this output would lose money: to get consumers to purchase S^* units of sewage service, the firm would charge a price of P^*, which is less than the average total cost of producing S^*. The deficit is shown by the shaded area.

The government has several options. First, it can provide the service itself, charge a price of P^* and cover the deficit with general tax revenue. Second, it can get a private firm to provide sewage service. If the government forces the firm to charge a price of P^*, subsidies are required to cover the deficit. A final option is to allow the private firm to charge P'' instead of P^*. At P'', average total cost equals the price, so the firm would cover all of its cost. Under this scheme, the output (S'') is less than the optimum output.

Local governments have the same options for other natural monopolies. Chapter 20 (Mass Transit) discusses the pricing and regulation of mass transit. For other natural monopolies (water systems, cable television networks, telephone networks), the government can either produce the service itself or regulate a private producer.

What level of government should operate or regulate a natural monopoly? Should sewage and transit services be run by local, metropolitan, regional, state, or national governments? The appropriate level of government is determined by the extent of scale economies: the greater the scale economies, the larger the political jurisdiction required to realize the scale economies associated with providing the service. Local governments are responsible for the provision and regulation of services for which scale economies are exhausted at the local level.

Externalities

One of the roles of government is to internalize externalities. An externality occurs if one person's consumption of a good generates benefits or costs for other people. The basic efficiency rule is that an activity should be increased to the point at which the marginal social benefit equals the marginal social cost. An externality causes a divergence between private and social benefits or between private and social costs. Individual consumers, who base their decisions on private benefits and costs, make choices that are inefficient from the social perspective. When this occurs, government intervention may promote efficiency.

Education Externalities.   Figure 16–4 shows the private and social benefits of education. Education generates private benefits (for the student himself) and external benefits (for the student's fellow workers and citizens). As a person becomes more educated, he becomes a better team worker: he understands instructions more readily and is more likely to suggest ways to improve production. In other words, education generates workplace externalities. In addition, a more educated citizen makes better

FIGURE 16–4   Externalities in the Consumption of Education

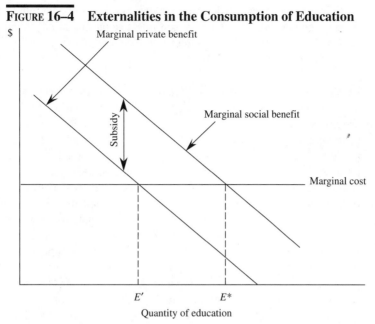

There are externalities in the consumption of education, so the marginal social benefit exceeds the marginal private benefit. In the absence of government involvement, the student chooses E' (where the marginal private benefit equals the marginal cost). The optimum level of education is E^*, which the student will choose if the government provides a subsidy equal to the gap between the marginal private and marginal social benefit.

choices on election day, generating external benefits for his fellow citizens. Because education generates workplace and civic externalities, the marginal social benefit of education exceeds the marginal private benefit. In the absence of government intervention, the worker-citizen ignores these external benefits, choosing E' units of education instead of the optimum (E^*).

The government has two options to solve the externality problem. The first is to take responsibility for providing the good. A system of free compulsory education could encourage citizens to consume more education. Alternatively, the government could subsidize education, encouraging citizens to consume more education while allowing them to choose their own schools. In Figure 16–4, the subsidy would be equal to the gap between the private and social benefits of education. The subsidy would increase consumption to E^* units of education. As discussed in Chapter 21 (Education), there is heated debate over whether the government should supplement the public school system with subsidies for private education (tuition tax credits and education vouchers).

What level of government should deal with education externalities? Should the public school system (or education subsidies) be managed by local, metropolitan, regional, state, or national governments? One factor in determining the optimum level of government is the geographical extent of the externalities. If people throughout the country benefit from the education of children in a particular school, national participation in education decisions (national schools or a national subsidy) may promote efficiency. If the benefits are confined to a particular city, local decision making may be efficient. As explained later in the chapter, there are other factors that affect the optimum level of government.

Public-Safety Externalities.   There are two types of externalities from spending on police services, positive and negative. Both externalities result from the fact that criminals are mobile: they can move freely from one jurisdiction to another. The positive externality occurs when one municipality uses its police budget to capture a criminal: by doing so, the municipality generates benefits for surrounding municipalities, so the marginal social benefit of police spending exceeds the marginal local (municipal) benefit. The negative externality occurs when one municipality's crime-fighting activities cause criminals to victimize people in surrounding municipalities. In other words, the police sometimes chase criminals from one municipality to another. In this case, police spending just moves crime around, so the marginal local benefit of police spending exceeds the marginal social benefit.

What is the optimum level of government for police protection? One factor is the geographical extent of the positive and negative externalities, which depends on the mobility of criminals. The greater the mobility of criminals, the larger the optimum jurisdiction. As explained later in the chapter, there are other factors that affect the optimum level of government. The typical response to these positive and negative externalities is to provide police services through municipal governments.

The other public-safety service, fire protection, also generates externalities. Fires can spread from one house to another, so the marginal social benefit of fire protection exceeds the marginal private benefit. In most metropolitan areas, fire protection is provided by local governments. Some municipalities contract with private firms to provide fire protection. For the trade-offs between public and private production, see Savas (1982) and Stevens (1984).

Characteristics of a Local Public Good

A local public good has three characteristics. First, it is **nonrivalrous** in consumption: several people consume the same good at the same time. Second, it is **nonexcludable:** it is impossible or impractical to exclude some people (e.g., those who do not pay for the good) from consuming the good. Third, the benefits of the good are confined to a relatively small geographical area.

Nonrivalrous Consumption (Joint Consumption).   Consider first the issue of rivalry in consumption. A private good (a hot dog) can be consumed by only one person. In contrast, a public good can be consumed by many people at the same time. For example, hundreds of people can watch a parade without interfering with each other's enjoyment of the parade. In other words, a parade is subject to **joint consumption:** everyone can consume the same good. The parade is a **pure local public good** if the marginal cost of an additional parade viewer is zero. This occurs if an additional viewer does not decrease the enjoyment of other parade viewers.

Many of the goods provided by local governments are semirivalrous. If the number of consumers becomes large enough, an individual consumer's benefit decreases. For example, if the city does not set up bleachers for parade viewers, tall people block the views of short people. This is a problem only if the number of parade viewers is large enough that short citizens do not get a front-row view. In this case, the parade is an **impure** or **congestable public good**. Other examples of impure public goods are city streets and highways: during the peak travel periods, travel speeds decrease as traffic volume increases, so the benefit of using the highway decreases as the number of consumers increases.

What about police and fire services? Although two citizens cannot use a police officer or a fire truck at the same time, public-safety systems are designed to respond quickly to emergencies. Most cities have enough police officers and fire trucks to simultaneously handle a reasonable number of calls for help. If everyone called at once, consumption would of course be rivalrous, but not everyone needs safety services at the same time.

Nonexcludability.   The second characteristic of a local public good is that it would be impractical to exclude some people from consuming the good. In other words, the good is nonexcludable. Consider the parade example. Although it may be possible to charge everyone for watching the parade and exclude those who don't pay, it would be very costly to do so. The government would have to first empty the streets and buildings along the parade route, and then admit people who paid a parade-viewing fee. If some people promised to not watch the parade, they might be permitted to enter a building along the route, but the government would have to find a way to prevent them from sneaking a look. Such a scheme would obviously be impractical.

What about streets and public parks? One way to charge people for using city streets would be to set up a system of toll booths, one on each corner. Such a system would be costly: the city would have to hire a large number of toll collectors, and road users would incur a substantial time cost in stopping at every corner to pay the tolls. Chapter 19 (Autos and Highways) describes a low-cost system for charging drivers for using streets and highways. There is little political support for such a system, so streets are likely to remain nonexcludable. The same argument applies to parks. Although it might be possible to install fences and turnstiles in city parks, such a system would be relatively costly.

What about public-safety services? For some safety activities, it would be easy to identify the beneficiaries and send them a bill for the safety services rendered. For example, the fire department could charge a fee for putting out fires, and the police could charge a fee for responding to burglaries and robberies. Under such a system, the fire and police departments would not provide services to people who could not afford the service fees. This system of user charges is politically infeasible because it would violate most people's notions of equity and fairness. For other types of safety activities, it would be more difficult to identify the beneficiaries and charge for the safety services. For example, when a city captures, prosecutes, and imprisons a criminal, every potential crime victim benefits. Other examples are crowd and traffic control. For these services, it would be impractical to exclude people who do not pay.

Localized Benefits.   The third characteristic of a local public good is that its benefits are confined to a relatively small geographical area. Unlike national defense, which generates benefits for the entire nation, most of the benefits of the local police force and local fire department go to local citizens. Similarly, local citizens get most of the benefits from local streets and highways. The appropriate size of the jurisdiction is determined by the "localness" of the public good (the geographical extent of the benefits from the public good): the more extensive the benefits, the larger the jurisdiction required to contain all the beneficiaries.

The Optimum Quantity of a Local Public Good

What is the optimum level of a local public good? According to the basic efficiency rule, the optimum level of an activity is the amount at which the marginal social benefit equals the marginal social cost. To determine the optimum level, we must determine the marginal social benefit of the local public good.

Consider a three-person city that must decide how many acres of public parks to provide. In Figure 16–5, the marginal-benefit curves show how much each citizen is

FIGURE 16–5   Optimum versus Equilibrium Provision of a Local Public Good

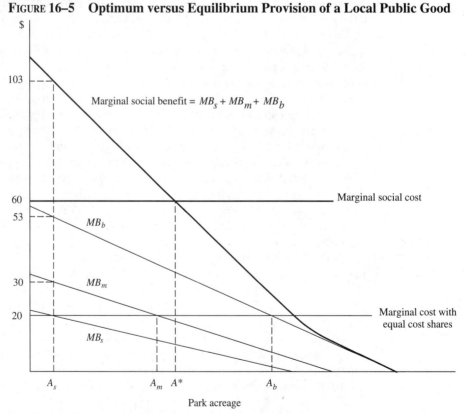

The marginal social benefit of park acreage is the sum of the private benefits of three citizens. The optimum park acreage is A^* (the amount such that the marginal social benefit equals the marginal social cost).

willing to pay for different amounts of parks: Sam has a low demand for parks and prefers relatively small parks (MB_s); Marian has a medium demand (MB_m); Bertha has a high demand and prefers big parks (MB_b). Suppose that city parks have the following characteristics:

1. **No congestion.** In the relevant range of park use, park acreage is non-rivalrous: park usage is low enough that there is no congestion.
2. **No intercity spillovers.** The city's park does not generate benefits or costs for people outside the city.

If these two conditions are satisfied, the park is a pure local public good. The social benefit of a given park size is the sum of the marginal benefits of Sam, Marian, and Bertha: if there is no congestion, the three citizens do not affect their fellow citizens' enjoyment of the park; if there are no spillovers, there are no other potential beneficiaries to worry about. For A_s acres of land, the marginal social benefit is $103 (Sam's marginal benefit is $20, Marian's is $30, and Bertha's is $53). The marginal-social-benefit curve is the vertical sum of the individual marginal-benefit curves.

At the optimum, the marginal social benefit of park acreage equals its marginal social cost. In Figure 16–5, the marginal cost is $60 per acre, so the optimum acreage is A^*. For any amount less than A^*, citizens in the city would be willing to pay more than $60 per additional acre, so an increase in size would increase social welfare. For example, suppose the city starts at A_s. At this point, the willingness to pay for parks (from the social-benefit curve) is $103 and the cost is only $60, so an increase in park acreage would generate a large net gain. Similarly, for any amount exceeding A^*, the willingness to pay would be less than the social cost, so a smaller park would be more efficient.

How do local governments decide how much of local public goods to provide? Chapter 17 discusses two methods for determining how much of a local public good to provide. One approach is to hold an election and let voters choose how much to spend on local public goods. Another approach is to allow citizens to vote with their feet by moving to the jurisdiction that provides the best combination of public services and taxes. One of the issues examined in Chapter 17 is whether either of these approaches generates the efficient amount of local public goods.

Federalism and the Optimum Level of Government

Under the federal system of government, the responsibility for providing public goods is divided between the federal, state, and local governments. Some goods, such as defense and space exploration, are provided at the national level. Others, such as education and police protection, are provided at the local level. Why are some public goods provided by local governments rather than state or federal governments?

Oates (1972) discusses the advantages and disadvantages of the local provision of public goods.

1. **Diversity in demand.** A system of small local governments allows communities to choose different levels of spending on public goods (parks,

public safety, education, libraries). Because local governments can accommodate the diverse demands for public goods, they promote efficiency.

2. **Externalities.** If the local jurisdiction is not large enough to contain all the people affected by its spending programs, there are externalities (benefit spillovers). Under a system of small local governments, local voters ignore the benefits that accrue to people outside the jurisdiction and therefore make inefficient choices.

3. **Scale economies.** If there are scale economies in the provision of public goods, a system of small local governments has a relatively high production cost.

The local provision of a public good is efficient if the advantages outweigh the disadvantages. In other words, local provision is efficient if (1) diversity in demand is relatively large, (2) externalities are relatively small, and (3) scale economies are relatively small.

Externalities versus Demand Diversity

Consider first the trade-off between internalizing externalities and accommodating diverse demands for local public goods. Suppose that because of interjurisdictional mobility, public education generates benefits for citizens outside the jurisdiction: once a citizen leaves her local school district, her co-workers and fellow workers in another jurisdiction benefit from her education. Because the municipality considers all the costs of the local public good but ignores some of the benefits, the local government provides the good at an inefficiently low level. The inefficiency occurs because the municipality is too small to contain all the beneficiaries of its spending program.

The same analysis applies to other local public goods that generate externalities. When the police capture a criminal, potential victims in surrounding municipalities benefit, so the social benefit of police spending exceeds the local benefit. If households cross municipal borders to use the services of other local governments, the social benefit of these services exceeds the local benefit. These interjurisdictional spillovers cause inefficient choices by municipalities and school districts.

One solution to the spillover problem is a system of subsidies from a higher level of government. If the municipality receives a subsidy equal to the marginal external benefit of the public good, it bases its spending decisions on the marginal social benefit of the good. The subsidy increases the municipality's benefit to the level of the marginal social benefit, so the municipality increases its spending to the optimum level. Chapters 18 (Local Taxes and Intergovernmental Grants) and 21 (Education) explore the effects of various types of intergovernmental grants on local spending.

An alternative response to the externality problem is metropolitan consolidation. The idea is that the jurisdiction could be expanded to include all the people affected by local-government policies. For example, a metropolitan area could consolidate all of its municipalities, school districts, and special districts into a single metropolitan government that would make spending decisions for the entire metropolitan area.

What are the trade-offs associated with metropolitan consolidation? The problem with a metropolitan government is that it chooses a single spending level for all households in the metropolitan area. Under the metropolitan government, externalities are internalized, but since a single spending level must be chosen, citizens are forced to compromise on their ideal spending levels. Metropolitan governments will be more efficient than municipal governments if interjurisdictional spillovers are large relative to diversity in demand. In this case, the advantages of small local governments (the ability to accommodate diverse demands for local public goods) are relatively small, and the disadvantages (the inefficiencies associated with externalities) are relatively large. Therefore, a metropolitan system of government will be more efficient.

Scale Economies versus Demand Diversity

There is also a trade-off between demand diversity and scale economies. Consider a metropolitan area with a single public good (fire protection) and two municipalities. The metropolitan area has the following characteristics:

1. **Diversity in demand.** The demand for fire protection is relatively high in municipality H and relatively low in municipality L.
2. **No externalities.** The benefits of fire protection do not cross municipal borders.
3. **Scale economies.** The average cost of fire protection decreases as the number of fire trucks increases. Therefore, a metropolitan fire department can produce fire protection at a lower average cost than a municipal fire department.
4. **Uniformity.** Under a metropolitan government, the two municipalities have identical fire-protection programs.

Under a system of municipal governments, each municipality makes its own decisions on fire protection. The decisions are based on the local benefits and costs of fire protection.

Suppose that municipality L has four fire trucks (low demand), while municipality H has eight fire trucks. The two municipalities merge to form a metropolitan government. Each community gets six fire trucks (the average number of fire trucks that would occur under municipal government) at a lower average cost. The switch to metropolitan government brings good news and bad news. The good news is that the average cost of fire protection decreases. The bad news is that both municipalities must compromise on their ideal level of fire protection, with H getting too few trucks (six instead of eight), and L getting too many (six instead of four). Metropolitan consolidation will be efficient if the savings in production cost are large relative to the losses resulting from the uniform provision of fire protection. In other words, consolidation will be efficient if scale economies are large relative to the diversity in demand for fire protection.

What are the facts on scale economies in the provision of local public goods? There have been dozens of studies of the relationship between production costs and jurisdiction sizes. The evidence suggests that there are moderate scale economies in the provision of water and sewage services. Because these services are capital-intensive, average cost decreases as population increases. In contrast, most studies of other local public goods (police protection, fire protection, schools) suggest that scale economies occur up to a population of about 100,000.

Metropolitan Consolidation

Should local governments be consolidated into metropolitan governments? Four arguments have been advanced in support of metropolitan consolidation.

Prevention of Suburban Exploitation

According to the suburban exploitation hypothesis, suburban commuters do not pay their "fair share" of the cost of central-city public services. Consider a worker who commutes from her suburban home to the city. Although she uses city services (streets, water, fire protection, police protection), she pays her property taxes to a suburban government. Does the commuter "exploit" central-city residents by using city services without paying for them?

The exploitation hypothesis ignores the fact that commuters pay taxes to the city. As shown in Chapter 18, over two fifths of municipal tax revenue comes from sales and income taxes, meaning that suburbanites who work and shop in the city center pay taxes to city governments. For large cities (population greater than 300,000), sales and income tax generate over half of municipal tax revenue. In addition, most cities have user fees for public services (tolls, admission prices for zoos and museums), so suburbanites pay directly for some city services. Most studies of the exploitation hypothesis suggest that suburbanites pay close to their share of the cost of city services (see Bradford and Oates, 1974, for a review of these studies).

Exploitation of Scale Economies

Another argument advanced in favor of consolidation is that a metropolitan government can exploit scale economies to provide public services at a lower cost. The scale-economy argument is incomplete. The switch to metropolitan government requires communities to compromise on their ideal levels of public goods, so the cost savings from scale economies must be compared to the welfare losses resulting from the uniform provision of public goods. Metropolitan consolidation will be efficient if scale economies are large relative to the diversity in demand.

Equalization of Tax Rates

Under a system of fragmented local government, municipalities with large tax bases often have relatively low tax rates. Under a metropolitan government, there would be a single property-tax base and thus a single tax rate. Therefore, the switch from a municipal system to a metropolitan government would increase tax rates in relatively wealthy communities and decrease tax rates in relatively poor communities.

To what extent does the equalization of tax rates redistribute income from the wealthy to the poor? Consider a metropolitan area with two municipalities, one with middle-income households and one with poor households. Everyone in the poor municipality lives in rental housing, and every household in the middle-income municipality owns the home it occupies. The poor community has a low tax base and a high tax rate, and the middle-income community has a large tax base and a low tax rate. Therefore, metropolitan consolidation increases property taxes in the middle-income community and decreases taxes in the poor community.

The changes in tax liabilities affect housing prices and property values in the two communities. In the poor community, the tax cut increases the profitability of housing, so the supply of housing increases and the price of housing (monthly rent) falls. Therefore, tenants benefit from the tax cut. Property owners also benefit: the decrease in the tax on rental housing increases the net income from rental property, increasing market values. This is the capitalization process: changes in tax liabilities are capitalized into property values. In the middle-income community, homeowners face higher tax liabilities, so their property values fall.

Who gains and who loses as a result of the equalization of taxes? Tenants and landlords in the poor community gain: the tenants pay lower rent, and the landlords have higher property values. Homeowners in the middle-income community lose because their property values fall. To predict the distributional effect of the equalization of tax rates, one needs information on the income levels of tenants, landlords, and homeowners. If landlords in the poor community are relatively wealthy, the equalization of tax rates could actually increase income inequality.

Equalization of Spending

Under the fragmented system of local government, spending varies within the metropolitan area, reflecting variation in the demands for public services. Consolidating local government would equalize spending on local public goods. Because spending on public services typically increases with income, metropolitan consolidation would narrow the spending gap between wealthy and poor communities.

Bradford and Oates (1974) explore the effects of metropolitan consolidation in northeastern New Jersey. They predict the effects of consolidating 58 local jurisdictions (5 central cities and 53 suburban governments) into a single metropolitan government.

Bradford and Oates evaluate the trade-offs associated with the equalization of educational spending. To explain their results, suppose that there are only two school districts, a wealthy one and a poor one. Before consolidation, the wealthy community spends $3,000 per pupil on education, and the poor one spends $2,600. Suppose that under the consolidated government, spending is equalized at $2,800 per pupil: spending increases by $200 in the poor district and decreases by the same amount in the wealthy district. According to Bradford and Oates, the extra $200 of education spending is worth only about $130 to the typical poor household: the household would be indifferent between receiving $200 in educational spending and $130 in cash. In contrast, the typical wealthy household would be indifferent between losing $200 in educational spending and giving up $230 in cash. Therefore, the equalization program produces a $130 benefit (to poor households) at a cost of $230 (to wealthy households).

Using the Bradford-Oates numbers, the equalization program seems to be foolish. Both the poor and the wealthy would be better off if the government used cash transfers—not education spending—to redistribute income. For example, if the government took just $130 from the wealthy and gave it to the poor, the poor would be just as well off, but the wealthy would be better off by $100.

This simplistic analysis is deceptive. As pointed out by Bradford and Oates, these calculations ignore the external benefits of education. As explained earlier in this chapter, education generates externalities, so individual households spend less than the optimum amount on education. The question is whether the external benefits of the equalization program are large enough to offset the private costs. Suppose that the equalization program increases the educational achievement of the poor by a relatively large amount. The *net external benefit* is defined as the external benefit of extra education for the poor less the external cost of less education for the wealthy. If the net external benefit is relatively large, the apparent inefficiency of the equalization program disappears: the equalization program would not be foolish, but would promote efficiency.

Another possible justification for the equalization program is that education may be a **merit good,** defined as a good that is assumed to be systematically undervalued by consumers. If individuals do not make rational choices concerning education, their willingness to pay for education understates the private value of education. In the example above, perhaps the poor don't realize that they would actually receive a benefit of $190 from the increase in education spending. If so, it wouldn't take much of an external benefit to make the equalization program socially efficient. The notion of a merit good can also be stated in terms of the willingness to donate: if the donors (the people in the wealthy school district) are allowed to make choices for the recipients (in the poor district), they are willing to donate more. They may be willing to give only $50 in cash, but $200 in extra education. If so, everyone is better off under the equalization program than they would be under the cash-transfer program.

Alternatives to Metropolitan Consolidation

An alternative to metropolitan consolidation is a **metropolitan federation**. Under a federated government, a metropolitan government would be responsible for the provision of goods with large scale economies (e.g., water and sewage systems, sanitation, highways, transit). Municipalities would continue to provide goods with relatively small scale economies (e.g., schools, police and fire protection, parks). The Toronto area established a federated government in 1954.

Another alternative to metropolitan consolidation is to contract with another level of government to provide public services. According to a recent survey conducted by the Advisory Commission on Intergovernmental Relations (1987), over half of all U.S. cities provided some public services under intergovernmental contracts (under which one unit of government arranges with another to provide a public service), and over half used joint-service contracts (under which two or more governmental units join to produce a public service). Both types of arrangements allow a relatively small jurisdiction to realize scale economies in the provision of public services.

The Growth in Local Spending

As mentioned earlier in the chapter, local spending rose from 5 percent of GDP in 1950 to around 8 percent in the 1980s. This section explores some of the reasons for this growth in local public spending. Because total spending equals the quantity of output times unit cost, an increase in spending could be caused by an increase in unit cost, an increase in the quantity produced, or increases in both cost and quantity.

Increases in Labor Cost: The Baumol Model

Baumol (1967) argues that rising labor cost has contributed to increases in local spending. To explain the Baumol model, consider an economy that produces manufactured goods (watches) and personal services (haircuts, public education). The labor market has the following characteristics:

1. **Manufacturing productivity.** The productivity of manufacturing workers increases over time, a result of innovations that allow the substitution of capital for labor.
2. **Service productivity.** The productivity of service workers (barbers and teachers) is constant. A haircut is a nonstandardized good: every head has a different shape, and every customer wants a unique haircut. Since a barber cannot be replaced by a machine, productivity is constant. Like the barber, the teacher provides a nonstandardized output: every child enters the classroom with a different set of skills and educational needs, and requires personal attention. In addition, every child requires a different educational output. Given the difficulty of capital substitution, teacher productivity is constant.
3. **Worker mobility and wages.** Workers move costlessly between manufacturing and service jobs. In equilibrium, all workers earn the same daily wage.
4. **Fixed labor supply.** The total supply of workers is fixed.

Figure 16–6 shows the market for labor in the two-sector economy. The demand curves for both manufacturing and services are negatively sloped. In the initial equilibrium (points *B* and *C*), the wage is $13.

Suppose that the productivity of manufacturing workers increases. An increase in productivity shifts the demand curve for manufacturing workers to the right: at every wage, more workers are demanded. In the short run, the supply of manufacturing workers is fixed, so the manufacturing wage rises to $17 (point *F*).

In the long run, the increase in the manufacturing wage causes some service workers to switch to manufacturing jobs. As the quantity of manufacturing workers

FIGURE 16–6   Effects of Increased Manufacturing Productivity on Wages in the Service Sector

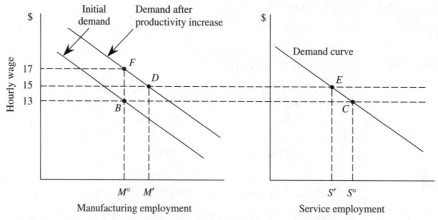

In the initial equilibrium (points *B* and *C*), the wage is $13. An increase in manufacturing productivity shifts the demand curve for manufacturing workers upward, causing excess demand for labor. As the manufacturing wage rises, service workers move to the manufacturing sector, causing a shortage in the service sector that increases the wage. In the new equilibrium (points *D* and *E*), the wage is $15.

increases, the manufacturing wage drops: the market moves downward along the new demand curve from point *F* toward point *D*. In addition, the decrease in the number of service workers causes a shortage of service workers, so the service wage increases: the market moves up the service demand curve, from point *C* toward point *E*. Equilibrium is restored when two conditions are satisfied. First, total employment in the two sectors equals the fixed supply of labor ($M° + S°$). Second, workers are indifferent between the two types of jobs. Workers will be indifferent if the two sectors pay the same wage. These two conditions are satisfied at points *D* and *E*.

What are the implications for the prices of manufacturing goods and services? Because the productivity of manufacturing workers increases over time, the increase in the wage is offset by increases in labor productivity, so production cost and market prices do not change. In contrast, the wages of service workers increase while their productivity is constant, so production cost and market prices increase over time. In other words, the price of haircuts and the unit cost of education increase over time.

Other local public goods share the personal-service features of haircuts and education. Consider the cost of police protection. Police officers interview witnesses and look for clues at the scenes of crimes. Neither of these tasks can be performed by a machine, so the growth in police productivity is relatively slow. The same is true for fire fighting: every fire presents a different set of circumstances, preventing the sort of capital substitution that occurs in the manufacturing sector. If the productivities of police and fire fighters are constant, an increase in wages (caused by an increase in the wage of manufacturers) increases the cost of police and fire protection.

Other Reasons for Rising Labor Cost

The Baumol model suggests that the labor cost of government increases because the government provides personal-service goods, not because public servants are lazy or greedy. There are two other possible reasons for increases in labor cost:

1. **Competition and innovation.** The nature of the public sector discourages innovation. Unlike a firm in a competitive market, the local government is shielded from competition, so there is less incentive to develop new labor-saving techniques. If this view is correct, the monopoly status of local government prevents innovations that would increase labor productivity.

2. **Union power.** Most government workers are represented by powerful labor unions. If unions use their power to increase the wages of government workers, public servants will be overpaid relative to their private-sector counterparts, increasing the cost of government. Freeman (1985) examined the wages of private and government employees. He compared the wages of public and private workers with similar qualifications (education, work experience, personal characteristics). He found that state and local administrators earn about 5 percent more than equally qualified private-sector workers, and public school teachers earn about 6 percent less than equally qualified private workers. On balance, it appears that the differences between private and government wages are relatively small. Freeman did not include pension plans in his analysis. Since public pension plans are generally more generous than private plans, the inclusion of pension benefits would increase public-sector wages relative to private-sector wages.

Increases in Quantity

An increase in local spending may be caused, in part, by an increase in the quantity of local services demanded. The Baumol model provides a useful framework for analyzing changes in the quantity of local public goods.

The quantity of education demanded changes over time for two reasons. The first is the **income effect.** The increase in manufacturing productivity increases the real income of the economy: the total output of the economy increases, increasing the purchasing power of its citizens. As real income increases, the citizens spend more on all normal goods, including education. In Figure 16–7, the demand curve for education shifts to the right: at every price, more education is demanded. At P', the quantity of education increases from $E°$ to E'.

The second reason the demand for education changes is the substitution effect. The **substitution effect** causes movement upward along the new demand curve. Because the productivity of manufacturing workers increases while the productivity of teachers is constant, the price of education increases relative to the price of other goods. As a result, consumers substitute manufactured goods for education (and other personal-service goods), decreasing the quantity of education demanded. In Figure

FIGURE 16–7   **Changes in the Quantity of Education Demanded**

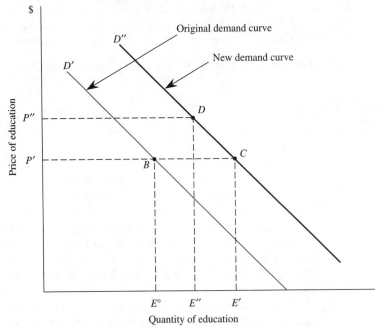

An increase in real income shifts the demand curve for education outward and increases the quantity demanded (the income effect: *B* to *C*). If the unit cost (price) of education increases from *P'* to *P''*, the quantity demanded decreases (the substitution effect: *C* to *D*). In this case, the income effect is large relative to the substitution effect, so the quantity demanded increases (*B* to *D*).

16–7, the price of education increases from *P'* to *P''*, and the substitution effect causes movement upward along the new demand curve from point *C* to *D*.

Figure 16–7 shows a net increase in the quantity of education demanded from *E°* to *E''*. The income effect (the outward shift of the demand curve) dominates the substitution effect (the upward movement along the new demand curve), so the equilibrium quantity of education increases. This occurs under the assumption that the income elasticity of demand for education is large relative to the price elasticity of demand. Total spending on education increases: the community consumes more education (*E''* instead of *E°*) at a higher unit cost (*P''* instead of *P'*).

Another possibility is that the quantity of education demanded decreases over time. If the income effect is small relative to the substitution effect (if the income elasticity is small relative to the price elasticity), the outward shift of the demand curve would be small relative to the movement up the new demand curve, and the quantity of education demanded would decrease. If this happens, total expenditures on education may either increase or decrease. If the decrease in the quantity demanded is large enough to offset the increase in unit cost, total expenditures would decrease. But if the decrease in quantity demanded is relatively small, total expenditures would increase.

Taxpayer Revolt: Expenditure Limits

As mentioned earlier, the share of GDP spent on local government has decreased since 1976. The decrease in the relative importance of local spending was caused in part by new restrictions on local taxes and spending. By 1981, a total of 30 states had tightened restrictions on local tax rates, tax revenue, and spending. According to Aronson and Hilley (1986), there is evidence that tax and expenditure limits have decreased local spending in Arizona, California, Colorado, Indiana, Iowa, and New Jersey.

Aronson and Hilley discuss the responses of local governments to the tax and expenditure limitations. Local governments have mitigated the effects of the limitations in four ways:

1. Local governments have shifted to user fees and taxes that are not subject to restrictions (income, sales, and business taxes).
2. Some spending programs have been transferred to special districts to evade the spending limits.
3. Intergovernmental grants from state governments have increased.
4. In cases where limits apply to specific spending categories, programs have been moved from restricted categories to unrestricted ones.

The debate over tax and spending limitations has been spirited. The supporters of limitations view local governments as inefficient monopolies. According to this view, the limitations force local governments to "cut out the fat" by increasing productivity and decreasing wages. According to Courant, Gramlich, and Rubinfeld (1987), many of the people who vote for tax and spending limitations hold this view.

The critics of tax and spending limitations believe that the Baumol model is applicable to the local public sector. They believe that the cost of local services has increased because of rising productivity in the private sector, not because public workers are lazy and wasteful. According to this view, there is little "fat" in the local public budget, so the spending limitations decrease the quantity of local public services. Another concern is that local tax limitations may increase the state involvement in local budget choices, decreasing local control of tax money.

Fiscal Health of Central Cities

Since the early 1970s, many cities have experienced serious fiscal problems. The most sensational episode was the near default of New York City in 1975. In many other cities, tax revenues have fallen short of the amount required to provide the typical or average level of public services, requiring either tax hikes or service cuts to prevent budget deficits. This part of the chapter explores some of the reasons for the fiscal problems experienced by central cities in the last few decades.

The most severe fiscal problems have been experienced by large, older cities in the northeastern and north-central states. There are several reasons for the fiscal problems of these cities:

1. **Suburbanization and the tax base.** The suburbanization of employment and population has decreased the city's tax bases (income, property, sales), decreasing tax revenue.

2. **Increase in production cost.** As the population of a city falls, the costs of urban services do not necessarily fall at the same rate. The reason is simple: if a city invests in plant and equipment for a city of 5 million, it pays the same capital cost for its streets, transit systems, schools, and fire stations even if its population drops to 4 million. A decrease in population increases per capita cost because there are fewer "capitas" to pay the cost.

3. **Inflexible labor force.** In some cities, labor unions are powerful enough to prevent layoffs when the city's population decreases. If a city maintains a constant work force as it shrinks, a fiscal squeeze is inevitable.

Peterson (1976) examined the sources of fiscal distress in declining cities during the 1970s. Compared to growing cities, declining cities had (1) larger public expenditures per capita, (2) more municipal employees per capita, (3) higher municipal wages, and (4) declining real tax bases. Why did declining cities have higher wages? According to Peterson, cities used the large federal grants of the 1960s and 1970s to increase the wages of municipal workers.

Ladd and Yinger (1989) developed an index of fiscal health and estimated the index for dozens of the nation's central cities. Figure 16–8 shows the values of the index for 19 cities. In the average city, the value of the index is zero. A city with a negative value is in worse shape than the average city; a city with a positive value is in better shape. The values of the index range from −87 in New Orleans to 49 in Greensboro, North Carolina. In the figure, cities are arranged, top to bottom, in decreasing order of total population. It's clear that the largest cities (at the top of the figure) are in the worst fiscal shape.

The Ladd-Yinger index is based on two assumptions. First, in each city, the tax system imposes the same burden on residents: residents of each city are assumed to pay 3 percent of their income in municipal taxes. Second, each city is assumed to provide the same level of public services. Under the assumption of a standardized package of taxes and services, this index shows the fiscal health of cities in the absence of intercity differences in taxes and spending.

The value of the fiscal health index indicates the fiscal deficit or surplus associated with the standard packages of taxes and services. If the value is negative, it indicates the percentage deficit resulting from the standard tax/service package. Alternatively, if the deficit is to be eliminated by intergovernmental grants, the index indicates the size of the transfer (as a percent of local revenue) required to fill the gap between local tax revenue and the cost of providing the standard service level. For example, New York's value is −83: to provide the standard level of public services with the standard tax system, the city would need a transfer equal to 83 percent of its tax revenue. If the value of the index is positive, it indicates the percentage surplus resulting from the standard tax/spending package. For example, High Point's value is 41: if the city were to provide the standard service package, the standard tax system would generate a surplus of 41 percent.

FIGURE 16–8   Standardized Fiscal Health of Selected Central Cities in 1988

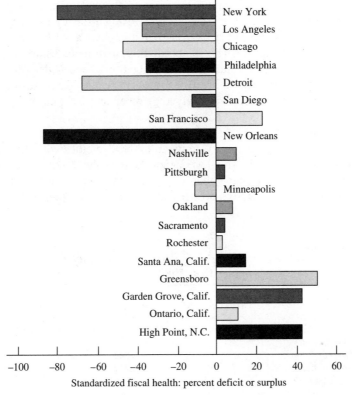

Standardized fiscal health: percent deficit or surplus

Definitions:

1. Negative value: percentage increase in revenue that a city would have to receive from an outside source to be able to provide the baseline quality at the standard tax burden.

2. Positive value: excess tax revenue (as a percent of total) after providing the baseline service quality at the standard tax burden.

SOURCE: Helen Ladd and John Yinger, *America's Ailing Cities: Fiscal Health and the Design of Urban Policy* (Baltimore: Johns Hopkins University Press, 1989), Table E.1.

The Ladd-Yinger index shows the effects of the economic environment on urban fiscal health. Since each city is assumed to provide the same services with the same tax system, fiscal problems are caused by either a relatively low tax base or a relatively high cost of providing the standard services. This approach ignores other possible sources of fiscal problems, including relatively low tax rates, relatively high service levels, or mismanagement. In the words of Ladd and Yinger, "We determine the fiscal cards each city is dealt; other approaches are needed to see how well each city plays its hand."

Revenue Capacity and Expenditure Needs

Ladd and Yinger examine both sides of the budget equation. The index of standardized fiscal health incorporates information about revenue-raising capacity and the cost of providing city services. A city's revenue-raising capacity is the amount of tax revenue generated by a tax system that imposes a burden on city residents equal to 3 percent of income. The standard tax system includes taxes on property, sales, and earnings. A city's standardized expenditure need is determined by the cost of providing the standard set of city services. To be considered healthy in a fiscal sense, a city must have either a relatively large revenue-raising capacity or a relatively low standardized expenditure need, or both.

Table 16–4 shows the characteristics of cities with small, medium, and large revenue-raising capacities. Compared to the five cities with the highest capacities, the five cities with the smallest capacities have about half the capacity. The second column of the table shows that, in general, there is a positive relationship between revenue-raising capacity and per capita income. The third column shows the em-

TABLE 16–4   Revenue-Raising Capacity and City Characteristics, 1982

	Revenue-Raising Capacity	Per Capita Income	Employment Ratio	Population (1,000)
Small Capacity				
Memphis, Tenn.	$282	$ 7,542	0.41	645
Jacksonville, Fla.	283	8,217	0.37	556
Philadelphia, Pa.	292	7,109	0.36	1,665
Portsmouth, Va.	306	7,382	0.22	105
Newark, N.J.	309	5,292	0.41	320
Medium Capacity				
Cleveland, Ohio	409	6,799	0.58	558
Akron, Ohio	409	8,106	0.46	231
Ontario, Calif.	409	7,967	0.21	96
Tampa, Fla.	427	7,855	0.63	276
High Point, N.C.	429	7,893	0.64	63
Large Capacity				
Rochester, N.Y.	527	8,072	0.73	243
Albany, N.Y.	565	8,305	0.60	100
Anaheim, Calif.	590	10,149	0.61	226
Salt Lake City, Utah	591	8,765	0.92	163
Ft. Lauderdale, Fla.	639	12,099	0.71	153
Average for small	294	7,108	0.35	658
Average for medium	417	7,724	0.50	245
Average for large	582	9,478	0.71	177

SOURCE: Helen Ladd and John Yinger, *America's Ailing Cities: Fiscal Health and the Design of Urban Policy* (Baltimore: Johns Hopkins University Press, 1989).

ployment ratios, defined as the number of private-sector jobs per city resident. A large employment ratio means that a large fraction of the city's work force lives outside the city but pays city taxes on sales and earnings. The payment of city taxes by outsiders increases the revenue raised by the standard tax system, so the revenue-raising capacity increases with the employment ratio. The fourth column shows that larger cities tend to have lower revenue-raising capacities. The larger the central city, the smaller the fraction of city taxes paid by outsiders, so the smaller the revenue raised by the standard tax system.

Consider next the standardized expenditure need. Table 16–5 shows the characteristics of cities with large, medium, and small expenditure needs. For the five cities with the largest expenditure needs, the average need is 2.4 times the average expenditure need of the five cities with the smallest needs. This index is derived from cost indices for three types of services: general services, police services, and fire services. The cost index shows the cost of providing the standard level of service relative to the cost incurred by the average city, with a value of 100 for the average city. For example, Newark's cost of general services was 2 percent above average, while its cost of police services was over seven times the average and its cost of fire services was over three times the average. Newark's value for standard expenditure need (170) suggests that its total costs were 70 percent above the average. In contrast, in Virginia Beach, the cost of the standard service package is about half the average cost.

Figure 16–9 shows the effects of various city characteristics on the cost of providing the standard service package. The cost elasticities provide a measure of the independent effects of the various characteristics on service costs. For example, the wage elasticity for general services is about 1.0, meaning that if two cities differ only in private-sector wages, a 10 percent difference in wages generates a 10 percent difference in the cost of providing general services. The elasticities of costs with respect to population are 0.14 for general services and 0.21 for police services. This means that a 10 percent difference in population between two cities causes a 1.4 percent difference in general costs and a 2.1 percent difference in police costs. These numbers suggest that in the cities studied by Ladd and Yinger, there are diseconomies of scale in providing general services and police services.

The cost of public services increases with the poverty rate and the fraction of the housing stock that is over 20 years old. In Figure 16–9, the elasticity of police costs with respect to the poverty rate is 1.1, meaning that a 10 percent difference in poverty rates between cities causes an 11 percent difference in the cost of police services. This occurs because crime rates and victimization rates are generally higher among the poor, so crime control is more costly. The elasticity of general costs with respect to the quantity of housing that is older than 20 years is 0.40: a 10 percent difference in the amount of old housing causes a 4 percent difference in general service costs. This occurs because cities with relatively old houses typically have relatively old public infrastructure as well, and old infrastructure has relatively high maintenance and repair costs. The elasticities for fire services (not shown in the figure) are 0.84 for the poverty rate and 0.40 for the amount of old housing. These elasticities reflect the fact that it is more costly to protect older, low-quality housing (typically occupied by the poor) from fire.

TABLE 16–5   Standard Expenditure Need and City Characteristics, 1982

	Standard Expenditure Need	General Cost	Police Cost	Fire Cost	Population (1,000)	Poverty Rate	Housing Over 20 Years Old	Metro Share	Employment Ratio
Large Need									
Newark, N.J.	170	102	710	344	320	44%	83%	17%	0.41
Cleveland, Ohio	145	151	300	218	558	29	89	29	0.58
Atlanta, Ga.	143	130	387	224	428	35	64	20	0.74
Detroit, Mich.	143	155	288	158	1,138	29	92	25	0.31
New York, N.Y.	141	124	474	113	7,086	26	79	86	0.41
Medium Need									
Milwaukee, Wis.	101	122	132	118	631	18	78	45	0.44
Sacramento, Calif.	100	121	123	125	288	19	57	26	0.41
Providence, R.I.	99	99	193	207	155	25	86	17	0.66
Indianapolis, Ind.	98	127	89	100	202	15	56	60	0.45
San Bernardino, Calif.	98	121	110	121	124	20	61	08	0.37
Small Need									
Pawtucket, R.I.	67	79	73	118	71	15	84	08	0.40
San Jose, Calif.	66	86	60	66	659	10	28	52	0.29
Garden Grove, Calif.	63	81	59	72	126	11	49	06	0.27
Hollywood, Fla.	58	74	51	70	122	09	35	10	0.43
Virginia Beach, Va.	52	70	38	43	282	11	21	37	0.19
Average large	148	132	432	211	1,906	33	81	35	0.49
Average medium	99	118	129	134	280	19	68	31	0.47
Average small	61	78	56	74	252	11	43	23	0.31

SOURCE: Helen Ladd and John Yinger, *America's Ailing Cities: Fiscal Health and the Design of Urban Policy* (Baltimore: Johns Hopkins University Press, 1989).

FIGURE 16–9   Elasticities of Service Costs with Respect to Various City Characteristics

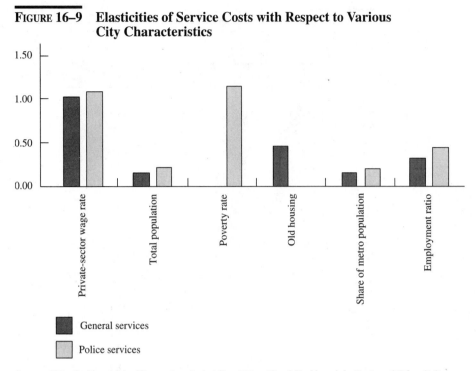

SOURCE: Helen Ladd and John Yinger, *America's Ailing Cities: Fiscal Health and the Design of Urban Policy* (Baltimore: Johns Hopkins University Press, 1989), Table 4.1.

The cost of providing the standard service package also depends on the role of the central city in the metropolitan economy. A central city that has a relatively small share of the metropolitan population has a higher cost because it provides services for its own residents as well as a relatively large number of commuters. The elasticities of general costs and police costs with respect to the metropolitan share of population are 0.14 and 0.19, respectively. The same phenomenon is reflected in the elasticities with respect to the employment ratio (jobs per city resident): a city with a large employment ratio provides services to more commuters and thus has a higher cost. The cost elasticities are 0.29 for general services and 0.40 for police and fire services.

The cost elasticities shown in Figure 16–9 are reflected in the data on standardized expenditure need in Table 16–5. Larger cities tend to have greater expenditure needs because of diseconomies of scale in providing public services. Cities with high poverty rates and relatively old housing have greater expenditure needs because they have higher police and fire costs. Finally, expenditure needs are higher in cities with relatively large numbers of commuters (cities with a small fraction of metropolitan population or large employment ratios).

Standard versus Actual Fiscal Health

Table 16–6 shows the characteristics of cities with low, medium, and high scores for standardized fiscal health. Larger cities and cities with relatively large numbers

TABLE 16–6   **Standard Fiscal Health and City Characteristics, 1982**

	Standard Economic Health	Population (1,000)	Per Capita Income	Poverty Rate	Housing Over 20 Years Old	Employment Ratio
Low Score						
Newark, N.J.	−110	320	$5,292	44%	83%	0.41
New York, N.Y.	−105	7,086	8,736	26	79	0.41
Detroit, Mich.	−92	1,138	7,090	29	92	0.31
New Orleans, La.	−73	564	8,017	33	73	0.39
Philadelphia, Pa.	−60	1,665	7,109	27	85	0.36
Medium Score						
Norfolk, Va.	−8	266	7,408	23	69	0.36
Pittsburgh, Pa.	−8	414	8,277	21	88	0.68
Omaha, Neb.	−6	328	9,194	14	64	0.51
Long Beach, Calif.	−5	371	9,978	18	74	0.36
St. Paul, Minn.	−3	275	9,173	14	75	0.55
High Score						
Warwick, R.I.	33	86	9,084	09	64	0.34
Anaheim, Calif.	33	226	10,149	10	36	0.61
Garden Grove, Calif.	44	126	9,668	11	49	0.27
Ft. Lauderdale, Fla.	45	153	12,099	18	43	0.71
Hollywood, Fla.	47	122	10,752	09	35	0.43
Average low	−88	2,155	7,249	32	82	0.38
Average medium	−6	331	8,806	18	74	0.49
Average high	40	143	10,350	11	45	0.47

SOURCE: Helen Ladd and John Yinger, *America's Ailing Cities: Fiscal Health and the Design of Urban Policy* (Baltimore: Johns Hopkins University Press, 1989).

of poor people have relatively small revenue-raising capacities and relatively large expenditure needs, so they have low scores for standardized fiscal health. Similarly, cities with relatively low per capita incomes and relatively high poverty rates have problems on both sides of the budget equation, so they have low scores for fiscal health. Ladd and Yinger estimate that 68 percent of the variation across cities in fiscal health scores results from differences in population, per capita income, and poverty rates. Other characteristics that affect fiscal health are (1) the fraction of the city's housing stock that is over 20 years old and (2) the central city's share of metropolitan population. In contrast, the employment ratio has a very weak effect on fiscal health: the presence of commuters is a mixed blessing. Although commuters pay taxes (and increase the city's revenue-raising capacity), they also require services (and increase the standard expenditure need). According to Ladd and Yinger, these two effects cancel each other out, so everything else being equal, an increase in the employment ratio does not have much effect on standardized fiscal health.

How do state and federal policies affect the fiscal health of cities? The policies of higher levels of government affect the fiscal circumstances of cities in three ways:

1. **Grants.** Cities receive grants from the states and the national government.

2. **Service responsibilities.** The states specify which public services will be provided by cities. For example, in some states, cities are responsible for providing education.

3. **Tax restrictions.** The states impose restrictions on city taxes. For example, some states prohibit city taxes on earnings (payroll taxes).

To estimate a city's actual fiscal health, Ladd and Yinger adjusted the scores for standardized fiscal health to incorporate the effects of these state and federal policies.

Figure 16–10 shows the effect of state and federal policies on the fiscal health of cities with low, medium, and high scores for standardized health. The computations are based on data from 1982, before the large decreases in state and federal grants. For the five cities with the lowest scores for standardized health, the average health score rises from −88 to −42. In other words, the gap between total revenue and the cost of providing the standard service package is cut in half. For cities with medium and high values of standardized health, the involvement of state and local governments decreases fiscal health: the positive effect of grants is more than offset by the greater service responsibilities and tax restrictions. In general, it is clear that state and federal policies decreased the intercity differences in fiscal health.

FIGURE 16–10   Effects of State and Federal Governments on the Fiscal Health of Cities

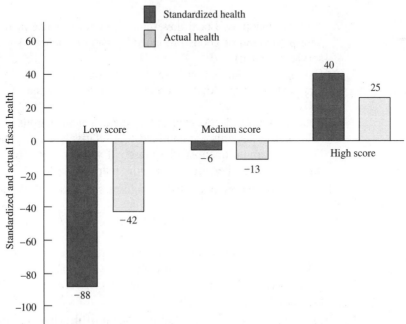

SOURCE: Helen Ladd and John Yinger, *America's Ailing Cities: Fiscal Health and the Design of Urban Policy* (Baltimore: Johns Hopkins University Press, 1989).

Between 1982 and 1988, two trends had conflicting effects on the fiscal health of cities. First, the national economy grew steadily and per capita income increased. In most cities, the increase in income increased the tax base and decreased service cost. Second, state and federal assistance from intergovernmental grants decreased. According to Ladd and Yinger, the positive effect of rising income was almost completely offset by the negative effect of less grant money, so there was little change in the average fiscal health of cities between 1982 and 1988.

Summary

1. There are over 86,000 local governments in the United States, including municipalities, school districts, counties, and special districts. Municipalities are responsible for about 33 percent of local-government spending, and school districts are responsible for about 30 percent. The largest spending program is education (42 percent of local-government spending).

2. In 1986, 37 percent of local revenue came from taxes on property, income, and sales, and 40 percent came from intergovernmental grants. The rest of local money comes from user fees and charges. The fraction of local funds from intergovernmental grants has decreased steadily since the late 1970s.

3. The national government is responsible for stabilization and redistribution policies.

4. Local governments are involved in resource allocation for three types of goods.
   a. Natural monopoly. Local governments either produce or regulate the private production of goods produced by natural monopolies (water, sewage services, transit).
   b. Externalities. One option is for the government to provide goods that generate externalities. Another option is to internalize the externality with a subsidy.
   c. Local public goods. A local public good is nonrivalrous and nonexcludable, and its benefits are confined to a relatively small geographical area. For the optimum quantity, the marginal social benefit (the sum of the marginal private benefits) equals the marginal cost.

5. There are advantages and disadvantages associated with the local provision of public goods.
   a. Local governments promote efficiency if there is diversity in demand for public goods.
   b. Local governments inhibit efficiency if the benefits or costs of public goods spill over into other jurisdictions (externalities).
   c. Local governments inhibit efficiency if there are scale economies in the production of public goods.

6. Local provision of a public good is efficient if the diversity in demand for local public goods is large relative to externalities and scale economies.

7. Metropolitan consolidation has been advocated as a way to prevent suburban exploitation, exploit scale economies, equalize tax rates, and equalize spending.

8. The Baumol model suggests that increases in the labor cost of personal services (haircuts and education) result from rising productivity in manufacturing, which pulls up the wages of all workers.
   a. Other theories of rising labor cost focus on the monopoly power of local governments and labor unions.
   b. The quantity of public services demanded will increase if the income effect (from rising productivity) is large relative to the substitution effect (from rising unit cost).

9. Between the late 1970s and 1981, a total of 30 states tightened restrictions on local tax rates, tax revenue, and spending.

10. Since the early 1970s, many cities have experienced serious fiscal problems. The most severe fiscal problems have been experienced by large, older cities with declining populations and employment.

11. The index of standardized fiscal health shows the fiscal health of cities in the absence of intercity differences in taxes and spending.

12. The cost of providing city services depends on the characteristics of the city.
    a. The elasticity of general costs with respect to population is 0.14, meaning there are diseconomies of scale in providing general services.
    b. The elasticity of police costs with respect to the poverty rate is 1.1: a 10 percent difference in poverty rates between cities causes an 11 percent difference in the cost of police services.
    c. The cost of providing the standard service package increases with the number of commuters working in the city.

13. Larger cities and cities with relatively large numbers of poor people have relatively small revenue-raising capacities and relatively large expenditure needs, so they have low scores for standardized fiscal health. About 68 percent of the variation across cities in fiscal health scores results from differences in population, per capita income, and poverty rates.

14. State and federal policies (grants, mandates, and tax restrictions) decrease the differences in fiscal health across cities.

Exercises and Discussion Questions

1. Why do we have public libraries? Why don't people rent books from firms, just as they rent trucks, Rototillers, and videos? If we have U-Haul, why not U-Read; if we have Captain Video, why not Captain Book?

2. Figure 16–5 showing the marginal social benefit of local parks assumes that there is no congestion in the use of the parks, that is, the good is literally nonrivalrous.

     a. Draw a new MSB curve under the assumption that congestion occurs.

     b. What are the implications for the optimum park acreage? Does it increase or decrease?

3. Consider Metro, a metropolitan area with three school districts, East, West, and North. There are externalities in the provision of education, but there are no scale economies in the provision of schools. Suppose that the three districts are consolidated into a single metropolitan school district. Will it be more or less efficient than the original arrangement?

4. Consider Metro, a metropolitan area with two municipalities, Sportville (high demand for parks) and Slothburg (low demand for parks). The provision of parks is subject to scale economies (the cost per acre of parks is lower under metropolitan management) and generates externalities. Suppose that the two municipalities are consolidated into a single metropolitan government. Under what circumstances will total expenditures on parks decrease?

5. Consider Metro, a metropolitan area with two municipalities, each of which has a small police force. The only activity of the police is chasing criminals: the police never capture criminals but simply cause them to move to another municipality.

     a. Suppose that the provision of police services is subject to scale economies. If the two municipal police forces are consolidated into a single metropolitan force, will total expenditures on police services increase, decrease, or stay the same?

     b. If you don't have enough information to answer the question, describe the information you need and explain how you would use it.

6. In the city of Crewville, everyone gets crew cuts: the output of the barber is standardized. The output of the teacher is also standardized: the only objective is to teach children how to add and subtract. Will the costs of haircuts and education increase relative to the cost of manufactured goods over time?

7. Consider the cost of admission to a performance by a popular rock band. Would you expect the relative cost of admission to increase over time (relative to the price of manufactured goods)?

References and Additional Readings

Overview

Advisory Commission on Intergovernmental Relations. *Significant Features of Fiscal Federalism.* Washington, D.C.: U.S. Government Printing Office, 1987.

Inman, Robert P. "The Fiscal Performance of Local Governments: An Interpretive Review." In *Current Issues in Urban Economics,* ed. Peter Mieszkowski and Mahlon Straszheim. Baltimore: Johns Hopkins University Press, 1979, pp. 270–321. Summarizes studies of the price and income elasticities of demand for local public goods and the elasticity of local expenditures with respect to intergovernmental aid.

Musgrave, Richard A., and Peggy B. Musgrave. *Public Finance in Theory and Practice.* New York: McGraw-Hill, 1980.

U.S. Bureau of the Census. *Census of Governments.* Washington, D.C.: Government Printing Office, 1987.

———. *City Government Finances.* Washington, D.C.: Department of Commerce, 1987.

———. *Statistical Abstract of the United States.* Washington, D.C.: U.S. Government Printing Office, 1990.

The Role of Local Government in the Federal System

Break, George. *Financing Government in a Federal System.* Washington, D.C.: Brookings Institution, 1980.

Oates, Wallace E. *Fiscal Federalism.* New York: Harcourt Brace Jovanovich, 1972. Analyzes the division of responsibilities between different levels of government, focusing on spillovers, scale economies, and diversity in demand.

Olson, Mancur. "The Principle of Fiscal Equivalence: The Division of Responsibilities among Different Levels of Government." *American Economic Review* 59 (1969), pp. 479–87. Argues that the federal system is required to control benefit spillovers.

Stigler, George J. "The Tenable Range of Functions of Local Government." In *Private Wants and Public Needs*, ed. Edmund S. Phelps. New York: Norton, 1965.

Municipal versus Metropolitan Government

Bahl, Roy, and David Puryear. "Regional Tax Base Sharing: Possibilities and Implications." *National Tax Journal* 29 (1976), pp. 328–35.

Bollens, John C., and Henry J. Schmandt. *The Metropolis.* New York: Harper & Row, 1982. Describes the metropolitan federation form of government, under which some public services are provided by a metropolitan government and others by small local governments.

Bradford, David, and Wallace E. Oates. "Suburban Exploitation of Central Cities and Government Structure." In *Redistribution through Public Choice*, ed. Harold Hochman and George Peterson. New York: Columbia University Press, 1974. Discusses the suburban exploitation hypothesis and predicts the effects of metropolitan consolidation on tax rates, expenditure levels, and income segregation.

Greene, Kenneth V., and Thomas J. Parliament. "Political Externalities, Efficiency, and the Welfare Losses from Consolidation." *National Tax Journal* 33 (1980), pp. 209–17. A study of the efficiency effects of metropolitan consolidation.

Reschovsky, Andrew. "An Evaluation of Metropolitan Area Tax Base Sharing." *National Tax Journal* 33 (1980), pp. 55–66. Describes the experience with tax-base sharing in Minneapolis–St. Paul.

Scale Economies in the Provision of Local Public Goods

Advisory Commission on Intergovernmental Relations. *Intergovernmental Service Arrangements for Delivering Local Public Services: Update 1983.* Washington, D.C.: U.S. Government Printing Office, 1985. A survey of the use of intergovernmental and joint-service contracts in the provision of local public services.

Gardner, John L. "City Size and Municipal Service Costs." In *Urban Growth Policy in a Market Economy*, ed. George S. Tolley, Philip E. Graves, and John L. Gardner. New York: Academic Press, 1979, pp. 51–61. Examines the relationship between public-service costs and city size, controlling for the fact that the demand for public services depends on income, which varies across cities. Concludes that cost per family increases with city size and decreases as population density increases.

Gyimahbrempong, K. "Economies of Scale in Municipal Police Departments—The Case of Florida." *Review of Economics and Statistics* 69 (1987), pp. 352–56.

Hines, Lawrence G. "The Long-Run Cost Function of Water Production for Selected Wisconsin Communities." *Land Economics* 45 (1969), pp. 133–40. Detects scale economies in the provision of water services.

Hirsch, Werner. "Expenditure Implications of Metropolitan Growth and Consolidation." *Review of Economics and Statistics* 41 (1959), pp. 234–35. Estimates the degree of scale economies for police, fire protection, and public schools. Did not detect scale economies for police services or public schools. Found scale economies for fire protection up to a population of about 100,000.

Neutze, G. M. *Economic Policy and the Size of Cities.* Canberra: Australian National University, 1965. Discusses scale economies in the provision of urban services.

Walzer, Norman. "Economies of Scale and Municipal Police Services: The Illinois Experience." *Review of Economics and Statistics* 54 (1972), pp. 431–38. Suggests that there are small scale economies in the provision of police services for small cities (up to 140,000 population).

Rising Cost of Government and the Tax Revolt

Aronson, J. Richard, and John L. Hilley. *Financing State and Local Governments.* Washington, D.C.: Brookings Institution, 1986. Chapter 12 discusses revenue and expenditure limits and the responses of local governments to the limits.

Baumol, William. "The Macroeconomics of Unbalanced Growth: The Anatomy of Urban Crisis." *American Economic Review* 65 (1967), pp. 414–26.

Bradford, David F.; R. A. Malt; and Wallace E. Oates. "The Rising Cost of Local Public Services: Some Evidence and Reflections." *National Tax Journal* 22 (1969), pp. 415–26.

Brennan, Geoffrey. "Tax Limits and the Logic of Constitutional Restrictions." Chapter 6 in *Tax and Expenditure Limitations*, ed. Helen Ladd and Nicholas Tideman. Washington, D.C.: Urban Institute, 1987, pp. 121–38.

Courant, Paul; Edward Gramlich; and Daniel Rubinfeld. "Why Voters Support Tax Limitation Amendments: The Michigan Case." Chapter 3 in *Tax and Expenditure Limitations,* ed. Helen Ladd and Nicholas Tideman. Washington, D.C.: Urban Institute, 1987, pp. 37–72.

Freeman, Richard B. "How Do Public Sector Waste and Employment Respond to Economic Conditions?" Working Paper no. 1653, National Bureau of Economic Research, Cambridge, Mass., 1985.

Ladd, Helen F. "An Economic Evaluation of State Limitations on Local Tax and Spending Powers." *National Tax Journal* 31 (1978), pp. 1–18. Explores the reasons behind tax revolts.

Ladd, Helen F., and Julie Boatwright Wilson. "Why Voters Support Tax Limitations: Evidence from Massachusetts' Proposition 2 1/2." *National Tax Journal* 35 (1982), pp. 137–40.

Musgrave, Richard. "Leviathan Cometh–Or Does He?" Chapter 5 in *Tax and Expenditure Limitations,* ed. Helen Ladd and Nicholas Tideman. Washington, D.C.: Urban Institute, 1987, pp. 77–120.

Oakland, William. "Proposition 13: Genesis and Consequences." *National Tax Journal* 32 (1979), pp. 387–409. Discusses the reasons for the tax revolt in the state of California.

Rabushka, A., and P. Ryan. *The Tax Revolt.* Stanford: Hoover Institution, 1982. Discusses the attempts by citizens to control government spending by tax and expenditure limitations.

Fiscal Health and Distress

Bradbury, Katharine L.; Anthony Downs; and Kenneth A. Small. *Urban Decline and the Future of American Cities.* Washington, D.C.: Brookings Institution, 1982. Discusses the reasons for the economic problems of cities.

Humphrey, Nance; George Peterson; and Peter Wilson. *The Future of Cleveland's Capital Plant.* Washington, D.C.: Urban Institute, 1979. Discusses the fiscal problems of Cleveland.

Ladd, Helen, and John Yinger. *America's Ailing Cities: Fiscal Health and the Design of Urban Policy.* Baltimore: Johns Hopkins University Press, 1989. A comprehensive study of the factors that determine a city's fiscal health.

Oakland, William H. "Central Cities: Fiscal Plight and Prospects for Reform." In *Current Issues in Urban Economics,* ed. Peter Mieszkowski and Mahlon Straszheim. Baltimore: Johns Hopkins University Press, 1979, pp. 322–58. Discusses the sources of central-city fiscal distress, suggesting that fiscal distress is caused in large part by the attempt of local governments to redistribute income. Suggests that intergovernmental grants should be designed to compensate local governments for the money spent on high-cost, low-revenue citizens.

Peterson, George E. "Finance." In *The Urban Predicament,* ed. William Gorham and Nathan Glazer. Washington, D.C.: Urban Institute, 1976. Provides a comprehensive analysis of the reasons for the fiscal crises of large cities and suggests ways to avoid future problems.

Reischauer, Robert; Peter Clark; and Peggy Cuciti. *New York City's Fiscal Problem.* Washington, D.C.: Congressional Budget Office, 1975. A detailed discussion of the fiscal problems experienced by New York City.

Privatization

Savas, E. S. *Privatizing the Public Sector.* Chatham, N.J.: Chatham House, 1982. Argues for shifting the responsibility for providing some public services to the private sector.

Stevens, Barbara J. *Delivering Municipal Services Efficiently: A Comparison of Municipal and Private Sector Delivery: Summary.* Report no. 3744, U.S. Department of Housing and Urban Development, Washington, D.C., June 1984. Compares the costs of providing municipal services by local governments and by private firms (through the contracting process). Concludes that government cost was substantially higher.

Voting with Ballots and Feet

This chapter discusses two ways that citizens express their preferences for local government. One option is to vote in budget elections and in other elections that pick mayors, city council members, and other local officials. The policy question is whether voting in local elections promotes efficiency in local government. Specifically, under majority rule, do local governments provide the optimum level of local public goods? A second option for citizens is to express their preferences by voting with their feet. The typical large metropolitan area, with its large number of local governments, provides citizens with a wide range of choices for local tax and spending programs. One way to get a better combination of local services and taxes is to move to another jurisdiction. The policy question is whether this foot voting promotes efficiency in local government. Specifically, would the consolidation of several municipalities into a metropolitan government improve the efficiency of the local public sector?

Voting with Ballots: The Median-Voter Rule

Local governments must decide how much of a local public good to provide. One approach to local decision making is to hold an election and let voters decide how much to spend on a local public good. Will voters choose the optimum amount of a local public good?

Recall the example (from the previous chapter) of the three-person city that must decide how many acres of public parks to provide. In Figure 17–1, the marginal-benefit curves show the willingness to pay for different amounts of parks: Sam has a low demand for parks and prefers them relatively small (MB_s); Marian has a medium demand and prefers medium-sized parks (MB_m); Bertha has a high demand and prefers big parks (MB_b). If there are no interjurisdictional spillovers, the marginal social benefit is the sum of the marginal benefits of the three citizens. At the optimum

FIGURE 17–1   Provision of Parks under Majority Rule and Benefit Taxation

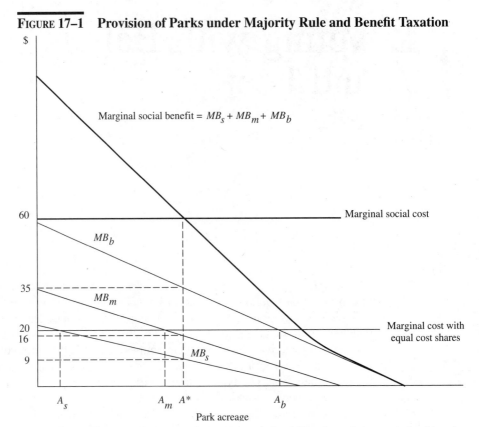

The optimum park acreage is A^* (the amount where the marginal social benefit equals the marginal social cost). If each household pays $20 per acre, the preferred amounts are A_s, A_m, and A_b. Under majority voting, the preferred size of the median voter (A_m) is chosen. Under a benefit tax, each household pays a tax (per acre) equal to its marginal benefit at the optimum park size (A^*), so there will be unanimous support for the optimum park size.

acreage, the marginal social benefit of park acreage equals its marginal social cost. In Figure 17–1, the marginal cost is $60 per acre, so the optimum acreage is A^*.

The city must pick a tax system to finance the provision of parks. Suppose that the city divides park costs equally among its three citizens. If the marginal cost is $60 per acre, every citizen pays $20 per acre of park land. What are the preferred park sizes for the three citizens? The preferred size of a particular voter is the acreage such that the marginal private cost equals the marginal private benefit. In Figure 17–1, the marginal private cost is the horizontal line at $20. For Sam, the cost curve intersects the benefit curve at a park size of A_s acres, so his preferred size is A_s acres. For the other two citizens, the preferred sizes are A_m and A_b.

Suppose that the city holds a series of elections in which citizens vote for one of two proposed park sizes. In an election between A_s and A_m, there is one vote for A_s (Sam), but two votes for A_m (Marian and Bertha), so A_m wins the election. A_m also wins an election against A_b: Sam and Marian vote for A_m. A_m wins both elections because it meets the preferred budget of the median voter (the voter that splits the rest of the voting public into two equal halves). The preferred budget of the median voter wins an election against a smaller size (as Bertha joins the median voter to make the vote 2 to 1) and any larger size (as Sam joins the median voter to make the vote 2 to 1). This is the **median-voter result:** if the spending level for a public good is determined by a majority vote, the winning budget is the preferred budget of the median voter.

In Figure 17–1, the size chosen by voters (A_m) is less than the optimum size (A^*). Is this an artifact of the election sequence, or would A_m win a direct election against the optimum? In an election between A_m and A^*, Sam would join Marian in voting for A_m because A_m is closer to Sam's preferred size. Therefore, A_m defeats the optimum size in a direct election.

The power—and inefficiency—of the median-voter result can be shown by considering the effects of changes in Bertha's preferences. Suppose that her marginal-benefit curve shifts upward by 100 percent: for every size, her willingness to pay for parks doubles. Because the marginal-social-benefit curve is the vertical sum of the individual marginal-private-benefit curves, the social-benefit curve would also shift upward, and the optimum park size would increase by a large amount. Nonetheless, voters still choose A_m: Sam joins with Marian to defeat any size above A_m. The same is true of changes in the other nonmedian benefit curve MB_s. The voting outcome depends only on the position of the median voter's marginal-benefit curve.

Benefit Taxation

Majority voting is inefficient because the costs of the public good are divided equally among the three voters. An alternative approach is to allocate park cost according to the willingness to pay for parks: the greater the citizen's willingness to pay, the higher the tax liability. This is the **Lindahl approach** to local decision making (named after Erik Lindahl): according to the **benefit principle,** tax liabilities are based on the benefits received from public goods.

Figure 17–1 shows how benefit taxes work. Suppose that the government knows the marginal-benefit curves of its citizens. It announces that Sam's tax liability per acre is $9, Marian's is $16, and Bertha's is $35. Given these private costs, all three citizens have the same preferred park size, A^*, which also happens to be the optimum size. In this case, the government is clever enough to figure out how much individual citizens are willing to pay for different levels of the local public good, and it sets each citizen's tax equal to his or her marginal willingness to pay. Sam (who prefers small parks) agrees to a larger park because he faces a lower tax liability: he pays $9 per acre instead of $20. Bertha (who prefers big parks) gets a larger park at a cost: she pays $35 per acre instead of $20. Under benefit taxation, citizens with larger benefits pay higher taxes.

Is the benefit principle practical? One problem with this approach is that the government doesn't know the shapes of the marginal-benefit curves of individual citizens, so it can't estimate the appropriate taxes for them. Moreover, there is little incentive for taxpayers with relatively high benefits to reveal their willingness to pay for local public goods: in doing so, they would be volunteering to pay higher taxes. It may be rational for high demanders to hide their true preferences in the hope that someone else will pay for the public good. This is the **free-rider problem:** citizens may understate their willingness to pay in an attempt to get a free ride.

Budget Elections and the Median Voter

The median-voter result is applicable to a wide variety of election formats. For example, if a school district holds a series of elections to determine its budget, the winning budget is the preferred budget of the median voter. To show this, consider a school district with the following characteristics:

1. **Citizens' preferences.** Citizens have different preferences for school spending. Table 17–1 shows the preferred budgets for seven voters in the school district. Voter A's preferred budget is $49, voter B's is $56, and so on.
2. **Series of elections.** The school board proposes a budget and holds an election in which citizens vote yes or no. If a given budget proposal fails to receive a majority of votes, the school board will decrease its proposed budget by $10 and hold another election. This process continues until a majority of citizens vote in favor of the budget.

Under this election scheme, the school district chooses the largest budget receiving majority support.

Suppose that the school board starts with a budget of $90. The voters know that if the $90 budget fails, the board will propose an $80 budget in the second election. A citizen votes yes if the $90 budget is better than an $80 budget (if the citizen's preferred budget is greater than $85). For example, voter F votes against the $90 budget because an $80 budget is closer to his preferred budget ($84). G is the only voter who votes for the $90 budget, so the first budget proposal loses by a vote of 6 to 1. The second proposal ($80) fails by a vote of 4 to 3: only citizens with preferred budgets greater than $75 vote yes.

TABLE 17–1   **The Median Voter in a Series of School Budget Elections**

Voter	Preferred Budget	Vote with $90 Budget	Vote with $80 Budget	Vote with $70 Budget
A	$49	N	N	N
B	$56	N	N	N
C	$63	N	N	N
D	$70	N	N	Y
E	$77	N	Y	Y
F	$84	N	Y	Y
G	$91	Y	Y	Y

A proposed budget of $70 wins an election by a vote of 4 to 3. All citizens with a preferred budget greater than $65 (citizens D, E, F, and G) vote for the $70 budget. The $70 budget proposal is successful because it's the preferred budget of the median voter. A $70 budget splits the voters into two equal halves, with half preferring a larger budget (E, F, G) and half preferring a smaller budget (A, B, C). By threatening to propose a smaller budget in the next election, the school board convinces citizens with preferred budgets above the median budget (E, F, G) to vote for the $70 budget; combined with the vote of the median voter (D), this generates a majority in favor of the proposed budget.

In this example, the school district decreases its proposed budget in $10 increments, from $90 down to the preferred budget of the median voter. The same result would occur if the board decreased the proposed budget in increments of $1. Similarly, the same result occurs if the school district reverses the direction of the budget sequence: if it starts out with a low budget and works its way upward, the median voter is still decisive.

The Median Voter in a Representative Democracy

In a **representative democracy,** decisions about budgets are made by elected officials. Citizens make budgetary decisions indirectly, by electing people whose budget philosophies are consistent with their own preferences. For example, Bill votes for the mayoral candidate whose expressed position on the city budget is closest to Bill's preferred budget.

To explain the budget choices in a representative democracy, consider a city that provides a single local public good (police services). The city has the following characteristics:

1. **Two candidates.** There are two candidates for mayor, Penny (a low spender) and Buck (a big spender).
2. **Single issue.** The only issue in the election is the police budget, which is set by the mayor.
3. **Citizen choice.** Every citizen votes for the candidate whose proposed police budget is closest to the citizen's preferred budget.
4. **Distribution of preferences.** Figure 17–2 shows the distribution of budget preferences. The horizontal axis measures the police budget, and the vertical axis measures the number of votes for a given budget. For example, 10 citizens have a preferred budget of $2, 15 have a preferred budget of $3, and so on. The distribution of budget preferences is symmetric, and the median budget (the budget that splits the rest of the voters into two equal halves) is $6.

Suppose that the candidates start out with different proposed police budgets: Penny proposes a budget of $4, and Buck proposes $8. Citizens with preferred budgets less than or equal to $5 vote for Penny (70 votes), and those with preferred budgets greater than or equal to $7 vote for Buck (70 votes). The two candidates split the 30 voters with a preferred budget of $6 (halfway between the two proposed budgets), so each candidate gets a total of 85 votes. The election results in a tie vote.

FIGURE 17–2   **The Median Voter in a Representative Democracy**

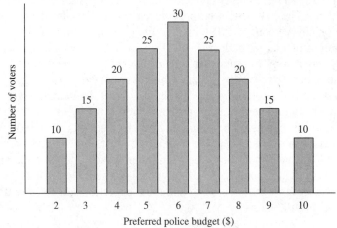

Citizens have different preferences for the police budget. If Penny proposes a budget of $4 and Buck proposes a budget of $8, the election will result in a tie vote: the two candidates split the votes of citizens with $6 preferred budgets, while Penny gets the votes of those with lower preferred budgets, and Buck gets the votes of those with higher budgets. By moving toward the median budget, Penny can increase her chances of being elected. In equilibrium, both candidates propose the budget of the median voter ($6).

Penny could increase her chance of being elected by increasing her proposed budget. Suppose that she proposes $5 instead of $4. She picks up all 30 votes of the citizens with a $6 preferred budget (Penny's $5 proposal is closer than Buck's $8), and she wins the election by a vote of 100 (10 + 15 + 20 + 25 + 30) to 70 (25 + 20 + 15 + 10). If Buck responds by decreasing his proposed budget to $7, the election results in a tie vote again. Penny and Buck will continue to revise their proposed budgets until each candidate's budget is close to the budget of the median voter ($6).

This example shows that the median-voter result occurs in a representative democracy. In equilibrium, both candidates propose a budget equal to the preferred budget of the median voter. Since both candidates have virtually the same proposed budget, it doesn't matter which candidate actually wins the election. In either case, the median voter determines the size of the police budget.

Implications of the Median-Voter Rule

There are four implications of the median-voter rule:

1. **Inefficient voting outcome.** There is nothing that guarantees that the preferred budget of the median voter is the optimum budget (the budget at which the marginal social cost of spending equals the marginal social benefit).

2. **Predicting election outcomes.** To predict the outcome of an election, one needs to (*a*) identify the median voter and (*b*) estimate his or her preferred budget. As a practical matter, it may be difficult to identify the median voter. One approach is to assume that the desired spending depends only on income. Under this assumption, the median voter is the voter with the median income. To the extent that desired spending depends on other variables (household size, age, political philosophy), this approach generates inaccurate predictions.

3. **Estimating the income elasticity.** Differences in income cause differences in spending on local public services. These differences can be used to compute the income elasticity of demand for local public services. To explain, consider two cities: city S has a small police budget ($100 per capita) and a low median income ($1,000), and city L has a large police budget ($125 per capita) and high median income ($1,200). Assume that the "price" of police services (the opportunity cost of money spent on police) is the same in the two cities. The income elasticity of demand for police services is defined as the percentage change in the police budget divided by the percentage change in income. City L, with 20 percent higher income, has a 25 percent larger police budget, so the income elasticity of demand is 1.25 (25 percent divided by 20 percent). Inman (1979) summarizes the results of empirical studies based on the median-voter model. As shown in Table 17–2, the income elasticities for most local goods are less than 1.0.

4. **Estimating price elasticity.** If there is variation across communities in the price of local public goods, the median-voter model can also be used to estimate the price elasticity of demand for public goods. To plot the demand curve for local spending, one needs information on price (the opportunity cost of local spending) and quantity (the local spending level). The price elasticity can then be computed from the demand curve. As shown in Table 17–2, the demands for local public goods are

TABLE 17–2   **Income and Price Elasticities of Demand for Local Public Goods**

Public Good or Service	Price Elasticity	Income Elasticity
Total expenditures	−0.23 to −0.56	0.34 to 0.89
Education	−0.07 to −0.51	0.24 to 0.85
Parks and recreation	−0.19 to −0.92	0.99 to 1.32
Public safety (police and fire)	−0.19 to −1.00	0.52 to 0.71
Public works	−0.92 to −1.00	0.79

SOURCE: Robert Inman, "The Fiscal Performance of Local Governments," in *Current Issues in Urban Economics*, ed. Peter Mieszkowski and Mahlon Straszheim (Baltimore: Johns Hopkins University Press, 1979).

price-inelastic: the price elasticities are all less than or equal to 1.0 (in absolute value). Some of the implications of these elasticities are discussed in Chapter 18 (Local Taxes and Intergovernmental Grants).

Qualifications of the Median-Voter Model

The median-voter model has a number of unrealistic assumptions. Although the model provides a useful framework for thinking about local-government decisions, it should be used with caution. There are three assumptions that limit the model's applicability:

1. **Ideology.** The politicians in the model care only about winning elections, so they slavishly adhere to voter preferences. An alternative assumption is that candidates base their positions on ideology. An ideological candidate uses the election campaign to persuade voters that her position is the correct one, playing the role of a leader, not a follower. In a model with ideological candidates, there is no reason to expect that the choice of the median voter will prevail.

2. **Single issue.** There is a single issue in the simple median-voter model. If there are several election issues (e.g., the police budget, the park budget, policies for the homeless), candidates offer package deals to voters. Unless the same citizen is the median voter on every issue, the winning budget is not the preferred budget of the median voter.

3. **All citizens vote.** In the median-voter model, all citizens vote. In the typical budget election, only a fraction of eligible voters actually cast ballots. A rational citizen abstains from voting if the cost of voting (the time and monetary costs of becoming informed and going to the polls) exceeds the benefit. The benefit of voting is relatively small if (a) the two proposed budgets are so close to one another that it makes little difference which person is elected (indifference), or (b) the proposed budget of the best candidate is so far from the citizen's preferred budget that the citizen is alienated from the election process (alienation). If some citizens abstain from voting, the median-voter result will not necessarily occur.

Voting with Feet: The Tiebout Model

Most metropolitan areas in the United States have dozens of municipalities, school districts, and other local governments. A model developed by Tiebout (1956) shows the role of consumer choice in the development of our fragmented system of local governments. The idea is that people vote with their feet, choosing the local government that provides the best combination of taxes and local public goods. One of the implications of the Tiebout model is that interjurisdictional mobility (voting with feet) may prevent the inefficiencies associated with majority voting.

The Simple Tiebout Model

There are five assumptions in the simple version of the Tiebout model:

1. **Jurisdictional choice.** A household "shops" for a local government and chooses the jurisdiction that provides the ideal level of local public goods. There are enough jurisdictions to ensure that every household finds the perfect jurisdiction.

2. **Information and mobility.** All citizens have access to all relevant information about the alternative jurisdictions, and moving is costless.

3. **No interjurisdictional spillovers.** There are no spillovers (externalities) associated with local public goods: all the benefits from local public goods accrue to citizens within the local jurisdiction.

4. **No scale economies.** The average cost of production is independent of output.

5. **Head taxes.** Local governments impose head taxes to pay for public goods: if you have a head, you pay the head tax.

Citizens in the Tiebout world sort themselves into municipalities and school districts according to their demands for local public goods. People with relatively low demand for parks choose a municipality with a relatively small park budget (and a relatively low head tax). Citizens with relatively high demand for parks choose a municipality with a relatively large park budget. Citizens vote with their feet: if they are dissatisfied with their current municipality, they move to another one.

Efficiency Effects of the Tiebout Process

The simple model suggests that shopping and sorting increase the efficiency of local governments. As explained earlier in the chapter, majority voting generates an inefficient level of local spending if the desired budget of the median voter differs from the optimum budget. One of the reasons for the inefficient outcome is that local citizens have different preferences for local public goods, so they disagree about the appropriate spending level. Under the Tiebout process, households sort themselves into homogeneous communities, so citizens agree on how much to spend.

To explain the efficiency effects of the sorting process, suppose that a region starts out with three identical municipalities. Each community has three citizens, one Sam-type citizen (who wants a small park), one Marian-type (medium-sized park), and one Bertha-type (big park). In other words, each municipality is heterogeneous with respect to the demand for parks. As shown in Figure 17–1, each heterogeneous municipality chooses A_m (the choice of the median voter), which is less than the optimum park size.

Suppose that the Tiebout process causes households to sort themselves into homogeneous municipalities. One municipality has three Sams (municipality S); one has three Marians (municipality M); one has three Berthas (municipality B). Figure 17–3 shows the spending choices in municipality S. The marginal-social-benefit

---

FIGURE 17–3   **Citizens in a Homogeneous Municipality Choose the Optimum Spending Level**

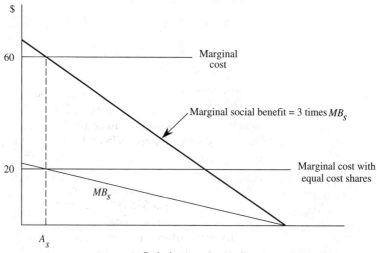

Municipality S has three Sam-type households (who want a small park), so the marginal social benefit is three times the marginal private benefit. If costs are divided equally between the three citizens, they all agree to a park size of A_s acres. The inefficiencies of majority voting are eliminated by the sorting of households into homogeneous municipalities.

curve is three times the marginal-benefit curve of Sam, and intersects the marginal-cost curve at a park acreage of A_s. If costs are divided equally between the three households, the marginal benefit equals the marginal cost at the optimum budget (A_s). All three households have the same preferences for parks, so there is unanimous support for the optimum park size.

The same analysis applies to decision making in the two other homogeneous communities. In each municipality, every household has the same marginal-benefit curve, so an equal sharing of park costs causes unanimous support for the optimum park size. In municipality M, the three Marians vote for a medium-sized park. In municipality B, the three Berthas vote for a big park. The potential inefficiencies of majority voting are avoided by the sorting of households into homogeneous communities.

Tiebout Model with Property Taxes

Hamilton (1975) made the Tiebout model more realistic by introducing property taxes into the model. His model assumes that local governments finance their spending programs with a property tax, not a head tax. To explain the effects of the property tax, consider a municipality with the following characteristics:

1. Every household demands $500 worth of park spending.

2. There are two income groups: the wealthy live in $75,000 houses, and the poor live in $25,000 houses.

3. Under a head tax, every household pays $500 in local taxes to support the parks.

Suppose the municipality switches from the head tax to a 1 percent property tax. Under the property tax, each wealthy household pays $750 in taxes (up from $500), and each poor household pays $250 (down from $500).

How does the property tax affect location choices? The wealthy, who now pay $750 for $500 worth of parks, will try to decrease their tax liabilities. One option is to set up a new municipality for wealthy households. If every household in the new wealthy municipality owns a house worth $75,000, a property tax of 0.667 percent generates a tax bill of $500 per household. In other words, if the wealthy households form an exclusive municipality, they again pay $500 in taxes for $500 worth of parks.

How do the wealthy establish their exclusive suburb? If it were legal, they might simply outlaw houses worth less than $75,000, thus guaranteeing that every household would pay at least $500 in taxes. Because this is illegal, they use **large-lot zoning**: the municipality establishes a minimum lot size for every dwelling. Since land and housing are complementary goods, the municipality can control housing consumption by controlling land consumption. One rule of thumb is that the market value of land is about one fifth of the total property value (the value of the structure and the land). If the price of land is $30,000 per acre, a half-acre lot ($15,000 worth of land) generates a property value of $75,000 (five times $15,000). Therefore, a minimum lot size of half an acre meets the target property value.

What about the poor people who remain in the original municipality? The wealthy households are eventually replaced by poor households in less expensive housing. The average property value in the original municipality decreases, requiring an increase in the tax rate to generate $500 of taxes per household. If the average property value falls to $25,000, the property tax rate rises to 2 percent.

The switch from the head tax to the property tax causes households to sort themselves with respect to housing consumption. There is one community for households with a large demand for housing and one for households with a small demand for housing. This sorting occurs because tax liabilities are based on housing consumption. If the municipalities were to tax Spam instead of housing, citizens would sort themselves into two communities—one where people consume large quantities of Spam and one where people consume small quantities.

The switch from a head tax to a property tax increases the equilibrium number of municipalities. Citizens sort themselves with respect to two characteristics: the demand for local public goods and the demand for housing. The equilibrium number of municipalities depends on the number of housing types and the number of public-good types. Suppose that there are three income groups (rich, middle-income, and poor) and three types of houses, large (occupied by the wealthy), medium (middle-income), and small (poor). Suppose further that for each income group there are two different levels of demand for public goods: some households in each income group have relatively high demands for local public goods, and others have relatively low demands. Given these assumptions, there will be six communities: three high-spending municipalities (one with large houses, one with medium houses, and one with small houses), and three low-spending municipalities. If local governments used a head tax instead of a property tax, there would be only two municipalities, a high-spending one and a low-spending one.

Capitalization and the Tiebout Model

Most municipalities are not homogeneous with respect to property values. The sorting of households with respect to property values is imperfect: there are some small houses in municipalities where most of the houses are large. A small house surrounded by large houses has a lower tax liability than a small house surrounded by small houses because the large-house community has a lower property tax rate. In the example above, a $25,000 house surrounded by $75,000 houses might have a tax rate of 0.667 percent, compared to a tax rate of 2 percent for a small house surrounded by small houses.

As explained in the chapter on housing, the market price of housing depends on the characteristics of the dwelling and the site. Among the site characteristics are the local tax liability and the quality of public services. Everything else being equal, a dwelling with a lower tax liability commands a higher price: the small house in the large-house (low-tax) municipality costs more than an equivalent house in a small-house (high-tax) municipality. In equilibrium, the consumers of small houses must be indifferent between the small houses in the two communities, and they bid up the price of the small house in the low-tax community until the price difference is large enough to offset the tax difference. In other words, lower taxes are **capitalized** into the market value of the small house.

The capitalization of taxes diminishes the incentive for free riding. If the small-house buyer moves to a community with a relatively large tax base and a low tax rate, he pays a premium for the small house. In other words, the benefits of low taxes are offset by higher housing costs.

Evidence of Shopping and Sorting

There is a good deal of evidence that citizens shop for municipalities and school districts. Using data for the New York metropolitan area, Oates (1969) estimated the relationship between house value, taxes, and school expenditures. He found that communities with relatively low tax rates had higher property values. This result suggests that people shop for school districts, bidding up the price of housing in areas with favorable combinations of taxes and local public goods. In other words, differences in taxes and expenditures are capitalized into house values.

There is also evidence that citizens sort themselves with respect to their demands for local public goods. Gramlich and Rubinfeld (1982) examined the tastes for local public goods in different metropolitan areas. In a metropolitan area with a single large municipality, households have no opportunity for shopping, so the single municipality contains households with a wide variety of demands for local public services. In contrast, if the metropolitan area has a large number of jurisdictions, each household can pick a municipality that provides the preferred level of public services, so households sort themselves into homogeneous communities. Using data from questionnaires, Gramlich and Rubinfeld concluded that the greater the number of municipalities to choose from, the more homogeneous the demand for local public goods within each municipality.

The Tiebout process is primarily a suburban phenomenon. In the suburbs, households can choose from dozens of municipalities and school districts. In the central city, there is typically a single large jurisdiction. One reason for the suburbanization of population is that the only option for central-city foot voters is to move to a suburban municipality. If large central-city governments were broken up into smaller municipalities, central-city residents would be able to vote with their feet without moving to the suburbs.

Critique of the Tiebout Model

Like any simple model, the Tiebout model can be criticized on a number of grounds. Some of its assumptions are unrealistic. For example, the model assumes that households are perfectly informed and perfectly mobile, so they can easily change jurisdictions if they become dissatisfied with their local government. This is clearly unrealistic: information about alternative locations is costly to acquire, and the cost of moving is high. As explained in Chapter 14 (Why Is Housing Different?), most households tolerate some dissatisfaction with their dwellings because moving is costly. In context of the Tiebout model, a household that is unhappy with its local government will switch jurisdictions only if the benefits from moving to a different jurisdiction are large enough to offset the associated moving cost. Although the shopping and sorting predicted by the Tiebout model certainly occur, the matching of households and jurisdictions is by no means perfect.

Another assumption of the Tiebout model is that there are enough local governments to allow every household to pick the ideal jurisdiction. In the Tiebout world, every household finds a local government that spends exactly the right amount on every public good. This is clearly unrealistic: there are simply not enough local jurisdictions to provide every household with the ideal level of every public good. This problem is complicated by the use of the property tax: if local governments use the property tax instead of a head tax, households must also sort themselves with respect to house value. If there are not enough jurisdictions to allow every household to choose the ideal jurisdiction, citizens compromise on their ideal tax-spending package, choosing a jurisdiction that comes closest to their ideal package. Households express their preferences for local public goods in local budget elections: after the household votes with its feet, it starts voting with ballots.

A final criticism of the Tiebout model concerns its efficiency implications. The model suggests that the fragmented system of local government is efficient because the sorting of households allows each household to consume its ideal level of local public goods. A key assumption of the model is that local public goods do not generate interjurisdictional externalities: all the benefits and costs of local public goods are confined within the local jurisdiction, regardless of the size of the jurisdiction. In the Tiebout world, even a one-person jurisdiction is efficient: the model assumes that all the benefits of spending on police, fire protection, sewerage, and education would be confined to the single person in the jurisdiction. Under this assumption, there is no real difference between local public goods and private goods. So the household's choice of a jurisdiction, however small, is as efficient as its choice of private goods.

The goods provided by local governments are indeed different from private goods. Some of the goods are nonrivalrous in consumption. For example, when a small municipality uses its police force to capture a criminal, people outside the municipality benefit. The municipality ignores these external benefits, and therefore spends too little on police services. Some goods provided by local governments generate externalities for people in surrounding areas. If a child educated in one city moves to another city as an adult, workers and citizens in the second city benefit from the education program of the first. An individual city ignores the benefits of its education program on outsiders, and therefore spends too little on education. In general, the goods provided by local governments are nonrivalrous and generate externalities, so Tiebout's fragmented system of local governments may be inefficient.

Metropolitan Consolidation and the Tiebout Model

The fragmented system of local government predicted by the Tiebout model has good points and bad points. On the positive side, citizens can choose from a wide variety of jurisdictions, so the fragmented system accommodates diversity in demand for local public goods. On the negative side, there are likely to be spillover benefits and costs that cause inefficiencies. Under what circumstances do the costs of the fragmented system dominate the benefits? Alternatively, under what circumstances would metropolitan consolidation improve the efficiency of local governments?

Inefficiency from Spillovers

Figure 17–4 shows the effects of benefit spillovers on the efficiency of municipal government. The marginal social benefit of parks equals the marginal local benefit (the benefit of citizens within the municipality) plus the marginal external benefit (the benefit of people outside the municipality). The municipality chooses the level at which the marginal social benefit equals the marginal cost (A_s). The optimum level is where the marginal local benefit equals the marginal cost (A^*). Because the municipality ignores the spillover benefits of its parks, it spends less than the optimum amount on parks. The inefficiency occurs because the municipality is too small to contain all the beneficiaries of its spending programs.

Figure 17–5 shows the inefficiency of municipal government in the metropolitan area with three municipalities, S (small parks), M (medium-sized parks), and B (big parks). Under the municipal system, there are spillovers: in each community, the marginal local benefit of spending is less than the marginal social benefit, so each municipality spends less than the optimum amount. For example, in community S, the marginal local benefit equals the marginal cost at a spending level S', which is less than the optimum level S^*. Similarly, M and B spend less than the optimum amounts ($M' < M^*$ and $B' < B^*$).

FIGURE 17–4   Interjurisdictional Externalities and Local Decision Making

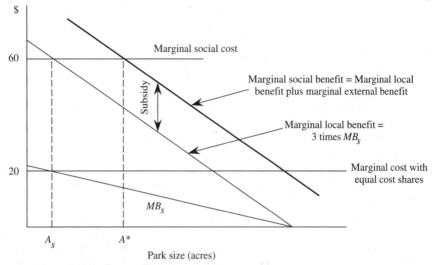

If municipal spending generates benefits for people outside the municipality, the marginal social benefit exceeds the marginal local benefit. The optimum spending level is A^*. Local voters, basing their decisions on local benefits and costs, choose less than the optimum spending level (A_s). A subsidy equal to the gap between the local benefit and the social benefit would cause the municipality to choose the optimum spending level.

FIGURE 17–5   Municipal versus Metropolitan System of Government

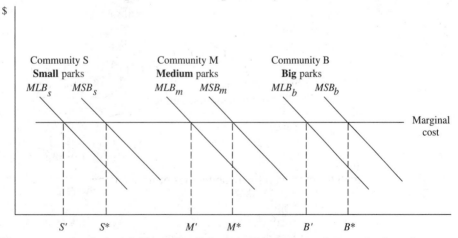

There are two options for local decision making. Under the municipal system, each community chooses its own level of spending, ignoring interjurisdictional spillover benefits. Municipality S chooses S', M chooses M', and B chooses B'. In each of the municipalities, spending falls short of the optimum spending level (S^*, M^*, B^*). Under a metropolitan government, the median voter (Marian in community M) picks the metropolitanwide spending level (M^*). The metropolitan spending level exceeds the optimum in community S ($M^* > S^*$) and falls short of the optimum in community B ($M^* < B^*$).

Effects of Consolidation

Suppose that the three municipalities are consolidated into a single metropolitan government. The metropolitan government is large enough to contain all the citizens affected by local spending, so citizens base their votes in the metropolitan election on the social benefits of parks. For example, citizens in community S base their votes on the marginal *social* benefits (MSB_s) not the marginal *local* benefits (MLB_s). Similarly, citizens in communities M and B base their votes on MSB_m and MSB_b. Given the marginal-cost curve, the preferred budgets for the three types of household are S^*, M^*, and B^*.

Suppose that the metropolitan government intends to build three parks, one in each community. The three parks will be the same size. If the metropolitan government holds an election to determine the size of the parks, the winning size is the size preferred by the median voter, M^*. Therefore, each community will get a park with M^* acres.

The spending under the metropolitan government is inefficient because it chooses a single park size for all three communities. The actual size (M^*) exceeds the optimum size for low-demand households (S^*) and falls short of the optimum size for the high-spending household (B^*). Under the metropolitan government, externalities are internalized, but two of the three communities are forced to compromise on their ideal park sizes.

Is the metropolitan system superior to the municipal system? The municipal system accommodates diversity in demand, but suffers from the externality problem. The metropolitan system solves the externality problem, but requires two of the communities to compromise on their ideal spending packages. It's not clear from Figure 17–5 which of the two systems of government is more efficient. Under both systems, the actual spending differs from the optimum combination (S^*, M^*, B^*) by large amounts: the municipal system generates a spending package of S', M', and B', and the metropolitan system generates a spending of M^* in all three communities.

If the diversity in demand is large relative to externalities, the municipal system will be more efficient than the metropolitan system. In Figure 17–6, interjurisdictional externalities are relatively small, so the gaps between the local- and social-benefit curves are relatively small. Therefore, under municipal decision making, the gaps between the equilibrium and optimum amounts of park acreage are relatively small. For example, the small-park municipality spends S', which falls short of the optimum spending S^* by a relatively small amount. Similarly, the gaps between M^* and M' and between B^* and B' are relatively small. In contrast, because diversity in demand is relatively large, the compromises associated with metropolitan government are relatively large. The gaps between M^* (the budget chosen under majority rule) and the optimum budget of community S ($M^* - S^*$) is relatively large. Similarly, the gap between M^* and B^* is relatively large. Therefore, the municipal system is more efficient than the metropolitan system.

In general, metropolitan government will be more efficient than municipal government if interjurisdictional spillovers are large relative to diversity in demand. In this case, the advantages of small local government (the ability to accommodate diverse demands for local public goods) are relatively small, and the disadvantages

FIGURE 17–6   **Superiority of the Municipal System if Diversity in Demand Is Large Relative to Externalities**

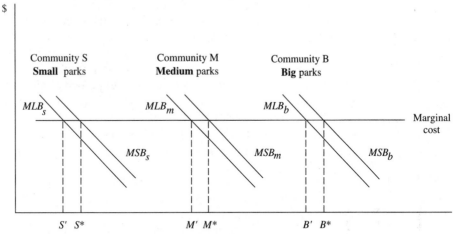

If externalities are relatively small, municipal decision making will be relatively efficient: the gaps between the equilibrium and optimum spending amounts ($S^* - S'$; $M^* - M'$; $B^* - B'$) will be relatively small. If the diversity in demand is relatively large, metropolitan decision making will be relatively inefficient: the gaps between the equilibrium (M^*) and optimum spending amounts ($M^* - S^*$; $B^* - M^*$) will be relatively large. If externalities (spillovers) are small relative to diversity in demand, the municipal system will be more efficient than the metropolitan system.

(the inefficiencies associated with externalities) are relatively large. Therefore, a metropolitan system of government will be more efficient.

Summary

1. The median-voter model predicts that the government adopts the preferred budget of the median voter (the voter that splits voters into equal halves, with one half preferring smaller budgets and the other half preferring larger budgets).
   a. Majority rule does not necessarily produce the optimum level of spending.
   b. The median voter is decisive in both a direct democracy and a representative democracy.
   c. Economists have used the median-voter model to estimate the elasticities of demand for local public goods.
2. The inefficiencies resulting from majority rule could be eliminated by the use of Lindahl taxes (tax equal to the marginal benefit of the local public good).
3. According to the Tiebout model, citizens shop for jurisdictions and sort themselves with respect to demands for local public goods. Because the

Tiebout model assumes that there are no externalities, the Tiebout process is just as efficient as shopping for private goods.

4. The property tax increases the equilibrium number of communities: households sort themselves with respect to both the demand for local public goods and housing consumption.
   a. The wealthy (consumers of large houses) use large-lot zoning to exclude the poor (consumers of small houses) from wealthy communities.
   b. Differences in taxes are capitalized into property values, so a small house in a wealthy community (with a low tax rate) costs more than a small house in a poor community (with a high tax rate).

5. There is a good deal of evidence for the Tiebout process.
   a. Citizens shop for local governments and sort themselves into relatively homogeneous communities.
   b. Most of the shopping is in the suburbs: large central-city governments limit the shopping options in the central city.

Exercises and Discussion Questions

1. In the example shown in Table 17–1, the school board started with a budget of $90 and worked its way downward until a majority of voters voted yes. Show that the same outcome would occur if the school board started with a budget of $10 and worked upward.

2. In the example shown in Table 17–1, the winning budget is $70. Explain the effects of the following changes on the winning budget. In each case, use as the starting point the distribution of voters shown in Table 17–1.
   a. Four elderly voters move into the school district. The elderly voters have preferred budgets of $20, $25, $30, and $35.
   b. In response to "A Nation at Risk," a report critical of educational programs, the desired spending of every household increases by $5.

3. Consider the effect of private schools on the local school election. Suppose that households F and G (in Table 17–1) enroll their children in private schools. Predict the effects of private schooling on the public school budget under the following two cases.
   a. F and G abstain from voting in the school election.
   b. F and G vote in the election. Their preferred budgets drop by $40 ($44 instead of $84 and $51 instead of $91).

4. Comment on the following: "If the median-voter model is correct, it's silly to mess around with elections. We should hire Mr. Gallup to identify the median voter and find out his or her preferred budget. Such a system would be cheaper than a series of budget elections."

5. You are the campaign manager for Dick Tracy, who is running for mayor. His opponent has committed herself to spending $500 per capita on police

services. You must decide how much Dick will propose for the police budget. What information would you collect, and how would you use it?

6. The conventional head tax is a fixed amount per head: if you have a head, you pay a $500 tax. Suppose that the head tax is based on head weight: the heavier your head, the larger your tax. Would you expect the switch from the conventional property tax to the head-weight tax to increase or decrease the equilibrium number of municipalities?

7. In Metro, there are three types of houses: E (expensive), M (medium), and C (cheap). A recent survey suggests that there are three types of preferences for fire protection: H (high), I (intermediate), and L (low). Mr. Wizard, an economic consultant to the city, recently made the following statement: "If my assumptions are correct, the shopping and sorting from the Tiebout process will generate three municipalities."
   a. Assume that Mr. Wizard's reasoning is correct. What are his assumptions?
   b. Suppose that the equilibrium number of municipalities turns out to be nine, not three. Where did Mr. Wizard go wrong? What set of assumptions would have given him the correct prediction?

8. Metro is a metropolitan area in which all households demand the same spending per pupil on public education. Education is produced with constant returns to scale. Because schools are financed with the property tax, there are dozens of school districts. According to Peabody, a fiscal analyst in Metro, "If my assumptions are correct, if we replace the property tax (a tax on market value) with a tax based on square footage (e.g., $2 per square foot of living space per year), the equilibrium number of school districts will decrease to one."
   What are Peabody's assumptions?

9. Under the traditional public school system, parents must send their children to the neighborhood school. In recent years, many people have suggested that parents be able to send their children to the public school of their choice, not necessarily the neighborhood school. Suppose that this change is implemented. Discuss the effects on the Tiebout shopping and sorting process. Would there be more or less income segregation?

10. In the example of the Tiebout model with a property tax, wealthy households established an exclusive suburb with a property tax rate of 0.667 percent, spending of $500, and a minimum lot size of 0.50 acres. Discuss the effects of the following changes on the property tax rate and the minimum lot size.
    a. The market value of houses is $100,000 instead of $75,000.
    b. The market value of land is $50,000 instead of $30,000 (and the market value of houses is $100,000).

11. Consider Metro, a metropolitan area with three school districts, East, West, and North. The optimum spending is $500 in East, $900 in West, and $700 in North. If the districts make independent decisions, spending will be $450

in East, $850 in West, and $650 in North. In other words, there are externalities in the provision of education, causing each district to spend too little. Suppose that the three districts are consolidated into a single metropolitan school district.

 a. Assume that there are no scale economies in the provision of schools. Will the metropolitan school district be more or less efficient than the original arrangement?

 b. How would your answer to (*a*) change if the expenditures under independent decision making were $200 (East) and $600 (West)?

 c. How would your answer to (*a*) change if there are scale economies in the provision of education?

12. The example shown in Figure 17–2 assumes that all citizens vote in the mayoral election. Suppose that some citizens refuse to vote if the proposed budgets of the two candidates are not very far apart (they abstain because of indifference). Specifically, suppose that if the difference between the candidates is less than $1, only 50 percent of citizens (of all budget preferences) vote.

 a. Will Buck increase his chances of being elected if he increases his proposed budget from $6 (the median budget) to $7?

 b. Will the median-voter result persist if there is indifference?

13. The example shown in Figure 17–2 assumes that all citizens vote in the mayoral election. Suppose that some citizens refuse to vote if the proposed budget of the closest candidate is too far from their preferred budget (they abstain because of alienation). Specifically, a voter abstains if the difference between the closest candidate and the citizen's preferred budget is greater than $3.

 a. Suppose that Penny decreases her proposed budget to $5. Does she increase or decrease her chances of being elected?

 b. Will the median-voter result persist if there is alienation?

References and Additional Readings

General

Inman, Robert. "The Fiscal Performance of Local Governments: An Interpretive Review." In *Current Issues in Urban Economics,* ed. Peter Mieszkowski and Mahlon Straszheim. Baltimore: Johns Hopkins University Press, 1979, pp. 270–321. Discusses various models of decision making in the local public sector, including the median-voter model and the dominant-party model. Summarizes studies of the price and income elasticities of demand for local public goods and the elasticity of local expenditures with respect to intergovernmental aid.

Median-Voter Model

Barr, J., and O. Davis. "An Elementary Political and Economic Theory of Local Governments." *Southern Economic Journal* 33 (1966), pp. 149–65.

Bergstrom, T., and R. Goodman. "Private Demand for Public Goods." *American Economic Review* 63 (1973), pp. 286–96. Derives the conditions under which the chosen budget is equal to the preferred budget of the median-income family.

Black, D. "On the Rationale of Group Decision Making." *Journal of Political Economy* 56 (1948), pp. 88–95.

Downs, Anthony. *An Economic Theory of Democracy.* New York: Harper & Row, 1956. Chapters 3, 8, and 14 discuss the rational voter and the median-voter model.

Edelson, N. "Budgetary Outcomes in a Referendum Setting." In *Property Taxation and the Finance of Education,* ed. R. Lindholm. Madison: University of Wisconsin Press, 1974.

Hotelling, Harold. "Stability in Competition." *Economic Journal* 39 (1929), pp. 41–57. The basis for the median-voter model. Shows why politicians are like ice-cream vendors.

Inman, Robert. "Testing Political Economy's 'As If' Proposition: Is the Median Voter Really Decisive?" *Public Choice* 33 (Winter 1978), pp. 45–65. Tested the median-voter model for local public schools and found that the decisive voter was in fact the median-income homeowner whose children attended public schools. The chosen budget moved away from the preferred budget of the median voter as the number of renters, elderly, and private-school families increased.

Rubinfeld, D. "Voting in a Local School Election: A Micro Analysis." *Review of Economics and Statistics* 59 (1977), pp. 30–42.

The Tiebout Model of Interjurisdictional Mobility

Bewley, T. "A Critique of Tiebout's Theory of Local Public Expenditures." *Econometrica* 49 (1981), pp. 713–40. Discusses the conditions under which the Tiebout process is efficient.

Eberts, Randall W., and Timothy J. Gronberg. "Jurisdictional Homogeneity and the Tiebout Hypothesis." *Journal of Urban Economics* 10 (1981), pp. 227–39. Discusses the problems associated with a limited supply of local jurisdictions.

Hamilton, Bruce W. "Capitalization of Interjurisdictional Differences in Local Tax Prices." *American Economic Review* 66 (1976), pp. 743–53. Explores the roles of zoning and capitalization in attaining a Tiebout equilibrium in a community whose citizens have different demands for housing.

———. "Zoning and Property Taxation in a System of Local Governments." *Urban Studies* 12 (1975), pp. 205–11. Discusses the role of zoning in maintaining the Tiebout equilibrium under property tax finance.

Hamilton, Bruce W.; Edwin S. Mills; and David Puryear. "The Tiebout Hypothesis and Residential Income Segregation." In *Fiscal Zoning and Land Use Controls,* ed. Edwin S. Mills and Wallace Oates. Lexington, Mass.: D. C. Heath, 1975. Discusses the effects of fragmented government on income segregation.

Henderson, J. V. "Theories of Group, Jurisdiction, and Size." In *Current Issues in Urban Economics,* ed. Peter Mieszkowski and Mahlon Straszheim. Baltimore: Johns Hopkins University Press, 1979, pp. 235–69. Discusses the allocation of population among local communities.

Oates, Wallace E. "On the Use of Local Zoning Ordinances to Regulate Population Flows and the Quality of Local Services." In *Essays in Modern Labor Market Analysis,* ed. Orley Ashenfelter and Wallace E. Oates. New York: John Wiley & Sons, 1977, pp. 201–19.

Pack, H., and J. Pack. "Metropolitan Fragmentation and Local Public Expenditure." *National Tax Journal* 31 (1978), pp. 349–62. Discusses the problems associated with a limited supply of local jurisdictions.

Tiebout, Charles. "A Pure Theory of Local Expenditures." *Journal of Political Economy* 64 (1956), pp. 416–24. The original statement of the Tiebout model.

Tests of the Tiebout Model

Gramlich, Edward M., and Daniel L. Rubinfeld. "Microestimates of Public Spending Demand Functions and Test of the Tiebout and Median-Voter Hypothesis." *Journal of Political Economy* 90 (1982), pp. 536–60. Found relatively small differences in the demands for local public goods in metropolitan areas where there are many local jurisdictions.

Oates, Wallace E. "The Effects of Property Taxes and Local Public Spending on Property Values: An Empirical Study of Tax Capitalization and the Tiebout Hypothesis." *Journal of Political Economy* 77 (1969), pp. 957–70. Estimates the effects of local taxes and expenditures on property values. Provides evidence that households shop for local jurisdictions.

Zodrow, George. *The Tiebout Model after Twenty-Five Years.* New York: Academic Press, 1983. A collection of papers on the Tiebout model.

Local Taxes and Intergovernmental Grants

The thing generally raised on city land is taxes.
Charles Dudley Warner

This chapter explores the revenue side of local government, discussing the economics of local taxes and intergovernmental grants. When a government imposes a tax, the people who pay the tax in a legal sense have the incentive to change their behavior to avoid the tax. By doing so, they shift it to someone else. The policy question is: after taxpayers have fully adjusted to the new tax, who actually pays the tax? The first two parts of the chapter answer this incidence question for the residential property tax, and the third part answers the incidence question for the tax on commercial and industrial property. The fourth part discusses the effects of the Tiebout shopping/sorting process on the distribution of the burden of the property tax. The fifth part discusses the administration of the property tax. The last three parts explore the economics of intergovernmental grants. The principal question is: how do local governments respond to state and federal grants? Do they spend all grants on additional local public goods, or do they use grants to cut local taxes?

Who Pays the Residential Property Tax?

The property tax is a tax on residential, commercial, and industrial property. This section considers the effect of the residential property tax, using a model of a residential city to explore the market effects of the tax. The analysis focuses on two principal questions about the residential property tax. First, how do property owners respond to the tax? Second, to what extent do property owners pass on the tax to consumers, landowners, and other property owners?

It is useful to divide rental housing into two components: the dwelling itself (the structure) and the land that comes with the dwelling. The annual rent on the residential property is the sum of dwelling rent and land rent. For example, an annual rent

511

of $5,000 can be broken down into $4,000 of dwelling rent and $1,000 of land rent. Similarly, the market value of residential property is the sum of the market values of the dwelling and the land. As explained in Chapter 7 (Introduction to Land Rent and Land Use), the market value of property equals the present value of the rental income from the property. If the market interest rate is 10 percent, the market value of the dwelling is $40,000 ($4,000/0.10), the market value of the land is $10,000 ($1,000/0.10), and the market value of the residential property (both dwelling and land) is $50,000.

The residential property tax is an annual tax based on the market value of the property. For example, under a 2 percent property tax, the owner of a $50,000 property would pay $1,000 per year in taxes. This can be broken down into an $800 tax on the dwelling itself (2 percent of a market value of $40,000) and a $200 tax on the land (2 percent of a market value of $10,000).

To explain the market effects of the property tax, consider the city of Taxville, where all land is used for rental housing. The city has the following characteristics:

1. **Identical dwellings.** The city has 900 identical rental housing units.
2. **Housing inputs.** There are two inputs to housing: land and improve-ments (the dwelling). Every dwelling occupies a quarter-acre lot.
3. **Capital mobility.** Dwellings are immobile in the short run, but can be moved from one city to another in the long run.
4. **Unit property tax.** The annual property tax is paid in legal terms by the property owner. The tax is $200 per quarter-acre lot and $800 per dwelling, regardless of the market values of land and improvements.

The fourth assumption means that the property tax is not based on market value, but is a fixed unit tax. This assumption simplifies the exposition without changing the analysis in any substantive way.

The Land Portion of the Property Tax

Consider first the effect of the land portion of the property tax. Figure 18–1 shows the city's land market. The supply of land is perfectly inelastic, with a fixed supply of 900 quarter-acre lots. The demand curve intersects the supply curve at point *B*, generating an annual rent of $1,000 per lot. If the market interest rate is 10 percent, market value of land is $10,000 per lot.

Can landowners shift the land tax onto land consumers? The property tax in-creases the property owner's tax liability by $200 per year. Suppose that the prop-erty owner increased land rent from $1,000 per year (point *B*) to $1,200 (point *C*). At point *C*, the quantity of land demanded (450 lots) is less than the fixed supply (900 lots), so some land is vacant. The excess supply of land causes landowners to cut prices to attract consumers. The price cutting continues until the gap between supply and demand is eliminated. In equilibrium, land rent falls to $1,000 and the net return to property owners drops to $800 ($1,000 less the $200 tax). Because the supply of land is fixed, the land tax is ultimately borne by landowners. The decrease in net rental income decreases the market value of land from $10,000 to $8,000 ($800/0.10).

FIGURE 18–1   Market Effects of the Land Tax

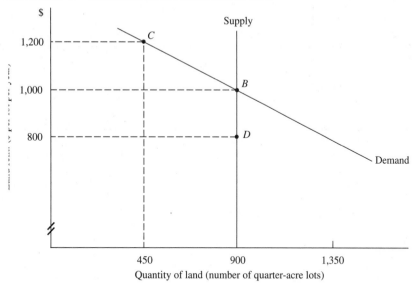

Land rent is $1,000 in the pre-tax equilibrium. Since the supply of land is fixed, the land tax decreases rent by the amount of the tax ($200). If the landowner tried to pass on the $200 annual tax to consumers, the net cost of land would rise to $1,200 (point *C*), and the quantity supplied (900) would exceed the quantity demanded (450). The surplus of land would cause rent to fall to $800.

The Improvement Tax: The Traditional View

The traditional analysis of the property tax examines the effects of the property tax on the city that imposes the tax. The traditional view is based on partial-equilibrium analysis. The analysis is "partial" in the sense that it ignores the effect of the tax on other cities.

Figure 18–2 shows the market for improvements (dwellings) in the taxing city. In the long run, the supply of dwellings is assumed to be perfectly elastic: the city is assumed to be a small part of a national market for dwellings, so the market price is unaffected by events in the city. Given the supply and demand curves, the initial equilibrium (point *B*) generates a dwelling rent of $4,000 per year and 900 dwellings. If the market interest rate is 10 percent, the market value of the rental dwelling is $40,000.

Why is the long-run supply curve perfectly elastic? One way to picture the long run is to imagine that property owners can put wheels on their dwellings and roll them to other cities. Although property owners do not literally move their dwellings from place to place, they can decrease the supply of housing in other ways. As explained in the chapter on housing, property owners can (1) decrease their investment in repair and maintenance, (2) abandon dwellings, (3) convert property to other uses, and (4) not respond to increases in the demand for housing. Given these four responses, property owners can decrease the effective supply of housing without actually moving their dwellings to another location. The house-on-wheels metaphor captures the idea that property owners can decrease the supply of housing in the long run.

FIGURE 18–2   **Partial-Equilibrium Effects of Improvement Tax**

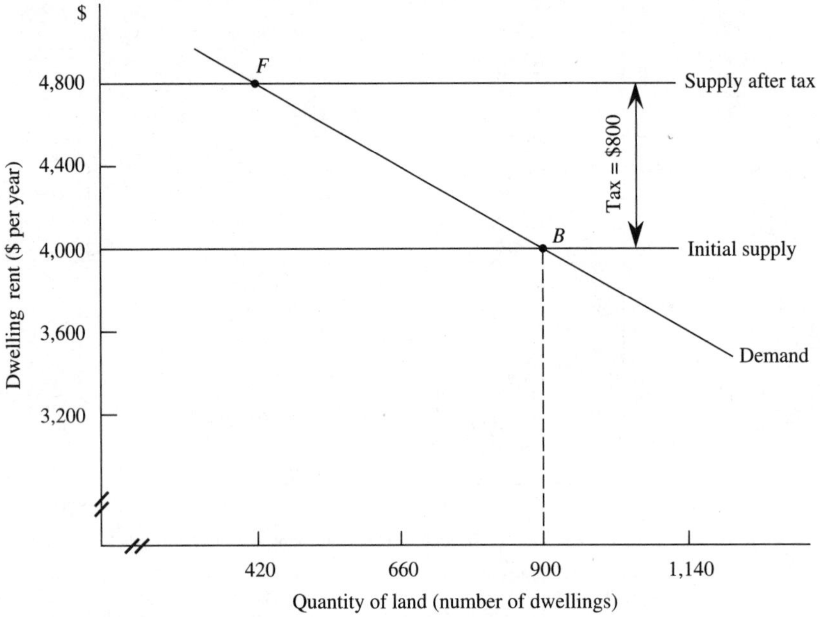

Before the dwelling tax, *B* is the equilibrium point (rent = $4,000 per year). The property tax is $800 per dwelling, so the supply curve shifts up by $800. Dwelling rent increases to $4,800 per year, and the number of dwellings decreases to 420.

The property tax generates an annual tax of $800 per dwelling. Because the property owner pays the improvement tax in a legal sense, the tax shifts the long-run supply curve up by the amount of the tax: the supply curve is a marginal-cost curve, and the tax increases the marginal cost of rental property by $800 per dwelling per year. The market moves from point *B* to *F:* the equilibrium rent rises by the full amount of the tax (from $4,000 to $4,800), and the quantity of dwellings drops from 900 to 420. Net rental income remains at $4,000: the property owner collects $4,800 in rent and pays $800 in taxes, leaving $4,000 in net income. The tenant pays the entire tax: the annual cost of rental housing rises by $800.

The improvement tax is borne by consumers because the supply of dwellings is perfectly elastic. The city is a small part of the national market for dwellings, so it takes the national rent of $4,000 as given: if the city's property owners were to receive anything less than $4,000 in net rental income, they would roll their dwellings out of town. In fact, the decrease in the supply of dwellings (from 900 to 420) increases dwelling rent by an amount large enough to restore the original net rental income of $4,000.

The New View of the Property Tax

The partial-equilibrium analysis explores the effects of the property tax on the markets for land and improvements in the taxing city. General-equilibrium analysis explores the effects of the property tax on markets outside the city, providing a new view of the property tax.

Suppose that Taxville shares a region with Notax, a residential city without a property tax. The region has the following characteristics:

1. **Fixed supply of dwellings.** The total number of dwellings in the region is fixed at 1,800.
2. **Capital mobility.** In the short run, dwellings cannot be moved between cities. In the long run, dwellings can be moved between cities at zero cost.
3. **Household mobility.** Households are immobile in the sense that they cannot move from one city to another.
4. **Equilibrium price.** Property owners move their dwellings to the city with the highest return (the highest annual rent). In equilibrium, the market rent on dwellings is the same in the two cities.

The regional dwelling market is shown in Figure 18–3. Each city has a negatively sloped demand curve, and the initial equilibrium occurs with points *B* (in Taxville) and *K* (in Notax). The equilibrium price of dwellings is $4,000, and each city has 900 dwellings.

In the short run, the property owner pays the improvement tax. In the short run, the supply of dwellings in each city is fixed. The property tax ($800 per year) decreases the net rental income in Taxville from $4,000 (point *B*) to $3,200 (point *T*). The property tax is borne by property owners because the supply of dwellings is perfectly inelastic. In the nontaxing city, rent stays at $4,000.

In the long run, property owners move their dwellings to the more lucrative market in Notax. Suppose that property owners move 120 dwellings from Taxville to Notax. In Figure 18–3, the Taxville market moves from point *B* (900 dwellings) to point *C* (780 dwellings), causing the rent on Taxville dwellings to rise from $4,000 to $4,200. The net income of Taxville's property owners increases from $3,200 ($4,000 rent less $800 tax) to $3,400 ($4,200 less $800). Taxville's loss is Notax's gain: the Notax market moves from point *K* to point *L* (an increase of 120 dwellings, from 900 to 1,020), and rent drops from $4,000 to $3,800.

Is the dwelling market in equilibrium with points *C* and *L?* Equilibrium occurs when two conditions are satisfied. First, the total number of dwellings in the two cities must equal 1,800 (the fixed supply). Second, property owners have no incentive to move their dwellings from one city to another: the net rental income must be the same in the two cities. For points *C* and *L*, the first condition is satisfied (720 + 1,020 = 1,800), but the second condition is violated: the net income in Taxville ($3,400) is still less than net income in Notax ($3,800). Therefore, the market will continue to move up the Taxville demand curve and down the Notax demand curve. The movements along the demand curves will continue until both equilibrium conditions are satisfied. Equilibrium occurs with points *D* and *M:* there are 660 dwellings in Taxville and 1,140 in Notax, and the net income is $3,600 per rental dwelling.

There are two lessons from the general-equilibrium analysis:

1. **Property owners pay the tax.** The tax decreases net rental income in both cities to $3,600. The movement of dwellings to the untaxed city

FIGURE 18–3 **General-Equilibrium Effects of Improvement Tax**

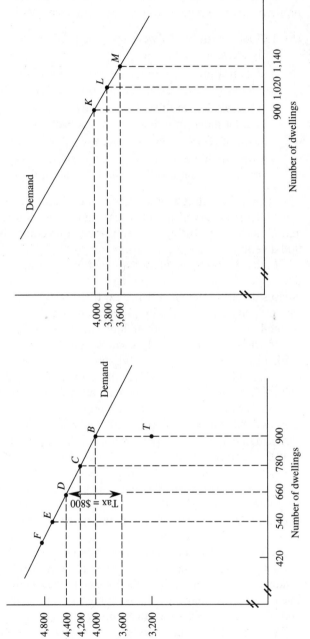

The initial (pre-tax) equilibrium is shown by points *B* and *K*. The improvement tax is $800 per dwelling per year. In the short run, dwellings are immobile, so dwelling rent is fixed at $4,000 and property owners pay the tax. In the long run, property owners move their dwellings to the nontaxing city, increasing dwelling rent in the taxing city (movement upward along the demand curve) and decreasing rent in the nontaxing city (movement down the demand curve). In long-run equilibrium, property owners receive the same net (post-tax) return, so Taxville rent exceeds Notax rent by the amount of the tax: with points *D* and *M*, Taxville rent is $4,400 (net return = $3,600) and Notax's rent is $3,600. The tax is shifted to property owners in the nontaxing city.

decreases rent in the untaxed city (to $3,600) and increases rent in the taxing city (to $4,400). The tax is paid by property owners throughout the region, not just property owners in the taxing city.

2. **Consumer effects.** Consumers in Taxville lose (they pay $4,400 instead of $4,000), and consumers in Notax gain (they pay $3,600). The changes in housing costs offset one another, so the tax does not change the average rent.

The general-equilibrium analysis suggests that the improvement tax is paid by property owners (the owners of dwellings). Because the total (regional) supply of dwellings is perfectly inelastic, property owners are unable to escape the tax. On the other side of the market, housing consumers as a class escape the tax: the losses of Taxville households are offset by the gains of Notax households. The improvement tax causes zero-sum changes in rent, so housing consumers are no worse off as a result of the tax.

Changing the Assumptions

The simple general-equilibrium model has a number of unrealistic assumptions. How does the analysis change when these assumptions are dropped?

More than Two Municipalities.   One of the key assumptions of the simple model is that only two municipalities share a fixed supply of dwellings. An alternative assumption is that Taxville is one of 100 cities in a region, so that Taxville shares a fixed supply of dwellings with 99 other cities.

When Taxville imposes a property tax, dwellings flee to 99 other cities, not just to Notax. Suppose that 240 dwellings leave Taxville (the market moves from point B to point D in Figure 18–3), so that each of the other 99 cities gets about 2.4 additional dwellings. Each city experiences a relatively small increase in dwellings, and thus a relatively small decrease in dwelling rent (e.g., from $4,000 to $3,996). Given the small decrease in rent, there is still a gap between the net income on dwellings in Taxville ($4,400 − $800 = $3,600) and net income elsewhere ($3,996). Therefore, point D in Figure 18–3 is not an equilibrium point in the 100-city case.

Dwellings continue to leave Taxville until the income gap is closed. Given the small price effect of fleeing dwellings, a large number of dwellings must leave the taxing city. The market moves a relatively long distance up Taxville's demand curve. In equilibrium, the market is near point F (dwelling rent is close to $4,800 and a total of 480 dwellings have left the taxing city). Suppose that 475 dwellings leave Taxville, meaning that the other 99 cities each gain about 4.8 dwellings. Dwelling rent is $4,792 in Taxville and $3,992 in the other 99 cities. At this rent, the net income of Taxville property owners ($3,992 = $4,792 − $800) equals the net income of property owners in other cities.

The 100-city case has the same aggregate effects as the 2-city case. The tax is paid by property owners: every property owner in the 100-city region receives $8 less per dwelling. The only difference is that there are 50 times as many dwellings in the 100-city case (100 cities full of dwellings instead of 2 cities), so the decrease in equilibrium rent in the nontaxing cities is one fiftieth as large ($8 instead of $400).

In the taxing city, the tax increases dwelling rent by a relatively large amount because a large number of dwellings leave the city.

Tax in Both Cities.   The simple model assumes that the property tax is imposed in only one city. Suppose that both cities impose a $400 improvement tax. In the short run, the improvement taxes decrease the net income of property owners to $3,600. Because both cities impose the tax, there is no incentive for property owners to move their dwellings to the other city. Therefore, the short-run effect is the same as the long-run effect: the tax decreases net income, but does not affect the market rent. Property owners pay the improvement tax, just as they did in the single-tax case. Because the tax does not change the equilibrium rent, it does not affect housing consumers. Housing consumers escape the tax because dwellings do not move from one city to another.

Variable Supply of Dwellings.   The simple model assumes that the total supply of dwellings is fixed. Although the tax decreases income from rental property, it does not decrease the total supply of dwellings. If the total supply of dwellings decreases as net rental income decreases, the analysis changes in three ways:

1. **Dwellings are withdrawn.** Only some of the dwellings that leave Taxville arrive in the untaxed city. Some of the dwellings are withdrawn from the regional housing market. Suppose that one third of the dwellings that leave Taxville are transferred to the untaxed city, and two thirds are withdrawn from the regional market. In Figure 18–3, equilibrium occurs with points *E* and *L* (compared to *D* and *M* if the total supply of dwellings is fixed). The quantity of dwellings in Taxville decreases to 540 (a reduction of 360), while the quantity of dwellings in Notax increases to 1,020 (an increase of only 120), and 240 dwellings are retired from the market.

2. **Property owners lose less.** The withdrawal of dwellings increases net rental income. At points *L* and *E*, dwelling rent is $3,800 in Notax and $4,600 in Taxville. The net income for property owners in both cities is $3,800 (compared to $3,600 with a fixed supply of dwellings). The tax causes a smaller decrease in rental income because property owners respond to the tax by decreasing the supply of dwellings.

3. **Tenants pay part of the tax.** The withdrawal of dwellings shifts part of the tax to housing consumers. The tax increases dwelling rent to $4,600 in Taxville and decreases rent in Notax to $3,800. In other words, the loss of Taxville tenants (rent increase of $600) exceeds the gain of Notax tenants (rent reduction of $200). The tax harms Taxville tenants more than it helps Notax tenants, so the tenant class is worse off. Because property owners decrease the supply of dwellings, they can shift part of the improvement tax to housing consumers.

Mobile Consumers.   One of the assumptions of the simple model is that tenants are immobile. When dwelling rent increases in the taxing city, none of the households leave the city. What happens if households can move to the nontaxing city?

If households can move costlessly between the two cities, they will leave the taxing city as long as it has a higher housing rent. If the market is at points *D* and *M* in Figure 18–3, housing rent (the sum of dwelling rent and land rent) is $5,400 in the taxing city ($4,400 for the dwelling plus $1,000 for the land) and $4,600 in the un-taxed city ($3,600 plus $1,000). When households leave the taxing city, the demand for Taxville land decreases, decreasing land rent and housing rent. For example, if land rent drops to $900, housing rent decreases to $5,300. At the same time, the migration of households to the untaxed city bids up land rent, increasing housing rent: if land rent increases to $1,100, housing rent increases to $4,700. In other words, migration from Taxville to Notax narrows the difference between housing rents in the two cities. In locational equilibrium, the two cities have the same housing rent. For example, if land rent drops to $600 in Taxville and rises to $1,400 in Notax, housing rent is $5,000 in both cities ($4,400 plus $600 in the taxing city and $3,600 plus $1,400 in the untaxed city).

The migration of households causes capital gains and losses for landowners. If the annual rent on Taxville land drops from $1,000 to $600, the market value of the land drops from $10,000 to $6,000. In contrast, if rent on Notax land rises to $1,400, its market value increases to $14,000. The migration of households eliminates the intercity differences in housing cost. Instead of differences in housing cost, there are differences in land rent and differences in the market values of land. In other words, the migration of households allows consumers to shift the benefits and the costs of the improvement tax to landowners.

Summary: Who Pays the Residential Property Tax?

The different views and models of the property tax are cleverly designed to baffle students. Who actually pays the property tax? The incidence of the land tax is straightforward: given the perfectly inelastic supply of land, the tax is paid by landowners. The incidence of the improvement tax is not so easily summarized, as it depends on one's perspective.

The Local Effects of a Local Tax

Tom is the mayor of a small city in a nation of 100 cities. To predict the effects of his city's improvement tax, he should use the partial-equilibrium model. Because his city is small, it does not affect the national market for dwellings, so the assumption of a perfectly elastic supply of dwellings is a good approximation of reality. Using the partial-equilibrium model, Tom would predict that an $800 improvement tax will increase dwelling rent by the full amount of the tax ($800): the tax will be borne entirely by housing consumers.

Tom's analysis is not literally correct, but it is a good approximation. In one of the examples in the previous section, an improvement tax in a 100-city region increased dwelling rent in the taxing city by $792 and decreased dwelling rent in the rest of the region by $8. Because Tom doesn't care about people outside his city, he can ignore the effects of the tax on outsiders. From Tom's perspective, all that matters is that his citizens pay *about* $800 more for dwelling rent.

TABLE 18–1   **Property Tax Incidence, Local and National Perspectives**

	Property Tax as Percent of Income	
Income ($)	*Local Perspective (partial equilibrium)*	*National Perspective (general equilibrium)*
0–5,000	7.9%	1.0%
5,000–10,000	3.0	0.6
10,000–15,000	2.4	0.9
15,000–20,000	2.1	0.9
20,000–25,000	2.1	1.0
25,000–30,000	2.1	1.2
30,000–50,000	2.2	1.4
50,000–100,000	2.3	2.2
100,000–500,000	2.2	3.9
500,000–1 million	2.2	5.2
Over 1 million	2.3	5.8

SOURCE: Joseph A. Pechman, *Who Paid the Taxes, 1966–1985?* (Washington, D.C.: Brookings Institution, 1985), Table 3–1.

Table 18–1 shows the distribution of the property tax burden from the local perspective (the traditional view). In computing the numbers, Pechman (1985) assumes that (1) the land tax is borne entirely by landowners and (2) the improvement tax is borne entirely by housing consumers. In other words, the computational results are based on partial-equilibrium analysis. Since the income elasticity of demand for housing (or improvements) is slightly less than 1.0, the improvement tax is regressive: the ratio of tax to income decreases as income increases. In contrast, land ownership rises rapidly with income, so the land portion of the property tax is progressive. In combination, the two components of the tax cause the property tax to be highly regressive for incomes less than $20,000 and roughly proportional for incomes above $20,000.

The National Effects of a Local Tax

Bertha, the president of a nation of 100 cities, wants to estimate the national effects of a property tax in a single city. She should use the general-equilibrium model. Under the assumption of a fixed national supply of dwellings, the improvement tax is paid by capitalists in the form of a lower return on capital (lower net income from rental property). The tax causes zero-sum changes in the cost of housing: consumers outside the taxing city gain at the expense of consumers in the taxing city.

Table 18–1 shows the distribution of the property tax burden from the national perspective (the new view). In computing the numbers, Pechman (1985) assumes that (1) the land tax is borne entirely by landowners and (2) the improvement tax is borne entirely by capitalists (property owners). In other words, the computational results are based on general-equilibrium analysis. Because capital and land ownership increase rapidly with income, the property tax is progressive: the tax burden as a fraction of income increases with income.

What if Bertha assumes that the supply of capital is not fixed? If the supply is not perfectly inelastic, part of the tax is shifted to housing consumers. The price of housing increases by a relatively large amount in the taxing city and decreases by a relatively small amount in the other 99 cities. As a result, the average cost of housing increases.

The Effects of a National Tax

Sam is the president of a nation in which all 100 cities have the same property tax. He wants to estimate the effect of the improvement tax. Because all cities impose the tax, it does not cause any movement of capital between cities. Under the assumption of a fixed national supply of capital, the tax is borne entirely by capitalists. The tax does not affect the cost of housing because there is nowhere for the dwellings to flee. Under the assumption that the supply of capital is not perfectly inelastic, the tax is split between housing consumers and capitalists, with the consumer share increasing as the elasticity of supply of capital increases.

TABLE 18–2   Who Pays the Property Tax?

Tax Imposed by a Small City
Welfare effects in the taxing city
   1. Immobile households: consumers pay higher dwelling rent.
   2. Mobile households: landowners receive lower land rent.

Welfare effects in a nontaxing city
   1. Immobile households: consumers pay lower dwelling rent.
   2. Mobile households: landowners receive higher land rent.

National welfare effects
   1. Property owners (capitalists) receive lower net rental income.
   2. Immobile households
       a. Fixed supply of dwellings: zero-sum changes in dwelling rent.
       b. Variable supply of dwellings: positive-sum changes in dwelling rent.
   3. Mobile households
       a. Fixed supply of dwellings: zero-sum changes in land rent.
       b. Variable supply of dwellings: negative-sum changes in land rent.

Tax Imposed by All Cities (A National Property Tax)
Welfare effects in the taxing cities
   1. Fixed supply of dwellings: housing consumers and landowners unaffected by the tax.
   2. Variable supply of dwellings: dwelling rent increases and land rent decreases.

National welfare effects
   1. Property owners receive lower net rental income.
   2. Fixed supply of dwellings: property owners pay the entire tax.
   3. Variable supply of dwellings: tax shared by property owners, consumers, and
      landowners.

Summary of Incidence Results

Table 18–2 (previous page) summarizes the results of the analysis of the property tax. It shows who pays the tax under different assumptions about the type of tax (a tax in a small city versus a national tax), household mobility, and the response of property owners to the tax (fixed versus variable supply of dwellings). It also discusses the welfare effects for three types of jurisdictions: the taxing city, the nontaxing cities, and the nation.

The Tax on Commercial and Industrial Property

Because Taxville has only residential property, the property tax is effectively a tax on residential property. This section discusses the effects of the general property tax (a tax on residential, commercial, and industrial property) in cities with all three types of property.

The General Property Tax

The analysis of the land portion of the general property tax is straightforward. Because the supply of land is perfectly inelastic, the tax is paid entirely by landowners. The land tax does not affect land rent, but simply decreases the annual rental income by the annual tax. The decrease in net rental income decreases the market value of the land.

What about the tax on improvements? Suppose that a city imposes a 2 percent tax on residential, commercial, and industrial structures. In the short run, the supply of structures is fixed, so the tax decreases the net income of the city's property owners. In the long run, property owners move their structures to Notax, the other city in the region. The movement of capital increases the rent on structures in the taxing city and decreases it elsewhere. For example, rent might rise from $4,000 to $4,400 in the taxing city and decrease to $3,600 elsewhere. The changes in structure rents increase the price of consumer goods in the taxing city and decrease prices elsewhere. The changes in structure rents also equalize net property income at $3,600.

Differential Tax Rates

Most jurisdictions impose the same nominal tax rate on residential and business property. Because assessment ratios differ across property types, however, effective tax rates often differ. Consider a city with the following characteristics:

1. There are two types of structures: houses and pizza parlors.
2. The city starts with the same effective tax rates on pizza parlors and houses.
3. The total capital in the city (the total number of structures) is fixed.
4. Structures can be used for either houses or pizza parlors.
5. In the initial equilibrium, the structure rent is $4,000.

Suppose that the city cuts the property tax rate on pizza parlors and increases the tax rate on housing. The change in tax policy is revenue-neutral: the loss of revenue from pizza parlors equals the gain in tax revenue from residences. The new tax policy causes the following changes in the city.

1. **Transfer of capital.** Property owners move capital from the residential sector to the more lucrative pizza sector.
2. **Increased dwelling rent.** The movement of capital out of the housing sector increases dwelling rent.
3. **Decreased pizza prices.** The movement of capital into the pizza sector decreases the price of pizza.

Who gains and who loses? The change in tax policy is revenue-neutral, so property owners are not affected by the change in tax policy. Housing consumers lose because the price of housing increases, and pizza consumers gain because the price of pizza decreases. This general-equilibrium analysis suggests that differences in effective tax rates are reflected in differences in consumer prices. If a city taxes residential property at a higher rate than business property, its citizens pay more for housing, but less for other goods.

What if nonresidential goods are consumed by people outside the city? The taxation of property used in the production of exports increases the export price, so part of the city's tax burden is borne by consumers outside the city. This is known as **tax exporting**: the city uses tax revenue from outsiders to pay for local government. Suppose that a large fraction of the city's pizza is consumed by outsiders. If the city wants to decrease the local tax burden, it could cut the residential tax rate and increase the tax rate on commercial property (including pizza parlors). Although pizza prices increase, partly offsetting the decrease in the cost of housing, local consumers are better off because a larger fraction of local taxes is shifted to outsiders.

What are the limits to tax exporting? The taxation of exports decreases the city's export volume: consumers respond to the increase in price by decreasing the quantity of exports demanded, so the city's tax base decreases. In addition, export firms have an incentive to move to cities with lower taxes. Because taxation decreases the city's tax base, there are limits to tax exporting. Tax exporting is more likely in a city that has a unique production advantage that makes it the dominant locational choice for export firms.

The Tiebout Model and the Property Tax

The Tiebout model, introduced in the previous chapter, suggests that citizens shop for municipalities and school districts. In equilibrium, households sort themselves with respect to (1) the demand for public goods and (2) housing consumption. This section discusses the implications of the Tiebout process for the incidence of the property tax.

To explain the effects of the property tax in the Tiebout world, consider Metro, a metropolitan area with the following characteristics:

1. **Local public good.** Municipalities provide a single public good (parks).
2. **Income and house value.** Half the households are wealthy and have $100,000 houses. Half are poor and have $50,000 houses.
3. **Park demands.** Half the households in each income group want a large park budget ($2,000), and half want a small park budget ($200).
4. **Municipalities and zoning.** Households can set up new municipalities, using large-lot zoning to establish minimum house values.

As shown in Table 18–3, households sort themselves with respect to park demands and property values, forming four municipalities. There are two wealthy communities, one with a large park budget (tax rate = 2.0%) and one with a small park budget (tax rate = 0.20%). Similarly, there are two poor municipalities.

Because the households in Metro sort themselves into homogeneous communities, the property tax is a user fee, not a conventional tax. The tax liability of a particular household depends on its park consumption, not on its housing consumption (property value). Every household pays a tax equal to its desired park budget, regardless of its property value: the poor pay a higher tax rate to generate the same park budget as their counterparts in the wealthy community; the low spenders pay a lower tax rate than their counterparts in the high-spending municipalities. In the Tiebout world, there is no link between property value and property tax liability. Instead, the tax liability depends strictly on park consumption.

In the Tiebout world, an increase in housing consumption does not affect property taxes. Suppose that a few of the wealthy, high-spending households decide to buy $200,000 homes. They will form a new community of high-spending households with $200,000 houses, and finance their $2,000 park program with a 1 percent property tax. The doubling of housing consumption cuts the property tax rate in half, so property taxes remain at $2,000. In general, a change in housing consumption causes the household to move to a community where other households have (1) the same demand for public goods and (2) the same housing consumption.

In the Tiebout world, the discussion of the incidence of the property tax is meaningless. If households are sorted into homogeneous communities, the property tax is a user fee, and every household gets exactly what it pays for. The "incidence" of a $200 tax liability is the same as the "incidence" of $1 paid for a hot dog: you pay the $1 to get the hot dog; you pay the $200 tax to get $200 worth of parks. Since the consumer's tax liability is independent of his housing choice, the property tax is a user fee, not a conventional tax.

TABLE 18–3   Tiebout Sorting and the Property Tax

Municipality	Property Value ($)	Park Budget ($)	Tax Rate (%)
Wealthy—Large budget	100,000	2,000	2.0%
Wealthy—Small budget	100,000	200	0.20
Poor—Large budget	50,000	2,000	4.0
Poor—Small budget	50,000	200	0.40

How realistic is the Tiebout model? The conditions required for Tiebout equilibrium are unlikely to be satisfied. There are simply not enough local governments to allow households to sort themselves into perfectly homogeneous communities. The Tiebout model is clearly inapplicable to central cities, where a single municipality serves a large and diverse population. Therefore, the central-city property tax is not a user fee, but a conventional tax. In the suburbs, where there is more sorting of households with respect to demands for public services and housing consumption, the property tax is closer to a user fee.

Administering the Property Tax

Because the property tax is based on the value of the property, the local government must periodically assess the value of the property. The annual tax liability of a piece of property is

$$\text{Tax} = \text{Nominal tax rate} \cdot \text{Assessed value} \qquad (18\text{--}1)$$

The assessed value is

$$\text{Assessed value} = \text{Assessment ratio} \cdot \text{Market value} \qquad (18\text{--}2)$$

If the assessment ratio is 25 percent, a house with a market value of $120,000 has an assessed value of $30,000. If the nominal tax rate is 10 percent, the tax liability is $3,000 (10 percent of the assessed value). The **effective tax rate**, defined as the tax liability divided by the market value, is only 2.5 percent ($3,000 divided by $120,000). The effective tax rate is less than the nominal tax rate because the assessed value is less than the market value.

Most local governments systematically underassess property. According to the *Census of Governments* (1987), the average assessment ratio was 0.40 in 1981, meaning that the typical property was assessed at 40 percent of its market value. If all property in a jurisdiction is subject to the same assessment ratio, underassessment does not affect tax liabilities or effective tax rates, but simply requires a higher nominal tax rate to generate the same tax revenue. In other words, a local government can offset a low assessment ratio with a higher nominal tax rate.

In most jurisdictions, assessment ratios also vary from one piece of property to another. Some of the variation is caused by random assessment errors, a reflection of the imperfections of the assessment process. Another reason for variation in assessment ratios is systematic assessment errors, that is, the assessment ratio varies systematically with property value. In many cities, the assessment ratio is inversely related to property value: as property value increases, the assessment ratio decreases. This practice of regressive assessment has been documented by Engle (1975), Black (1977), Ihlanfeldt (1982), and Netzer (1980).

Table 18–4 illustrates the effects of regressive assessment. There are three households, poor, middle-income, and wealthy. Each owns a home with a market value equal to three times its income. The nominal tax rate is 10 percent. Under a proportional assessment scheme, all properties are assessed at 50 percent of market value, and tax liabilities are proportional to income. The poor household pays a

TABLE 18–4   **Systematic Assessment Errors**

	Poor	*Middle-Income*	*Wealthy*
Income	$20,000	$30,000	$ 40,000
Market value of house	$60,000	$90,000	$120,000
Proportional Assessment			
Assessment ratio	50%	50%	50%
Assessed value	$30,000	$45,000	$ 60,000
Nominal tax rate	10%	10%	10%
Tax liability	$ 3,000	$ 4,500	$ 6,000
Effective tax rate	5%	5%	5%
Tax as fraction of income	15%	15%	15%
Regressive Assessment			
Assessment ratio	60%	50%	40%
Assessed value	$36,000	$45,000	$ 48,000
Nominal tax rate	10%	10%	10%
Tax liability	$ 3,600	$ 4,500	$ 4,800
Effective tax rate	6%	5%	4%
Tax as fraction of income	18%	15%	12%

10 percent tax on an assessed value of $30,000, generating a tax liability of $3,000, which is 15 percent of its $20,000 income. The other households also pay 15 percent of their income in property taxes, so the property tax is a proportional tax. Note that this example adopts the traditional view of the property tax: housing consumers pay the tax.

Under a regressive assessment policy, the poor, who occupy low-value housing, face an assessment ratio of 60 percent, compared to assessment ratios of 50 percent for middle-income households and 40 percent for the wealthy. The switch to regressive assessment increases the tax liability of the poor from $3,000 to $3,600 and decreases the tax liability of the wealthy from $6,000 to $4,800. Under regressive assessment, the property tax is a regressive tax; the fraction of income spent on property taxes is a decreasing function of income: the poor pay 18 percent of their income on the property tax, while the middle-income households pay 15 percent, and the wealthy pay 12 percent.

There are two reasons for regressive assessment practices. First, assessors do not always keep up with changes in property value: unless property is reassessed as it increases in value, the assessment ratio decreases over time. Since market values typically rise more rapidly in wealthy neighborhoods, the assessment ratio of high-income housing decreases relatively fast over time (see Engle, 1975). Second, assessors sometimes discriminate against multiple-family properties, assessing them at higher rates than single-family properties. Since a large fraction of the poor live in multiple-family buildings, the poor face higher effective tax rates. This phenomenon is discussed by Aaron (1975) and Netzer (1980).

Other Taxes

Property taxes generate less than half of municipal tax revenue. As was shown in Figure 16–1, the sales tax raises about three tenths of municipal tax revenue, and the income tax raises about one sixth of municipal revenue. Larger cities rely to a greater extent on the municipal income tax: the income tax generates about one fifth of tax revenue in cities with populations greater than 300,000. This section discusses the incidence of the municipal sales tax and income tax.

Municipal Sales Tax

Who pays the municipal sales tax? According to the theory of tax incidence, the distribution of the tax burden depends on the elasticities of supply and demand: the relatively inelastic side of the market pays a relatively large share of the tax.

Figure 18-4 shows the effects of a 25 percent general sales tax. The market starts at point *B*, with an equilibrium price of $8 and an equilibrium quantity of 30 units. If the tax is paid, in legal terms, by the city's merchants, their costs increase by

FIGURE 18–4   Market Effects of a Municipal Sales Tax

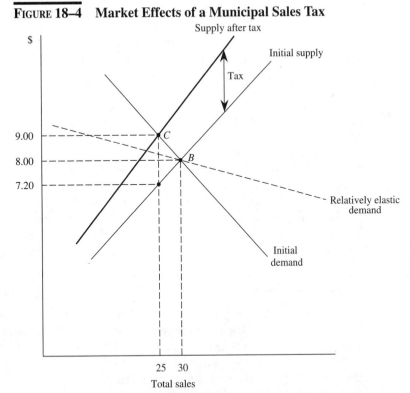

Before the sales tax, *B* is the equilibrium point. A 25 percent sales tax shifts the supply curve upward by 25 percent, generating a new equilibrium at point *C*. The consumer price rises from $8.00 to $9.00, and the revenue of the merchant (price less tax) drops from $8.00 to $7.20.

25 percent, shifting the supply curve upward. The equilibrium net price (the price charged by the merchant plus the tax) increases to $9.00, and total output decreases to 25 units (point *C*). Merchants charge consumers $9.00 and pay the government $1.80 in taxes, leaving them with $7.20. In this example, consumers pay about 55 percent of the tax (the $1 increase in price divided by the $1.80 tax).

How does a change in the elasticity of demand affect the distribution of the tax burden? Suppose that the demand curve in Figure 18–4 becomes more elastic: its slope decreases and it pivots around point *B*. The flatter demand curve (shown by the dashed line) intersects the post-tax supply curve at a lower net price, so consumers pay a smaller fraction of the tax. A relatively elastic demand means that consumers can more easily change their behavior, so they are better able to escape the tax.

How does a change in supply elasticity affect the distribution of the tax burden? For example, suppose the initial supply curve in Figure 18–4 is horizontal (perfectly elastic). The sales tax shifts the supply curve up by the amount of the tax, and the post-tax supply curve intersects the demand curve at a price equal to the original price plus the tax. In other words, if supply is perfectly elastic, the consumer bears the entire tax. In general, the more elastic the supply curve (the flatter the curve), the smaller the supplier burden and the larger the consumer burden.

The sales tax also affects the urban land market. As the city's sales volume decreases, the demands for all inputs (labor, land, capital) decrease: merchants need fewer laborers, machines, buildings, and land. In the short run, the prices of these inputs decrease. In the long run, inputs that are mobile (labor and capital) leave the taxing city, and the prices of the mobile inputs recover. In contrast, land is immobile, so the tax-induced decrease in the demand for land causes a permanent decrease in the price of land. Therefore, part of the sales tax is borne by landowners. Although merchants receive a lower net price ($7.20 instead of $8.00), they can still make zero economic profit (normal accounting profit) because they pay less for immobile inputs (e.g., land).

This discussion of the city's input markets shows the link between tax policy and economic development. The sales tax increases the net price of the city's products, so the city produces less output and uses less capital, labor, and land. In other words, the tax decreases output and employment. The local economy is particularly sensitive to changes in taxes because firms and households can easily move between jurisdictions. Because of the high degree of intercity mobility, relatively small differences in tax rates can cause relatively large changes in the level of economic activity.

Municipal Income Tax

As shown in the first chapter on the local public sector, the income tax generates about one sixth of municipal tax revenue. It will be useful to compare the municipal income tax to a national income tax. Figure 18–5 shows the effect of a national income tax. In the initial equilibrium (point *B*), the wage is $8 and the quantity of labor is N_o. Suppose that the federal government imposes an income tax of $2 per hour, which is paid in legal terms by the employer. The tax shifts the demand curve down by $2, decreasing the market wage (paid to employees) from $8.00 to $6.10. The net cost of labor (the wage plus the employer's tax liability) rises from $8.00

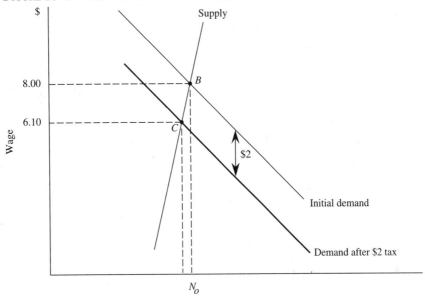

FIGURE 18–5 Market Effects of a National Income Tax

The initial equilibrium is point *B*. A $2 labor tax (paid by the employer) shifts the demand curve down by the amount of the tax, generating a new equilibrium at point *C*. The equilibrium wage (paid to laborers) drops from $8.00 to $6.10, meaning that workers pay about 95 percent of the $2 tax.

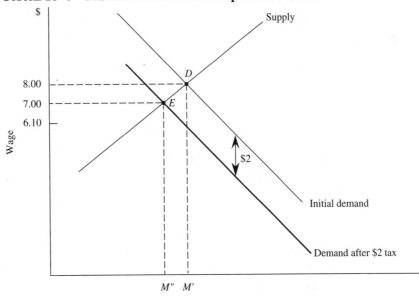

FIGURE 18–6 Market Effects of Municipal Income Tax

The initial equilibrium is point *D*. A $2 labor tax (paid by the employer) shifts the demand curve down by the amount of the tax, generating a new equilibrium at point *E*. The equilibrium wage (paid to laborers) drops from $8 to $7, meaning that suppliers pay only about half of the $2 tax. Workers pay a smaller portion of the municipal tax because the municipal supply of labor is more elastic than the national supply.

to $8.10. Workers pay almost the entire tax because the supply of labor is relatively inelastic.

Figure 18–6 shows the effect of a municipal income tax. Since laborers can move easily from one municipality to another, the municipal supply curve is more elastic than the national supply curve. When the municipality imposes a $2 income tax, the demand curve shifts down by $2, decreasing the market wage from $8 to $7. Compared to the national income tax, the municipal tax causes a smaller decrease in the market wage ($1.00 instead of $1.90) because it is easier to escape the municipal tax. Because intercity migration is less costly than international migration, laborers bear a smaller fraction of the municipal tax.

The municipal income tax increases the net cost of labor from $8 to $9. In other words, the demander's share of the tax is $1. If all firms make zero profits, who actually pays this part of the tax? The tax is paid by the owners of immobile resources: it is paid by owners of inputs that cannot be moved to other cities with the fleeing laborers. As the level of economic activity in the taxing city decreases (the number of laborers decreases from M' to M''), the demand for land decreases, lowering the price of land. Although firms pay a higher net wage ($9 instead of $8), they also pay less for land, so they can still make zero economic profits.

Intergovernmental Grants

As was shown in Table 16–3, intergovernmental grants provide about two fifths of local-government revenue. The spending programs receiving the largest amount of grant money are education, public welfare, housing and community development, highways, and health and hospitals.

Why Intergovernmental Grants?

Why don't local governments pay their own way, supporting their spending programs with local taxes? There are two principal reasons. First, intergovernmental grants can be used to internalize interjurisdictional spillovers, as discussed in Chapter 16. Second, local tax instruments are relatively inflexible, causing mismatches between local tax revenue and local expenditures.

The mismatch problem occurs if the desired spending on local public goods rises faster than the tax base. Figure 18–7 shows the mismatch problem for a city with the following characteristics:

1. Local public goods are financed with the residential property tax.
2. Income is rising twice as fast as property values.
3. The desired spending on local public goods is proportional to income: the income elasticity of demand for local public goods is 1.0.

At the start of the decade, the desired spending equals the average property tax liability. Because income increases at twice the rate of property values, the desired spending increases twice as fast as the average tax liability. By the end of the decade, there

FIGURE 18–7   Mismatch between Desired Spending and Tax Revenue

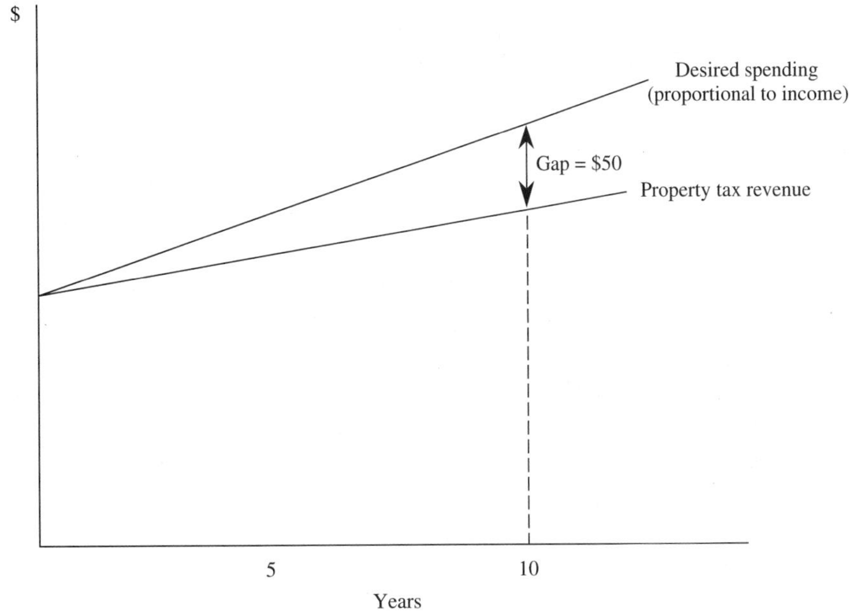

If income rises twice as fast as property values, the desired spending rises twice as fast as property tax revenue. The gap between tax revenue and desired spending grows to $50 by the end of the decade. An increase in the tax rate would close the gap.

is a $50 gap between desired spending and taxes. The mismatch occurs because (1) property values are relatively sluggish and (2) the tax rate is fixed.

There are two possible responses to the mismatch between taxes and desired spending. The obvious response is to increase the tax rate. The alternative approach is to transfer surplus federal tax revenue to the local government. The federal income tax will generate a surplus if (1) the income tax has a progressive rate structure and (2) federal spending is a constant fraction of income. In Figure 18–7, a federal transfer of $50 per capita would solve the local mismatch problem.

Unconditional Grants

An unconditional grant is a lump-sum grant with no strings attached. An example of an unconditional grant is general revenue sharing, under which the federal government provides unrestricted grants to localities. The local response to an unconditional grant can be predicted by examining the effects of the grant on the preferences of the median voter.

Figure 18–8 shows the budget lines and indifference curves of Marian, the median voter in city G. The city provides a number of local public goods and pays for them with local taxes: for every dollar spent on public goods there is one dollar of taxes, so there is one less dollar to spend on private goods. The indifference curves, which show Marian's subjective trade-off between public and private goods,

FIGURE 18–8   **Effects of a $20 Unconditional Grant**

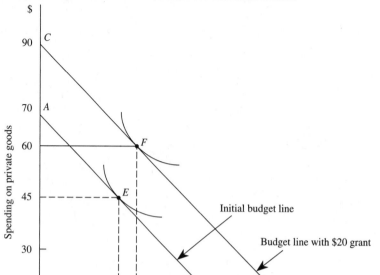

An unconditional grant of $20 per capita shifts the budget line of the median voter from *AB* to *CD*. The utility-maximizing combination of public and private goods moves from point *E* to point *F*. Spending on local public goods increases by $5, and spending on private goods increases by $15. The local government responds to the grant by cutting local taxes, allowing citizens to spend three fourths of the grant on private goods.

are convex, reflecting the diminishing marginal rate of substitution between public and private goods. Given the initial budget line (*AB*) and her indifference curves, Marian's utility is maximized at point *E*. According to the median-voter model described in the previous chapter, the city chooses the preferred budget of the median voter, so the city spends $25 per household on public goods, leaving Marian $45 for private goods.

Suppose that the state gives the city an unconditional grant of $20 per household. The city makes the following announcement to its citizens: "The state has just given us $20 per household. Tell us how much to spend on public services, and we'll cut taxes to distribute the rest of the grant to you." The grant shifts Marian's budget line upward, from *AB* to *CD*, increasing her desired spending on public goods to $30 (point *F*). The city, adhering to the preferences of the median voter, increases its budget by $5 and cuts taxes, thus distributing the rest of the grant ($15) to its citizens. The tax cut allows Marian to increase private consumption to $60.

One of the predictions of the median-voter model is that an unconditional grant has the same effect on local spending as an equal increase in per capita income. In fact, there is conclusive evidence that cities spend a relatively large fraction of an unconditional grant on public goods, meaning that a grant is not equivalent to an increase in income. This phenomenon is known as the **flypaper effect:** the grant money sticks where it first hits (the local government).

Some of the theories of the flypaper effect assume that city officials either confuse or deceive their citizens. In a model developed by Filimon, Romer, and Rosenthal (1982), the objective of city bureaucrats is to maximize the city budget. If bureaucrats do not publicize the grant, citizens are unlikely to demand tax cuts, so a large fraction of the grant can be used to increase government spending.

Lump-Sum Conditional Grants

The money from a **conditional grant** or **categorical grant** must be spent on a specific program. Conditional grants are provided for education, public welfare, health and hospitals, highways, housing, and community development. There are program-specific grants within each expenditure group. For example, the $1.5 billion in education grants is composed of specific grants for remedial reading, school libraries, special education, and other programs.

Suppose that the state gives the city a lump-sum grant of $20 per capita for special-education programs. Figure 18–9 shows Marian's preferences for special education and all other goods. "Other goods" includes private goods and other local public goods. The grant shifts Marian's budget line from *AB* to *AGD*. Point *G* is in the new budget set because Marian could spend all of her own money on other goods and use the $20 grant to support special education. As spending on special education increases above $20, there is a dollar-for-dollar trade-off between spending on special education and other goods, so the slope of the budget line is 1.0.

The grant increases Marian's desired spending on both special education and other goods. If the city adheres to the preferences of the median voter, spending on special education increases from $25 to $30 and spending on other goods increases from $45 to $60. One quarter of the grant is spent on special education, and three fourths is spent on other goods.

The city can spend part of the grant on other goods because it decreases its own contribution to special education. Before the grant, $25 of local tax money was spent on special education. After the grant, spending on special education is $30, and the city can pay for its special-education program with the $20 grant and $10 of local tax money. The grant frees up $15 worth of local tax money, which can be spent on other local public goods and private goods.

In Figure 18–9, the conditional grant is equivalent to an unconditional grant. Because the desired spending exceeds the grant, the community can replace its own spending on special education with the grant: in effect, the grant has no strings attached. In graphical terms, the budget lines of the two grants are identical as long as the desired spending exceeds the grant (as long as the city chooses a point to the right of *G*).

FIGURE 18–9 **Effects of a $20 Conditional Grant**

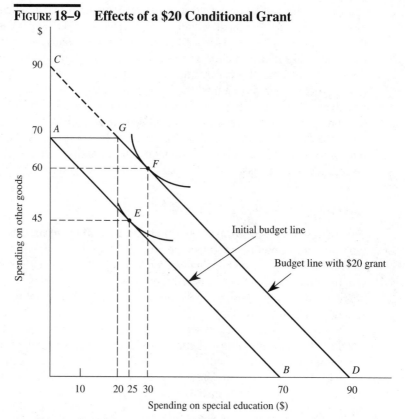

A conditional grant of $20 per capita shifts the budget line of the median voter from *AB* to *AGD*. The utility-maximizing combination moves from point *E* to point *F:* one fourth of the grant is spent on special education. The city uses the grant to decrease its contribution to special education, providing more money to spend on other goods. Because the desired spending on special education exceeds the grant, the conditional grant is equivalent to an unconditional grant.

The conditional grant is not equivalent to the unconditional grant if the desired spending on special education is less than $20. Suppose that the city starts with spending of $5 on special education, and the desired spending increases to $10 under the unconditional grant. In other words, the city moves to a point midway along the segment *CG*. In contrast, the city is likely to choose point *G* under the conditional grant. Since the city wishes to spend less than $20 on special education, it cannot substitute the conditional grant for its own spending on special education, so a conditional grant is not equivalent to an unconditional grant. The unconditional grant generates a higher utility level for voters in the city. The conditional grant causes a larger increase in spending on special education.

Matching Grants: Open-Ended

Under a matching grant, the government contributes $$m$ for every $1 of local spending on a program. One possibility is a one-for-one matching grant: every $1 of local spending generates $1 in grant money, so $1 of local spending buys $2 worth of local public goods. There are two types of matching grants, open-ended and closed-ended.

Figure 18–10 shows the effect of a one-for-one matching grant for special education. The grant decreases the slope of Marian's budget line from 1.0 to 0.50: instead of a dollar-for-dollar trade-off, Marian gets $2 worth of special education for every $1 she diverts from other goods. Given the new budget line, Marian's optimum point moves from point *E* to point *H*. If the city adheres to the preferences of the median voter, spending on special education increases from $25 to $40 and spending on other goods increases from $45 to $50. Half of the city's $40 special-education budget comes from the state government, so the local contribution to special education is $20, leaving $50 for spending on other goods. In other words, the city spends one quarter of the matching grant on other goods.

The matching grant provides a greater stimulus to special education than an equivalent lump-sum conditional grant. Although the state spends the same amount on each type of grant ($20), the matching grant increases spending on special education to $40, while the lump-sum grant increases spending to only $30 (see Figure 18–9). The matching grant has a relatively large stimulative effect because it has

FIGURE 18–10   Effects of an Open-Ended Matching Grant

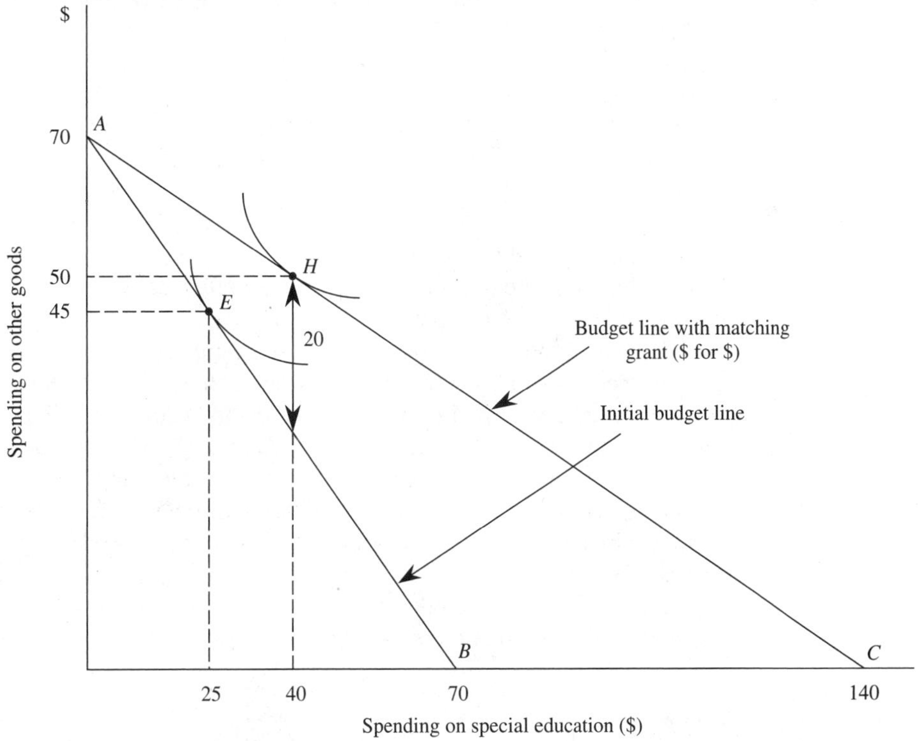

An open-ended matching grant shifts the budget line of the median voter from *AB* to *AC*. The utility-maximizing combination moves from point *E* to point *H:* three fourths of the grant is spent on special education. The matching grant decreases the opportunity cost of spending on special education, providing a greater stimulus to special education than an equivalent lump-sum grant.

both an income effect and a substitution effect. Both grants increase real income by $20 per capita, increasing the demand for all normal goods, including special education (the income effect). The matching grant also has a substitution effect: the matching grant cuts the relative price of special education in half (from 1.0 to 0.50), causing the substitution of special education for other goods. Since the matching grant has a substitution effect as well as an income effect, it increases spending by a larger amount.

The information in Figure 18–10 could be used to plot two points on the city's demand curve for special education. Before the matching grant, the "price" of special education is $1: there is a dollar-for-dollar trade-off between special education and other goods. At a price of $1, the quantity of special education demanded is $25 (point *E*). The matching grant decreases the price to $0.50, and increases the quantity demanded to $40 (point *H*). Since the grant does not affect the other determinants of demand (income and other prices), points *E* and *H* identify two points on the demand curve: ($1, $25) and ($0.50, $40).

Matching Grants: Closed-Ended

Under a closed-ended matching grant, the government specifies a maximum grant. In Figure 18–11, the maximum grant is $30: the government provides matching funds up to a total of $30. The budget line has a kink at the point at which the grant limit sets in. Given a one-for-one matching grant, the kink occurs when spending on special education (the sum of city spending and grant money) reaches $60. For spending above $60 (below point *D*), every additional dollar spent on special education decreases local spending on other goods by $1, so the slope of the budget line is 1.0.

In Figure 18–11, the city's response to the closed-ended grant program is the same as its response to the open-ended program. Since the desired spending level ($40), is less than the limit, the grant limit is irrelevant. Therefore, the closed-ended grant is equivalent to the open-ended grant.

The two grants are not equivalent if the desired spending under the open-ended grant exceeds $60. In Figure 18–11, the open-ended budget line is the line *ADC*, and the closed-ended budget line is *ADI*. If the desired spending under the open-ended grant exceeds $60, the city will choose a point along the segment *DC*. In this region, the open-ended budget line (segment *DC*) lies above the closed-ended grant (segment *DI*). Spending is higher under the open-ended grant for two reasons. First, real income is higher under the open-ended grant, producing an income effect that increases spending on all normal goods, including special education. Second, the opportunity cost of special education is lower under the open-ended grant, producing a substitution effect that increases spending on special education.

Block Grants

Under a block grant program, dozens of conditional grants are consolidated into a single general grant. For example, all grants for education (special education, reme-dial reading, kindergartens, libraries, and so on) could be consolidated into a single

FIGURE 18–11   Effects of a Closed-Ended Matching Grant

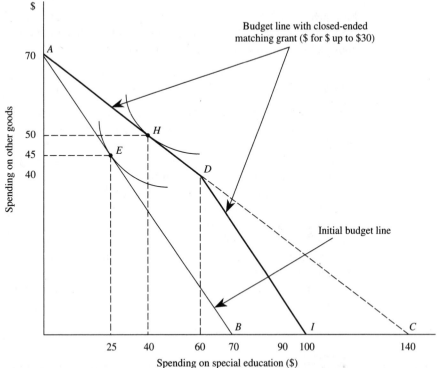

A closed-ended matching grant shifts the budget line of the median voter from *AB* to *ADI*. The utility-maximizing combination moves from point *E* to point *H*. Since the desired spending level ($40) is less than the limit ($60), the grant limit is irrelevant, and the closed-ended grant is equivalent to the open-ended grant. If desired spending exceeded the limit, the city would spend less under the closed-ended grant than under the open-ended grant.

block grant for education. The block grant is a compromise between unconditional and conditional grants. Although the city is forced to spend the entire education block grant on education, it can choose how to allocate the money between special education, remedial reading, kindergartens, and libraries. This greater flexibility is welcomed by local officials, but is often opposed by state and federal officials, who lose some control over grant money.

Summary: The Stimulative Effects of Grants

As explained earlier, local governments use intergovernmental grants to increase local expenditures and to cut local taxes. The tax cuts allow local citizens to spend part of the grant on private goods. The empirical question is: what fraction of grant money is used for additional local spending, and how much is used to cut taxes? Inman (1979) summarizes the results of several studies of the local response to grants. He concludes that local-government spending increases by about 30 cents per dollar of grant money, leaving 70 cents per dollar for tax relief.

Capitalization and the Distributional Effects of Grants

Intergovernmental grants are often used to promote income redistribution. Grants are targeted to two types of communities: those with a large number of low-income households and those with relatively high tax rates.

Grants to Low-Income Communities

Consider a state with two cities, a wealthy one and a poor one. In the poor city, all households rent housing for $400 per month. In an attempt to redistribute income from the rich to the poor, the state imposes a tax on the wealthy city and uses the tax revenue to support a grant to the poor city of $100 per household. Suppose that the poor city responds to the grant by cutting its income tax by $100 per household.

Figure 18–12 shows the effect of the grant program on the housing market in the poor city. The decrease in local taxes increases the relative attractiveness of the city, causing migration to the city that shifts the demand curve for housing upward. The equilibrium price of housing increases, from $400 to $435. Because the grant increases the price of housing, the net benefit per household is only $65 ($100 less the $35 increase in rent).

The intergovernmental grant is a blunt instrument for income redistribution for two reasons. First, the grant is tied to a location, not to a poor household. The grant

FIGURE 18–12   Grant to Poor City and the Price of Housing

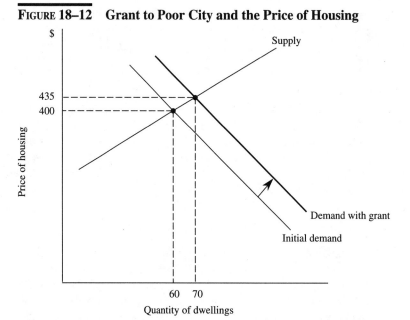

A grant to a poor community increases the relative attractiveness of the community, increasing the demand for housing and housing prices. The grant is capitalized into housing prices, so some of the benefits of the grant accrue to property owners.

increases the market value of land and housing in the poor city, generating benefits for property owners. In other words, the grant is capitalized into housing and land prices. Second, although part of the grant goes to households in the recipient city, all households in the city benefit, not just poor households.

Grants to High-Tax Communities

Under some grant programs, the size of the grant depends on "local tax effort." A city with relatively high tax rates receives a relatively large grant. Is this equitable?

Suppose that there are two cities in a region, North and South. North has harsh winters, so the city has high taxes to support large expenditures on highway maintenance. In contrast, South has mild winters and a relatively low tax rate. In equilibrium, people must be indifferent between living in the two cities, so the differences in tax rates are capitalized into property values. The residents of North pay high taxes, but are able to buy inexpensive land and housing. Similarly, the low taxes in South are offset by relatively high land and housing prices.

Suppose that highway grants are based on local tax effort, so North receives a larger highway grant. Is the grant policy equitable? Before the highway grant, households were indifferent between the two cities, with differences in tax rates capitalized into housing prices. Because citizens in the two cities achieve the same utility level before the grant, a larger grant to North does not necessarily promote "fairness." On the contrary, the relatively large grant to North increases property values in the city, generating capital gains for property owners.

Tax Expenditures: Implicit Grants

The federal government uses its tax code to influence local government spending. Two provisions of the federal income tax code affect local spending: the deductibility of local taxes and the exemption of interest from municipal bonds.

Deductibility of Local Taxes

Federal taxpayers can deduct local and state taxes on income and property from their taxable income. Consider a city with the following characteristics:

1. Marian, the median voter in the city, itemizes her deductions on her federal tax form.
2. Marian has a marginal tax rate of 28 percent.
3. All local taxes are deductible.

Figure 18–13 shows Marian's spending choices. In the absence of the deduction for local taxes, the opportunity cost of $1 of public spending is $1 of private spending, so the budget line is *AB*. The deductibility of local taxes decreases the opportunity cost of local spending to 72 cents on the dollar: every dollar of local taxes decreases Marian's federal tax liability by 28 cents, so she gives up only 72 cents worth of

FIGURE 18–13   **Deductibility of Local Taxes and Local Spending**

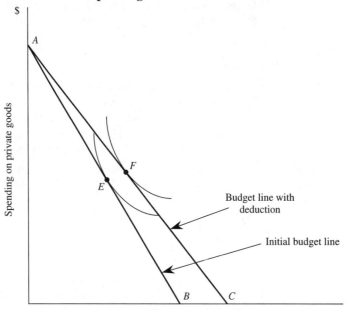

The deduction for local taxes decreases the opportunity cost of local spending, increasing the desired spending of the median voter. The deduction is equivalent to an open-ended matching grant.

private goods to consume $1 worth of local public goods. The deduction shifts the budget line from *AB* to *AC,* shifting Marian's preferred point from *E* to *F*. If the city adheres to the preferences of its median voter, it chooses point *F*.

The deduction for local taxes is equivalent to an open-ended matching grant. This can be seen by comparing Figures 18–13 and 18–10. The deduction is an example of a **tax expenditure:** the federal government stimulates local spending indirectly, providing tax cuts with the expectation that part of the tax cut will be spent on local public goods. Instead of giving the locality an intergovernmental grant of $20 per capita, the federal government gives local citizens a $20 tax cut. In other words, the federal government uses local taxpayers as intermediaries in its subsidization of local spending.

The stimulative effect of the federal tax deduction varies across cities. If the median voter in a middle-income city has a marginal tax rate of 15 percent, the city's federal subsidy is 15 cents per dollar of local spending. If the median-income voter in a higher-income city has a marginal tax rate of 28 percent, the city's federal subsidy is 28 cents per dollar. If the median voter in a low-income city does not itemize his deductions, the city's federal subsidy is zero.

Exemption of Interest on Local-Government Bonds

Because the interest earned on local-government bonds is not subject to the federal income tax, local governments can pay bondholders a relatively low interest rate. Consider Bill, whose marginal tax rate is 28 percent. Suppose that the market interest rate for private bonds is 12 percent. Since Bill declares his interest earnings on private bonds as taxable income, every $1 of interest income increases his federal tax liability by 28 cents. Therefore, the net return on private bonds is about 9 percent, not 12 percent. If the interest on local-government bonds is not taxable, the net return on a government bond is equal to its gross return. The local government can compete with private bonds by setting the interest rate on government bonds at about 9 percent. The tax exemption allows local governments to finance their capital projects at a fraction of the cost of private projects, so it stimulates local spending. The exemption is another example of a tax expenditure: the federal government stimulates local spending by giving up tax revenue, not by providing money directly to local governments.

Summary

1. The property tax is a tax on land and improvements (capital). Since the supply of land is fixed, the land tax is borne by landowners. There are two perspectives on the incidence of the improvement tax.
   a. The traditional view takes a partial-equilibrium approach, focusing on the effect of the improvement tax on the taxing jurisdiction. The supply of dwellings is perfectly elastic, so the tax is paid by housing consumers.
   b. The new view takes a general-equilibrium approach, focusing on the effect of the tax on people inside and outside the taxing jurisdiction. Property owners throughout the region bear the tax, and consumers outside the taxing city gain at the expense of consumers in the taxing city.
2. The incidence of the improvement tax depends on one's perspective.
   a. A mayor should use the partial-equilibrium model (the traditional view) to estimate the effects of the city's property tax. From the local perspective, the tax is paid by local housing consumers.
   b. The president of a nation should use the general-equilibrium model to estimate the national effect of one city's tax. Because the tax causes zero-sum changes in housing rent, the president can ignore the effects on housing consumers. The tax is paid by the nation's capitalists.
   c. If all cities in the nation have the same property tax rate, the tax is paid by capitalists. There are no housing-price effects because there is nowhere for capitalists to move their capital.
3. The simple model of the property tax assumes that the national supply of capital is fixed. If the supply of capital is responsive to changes in net returns, capitalists shift part of the tax onto housing consumers in the form of higher housing prices.

4. The simple model assumes that households are immobile. If they can leave the taxing jurisdiction, they pass the tax onto landowners.

5. The analysis of the general property tax (on residential, commercial, and industrial property) is the same as the analysis of the residential property tax.
   a. According to the general-equilibrium model, the tax decreases the return on capital; consumer prices increase in the taxing city and decrease elsewhere.
   b. If a city imposes a higher effective tax rate on residential property, consumers pay more for housing, but less for other goods (e.g., pizza, clothes).

6. In the Tiebout world, a household's property tax bill is independent of its housing consumption: households sort themselves into homogeneous communities, so a household's tax bill depends only on its consumption of public goods.

7. Assessment practices cause differences between nominal and effective property tax rates.
   a. Because of underassessment, the nominal property tax rate exceeds the effective tax rate.
   b. Some cities systematically overassess low-value property and underassess high-value property, so the poor face a relatively high effective tax rate.

8. Taxes on sales and income are paid in part by landowners.
   a. The municipal sales tax is paid by consumers, who pay higher prices, and landowners, who receive less rent.
   b. The municipal income tax is paid by laborers, who receive lower wages, and landowners. Because labor is more mobile between municipalities than between nations, labor's share of a municipal income tax is smaller than its share of a national income tax.

9. The states provide the bulk of grants to local governments (86 percent of all grants). Grants are used to internalize externalities and solve the mismatch problem (desired spending rising faster than tax revenue).

10. The local response to an intergovernmental grant can be predicted by examining the effects of the grant on the budget choices of the median voter.
    a. Local governments respond to grants by cutting local taxes, so part of the grant money is spent on private goods.
    b. If citizens don't know about grants, government spending may increase by a relatively large amount (the flypaper effect).
    c. A conditional grant is equivalent to an unconditional grant if the desired spending exceeds the grant: the local government can replace its own spending with the grant money, so the conditional grant is the same as a cash payment.
    d. A matching grant has a relatively large stimulative effect because it has a substitution effect and an income effect.

11. Under a block grant program, dozens of conditional grants are consolidated into a single general grant.

12. Intergovernmental grants are capitalized into property values, so part of a grant to a low-income community ends up in the pockets of property owners. Similarly, grants to high-tax communities generate benefits for property owners.

13. The federal government uses tax expenditures to stimulate local spending. Taxpayers act as intermediaries in the stimulation of local spending.
    a. The deduction for local taxes decreases the opportunity cost of government spending.
    b. The exemption of interest on local bonds decreases the cost of government borrowing.

Exercises and Discussion Questions

1. Consider the new view of the property tax. Based on the Taxville example, compute the long-run effects of Taxville's property tax on the following individuals. How much do they gain or lose?
   a. Ms. Partial rents a house in Taxville.
   b. Mr. Wash is a traveling salesman who rents one dwelling in Taxville and one in Notax.
   c. Ms. Capitalist owns five dwellings in Taxville.
   d. Mr. Capitalist owns five dwellings in Notax.

2. In the Taxville example, a 2 percent property tax decreased net rental income by $400 in each city. Suppose that the region has four cities instead of just two.
   a. By how much will the property tax increase dwelling rent in the taxing city?
   b. By how much will the tax decrease net rental income?

3. Choose the word in parentheses that makes the following statement correct, and then explain your choice: As the moving cost of households decreases, the tax-induced increase in Taxville's dwelling rent (*increases, decreases*).

4. Mr. Javelin is the economic forecaster for the city of Drip, Oregon. You are his research assistant and do all of his computations. The city is considering a tax of $2 per raincoat. In estimating the revenue from the raincoat tax, you make the following assumptions:
   i. The supply of raincoats to the city is perfectly elastic.
   ii. The current price of raincoats is $20, and the current quantity of raincoats demanded is 1,000 per week.
   iii. The price elasticity of demand for raincoats is −2.0.
   a. Estimate the tax revenue from the raincoat tax.
   b. When Mr. Javelin sees your computations, he says: "Those revenue projections look pretty low. You know, the state imposed a $2 raincoat tax several years ago and it raised $39,000 per week. Since about 5 percent of the state's raincoats are bought in Drip, I would expect that we would

raise about 5 percent of the revenue raised by the state tax. If your revenue projection is less than $1,950, it's wrong." Is Mr. Javelin correct? If so, what is your mistake? If not, what is wrong with his analysis?

5. The city of Tinytown is one of 10 municipalities in a large metropolitan area. Compare the incidence of a Tinytown income tax to the incidence of a metropolitan income tax.

6. Suppose Collegetown eliminates its tax on pizza parlors and increases its tax on residential property. Under what conditions will the change in tax policy decrease the tax liability of Joe College?

7. Consider a school district with a total budget of $500,000. The district is currently spending $250,000 on special-education programs for disadvantaged students (SE programs). There are three types of federal grants for SE programs:

Grant A: Unconditional grant of $100,000 to the school district.

Grant B: Categorical grant (money to be spent on SE programs) of $100,000. To ensure that the categorical grant is spent on SE, the federal government gives 100,000 marked dollar bills to the school district. On each dollar bill is written: "This dollar must be spent on special education."

Grant C: Categorical matching grant (dollar for dollar) with a maximum subsidy of $100,000. For each $1 spent by the school district on SE, the federal government gives it $1.

   a. Use diagrams to illustrate the district's responses to the three types of grants.

   b. How would the district's responses differ if the pre-grant expenditures on SE were only $50,000?

School District	Type of Grant	Educational Spending
E	None	$50
F	$1 grant for $1 local	70
G	$0.33 grant for $1 local	60

8. The state of Grantland has experimented with different types of matching grants for education. The state picked three identical school districts and used three different matching grants. The results are shown in the table above.

   a. Map the demand curve for education—different combinations of price (opportunity cost) and quantity (educational spending).

   b. Using the data for school districts E and F, compute the price elasticity of demand for education.

9. If the flypaper effect occurs, will the deductibility of local taxes still be equivalent to a matching grant? Which policy will generate a larger increase in local-government spending?

10. The discussion of the mismatch between local tax revenue and desired spending assumes that the desired spending on local public goods is proportional to income: the income elasticity of demand for public spending is 1.0. Another implicit assumption is that the unit cost of local public goods is constant. Draw the spending and tax lines for the following two cases:

    a. The income elasticity of demand for local spending is 2.0. Does the larger income elasticity generate a larger or a smaller gap between desired spending and tax revenue?

    b. The income elasticity of demand for local spending is 1.0, but the unit cost of local public goods increases by 25 percent over the course of the decade. Does rising cost generate a larger or a smaller gap between desired spending and tax revenue?

11. Consider the distributional effects of intergovernmental grants. In the example shown in Figure 18–12, the $100 grant to the poor city decreased the city's income taxes, generating benefits for both tenants (the poor) and landowners. Suppose that instead of cutting taxes, the city increases spending on schools, police, fire protection, and parks. Will the benefits of the grants still be shared by tenants and landowners?

References and Additional Readings

Revenue Facts

U.S. Bureau of the Census. *Census of Governments.* Washington, D.C.: Department of Commerce, 1987.

U.S. Bureau of the Census. *Government Finances in 1984–85.* Washington, D.C.: Department of Commerce, 1987.

Property Tax Incidence

Aaron, Henry J. *Who Pays the Property Tax? A New View.* Washington, D.C.: Brookings Institution, 1975. Discusses the traditional and new views of the property tax. Describes the administrative problems of the property tax, including assessment errors.

Aronson, J. Richard, and John L. Hilley. *Financing State and Local Governments.* Washington, D.C.: Brookings Institution, 1986.

Boskin, Michael. "Taxation, Saving, and the Rate of Interest." *Journal of Political Economy* 86 (1978), pp. S3–S28. Estimates that the supply of savings is responsive to the rate of return, with an elasticity between 0.20 and 0.60.

Freeman, Richard B. "How Do Public Sector Waste and Employment Respond to Economic Conditions?" Working Paper no. 1653, National Bureau of Economic Research, Cambridge, Mass., 1985.

Mieszkowski, Peter. "The Property Tax: An Excise Tax or a Profits Tax?" *Journal of Public Economics* 1 (1972), pp. 73–96. Discusses the new view of the property tax.

Pechman, Joseph A. *Who Paid the Taxes, 1966–1985?* Washington, D.C.: Brookings Institution, 1985. Estimates the incidence of the property tax under the traditional view and the new view.

Property Tax: Administration and Reform

Aaron, Henry J. *Who Pays the Property Tax? A New View.* Washington, D.C.: Brookings Institution, 1975. Chapter 4 discusses the administrative problems of the property tax, including assessment errors. Chapters 5 and 6 discuss reform proposals.

Aronson, J. Richard, and John L. Hilley. *Financing State and Local Governments.* Washington, D.C.: Brookings Institution, 1986. Chapter 7 discusses some of the assessment problems associated with the property tax.

Black, David E. "Property Tax Incidence: The Excise-Tax Effect and Assessment Practices." *National Tax Journal* 30 (1977), pp. 429–34. Discusses the effects of regressive assessment practices on the incidence of the property tax.

Engle, Robert F. "De Facto Discrimination in Residential Assessments: Boston." *National Tax Journal* 28 (1975), pp. 445–51. Shows that assessment ratios are inversely related to market values.

Ihlanfeldt, Keith. "Property Tax Incidence on Owner-Occupied Housing: Evidence from the Annual Housing Survey." *National Tax Journal* 35 (1982), pp. 89–97. A study of regressive assessment in Philadelphia and Atlanta.

Netzer, Richard. *Real Property Tax Policy for New York City.* New York: New York University, 1980. Shows that assessment ratios are relatively low for one-family and two-family houses.

Peterson, George E. *Property Tax Reform.* Washington, D.C.: Urban Institute, 1973.

Income and Sales Taxes

Aronson, J. Richard, and John L. Hilley. *Financing State and Local Governments.* Washington, D.C.: Brookings Institution, 1986. Chapter 8 discusses the local sales tax, the income tax, and user fees.

Intergovernmental Grants: Reasons, Types, and Effects

Aronson, J. Richard, and John L. Hilley. *Financing State and Local Governments.* Washington, D.C.: Brookings Institution, 1986. Chapter 3 discusses federal intergovernmental grants, and Chapter 4 discusses state grants.

Courant, Paul N.; Edward M. Gramlich; and Daniel Rubinfeld. "The Stimulative Effect of Intergovernmental Grants, or Why Money Sticks Where It Hits." In *Fiscal Federalism and Grants-in-Aid,* ed. Peter Mieszkowski and William Oakland. Washington, D.C.: Urban Institute, 1979. Discusses the flypaper effect.

Filimon, R., T. Romer, and H. Rosenthal. "Asymmetric Information and Agenda Control: The Bases of Monopoly Power and Public Spending." *Journal of Public Economics* 17 (1982), pp. 51–70.

Gramlich, E. M. "Intergovernmental Grants: A Review of the Empirical Literature." In *The Political Economy of Fiscal Federalism,* ed. Wallace E. Oates. Lexington, Mass.: Lexington Books, 1977. Reviews the literature on the effects of grants on local spending. Concludes that matching grants are more stimulative than lump-sum grants, and the categorical grant has a larger stimulative effect than an equivalent increase in private income.

Inman, Robert P. "The Fiscal Performance of Local Government: An Interpretive Review." In *Current Issues in Urban Economics,* ed. Peter Mieszkowski and Mahlon Straszheim. Baltimore: The Johns Hopkins University Press, 1979, pp. 270–321.

Ornstein, Norman J. "Chipping Away at the Old Blocks." The *Brookings Bulletin* 18 (1982), pp. 11–15. Discusses the reasons for categorical and block grants.

Tax Expenditures

Ladd, Helen F. "Federal Aid to State and Local Governments." In *Federal Budget Policy in the 1980s,* ed. Gregory V. Mills and John L. Palmer. Washington, D.C.: Urban Institute, 1984. Discusses the role of tax expenditures in intergovernmental finance.

CHAPTER 19 Autos and Highways

The home is where part of the family waits until the others are through with the car.

Herbert Prochnow

This is the first of two chapters on urban transportation. It discusses the most popular travel mode, the automobile, which is used by about 83 percent of U.S. commuters. It examines three transportation problems caused by the automobile: congestion, air pollution, and highway accidents. Congestion during rush hours is inevitable, and a certain level of congestion is actually efficient. Just as it would be inefficient to eliminate all air pollution, it would be inefficient to eliminate all congestion. The question is whether congestion is at the optimum level. If not, there are a number of policies that could decrease congestion, including various taxes on auto travel, subsidies for mass transit, and highway construction. The second problem, air pollution, is controlled by the federal government through its auto emissions policies. The question is whether other pollution-control policies such as pollution taxes or gas taxes might be more efficient in controlling pollution. The third transportation problem is auto safety. Traffic accidents injure and kill people, and also disrupt traffic flow, contributing to the congestion problem. The policy question is: how do government policies affect highway death rates and accident rates?

Table 19–1 shows commuting patterns and auto usage in U.S. cities in 1980. (The relevant data from the 1990 census (in *Journey to Work*) was not available at the time this book was published.) About one third of workers commute within the central city, and about one fifth commute from a suburban residence to a central-city job. The most frequent commuting trip is from a suburban residence to a suburban job, a trip made by about 40 percent of commuters. Over four fifths of commuters travel to work by car, truck, or van, and about two thirds of these commuters drive to work alone. The private vehicle is most popular among suburbanites: it is used by over 90 percent of the workers who commute between the suburbs and the city center and over 87 percent of the workers who commute from one suburb to another.

TABLE 19–1   Commuting Patterns and Auto Use

Type of Commute	Percent of All Trips	Percent Using Car, Truck, or Van	Percent Driving Alone	Percent in Carpools
Central city to central city	33.1%	72.4%	56.1%	16.3%
Central city to suburb	6.8	91.3	69.2	22.1
Suburb to central city	20.1	90.3	68.1	22.2
Suburb to suburb	40.1	87.5	69.7	17.8
Total	100.0	83.3	64.9	18.5

SOURCE: U.S. Bureau of the Census, *1980 Census of Population: Journey to Work—Metropolitan Commuting Flows* (Washington, D.C.: U.S. Government Printing Office, 1984).

Congestion: Equilibrium versus Optimum Traffic Volume

Most cities suffer from traffic congestion during the morning and evening rush hours. To explain the congestion phenomenon, consider a city with the following characteristics:

1. **Radial highway.** There is a two-lane highway from the suburbs to the city center (a distance of 10 miles).
2. **Monetary travel cost.** The monetary cost of auto travel is 20 cents per mile.
3. **Time cost.** The opportunity cost of travel time is 10 cents per minute.

The total cost of a commuting trip is the sum of the monetary and time costs of the 10-mile trip. The monetary cost is $2 (10 miles times 20 cents per mile). The time cost depends on travel time: a trip that takes 30 minutes has a time cost of $3 (30 minutes times 10 cents per minute); a 20-minute trip has a time cost of only $2. Therefore, the total cost of a 30-minute trip is $5 ($2 plus $3), and the total cost of a 20-minute trip is $4.

The Demand for Urban Travel

Consider first the demand side of the urban travel market. Figure 19–1 shows the demand curve for travel along the radial highway. The horizontal axis measures the number of vehicles per lane per hour. The vertical axis measures the cost of the commuting trip, the sum of the monetary and time costs of the 10-mile trip. The demand curve shows, for each trip cost, how many travelers use the highway. For example, if the trip cost is $12.80, there are 1,200 people for whom the benefit of the trip exceeds the cost, so the traffic volume is 1,200 vehicles per lane per hour. As the cost of the trip decreases, there are more people for whom the benefit exceeds the cost, so the city moves downward along the travel demand curve: there are 1,400 vehicles at a cost of $9.14, and 1,600 vehicles at a cost of $5.48.

FIGURE 19–1   Congestion Externalities and the Congestion Tax

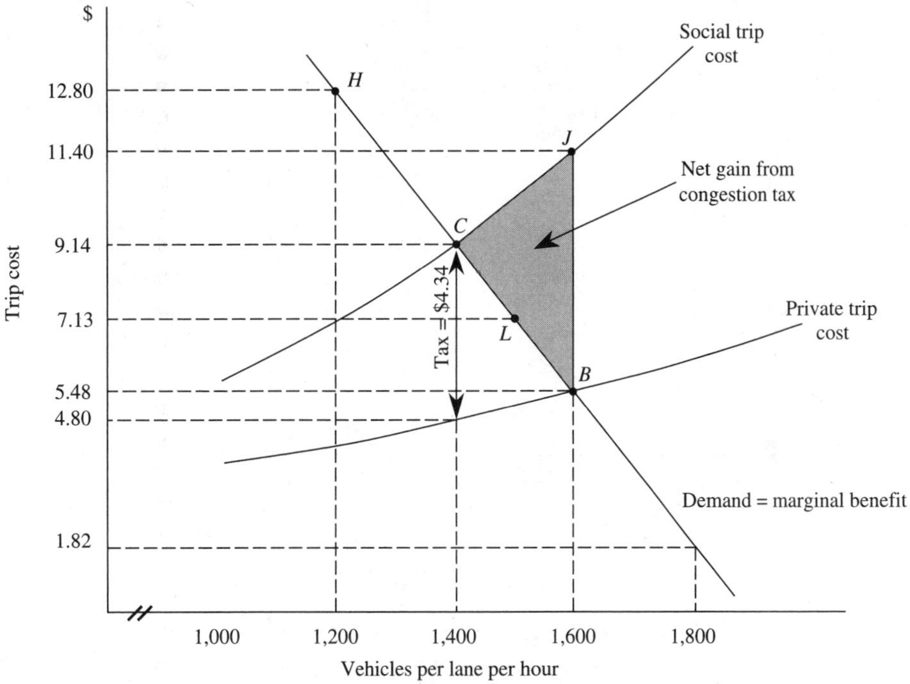

Drivers use the highway as long as the marginal benefit (shown by the demand curve) exceeds the private trip cost, so the equilibrium traffic volume is 1,600 vehicles per lane per hour. At the optimum, the marginal benefit equals the marginal social cost (the social trip cost). The equilibrium volume (1,600) exceeds the optimum volume (1,400) because drivers ignore the external costs of their trips. A congestion tax of $4.34 internalizes the congestion externality, generating the optimum traffic volume.

The demand curve is a **marginal-benefit curve**. For each traffic volume, it shows how much the marginal traveler is willing to pay for the highway trip. Suppose that the city starts with a trip cost of $9.15 and a traffic volume of 1,399. If the trip cost decreases to $9.14, traffic volume increases to 1,400, meaning that the 1,400th driver is willing to pay $9.14 to make the trip; at any cost above $9.14, the trip would not be worthwhile. The demand curve shows that the marginal benefit of the 10-mile trip decreases from $12.80 for the 1,200th driver to $1.82 for the 1,800th driver.

The Private and Social Costs of Travel

Table 19–2 shows the relationships between traffic volume and travel time. Column B lists the trip time (the travel time per driver) for different traffic volumes. For traffic volumes up to 400 vehicles per lane per hour, there is no congestion: everyone travels at the legal speed limit of 50 miles per hour, and the 10-mile trip takes 12 minutes.

TABLE 19–2   Traffic Volume, Travel Time, Travel Cost, and Congestion Externalities

A	B	C	D	E	F	G	H
		Increase in	Increase in				
Traffic		Travel Time	Total Travel	External	Private	Social	Marginal
Volume	Trip Time	per Driver	Time	Trip Cost	Trip Cost	Trip Cost	Benefit
(vehicles)	(minutes)	(minutes)	(minutes)	($)	($)	($)	(demand)
200	12.0	0	0	0	3.20	3.20	31.10
400	12.0	0	0	0	3.20	3.20	27.44
600	12.8	0.007	4.2	0.42	3.28	3.70	23.78
800	14.8	0.013	10.4	1.04	3.48	4.52	20.12
1,000	18.0	0.019	19.0	1.90	3.80	5.70	16.46
1,200	22.4	0.025	30.0	3.00	4.24	7.24	12.80
1,400	28.0	0.031	43.4	4.34	4.80	9.14	9.14
1,600	34.8	0.037	59.2	5.92	5.48	11.40	5.48
1,800	42.8	0.043	77.4	7.74	6.28	14.02	1.82
2,000	52.0	0.049	98.0	9.80	7.20	17.00	

For traffic volume above 400 vehicles, the computations are based on the following formula:

$$\text{Trip time} = 12.0 + 0.001 \cdot (\text{Volume} - 400) + 0.000015 \cdot (\text{Volume} - 400)^2 \quad (19\text{–}1)$$

When the 401st driver enters the highway, the congestion threshold is crossed. As the highway becomes crowded, the space between vehicles decreases and drivers slow down to maintain safe distances between cars. As more and more drivers enter the highway, travel speeds decrease and travel times increase: the trip takes 12.8 minutes if there are 600 vehicles, 22.4 minutes for 1,200 vehicles, and 52.0 minutes for 2,000 vehicles.

Columns C and D show the effects of the marginal driver on the travel times of other drivers. For low traffic volumes (below 400 vehicles), an additional driver does not affect speeds or travel times. For volumes above 400 vehicles, however, an additional driver slows traffic and increases travel times. For example, the 600th driver increases the travel time *per driver* by 0.007 minutes (column C): when the driver enters the highway, the trip time increases from 12.793 to 12.80. The increase in total travel time is simply the extra time per driver (0.007) times the number of other drivers (599), or 4.2 minutes (column D). This is the **congestion externality:** the marginal driver slows traffic and increases travel time, forcing other drivers to spend more time on the road. The congestion externality increases with traffic volume: the 1,200th driver increases travel time by 30 minutes (0.025 minutes times 1,199), and the 1,600th driver increases travel time by 59.2 minutes (0.037 times 1,599).

The **external trip cost** equals the monetary value of the congestion externality. The figures in column E are based on the assumption that the opportunity cost of travel time is 10 cents per minute. For the 600th driver, the external trip cost equals the increase in total travel time (4.2 minutes) times 10 cents per minute, or 42 cents. The external trip cost increases with traffic volume, rising to $3.00 for the 1,200th driver, $5.92 for the 1,600th driver, and $9.80 for the 2,000th driver.

Columns F and G show the private and social costs of travel. The **private trip cost** is the travel cost incurred by the individual commuter, defined as the sum of the monetary cost ($2.00) and the private time cost. To compute the private time cost, multiply the trip time by the opportunity cost of travel time: the opportunity cost is 10 cents per minute, so the private time cost is $1.20 for a volume of 200 vehicles, $1.28 for 600 vehicles, and so on. Therefore, the private trip cost is $3.20 for 200 vehicles, $3.28 for 600 vehicles, and so on. The **social trip cost** is the sum of the private trip cost (column F) and the external trip cost (column E). Figure 19–1 shows the cost curves for private trip cost and social trip cost. The social-cost curve lies above the private-cost curve, with the gap between the two curves equal to the external trip cost.

There are some alternative labels for private and social trip costs. An alternative label for private trip cost is **average travel cost**, defined as total travel cost divided by the number of drivers. Since each driver travels at the same speed and thus has the same travel cost, the average travel cost equals the private trip cost. An alternative label for social trip cost is **marginal travel cost**, defined as the increase in the total cost of travel resulting from adding one more traveler. Since the social trip cost equals the trip cost incurred by the marginal driver plus the external cost he imposes on other drivers, the social trip cost is the same as the marginal travel cost.

Equilibrium versus Optimum Traffic Volume

What is the equilibrium number of drivers? A driver uses the highway if the marginal benefit of a trip (from the demand curve) exceeds the private trip cost. In Figure 19–1, the demand curve intersects the private-trip-cost curve at 1,600, so the equilibrium number of vehicles is 1,600 and the equilibrium private trip cost is $5.48. The 1,601st driver does not use the highway because the marginal benefit of using the highway is less than the trip cost.

What is the optimum number of drivers? The basic efficiency rule is that an activity should be increased as long as the marginal social benefit exceeds the marginal social cost; at the optimum level, the marginal benefit equals the marginal cost. In Figure 19–1, the marginal social benefit is shown by the demand curve, and the marginal social cost is shown by the social-trip-cost curve. The demand curve intersects the social-trip-cost curve at a volume of 1,400, so the optimum traffic volume is 1,400 vehicles. For the first 1,400 drivers, the social benefit of travel exceeds the social cost, so their use of the highway is efficient. For the 1,401st driver, the social cost exceeds the benefit, so her use of the highway is inefficient.

The equilibrium volume exceeds the optimum volume because drivers ignore the costs they impose on other drivers. An additional driver slows traffic, forcing other drivers to spend more time on the road. Suppose that Carla, the 1,599th driver, has a private benefit of $5.49. From column F in Table 19–2, the private trip cost for 1,599 vehicles is about $5.48, so Carla uses the highway. Her use of the highway is inefficient because the benefit of the trip ($5.49) is less than the social cost of the trip ($11.40, equal to the sum of Carla's private cost of $5.48 and the external trip cost of $5.92). Because Carla ignores the $5.92 external cost, she makes an inefficient choice.

The Policy Response: Congestion Tax

The government could use a congestion tax to generate the optimum traffic volume. A tax equal to the external trip cost would internalize the congestion externality, generating the optimum number of drivers. In Figure 19–1, a congestion tax of $4.34 per trip would shift the private-trip-cost curve upward by $4.34, decreasing the equilibrium number of drivers from 1,600 to 1,400. The 1,401st driver would not use the road because the benefit of the trip ($9.13) would be less than the full cost of the trip ($9.14, the sum of the $4.80 private cost and the $4.34 congestion tax). Because the congestion tax closes the gap between private and social costs, the individual driver bases his travel decision on the social cost of travel. Therefore, the highway is used efficiently.

Benefits and Costs of Congestion Taxes

From the perspective of the individual traveler, the imposition of congestion taxes generates good news and bad news. People who continue to use the highway after the tax is imposed pay the tax, but also have a lower time cost: the tax decreases traffic volume, which decreases travel times. People who stop using the highway avoid the tax, but forgo the benefits associated with using the highway. In other words, there are costs and benefits for both types of people. Do the benefits outweigh the costs?

A key consideration in the evaluation of the congestion tax is the disposition of the revenue it generates. The government does not throw the tax revenue away, but presumably uses it to finance public services or to decrease other local taxes. In fact, as explained later in the chapter, the total revenue from the congestion tax is just enough to pay for the optimum highway. Therefore, the government could substitute congestion taxes for the gasoline tax, which is currently used to finance highways. To simplify matters, suppose that the government redistributes the tax revenue, in equal shares, to all of the households who use the highway before the congestion tax is imposed. In Figure 19–1, the pre-tax traffic volume is 1,600, so there are 1,600 highway users. The total tax revenue is $6,076 (1,400 vehicles at $4.34 per vehicle), so the transfer per household is $3.79 ($6,076/1,600).

Table 19–3 shows the costs and benefits for two travelers. Helen has a relatively large willingness to pay for highway use, so she uses the highway even after the congestion tax is imposed. In Figure 19–1, her position on the demand curve is shown by point H. Louis has a relatively small willingness to pay, so he stops using the highway after the tax is imposed (point L in Figure 19–1). What are the benefits and costs for the two travelers?

1. Helen pays a tax of $4.34 and receives a refund of $3.79, for a 55-cent net increase in taxes. The congestion tax decreases the private trip cost from $5.48 (at a volume of 1,600) to $4.80 (at a volume of 1,400), for a savings of 68 cents. The net benefit is 13 cents: a benefit of 68 cents less the tax increase of 55 cents.

2. Louis doesn't use the highway after the congestion tax is imposed. Before the tax, his benefit from using the highway equaled the gap between his willingness to pay (from the demand curve) and the private trip cost.

TABLE 19–3   **Benefits and Costs of Congestion Taxes**

	Congestion Tax	Tax Refund	Net Transfer	Time Savings	Consumer Surplus Lost	Net Benefit
Helen (H)	$4.34	$3.79	−$0.55	$0.68	—	+$0.13
Louis (L)	—	3.79	+ 3.79	—	$1.65	+ 2.14

Definitions

1. Total tax revenue = Tax per driver × Volume: 1,400 × $4.34 = $6,076.
2. Transfer payment = Total tax revenue ÷ Number of citizens: $6,076/1,600 = $3.79.
3. Net transfer = Refund − Congestion tax (if any).
4. Consumer surplus lost = Willingness to pay (from demand curve) − Private trip cost (before congestion tax).

This gap is his **consumer surplus** from using the highway. From Figure 19–1, Louis was willing to pay $7.13 for a trip with a private trip cost of $5.48, so his consumer surplus was $1.65 ($7.13 − $5.48). After the congestion tax, Louis does not use the highway, so he loses this surplus. Because the tax also provides a transfer payment of $3.79, Louis is better off after the congestion tax by $2.14: the transfer payment more than offsets his loss of consumer surplus.

In this example, both citizens benefit from the imposition of congestion taxes. A more rigorous analysis of the benefits and costs would show that some people in the city would be harmed by the congestion tax policy: for some travelers, the savings in travel costs and the transfer payment would not be large enough to offset the congestion tax or the loss in consumer surplus.

A more rigorous analysis would also show that the winners' benefits exceed the losers' costs. In other words, the move from the equilibrium to the optimum generates a net gain for society. In Figure 19–1, the net gain is shown by the shaded area, the area between the demand curve (the marginal-benefit curve) and the social-trip-cost curve. To explain this, suppose the city starts with the equilibrium volume (1,600 vehicles) and somehow persuades the 1,600th driver to not use the road. What are the benefits and costs of diverting the driver? On the benefit side, total travel cost decreases by the social trip cost for the 1,600th driver (about $11.40 at point J). On the cost side, the driver loses the benefits of the highway trip; the willingness to pay for the trip is shown by the demand curve (about $5.48 at point B). The net benefit from diverting the driver is the difference between the social trip cost and the willingness to pay, or $5.92. The social gain from diverting the 1,599th driver is slightly lower than this because the social trip cost is lower (the city starts lower on the cost curve) and the willingness to pay is higher (the city starts further up the demand curve). The net gain to society from moving from the equilibrium (point B) to the optimum (point C) is the sum of the differences between the social trip cost and the willingness to pay (from the demand curve) for the 1,600th through the 1,401st drivers. In other words, it is the area between the two curves, shown by the area of triangle CJB. Because there is a net gain from the move to the optimum point, the government could, in principle, redistribute income from the winners to the losers to ensure that everyone is made better off by the congestion tax.

Peak versus Off-Peak Travel

To be efficient, the congestion tax must vary across time and space. The tax should be higher on congested highways. The most congested highways are the ones leading to and from employment centers. Most congestion occurs during the morning and evening rush hours. According to Straszheim (1979), about a quarter of all trips are made during the rush hours. McConnell-Fay (1986) reports that 64 percent of the trips from homes to workplaces in the San Francisco Bay area occur between 6:30 and 8:30 A.M., and 57 percent of the workplace-home trips occur between 4:30 and 6:30 P.M. Figure 19–2 shows the demand curves and congestion tolls for the peak period and the off-peak period. Given the high volume of traffic during the peak period (V_p, compared to V_o during the off-peak period), the peak-period congestion toll is higher.

Estimates of Congestion Taxes

What is the optimum congestion tax? In a study of the San Francisco Bay area, Keeler and Small (1977) estimate congestion taxes for different locations and times. Pozdena (1988) updated the Keeler and Small estimates, and he estimates that during the

FIGURE 19–2   Congestion Tax during Peak and Off-Peak Periods

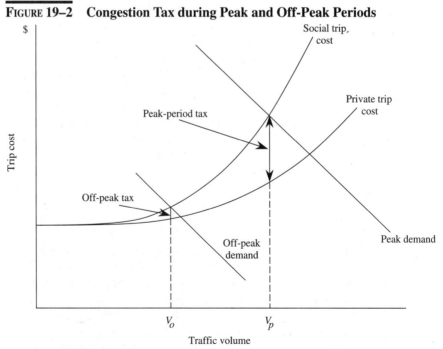

During the off-peak period, the demand for travel is relatively low, generating a low traffic volume (V_o, compared to V_p during the peak period), so the optimum congestion tax is relatively low.

peak travel periods, the congestion tax would be 65 cents per mile on central urban highways, 21 cents per mile on suburban highways, and 17 cents per mile on fringe highways. During the off-peak periods, the taxes would be between 3 and 5 cents per mile at all locations. Because the Bay area is more congested than most metropolitan areas, the optimum congestion taxes would be lower in most other metropolitan areas.

Suppose the Bay area implemented such a system of congestion tolls. How much would different types of commuters pay for travel during the peak periods? Consider first a suburban commuter who travels seven miles on suburban highways and three miles on central urban highways to a job in the central city. The commuter's one-way congestion bill would be $3.42 (seven miles times 21 cents plus three miles times 65 cents), so the daily congestion tax would be $6.84. Consider next a suburban commuter who travels eight miles to a job in another suburb. The commuter's one-way congestion tax would be $1.68 (eight miles times 21 cents per mile).

Implementing the Congestion Tax

How would the government collect the congestion tax? One possibility is to install toll booths on every road and collect the tax directly from drivers. This option is impractical because the collection process slows traffic, causing more congestion. The high-technology version of toll booths is a vehicle-identification system (VIS). Under a VIS, every car is equipped with an electronic device that allows sensors along the road to identify the car as it passes. The system records the number of times a vehicle uses the congested highway and sends a congestion bill to the driver at the end of the month. For example, a driver who travels 10 miles along a congested highway 20 times per month would pay a monthly congestion bill of $86.80 (20 times $4.34 as shown in Figure 19–1).

Why haven't cities used the VIS to impose congestion taxes? The systems are relatively inexpensive, so the opposition is not based on the costs of installing and running the system. Some people oppose VIS because they oppose congestion taxes in any form. A common complaint is that congestion taxes would be "regressive" (the poor would pay a larger fraction of their income for taxes). There is no evidence to support this view. Even if congestion taxes were regressive, the government could presumably adjust other taxes to offset the undesirable distributional effects of tolls. Other people oppose VIS because they are troubled by the potential threat to civil liberties: the information gathered from VIS might be used by an inquisitive government to spy on its citizens.

Alternatives to a Congestion Tax: Taxes on Auto Use

Given the practical difficulties in imposing a congestion tax, a number of alternative policies have been proposed. One set of policies discourages auto use by increasing the cost of auto travel. Three of the pricing options are gasoline taxes, parking taxes, and congestion-zone taxes. How effective are these policies compared to the congestion tax?

To set the stage for a discussion of the efficacy of the alternative policies, it will be useful to list the four ways that the congestion tax decreases traffic volume:

1. **Modal substitution**. The tax increases the cost of auto travel relative to carpooling and mass transit (buses, subways, light rail), causing some travelers to switch to these other travel modes.

2. **Time of travel**. The tax is highest during the peak travel periods, causing some travelers to travel at different times. Because work and study schedules are relatively inflexible, commuters and students would be less likely to change their travel times than other travelers (e.g., shoppers). Nonetheless, firms would have a greater incentive to change work schedules to allow their workers to avoid costly travel during the peak period. The institution of "flex-time" and the rearrangement of shift times would cause some workers to change their travel times.

3. **Travel route**. The congestion tax is highest on the most congested routes, causing some travelers to switch to alternative routes.

4. **Location choices**. The congestion tax increases the unit cost of travel (travel cost per mile), causing some commuters to decrease their commuting distances. Some workers may move closer to their jobs, and others may switch to jobs closer to their residences.

These four changes cause the city to move up the travel-demand curve as the cost of travel increases. In Figure 19–1, the congestion tax decreases traffic volume from 1,600 to 1,400 because it changes travel modes, times, routes, and distances.

Gasoline Tax

One alternative to the congestion tax is a gasoline tax. The simple idea is that if travel is more expensive, traffic volume decreases. The problem is that the gas tax increases the costs of all automobile travel, not just travel along congested routes during peak periods. In contrast with the congestion tax, which changes travel times and routes, the gas tax does not encourage drivers to switch to other travel times or routes.

Suppose the government wants to use the gasoline tax to decrease the peak-period traffic volume to its optimum level. What is the required gasoline tax? To have the same effect as the congestion tax in Figure 19–1, the gas tax must increase the cost of travel by 43.4 cents per mile ($4.34 per 10-mile trip). If the typical car gets 25 miles per gallon of gasoline, the required gas tax is $10.85 per gallon (43.4 cents times 25); if gas mileage is only 10 miles per gallon, the tax is $4.34 per gallon. Even if a gas tax at this level were feasible, it would be inefficient because it also increases the cost of off-peak travel by 43.4 cents per mile.

Parking Tax

A number of cities use parking taxes to discourage driving to CBD jobs. In an experiment in Madison, Wisconsin, a tax surcharge of $1 was imposed on drivers who arrived at parking garages during the peak travel period (7 A.M. to 9 A.M.) and left their cars for more than three hours. As explained by Parody (1984), the surcharge decreased traffic volume because (1) some commuters switched to carpools and mass transit and (2) some changed their travel times. In Washington, D.C., the government increased parking costs for its employees, causing some workers to switch to carpools and mass transit (Miller and Everett, 1982). In Ottawa, Canada, the government increased parking rates for government employees from zero to 70 percent of the commercial rate, causing (1) a 23 percent decrease in the number of workers driving to work, (2) a 6 percent increase in the auto occupancy rate (from 1.33 to 1.41), and (3) a 16 percent increase in bus ridership (DiRenzo, Cima, and Barber, 1981). In a series of experiments in Los Angeles, the elimination of free parking decreased the number of solo drivers by 18 percent to 83 percent. When one Los Angeles firm increased its parking fee from zero to $28.75 per month, the number of solo drivers dropped by 44 percent; when the firm increased the monthly fee to $57.50, solo driving decreased 81 percent (Small, 1992).

There are three potential problems with using parking taxes to decrease congestion. The first is that the taxes must be imposed only on peak-period commuters: drivers who travel during the off-peak period should be exempt from the tax. As shown by the Madison experiment, this problem can be solved by imposing a surcharge for drivers who arrive at parking garages during the peak travel period. Second, in contrast with the congestion tax, which increases the unit cost of travel and decreases travel distances, the parking tax does not depend on the distance traveled. Therefore, there is less incentive for commuters to economize on travel cost by living closer to their workplaces. Third, because much of the congestion problem is caused by cars that do not park in congested areas, the tax does not force all peak-period travelers to pay for the congestion they cause.

Shoup (1982) suggests that the subsidization of parking by private employers contributes to the congestion problem. Using data from the 1970s, he shows that over 90 percent of commuters parked for free. Shoup estimates that if private parking subsidies were eliminated, about 20 percent of drive-alone commuters would switch to some sort of ride sharing or mass transit. A recent study of Los Angeles (Willson, 1988) suggests that subsidies are widespread and large. Only 14 percent of employers in the city did not offer any subsidies, and the median subsidy was $3.71 per day (compared to a median parking cost of $5 per day). If employers replaced the parking subsidies with cash payments, the increase in the parking cost would encourage some workers to carpool or use mass transit.

Congestion Zones and Permits

A third congestion policy involves the establishment of congestion zones, areas where access would be limited to drivers who paid a special fee. Under a scheme proposed for London in 1974, all vehicles using the inner streets between 8 A.M. and 6 P.M. were to pay a flat fee (Altshuler, 1979). The scheme generated heated debate and was never implemented. Singapore implemented a congestion-zone scheme in 1975. To drive in the central area of the city between 7:30 and 10:15 A.M., auto drivers must buy a permit costing about $1.30 per day. Travel within the control area is free to buses, motorcycles, and carpools.

Singapore's zone policy generated some interesting results. During the morning hours, auto traffic in the control zone decreased by 74 percent and travel speeds increased by 22 percent (Altshuler, 1979). Many commuters drove their cars to the edge of the control area and then rode buses to their downtown workplaces. During the afternoon rush hours (when driving permits were not required), the changes in traffic volume and travel speeds were relatively small. Some commuters took public transit to central-city workplaces in the morning, but were picked up at the end of the day by family members. Through traffic, which used circumferential routes during the morning control period, resumed its radial travel pattern in the afternoon.

Alternatives to Auto Taxes

The congestion policies discussed so far decrease congestion by increasing the cost of driving. There are several alternative approaches. One option is to increase the carrying capacity of the highway, and another is to subsidize transit ridership.

Capacity Expansion and Traffic Design

One response to the congestion problem is to widen the highway to increase its carrying capacity. Figure 19–3 shows the effects of such a policy on travel times and traffic volume. The wider road reaches the congestion threshold at a higher traffic volume and has a lower private trip cost at all volumes above the original congestion threshold ($V = 400$). The decrease in trip costs increases traffic volume as the city moves down the demand curve from point D to E.

Under what conditions would the widening of the highway be efficient? One way to measure the total benefit is with consumer surplus. As explained earlier, consumer surplus equals the excess of the willingness to pay (from the demand curve) over the actual cost of travel. Widening the highway decreases the trip costs of all drivers, so it increases consumer surplus. The increase in consumer surplus is shown as the shaded area in Figure 19–3. For the original drivers (Volume $= V_o$), the consumer surplus per driver increases by the savings in private trip cost ($C_o - C_w$). The increase in consumer surplus is the rectangular area with a width of ($C_o - C_w$) and a length of V_o. The decrease in trip cost also increases traffic volume from V_o to V_w. The consumer surplus of the new drivers equals the area of the triangle DEF. The benefit of widening the highway exceeds the cost if the increase in consumer surplus (the sum of the rectangle and the triangle) exceeds the cost of widening the highway. This analysis ignores pollution cost, which is discussed later in the chapter.

The city could also improve the flow of traffic on the existing highway. Street lights can be synchronized to keep traffic flowing at a steady speed. Designating one-way streets and restricting on-street parking increase the carrying capacity of streets. Some cities have placed stoplights on expressway on-ramps, thus smoothing the flow of vehicles onto expressways. In the language of transportation engineers, the ramp lights decrease the "turbulence" caused by entering vehicles, thus increasing travel speeds. In Los Angeles, the installation of such a system on the Harbor Freeway increased average travel speeds from 15 miles per hour to 40 miles per

---

FIGURE 19–3   **Effects of Widening the Highway**

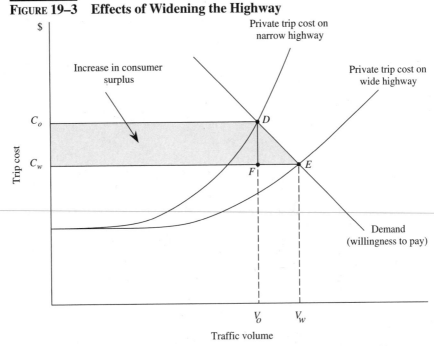

The widening of the highway shifts the private trip cost to the right: the congestion threshold increases, and trip cost is lower at every traffic volume above the original threshold volume. The decrease in trip cost increases traffic volume from V_o to V_w. The benefit of the widening is the increase in consumer surplus (the shaded area).

hour. A similar system in Dallas increased travel speeds from 14 miles per hour to 30 miles per hour.

Subsidies for Transit

Another alternative to the taxation of auto travel is the subsidization of mass transit (buses, subways, commuter trains, light rail). Transit and autos are substitute travel modes, so a decrease in the cost of transit causes some consumers to switch from autos to transit. In other words, a transit subsidy decreases the auto volume, narrowing the gap between the equilibrium and optimum traffic volumes.

Figure 19–4 shows the interactions between the auto and transit markets. Under a system of optimum congestion taxes, the auto market reaches point *B*, with traffic volume of A^* (where the demand curve intersects the social-trip-cost curve), and the transit market reaches point *Q*, with ridership of T^* (where the demand curve intersects the marginal-social-cost curve). In the presence of congestion taxes, both markets are at their optimum points, defined as the points at which the marginal social benefit (from the demand curve) equals the marginal social cost.

What if there are no congestion taxes? The auto market reaches point *C*, where the demand curve intersects the private-trip-cost curve, generating an equilibrium

FIGURE 19–4 Effects of Transit Subsidies on Auto Volume and Transit Ridership

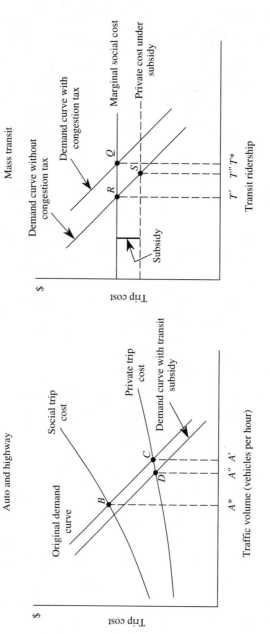

In the optimum situation, auto drivers pay a congestion tax, so auto volume is A^* and transit ridership is T^*. If there is no congestion tax, the auto volume is A' and the transit ridership is T' (the underpricing of auto travel shifts the demand curve for transit downward). A transit subsidy increases transit ridership to T'' and decreases auto volume to A'' (the subsidy shifts the auto-demand curve downward). The subsidy narrows the transit gap faster than it narrows the auto gap.

traffic volume of A'. The underpricing of auto travel shifts the demand curve for transit (a substitute good) downward. The equilibrium is shown by point R, with ridership of T'. If auto travel is underpriced, the auto volume exceeds the optimum volume and transit ridership is less than the optimum ridership.

A small transit subsidy moves both markets closer to their optimum points. In the transit market, the subsidy decreases the cost of transit, causing movement down the demand curve to point S: ridership increases to T'', closing about two thirds of the gap between the equilibrium and the optimum volume. In the auto market, the decrease in the price of transit shifts the auto-demand curve downward, moving the market from point C to point D. The equilibrium volume decreases from A' to A'', closing about one quarter of the gap between the equilibrium and the optimum volume. The subsidy narrows—but does not eliminate—the gaps between the optimum and equilibrium volumes: A^* is still less than A'' and T'' is still less than T^*.

Would it be possible to eliminate both the auto gap and the transit gap? In Figure 19–4, the transit gap is closing faster than the auto gap: the subsidy closes two thirds of the transit gap, but only one quarter of the auto gap. In other words, the subsidy increases transit ridership by more than it decreases auto volume. This occurs because in addition to diverting some drivers from cars to transit, the subsidy also attracts new travelers to transit. For example, suppose that the subsidy causes 250 drivers to switch from autos to transit ($A' - A'' = 250$) and also generates 280 new travelers. The total increase in transit ridership is 530 ($T'' - T' = 530$), the sum of the diverted auto drivers and the new transit riders. Because the transit gap is closing faster than the auto gap, if the city decides to eliminate the transit gap, the city will be left with an auto gap. Alternatively, if it decides to eliminate the auto gap, the city will "overshoot" the transit gap: transit ridership will exceed the optimum ridership. The city can close one—but not both—gaps.

The fundamental problem of the transit subsidy is that it underprices transit, increasing ridership above its optimum level. In the absence of congestion taxes, a transit subsidy may improve the efficiency of the transportation system, but the subsidy will never be as efficient as a system of congestion taxes. The policy question is whether the benefit of the transit subsidy (the diversion of drivers from underpriced and congested roads) is larger or smaller than the cost (excessive transit ridership).

Highway Pricing and Traffic Volume in the Long Run

This section shows how the government could pick both the optimum traffic volume and the optimum road width. The long-run analysis of highway pricing and investment has four steps:

1. Derive the average total-cost curves for different highway widths.
2. Derive the long-run cost curves (average and marginal).
3. Pick the optimum traffic volume and road width.
4. Pick the congestion tax that generates the optimum traffic volume on the optimum road.

Average Total Cost for Two-Lane and Four-Lane Highways

The average total cost of travel is the sum of the trip cost and the **average road cost**. Figure 19–5 shows the trip-cost curves for both the two-lane and the four-lane highways: the cost curves are horizontal up to the point at which congestion sets in; the congestion threshold is V_2 vehicles per hour for the two-lane highway and V_4 vehicles for the four-lane highway. The average road cost equals the total cost of building the highway divided by the number of trips.

The average total-cost curves are U-shaped. An increase in traffic volume has two effects on average total cost. First, an increase in volume spreads construction cost over more drivers, so the average road cost decreases (the road-cost effect). Second, an increase in volume may increase congestion, increasing travel times and the trip cost (the trip-cost effect). At traffic volumes below the congestion threshold (V_2 for the two-lane highway and V_4 for the four-lane highway), there is no trip-cost effect, so the average total-cost curve is negatively sloped. At high traffic volumes, the average road cost is relatively low and congestion is severe, so the trip-cost effect dominates the road-cost effect. Therefore, the average total-cost curve is positively sloped. In Figure 19–5, the average total-cost curve for the two-lane highway reaches its minimum point at a volume of V' drivers, indicating that the road-cost effect

FIGURE 19–5   Average Cost for Two- and Four-Lane Highways

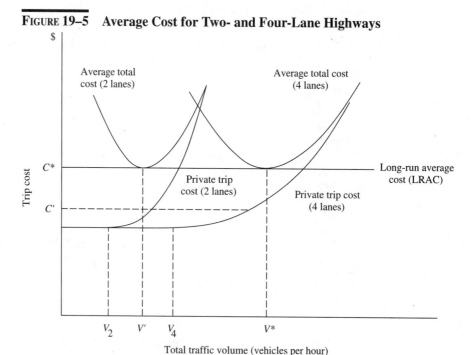

The average total cost of travel is the sum of private trip cost and average road cost. The average total-cost curves are U-shaped. If there are constant returns to scale in road building, the two average total-cost curves reach the same minimum cost C^*, but the four-lane highway reaches this cost with twice the traffic volume (V^* instead of V'). The long-run average cost is composed of the minimum points of the average total-cost curves.

dominates for volumes up to V' drivers and the trip-cost effect dominates for higher volumes. For the four-lane highway, the trip-cost effect dominates for volumes above V^* drivers.

The cost curves in Figure 19–5 are drawn under the assumption of constant returns to scale in highway building. If there are constant returns to scale, a doubling of construction cost (to build four lanes instead of two) doubles the carrying capacity of the highway. The congestion threshold of the four-lane highway (V_4) is double that of the two-lane highway (V_2). Similarly, it takes twice as many drivers on the four-lane road to reach a given private trip cost: to reach the private trip cost C', the four-lane highway requires twice the traffic volume. The two total-cost curves reach the same minimum cost (C^*), but the four-lane highway reaches this point with twice the traffic volume (V^* instead of V').

Long-Run Average Cost and Marginal-Cost Curves

The long-run average cost curve (LRAC) shows the minimum average total cost for each traffic volume. The curve is drawn by answering the following question: for a given traffic volume, what is the average total cost of the *most efficient* highway? Figure 19–5 shows two points on LRAC: for a volume of V' drivers, the two-lane highway minimizes average cost at an average cost of C^*; for a volume of V^* drivers, the four-lane highway minimizes average cost at the same cost. The LRAC curve is made up of the minimum points of the average total-cost curves for different highway widths, so it indicates the average total cost under the assumption that the government builds the optimum highway for each traffic volume. Given the assumption of constant returns to scale, LRAC is horizontal, with an average total cost (the sum of average road cost and average trip cost) of C^*. The long-run marginal-cost curve (LRMC) indicates the marginal social cost of an additional driver, including the cost of widening the road to accommodate the new driver. In Figure 19–5, LRAC is horizontal (a result of constant returns to scale), so LRMC is the same as LRAC (if the average is constant, the marginal equals the average).

Optimum Volume and Road Width

For the optimum traffic volume, the marginal benefit of travel equals the long-run marginal cost of travel. In Figure 19–6, the demand curve shows the marginal benefit of travel, and the LRMC shows the long-run marginal cost of travel. The two curves intersect at V^*, so the optimum traffic volume is V^* drivers. From Figure 19–5, the four-lane highway generates the minimum average total cost for a volume of V^* drivers, so the optimum road width is four lanes.

How does the city persuade the optimum number of drivers to use the highway? From the demand curve, a total of V^* drivers will use the road if the cost of the trip is C^*. Drivers will face a cost of C^* only if the city imposes a congestion tax. If the city builds a four-lane road but does not impose a congestion tax, there will be V_o drivers (volume at which the demand curve intersects the private-trip-cost curve) instead of V^*. If the government adds a congestion tax ($C^* - C'$), the traffic volume will be V^* (volume at which the demand curve intersects the social-trip-cost curve).

FIGURE 19–6   **Optimum Road Width and Congestion Tax**

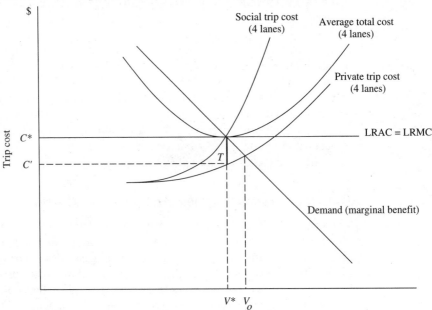

Total traffic volume (vehicles per hour)

The optimum traffic volume (V^*) is the volume such that the marginal benefit of travel (shown by the demand curve) equals the long-run marginal cost of travel (LRMC). The four-lane highway minimizes the average total cost of travel for V^* drivers, so the optimum road width is four lanes. The appropriate price of travel is C^*, so a congestion tax of T is added to the private trip cost of C'. The congestion tax equals the average road tax, so congestion taxes cover the cost of the optimum road.

Congestion Tolls Pay for the Optimum Road

If there are constant returns to road building, the revenue from the congestion tax covers the cost of building the road. In Figure 19–6, the congestion tax equals the gap between the social trip cost and the private trip cost ($C^* - C'$). Because the long-run average cost is the sum of the private trip cost and the average road cost, the gap between the LRAC and the private trip cost is the average road cost ($C^* - C'$). Because the congestion tax equals the average road cost, a system of congestion tolls pays for the optimum road.

Is this a fluke, or is there something systematic about congestion tolls and road costs? The expressions for average road cost and the congestion tax are as follows:

$$\text{Average road cost} = \text{Average total cost} - \text{Private trip cost} \qquad (19\text{–}2)$$

$$\text{Congestion tax} = \text{Social trip cost} - \text{Private trip cost} \qquad (19\text{–}3)$$

Therefore, the average road cost equals the congestion tax if the average total cost (ATC) equals the social trip cost (STC). STC is actually the short-run marginal cost of driving; it shows the increase in social cost from one additional driver. The marginal-cost curve (STC) intersects the ATC curve at its minimum point. If the government builds the optimum highway, the market reaches the minimum point of some ATC curve, so STC equals ATC. Therefore, the average road cost equals the congestion tax, meaning that the revenue from congestion taxes covers the cost of the road.

The revenue from a congestion tax provides an important signal to road builders. If tax revenue exceeds the total cost of building the road, the road should be widened. In other words, any surplus tax revenue should be spent on widening the road. To explain, suppose that the city builds a two-lane highway and imposes a congestion tax of $4.34 (see Figure 19–1). If the total revenue from the tax ($4.34 times 1,400 drivers) exceeds the total cost of building the road, the road should be widened.

Who Pays for Highways?

Highways are financed through various user fees. Auto drivers pay federal and state taxes on gas, oil, and auto parts. In addition to these normal user taxes, truck drivers also pay user fees based on mileage and weight.

Since the early 1970s, user taxes have failed to cover the cost of building and maintaining roads (Meyer and Gómez-Ibáñez, 1981). During the 1960s, revenue from user taxes exceeded the highway cost by about 25 percent. During the 1970s, revenue from the gas tax did not keep pace with inflation because the gas tax is a fixed amount per gallon, not a fixed percentage of the price. By 1975, there was a deficit of about 25 percent. Urban road users actually paid more than their share of the highway cost: the tax revenue collected from urban road users exceeded the cost of urban roads by about 14 percent. In contrast, rural travelers paid only about 56 percent of the cost of rural roads.

Congestion and Land-Use Patterns

This section explores the effects of congestion externalities and congestion taxes on urban land-use patterns. It uses the concepts developed in Part II (Land Rent and Urban Land Use Patterns) to show how a system of congestion taxes would change residential land use and city size. The land-use effects can be divided into partial-equilibrium effects and general-equilibrium effects.

Partial-Equilibrium Effects

The congestion tax increases the slope of the residential bid-rent function. The congestion tax increases the unit cost of commuting: in Figure 19–1, the congestion tax adds 43.4 cents per mile to commuting cost. As explained in Chapter 8 (Land Use in the Monocentric City), an increase in the unit cost of commuting increases the slopes of the housing-price function and the residential bid-rent function. Figure 19–7 shows three residential bid-rent functions. The relatively flat curve (R_o) is the initial bid-rent function (before the imposition of congestion tax). After congestion tax is imposed, the bid-rent function shifts to R_c if (1) the government throws the tax money away and (2) the congestion tax does not change traffic volume or travel times. Under these two assumptions, the congestion tax decreases the bid rent at all locations, with the gap between R_o and R_c increasing with distance to the city center: the longer the commuting distance, the larger the decrease in the bid-rent for land.

FIGURE 19–7   Partial-Equilibrium Effects of Congestion Taxes

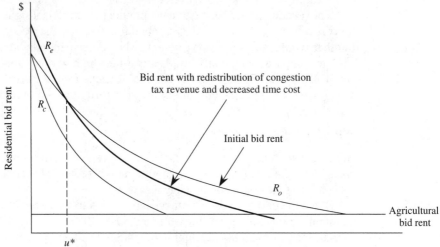

The imposition of congestion taxes shifts the bid-rent function from R_o to R_c if the tax revenue is not redistributed to the city's households. The redistribution of tax revenue (combined with the decreases in travel times caused by decreases in traffic volume) shifts the bid-rent function upward from R_c to R_e. The bid rent rises above the original bid rent for distances up to u^* miles and drops below the original bid rent for locations beyond u^*.

The third bid-rent function, R_e, shows the actual effect of congestion taxes. It lies above R_c for two reasons. First, if the government uses the congestion tax revenue to cut other taxes, residents are willing to pay more for housing and land at all locations. Second, the congestion tax decreases traffic volume, increasing travel speeds and decreasing travel times. The decrease in the time cost decreases the unit cost of travel, partly offsetting the effects of the congestion tax on the slope of the bid-rent function. By comparing R_e to the original bid-rent function, R_o, we can see that the congestion tax increases bid rents within u^* miles of the city center and decreases bid rents beyond u^*. Locations near the city center become more attractive because the congestion tax bill is relatively low, so the bad news (increase in congestion taxes) is dominated by the good news (decrease in other taxes and lower time cost). In contrast, locations far from the city center become less attractive because the congestion tax bill is relatively large. To summarize, the congestion tax increases the relative attractiveness of locations close to the city center, increasing the slope of the bid-rent function.

Figure 19–8 shows the effect of congestion taxes on the residential density function. The density function shows population density (people per acre) at different locations. As explained in Chapter 8, density increases as one approaches the city center: land is more expensive, and people economize on the relatively expensive land by consuming less of it (they live in smaller dwellings on less land), so there are more residents per acre. The congestion tax shifts the density function from D_o to D_e: in locations where land rent rises (distance less than u^*), households consume less land, so density increases; beyond u^*, where land rent falls, households consume more land, so density decreases.

FIGURE 19–8   Congestion Taxes and Residential Density

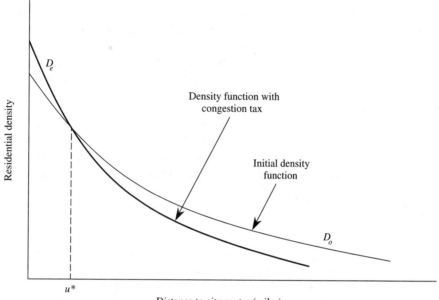

The congestion tax increases residential density up to u^* miles from the city center and decreases density beyond u^*.

The change in the density function shows that the congestion tax generates a more compact city. After the tax, the city has a larger fraction of its population living within a given distance of the city center, so it has shorter commuting distances and travel times. As explained earlier in the chapter, the congestion tax causes the city to move up its travel-demand curve: the increase in travel cost decreases traffic volume. One reason for the decrease in traffic volume is that workers have shorter commuting distances. This is shown by the change in the population density function: the congestion tax increases the fraction of households living within a given distance of the city center, so the average commuting distance decreases.

General-Equilibrium Effects

Figures 19–7 and 19–8 show the partial-equilibrium effects of the congestion tax. In other words, they show the effects of the congestion tax on the residential land market, ignoring the effects on other markets in the city. As explained in Chapter 9 (General-Equilibrium Land Use), general-equilibrium analysis examines the effects of changes in the land market on the city's labor market.

Does the congestion tax increase or decrease total labor supply? The tax increases total labor supply because it increases the efficiency of the city's transportation system and increases the welfare of city residents. The switch to the optimum pricing scheme makes highway travel more efficient, generating a net increase in the welfare of city residents. As shown in the example in Table 19–3, the congestion tax makes both Helen (the typical highway user) and Louis (the typical nonuser) better off. In Figure 19–1, the net gain from the congestion tax is the shaded area *CJB*. Because the congestion tax generates a net gain for city residents, it increases the relative attractiveness of the city, increasing total labor supply.

How does the congestion tax affect the labor market and the city's wage? The initial increase in total labor supply causes excess supply of labor, so the city's wage decreases. Firms respond to the wage cut by increasing the quantity of labor demanded, narrowing the gap between labor supply and demand. The wage continues to drop until labor supply equals labor demand. Equilibrium is restored with a lower wage and a larger work force.

How will the city look after general equilibrium is restored? One way to answer this question is to use a computer to generate two pictures of the urban economy, one before the congestion tax and one after the economy has adjusted to the new tax. An urban general-equilibrium computer model allocates different plots of land in a hypothetical city to firms and households. If a particular allocation does not satisfy the conditions for general equilibrium, the computer tries a different one. This groping process continues until an equilibrium allocation of land is found. The computer model can be designed to compute a pre-tax equilibrium and a post-tax equilibrium. To see the general-equilibrium effects of the congestion tax, one compares the "before" and "after" snapshots of the urban economy.

Sullivan (1983) used a computer model to simulate the effects of congestion taxes in a monocentric city. The results of the study are listed in Table 19–4. The hypothetical city has an initial population of 518,000 and a wage of $6.00 per hour. The average commuter travels 3.72 miles to work and spends 3.73 hours per week commuting. As shown in the second column of the table, the congestion tax increases the city's population and decreases its wage. The changes in population and wages are relatively large because the hypothetical city is highly congested, much more so than the typical U.S. city. The congestion tax causes households to move closer to their workplaces: the average commuting distance drops from 3.72 miles to 3.42 miles, and the average weekly commuting time drops by 0.32 hours. Another change occurs in the transportation network: the decrease in traffic volume allows the city to build narrower roads, so it uses less of its land for highways (16.2 percent instead of 17.9 percent).

TABLE 19–4   General-Equilibrium Effects of Congestion Taxes

Variable	Initial City	Congestion Tax City
Population	518,000	561,000
Wage ($ per hour)	6.00	5.31
Commute distance (miles)	3.72	3.42
Commuting time (hours per week)	3.73	3.41
Percent of land used for transportation	17.9	16.2

SOURCE: Arthur M. Sullivan, "The General Equilibrium Effects of Congestion Externalities," *Journal of Urban Economics* 14 (1983), pp. 80–104.

The analysis of congestion taxes provides an important lesson about urban problems and policies. Congestion is truly an urban problem in the sense that the largest cities usually have the most severe congestion. Nonetheless, a city that imposes a congestion tax is likely to grow, not shrink. Because the congestion tax internalizes the congestion externality, it improves the efficiency of the city's transportation network and thus increases the relative attractiveness of the city. The lesson is that solving an urban problem is likely to cause economic growth, not decline.

Autos and Air Pollution

Another urban transportation problem is air pollution. Autos and trucks contribute to air pollution in a number of ways.

1. **Photochemical smog.** Smog results from the combination of hydrocarbons, nitrogen oxides, sunlight, and heat. In the typical city, autos and trucks generate about 40 percent of hydrocarbons and about 40 percent of nitrogen oxides. For healthy people, smog causes physical discomfort, coughing, and nausea. For people who suffer from respiratory disease, smog causes more serious health problems.

2. **Carbon monoxide.** About 83 percent of carbon monoxide is generated by motor vehicles. In high concentrations, carbon monoxide decreases the breathing capacity and alertness of healthy individuals and causes pain and discomfort for people who suffer from cardiovascular disease.

3. **Lead.** About 88 percent of lead comes from motor vehicles. If lead is absorbed into the blood at high concentrations, it can cause serious health problems.

4. **Suspended particulates.** About 9 percent of particulate matter comes from motor vehicles. Some particulates cause respiratory problems, and others are suspected of causing cancer.

5. **Nitrogen oxides.** Autos and trucks generate about 40 percent of nitrogen oxides. The experts disagree about the health effects of nitrogen oxides.

Although everyone agrees that automobiles and trucks are important sources of air pollution, there is disagreement about what should be done about the problem.

The Economic Approach: Effluent Fees

The economic approach to air pollution starts with a description of the externality problem. Drivers base their travel decisions on the marginal private cost of driving, which is less than the marginal social cost because autos and trucks cause air pollution. The pollution externality causes people to (1) drive cars that generate a relatively large amount of pollution per mile driven and (2) drive too many miles. To an economist, the obvious response is to force people to pay for pollution, that is, to internalize the externality.

One approach would be to install a monitoring device in every car. Such a device would measure the car's emissions, allowing the government to tax the car owner for the air pollution caused by the car. For example, if the estimated pollution cost per unit of carbon monoxide is one cent, the monthly bill would be $2 for a vehicle that emits 200 units per month, and $3 for a vehicle that emits 300 units. Such a scheme is obviously impractical, but it illustrates the basic objective of policy: drivers should pay for the pollution their cars generate. The trick is to estimate how much pollution each car generates.

An alternative approach is to impose a one-time pollution tax on automobiles. The government could estimate (1) the lifetime emissions of a particular car model and (2) the cost per unit of pollution. The pollution tax for a particular model would be set equal to the product of total emissions and the unit cost. For example, if model B is expected to emit 5,000 units of carbon monoxide (CO) over its lifetime and the unit cost of CO is one cent, its CO tax would be $50. If the same car is expected to emit 400 units of lead and the unit cost of lead pollution is 50 cents, its lead tax would be $200. The car's total pollution tax would equal the sum of the taxes for CO, lead, nitrogen oxides, hydrocarbons, and particulates. Under this scheme, car buyers would pay more for cars that generate more pollution, so consumers would have the incentive to buy cleaner cars.

Another approach is to use a gasoline tax to increase the private cost of auto travel. The tax would increase the cost per mile driven, so it would decrease the total miles driven, thus decreasing air pollution. The problem with the gas tax is that every driver would pay the same tax, regardless of how much pollution his or her car generates. In other words, there would be no practical way to impose a higher tax on cars that generate more pollution. Such a tax would decrease pollution by decreasing miles driven, not by persuading people to drive cleaner cars.

What is the marginal external cost of auto driving? Straszheim (1979) summarizes the results of a number of studies of auto-related air pollution. In the 1970s, the cost of auto pollution was between 0.50 and 0.80 cents per mile driven. Since then, auto emissions rates have decreased as a result of federal emissions policy, pulling down the cost per mile driven. Between 1970 and 1983, hydrocarbon emissions per mile dropped by two thirds, carbon monoxide dropped by three fifths, and nitrogen oxides dropped by one third (Crandall et al., 1986). The net effect is a moderate increase in the cost per mile driven. If the cost per mile is 1 cent and the typical car gets 25 miles per gallon, the appropriate gasoline tax would be about 25 cents per gallon.

Transit Subsidies

An alternative approach for controlling auto pollution is to subsidize mass transit. Although both autos and mass transit generate air pollution, the pollution per passenger is lower on mass transit. If there are no pollution taxes, auto travel is underpriced relative to transit. As explained earlier in the case of congestion externalities, the underpricing of autos generates an excessive traffic volume (the equilibrium auto volume exceeds the optimum volume) and too little transit ridership (the equilibrium transit ridership is less than the optimum ridership). One response to the underpricing of autos is to subsidize transit, the substitute good.

As shown in Figure 19–4, transit subsidies can be used to move the auto and transit markets closer to their optimum points (A^* and T^*). As explained for the case of congestion externalities, the basic problem with transit subsidies is that they decrease the cost of transit below the marginal social cost, causing too much transit travel. The excessive amount of travel is costly because society's productive resources (labor, capital, fuel) are used inefficiently: the transit system will use an excessive number of drivers, mechanics, and buses, and consume an excessive amount of fuel. If the pollution cost per auto passenger exceeds the pollution cost per transit rider by a wide margin, there are large air-quality benefits from transit subsidies. The real question is whether the air-quality benefits dominate the resource cost of the policy.

Regulatory Policy

The Environmental Protection Agency (EPA) has adopted a two-part strategy for controlling air pollution. First, the EPA has established emissions standards for autos and trucks. The standards control four pollutants: nitrogen oxides (NOX), carbon monoxide (CO), hydrocarbons (HC), and lead. Second, the EPA has established standards for ambient air quality, specifying maximum concentration (parts per million) for NOX, CO, lead, sulfur oxides (SOX), and particulate matter.

Emissions Policy.   The national emissions policy started with the Motor Vehicle Pollution Control Act of 1965. In 1963, the state of California set maximum emission levels for CO, HC, and NOX. The emissions standards were first applied to the 1966 model year. In 1965, the federal government extended the California standards to the rest of the nation, with the standards applied to the 1968 model year. In 1970, the amendments to the Clean Air Act mandated 90 percent reductions in CO, HC, and NOX by 1975. Automakers were unable to meet the deadlines for the emissions standards, so the EPA relaxed the standards and extended the deadlines. By 1980, new-car emissions of HC and CO had been reduced to the target levels. The NOX emissions proved more difficult to control: by 1980, they had been reduced by half. The 1990 amendments to the Clean Air Act imposed even stricter regulations for automobile exhaust.

The emission program has decreased auto emissions considerably. Although the total miles driven increased between 1970 and 1983, total emissions decreased. In 1983, the volume of hydrocarbons generated per mile was only 33 percent of the corresponding figure for 1970 (Crandall et al., 1986). The 1983 figure for carbon monoxide was 40 percent of the 1970 figure, and the 1983 figure for nitrogen oxides was 65 percent of the 1970 figure.

Costs and Benefits of Emissions Policy.   What are the benefits of the emissions policy? Freeman (1982) estimates the benefits that would occur if all auto-related pollution were eliminated. He divides the benefits of cleaner air into health benefits (e.g., decreased risk for cardiac patients), the reduction of damage to vegetation (e.g., increased crop and forest yields), and aesthetic benefits (e.g., increased visibility). He estimates that the total benefit from eliminating air pollution from autos would be about $8.3 billion per year (in 1984 dollars).

What is the cost of the emissions policy? Crandall et al. (1986) estimate that the national emissions standards added $1,601 to the cost of a 1984 car, including $592 in additional equipment and $1,009 in additional fuel and maintenance cost. Based on this figure, they estimate that the total cost of emissions standards was about $16.8 billion per year. In other words, the total cost of the 1984 emissions policy, which decreased but did not eliminate auto pollution, is about twice the estimated benefit that would occur if all auto-related pollution were eliminated ($8.3 billion).

It's important to note that there is a great deal of uncertainty about the health effects of air pollution. Therefore, it is difficult to estimate the benefits of pollution abatement, and Freeman's estimates should be used with caution. In addition, the estimates do not take into account the greenhouse effect or the depletion of the ozone, two phenomena that scientists are only beginning to explore. Nonetheless, the available evidence suggests that the costs of the current emissions program far outweigh the benefits we know about and can quantify. There is heated debate in policy circles about some subtle health effects of air pollution that are not included in benefit-cost studies.

Ambient Air-Quality Standards.   As part of the Clean Air Act and amendments to the Act, the EPA established standards for ambient air quality. The individual states are responsible for meeting the standards. The states have used various policies to decrease auto pollution, including vehicle inspection and repair programs, restrictions on parking, and "cash for clunkers" (paying people for old cars and then crushing the cars).

Amendments to the Clean Air Act (in 1977 and 1990) included one innovative feature for the control of stationary pollution sources. In cities where the EPA standards were exceeded, new pollution sources were allowed if two conditions were satisfied. First, the new sources had to adopt the most effective abatement technology. Second, existing sources had to decrease their emissions to ensure that there was a net improvement in air quality. This policy set the stage for the development of a market for pollution rights, in which new firms purchase pollution rights from existing firms. Because this "offset" policy mimics a system of effluent fees, it generates efficient abatement activity.

Auto Safety

The third transportation problem is auto safety. Traffic accidents generate two types of costs. First, people involved in accidents are often injured or killed: traffic accidents kill about 50,000 people per year and injure another 2 million. About a third of the deaths and about three fifths of the injuries occur in urban areas. Second, traffic accidents during rush hours disrupt traffic flows and contribute to congestion.

This section explores the effects of various public policies on auto safety and traffic accidents. Federal safety legislation requires automakers to install a number of safety features (e.g., seatbelts, shatterproof windshields). One policy issue concerns the effects of these regulations on highway death rates and accident rates. Another issue concerns the effects of congestion and pollution policies on traffic safety. For example, policies that encourage the switch to smaller cars decrease the congestion problem (smaller cars take up less space on the highway) and the pollution problem (small cars use less fuel and generate less pollution). Unfortunately, smaller cars are less safe (injuries are more severe in collisions involving small cars), so there are trade-offs between safety, congestion, and pollution.

The Effects of Safety Regulations

The Vehicle Safety Act of 1966 established safety standards for new cars. Automakers were forced to install head restraints, padded dashboards, seatbelts, shatterproof windshields, dual braking systems, and collapsible steering columns. Most of the standards were met in the 1968 model year. Figure 19–9 shows the trend in highway deaths per 100 million vehicle miles. The death rate decreased between 1947 and 1961, increased from 1961 to 1965, and then decreased from 1965 to 1983. In other words, highway death rates have decreased steadily since the safety standards were implemented.

The data on highway death rates raise two questions. First, to what extent did the safety regulations contribute to the decrease in highway death rates? Crandall et al. (1986) have studied the effects of various factors on highway death rates. They estimate that safety regulations decreased the number of highway fatalities by about 30 percent, saving about 20,000 lives per year.

The second question concerns the response of drivers to safety regulations. Peltzman (1975) argues that because safety regulations make people feel safer, they drive more recklessly and are therefore involved in more collisions. This is the **theory of risk compensation.** This theory suggests that safety regulations generate benefits

FIGURE 19–9   **Highway Deaths per 100 Million Vehicle Miles**

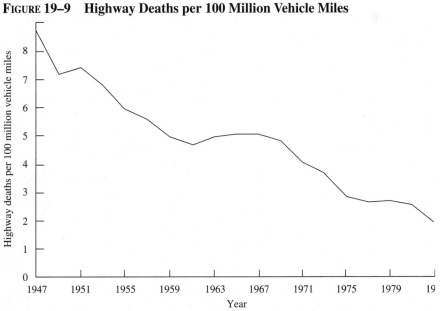

SOURCE: Robert W. Crandall, Howard K. Gruenspecht, Theodore E. Keeler, and Lester B. Lave, *Regulating the Automobile* (Washington, D.C.: Brookings Institution, 1986), p. 46.

(greater safety in the event of a collision) and costs (more collisions). If the regulations increase the number of collisions, the death rates of nonoccupants (pedestrians and bicyclists) are likely to increase. In addition, an increase in the number of accidents increases the congestion problem on crowded urban highways.

The Optimum Speed.   To explain a driver's response to safety equipment, consider Duke, who lives in Hazard City. Every Saturday night, Duke must decide how fast to drive from his suburban home to the dance hall in the city center. The benefit of fast driving is that he spends less time on the road, giving him more time to dance with Betty Lou. Figure 19–10 shows the marginal-benefit curve for speed. The curve indicates how much Duke benefits from a one-unit increase in speed. When his speed increases from 45 m.p.h. to 46 m.p.h., he can spend more time dancing, and he is willing to pay $16 for the additional dance time. The benefit curve is negatively sloped, reflecting the diminishing marginal utility of dancing.

Table 19–5 shows the expected cost of crashing at different speeds. As the speed increases, the probability of crashing increases: the probability is only 0.001 for a speed of 45 m.p.h., but rises to 0.011 for a speed of 55 m.p.h. Faster driving also causes more damage to Duke and his car. If he crashes at a speed of 45 m.p.h., his total crash cost (medical bills plus auto-repair costs) will be $2,000. If he crashes at a speed of 55, his total crash cost will be $12,000. The **expected crash cost** is the probability of crashing times total crash cost. The expected crash cost rises from $2 for a speed of 45 m.p.h. (0.001 times $2,000) to $132 for a speed of 55 m.p.h. (0.011 times $12,000). The **marginal cost of speed** is the change in the expected

FIGURE 19–10   Optimum Speed and Safety Regulations

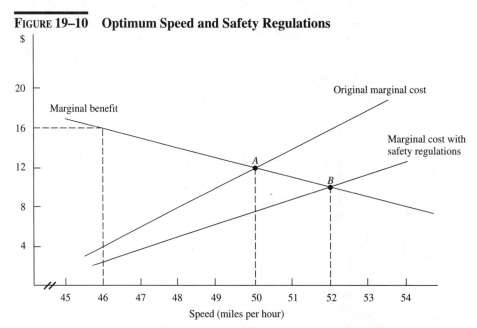

The optimum speed is the speed at which the marginal benefit of speed (value of decreased travel time) equals its marginal cost (increased expected accident costs). In the absence of safety regulations, Duke chooses point *A* (50 m.p.h.). Safety regulations decrease the expected cost of collisions, shifting the marginal-cost curve downward, increasing the optimum speed to 52 m.p.h. (point *B*).

TABLE 19–5   **Crash Costs and Optimum Speed**

Speed (m.p.h.)	Probability of Crash	Crash Cost ($)	Expected Crash Cost ($)	Marginal Cost of Speed ($)	Marginal Benefit of Speed ($)
45	0.001	2,000	2	0	17
46	0.002	3,000	6	4	16
47	0.003	4,000	12	6	15
48	0.004	5,000	20	8	14
49	0.005	6,000	30	10	13
50	0.006	7,000	42	12	12
51	0.007	8,000	56	14	11
52	0.008	9,000	72	16	10
53	0.009	10,000	90	18	9
54	0.01	11,000	110	20	8
55	0.011	12,000	132	22	7

---

crash cost for a one-unit increase in speed. An increase in speed from 45 m.p.h. to 46 m.p.h. increases the expected crash cost from $2 to $6, so the marginal cost of speed is $4 for a speed of 46 m.p.h. The marginal cost of speed increases with the speed, reaching $22 for a speed of 55 m.p.h.

What is the optimum travel speed? Duke increases his speed as long as the marginal benefit of speed (the value of the increase in dance time) exceeds the marginal cost (the increase in the expected crash cost). In Figure 19–10, the optimum speed (where the marginal-benefit curve intersects the marginal-cost curve) is 50 m.p.h. Table 19–5 shows that a speed of 50 m.p.h. generates a marginal cost of $12 and an expected crash cost of $42.

What are the effects of safety regulations on the expected crash cost? Suppose that Duke is forced to buy a car with seatbelts and a shatterproof windshield. If he crashes in his new car, he is less likely to suffer serious injuries, so the expected cost of crashing at each speed decreases. In Figure 19–10, the decrease in the expected crash cost shifts the marginal-cost curve downward, increasing his optimum speed from 50 m.p.h. to 52 m.p.h. Because the safety regulations protect Duke in an accident, they cause him to take more risks, so the probability of crashing increases. The net effects of the safety regulations are smaller than they would be if his speed did not change: he has a lower injury cost if he crashes, but he is also more likely to crash.

Evidence of Risk Compensation.   Peltzman (1975) uses two observations to support his theory of increased risk-taking. First, collision rates were higher than expected in the years following the implementation of safety regulations. Second, pedestrian death rates were also higher than expected. If people drive faster and more recklessly in their safer cars, they take more risks for themselves and others and may kill more pedestrians.

The results of Crandall et al. (1986) provide support for the risk compensation theory. The death rates for pedestrians and bicyclists are inversely related to an index of safety features, suggesting that drivers in safe cars take more risks and endanger others. Because the decrease in driver deaths exceeds the increase in nondriver deaths, safety regulations produce a net decrease in highway deaths.

Small Cars and Safety

A second safety issue concerns the costs and benefits of shifting to a fleet of smaller cars. A greater reliance on small cars would provide some relief from transportation problems because small cars use less fuel and generate less air pollution. In addition, small cars take up less space on streets and highways, so a switch to smaller cars would increase the carrying capacity of the road system, reducing congestion. On the other hand, travel in small cars is less safe. The policy issue is whether the decreases in energy consumption, pollution, and congestion are worth the cost (the increase in traffic injuries and deaths).

The occupants of small cars are more likely to suffer serious injuries in a collision. The state of New York has estimated the injury rates for different car types (Meyer and Gómez-Ibáñez, 1981). In a collision between two large cars (weight greater than 3,500 pounds), the rate of serious injury is 5.2 per hundred million vehicle miles. In a collision between a large car and a small car (weight less than 2,000 pounds), the injury rate is 3.7 for the occupants of the large car and 13.8 for the occupants of the small car. The combined injury rate for such a collision is 8.8. In a collision between two small cars, the injury rate is 9.7 for the occupants of each car. In other words, a collision between two small cars is more lethal than a collision involving a small and a large car.

Are small cars more or less likely to be involved in collisions? Studies of the accident rates of different car sizes have generated mixed results: some studies found higher collision rates for small cars, while others found no significant differences in accident rates. Overall, it appears that small-car occupants are just as likely to be involved in collisions and more likely to suffer serious injuries. Therefore, travel in small cars is more dangerous than travel in large cars.

A shift toward a small-car fleet is likely to increase injury and death rates. As the fraction of small cars increases, the fraction of collisions involving small cars increases, increasing the rate of serious injury. According to Meyer and Gómez-Ibáñez (1981), if the percent of small cars in the fleet increases from 20 percent to 70 percent, the percent of dangerous accidents (between a large and a small car, or between two small cars) will increase by 50 percent to 95 percent. The increase in the fraction of dangerous accidents increases traffic death rates. These numbers suggest that there is a considerable cost associated with the switch to smaller cars. The policy question is whether the benefits (less congestion and pollution) are greater than the cost.

Meyer and Gómez-Ibáñez point out two additional factors that must be taken into account in predicting the safety effects of small cars. First, about 37 percent of urban traffic deaths involve pedestrians and bicyclists. If small cars are less lethal for pedestrians and bicyclists, there would be fewer pedestrian and bicycle deaths. Second, about 11 percent of urban traffic deaths result from single-car crashes (a car hitting a fixed object). Since small cars are about as safe as large cars in this type of accident, a shift to small cars is unlikely to increase the number of single-car fatalities.

The switch to small cars is also likely to change driving habits. A driver who switches to a smaller, more dangerous car is likely to drive more cautiously to mitigate the risk of serious injury. If Duke switches to a small car, his expected injury cost would increase, shifting his marginal-cost curve upward. As a result, he decreases his speed, partly offsetting the increase in the severity of accidents by decreasing the probability of crashing. In addition, Duke would be more likely to fasten his seatbelt, thus decreasing the severity of injuries.

Summary

1. The three most popular commuting trips are between suburbs (40 percent of commuters), within the central city (33 percent), and from a suburb to the central city (20 percent). About 4 of 5 workers (and 9 of 10 suburbanites) commute by auto, truck, or van.

2. The demand for travel depends on the private cost of travel, the sum of the monetary and time costs of the trip. The larger the trip cost, the fewer the drivers.

3. Auto travel is subject to congestion externalities.
   a. The external cost of travel is the time cost imposed on other drivers: the marginal driver slows down traffic, forcing other drivers to spend more time on the highway.
   b. The social trip cost is the sum of the private and external trip cost.
   c. Drivers base their travel decisions on private—not social—costs, so the equilibrium volume exceeds the optimum volume.
   d. A congestion tax internalizes the congestion externality, generating the optimum traffic volume.
   e. The congestion tax would be higher during peak travel periods and along more congested routes.
   f. Estimates for the San Francisco Bay area suggest that the congestion tax for travel during the peak period would be 65 cents per mile on central highways, 21 cents on suburban highways, and 17 cents on fringe highways.

4. One way to implement congestion taxes is with a vehicle identification system, under which every car is equipped with an electronic device that allows sensors along the road to identify the car as it passes.

5. There are several alternatives to the congestion tax.
   a. The gas tax is inappropriate because it would be the same on all routes at all times.
   b. Experiences with parking taxes suggest that they decrease traffic volume by encouraging auto drivers to carpool and take mass transit. One problem is that the tax does not depend on distance traveled.

    c. The supply response to congestion is to increase highway capacity. The benefit of capacity expansion is the increase in consumer surplus.

    d. A transit subsidy would cause some auto drivers to switch to transit, decreasing the congestion problem. The problem is that the subsidies may increase transit ridership above the optimum level.

6. In the long run, the optimum road width and traffic volume are determined simultaneously.

    a. The optimum volume is where the demand (marginal-benefit) curve intersects the long-run marginal-cost curve.

    b. A congestion tax will generate the optimum traffic volume.

    c. The congestion tax will pay the full cost of the optimum highway. If the revenue from congestion taxes exceeds the cost of the road, the road should be widened.

7. A congestion tax increases the efficiency of the city's transportation system, decreases commuting distances, and increases city size.

8. Autos and trucks generate several types of air pollution, including smog, carbon monoxide, lead, suspended particulates, and nitrogen oxides.

    a. One response to the auto pollution problem is to impose pollution taxes on new cars.

    b. Another option is to impose a gasoline tax equal to the average external cost.

    c. A third option is to subsidize transit, a policy that decreases pollution but also increases transit ridership above its optimum level.

    d. The EPA sets emission standards for carbon monoxide, hydrocarbons, and nitrogen oxides. Emissions controls have decreased total emissions despite an increase in total miles driven. The estimated cost of the current emissions policy, which decreases but does not eliminate auto pollution, is about twice the estimated benefit of eliminating all auto pollution.

9. There are trade-offs associated with safety regulations: the regulations decrease death rates of accident victims in autos, but increase death rates of nonoccupants (pedestrians and bicyclists) and increase collision rates.

10. A shift toward small cars is likely to increase injury and death rates: small-car collisions are more lethal than large-car collisions, and small cars seem to be just as likely to be involved in accidents. The policy question is whether the benefits of small cars (less pollution and congestion) are greater than the safety cost.

Exercises and Discussion Questions

1. Suppose that the relationship between traffic volume and travel time is

$$\text{Trip time} = 12.0 + 0.001 \cdot (\text{Volume} - 400) + 0.00001 \cdot (\text{Volume} - 400)^2$$

The marginal benefit (demand) is \$22.12 for a volume of 200 and drops by \$2.48 for every additional 200 drivers.

a. Use this equation to derive a table like Table 19–2.

b. What is the equilibrium traffic volume? What is the optimum volume?

c. What is the appropriate congestion tax?

2. You have been assigned the task of estimating the external trip cost at a traffic volume of 1,600 vehicles per lane per hour for a one-mile section of an urban freeway between two exits. You have traffic data for the relevant stretch of highway for the last year. Outline your strategy for computing the external trip cost. What information would you collect and how would you use it?

3. In estimating the congestion tax for peak-period travel, Keeler and Small (1977) assumed that the imposition of a congestion tax would not affect traffic volume.

a. Depict graphically the model of auto travel underlying this assumption.

b. Did Keeler and Small overestimate or underestimate the congestion tax? In other words, if the assumption of a fixed traffic volume were dropped, would the estimated congestion tax increase or decrease?

4. Consider the following quote from Peabody and Associates, a transportation consulting firm: "According to the Peabody principle, an increase in highway capacity increases traffic volume by an amount sufficient to leave the private trip cost unchanged."

a. Use a graph to depict a situation in which the Peabody principle is correct.

b. Choose the word in parentheses that makes the following statement correct and then explain your choice of words: "As the price elasticity of demand for highway travel (*increases, decreases*) in absolute value, the Peabody principle becomes a more accurate prediction of reality."

5. Sinead commutes from her suburban residence to the city center. When asked her opinion of a proposed congestion tax of $5.00 per trip, she says, "Of course I oppose the congestion tax. It would make me worse off by $5.00 per trip. What do you think I am, stupid?" Critically appraise Sinead's statement.

6. A city has announced plans to widen a radial highway. The demand curve for the typical traveler is $T = 40 - P$, where T is the number of trips per month and P is the cost per trip (in cents). For example, if the cost is 10 cents, the typical traveler will make 30 trips per month. If the new highway is built, the cost per trip would decrease from 30 cents to 20 cents and the taxes of the typical traveler would increase by $1.25 per month. Will the typical traveler support the construction of the new highway? Explain.

7. In Figure 19–3, the widening of the road decreased trip cost and increased traffic volume.

a. Compute the increase in consumer surplus if $C_o = \$5$, $C_w = \$4$, $V_o = 1,600$, and $V_w = 1,800$. If the widening project costs $1,400, is it worthwhile?

b. How would your answer change if every auto using the stretch of highway generates $2 worth of air pollution?

c. What is the lesson from this exercise?

8. Consider a city that has both a congestion problem (it does not have a congestion tax) and an auto pollution problem (drivers do not pay for the pollution they generate).
   a. Draw the private-trip-cost curve and the social-trip-cost curve. How do your cost curves differ from those in Figure 19–1?
   b. Label the optimum volume V^* and the equilibrium volume V'.
   c. Suppose that the city builds a light-rail transit system and subsidizes light-rail fares. Depict graphically a situation in which the subsidized light-rail system generates an auto volume of V^*.
   d. Does the fact that the light-rail system generates the optimum auto volume mean that it is an efficient policy?

9. Using the data in Table 19–5, compute the effects of the following events on Duke's optimum speed. Illustrate your answers with a graph (like Figure 19–10).
   a. Betty Lou is grounded for make-up violations, leaving Duke without his favorite dance partner. The marginal benefit of speed decreases by $9 for every speed.
   b. The normal country western band is replaced by Adam Smith and the Invisible Hands, a punk rock band. Although Duke and Betty Lou en-joy slam-dancing, it generates one quarter of the utility of the two-step (a country western dance).
   c. The legal speed limit decreases to 46 m.p.h. The expected cost from speeding tickets increases by $3 for every 1 m.p.h. over the speed limit: $3 for 47 m.p.h., $6 for 48 m.p.h., $9 for 49 m.p.h., and so on.
   d. Highway improvements cut the probabilities of crashing in half.

10. Duchess, a resident of Hazard City, has the same marginal-benefit curve as Duke (Table 19–5), but her marginal-cost curve is horizontal.
    a. Suppose that the marginal cost of speed without air bags is $14. What is her optimum speed?
    b. Suppose that an air-bag system would decrease the marginal cost of speed to $8. If the air-bag system costs $300, should Duchess buy the system?

11. Chopperville is evaluating the merits of using helicopters to clear up high-way accidents. Suppose that an accident simply stops traffic from the time the accident occurs to the time the disabled vehicles are removed from the highway. During rush hours, the typical accident stops traffic for 7,000 cars. Under the current tow-truck system, the typical rush-hour accident stops traffic for 20 minutes. Under a helicopter system, the typical rush-hour accident would stop traffic for only eight minutes. Suppose that the cost of operating the tow-truck system (including the costs of labor, fuel, and equipment) is $200 per accident and the cost of operating the helicopter system (including the costs of labor, fuel, and equipment) would be $3,000 per accident. Your task is to determine whether the helicopter system is superior to the tow-truck system.

    a. Is there enough information to determine which system would be superior? If not, what additional information do you need, and how would you use it?

    b. If possible, specify "reasonable" values for the missing bits of information and compute the benefits and costs of switching to the helicopter system.

    c. Suppose that it is possible, for each accident, to instantaneously determine which driver is at fault, and that the responsible driver must pay for either a helicopter or a tow truck to clear up the accident (at a cost of $200 for the truck or $3,000 for the helicopter). Describe a simple public policy that would provide the incentive for drivers to freely choose the socially efficient method of clearing up the accident (either the truck or helicopter).

References and Additional Readings

General

Kraft, Gerald, and Thomas A. Domencich. "Free Transit." In *Readings in Urban Economics,* ed. Matthew Edel and Jerome Rothenberg. New York: Macmillan, 1972, pp. 459–80. Reports estimates of the elasticities of demand for auto travel.

Meyer, John R., and José A. Gómez-Ibáñez. *Autos, Transit and Cities.* Cambridge, Mass.: Harvard University Press, 1981.

Small, Kenneth A. *Urban Transportation Economics.* Philadelphia, Penn.: Harwood Academic Publishers, 1992. A comprehensive survey of the economics of urban transportation.

U.S. Bureau of the Census. *1980 Census of Population: Journey to Work—Metropolitan Commuting Flows.* Washington, D.C.: U.S. Government Printing Office, 1984.

Congestion

Altshuler, Alan A. *The Urban Transportation System.* Cambridge, Mass.: Joint Center for Urban Studies of MIT and Harvard, 1979. Chapter 9, pp. 317–73.

Downs, Anthony. *Stuck in Traffic: Coping with Peak-Hour Traffic Congestion.* Washington, D.C.: The Brookings Institution, 1992. Explores the effects of adopting several anticongestion remedies, including gasoline taxes, highway expansion, high-occupancy lanes, and increased employment and population density.

Keeler, Theodore E., and Kenneth A. Small. "Optimal Peak-Load Pricing, Investment and Service Levels on Urban Expressways." *Journal of Political Economy* 85 (1977), pp. 1–25. Develops a long-run model of highway pricing and investment and uses the model to estimate optimum congestion taxes.

Keeler, Theodore E.; Kenneth A. Small; George S. Cluff; and Jeffrey K. Finke. "Optimal Peak-Load Pricing, Investment and Service Levels on Urban Expressways." Working Paper no. 253, Institute of Urban and Regional Development, University of California, Berkeley, 1975. Develops a long-run model of highway pricing and investment and uses the model to estimate optimum congestion taxes.

McConnell-Fay, Natalie. "Tackling Traffic Congestion in the San Francisco Bay Area." *Transportation Quarterly* 40 (1986), pp. 159–70. A planner's view of the congestion problem and alternative policy responses.

Meyer, John R., and José A. Gómez-Ibáñez. *Autos, Transit and Cities.* Cambridge, Mass.: Harvard University Press, 1981. Chapter 11, pp. 185–229.

Moore, Terry, and Paul Thorsnes. *The Transportation/Land Use Connection.* Chicago: American Planning Association, 1994. Explores the effects of public policy on transportation systems and land-use patterns.

Pozdena, Randall J. "Unlocking Gridlock." *Federal Reserve Bank of San Francisco Weekly Letter,* December 1988, pp. 1–5. Updates the Keeler and Small (1977) estimates of congestion tolls.

Sullivan, Arthur M. "The General Equilibrium Effects of Congestion Externalities." *Journal of Urban Economics* 14 (1983), pp. 80–104. Uses a general-equilibrium computer model to simulate the effects of optimum congestion externalities on land rent, land use, and city size.

Vickrey, William S. "Pricing in Urban and Suburban Transport." *American Economic Review* 53 (1963), pp. 452–65. Reprinted in *Urban Economics: Readings and Analysis,* ed. Ronald E. Grieson. Boston: Little, Brown, 1973, pp. 106–18.

Walters, A. A. *The Economics of Road User Charges.* Baltimore: Johns Hopkins University Press, 1968. Chapters 2 and 3.

Watson, Peter L., and Edward P. Holland. "Congestion Pricing—The Example of Singapore." In *Urban Transportation Economics, Special Report 181.* Washington, D.C.: Transportation Research Board, 1978, pp. 27–30. Reprinted from *Finance and Development* 13 (March 1976), pp. 20–24.

Williams, Stephen R."Getting Downtown, Relief of Highway Congestion through Pricing." In *Urban Economic Issues,* ed. Stephan Mehay and Geoffrey Nunn. Glenview, Ill.: Scott, Foresman, 1984. Discusses the efficiency and equity effects of congestion tolls and describes Singapore's congestion policy.

Wohl, Martin. "Congestion Toll Pricing for Public Transport Facilities." In *Public Prices for Public Products,* ed. Selma Mushkin. Washington, D.C.: Urban Institute, 1972, pp. 245–46.

Parking Taxes and Other Alternatives to Congestion Taxes

DiRenzo, J.; B. Cima; and E. Barber. "Parking Management Tactics." Vol. 3, *Reference Guide.* Washington, D.C.: U.S. Department of Transportation, 1981. Reports the results of the increase in parking cost in Ottawa, Canada.

Kulash, Damian. *Parking Taxes as Roadway Prices: A Case Study of the San Francisco Experience.* Washington, D.C.: Urban Institute, 1973, pp. 25–28.

McElhiney, Paul T. "Evaluating Freeway Performance in Los Angeles." *Traffic Quarterly* 14, no. 3 (July 1960), pp. 296–312.

Miller, Gerald K., and Carol T. Everett. "Raising Commuter Parking Prices—An Empirical Study." *Transportation* 11 (1982), pp. 105–29. Examines the result of an increase in parking cost for government employees in Washington, D.C.

Mohring, Herbert. "The Benefits of Reserved Bus Lanes, Mass Transit Subsidies, and Marginal Cost Pricing in Alleviating Traffic Congestion." Chapter 6 in *Current Issues in Urban Economics,* ed. Peter Mieszkowski and Mahlon Straszheim. Baltimore: Johns Hopkins University Press, 1979, pp. 165–95.

Parody, Thomas E. "Implementation of a Peak-Period Pricing Strategy for CBD Parking." *Transportation Quarterly* 38 (1984), pp. 153–69. Describes the results of an experiment with peak-period parking taxes in Madison, Wisconsin.

Shoup, Donald C. "Cashing Out Free Parking." *Transportation Quarterly* 36 (1982), pp. 351–64.

Willson, Richard W. "Parking Subsidies and the Drive-Alone Commuter: New Evidence and Implications." Paper presented at the Transportation Research Board Annual Meeting, 1988. Reports the results of a survey of parking subsidies in Los Angeles.

Highway Investment

Downs, Anthony. "The Law of Peak Hour Expressway Congestion." *Traffic Quarterly,* July 1962, pp. 393–409. Reprinted in Anthony Downs, *Urban Problems and Prospects,* 2nd ed. Skokie, Ill.: Rand McNally, 1976, pp. 185–99.

Keeler, Theodore E., and Kenneth A. Small. "Optimal Peak-Load Pricing, Investment and Service Levels on Urban Expressways." *Journal of Political Economy* 85 (1977), pp. 1–25. Develops a long-run model of highway pricing and investment and uses the model to estimate optimum congestion taxes.

Keeler, Theodore E.; Kenneth A. Small; George S. Cluff; and Jeffrey K. Finke. "Optimal Peak-Load Pricing, Investment and Service Levels on Urban Expressways." Working Paper no. 253, Institute of Urban and Regional Development, University of California, Berkeley, 1975. Develops a long-run model of highway pricing.

Kraus, Marvin. "Scale Economies Analysis for Urban Highway Networks." *Journal of Urban Economics* 9 (1981), pp. 1–22.

Mohring, Herbert. "Urban Highway Investments." In *Measuring Benefits of Government Investments,* ed. Robert Dorfman. Washington, D.C.: Brookings Institution, 1965.

Auto Safety

Altshuler, Alan A. *The Urban Transportation System.* Cambridge, Mass.: Joint Center for Urban Studies of MIT and Harvard, 1979. Chapter 7, pp. 210–51.

Case, H. W.; A. Burg; and J. D. Baird. "Vehicle Size and Accident Involvement: A Preliminary Study." *Journal of Safety Research* 5 (1973), pp. 26–35.

Crandall, Robert W.; Howard K. Gruenspecht; Theodore E. Keeler; and Lester B. Lave. *Regulating the Automobile.* Washington, D.C.: Brookings Institution, 1986. Chapter 4 discusses the effects of safety regulations on highway death rates. Chapter 3 explores the cost of safety regulations. Chapter 7 discusses the conflicting goals of regulations on auto safety, auto emissions, and fuel economy.

Meyer, John R., and José A. Gómez-Ibáñez. *Autos, Transit and Cities.* Cambridge, Mass.: Harvard University Press, 1981. Chapter 13, pp. 254–76.

Peltzman, Sam. *Regulation of Automobile Safety.* Washington, D.C.: American Enterprise Institute, 1975. Explores the effect of auto safety regulation on driver behavior.

Auto Pollution

Ackerman, Bruce. "Clean (Cough) Air." *New York Times,* August 20, 1977, p. 21.

Altshuler, Alan A. *The Urban Transportation System.* Cambridge, Mass.: Joint Center for Urban Studies of MIT and Harvard, 1979. Chapter 6, pp. 172–209.

Crandall, Robert W.; Howard K. Gruenspecht; Theodore E. Keeler; and Lester B. Lave. *Regulating the Automobile.* Washington, D.C.: Brookings Institution, 1986. Chapter 5 discusses the effects of emissions policy on air pollution. Chapter 3 explores the cost of emissions controls. Chapter 7 discusses the conflicting goals of regulations on auto safety, auto emissions, and fuel economy.

Freeman, A. Myrick. *Air and Water Pollution Control: A Benefit-Cost Assessment.* New York: John Wiley & Sons, 1982. Estimates the benefits and costs of air pollution programs.

Gómez-Ibáñez, José A., and Gary R. Fauth. "Downtown Auto Restraint Policies: The Costs and Benefits for Boston." *Journal of Transport Economics and Policy* 14 (1980), pp. 133–53.

Meyer, John R., and José A. Gómez-Ibáñez. *Autos, Transit and Cities.* Cambridge, Mass.: Harvard University Press, 1981. Chapter 9, pp. 149–70.

Mills, Edwin S., and Lawrence J. White. "Government Policies toward Automotive Emissions Control." In *Approaches to Controlling Air Pollution,* ed. Ann F. Friedlaender. Cambridge, Mass.: MIT Press, 1978, pp. 348–409.

National Academy of Sciences and National Academy of Engineering. *Air Quality and Automotive Emission Control.* Vol. 4, *The Costs and Benefits of Automobile Emission Control.* Prepared for the Senate Committee on Public Works. Washington, D.C.: U.S. Government Printing Office, 1974.

Straszheim, Mahlon R. "Assessing the Social Costs of Urban Transportation Technologies." In *Current Issues in Urban Economics,* ed. Peter Mieszkowski and Mahlon Straszheim. Baltimore: Johns Hopkins University Press, 1979. Reviews the literature on the externalities associated with automobiles and highways.

Mass Transit

> While real trolleys in Newark, Philadelphia, Pittsburgh, and Boston languish
> for lack of patronage and government support, millions of people flock to
> Disneyland to ride fake trains that don't go anywhere.
> Kenneth T. Jackson

This chapter addresses five questions about urban mass transit, devoting one section to each question. First, how does a commuter choose a travel mode, and why do so few commuters use mass transit? Second, how does the cost of a bus system compare to the costs of a heavy rail system and an auto-based system? Third, how do the costs of the new light-rail systems compare to the costs of alternative transit systems? Fourth, why do most transit systems generate large operating deficits? Finally, should the private sector play a greater role in the provision of mass transit?

Mass Transit Facts

Table 20–1 shows commuting patterns and transit ridership in U.S. metropolitan areas. Public transit includes buses, streetcars, subways, elevated trains, and railroads. Public transit is most popular among workers who commute within the central city, being used by 15.8 percent of city commuters. Transit is less popular among workers who commute from a suburban residence to a central-city job: only 8 percent of these commuters use transit. For the most frequent commuting trip (from suburb to suburb), only 1.5 percent of commuters use public transit.

Table 20–2 shows trends in transit ridership. Between 1950 and 1990, the total number of transit trips decreased by about 50 percent. Transit ridership reached its low point in the early 1970s and has recovered since then. The trolley coach (a bus powered by overhead electric wires) reached its peak in 1950 and has declined since then. The use of light-rail systems (streetcars) decreased steadily between 1940 and 1980, but has recently staged a recovery: systems have recently been built or restored

TABLE 20–1   Commuting Patterns and Public Transit Use

Commute Pattern	Percent of Trips	Percent Using		
		Public Transit	Bus or Streetcar	Heavy Rail
Central-City Residents				
Job in central city	33.1	15.8	10.0	5.8
Job in suburb	6.8	5.5	4.9	0.6
Suburban Residents				
Job in central city	20.1	8.0	5.0	3.0
Job in suburb	40.1	1.5	1.4	0.1
Total	100.0	7.8	5.2	2.6

Definitions

1. Public transit: buses, streetcars, subways, elevated trains, and railroads.
2. Heavy rail: subways, elevated trains, and railroads.

SOURCE: U.S. Bureau of the Census, *1980 Census of Population: Journey to Work—Characteristics of Workers* (Washington, D.C.: U.S. Government Printing Office, 1984), Table 1.

in Portland, San Jose, Sacramento, Buffalo, San Diego, and Pittsburgh. In Canada, there are new light-rail systems in Edmonton and Calgary.

There is substantial variation in transit ridership between metropolitan areas. In 1980, the percentage of workers riding transit was 45 percent in New York, but no more than 18 percent in any other metropolitan area. In the 25 largest metropolitan areas, there were 4 areas with transit ridership between 15 and 18 percent (Chicago, San Francisco-Oakland, Washington, D.C., and Boston) and 5 with transit ridership between 10 and 15 percent (Philadelphia, Baltimore, Pittsburgh, Cleveland, and New Orleans). In the remaining 16 metropolitan areas, less than 10 percent of commuters took mass transit. Among the areas with the lowest transit ridership were Detroit (3.7 percent), Dallas (3.4 percent), Houston (3 percent), and San Diego (3.3 percent).

TABLE 20–2   Public Transit Ridership, 1940–1990
(Numbers in millions)

Year	Total Rides	Heavy Rail	Light Rail	Trolley Coach	Motor Bus
1940	13,098	2,382	5,943	534	4,239
1950	17,246	2,264	3,904	1,658	9,420
1960	9,395	1,850	463	657	6,425
1970	7,332	1,881	235	182	5,034
1980	8,567	2,388	133	142	5,837
1990	8,873	2,346	176	126	5,784

SOURCE: American Public Transit Association, *Transit Fact Book* (Washington, D.C., 1991).

What are the elasticities of demand for mass transit? By how much would transit ridership increase when transit fares decrease or transit service improves? There are four general conclusions from empirical studies of transit ridership:

1. **Price elasticity.** The demand for transit is price-inelastic, with a price elasticity between −0.20 and −0.50 (Beesley and Kemp, 1987). A common rule of thumb is that a 10 percent increase in fares decreases ridership by about 3.3 percent, meaning that the price elasticity is −0.33. According to Small (1992), the price elasticity is relatively large for off-peak trips and trips by high-income commuters.

2. **Time elasticities.** The demand for transit is more responsive to changes in travel time. For the **line-haul** portion of the trip (time spent in the vehicle), Domencich, Kraft, and Valette (1972) estimate an elasticity of −0.39: a 10 percent increase in line-haul time decreases ridership by about 3.9 percent. For access time (time spent getting to the bus stop or transit station), they estimate an elasticity of −0.71.

3. **Value of travel time.** According to Small (1992), the average commuter values the time spent in transit vehicles at about half the wage: the typical commuter would be willing to pay half of his hourly wage to avoid an hour on the bus or train. The value of time spent walking and waiting is two to three times larger: the typical commuter would be willing to pay between 1.0 and 1.5 times his hourly wage to avoid an hour of walking or waiting time. The value of travel time increases less than proportionately with income: a 50 percent difference in income generates less than a 50 percent difference in the value of travel time.

4. **Noncommuting trips.** The elasticities of demand for noncommuting travel are higher than the elasticities for commuting trips.

There are three principal implications from these empirical results. First, an increase in transit fares increases total fare revenue. A fare increase decreases ridership by a relatively small amount, so total revenue (fare times ridership) increases. Second, a simultaneous improvement in service and fares may increase ridership. Suppose that a transit authority increases the frequency and speed of buses and finances the improved service with increased fares. Because people are more sensitive to changes in time cost than changes in fares, ridership may increase. Third, service improvements that decrease walking and waiting time (more frequent service, shorter distances between stops) generate larger increases in ridership than improvements that decrease line-haul time.

Choosing a Travel Mode: The Commuter

This section discusses modal choice from the perspective of the commuter. The commuter chooses the mode that minimizes the total cost of travel (the sum of time and monetary costs). Suppose that a commuter has three travel options: the automobile, the bus, and a fixed-rail transit system such as San Francisco's Bay Area Rapid Transit (BART) or Washington, D.C.'s, Metro.

The commuting trip can be divided into three parts. The **collection phase** involves travel from the home to the main travel vehicle. The auto mode has no collection cost because the driver uses his own vehicle. The bus mode has a moderate collection cost because the rider must walk from his home to the bus stop. The fixed-rail system has the highest collection cost because there is a relatively long average distance between transit stations, so riders must either walk a long distance or take another mode (e.g., auto or bus) from the home to the transit station. The **line-haul phase** is the part of the trip spent on the main travel vehicle. The heavy-rail mode has the shortest line-haul time because it has an exclusive right-of-way, so it avoids rush-hour congestion. Although the bus and the auto both travel on congested streets and highways, the auto is faster because the bus must stop to pick up passengers along the way. The **distribution phase** involves travel from the end of the vehicular trip (at the downtown transit station, parking garage, bus stop) to the workplace. If parking is available near the workplace, the auto has the shortest distribution time, followed by the bus and the fixed-rail system.

An Example of Modal Choice

Table 20–3 lists the monetary and time costs of the three travel modes for Carla, a commuter who travels 10 miles from her suburban home to a job in the central city. The computations are based on the assumption that Carla values the time spent on the transit vehicle at half her wage rate and values time spent walking and waiting at 1.5 times her wage rate. If her wage is $12 per hour, she is willing to pay $6 to avoid one hour of in-vehicle time and $18 to avoid one hour of walking and waiting time. Therefore, the cost of walking and waiting time is 30 cents per minute, and the cost of in-vehicle time is 10 cents per minute.

1. **Collection time cost.** Carla walks to the bus stop or the BART station. Since the bus stop is closer to her home, the bus has a lower collection cost.
2. **Line-haul time cost.** BART is the fastest mode (it operates on an exclusive right-of-way), followed by autos (which travel on congested streets) and buses (which travel on congested streets and stop to pick up passengers).
3. **Distribution cost.** Carla parks her auto in a company parking lot under her office building, so the distribution cost of the auto trip is zero. The bus stop is relatively close to the office, so the bus has a lower distribution cost than BART.
4. **Monetary cost.** The monetary cost of the auto trip is $0.20 per mile, or $2.00. The bus fare is $1, and the BART fare is $1.50. Half of the $6.00 parking cost is allocated to the morning commute.

The cost of driving is less than the cost of the bus and BART. Although the monetary cost of driving exceeds the monetary cost of the bus by $4, the lower time cost of the auto more than offsets its higher monetary cost. Similarly, the auto is more expensive but faster than BART. The largest difference in time cost is for collection and distribution costs, where the auto has a cost advantage of $4.50 over the

TABLE 20–3   **Costs of Travel Modes and Modal Choice**

	Auto	*Bus*	*BART*
Collection Time Cost			
Collection time (minutes)	0	10	15
Cost per minute ($)	0.30	0.30	0.30
Collection time cost ($)	0.00	3.00	4.50
Line-Haul Time Cost			
Line-haul time (minutes)	40	50	30
Cost per minute ($)	0.10	0.10	0.10
Line-haul time cost ($)	4.00	5.00	3.00
Distribution Time Cost			
Distribution time (minutes)	0	5	9
Cost per minute ($)	0.30	0.30	0.30
Distribution time cost ($)	0.00	1.50	2.70
Monetary Cost			
Operating cost or fare ($)	2.00	1.00	1.50
Parking cost ($)	3.00	0.00	0.00
Total Monetary Cost ($)	5.00	1.00	1.50
Total Time Cost ($)	4.00	9.50	10.20
Total Cost ($)	9.00	10.50	11.70

bus ($3.00 for collection + $1.50 for distribution), and $7.20 over BART ($4.50 + $2.70). Since the auto has a lower total cost than both the bus and BART, Carla drives to work.

What would it take to persuade Carla to switch from her auto to mass transit? There are several possibilities:

1. **Subsidized transit.** If the bus and BART were free, Carla would still drive. To get her to switch to the bus, she would have to be paid a bribe of 51 cents per bus ride. A bribe of $1.21 would cause her to switch to BART. Transit fares must decrease by relatively large amounts to offset the time-cost advantages of the automobile.

2. **Line-haul time.** If the line-haul time of the bus decreased from 50 minutes to less than 35 minutes, Carla would ride the bus. She would take BART if its line-haul time decreased to less than 3 minutes.

3. **Collection and distribution time.** Carla would ride the bus if its collection and distribution time decreased from 15 minutes to less than 10 minutes and would switch to BART if its collection and distribution time decreased from 24 minutes to less than 15 minutes.

4. **Auto monetary cost.** Carla would ride the bus if the car's unit cost increased from 20 cents to 36 cents per mile. As reported in Chapter 19, estimates

of congestion tax are in the range of 21 to 65 cents per mile for rush-hour traffic, so the imposition of a congestion tax would cause her to switch to the bus. Similarly, if the city imposed a pollution tax of at least 16 cents per mile, Carla would stop driving.

5. **Parking cost.** Carla would ride the bus if the parking cost rose to at least $4.50 ($9 per day).

6. **Wage.** If Carla's wage dropped to $8, the bus would be less costly than the auto, and if her wage dropped to $6, BART would be less costly than the auto. As the wage decreases, the opportunity cost of travel time decreases, increasing the relative attractiveness of the modes with relatively low monetary cost and high time cost.

To summarize, to get Carla to switch to transit, the changes in either the monetary cost or the line-haul time cost would have to be relatively large. On the other hand, she would switch to transit with relatively small changes in collection and distribution time costs. These conclusions are consistent with the transit elasticities discussed earlier in the chapter.

What type of commuters take mass transit instead of driving? There are five possibilities:

1. **Proximity to stops and stations.** A person who lives near a bus stop or a rail station has a relatively low collection cost for transit and is more likely to take the bus or BART.

2. **Low opportunity cost.** For a person who has a low opportunity cost of travel time (a worker with a low wage, a student, a retired person), the time cost of travel is relatively low. As a result, the advantages of transit (lower monetary cost) dominate the disadvantages (longer commuting time). Such a person is more likely to choose transit.

3. **Low walking cost.** A person who enjoys walking has relatively low collection and distribution costs and is more likely to choose transit.

4. **Disutility of driving.** A person who dislikes the hassle and anxiety of driving is more likely to choose transit. In terms of the numerical example, such a person has a relatively high cost for in-vehicle auto time and is more likely to take the bus or BART. In contrast, a person who considers driving a challenging form of athletics will buy a pair of gloves and drive to work.

5. **No automobile.** Many of the poor do not have access to an auto, so their only option is to use public transit.

Transit Service and Modal Choice

How do changes in transit design and scheduling affect ridership? Transit ridership increases as a result of service improvements that decrease the time cost of transit. As explained earlier, commuters are most responsive to changes in collection and distribution time (walking and waiting time).

Designing the Bus System.   Consider first the bus system. The bus company affects time cost in two ways. First, it chooses the bus headway, the period of time between buses on the bus route. As the headway decreases, riders spend less time waiting at the bus stop, so their time cost decreases. Second, the bus company chooses the frequency of stops in the residential collection area. An increase in the frequency of stops decreases walking distances and collection cost. Similarly, the more frequent the stops in the downtown distribution area, the lower the distribution cost. An increase in the frequency of stops also increases line-haul (in-vehicle) time: more time is spent picking up and dropping off passengers, so the trip takes longer.

Designing the Fixed-Rail System.   Consider next the design of a fixed-rail system. San Francisco's BART provides a nice illustration of the trade-offs associated with the design of a rail transit system. There are two basic design trade-offs:

1. **Mainline versus integrated system.** BART is considered a mainline system because it relies on other transit systems to collect its riders from residential neighborhoods. Riders must either walk, drive, or ride a bus to the BART station. The alternative to the mainline system is an integrated system, under which commuters make the entire commute trip on a single transit mode.

2. **Spacing between stations.** BART has widely spaced stations (about 2.5 miles apart), so there are few stops on the way to the city center. As a result, travel time from the suburban station to the downtown station (line-haul time) is relatively short, and in-vehicle time cost is relatively low. On the other hand, the average commuter must travel a relatively long distance from home to one of the widely spaced transit stations, so collection cost (by foot, bus, or car) is relatively high.

BART was designed to compete with the line-haul portion of the automobile trip. It achieves this objective, providing comfortable, speedy service from the suburban stations to the city center. There is a trade-off, however: collection cost is relatively high because BART is a mainline system with widely spaced stations. Because walking and waiting time is more costly than in-vehicle time, the negative attribute (high collection cost) dominates the positive one (comfortable, speedy line-haul travel), so the full cost of a BART trip is relatively high and BART has diverted a relatively small number of auto commuters.

Bus and Carpool Lanes.   Another design issue concerns the treatment of high-occupancy vehicles (HOV) such as carpools and buses. When a city establishes a "diamond" lane for the exclusive use of buses and carpools, the line-haul times of buses and carpools decrease. Under the diamond-lane approach, buses and carpools have the advantages of the fixed-rail system (faster line-haul times) without the disadvantages (high collection and distribution costs). As a result, the diamond lane causes some drivers to switch to a bus or a carpool. Given the moderate elasticity of transit demand with respect to line-haul time (-0.39), there will be a moderate diversion of auto traffic.

What are the effects of diamond lanes on commuters who continue to drive? There is good news and bad news. The good news is that some auto drivers switch to buses and carpools, so there is less auto traffic. In Figure 20–1, the diamond lanes shift the demand curve to the left, decreasing trip cost for the original trip-cost curve. The bad news is that there are fewer lanes for the remaining autos: the diamond lanes decrease the amount of road space, so the congestion threshold decreases and the trip-cost curve shifts to the left. In this example, the shift of the demand curve is small relative to the shift of the cost curve, so the trip cost increases from $5 to $6. If shift of the demand curve were relatively large, the trip cost would decrease.

Figure 20–1 accurately depicts recent experiences with diamond lanes. The first experiment with diamond lanes occurred along the Santa Monica Freeway in Los Angeles. The diamond lanes increased the average trip cost of a vociferous group of auto commuters, and the experiment was short-lived. The city of Boston experienced similar problems when it set up diamond lanes along the Southeast Expressway.

Some cities have built new lanes for buses and carpools. Among the cities that have built new diamond lanes are Miami (along Interstate 95), Washington, D.C. (along the Shirley Expressway), and Los Angeles (along the San Bernardino Freeway). By building new lanes instead of taking away auto lanes, these cities did not

FIGURE 20–1   Diamond Lanes and Auto Trip Costs

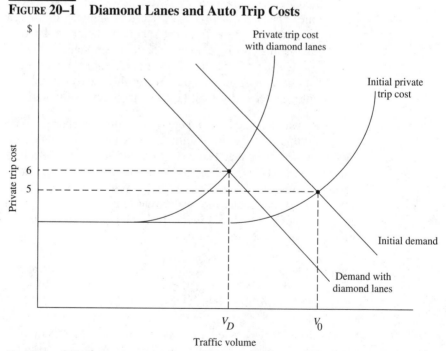

The addition of diamond lanes (reserved for buses and carpools) affects travel in nondiamond lanes in two ways: there are fewer vehicles in nondiamond lanes, so the demand curve shifts to the left; there are fewer lanes, so the trip-cost curve shifts to the left. If a relatively small number of vehicles are diverted to the diamond lanes, the net cost of travel in nondiamond lanes increases from $5 to $6.

impose any explicit cost on auto drivers, so there was little opposition to the diamond lanes. The new diamond lanes do, however, impose an implicit cost on drivers: if the new lanes were opened to auto traffic, the trip cost curve would shift to the right, decreasing travel times for auto commuters.

Choosing a System: The Planner's Problem

This section discusses modal choice from the perspective of a transportation planner. The planner must decide what type of transportation system to build. There are three options: an auto-based highway system, an integrated bus system, and a fixed-rail system like BART or Metro. Estimates of the cost of these alternative systems are provided by a study of transportation options in the San Francisco Bay area (Keeler, Merewitz, Fisher, and Small 1975).

Keeler et al. estimated the cost of three different commuting systems: an auto-based system, an integrated bus system, and BART. The principal conclusions of their study are shown in Figure 20–2. The horizontal axis measures the number of commuters traveling through a transportation corridor during the one-hour peak period. The vertical axis measures the long-run average cost of a "typical" commuting

FIGURE 20–2   Costs of Alternative Transit Systems

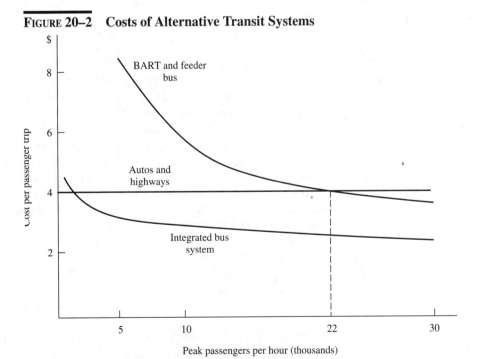

Peak passengers per hour (thousands)

The average cost of auto traffic is independent of auto volume, but the average costs of an integrated bus system and BART decrease as volume increases. The bus system is more efficient than BART for all volumes studied and more efficient than an auto-based system for volumes exceeding 1,100 passengers per hour.

trip (a six-mile line haul and additional time spent in residential collection and down-town distribution). The cost curves show that the bus system is more efficient than the auto system for volumes above 1,100 passengers per hour and is more efficient than BART for all traffic volumes. The auto system is more efficient than BART for volumes up to about 22,000 passengers per hour.

Cost of the Auto System

The cost of the auto system is the sum of the driver's time and operating cost and the public cost of auto traffic. The public cost includes the cost of building the optimum road system. As explained in the previous chapter, the revenue from the optimum congestion tax equals the cost of building the optimum road, so congestion taxes can be used to both internalize congestion externalities and pay for the roads. The public cost also includes the cost of air and noise pollution.

The average cost curve is horizontal for two reasons. First, Keeler et al. assume that the average operating cost and the average pollution cost (cost per mile) do not depend on traffic volume. Second, the trip time (and private trip cost) does not depend on traffic volume: as volume increases, the road is widened to accommodate the increased traffic without any reduction of travel speeds. Given constant returns to scale in highways, a doubling of highway capacity doubles traffic volume without changing the trip time. Using data for 1972, Keeler et al. estimate that the full cost of an auto trip with a six-mile line haul is $4.15.

Cost of the Bus System

The cost of the integrated bus system is the sum of time cost, agency cost, and the public cost of the bus system. The agency cost includes both the operating cost and the capital cost. Included in the public cost are (1) the cost of modifying the roadway to accommodate buses and (2) pollution cost.

The average cost curve is negatively sloped for two reasons. First, as ridership increases, the fixed cost of administering the bus system is spread over more riders. Second, as ridership increases, collection and distribution times decrease. An increase in ridership decreases headways (the time between buses) and decreases the space between bus stops, so riders spend less time walking to and waiting for the bus. In addition, an increase in ridership allows a bus to fill up with a shorter collection route. Less time is spent picking up passengers, so in-vehicle time decreases. According to Keeler et al., if the traffic volume along the corridor exceeds 1,100 passengers, the integrated bus system is less costly than the auto system.

Cost of BART

The BART option involves the mainline heavy-rail system and feeder buses to bring commuters to the BART stations. The time cost of the BART option is the sum of walking and waiting time costs and in-vehicle time cost. The agency cost is the sum of the operating and capital costs of the feeder buses and BART. Given the substantial investment in tracks and right-of-ways, the capital cost of the BART option is large.

The cost curve is negatively sloped for three reasons. First, the system has a substantial fixed cost, which is spread over more riders as ridership increases. Second, as ridership increases, BART headways decrease, decreasing waiting time. Third, an increase in bus ridership decreases the time and monetary cost of feeder-bus service.

BART is more costly than the bus system for three reasons. First, given its design as a mainline system with widely spaced stations, the collection and distribution costs are relatively high. Second, its capital cost is very large: the fixed cost of the system was $1.6 billion. According to Webber (1976), BART could buy enough buses to carry its passengers for only $40 million (2.5 percent of BART's capital cost). Third, BART has a surprisingly high operating cost: in 1975, the operating cost was 15.7 cents per passenger mile, compared to 13.6 cents for a bus. Most planners were surprised to discover that the large investment in capital equipment did not generate large savings in operating cost.

System Choice

The Keeler et al. study provides important information for transit planners. For all corridor volumes studied (up to 30,000 passengers per hour), BART was more costly than an integrated bus system. At a peak volume of 30,000 passengers per hour, BART is 50 percent more costly than the bus system. In 1984, BART's peak ridership through the transbay tube was 15,300 passengers per hour. The lesson for planners is clear: with the possible exceptions of New York City and Chicago, which have corridor volumes exceeding 30,000 passengers per hour, an integrated bus system is likely to be more efficient than a modern fixed-rail system like BART.

Experiences with new heavy-rail systems in other metropolitan areas are similar to the BART experience. The Metro system in Washington, D.C., would have to charge a one-way fare of $8 (Gordon and Richardson, 1989) to cover its operating and capital costs. Ridership on the new systems in Atlanta, Miami, and Baltimore have fallen well short of the projected levels. The problems with heavy-rail systems should not be surprising in light of Keeler et al.'s conclusion that corridor volumes must exceed 30,000 to make a heavy-rail system competitive with a bus system.

Light Rail

In recent years, many medium-sized cities have built light-rail transit systems. Light rail is the modern version of the trolley and streetcar systems that were built in the late 1800s and early 1900s. The first modern light-rail system opened in Edmonton in 1978. Since then, new systems have opened in San Diego, Calgary, Buffalo, Portland, Vancouver, Sacramento, and San Jose. Many other cities are planning to build new systems or extend old streetcar and trolley systems.

How does light rail compare to buses and heavy rail? Gómez-Ibáñez (1985) has studied the cost and performance of new light-rail systems in San Diego, Edmonton, and Calgary, and has come to the following conclusions:

1. **Capital cost.** The capital cost of light rail includes the costs of the vehicles, the track, and the power distribution system. These costs make light rail more costly than a bus system, which uses less expensive vehicles and travels along regular streets and highways. Light rail is much less costly than heavy rail: the cost per mile is $7 million to $20 million, compared to $50 million to $200 million per mile for heavy rail. Light rail is less expensive because it typically uses surface streets (instead of requiring subways or elevated guideways) and is designed for lower speeds.

2. **Operating cost.** Compared to a bus system, light rail has a lower labor cost because it needs fewer operators: a three-car train can be operated by one person and can carry about 10 times as many riders as a standard bus. Because light rail has a higher maintenance cost on its vehicles and its right-of-way, however, its total operating cost is equal to or greater than the operating cost of buses.

3. **Performance.** Most light-rail systems consist of one or two radial rail lines, with feeder buses for the collection and distribution phases of the transit trip. Like the heavy-rail systems, the light-rail systems have higher collection and distribution costs than a bus system. Light rail also has shorter line-haul times and provides a more comfortable ride than a bus.

Table 20–4 compares the cost of the San Diego light-rail system to the bus routes it replaced. The total cost per light-rail passenger was $3.11, compared to $1.16 for the bus system. Light rail has a moderately higher operating cost and a much higher capital cost. The light-rail system seems to have increased transit ridership: ridership in the area served by the system increased from 3.4 million to 4.8 million per year. According to Gómez-Ibáñez, much of the increased ridership was caused by population growth in the corridor served by light rail. If one assumes that the entire increase in ridership was caused by the introduction of the light-rail system, the cost per additional rider was $5.47. The San Diego experience suggests that although light rail may increase ridership, it does so at a relatively high cost.

TABLE 20–4   Comparison of San Diego's Light-Rail and Bus Systems

	Bus System	Light-Rail System
Costs per passenger		
Operating cost	$0.82	$1.02
Capital cost	$0.34	$2.09
Total cost	$1.16	$3.11
Ridership (thousands per year)	3,398	4,845
Cost per new light-rail passenger		$5.47

SOURCE: José A. Gómez-Ibáñez, "A Dark Side to Light Rail?" *Journal of the American Planning Association* 51 (Summer 1985), pp. 337–51.

Subsidies for Mass Transit

In 1985, passenger fares covered only about 39 percent of the operating cost of mass transit. As shown in Figure 20–3, the remainder of operating cost was covered by local governments (providing 22 percent of revenue), state governments (13 percent), and the federal government (12 percent). Can transit subsidies be justified on efficiency grounds?

Justification for Transit Subsidies

There are two justifications for the subsidization of mass transit. First, there are substantial scale economies in the provision of transit, so transit systems have the characteristics of a natural monopoly. As explained in Chapter 16 (Overview of Local Government), the subsidization of a natural monopoly promotes efficiency. Figure 20–4 shows the long-run average cost and marginal-cost curves for a transit system. The curves are negatively sloped because (1) there is a substantial fixed cost associated with setting up the system and (2) the marginal cost of adding another rider is relatively small. The optimum ridership (R^*) is where the marginal social benefit (from the demand curve) equals the marginal cost. To generate this level of ridership, the price must be P^*, which is less than the average total cost. The deficit associated with marginal-cost pricing is shown by the shaded area. If the transit system were forced to cover all its costs, it would charge a price of P' and generate a ridership of R', which is less than the optimum level.

FIGURE 20–3   Transit Revenue Sources, 1985

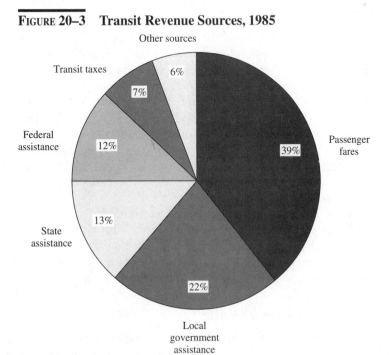

Other sources

Transit taxes

6%

7%

Federal assistance

12%

Passenger fares

39%

State assistance

13%

22%

Local government assistance

FIGURE 20–4   Transit Subsidies for a Natural Monopoly

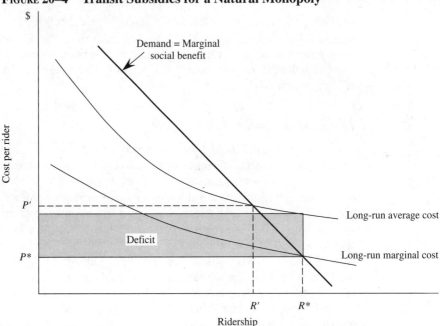

Mass transit is a natural monopoly: scale economies generate a negatively sloped long-run average cost curve. The optimum output is where the demand curve (the marginal-benefit curve) intersects the marginal-cost curve. At the optimum ridership (R^*), the price (P^*) is less than the average total cost, so the system generates a deficit. The system would cover its cost at a price of P', but ridership (R') would be below the optimum level.

The second justification of transit subsidies is explained in Chapter 19 (Autos and Highways). Auto travel is underpriced because drivers do not pay the external costs associated with highway congestion and air pollution. Therefore, transit is overpriced relative to auto travel, and transit subsidies can be used to offset the artificially low price of autos. As explained in Chapter 19, there are trade-offs with transit subsidies: although the subsidies discourage auto use, decreasing congestion and pollution, they also cause the underpricing of urban travel in general, leading to an excessive amount of travel. The policy question is whether the benefit of the subsidy (decreased congestion and air pollution) exceeds the cost (too many resources used in transportation).

How large a transit subsidy would be required to offset the underpricing of auto travel? Suppose that the appropriate congestion tax is, on average, 43 cents per mile and the pollution cost is 1 cent per mile. If the typical auto commute is 10 miles, the commuter avoids $4.40 worth of taxes per trip. A transit subsidy of this amount would eliminate the artificial cost advantage of the automobile.

Reasons for Transit Deficits

Table 20–5 shows recent trends in transit revenues and costs. All dollar figures are in 1980 dollars. In 1965, the fare-box ratio (the ratio of fare revenue to operating cost)

TABLE 20–5   Transit Revenue, Costs, and Deficits, 1960–1980

	1960	*1965*	*1970*	*1975*	*1980*
Fare-box ratio	1.02	0.99	0.86	0.54	0.42
Revenue					
Operating revenue per vehicle mile ($)	1.71	1.72	1.77	1.33	1.23
Fare per passenger ($)	0.46	0.47	0.54	0.47	0.40
Passengers (millions)	9,345	8,253	7,332	6,972	8,235
Cost					
Operating cost per vehicle mile ($)	1.65	1.72	2.06	2.67	2.98
Vehicle miles (millions)	2,143	2,008	1,883	1,990	2,093
Employees (thousands)	156	145	138	160	187
Vehicle miles per employee	13,737	13,848	13,645	12,438	11,193
Passengers per employee	59,904	56,917	53,130	43,575	44,519
Federal funds (million $)	0	27	299	1,608	3,367

SOURCE: Gordon J. Fielding, *Managing Public Transit Strategically: A Comprehensive Approach to Strengthening Service and Monitoring Performance* (San Francisco: Jossey-Bass, 1987), Tables 2 and 3.

was 0.99, meaning that transit riders covered most of the operating cost of transit. By 1980, the fare-box ratio decreased to 0.42, meaning that transit riders paid only 42 percent of operating cost.

One reason for the growth in the transit deficit is that operating revenue decreased over time. Between 1965 and 1980, operating revenue per vehicle mile decreased from $1.72 to $1.23 (in 1980 dollars). Three factors contributed to the decline in revenue. First, the average passenger fare decreased from 47 cents in 1965 to 40 cents in 1980. Second, total ridership decreased slightly, from 8.25 billion to 8.23 billion. Third, the total vehicle miles increased, from 2.01 billion miles to 2.09 billion miles. The number of riders decreased while vehicle miles increased, so the number of riders per vehicle mile decreased. Since there were fewer riders paying lower fares, revenue per vehicle mile decreased.

The primary reason for the growth of the deficit is rising cost. Between 1965 and 1980, the operating cost per vehicle mile increased from $1.72 to $2.98 (in 1980 dollars). Operating cost increased because of rising wages, increased energy cost, and decreased labor productivity. One of the reasons for rising wages is explained in the first chapter on local government: the Baumol model shows that the wages of service workers increase over time because of rising productivity (and wages) in manufacturing.

The simple facts on labor productivity are startling. Between 1965 and 1980, total transit employment increased from 145,000 to 187,000. Since the number of vehicle miles increased by a smaller amount, the number of vehicle miles per employee decreased from 13,848 to 11,193. While the number of transit workers increased, the number of transit riders decreased, so the number of passengers per transit worker decreased from 56,917 to 44,519.

Why did the number of passengers per employee decrease? According to Fielding (1987), an important factor was an increase in the fraction of transit trips taken during peak periods. To explain the peaking problem, consider a city where transit ridership is uniform throughout an eight-hour workday: the city can serve its transit riders with a single bus running all day. Suppose that all the riders suddenly decide to travel to work during two morning rush hours: traffic volume during the two rush hours quadruples. The city will no longer be able to serve its transit riders with a single bus and a single bus driver, but will be forced to buy three more buses and hire more drivers.

What are the effects of the shift to peak ridership on the city's labor productivity and labor cost? Consider first the possibility that the city hires part-time drivers. If the city hires drivers by the hour, productivity does not change: the city hires four part-time drivers instead of one full-time driver. On the other hand, if the city must hire four full-time drivers (who will be idle for six hours per day), its labor productivity decreases and its labor cost rises. In other words, if the shift to peak-period travel is combined with restrictive work rules that prevent part-time workers and split shifts, labor productivity decreases and labor cost increases.

Pickerell (1983) examined the relative importance of five factors that contributed to the growth of the transit deficit between 1970 and 1980. The factors, and their contributions to the growing deficit, are as follows:

1. Decrease in fares: responsible for 28 percent of the growth in the deficit.
2. Increase in wages: 25 percent.
3. Decrease in labor productivity: 18 percent.
4. Increased transit mileage: 16 percent.
5. Increase in energy cost: 12 percent.

Pickerell's results suggest that many factors contributed to the growing deficit. It's important to note that two of the contributing factors (the decrease in fares and the increase in mileage) were integral parts of transportation policy: in an attempt to divert commuters from polluting autos on congested highways, the government has improved transit service while keeping fares relatively low. As explained earlier, an alternative policy would be to force auto drivers to pay the full cost of travel, including the costs of congestion and air pollution.

History of Federal Assistance

Federal assistance to mass transit grew from only $27 million in 1965 to $2.84 billion in 1985 (Fielding, 1987). The Urban Mass Transit Act of 1964 established a program of capital subsidies for transit. For the first several years, most of the federal money was used to purchase unprofitable bus companies. Later, the money was used to invest in new capital equipment (buses, rail vehicles, tracks, and right-of-ways). Before 1973, the federal government paid two thirds of the cost of new transit projects. In 1974, the federal contribution increased to four fifths of the project cost.

Federal assistance for operating costs started with the National Mass Transportation Act of 1974. By 1984, a total of $5.3 billion of operating assistance was provided by all levels of government, with about half of the money coming from local governments, one third from state governments, and one sixth from the federal government. Federal operating subsidies were originally allocated to cities on the basis of total population. This allocation scheme caused large cities to receive relatively small subsidies per transit rider. Suppose that every city receives a 1-cent subsidy per citizen. A large city (e.g., New York), in which 25 percent of the population uses mass transit, would receive a subsidy of four cents per transit rider. A small city (e.g., Santa Barbara), in which 2 percent of the population uses mass transit, would receive a subsidy of 50 cents per rider. To solve this problem, allocations are now based primarily on transit ridership.

Since 1983, a portion of the revenue from the federal gasoline tax has been funneled to mass transit. When the gas tax was increased by five cents per gallon, one cent of the increase was earmarked for a mass-transit fund. In 1984, a total of $1.2 billion was generated by the gas tax. The money was used to support bus systems ($300 million), existing rail systems ($500 million), and new transit systems ($400 million). A city receiving money from the transit fund must either use the money for mass transit or lose it. This creates the incentive to undertake transit projects when other projects (e.g., highway improvements) might be more efficient.

Deregulation: The Private Provision of Transit

In most cities, mass transit is provided by the public sector. To shield the public transit system from competition, private transit activity (e.g., taxis and private bus service) is heavily regulated. Given the large deficits generated by public transit authorities, an obvious question is whether private industry could provide transit services more efficiently. There are two possible strategies for transit deregulation: the private provision of transit services through service contracts, and free entry into the mass transit market.

Contracting for Transit Services

Under the first type of deregulation, the local transit monopoly would be granted to a private firm instead of a government agency. Under a contracting arrangement, the local government specifies the service characteristics of the transit system (e.g., headways, travel times, location of bus stops, fares) and then accepts bids from private firms for the transit service. The transit monopoly is granted to the firm that provides the service at the lowest cost.

The experiences with contracting arrangements are discussed by Lave (1985), Echols (1985), and Rosenbloom (1985). The city of Tidewater, Virginia, contracted for bus service to low-density areas. The private transit company provided the same transit service at a fraction of the cost of public bus service. Along one route, the deficit per passenger decreased from $4.75 to $1.63. Other cities using transit contracts have had similar experiences: the typical private bus company provides transit service for about half the cost of the public bus system. Contracts are also used for subsidized dial-a-ride services: in 1983, the city of Phoenix paid a local taxi company $104,425 to provide dial-a-ride services on Sundays, about one sixth of the cost of using city buses for Sunday service.

Private firms provide transit services for a lower cost for three reasons. First, they pay lower wages. Second, they have more flexible work rules. They have split shifts and use part-time workers, so they don't pay idle workers during the off-peak periods. Third, they use minibuses on low-density routes. In Phoenix, the private bus company uses minibuses with an operating cost of $1.22 per mile, compared to $2.86 per mile for the standard bus.

Entry and Competition

Most cities grant monopoly power to the local transit authority and protect the transit authority from competition. There are two rationales for restricting entry:

1. **Cross subsidization.** The city sets a single transit fare and then forces the transit authority to cover all routes, including some unprofitable ones. For some routes, fares exceed the cost, providing a surplus that is used to subsidize service along unprofitable routes. If entry were allowed, a new firm would provide service along the lucrative routes, underpricing the public transit and capturing its riders. The transit authority would make less money along the profitable routes, destroying the cross-subsidization scheme.

2. **Scale economies.** As explained earlier, there is a substantial fixed cost in providing mass transit, so transit service is a natural monopoly. Although fixed-rail systems are certainly natural monopolies, the case is not so clear for bus systems. Walters (1982) and Morlok and Viton (1985) suggest that scale economies in bus transit are exhausted at a ridership level well below the volume of the typical medium-sized city.

Some cities allow private bus companies to compete with the public bus authority. The experiences with private bus companies are discussed by Johnson and Pilarsky (1985) and Walder (1985). In the city of Chicago, commuter bus clubs provide subscription bus service. In 1981, the full cost (including vehicle cost) of a private bus trip was $1.15, compared to a partial cost (excluding vehicle cost) of $1.44 for a public bus trip. In New York City, private commuter vans travel from Staten Island to Manhattan. The private vans charge the same fare as the public bus, but cover all of their cost and take less time to make the trip.

Would deregulation increase fares along some routes? Under deregulation, a route would not be served unless its total revenue exceeds its total cost. Therefore, transit fares along low-volume routes would increase. If policymakers are concerned about poor households along low-volume routes, they could give money to the poor to compensate for the higher fares. The problem with cross-subsidization is that the transit subsidies go to rich and poor alike. Another option is to provide explicit subsidies for service along low-volume routes, a strategy adopted by Phoenix and other cities.

A second proposal for deregulation is to allow taxis to serve as transit vehicles. Under current regulations, a taxi cannot serve as a common carrier: the taxi can carry an individual or a small group of people traveling together, but cannot give rides to strangers in transit. If taxis were deregulated, they could pick up customers along routes of their own choice, serving as flexible transit vehicles.

The proposals for taxi deregulation have revived the *jitney* concept. Between 1915 and 1920, private cars were used as transit vehicles. The fare was five cents and the slang word for a nickel was *jitney*, so the private vehicles were called *jitneys*. Most jitneys operated during rush hours, allowing the driver to work at another job during the off-peak hours. Some jitneys operated as carpools: the driver posted his workplace on his windshield and picked up riders along his way to work. Other jitney drivers started driving without a specific destination and then modified their routes as they picked up passengers. If taxis were deregulated to serve as common carriers, they would operate much like the jitneys of the early 1900s.

British Experience with Deregulation

In Great Britain, the transit industry was deregulated under the British Transport Act of 1985. As explained by Gómez-Ibáñez and Meyer (1990), the act relaxed controls on entry into the transit industry, reorganized most public transit authorities as for-profit organizations, and introduced competitive bidding for certain transit services. Local governments can continue to subsidize transit services as long as the subsidized service is provided by the low bidder in a competitive auction. Although the London area was not covered under the Transport Act, contracting out is used extensively in the metropolitan area, and full deregulation is expected sometime in the 1990s.

Britain's new transit policy combined deregulation with substantial cuts in transit subsidies. For example, transit subsidies were cut by about 23 percent in the metropolitan counties and about 6 percent in other counties. The decrease in transit subsidies generated pressure to increase fares and cut services. Gómez-Ibáñez and Meyer (1990) and Small (1992) summarize some of the results of the new transit policy:

1. **Service.** In the first full year following deregulation, total mileage was up by 3.3 percent in the metropolitan counties and 16.5 percent in other counties. The use of minibuses (with 12 to 25 seats) increased dramatically. Some unprofitable services were curtailed: for example, some off-peak and low-density routes were abandoned.

2. **Fares.** Transit fares increased by about 35 percent in real terms over a two-year period.

3. **Ridership.** Ridership decreased by about 14 percent.

4. **Production cost.** Production cost fell as a result of labor concessions (relaxed work rules and lower compensation), the introduction of minibuses, and the elimination of excess capacity. According to Heseltine and Silcock (1990), unit cost fell by between 15 percent and 30 percent.

Gómez-Ibáñez and Meyer discuss three lessons from the British experience with the deregulation of transit. First, it is possible to have both competition in the local bus industry and subsidies for unprofitable services. By using competitive bidding to pick a firm to provide the subsidized services, the public sector can provide the services at the lowest possible cost. Second, in addition to cutting cost and increasing productivity, deregulation generates service innovations: the private bus companies introduced minibuses, and local governments improved the services along unprofitable routes. Third, because most of the benefits from deregulation come from competition among transit firms, the public sector must develop policies to ensure competition.

Transportation and Land-Use Patterns

Part II of this book (Land Rent and Urban Land-Use Patterns) discusses the effects of changes in transportation technology on urban land-use patterns. The development of the internal-combustion engine allowed the development of new travel modes (the car and the truck) that were more flexible and less costly than streetcars and horse-drawn wagons. The new modes decreased the reliance of firms and households on the central area of the city, allowing the decentralization of employment and residents. This section discusses two types of changes in transportation: an increase in gasoline cost and the construction of fixed-rail transit systems.

Gasoline Prices

Suppose that the real cost of gasoline increases. How will the increased cost of auto travel affect housing and land prices? As explained in Part II, increase in transportation cost increases the slopes of the housing-price function and the residential bid-rent function. Studies by Small (1986) and Coulson and Engle (1987) confirm these theoretical predictions: an increase in the price of gasoline increases the relative attractiveness of locations near employment centers, increasing the prices of housing and land.

How will an increase in the cost of gasoline affect the distributions of employment and population? The changes are likely to be relatively small for three reasons. First, the cost of gasoline is a relatively small part of the cost of travel. Second, other responses to an increase in gasoline prices (buying more fuel-efficient cars, carpooling, switching to public transit) allow drivers to decrease travel cost without changing residences or workplaces. For these two reasons, the changes in the prices of housing and land are likely to be relatively small. Even if the changes in price were relatively large, it would take a long time before there would be changes in population density near employment centers because structures last a long time and are costly to demolish. Small (1985) estimated that a $1 per gallon increase in the price of gasoline would cause a relatively small number of suburban households to move to the central city.

Fixed-Rail Systems and Land Use

How do fixed-rail systems affect land rent and land-use? Dewees (1976) examined the effect of Toronto's subway on housing prices near the new transit stations and concluded that the subway increased the price of housing within one third of a mile of the stations. The largest increases in prices occurred for the locations closest to the stations.

Do fixed-rail systems affect land-use patterns? Webber (1976) studied the effects of BART on land-use patterns in the San Francisco Bay area. His conclusions are as follows:

1. There was a boom in downtown office construction during the construction of BART. The office boom was caused by several factors, and it is impossible to identify BART's contribution.

2. There is no evidence that downtown office development would have been any slower if transit authorities had expanded bus service instead of building BART.

3. There has been little development of activities around the suburban train stations.

In a different study, Dyett and Escudero (1977) concluded that BART caused some clustering of activities within the central city.

In summarizing the results from several studies of the effects of rail systems on land-use patterns, Altshuler (1979) makes two observations:

1. In a growing economy, rail transit contributes to the clustering of activities near downtown stations. These clustering effects are usually negligible outside the CBD.

2. Investment in rail transit is sensible only if it is used in concert with more powerful land-use instruments such as zoning and property taxation. If the government uses its zoning and tax policies to generate high-density development, rail transit provides an efficient means of delivering a large number of workers to the dense central area.

In general, there is evidence that fixed-rail systems cause small changes in the spatial distribution of employment. The primary effect of transit is an increase in downtown employment.

Summary

1. Mass transit is most popular among workers who commute within the central city (used by 15.8 percent of commuters) and least popular among workers who travel from one suburb to another (used by 1.5 percent).

2. Transit ridership is relatively unresponsive to changes in monetary cost (fares), but responsive to changes in time cost, especially waiting and walking costs. On average, commuters value in-vehicle time at about half their wage rate and collection and distribution time at between 1.0 and 1.5 times the wage rate.

3. The time cost of a trip is the sum of collection cost, in-vehicle cost, and distribution cost. Commuters choose the mode that minimizes the sum of monetary and time costs. Mass transit has a lower monetary cost than autos, but higher collection and distribution time costs.

4. There are trade-offs associated with bus service: a decrease in the headway or an increase in the frequency of stops decreases collection and distribution costs, but increases line-haul cost.

5. There are two basic trade-offs in the design of a fixed-rail system.
    a. A mainline system forces commuters to use other travel modes in the collection and distribution phases of the trip. An alternative is an integrated system, which allows commuters to take the entire trip on a single mode.
    b. A system with widely spaced stations has shorter line-haul times but higher collection and distribution costs.
    c. BART is a mainline system with widely spaced stations. Because its collection and distribution costs are relatively high, it caused a relatively small number of commuters to switch from autos to transit.

6. Diamond lanes cause a moderate number of commuters to switch from autos to buses. The decrease in the number of auto lanes increases congestion, increasing the time cost of auto commuters.

7. A study of alternative transport systems for the San Francisco Bay area generated the following conclusions.
    a. For all corridor volumes studied, BART was more costly than an integrated bus system.
    b. For corridor volumes exceeding 1,100 vehicles per hour, an integrated bus system was less costly than an auto-based system.

8. In 1985, passenger fares covered only about 39 percent of the operating cost of transit. Transit subsidies can be justified on efficiency grounds because transit is a natural monopoly and automobile travel is underpriced. Transit deficits have increased over the last few decades, a result of decreases in fares and productivity and increases in wages, energy cost, and transit mileage.

9. Deregulation of transit could take two forms: the private provision of transit through service contracts and free entry into the transit market. Contracting arrangements have decreased the cost of providing transit services in a number of cities. Free entry could involve private buses or taxis serving as common carriers.

10. Increases in gasoline prices change housing and land prices, but do not cause large changes in location patterns.

11. Fixed-rail systems increase land rent for locations near the stations, but cause relatively small changes in location patterns. If the government uses its zoning and tax policies to generate high-density development, rail transit can provide an efficient means of delivering workers to the high-density areas.

Exercises and Discussion Questions

1. Fill in the blanks in the following table.

	Auto	Bus	BART
Collection Time Cost			
Collection time (minutes)	0	12	16
Cost per minute ($)	0.20	0.20	0.20
Collection time cost ($)	——	——	——
Line-Haul Time Cost			
Line-haul time (minutes)	30	40	20
Cost per minute ($)	0.15	0.15	0.15
Line-haul time cost ($)	——	——	——
Distribution Time Cost			
Distribution time (minutes)	0	4	11
Cost per minute ($)	0.20	0.20	0.20
Distribution time cost ($)	——	——	——
Monetary Cost			
Operating cost or fare ($)	3	1.5	2
Parking cost ($)	4	0	0
Total monetary cost ($)	——	——	——
Total time cost ($)	——	——	——
Total cost ($)	——	——	——

2. Buster has proposed that the distance between bus stops along a certain route be shortened to decrease the walking distance for the typical rider from 10 blocks to 8 blocks. The decrease in bus-stop distance will increase line-haul time from 50 to 55 minutes and increase the total operating cost of the route by 10 percent.

   a. Given the available evidence concerning the size of the relevant elasticities, is ridership likely to increase or decrease?

   b. Suppose that the transit authority passes on the higher operating cost in the form of an increased fare. Given the available evidence concerning the relevant elasticities, is ridership likely to increase or decrease?

3. Marta the transportation planner recently proposed that bus headways (the time between buses) along a high-density route be shortened from 20 minutes to 10 minutes. Your mission is to estimate the effects of such a policy on bus ridership. Assume that any increase in operating costs will be passed on to riders in the form of a higher fare.

   a. What information would you collect, and how would you use it?

   b. Provide a numerical example of a situation in which ridership will increase.

4. Figure 20–2 shows average cost curves for three types of travel systems: an auto system, an integrated bus system, and a heavy-rail system.
   a. Contrast the auto curve in Figure 20–2 to the cost curves in Figure 19–1. Why is the cost curve in 20–2 flat while the cost curves in 19–1 are positively sloped?
   b. Suppose that public opposition prevents the expansion of the highway network. Draw a new pair of cost curves for Figure 20–2, one for the auto system and one for the BART system. Explain any differences between the new curves and the old ones.

5. The cost curves in Figure 20–2 were derived by Keeler et al. (1975) under a number of assumptions about the disutilities of walking, waiting, and in-vehicle time. Draw a new set of curves for the following changes:
   a. Decrease in the disutility of walking and waiting time.
   b. Increase in the disutility of line-haul time.

6. In drawing the cost curves in Figure 20–2, Keeler et al. assumed that the disutility of time spent riding a bus is the same as the disutility of time driving a car.
   a. Based on your own preferences, is this a realistic assumption?
   b. Draw a new set of cost curves consistent with your preferences.

7. In drawing the cost curves in Figure 20–2, Keeler et al. assumed that the interest rate was 6 percent. Draw a new set of cost curves under the assumption that the interest rate is 12 percent.

8. Use a graph like Figure 20–2 to show the long-run average cost of a light-rail system. Draw the light-rail curve along with the curves for BART and a bus system. Explain your placement of the light-rail curve.

9. Zirconium City just converted one of the four lanes on its freeways to a diamond lane. The conversion shortened the line-haul time of buses by 10 minutes and increased the line-haul time of autos by 3 minutes. Consider the responses of two commuters: Maeve switched from driving to taking the bus, but Cormac continues to drive. Explain these different responses to the changes in travel times caused by the diamond lane. How does Maeve differ from Cormac?

10. In Weather City, the winters are cold and the summers are hot and humid. In Mild City, the winters and summers are mild. Except for the differences in weather, the two cities are similar. Would you expect the distance between bus stops to be longer or shorter in Mild City?

11. The city of Congestville is examining alternative policies to deal with its congestion problem. One of the options is free rush-hour bus service. Depict graphically the effects of free bus service on auto congestion and auto trip costs.

12. Consider the effects of dropping a planner's bomb on the San Francisco Bay area. A planner's bomb doesn't hurt any people, but destroys everything except the BART infrastructure (tracks, vehicles, and station). Most important, it destroys all buildings, so the metropolitan area must be completely rebuilt. Design a set of public policies that will ensure that in the rebuilt

Bay area, BART ridership will be high enough that BART is as efficient as an integrated bus system.

13. In the city of Phoenix, private companies provide bus services on low-volume routes at a fraction of the cost of the public bus agency. In New York City and Chicago, private companies provide bus service on high-volume (peak-period) routes at a fraction of the cost of the public bus agency. If private firms can underprice the public sector on high-volume and low-volume routes, what, if anything, should be the role of the public sector in the provision of transit services?

14. Suppose that the purpose of cross-subsidization is to increase the welfare of people along low-volume routes. Discuss some alternative means of improving their welfare.

References and Additional Readings

General

Altshuler, Alan A. *The Urban Transportation System*. Cambridge, Mass.: Joint Center for Urban Studies of MIT and Harvard, 1979.

American Public Transit Association. *Transit Fact Book*. Washington, D.C., 1991.

Cervero, R. "Efficiency and Equity Impacts of Current Transit Fare Policies." *Transportation Research Record* 790 (1981), pp. 7–15.

Cherwony, W., and S. R. Mundle. "Peak-Base Cost Allocation Models." *Transportation Research Record* 663 (1978), pp. 52–56.

Dewees, Donald. "Travel Cost, Transit, and Urban Motoring." *Public Policy* 24 (Winter 1976), pp. 59–79.

Kemp, Michael A., and Melvyn D. Cheslow. "Transportation." In *The Urban Predicament*, ed. William Gorham and Nathan Glazer. Washington, D.C.: Urban Institute, 1976, pp. 321–24.

Lave, Charles A. "The Demand for Urban Mass Transportation." *Review of Economics and Statistics* 52 (1970), pp. 320–23.

———. "Transportation and Energy: Some Current Myths." *Policy Analysis* 4 (Summer 1978), pp. 297–315.

Meyer, John R., and José A. Gómez-Ibáñez. *Autos, Transit and Cities*. Cambridge, Mass.: Harvard University Press, 1981.

Meyer, John; John Kain; and Martin Wohl. *The Urban Transportation Problem*. Cambridge, Mass.: Harvard University Press, 1965.

Mohring, Herbert. *Transportation Economics*. Cambridge, Mass.: Ballinger, 1976.

Small, Kenneth A. *Urban Transportation Economics*. Philadelphia: Harwood, 1992. A comprehensive summary and review of the economics of urban transportation.

U.S. Bureau of the Census. *1980 Census of Population: Journey to Work—Characteristics of Workers*. Washington, D.C.: U.S. Government Printing Office, 1984.

Buses and Scale Economies

Mohring, Herbert. "Minibuses in Urban Transportation." *Journal of Urban Economics* 14 (1983), pp. 293–317.

————. "Optimization and Scale Economies in Urban Bus Transportation." *American Economic Review* 62 (1972), pp. 591–604.

Morlok, Edward K., and Philip A. Viton. "The Comparative Costs of Public and Private Providers of Mass Transit." Chapter 10 in *Urban Transit: The Private Challenge to Public Transportation,* ed. Charles Lave. Cambridge, Mass.: Ballinger, 1985; pp. 233–50.

Walters, A. A. "Externalities in Urban Buses." *Journal of Urban Economics* 11 (1982). Discusses the advantages of small buses.

Demand Elasticities

Beesley, Michael E. "The Value of Time Spent Traveling: Some New Evidence." In *The Demand for Travel: Theory and Measurement*, ed. Richard Quandt. Lexington, Mass.: D. C. Heath, 1970.

Beesley, Michael E., and Michael A. Kemp. "Urban Transportation." Chapter 26 in *Handbook of Regional and Urban Economics.* Vol. 2 of *Urban Economics*, ed. Edwin S. Mills. Amsterdam: North Holland, 1987.

Domencich, T.; G. Kraft; and J. Valette. "Estimation of Urban Passenger Travel Behavior." In *Readings in Urban Economics*, ed. M. Edel and J. Rothenberg. New York: Macmillan, 1972.

Domencich, Thomas, and Daniel McFadden. *Urban Travel Demand.* Amsterdam: North Holland, 1975.

Kemp, Michael A. "Some Evidence of Transit Demand Elasticities." *Transportation* 2 (1973).

Kraft, Gerald, and Thomas Domencich. "Free Transit." In *Readings in Urban Economics*, ed. Matthew Edel and Jerome Rothenberg. New York: Macmillan, 1972, pp. 459–80.

Lago, Armando M., Patrick Mayworm, and J. Matthew McEnroe. "Transit Service Elasticities." *Journal of Transport Economics and Policy* 15 (1981), pp. 99–119.

Meyer, John, and Mahlon R. Straszheim. *Pricing and Project Evaluation.* Vol. 1 of *Techniques of Transport Planning.* Washington, D.C.: Brookings Institution, 1971. Chapter 7.

Improving Mass Transit

Fielding, Gordon J. *Managing Public Transit Strategically: A Comprehensive Approach to Strengthening Service and Monitoring Performance.* San Francisco: Jossey-Bass, 1987.

Hamer, Andrew Marshall. *The Selling of Rail Rapid Transit.* Lexington, Mass.: D. C. Heath, 1976, pp. 61–67, 75–77.

Kain, John F. "How to Improve Urban Transportation at Practically No Cost." *Public Policy* 20 (Summer 1972), pp. 335–58.

————. "Toward Better Urban Transport Pricing: Using What Is Known and Exploring What Is Not Known." In *Urban Transportation Pricing Alternatives.* Washington, D.C.: Transportation Research Board, 1976.

Meyer, John R., and José A. Gómez-Ibáñez. *Improving Urban Mass Transportation Productivity.* Washington, D.C.: U.S. Department of Transportation, Urban Mass Transportation Administration, 1977.

Webber, Melvin W. "The BART Experience—What Have We Learned?" *The Public Interest*, Fall 1976, pp. 79–108.

Transit Deficits

Hilton, George. *Federal Transit Subsidies*. Washington, D.C.: American Enterprise Institute for Public Policy Research, 1974.

Pickerell, Don H. "The Causes of Rising Transit Operating Deficits." *Transportation Research Record* 915 (1983), pp. 18–24.

Pucher, John; Anders Markstedt; and Ira Hirshman. "Impacts of Subsidies on the Costs of Urban Public Transport." *Journal of Transport Economics and Policy* 17 (1983), pp. 155–76.

Comparative Costs: Auto versus Bus versus Rail

Keeler, Theodore E.; L. Merewitz; P. Fisher; and K. Small. *The Full Costs of Urban Transport*. Monograph 21, part 3, Institute of Urban and Regional Development, University of California, Berkeley, 1975. Estimates the costs of alternative travel modes.

Straszheim, M. "Assessing the Social Costs of Urban Transportation Technologies." Chapter 7 in *Current Issues in Urban Economics*, ed. Peter Mieszkowski and Mahlon Straszheim. Baltimore: Johns Hopkins University Press, 1979, pp. 196–232.

Public Transit

Glaister, Stephen. "Competition on an Urban Bus Route." *Journal of Transport Economics and Policy* 19 (1985), pp. 65–81.

Gómez-Ibáñez, José A. "A Dark Side to Light Rail?" *Journal of the American Planning Association* 51 (Summer 1985), pp. 337–51. Compares the cost of new light-rail systems to the cost of conventional bus systems.

Gordon, Peter, and Harry Richardson. "Notes from Underground: The Failure of Urban Mass Transit." *The Public Interest* 94 (1989), pp. 77–86.

Hilton, George W. "The Rise and Fall of Monopolized Transit." Chapter 2 in *Urban Transit: The Private Challenge to Public Transportation*, ed. Charles Lave. Cambridge, Mass.: Ballinger, 1985.

Kemp, Michael A., and Ronald F. Kirby. "Government Policies Affecting Competition in Public Transportation." Chapter 12 in *Urban Transit: The Private Challenge to Public Transportation*, ed. Charles Lave. Cambridge, Mass.: Ballinger, 1985.

Savas, E. S. "Municipal Monopolies vs. Competition in Delivering Public Services." *Urban Analysis* 2 (1974), pp. 93–116.

Wilson, James Q. "The Dead Hand of Regulation." *The Public Interest* 49 (Fall 1977), pp. 39–58.

Cost Comparisons: Public versus Private Transit

Echols, James C. "Use of Private Companies to Provide Public Transportation Services in Tidewater, Virginia." Chapter 4 in *Urban Transit: The Private Challenge to Public Transportation*, ed. Charles Lave. Cambridge, Mass.: Ballinger, 1985.

Giuliano, Genevieve, and Roger F. Teal. "Privately Provided Commuter Bus Services: Experiences, Problems, and Prospects." Chapter 7 in *Urban Transit: The Private Challenge to Public Transportation*, ed. Charles Lave. Cambridge, Mass.: Ballinger, 1985.

Gómez-Ibáñez, José A., and John R. Meyer. "Privatizing and Deregulating Local Public Services: Lessons from Britain's Buses." *Journal of the American Planning Association* 56 (Winter 1990), pp. 9–21. Discusses Britain's experience with the deregulation of the bus industry, focusing on the effects of deregulation on service, fares, ridership, and production cost.

Heseltine, P. M., and D. T. Silcock. "The Effects of Bus Deregulation on Costs." *Journal of Transportation Economics and Policy* 24 (1990), pp. 239–54. Discusses the effects of the deregulation of the British bus industry on production cost.

Johnson, Christine M., and Milton Pilarsky. "Toward Fragmentation: Transportation in Chicago." Chapter 3 in *Urban Transit: The Private Challenge to Public Transportation*, ed. Charles Lave. Cambridge, Mass.: Ballinger, 1985.

Lave, Charles A. "The Private Challenge to Public Transportation—An Overview." Chapter 1 in *Urban Transit: The Private Challenge to Public Transportation*, ed. Charles Lave. Cambridge, Mass.: Ballinger, 1985.

Morlok, Edward K., and Philip A. Viton. "The Comparative Costs of Public and Private Providers of Mass Transit." Chapter 10 in *Urban Transit: The Private Challenge to Public Transportation*, ed. Charles Lave. Cambridge, Mass.: Ballinger, 1985.

———. "Recent Experience with Successful Private Transit in Large U.S. Cities." Chapter 6 in *Urban Transit: The Private Challenge to Public Transportation*, ed. Charles Lave. Cambridge, Mass.: Ballinger, 1985, pp. 121–48.

Pagano, Anthony M. "Private Sector Alternatives for Public Transportation." *Transportation Quarterly* 38 (1984), pp. 433–47.

Rosenbloom, Sandra. "The Taxi in the Urban Transport System." Chapter 8 in *Urban Transit: The Private Challenge to Public Transportation*, ed. Charles Lave. Cambridge, Mass.: Ballinger, 1985.

Simpson, Anthony U. "Implications of Efficiency Incentives on Use of Private Sector Contracting by the Public Transit Industry." Chapter 13 in *Urban Transit: The Private Challenge to Public Transportation*, ed. Charles Lave. Cambridge, Mass.: Ballinger, 1985.

Walder, Jay H. "Private Commuter Vans in New York." Chapter 5 in *Urban Transit: The Private Challenge to Public Transportation*, ed. Charles Lave. Cambridge, Mass.: Ballinger, 1985, pp. 101–18.

Taxis and Jitneys

Eckert, Ross, and George Hilton. "The Jitneys." *Journal of Law and Economics* 15 (1972), pp. 293–325.

Kirby, Ronald F. *Paratransit: Neglected Options for Future Mobility*. Washington, D.C.: Urban Institute, 1974.

Rosenbloom, Sandra. "Taxis, Jitneys, and Poverty." *Transaction* 7 (1970), pp. 47–54.

Wohl, Martin. "The Taxi's Role in Urban America: Today and Tomorrow." *Transportation* 4 (1975).

Transportation Systems and Land Use

Anas, Alex, and Leon N. Moses. "Transportation and Land Use in the Mature Metropolis." In *The Mature Metropolis*, ed. C. L. Levin. Lexington, Mass.: D. C. Heath, 1978, p. 161.

Coulson, N. Ed, and Robert F. Engle. "Transportation Costs and the Rent Gradient." *Journal of Urban Economics* 21 (1987), pp. 287–97.

De Leuw, Cather, and Company. "Land Use Impacts of Rapid Transit: Implications of Recent Experience." Washington, D.C.: U.S. Department of Transportation, August 1977.

Dewees, D. N. "The Effect of a Subway on Residential Property Values in Toronto." *Journal of Urban Economics* 3 (1976), pp. 357–69. Estimates the effects of Toronto's subway on property values along the transit line and around the transit stations.

Downs, Anthony. *Stuck in Traffic: Coping with Peak-Hour Traffic Congestion.* Washington, D.C.: The Brookings Institution, 1992.

Dyett, Michael V., and Emilio Escudero. "Effects of BART on Urban Development." 1977. Mimeo.

Goldstein, Gerald, and Leon Moses. "Transport Controls, Travel Costs, and Urban Spatial Structure." *Public Policy* 23 (Summer 1975), pp. 355–80.

Heenan, Warren G. "The Economic Effect of Rapid Transit on Real Estate Development." *Appraisal Journal* 36 (April 1968), pp. 213–24.

Hilton, George W. "Rail Transit and the Pattern of Modern Cities: The California Case." *Traffic Quarterly* 21 (July 1967), pp. 379–93.

Moore, Terry, and Paul Thorsnes. *The Transportation/Land Use Connection.* Chicago: American Planning Association, 1994. Explores the effects of public policy on transportation systems and land-use patterns.

Small, Kenneth. "Transportation and Urban Change." In *The New Urban Reality*, ed. P. Peterson. Washington, D.C.: Brookings Institution, 1985, pp. 197–223.

———. "The Effect of the 1979 Gasoline Shortages on Philadelphia Housing Prices." *Journal of Urban Economics* 19 (1986), pp. 371–81.

Smerk, George M. "The Streetcar: Shaper of American Cities." *Traffic Quarterly* 21 (October 1967), pp. 569–84.

Warner, Samuel B., Jr. *Streetcar Suburbs: The Process of Growth in Boston, 1870–1900.* Cambridge, Mass.: Harvard University Press, 1932.

Webber, Melvin W. "The BART Experience—What Have We Learned?" *The Public Interest,* Fall 1976, pp. 79–108.

Future Transit Systems

Anderson, Edward J. *Personal Rapid Transit.* Minneapolis: University of Minnesota, Department of Audio Visual Extension, 1972.

———. *Personal Rapid Transit II.* Minneapolis: University of Minnesota, Department of Audio Visual Extension, 1974.

Fisher, Ronald J. " 'Megatrends' in Urban Transport." *Transportation Quarterly* 38 (1984).

Kain, John F. "The Unexplored Potential of Freeway Rapid Transit in Regional Transportation Planning: An Atlanta Case Study." In *Unorthodox Approaches to Urban Transportation: The Emerging Challenge to Conventional Planning*, ed. Andrew Hamer. Atlanta: Georgia State University, Bureau of Business and Economic Research, 1972, pp. 38–51.

Skinner, Robert E., Jr., and Thomas B. Deen. "Second Generation U.S. Rail Transit Systems: Prospects and Perils." *Transportation* 8 (1980).

Benefit-Cost Analysis

Beesley, M. E. *Urban Transport: Studies in Economic Policy.* London: Butterworths, 1973.

Foster, C. D., and M. E. Beesley. "Estimating the Social Benefit of Constructing an Underground Railway in London." *Journal of the Royal Statistical Society* 126 (1963), pp. 46–92.

Meyer, John, and Mahlon R. Straszheim. *Pricing and Project Evaluation.* Volume 1 of *Techniques of Transport Planning.* Washington, D.C.: Brookings Institution, 1971. Chapters 11 and 12.

Peterson, Thomas C. "Cost-Benefit Analysis for Evaluating Transportation Proposals: Los Angeles Case Study." In *Urban Economic Issues,* ed. Stephan Mehay and Geoffrey Nunn. Glenview, Ill.: Scott, Foresman, 1984. Critique of a cost-benefit study that was used to justify the construction of a fixed-rail transit system in Los Angeles.

CHAPTER 21 Education

Human history becomes more and more a race between education and catastrophe.

H. G. Wells

This chapter explores some of the spatial aspects of elementary and secondary education. Given the large number of school districts in most metropolitan areas, households can choose from a wide variety of schools, each of which provides a different combination of teaching philosophies, educational quality, and tax costs. As explained in the chapter on voting, the Tiebout process causes households to sort themselves geographically with respect to desired spending on local public goods, property values, and income. This chapter explains how this sorting process contributes to inequalities in educational spending and achievement, and discusses the effects of various public policies on spending and achievement inequalities.

What's special about education? Spending inequalities occur for other local public goods: poor municipalities spend less on parks, recreation, and fire protection. Education is special because a good education is necessary for economic survival. A person with an inferior education is unlikely to find a well-paying job and is therefore more likely to be poor and more likely to turn to crime. One approach to solving the problems of poverty and crime is to improve the educational opportunities for poor children in the central city.

The chapter is organized as follows. The first section discusses the education production function, which is used to estimate the relative importance of various inputs to the education process. The most important factors in educational achievement are the home environment of the student and the intelligence and motivation of his fellow students. The second section explains the effects of the Tiebout sorting process on the educational system, showing how the sorting process causes inequalities in educational spending, racial and income segregation, and inequalities in educational achievement. The third and fourth sections discuss two policy responses to these inequalities: grants can be used to equalize educational spending, and desegregation

617

can be used to integrate students with respect to race and income. The question is whether these policies actually decrease spending inequalities and segregation. The final section explores the effects of education vouchers on the educational system.

The Education Production Function

The production function summarizes the relationship between the inputs to the educational process and the output (achievement). The production-function approach can be used to estimate the relative importance of the various inputs to the education process.

Inputs and Outputs of the School

What is the output of a school? The purpose of education is to develop cognitive, social, and physical skills. The basic cognitive skills (reading, writing, mathematics, logic) are necessary for employment and participation in a democracy. Cognitive skills also increase the enjoyment of leisure activities: they allow people to read books, understand jokes, and compute bowling scores. Schools also develop social skills: they teach children how to exchange ideas and make group decisions. Finally, schools develop physical skills: they teach children how to exercise and play games.

Education is different from other production activities because the output (educational achievement) is difficult to measure. While tests have been developed to measure basic cognitive skills, it is virtually impossible to accurately measure social and physical skills. Consequently, any empirical study of schools can, at best, measure only one component of the output of schools. Because empirical studies ignore social and physical skills, they provide an incomplete picture of the education process and must be interpreted with caution.

The production-function approach explores the contributions of different inputs to the cognitive achievement of students. Cognitive achievement is measured by scores on standardized achievement tests. Suppose that achievement is defined as the change in the test score of a particular child over a one-year period. If the output of the school is defined as the change in the test score, the production function can be written as

$$\text{Achievement} = f(C, E, T, H, P) \qquad (21\text{--}1)$$

where

C = School curriculum
E = Quantity of instructional equipment of the school
T = Quantity of labor input (teacher) per student
H = Home environment of the child
P = Average achievement level of other students in the class

Achievement depends on five inputs: the school's curriculum and educational equipment, the classroom teacher, the home environment, and the achievement level of the child's classmates.

These five inputs to the production function can be divided into three groups:

1. **School resources.**   The school has control over three inputs: curriculum, instructional equipment, and classroom teachers. Under the supervision of the local school district, the school designs a curriculum, purchases instructional equipment (building, books, science labs, computers) and hires teachers. An increase in the number of teachers decreases class size, increasing the teacher input per student.

2. **Home environment.**   Educational achievement is influenced by the home environment of the child in three ways. First, parents set the rules of the household, establishing an environment that is either favorable or unfavorable to education. For example, an unfavorable environment is one in which children watch television instead of reading books or doing their homework. Second, parents can motivate their children by encouraging reading, helping with homework, and rewarding success. Third, parents can provide instructional materials such as books and home computers, encouraging independent learning. The quality of the home environment depends in part on the income and education level of the parents. The children of wealthy and educated parents learn more because they receive more encouragement and assistance at home, and also pick up verbal and quantitative skills in everyday interactions with their parents. In contrast, children from poor and less-educated families learn less because there is often less encouragement to achieve and less learning from parents. In addition, children living in poverty are often malnourished, inhibiting their ability to learn.

3. **Peer group effects.**   The final input to the production process is the peer group of the child. A child learns more if he or she is surrounded by smart and motivated children. Smart peers promote achievement because of cooperation (children learn from one another) and competition (children compete with one another). Motivated peers promote achievement because the teacher can spend less time disciplining and motivating students, and more time teaching them. In addition, an unmotivated student provides an undesirable role model for other students.

The Coleman Report

Which inputs to the production process are the most important? Using the production-function approach, educators and economists have estimated the contributions of the various inputs to the education process. The Coleman report (Coleman et al., 1966), was the first attempt to estimate the education production function. The conclusions of the report are as follows:

1. The most important inputs are the home environment of the student and the characteristics of the peer group.

2. High-income families have more favorable home environments, so children from wealthy families learn more than children from poor families.

3. Children from wealthy families provide a more favorable peer group, so children with wealthy classmates learn more than children with poor classmates.

4. School inputs (curriculum, instructional equipment, teachers, and class size) do not affect achievement.

The Coleman report shocked the education community. The report was disturbing and perplexing for three reasons. First, it implies that schools don't matter, that educational achievement is determined by factors beyond the control of educators. This was a surprise to teachers and educators, who assumed that they contributed to the education process. Second, the report suggests that education cannot be used to lift children out of poverty. If achievement depends exclusively on the child's home environment and peer group, children in poor areas are trapped: they receive inferior education precisely because they come from poor families (with inferior home environments) and live in poor neighborhoods (with inferior peer groups). If school resources do not affect achievement, the government cannot compensate for inferior home and peer environments by spending more money on the education of poor students. Third, the report suggests that teachers do not matter, that all teachers are equally effective, regardless of education, experience, innate intelligence, and motivation. In other words, a teacher is a standardized input like a blackboard: put one in the classroom and it works just as well as any other teacher.

To put the conclusions of the Coleman report in perspective, suppose that you are a parent choosing a school for your child. What questions would you ask about a prospective school? According to the Coleman report, you need to ask only one question: what is the average income level of students in the school? It would be senseless to ask questions about curriculum, instructional equipment, and teachers because, according to the Coleman report, these inputs do not affect achievement.

The Coleman report precipitated a flood of criticism. As several researchers pointed out, the statistical methods of the report were flawed by two basic problems:

1. **Unit of observation.** Coleman et al. (1966) chose the school, not the individual student, as the unit of observation. The report explores the relationship between the average achievement level of a school and the average school inputs (e.g., average class size, average level of teacher experience, average income) and found that schools with different inputs did not have different achievement levels. The alternative approach is to examine the relationship between the achievement level of an individual child and the quantities of inputs experienced by that child (e.g., the size of the child's class, the teacher's experience and education level, the family income). Because Coleman et al. use schoolwide data, their approach obscures important differences between students in a given school and may generate inaccurate assessments of the relative importance of education inputs.

2. **Robustness of results.** The second problem is that the Coleman results are not robust: they change with small changes in the statistical methodology. Their results are sensitive to the order in which the various inputs (home environment, peer environment, and school resources) are incorpo-

rated into the statistical analysis. If the home variables enter the analysis before the school variables, it appears that school inputs don't matter. If, however, the school variables are entered first, it appears that school inputs affect achievement. Since the Coleman results are sensitive to the order in which inputs are included in the study, the results are of questionable validity.

Other Studies of the Production Function

Researchers did more than criticize the statistical methods of the Coleman report. Using superior data and more sophisticated statistical methods, they generated new estimates of the education production function. The new results cast doubts on some of the conclusions of the Coleman report. The results of these new studies are by no means definitive, so many issues remain unresolved. There is a consensus emerging, however, on the influences of the home environment, the peer group, and teachers.

Home Environment and Peer Group Effects.   Most researchers agree that the home environment has an extraordinary effect on achievement. Wealthy and well-educated parents provide a more favorable home environment. Researchers also agree about the effects of the peer group on achievement: a student learns more if she is surrounded by smart and motivated students. There is some evidence that the largest peer group effects are experienced by low achievers: the students at the bottom of the class have the most to gain from adding smart and motivated students to the class. There is also evidence that these peer effects are most important in the middle and upper grades (grades 5 through 12).

The Effectiveness of Teachers.   There is also agreement that teachers matter. Contrary to the conclusions of the Coleman report, teachers are not like blackboards, but in fact vary in effectiveness. The most effective teachers are the ones that are smart, motivated, innovative, and flexible.

While researchers agree that some teachers are more effective than others, they do not agree on what makes a good teacher. In looking for teacher characteristics that explain differences in effectiveness, researchers have focused on education level (years of postgraduate study), communication skills (verbal ability), and experience (years of teaching). The results of the studies are as follows:

1. **Education level.** There is no evidence that teachers increase their teaching skills by going to graduate school. It appears that students do not learn more from teachers with advanced degrees.

2. **Verbal skills.** The most effective teachers have superior communication skills. Students learn more from teachers that score high on standard tests of verbal ability.

3. **Experience.** There is some disagreement about the effects of experience on teaching skills. Murnane (1975, 1983, 1985) suggests that teaching effectiveness increases for the first few years of teaching and then levels off. In contrast, Hanushek (1971, 1981) suggests that teaching skills are

independent of teaching experience. Summers and Wolfe (1977) found that low achievers learn more from inexperienced teachers, while high achievers learn more from experienced teachers. Given these conflicting results, the link between teacher experience and effectiveness is still an open question.

Curriculum and Instructional Equipment.   There is evidence that curriculum matters. One of the most important factors in the highly publicized decline in SAT test scores during the 1970s and 1980s was the relaxation of graduation requirements. Under the "smorgasbord" approach to education, students were allowed to choose from a wide variety of courses, many of which were not academic in nature. The typical student took fewer rigorous academic courses, and academic achievement declined. This is the "Twinkie" effect: students skipped the meat and vegetable courses (academic courses) and filled up on the Twinkie courses.

Researchers agree that differences in achievement are not caused by differences in instructional equipment. In other words, students do not learn more in schools that spend a relatively large amount on books, projectors, and buildings. This does not mean that achievement would be unaffected if society returned to the days of log schoolhouses and shared books. It means that, given the current levels of spending on books and buildings, small changes in spending are unlikely to affect achievement.

Class Size.   There is some disagreement about the effects of class size on achievement. As Hanushek (1981) points out, there have been 112 studies of the relationship between class size and achievement, with 9 studies finding a negative relationship, 14 studies finding a positive relationship, and 89 studies finding no significant relationship. Summers and Wolfe (1977) suggest that low achievers learn more in small classes, and high achievers learn more in large classes. Given these conflicting results, the link between class size and achievement is still an open question. The issue is not whether class size matters at all, but whether small changes from the current class size affect achievement. No one doubts that achievement would decline if the average class size increased from 20 to 60 students.

The Tiebout Process and Inequalities in Achievement

How does the Tiebout sorting process affect educational spending and educational achievement? Under the Tiebout process, households sort themselves with respect to three characteristics: desired spending on schools, property values, and peer group characteristics.

Consider first the sorting with respect to educational spending. The desired spending on education varies across households, reflecting differences in income and preferences for education. Households sort themselves into high-spending and low-spending school districts. In this case, spending inequalities result from the simple fact that the wealthy spend more on education, just as they spend more on clothes, cars, and housing. The spending inequalities cause inequalities in educational opportunity: the low-spending school districts have less money for teachers, so they may have lower achievement levels.

Because local schools are financed with the property tax, households also sort themselves with respect to property values. Because housing is a normal good (positive income elasticity), the sorting with respect to house value causes sorting with respect to income. Suppose that all the households in a city, wealthy and poor, have the same desired spending on education. Under the property tax, the city has two school districts, one for the wealthy (who live in large houses) and one for the poor (small houses). Although the two school districts have the same per pupil spending, achievement is likely to be higher in the wealthy school district for two reasons. First, achievement is positively related to household income, so the average achievement is higher in the wealthier school district. Second, because of the more favorable peer environment in the wealthy district, a given child will reach a higher achievement level in the wealthy district. Income segregation deprives poor students of the possible benefits of being surrounded by smart and motivated students.

Consider finally the effects of student peer groups on location choices. Parents care about educational achievement, not simply educational spending. Given the importance of the peer group in achievement, the household looks for a school with smart and motivated students. In practical terms, this means that the household looks for a neighborhood full of high-income, well-educated parents who provide a favorable home environment. The shopping for a peer group reinforces income segregation. Suppose that a poor household has the same desired spending on education as middle-income households and occupies a house with the same market value (same tax liability). In the absence of peer group effects, middle-income households would welcome the poor household into their school district. However, because the poor student is likely to have a below-average achievement level, middle-income households have an incentive to exclude the child from their school. In general, the peer group effect adds another item to the household's shopping list, increasing the pressures for segregation with respect to income, race, and social status. As a result, it widens the spatial inequalities in educational achievement. Poor households are denied access to schools that provide a favorable peer environment.

Spending Inequalities

By how much does educational spending vary across school districts in a particular state? Figure 21–1 shows the spending inequalities in four states where the courts have recently declared school finance systems unconstitutional. For each state, the figure shows the average spending per pupil in the 10 highest-spending districts and in the 10 lowest-spending districts. In three of the four states, the high-spending districts spend more than twice as much as the low-spending districts. As shown by Katz (1991), spending ratios above 1.5 are common among other states as well.

Segregation and Achievement Inequalities

How segregated is the U.S. school system? Figure 21–2 shows the percentages of minority students (blacks, Hispanics, and other minorities) in schools with different degrees of segregation. Almost half of minority students (46 percent) attended highly segregated schools (where over 80 percent of the students were minorities).

FIGURE 21–1   **Inequalities in Spending per Pupil in Selected States, 1986–1987**

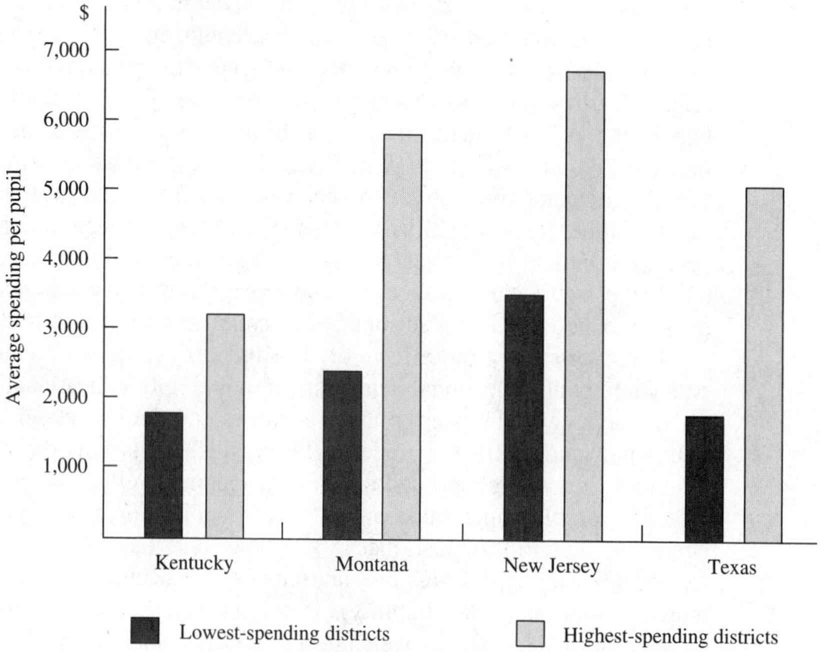

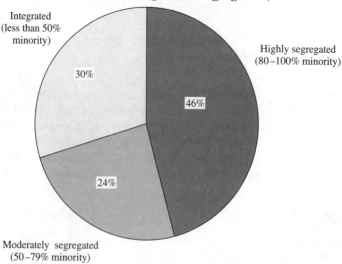

SOURCE: Jeffrey Katz, "The Search for Equity in School Funding," *Governing*, August 1991, pp. 20–22.

FIGURE 21–2   **Percent of Minority Students in Schools with Different Degrees of Segregation, 1986**

SOURCE: Bradley Schiller, *The Economics of Poverty and Discrimination*, 5th ed. (Englewood Cliffs, N.J.: Prentice Hall, 1989).

About a quarter (24 percent) of minority students attended schools that were moderately segregated (50 percent to 79 percent of the students were minorities). Only 30 percent of minority students attended schools where they were a minority of the student body.

According to a recent report from the U.S. Department of Education (1987), classrooms are even more segregated than schools. Under the **ability-tracking system,** students are segregated with respect to ability and achievement: the high achievers are put in one class, and the low achievers are put in another class. Because minority students quickly fall behind white students in the early grades, ability tracking in the later grades contributes to racial segregation within the schools.

How does the educational achievement of blacks and Hispanics compare to that of whites? At age nine, black and Hispanic students are, on average, 25 percent behind their white counterparts in reading, science, and math; by age 17, the achievement gap grows to 30 percent (National Center for Education Statistics, 1982). Although there has been some progress in the last 20 years in decreasing these achievement gaps, the gaps continue to be rather large.

Two other measures of educational achievement are the completion rates for high school and college. According to the Department of Education (1987), in 1985, only 63 percent of blacks had completed high school by age 19 (up from 56 percent in 1974), compared to 77 percent of whites (up from 76 percent in 1974). Although the gap in high school completion rates has narrowed, it is still large. In 1986, only 11 percent of Hispanics and 12 percent of blacks between the ages of 24 and 29 had completed at least four years of college, compared to 23 percent of whites (Schiller, 1989).

Programs to Decrease Spending Inequalities

Under the traditional system of education finance, school districts finance their education programs with the local property tax. Therefore, spending per pupil depends on local property values, which of course vary across school districts. In response to spending inequalities, states have developed a number of programs that redistribute money to school districts with relatively low tax bases. Figure 21–3 shows the contributions of the three levels of government to local education. In 1985, state governments provided about half of the funds for education.

Flat Grants

At the turn of the century, 38 states distributed funds to local school districts in the form of flat grants. Under a system of flat grants, the state gives each school district a fixed amount per student, thus guaranteeing a minimum level of spending.

Figure 21–4 shows the tax and spending options of two school districts before and after a program of flat grants. The horizontal axis measures the local property tax rate, and the vertical axis measures spending per pupil. The wealthy district has $60,000 of property per student, so per pupil spending increases by $600 for every one percent of property tax. The poor district has $30,000 per student, so for a given tax rate, it raises half as much tax revenue as the wealthy district. The poor district

FIGURE 21–3   **Sources of Education Funding, 1930–1985**

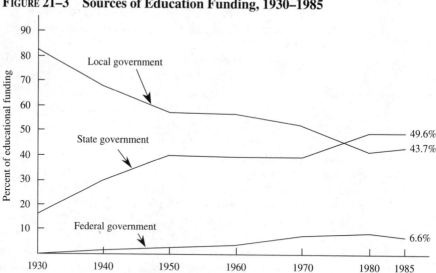

SOURCES: Advisory Commission on Intergovernmental Relations, *State Aid to Local Governments* (Washington, D.C.: U.S. Government Printing Office, 1969); U.S. Census Bureau, *Statistical Abstract of the United States* (Washington, D.C.: U.S. Government Printing Office, 1987).

might choose point *P*, spending $900 per pupil with a tax rate of 3 percent, while the wealthy district might choose point *W*, spending $1,200 per pupil with a tax rate of only 2 percent. In other words, children in poor school districts often receive less education while their parents pay relatively high tax rates.

A flat grant of $200 shifts the spending lines upward by $200, providing both districts with more tax-spending options. Before the grant, a 1 percent tax generates $600 in the wealthy district and $300 in the poor district. After the grant, the same tax rate generates $800 in the wealthy district and $500 in the poor district.

How does a flat grant affect spending in the two school districts? Suppose that each school district adopts the preferred budget of its median voter, as explained in Chapter 17 (Voting with Ballots and Feet). Figure 21–5 shows the budget lines and indifference curves of Marian the median voter. The horizontal axis measures per pupil education spending, and the vertical axis measures spending on other goods (on a per pupil basis). The budget line *BC* shows the trade-off between education and other goods: Marian has a total of $1,000 per pupil to spend on education and other goods, and every dollar spent on education decreases spending on other goods by one dollar. Before the flat grant, Marian chooses point *E*. Assuming that the school district adopts the preferred budget of the median voter, its initial spending on education is $400 per student.

The flat grant shifts Marian's budget line outward from *BC* to *BDF*. Point *D* is in the new budget set because Marian can use the grant to get $200 worth of education while spending all of her own money ($1,000) on other goods. The points along the line connecting *D* and *F* are in the new budget set: starting from point *D*,

FIGURE 21–4   **Tax-Spending Options for Different Tax Bases with and without a Flat Grant**

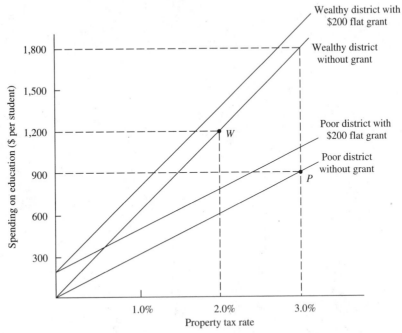

Poor district: Property value per student = $30,000.
Wealthy district: Property value per student = $60,000.

The tax-spending lines show education spending for different tax rates. The wealthy district has twice as much property value per student, so a given tax rate generates twice as much revenue per student. At point *W*, the wealthy district has a tax rate of 2 percent and spending of $1,200 per student. At point *P*, the poor district has a tax rate of 3 percent and spending of only $900 per student. A $200 flat grant shifts both tax-spending lines upward by $200.

Marian still faces a dollar-for-dollar trade-off between education and other goods. The shift of the budget line moves Marian's utility-maximizing point from *E* to *G*. If the school district adopts the preferred budget of the median voter, the flat grant increases education spending by $50 (to $450) and increases spending on other goods by $150 (to $750).

How does the school district increase spending on other goods? The district can fund its $450 spending program with the $200 grant and $250 of local tax revenue. The grant decreases the local contribution to education from $400 to $250, so the school district cuts local taxes by $150, thus allowing its citizens to spend $150 of the grant on other goods. From the perspective of local citizens, the flat grant is equivalent to an increase in consumer income, which increases the demand for all normal goods, including education and other goods. In cutting taxes, the school district is simply responding to the demands of its citizens.

Will a system of flat grants narrow the gap between the spending of wealthy and poor communities? Since every school district receives the same $200 grant,

FIGURE 21–5   Flat Grant and Spending per Student

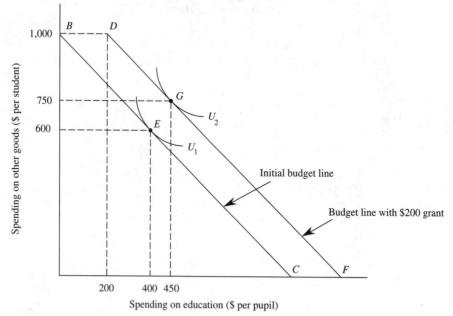

A \$200 flat grant shifts the budget line of the median voter from *BC* to *BDF*, and the utility-maximizing point moves from *E* to *G*. One fourth of the grant is spent on education, and the remaining \$150 is spent on other goods. The school district cuts taxes, allowing citizens to spend part of the grant on other goods.

spending on education increases in every district. The grant program will decrease spending inequalities only if the wealthy school district spends a smaller fraction of its \$200 grant on education. This occurs if citizens in the wealthy school district have a relatively low income elasticity of demand for education. There is no reason to think that this is the case.

Foundation Grants

In the 1920s, some states switched from flat grants to foundation grants. Under the foundation program, the education grant is inversely related to the property wealth of the school district. The grant for a particular school district is

Grant = Transfer rate · (Threshold property value − Property value per student)

$$(21\text{–}2)$$

If the district's property value per student is less than the threshold property value, the district is eligible for a foundation grant. The grant is computed as the transfer rate times the gap between the threshold and the actual property value. For example, suppose that the threshold property value is \$80,000 and the transfer rate is 0.01. A school district with property value per student of \$30,000 has a property-value gap of \$50,000 (\$80,000 − \$30,000) and receives \$500 per pupil (0.01 times \$50,000). A school district with property value per student of \$60,000 receives \$200 per pupil.

The only difference between the foundation grant and the flat grant is that the foundation grant is a decreasing function of the local tax base. In contrast with the flat grant, which is the same for all school districts, the foundation grant decreases as the local tax base increases. In Figure 21–4, the foundation plan in this example would shift the tax spending line of the poor school district up by $500 and shift the tax-spending line of the wealthy district up by only $200. The two tax-spending lines would intersect at a 1 percent tax rate: if both districts were to impose a 1 percent tax, they would each spend $800 on education. The poor district would combine its $500 grant with $300 of local taxes, and the wealthy community would combine its $200 grant with $600 of local taxes. For tax rates below 1 percent, the poor district would spend more than the wealthy district, and for tax rates above 1 percent, the poor district would spend less than the wealthy district.

Most states that use foundation plans have experienced relatively small changes in spending inequalities. The foundation plans have failed to significantly narrow spending inequalities for two reasons. First, most foundation programs provide relatively small grants. Second, school districts spend a small fraction of their grants on education, using the rest of the grant to increase spending on other goods. Because foundation plans do not stimulate education spending by very much, they have not narrowed spending inequalities very much.

The Legal Mandate to Equalize Expenditures

State courts became involved in the financing of education in the 1970s. In response to persistent inequalities in education spending, parents from poor school districts sued state governments, claiming that the spending inequalities violated state constitutions. In a number of states, the courts ruled in favor of the parents, finding that inequalities in educational spending violated the equal-protection clauses of state constitutions. Education is considered a fundamental right of citizens of the state, meaning that all citizens are to receive the same quality of education. The courts developed the **principle of fiscal neutrality**:

> The quality of education may *not* be a function of the wealth of the local community.

In other words, children from poor school districts must receive the same quality of education as children from wealthy school districts. The courts directed state governments to equalize spending on primary and secondary education.

***Serrano* v. *Priest*.**   The most frequently cited court case is *Serrano* v. *Priest*, decided in 1974 by the California Supreme Court. When John Serrano complained about the low quality of the local high school's education program, the school's principal suggested that Serrano move his family to a school district where per pupil spending was higher. Instead of moving, Serrano sued the state of California, arguing that spending inequalities were unconstitutional.

To illustrate the spending disparities, Serrano cited the differences between two school districts in the Los Angeles area, Beverly Hills and Baldwin Park. As shown in Table 21–1, Beverly Hills used its larger property tax base to spend more per student while charging a lower tax rate. In ruling in favor of Serrano, the court ruled that the property tax system violated the equal-protection clause of the state's

TABLE 21–1   **Taxes and Spending in Baldwin Park and Beverly Hills**

	Baldwin Park	Beverly Hills
Property value per student	$4,169	$49,501
Property tax rate	3.34%	2.55%
Educational spending per student	$272	$1,535

SOURCE: James Guthrie, "United States School Finance Policy 1955–1980."
In *School Finance Policies and Practices,* ed. James Guthrie (Cambridge,
Mass.: Ballinger, 1980), p. 14.

constitution. The court ordered the state legislature to develop a financing system under which per pupil spending would vary by no more than $100.

There have been similar court cases in dozens of other states. Between 1970 and 1983, the school finance systems of more than half the states were challenged, but only seven finance systems were declared unconstitutional during that period. In 1989 and 1990, the courts struck down the the school finance systems of four states: Kentucky, Montana, New Jersey, and Texas.

Limits on Reform.   Two court cases established the limits on education reform. In *McInnis* v. *Ogilvie*, the plaintiffs argued that the Constitution guarantees the right to equal educational *outcomes* rather than equal educational *spending*. They argued that government should eliminate inequalities in educational achievement, spending more on low-achieving students to bring them up to the level of high achievers. The court ruled against the plaintiffs, arguing that there was no practical way to enforce an equal-achievement standard. Given this decision, the objective of reform efforts is to equalize spending, not achievement.

Another case, *San Antonio Independent School District* v. *Rodriguez*, established the limits for federal involvement in school finance. The court ruled that education is not a fundamental right guaranteed to U.S. citizens. This ruling is based on the fact that education is not mentioned in the U.S. Constitution. Consequently, the equal-protection clause of the U.S. Constitution does not apply to education, and variation in per pupil spending is not proscribed by the U.S. Constitution. There are two implications from the *San Antonio* decision. First, any reform of the school-finance system must come from state governments, not the federal government. Second, although the court system may promote equalization of spending within individual states, the courts will do nothing to promote equalization of spending across states.

The Guaranteed Tax-Base Plan

The court cases of the 1970s demonstrated that the conventional grant programs had failed to reduce spending inequalities to tolerable levels. In response to court orders, states adopted new programs to decrease spending inequalities. Under the **guaranteed tax-base** (GTB) plan (also called *district power equalizing*), every school district has access to the same *effective* tax base. If the guaranteed tax base is $50,000 per student, every school district would receive $500 for every 1 percent of the local tax rate: $500 for a 1 percent tax rate, $1,000 for a 2 percent tax rate, and so on. Every school district has the same taxing power, regardless of its local tax base.

GTB Plan and the Poor School District.   Figure 21–6 shows the effect of a guaranteed tax base on the tax and spending options of a poor school district. The upper line is the guaranteed tax revenue for different local tax rates, given a guaranteed tax base of $50,000 per student. The lower line is local tax revenue, given a local tax base of $30,000 per student. The state grant is the difference between the guaranteed tax revenue and local tax revenue. For a 1 percent local tax, the school district is guaranteed a total of $500. The local district raises $300 locally, and the state provides the $200 difference between the guaranteed revenue and local revenue. For a 3 percent tax, the district receives a total of $1,500 ($900 from local taxes and $600 from the state).

The GTB plan decreases the opportunity cost of spending on education. Before the grant program, there is a dollar-for-dollar trade-off between spending on education and other goods: every dollar spent on education requires $1 of local taxes, so every dollar of education decreases spending on other goods by $1. Under the GTB plan, the trade-off is $1 for 60 cents. In Figure 21–6, the district can increase spending on education from 0 to $500 by imposing a 1 percent tax. A 1 percent tax

FIGURE 21–6   Guaranteed Tax Base: Poor School District

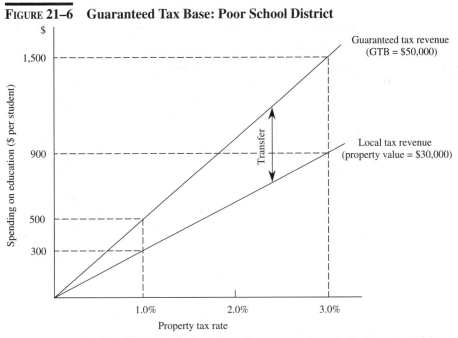

Under a guaranteed tax-base (GTB) plan, all school districts have access to the same effective tax base. If the GTB is $50,000 per student, the district is guaranteed tax revenue of $500 for every 1 percent of local tax rate. If the district imposes a 3 percent tax rate, it is guaranteed a total of $1,500 of tax revenue, so the state supplements the $900 of local revenue with a $600 grant. In this case, the GTB plan decreases the opportunity cost of education spending from $1 to 60 cents.

generates $300 of local tax revenue and a $200 grant, so the district gives up only $300 worth of other goods to get $500 worth of education. On average, the school district can get a dollar of education by sacrificing only 60 cents worth of other goods. The GTB program is equivalent to a matching grant with a matching rate of two thirds ($300 of local taxes generates a $200 grant).

How does the GTB plan affect the choices of the median voter? In Figure 21–7, the plan pivots Marian's budget line from *BC* to *BD*. The slope decreases because the grant decreases the opportunity cost of education spending from $1 to 60 cents. Marian chooses point *F* instead of point *E*. If the school district adheres to the preferences of the median voter, it increases school spending from $400 to $500.

A GTB grant has a larger stimulative effect than a flat grant because the GTB grant has both an income effect and a substitution effect. Like a flat grant, the GTB grant increases Marian's real income, increasing her desired spending on all normal goods, including education. This is the income effect. The GTB grant also decreases the opportunity cost of education spending from $1 to 60 cents, causing Marian to substitute education for other goods. This is the substitution effect. In Figure 21–5, a $200 flat grant increases education spending by $50 (from $400 to $450). In Figure 21–7, a $200 GTB grant increases spending by $100 (from $400 to $500).

GTB Plan and the Wealthy School District.   How would the GTB plan affect the tax-spending options of a wealthy school district? Suppose that the wealthy district

FIGURE 21–7   GTB and Spending and the Poor School District

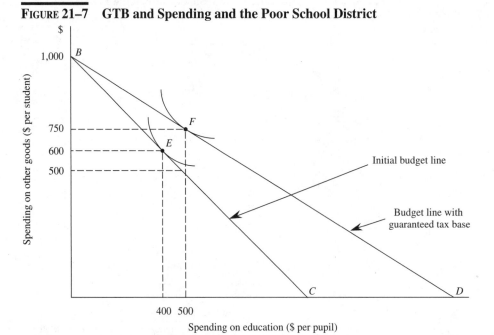

The GTB plan shifts the budget line of the median voter from *BC* to *BD*. The opportunity cost of education spending decreases, causing both an income effect and a substitution effect. Desired spending on education rises from $400 to $500.

has $60,000 of property value per student, compared to a guaranteed tax base of $50,000. The local tax revenue exceeds the guaranteed tax revenue: the surplus tax revenue is $100 for a 1 percent tax, $200 for a 2 percent tax, and so on. Under a pure GTB plan, the state collects this surplus tax revenue.

The GTB plan increases the opportunity cost of education spending in the wealthy district. If the district imposes a 1 percent tax, it raises $600 of local tax revenue, decreasing spending on other goods by $600. Since $100 of the $600 tax revenue is collected by the state, only $500 is left for local education. On average, the district must give up $1.20 worth of other goods to get $1 worth of education, so the GTB plan increases the opportunity cost of education from $1 to $1.20.

In the wealthy district, the income and substitution effects of the GTB plan combine to decrease spending on education. The GTB plan decreases the real income of the median voter, decreasing the desired spending on all normal goods, including education (the income effect). It also increases the opportunity cost of education, causing the median voter to substitute other goods for education (the substitution effect). If the school district adheres to the preferences of its median voter, the district will decrease spending on education and cut taxes.

GTB as an Equalization Tool.   Compared to the foundation plan, the pure GTB plan is a more powerful equalization tool. The GTB is more powerful for two reasons. First, the GTB plan has a Robin Hood feature: it takes from wealthy school districts and gives to poor ones. The resulting income effects decrease spending in wealthy districts and increase spending in poor ones. Second, the GTB plan increases the opportunity cost of education in wealthy districts and decreases the opportunity cost in poor districts. The resulting substitution effects reinforce the income effects, narrowing the spending gaps.

Would a pure GTB plan equalize spending on education? The GTB plan provides each school district with the same effective tax base. If every community chooses the same tax rate, education spending would be the same in all districts. If, however, communities choose different tax rates, spending inequalities would persist. Under a pure GTB plan, any remaining differences in education spending are the result of differences in chosen tax *rates*, not differences in tax *bases*.

Most states with GTB plans have adopted an impure version of GTB. School districts are allowed to raise and spend more than the guaranteed tax revenue. In the language of local government, states do not "recapture" or recycle the surplus tax revenue of wealthy school districts. Because the impure GTB plan does not recapture surplus tax revenue, it is a relatively weak equalization tool: the plan increases spending in poor school districts, but does not decrease spending in wealthy school districts. According to Carroll (1979), GTB plans have had relatively small effects on spending inequalities.

Michigan's Equalization Plan

Michigan adopted an equalization plan that combined the features of a foundation plan and a GTB plan. The state's 531 school districts were divided into three groups, according to local tax rates and tax bases:

1. **GTB districts.** About one third of the school districts were included in a GTB plan. The GTB districts had tax rates less than 2.2 percent and tax bases less than $38,000 per student. The guaranteed tax base was $38,000.

2. **Foundation districts.** About three fifths of the school districts were included in a foundation plan. The foundation districts had tax rates greater than 2.2 percent and property values less than $38,000 per student. The transfer rate was 2.2 percent and the threshold property value was $38,000.

3. **Ineligible districts.** The remaining school districts had tax bases greater than $38,000 per student and received no state aid.

The Michigan program had a relatively small effect on spending inequalities. Three factors contributed to its limited effect. First, only about one third of the school districts—those eligible for the GTB plan—experienced significant changes in state support. The districts eligible for foundation grants continued to receive about the same level of state support. Second, the state did not recapture the surplus tax revenue of the relatively wealthy school districts, so the plan did not decrease the spending of wealthy districts. Third, the GTB school districts increased their spending on education by relatively small amounts. The Michigan program failed to equalize spending because it caused relatively small effects in about two thirds of the state's school districts.

The California Equalization Program

Under the California equalization plan, the state has equalized expenditures by assuming complete control of education finance. The state of California responded to the *Serrano* decision by establishing spending limits for local school districts. The state limited the rate at which each district could increase its per pupil spending. Because the state allowed low-spending districts to increase their spending more rapidly than high-spending districts, the spending limits narrowed the spending gaps over time. Until 1979, a school district could override its spending limit if it received the approval of two thirds of its voters. Starting in 1979, the spending limits could not be exceeded under any circumstances.

The state's equalization plan received a boost from the tax revolt. In 1978, California voters approved Proposition 13, which imposed strict limits on local property tax rates. The state made the following offer to every school district: if the district imposed a property tax of 1 percent (the maximum allowable under Proposition 13), the state would make up the difference between local tax revenue and the district's state-imposed spending limit. If the school district agreed to the deal, its actual spending would equal its maximum spending. Since every school district accepted the state's offer, the state is now in full control of education spending: every school district spends the maximum amount allowed by the state.

The California equalization plan has sharply reduced spending inequalities. The *Serrano* decision directed the state to decrease spending inequalities to no more than $100 per student. The court would be satisfied, for example, if all school districts spent between $4,000 and $4,100 per student. Since 1974, the percentage of students within the $100 interval increased from 50 percent to more than 90 percent. The equalization program increased state support of education: the state's share of education spending increased from about two fifths in 1974 to about two thirds in 1984.

Desegregation Policy

What causes racial segregation in the schools? One reason for segregation is racial prejudice. Some white parents are unwilling to let their children be educated with racial minorities, regardless of the achievement level of the minority children (and their peer group effects). Others use race as a signal about the likely achievement level of students: if minority children have, on average, a lower achievement level, a simple way to produce a more favorable peer group is to exclude all racial minorities.

Racial segregation can be accomplished in a number of ways. The first approach is to use explicit segregation, a method used in many southern cities until the early 1970s. A more subtle approach, used by many northern cities, is to manipulate attendance boundaries to send most black children to predominantly black schools. The third approach is to set up neighborhood schools and let households sort themselves with respect to race: households interested in sending their children to white schools can move to wealthy suburban school districts that exclude blacks. A final approach to segregation is to send children to private schools, which are typically too expensive for many minority households.

Court-Ordered Desegregation

The courts have outlawed the first two methods of segregation. In *Brown* v. *Board of Education of Topeka* (1954), the Supreme Court declared that explicit racial segregation is unconstitutional. This *Brown* case reversed *Plessy* v. *Ferguson* (1896), which established the constitutionality of "separate but equal" schools. The *Brown* decision required the desegregation of schools only in areas where local governments pursued a policy of explicit segregation. Most of the cities forced to desegregate their schools under the *Brown* decision were in the South. As pointed out by Clotfelter (1979), the mandate for desegregation was extended in the 1970s to northern cities that used attendance boundaries and other subtle techniques to promote segregation. The courts ordered several large northern and western cities to desegregate their schools. The objective was to integrate the schools to the extent that would have occurred in the absence of earlier government policies that had encouraged segregation. In other words, the court did not require the cities to develop a truly integrated school system, only one in which government policy had a neutral effect. The segregation that results from the individual location choices of households (the Tiebout shopping process) is considered constitutional.

How did white households respond to forced desegregation? One of the lessons from the history of desegregation policy is that it often increases rather than decreases segregation. There are powerful forces behind segregation that are not neutralized by court-ordered desegregation, and households can take a number of actions to counteract desegregation plans. There are two responses that weaken or reverse the effects of desegregation: households can move from the integrating school district to an all-white school district, or parents can enroll their children in private schools.

Moving to Another School District

Consider first the possibility of moving to another school district. In the South, many central cities had marbled spatial distributions of households: black areas were interspersed within white areas. The cities used explicit segregation to send whites and blacks living in the same area to different schools. When the courts outlawed explicit segregation, many central-city white families moved to the predominantly white suburbs to keep their children in all-white schools.

Clotfelter (1979) examined the various responses to desegregation in Baltimore and Atlanta and came to the following conclusions:

1. The fleeing of whites to the suburbs decreased the demand for central-city housing and decreased housing prices. In stable neighborhoods, the price of central-city housing decreased by about 4.7 percent for a 10 percent increase in the proportion of blacks in local public schools.
2. Families with school-age children were the most likely to move to the suburbs when central-city schools were integrated.

The same phenomenon occurred in other cities that used busing to integrate their schools: some white households moved from desegregating school districts to predominantly white school districts.

Switching to Private Schools

Another option for parents in a desegregating school district is to enroll their children in private schools. To evaluate the effects of desegregation on private-school enrollment, it will be useful to develop a model of the choice between private and public schools.

The Choice between Public and Private Schools.   In choosing between public and private schools, parents face a trade-off between the consumption of education and other goods. Private schools charge tuition, but also provide a better education, on average, than a public school. Parents send a child to a private school only if the increase in educational achievement is worth the sacrifice of other goods.

Figure 21–8 shows the options faced by the Smith family. The horizontal axis measures the consumption of education (measured by the achievement level of the child), and the vertical axis measures consumption of other goods (in dollars). The family faces a binary choice: it chooses either a public-school education *or* a private-school education, not a mixture of the two. Therefore, the budget set consists of two points, V (private education) and B (public education). If the family has \$2,000 to spend on education and other goods, the public-school option in the absence of desegregation is point B: if the family chooses public education, it receives E_b units of free public education, leaving \$2,000 for other goods. If private-school tuition is

FIGURE 21–8   **Desegregation Causes Switch from Public to Private Education**

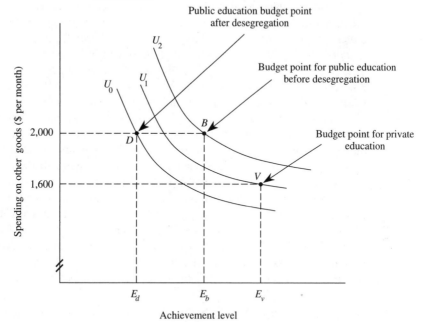

The initial budget points are *B* (public education) and *V* (private). Given its indifference curves, the household is not willing to sacrifice $400 worth of other goods to increase achievement by $E_v - E_b$, so it chooses public education. Desegregation decreases achievement in public schools (the budget point shifts from *B* to *D*), causing a switch to private schools.

$400, the family could get E_v units of education at a cost of $400, leaving $1,600 to spend on other goods (point *V*).

The Smiths choose public education over private education. The household's negatively sloped indifference curves (U_1 and U_2) reflect its subjective trade-off between education and other goods. The indifference curves show that the family is willing to sacrifice only a small amount of noneducation goods to increase educational achievement. Given the indifference curves and the budget points, the utility level from public education (U_2) exceeds the utility level from private education (U_1), so the family chooses public education. The benefit of increased achievement (from E_b to E_v) is outweighed by the loss of $400 worth of other goods.

Differences in Achievement?   Why do students in private schools learn more than their counterparts in public schools? According to Murnane (1986), private schools are superior in part because they have more favorable peer group effects. As discussed earlier in this chapter, a particular student learns more if he is surrounded by smart and motivated classmates, and the smartest and most motivated students come from high-income families. Since a large fraction of private-school children come from high-income families, the peer groups in private schools are superior to the peer groups in public schools. According to Murnane, the favorable peer group effects explain over half of the difference between the achievement levels of public and private students.

Murnane quantifies the peer group effect by predicting student test scores under different circumstances. The first question he poses is: *how would the test score of the typical public-school student change if the student transferred from the public school to a private school?* The answer is that the student's score would increase from 24.4 to 26.1. By transferring to a private school, the typical student would experience a 7 percent increase in achievement. The second question posed by Murnane is: *how would the test score of the typical public-school student change if the student, along with his public-school classmates, transferred from the public school to a private school?* The answer is that the student's score would increase from 24.4 to 25.1, an increase of about 2.9 percent. If the student brings his public-school peers along with him to the private school, he experiences less than half the achievement gain that occurs if he leaves his public-school peers behind.

Murnane's results suggest that a large part of the difference between public and private schools is caused by peer group effects. A student in a private school is surrounded by smarter and more motivated students and therefore learns more. The other half of the achievement difference is presumably caused by differences in curriculum, teachers, educational methods, and discipline. An important advantage of private schools is that they have more flexibility in expelling troublemakers.

Desegregation and Private Schools.   How does desegregation affect the household's choice between private and public schools? Suppose that desegregation enrolls more poor children in the public schools and decreases the average achievement level of the Smiths' public school. In Figure 21–8, the budget point for public education would shift to the left, from B to D. For the Smiths, who chose the public school before desegregation, the utility generated by the public school is now less than the utility from private schools: the achievement gap is larger, so the increase in achievement generated by a switch from the public to the private school is now worth the $400 sacrifice of other goods. In this case, desegregation causes a switch to a private school.

There is conclusive evidence that desegregation causes "white flight" to private schools. Clotfelter (1976) hypothesizes the following relationship:

$$E = f(S, I, B) \tag{21–3}$$

where

E = Proportion of whites enrolled in private schools
S = Family size
I = Household income
B = Percent of public-school students who are black

Using data from Mississippi, he concludes that white enrollment in private schools increased with the number of blacks in the neighborhood public school. The relationship is especially strong when black enrollment in the neighborhood public school exceeds 50 percent. For B less than 50 percent, a one-unit increase in B (one percentage point increase) increased E by 0.40 percentage points; for B greater than

50 percent, a one-unit increase in B increased E by 2.8 percentage points. In other words, the **tipping point** (where the relationship between B and E suddenly becomes much stronger) is about 50 percent.

Tiebout-Based Segregation

The segregation that results from the individual location choices of households (the Tiebout shopping process) is considered constitutional. What sort of government actions would diminish this type of segregation? In other words, what policies diminish the incentives for households to sort themselves with respect to income and race?

One approach would be to consolidate local school districts into a metropolitan school district or a statewide school authority. Such a policy would generate a uniform spending level and a single tax base, so there would be less incentive for households to sort themselves with respect to desired school spending and property values. As explained in the chapters on local government, there are some trade-offs with this policy: to the extent there is diversity in demand for education, the large jurisdiction—with its uniform provision of education—will be less efficient than the system of smaller jurisdictions. Moreover, as pointed out by Bradford and Oates (1974), such a policy would not eliminate segregation because parents will still seek a school that provides a favorable peer group for their children. Middle-income households still have an incentive to exclude poor children from their neighborhoods and schools because the poor have lower average achievement levels.

A less drastic approach would be to use intergovernmental grants to equalize spending. This policy has an advantage over consolidation because it gives the local school district greater control over how to spend its fixed budget. It eliminates the incentive for fiscally based sorting (sorting with respect to desired spending levels and property values), but would not affect sorting motivated by peer group effects. State governments have tried a number of grant programs, none of which has narrowed spending gaps significantly. The only equalization policy that worked was the California program, under which the state assumed complete control of education funding.

Is there any way to diminish the sorting motivated by peer group effects? Suppose that state grants were tied to students (they traveled with the student to her school) and were inversely related to the income level of the student's family. By admitting a low-income student, a school would increase its grant revenue; it could use the extra money to improve its education program (e.g., decrease class sizes, hire better teachers). Such a scheme would decrease the incentive for middle-income and wealthy households to exclude poor students, so it would promote integration. To the extent it fails to integrate the schools, a school full of poor (highly subsidized) students could at least use the extra money to provide a better education program.

Subsidies for Private Education: Education Vouchers

Should the government subsidize students who attend private as well as public schools? The advocates of private-school subsidies view the public school system as an inflexible and inefficient monopoly. They argue that a subsidy for private education would force public schools to compete with private schools for students, so public schools would be more concerned about efficiency and more responsive to parental concerns. Would the public support of private schools lead to greater inequalities in educational achievement?

Under a voucher system, every child is issued a coupon that can be used to pay for either public or private education. The typical voucher plan has the following features:

1. The state gives each child an educational voucher with a face value equal to the current per pupil spending in public schools (for example, $2,500).
2. The family uses the voucher to pay for tuition at a qualifying school, public or private. The school redeems the voucher with the state government.
3. Public schools charge tuition equal to $2,500, making public education effectively free.
4. To qualify for the voucher program, a school must teach basic cognitive skills and civics and must admit students without regard for race, sex, or religion.
5. The family is free to supplement the voucher with its own funds, so the child is free to attend a school charging more than $2,500 in tuition.
6. The government collects and disseminates information on the teaching methods, curriculum, and test scores of qualifying schools.

The voucher program involves a mixture of subsidies and regulations. The subsidies place private and public schools on equal footing with respect to governmental support. The regulations prevent explicit racism and sexism and force private schools to teach basic cognitive skills and civics. The government's information program helps parents choose among the alternative schools.

The debate over education vouchers has been spirited. Like most policy proposals, the voucher plan has both good and bad points. Because a true voucher plan has never been tried, there is a great deal of uncertainty about its possible effects. The obvious response is to experiment with voucher systems in one or more school districts.

The advocates of education vouchers stress two points in their arguments for vouchers:

1. **Competition**. The voucher plan would allow private schools to compete more effectively for students. Competition would improve the efficiency of the educational system, increasing educational achievement per dollar spent.
2. **Diversity**. The voucher plan would encourage diversity in educational philosophy and methods, providing parents with more options.

Voucher advocates argue that vouchers would break up the public-school monopoly, leading to greater efficiency and wider consumer choice.

The opponents of education vouchers stress four points in their arguments against vouchers:

1. **Unequal educational opportunities.** Under a voucher system, wealthy families may supplement the voucher with their own money, sending their children to expensive (and high-quality) schools. The children from poor families would receive inferior education.

2. **Income segregation.** Under the voucher system, there would be low-cost schools (patronized by poor families) and high-cost schools (patronized by wealthy families). The educational system would be stratified with respect to income.

3. **Pluralist decision making.** Children educated in a stratified educational system would be less aware and tolerant of other viewpoints and lifestyles, so decision making in today's pluralist society would become more difficult.

4. **Occupational choices.** Children educated in a stratified system would be more likely to choose the same occupations and social status as their parents: the educational system would inhibit occupational and social mobility between generations.

The opponents of vouchers consider the public school system a necessary component of a pluralist, democratic society. Education in public schools forces children from different social classes to interact, resulting in citizens who are more tolerant and flexible. If the voucher system generates a more stratified educational system, children from different social classes would not have the opportunity to interact, so they would not develop the traits necessary for managing in a pluralist democracy.

There are clearly trade-offs associated with the voucher scheme. A system of vouchers would improve the efficiency of the school system by fostering competition between schools and providing more choice. The plan may also increase inequalities in educational spending, causing greater inequalities in educational achievement. In addition, it may increase income segregation, causing the school system to produce citizens who are less tolerant of alternative viewpoints and lifestyles. Given the lack of experience with voucher plans, these trade-offs cannot be quantified, so it is difficult to make an informed policy decision.

Summary

1. The production function summarizes the relationship between education inputs and achievement.
   a. There are five inputs to education: curriculum, educational equipment, teachers, the home environment, and the peer group.
   b. The home environment has an extraordinary effect on achievement.
   c. A child learns more when he is surrounded by smart and motivated peers.

        d. Teachers vary in effectiveness. Teacher productivity increases with communication skills, but is not affected by graduate education. Some researchers suggest that productivity increases for the first few years of teaching, while others suggest that productivity is independent of teaching experience.

        e. The link between class size and achievement is still an open question. If there is a negative relationship, it seems to be a weak one.

2. Under the Tiebout process, households sort themselves with respect to three characteristics: desired spending on schools, property values, and peer group traits.

3. Education spending varies considerably across school districts, a result of differences in desired spending and differences in property tax bases.

4. U.S. schools are highly segregated: in 1986, almost half of minority students attended schools in which over 80 percent of the students were minorities. Under the ability-tracking system, classrooms are even more segregated than the schools.

5. Blacks and Hispanics have relatively low achievement levels: at age 17, they are 30 percent behind white students. In the last few decades, the test scores of blacks and Hispanics have increased relative to whites, with the largest improvements experienced by nine-year-olds. In 1985, the high school completion rate was 63 percent for blacks, compared to 77 percent for whites.

6. The traditional education grants (flat grants and foundation grants) are lump-sum grants. Under a flat-grant program, the state gives the same per pupil grant to every school district. Under a foundation plan, the grant is inversely related to the district's tax base per pupil.

        a. The grant increases spending on education and also decreases taxes, so households can spend part of the grant on other goods.

        b. Foundation plans have had small effects on spending inequalities because the grants are small and school districts spend a relatively small fraction of each grant on education.

7. In the 1970s, state courts declared that intrastate spending inequalities were unconstitutional. The states responded by developing new grant programs.

        a. Under the guaranteed tax-base (GTB) plan, every school district has access to the same effective tax base.

        b. The pure version of GTB would decrease spending inequalities by a relatively large amount because it (i) decreases the tax base of wealthy districts and increases the tax base of poor districts and (ii) increases the opportunity cost of education in the wealthy district and decreases the opportunity cost in the poor district.

        c. Most states have adopted an impure version of GTB, under which wealthy districts keep the excess of local taxes over the guaranteed tax revenue.

8. In California, the state government has assumed complete control for education finance and has virtually eliminated spending inequalities.

9. The Supreme Court outlawed segregation based on explicit and implicit government actions and ordered many cities to desegregate their school systems.

   a. Many white households moved from central-city school districts to all-white school districts in the suburbs.

   b. Other white households switched to private schools.

10. In choosing between public and private schools, parents face a trade-off between the consumption of education and other goods.

    a. Achievement is higher in private schools, a result of more favorable peer groups and other factors.

    b. Desegregation causes some households to switch to private schools if the integration of public schools decreases achievement.

11. Under a voucher system, every child is issued a coupon to pay for either public or private education. The voucher plan has advantages and disadvantages.

    a. Competition among schools would increase, improving efficiency and increasing consumer choice.

    b. Spending inequalities may increase, violating the principle of equal educational opportunity.

    c. Income segregation may increase, causing the school system to produce citizens who are less tolerant of alternative viewpoints and lifestyles.

Exercises and Discussion Questions

1. According to Summers and Wolfe (1977), low achievers learn more in small classes and with inexperienced teachers, while high achievers learn more in large classes with experienced teachers. Why?

2. Consider a school district that can hire teachers from a large pool of applicants that differ in their verbal abilities and the number of credit hours of graduate study in education. Under the current salary structure, a teacher's annual salary increases by $100 for a one-unit increase in credit hours and increases by $200 for a one-unit increase in verbal ability. Suppose that the district's objective is to minimize the cost of providing a given educational output. Use the standard isoquant-isocost analysis (covered in intermediate microeconomics) to show the district's choice (the cost-minimizing combination of verbal ability and hours of graduate study):

   a. Use the available empirical evidence to draw the education isoquant, with verbal ability on the horizontal axis and graduate credit hours on the vertical axis.

   b. Show the cost-minimizing combination of verbal ability and graduate education. Provide a brief explanation of your choice.

3. The objective of the state of Egalitaria is to equalize educational opportunity (defined as the same average achievement level in every school). Comment

on the following: "To achieve its objective, the state must equalize educational spending (spending the same amount per student in every school)."

4. Your task is to predict the effects of a state's foundation plan on the school district and the state budget. The transfer rate (t) is 2 percent, and the maximum property value per student (V') is $60,000. The income elasticity of demand for education is +0.50.

a. Fill in the blanks in the following table.

	District E	District F
Tax base per pupil	$40,000	$50,000
Initial spending per pupil	$600	$800
Tax rate	_____	_____
Foundation grant	_____	_____
Initial income of median voter	$1,600	$2,000
Percentage change of median-voter income	_____	_____
New (postgrant) spending per pupil	_____	_____
Local contribution to education (per pupil)	_____	_____
New tax rate	_____	_____

b. If each school district has 1,000 students, how much does the foundation plan cost the state?

c. What is the bang (increase in education spending) per buck of the foundation grant in District E?

5. Suppose that a school district has a tax base per student of $40,000 and per pupil spending of $600.

a. Draw the district's tax-spending line, and label its chosen point *A*.

b. Suppose the state gives the school district a foundation grant of $400. Using the same graph, draw the new tax-spending line. The district responds by increasing its spending to $800. Label its new choice point *B*.

c. Suppose that the state offers the school district a GTB plan with a guaranteed tax base of $80,000. Map the new tax-expenditure line. If the school district must choose between the foundation plan and the GTB plan, which will it choose?

6. Compute the price elasticity of demand for education given the following facts:

a. The local school district has a property value per student of $30,000.

b. The state institutes a guaranteed tax-base plan with GTB = $40,000.

c. As a result of the GTB, the school district increases spending per student from $2,000 to $2,100.

7. Suppose that you are the budget analyst for the state government. Your task is to estimate the fiscal impact of a guaranteed tax-base plan. Assume the following:

  i. The price elasticity of demand for education is -0.80.

  ii. The guaranteed tax base is $40,000.

  iii. The typical school district has 100 students and a property tax base of $30,000 per student, and initially spends $600 per student.

Compute the effects of the GTB on the following:

a. Spending per pupil.

b. The local contribution to education (per pupil) and the local tax rate.

c. The state contribution to education (per pupil) and the total budgetary cost of the GTB plan.

d. The bang (increase in education spending) per buck (budgetary cost).

8. Use the median-voter model (see Chapter 17) to predict the effects of desegregation on spending (per pupil) in public schools. Will spending increase or decrease?

9. One of the criticisms of a voucher program for education is that it would increase spending inequalities and achievement inequalities. Design a new voucher plan that would narrow—rather than widen—spending and achievement differences across schools. How would you change the conventional voucher proposal to decrease spending and achievement inequalities?

10. Consider Creditland, a state that recently implemented a system of income-tax credits for private schools. The characteristics of the state and the program are as follows:

  i. Each family has one child in school.

  ii. The government spends $4,000 on each child in the public schools.

  iii. Tuition in private schools is $3,500.

  iv. The tuition tax credit is 50 percent of private-school tuition.

a. What additional information do you need to compute the fiscal effects of the tax credit program?

b. Make up some numbers and compute the fiscal effect.

c. Choose the word in parentheses that makes the following statement correct and then explain your choice: "The net budgetary cost of the tax-credit plan increases as the price elasticity of demand for private education (*increases, decreases*) in absolute value."

References and Additional Readings

Overview

Garms, Walter I.; James W. Guthrie; and Lawrence C. Pierce. *School Finance: The Economics and Politics of Public Education.* Englewood Cliffs, N.J.: Prentice Hall, 1978. Chapter 3 discusses the reasons for government intervention in education. Chapter 4 discusses the roles of the federal, state, and local governments.

Murnane, Richard J. "An Economist's Look at Federal and State Education Policies." In *American Domestic Priorities: An Economic Appraisal*, ed. John Quigley and Daniel Rubinfeld. Berkeley and Los Angeles: University of California, 1985.

Discusses a number of issues in public education, including trends in achievement scores, merit pay, the restrictive effects of state certification requirements, and curriculum reforms.

Education Facts

Advisory Commission on Intergovernmental Relations. *State Aid to Local Governments.* Washington, D.C.: U.S. Government Printing Office, 1969.

Brown, L.; A. Ginsberg; J. Killalea; R. Rosthal; and E. Tron. "School Finance Reform in the Seventies: Achievements and Failures." *Selected Papers in School Finance, 1978.* Washington, D.C.: U.S. Department of Health, Education, and Welfare, 1978.

Congressional Budget Office. *Trends in Educational Achievement.* Washington, D.C.: U.S. Congress, 1986. Reports trends in test scores.

Katz, Jeffrey. *Three National Assessments of Science: Changes in Achievement, 1969–77.* Denver: Education Commission of the States, 1978. Reports trends in science scores for 9-, 13-, and 17-year-olds.

———. *Has Title I Improved Education for Disadvantaged Students? Evidence from Three National Assessments of Reading.* Denver: Education Commission of the States, 1981a. Evaluates the effects of federal support programs.

———. *Three Assessments of Reading: Changes in Performance, 1970–1980.* Denver: Education Commission of the States, 1981b. Reports trends in reading scores for 9-, 13-, and 17-year-olds.

———. *The Third National Mathematics Assessment: Results, Trends, and Issues.* Denver: Education Commission of the States, 1982. Reports trends in math scores for 9-, 13-, and 17-year-olds.

———. "The Search for Equity in School Funding." *Governing,* August 1991, pp. 20–22.

National Center for Education Statistics. *Digest of Education Statistics, 1982.* Washington, D.C.: U.S. Government Printing Office, 1982. Documents the differences in achievement between whites, blacks, and Hispanics.

Office of Civil Rights, Department of Education. *1986 Elementary and Secondary School Civil Rights Survey: National Summaries.* Washington, D.C.: U.S. Government Printing Office, 1987. Shows that classrooms are more segregated than schools.

Schiller, Bradley. *The Economics of Poverty and Discrimination.* 5th ed. Englewood Cliffs, N.J.: Prentice Hall, 1989.

U.S. Census Bureau. *Statistical Abstract of the United States,* 1987. Washington, D.C.: U.S. Government Printing Office.

U.S. Department of Education. *The Condition of Education: A Statistical Report, 1983, 1985, 1986.* Washington, D.C.: U.S. Government Printing Office, 1987. Reports the facts on education, including information on student performance, fiscal resources, teacher characteristics, public opinion of the schools, and governance.

Production Function

Brown, B. "Achievement, Costs, and the Demand for Public Education." *Western Economic Journal* 10 (1972), pp. 198–219. Suggests that an increase in the teacher-pupil ratio does not affect achievement, but an increase in teacher quality (experience and training) increases achievement.

Brown, B., and D. Sachs. "The Production and Distribution of Cognitive Skills within Schools," *Journal of Political Economy* 83 (1975), pp. 571–94.

Coleman, James S.; E. Q. Campbell; C. J. Hobson; J. McPartland; A. M. Mood; F. D. Weinfield; and R. L. York. *Equality of Educational Opportunity.* Washington, D.C.: U.S. Government Printing Office, 1966. The controversial "Coleman report," which was interpreted to mean that schools and teachers do not matter.

Hanushek, Eric A. "The Economics of Schooling: Production and Efficiency in Public Schools." *Journal of Economic Literature* 24 (1986), pp. 1141–77. A survey of research on education, focusing on production and efficiency. Discusses the results of studies that have estimated the education production function.

———. "Throwing Money at Schools." *Journal of Policy Analysis and Management* 1 (1981), pp. 19–41. Summarizes the results of estimates of the production function, focusing on the effects of teachers on achievement. Concludes that teachers do in fact matter, with teachers of higher verbal ability doing better in terms of student achievement. Suggests that spending more money on schools does not increase achievement; argues for the development of direct performance incentives.

Murnane, Richard J. *The Impact of School Resources on the Learning of Inner City Children.* Cambridge, Mass.: Ballinger, 1975. Surveys the results of previous studies and provides new estimates of the education production function. Concludes that teacher experience matters for the first few years of teaching.

Summers, Anita, and Barbara Wolfe. "Do Schools Make a Difference?" *American Economic Review* 67, no. 4 (1977), pp. 639–52. Estimates the education production function, showing that achievement depends on teacher characteristics and class size, with different effects on high achievers and low achievers.

Teachers: Productivity and Class Size

Eberts, Randall W., and Joe Stone. "Wages, Fringe Benefits, and Working Conditions: An Analysis of Compensating Differentials." *Southern Economic Journal* 52, no.1 (1985), pp. 274–79. Estimates the responsiveness of teacher salaries to changes in working conditions, including changes in class size.

Hanushek, Eric A. "Teacher Characteristics and Gains in Student Achievement: Estimates Using Micro Data." *American Economic Review* 61, no. 2 (1971), pp. 280–88. Estimates the education production function, showing that achievement depends on the general ability of teachers (as measured by scores on verbal tests) and how recently the teacher has received formal training.

Murnane, Richard J. "Understanding the Sources of Teaching Competence: Choice, Skills, and the Limits of Training." *Teachers College Record* 84 (1983), pp. 564–69. Discusses the evidence about which teacher characteristics matter (verbal ability and experience) and which do not (formal education) and the policy implications of these findings.

Decline of Test Scores

Advisory Panel on the Scholastic Test Score Decline. *On Further Examination.* New York: College Entrance Examination Board, 1977. Discusses some of the reasons for the decline in SAT scores.

Harnischfeger, Annegret, and David E. Wiley. *Achievement Test Score Decline: Do We Need to Worry?* Chicago: Cemrel, 1975.

———. *Time and Learning in California Schools.* Sacramento: California Testing Program, 1984. Suggests that student achievement depends on the number of academic courses completed.

Spending Inequalities

Berne, Robert, and Leanna Stiefel. *The Measurement of Equity in School Finance.* Baltimore: Johns Hopkins University Press, 1984.

Coons, John E.; William H. Clune; and Stephen D. Sugarman. *Private Wealth and Public Education.* Cambridge, Mass.: Harvard University Press, 1970. Developed the notion of fiscal neutrality.

Guthrie, James W. "United States School Finance Policy 1955–1980." Chapter 1 in *School Finance Policies and Practices,* ed. James W. Guthrie. Cambridge, Mass.: Ballinger, 1980. Relates the history of school finance, focusing on court cases that forced states to reform their financing policies.

McDonald, M. Brian. "Educational Equity and the Fiscal Incidence of Public Education." *National Tax Journal* 33 (1980), pp. 45–54. Shows that there is an inverse relationship between income and the net benefits from education.

Equalization Policies

Bradford, David, and Wallace E. Oates. "Suburban Exploitation of Central Cities and Government Structure." In *Redistribution through Public Choice,* ed. Harold Hochman and George Peterson. New York: Columbia University Press, 1974. Discusses the suburban exploitation hypothesis and predicts the effects of metropolitan consolidation on tax rates, expenditure levels, and income segregation.

California Department of Education. *Selected Financial and Related Data for California Public Schools, K–12, 1984.* Sacramento: State of California, 1985.

Carroll, Stephen J. *The Search for Equity in School Finance: Summary and Conclusions.* Santa Monica: Rand Corporation, 1979. Discusses the reasons why GTB plans have not had a significant effect on spending inequalities.

Courant, Paul N.; Edward M. Gramlich; and Daniel Rubinfeld. "The Stimulative Effect of Intergovernmental Grants, or Why Money Sticks Where It Hits." In *Fiscal Federalism and Grants-in-Aid,* ed. Peter Mieszkowski and William Oakland. Washington, D.C.: Urban Institute, 1979. Discusses the flypaper effect of intergovernmental grants.

Gramlich, E. M. "Intergovernmental Grants: A Review of the Empirical Literature." In *The Political Economy of Fiscal Federalism*, ed. Wallace E. Oates. Lexington, Mass.: Lexington Books, 1977. Reviews the literature on the effects of grants on local spending. Concludes that matching grants are more stimulative than lump-sum grants and the categorical grant has a larger stimulative effect than an equivalent increase in private income.

Neenan, William B. "Fiscal Relations between State of Michigan and Southeastern Michigan." In *Financing the Metropolis,* ed. Kent Mathewson and William B. Neenan. New York: Praeger, 1980.

Public versus Private Schools

Barzel, Y. "Private Schools and Public School Finance." *Journal of Political Economy* 81 (1973), pp. 174–86. Analyzes the exit of wealthy households to private schools when the achievement levels of public schools decrease.

Coleman, James S.; Thomas Hoffer; and Sally Kilgore. *Achievement in High School: Public and Private Schools Compared.* New York: Basic Books, 1981. Shows that students in private schools have higher test scores than students in public schools.

Also suggests that achievement depends on the number of academic courses completed.

Inman, Robert. "Optimal Fiscal Reform of Metropolitan Schools: Some Simulation Results." *American Economic Review* 68 (1978), pp. 107–22. Discusses the choice between private and public schools and the implications for education finance.

Murnane, Richard J. "Comparisons of Private and Public Schools: The Critical Role of Regulations." Chapter 4 in *Private Education: Studies in Choice and Public Policy,* ed. Daniel C. Levy. Oxford: Oxford University Press, 1986a.

———. "Comparisons of Private and Public Schools: What Can We Learn?" Chapter 5 in *Private Education: Studies in Choice and Public Policy,* ed. Daniel C. Levy. Oxford: Oxford University Press, 1986b.

School Problems: Desegregation and Busing

Clotfelter, Charles T. "The Effect of School Desegregation on Housing Prices." *Review of Economics and Statistics* 57 (1975), pp. 446–51. Shows that desegregation in the South decreased the demand for central-city housing, decreasing housing prices.

———. "School Desegregation, Tipping, and Private School Enrollment." *Journal of Human Resources* 11 (1976), pp. 28–50. Shows that an increase in black enrollment in public schools increases the proportion of whites enrolled in private schools.

———. "School Desegregation as Urban Public Policy." In *Current Issues in Urban Economics,* ed. Peter Mieszkowski and Mahlon Straszheim. Baltimore: Johns Hopkins University Press, 1979, pp. 359–88. Describes the evolution of desegregation policy, explores the "white flight" phenomenon, and discusses the effects of desegregation on achievement.

Coleman, James, and Sara Kelly. "Education." In *The Urban Predicament,* ed. William Gorham and Nathan Glazer. Washington, D.C.: Urban Institute, 1976. Analyzes racial segregation in schools between 1968 and 1973.

Giles, Michael W.; Douglas Gatlin; and Everett F. Cataldo. "White Flight and Percent Black: The Tipping Point Re-Examined." *Social Science Quarterly* 56 (1975), pp. 85–92. Using data for Florida, estimates that the tipping point for white enrollment in private schools is about 30 percent black enrollment in public schools.

Education Vouchers

Bridge, Gary. "Citizen Choice in Public Services." In *Alternatives for Delivering Public Services,* ed. E. S. Savas. Boulder, Colo.: Westview Press, 1977. Suggests that parents are likely to pick education programs for their children that prepare them for the same type of occupation.

Coons, John E., and Stephen D. Sugarman. *Education by Choice: The Case for Family Control.* Berkeley and Los Angeles: University of California, 1978. Discusses the voucher program, arguing that a voucher system would provide better education because parents and students would have greater opportunity for educational choice.

Levin, Henry M. "Educational Vouchers and Social Policy." In *School Finance Policies and Practices,* ed. James W. Guthrie. Cambridge, Mass.: Ballinger, 1980. Relates the history of the voucher proposal and describes the features of the most recent voucher proposals. Discusses the role of integrated classrooms for the promotion of occupational mobility and the functioning of a pluralist democracy and suggests that a voucher scheme is likely to cause a stratification of the education system.

Crime and Punishment

I don't worry about crime in the streets; it's the sidewalks I stay off of.
Johnson Letellier

This chapter presents the economic approach to crime and crime prevention. The economic approach assumes that both criminals and victims are rational in the sense that they base their choices on the expected benefits and costs of alternatives. A rational person commits a property crime if the expected benefit of the crime exceeds the expected cost. Similarly, potential victims use their resources to prevent crime if the expected benefit of prevention exceeds the expected cost. The economic approach leads logically to a discussion of the optimum amount of crime: because crime is costly to prevent, it is rational to allow some crime to occur.

Why study crime? The analysis of crime is an important part of urban economics for three reasons. First, most crime occurs in metropolitan areas, and crime rates are highest in central cities. Second, households are sensitive to crime rates, so their location decisions are affected by local crime rates. In other words, crime affects the spatial distribution of people within and between cities. Because households are attracted to areas with low crime rates, an area with a relatively low crime rate has relatively high housing prices. Third, the relatively high crime rates in central cities have contributed to the suburbanization of population: many households have moved to the suburbs to escape central-city crime.

Crime Facts

Most crime data come from the FBI's *Uniform Crime Reports*. The FBI collects data from local police departments on seven **index crimes**. The index crimes are divided into personal crimes and property crimes.

1. **Personal crime.** The victim of a personal crime is placed in physical danger. For some personal crimes, the criminal's objective is to injure the victim (homicide, rape, aggravated assault). For other personal crimes, the objective is to steal property, but the criminal uses a show of force to coerce the victim (robbery).

2. **Property crime.** Property crimes are crimes of stealth, not force. Examples are burglary (illegal entry of a building), larceny (purse snatching, pocket picking, and bicycle theft), and auto theft.

The FBI data provide a partial picture of the crime scene. Among the crimes omitted in the *Uniform Crime Reports* are disorderly conduct, shoplifting, arson, employee theft, and drug-related offenses (possession and sale of narcotics, public drunkenness, drunk driving).

Table 22–1 lists the crime rates for the seven index crimes for the last few decades. The crime rates are expressed as the number of crimes per 100,000 population. Most of the reported index crimes are economically motivated. In 1990, the four economic crimes (robbery, burglary, larceny, and auto theft) made up about 90 percent of total reported crimes. The total crime rate rose from 1,870 in 1960 to 5,950 in 1980, and then fell to 5,820 in 1990.

Because the FBI data include only the crimes that are reported to the police, they may be deceptive. In 1986, the reporting rates were 54 percent for robberies, 46 percent for assaults, 27 percent for personal larceny, 50 percent for burglary, 27 percent for household larceny, and 71 percent for auto theft. Given the low reporting rates

---

TABLE 22–1   FBI Index Crimes, 1960–1990

	Number of Crimes per 100,000 People			
	1960	*1970*	*1980*	*1990*
Personal Crime				
Murder	5.0	7.8	10.2	9.4
Rape	9.5	18.6	36.8	41.2
Aggravated assault	85.2	176.9	298.5	424.1
Robbery	59.5	187.2	251.1	257.0
Property Crime				
Auto theft	182	457	502	658
Larceny	1,024	2,124	3,167	3,184
Burglary	504	1,152	1,684	1,236
Total index crimes	1,870	3,949	5,950	5,820

Source: U.S. Federal Bureau of Investigation, *Crime in the United States, 1990* (Washington, D.C.: U.S. Government Printing Office, 1991).

for most crimes, the FBI data may be misleading: a change in the FBI crime rate could be caused by a change in actual crime or a change in reporting rates. In 1988, the overall reporting rate was 36 percent, which was 12 percent higher than the 1973 rate.

Since 1973, the Justice Department has collected crime data from its semi-annual victimization surveys. The surveys suggest that crime rates decreased between 1973 and 1988. The percentage reductions of property crime were 24 percent for robbery, 32 percent for burglary, 26 percent for larceny, and 5 percent for motor-vehicle theft.

The Victims of Crime

Who are the victims of crime? Victimization rates vary with income, place of residence, and race.

1. **Crime and income.** Figure 22–1 shows victimization rates for different income levels. The victimization rates for crimes of violence (rape, robbery, and assault) decrease as income increases: the poor are more likely to be victims of violent crime. In contrast, the victimization rates for crimes of theft (larceny) are highest at the two ends of the income distribution and increase with income for households with annual income between $7,500 and $30,000.

FIGURE 22–1   Victimization Rates and Income

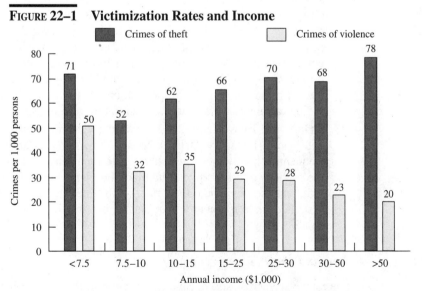

SOURCE: U.S. Department of Justice, Bureau of Justice Statistics, *Criminal Victimization in the United States, 1989,* National Crime Survey Report NC-J-129391 (Washington, D.C.: U.S. Department of Justice, 1991).

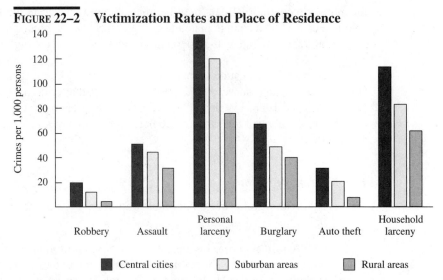

FIGURE 22–2   **Victimization Rates and Place of Residence**

SOURCE: U.S. Department of Justice, Bureau of Justice Statistics, *Criminal Victimization in the United States, 1989,* National Crime Survey Report NC-J-129391 (Washington, D.C.: U.S. Department of Justice, 1991), Tables 1 and 2.

2. **Crime and place of residence.** Figure 22–2 shows victimization rates for different residential locations. Crime rates are higher in metropolitan areas than in nonmetropolitan areas, and higher in central cities than in suburbs. The largest difference in crime rates is for robbery: the central-city robbery rate is over five times the rural rate and almost three times the suburban rate. Crime is concentrated in cities for three reasons. First, poverty is concentrated in cities. Because a large fraction of criminals come from poor households, the cities have a large supply of potential criminals. Second, wealth is concentrated in cities, and criminals are attracted by urban loot. Third, population density is higher in cities, providing criminals with a large concentration of targets.

3. **Crime and race.** Figure 22–3 shows the victimization rates for whites and blacks. For four of the six crimes shown, blacks are victimized more frequently than whites: the robbery rate for blacks is about three times the robbery rate for whites; the black burglary rate is 1.7 times the white rate; and the black auto-theft rate is 1.8 times the white rate. Whites are assaulted more frequently than blacks, but the difference is relatively small.

Crime and the Price of Housing

Crime rates vary across space, causing variation in the price of housing. Gray and Joelson (1979) studied the relationship between crime rates and property values in Minneapolis. In 1970, the burglary rate varied considerably across the city's census

FIGURE 22–3   Victimization Rates and Race

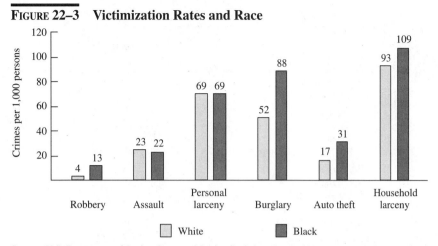

SOURCE: U.S. Department of Justice, Bureau of Justice Statistics, *Criminal Victimization in the United States, 1989,* National Crime Survey Report NC-J-129391 (Washington, D.C.: U.S. Department of Justice, 1991), Tables 1 and 2.

tracts, from 1 percent of dwellings per year in the lowest-crime tract to 14 percent in the highest. A one-unit increase in the crime rate (an additional percentage point) decreased the average property value by $336. The vandalism rate varied from less than 1 incident to 30 incidents per 1,000 population. A one-unit increase in the vandalism rate (an additional incident per 1,000 population) decreased the average property value by $117. In another study, Thaler (1978) estimated the elasticity of property values with respect to crime rates as −0.067: a 10 percent increase in the crime rate decreased the market value of housing by about 0.67 percent.

The Costs of Crime

Criminal activity imposes two types of costs on society. The direct costs are the cost incurred by the physical victims of crime: the victims of personal crimes are injured or killed, and the victims of property crime lose their property. The indirect costs are the costs incurred by potential victims in trying to prevent crime: people spend money on locks, guard dogs, and other prevention measures and also pay taxes to support society's crime prevention programs (the police, the court system, and prisons). The opportunity cost of crime prevention is the value of the resources in alternative uses: if there were less crime to prevent, locks could be melted into plows; lawyers could build bridges; and prison cells could be converted to condominiums.

Reynolds (1986) has estimated the direct and indirect cost of personal and property crime, using data from several sources. He estimated the nationwide cost of crime in 1983 and then divided that by the number of households to get the crime cost per household. As shown in Table 22–2, Reynolds estimated that the total cost of crime was $2,331 per household in 1983.

TABLE 22–2   The Costs of Crime in 1983

	Cost per Household ($ per year)
Direct Costs	
Personal losses	
Homicide	$ 72
Rape	89
Assault	192
Robbery (cost of injury)	82
Property losses	
Burglary	93
Larceny theft	81
Robbery (property losses)	8
Motor-vehicle theft	56
Business losses	
Arson	22
Shoplifting	300
Employee theft	125
Business fraud	600
Indirect Costs	
Prevention costs	
Business	81
Household	106
Criminal justice system	
Police	200
Courts and legal services	87
Corrections	87
Opportunity cost of imprisonment	50
Total Cost	$2,331

Direct Costs.   There are three types of direct cost from crime: personal losses, property losses, and losses from business crime:

1. **Personal losses.** To estimate the social cost of crimes against people, one must place dollar figures on the cost of injuries and death. Reynolds assumed that the cost per homicide was $300,000, the cost per rape was $30,000, the cost per serious assault was $12,000, and the injury cost per robbery was $6,600. As shown in Table 22–2, the estimated annual cost per household ranges from $72 for homicide to $192 for assault.

2. **Property losses.** Property losses occur as a result of burglary, larceny, robbery, and motor-vehicle theft. The estimated value of property losses in 1983 was $238 per household.

3. **Losses from business crime.** There are four types of business crime. Arson generated losses of $1.8 billion, or $22 per household. Reynolds assumed that the loss from shoplifting was 2 percent of retail sales, or

$300 per household, and the loss from employee theft was $125 per household. Business fraud, which generated total losses of $600 per household, includes credit card theft (losses of $1 billion per year), securities theft ($8 billion), bad checks ($2 billion), insurance fraud ($4 billion), mail and bank fraud ($1 billion), deceptive practices ($18 billion), bribes and kickbacks ($6 billion), and fencing of stolen property ($7 billion).

Indirect Costs.   There are two types of indirect cost: prevention cost and the cost of the criminal justice system. According to Reynolds, the total indirect cost was $611 per household in 1983.

1. **Prevention cost.** Reynolds estimated that firms spent a total of $6.5 billion on crime prevention measures in 1983, most of it on private security guards. Households spent an additional $8.5 billion on prevention measures, so the total cost of crime prevention was $15 billion, or $187 per household.

2. **Cost of the criminal justice system.** Reynolds estimated that spending on police, courts, and corrections facilities was $374 per household. Another cost of the criminal justice system is the opportunity cost of time spent in prison. Reynolds assumed that each prisoner could produce $10,000 worth of goods if he or she were gainfully employed. Based on this assumption, the opportunity cost of imprisonment was $50 per household. The total cost of the criminal justice system was therefore $424 per household in 1983.

The Rational Criminal and the Supply of Crime

The economic model of crime assumes that the criminal commits a crime if the expected benefit of the crime exceeds its expected cost. The model of the rational criminal is relevant for economically motivated crimes (property crimes), but not for crimes of passion and violence.

A Numerical Example of Burglary

Consider Boris, who must decide whether to spend a day planning and executing a burglary. Boris will commit the burglary if the expected net benefit of burglary exceeds the expected benefit of spending the day in some legal activity. The costs and benefits of the two activities are listed in Table 22–3.

1. **The expected loot.** The expected value of the burglary loot is the probability that Boris succeeds in the burglary (P_s) times the monetary value of the loot:

$$EL = P_s \cdot \text{Loot} \tag{22–1}$$

TABLE 22–3   Expected Benefits and Costs for a Burglary

	Benefits and Costs
Burglary Activity	
Expected loot	
Loot	$ 600
Probability of success (P_s)	0.80
Expected loot ($EL = P_s \cdot$ Loot)	$ 480
Expected cost	
Probability of punishment ($P_i = P_a \cdot P_p$)	0.02
Opportunity cost of prison time	
Daily wage (W)	$ 40
Expected workdays per year (D)	150
Forgone income per year ($I = W \cdot D$)	$6,000
Cost of lost freedom per year (F)	$2,000
Opportunity cost per year ($C = I + F$)	$8,000
Expected cost ($EC = P_i \cdot C$)	$ 160
Expected benefit of burglary ($B = EL - EC$)	$ 320
Legal Activity	
Daily income if employed (W)	$ 40
Net return from burglary ($R = B - W$)	$ 280

If the probability of success is 80 percent and the resale value of the stolen property is $600, the expected value of the loot is $480.

2. **Expected cost.** On the cost side, Boris faces the possibility of being sent to prison for committing the burglary. The expected value of the penalty for burglary is the probability of being imprisoned (P_i) times the opportunity cost of time spent in prison.

   a. **Probability of imprisonment.** The probability of being imprisoned is determined by the police and the court system. The probability of imprisonment (P_i) is the probability of being arrested (P_a) times the probability of being sentenced to prison once arrested (P_p).

$$P_i = P_a \cdot P_p \qquad (22-2)$$

   In the 1970s, about 16 percent of index crimes resulted in an arrest, so P_a is about 0.16; about 13 percent of arrestees were sent to prison, so P_p is about 0.13 (Wilson and Boland, 1976). If Boris faces similar chances of arrest and sentencing, the probability of being imprisoned is about 0.02 (0.16 times 0.13).

   b. **The opportunity cost of prison time.** The opportunity cost of time spent in prison equals the annual opportunity cost times the length of the prison sentence. Suppose that Boris is a relatively low-skilled worker who can find work only about 150 days per year and is paid $40 per day. For every year in prison, he gives up $6,000 in income

(150 times $40). Another cost of imprisonment is the loss of liberty
and freedom. If he values his freedom at $2,000 per year, the annual
opportunity cost of prison is $8,000 ($6,000 in forgone wages plus
$2,000 in lost freedom). If the prison sentence for burglary is one
year, the opportunity cost of imprisonment is $8,000.

   c. **Expected cost.** The expected cost is $160 [the probability of being
imprisoned (0.02) times the opportunity cost of imprisonment for burglary ($8,000)].

3. **Expected benefit from burglary.** The expected benefit from burglary is
the expected loot ($480) less the expected cost ($160), or $320.

4. **Net return from burglary.** The alternative to burglary is to spend the
day in a legal job. The net return from a burglary is the expected benefit of the burglary ($320) less the money Boris could earn in a legal job
($40), or $280. The net return is positive, so if Boris bases his decision
exclusively on the expected benefits and costs of burglary, he will commit the burglary.

Morality and Aversion to Crime?   Most people have an underlying aversion to
committing crime. For the typical person, crime is unattractive at any price. For other
people, the net return on crime must be high enough to overcome their underlying
aversion to it. One way to incorporate the aversion to crime into the benefit-cost
analysis is to estimate a person's **anguish cost,** defined as the cost associated with
engaging in antisocial activity. If Gabriel has a strong aversion to crime, his anguish
cost may be $10,000, meaning that he will commit a crime only if the net return
exceeds $10,000. If Lucifer is less averse to crime, his anguish cost is only $10, so
he will commit a crime if the net return exceeds $10. Returning to the example in
Table 22–3, Boris will commit the burglary if his anguish cost is less than the net
return of the burglary ($280).

Who Commits Crimes?   The model of the rational criminal provides three reasons why some people commit crimes. First, some people are relatively skillful at
committing crime and escaping punishment. For such people, the expected loot is
relatively large and the expected cost of crime is relatively small. Second, some people have a relatively low opportunity cost of time spent committing crime and time
spent in prison, so the expected cost of crime is relatively low. For example, the poor
may have a lower opportunity cost because they are unemployed or earn low wages.
Third, some people have less respect for society and are less averse to committing
crimes, so they need a relatively small net return to make crime worthwhile. For
most people, the moral anguish associated with crime is large enough to make crime
unattractive at almost any price.

The Crime-Supply Curve

The model of the rational criminal can be used to derive the supply curve for burglary.
The supply curve shows the relationship between the net return or "price" of burglary
and the number of burglaries committed.

FIGURE 22–4   **The Supply Curve for Burglary**

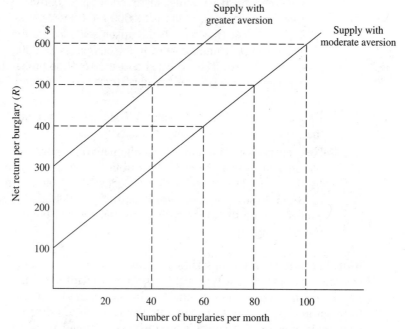

The supply curve shows the number of burglaries for different net returns (R) on crime. It has a positive intercept because of anguish cost and is positively sloped because an increase in the net return increases the number of burglars and increases the number of burglaries per burglar. An increase in the aversion to crime shifts the supply curve upward.

Figure 22–4 shows a city's supply curve for burglary. The horizontal axis measures the number of burglaries committed in the city per month, and the vertical axis measures the net return (R) of burglary. The supply curve for moderate aversion has a positive intercept of $100 because of anguish cost: for the first burglary, the net return must be high enough to exceed the anguish cost of the first burglary ($100). The curve is positively sloped: as the net return on burglary increases, more burglaries are committed because (1) the net return exceeds the anguish cost for more potential criminals, so more people become burglars and (2) burglars commit more crimes per month. When the net return increases from 400 to 600, the number of burglaries increases from 60 per month to 100.

The supply curve shows the effects of crime-fighting policies on the crime rate. Suppose that the city increases its police force and thus increases the probability of a burglar being arrested. The increase in the probability of arrest decreases the net return on burglary, so the city moves down its supply curve to a lower crime rate. The crime rate decreases as (1) each criminal commits fewer offenses and (2) some criminals exit from the crime business because the net return of crime falls short of their anguish cost. Marginal criminals "go straight" if the return on crime is not high enough to offset their underlying aversion to crime.

The aggregate supply curve shifts when the underlying aversion to crime changes. In Figure 22–4, an increase in the aversion to committing crime shifts

the supply curve upward: there are fewer crimes at each net return. For example, the crime rate for a net return of $500 drops from 80 to 40. Because an individual's aversion to crime depends in part on age, changes in the age distribution of the population shift the supply curve. Young males commit more than their share of crimes. Therefore, a society with a relatively large number of young males will have relatively high crime rates. Recent shifts in the age distribution of the U.S. population have decreased the proportion of young males. As the proportion of the population in the crime-prone years decreased, crime rates fell.

Optimum Amount of Crime

Because crime prevention is costly, the optimum amount of crime is positive. In other words, it is rational to tolerate some crime. How much crime should be allowed?

Victim Cost and Prevention Cost

The social costs of crime can be divided into **victim cost** and **prevention cost**. The victims of property crime lose property and are sometimes injured in the process. Figure 22–5 shows total victim cost as a function of the number of burglaries. The victim-cost curve is positively sloped and linear, reflecting the assumption that the victim cost per burglary is independent of the number of burglaries: if the number of burglaries doubles, victim cost also doubles.

Although society can decrease crime by decreasing the net return on burglary, crime prevention is costly. There are a number of options for crime prevention:

1. **Hardening the target.** Victims can decrease the expected loot by decreasing the probability of successful burglary (e.g., installing locks and using guard dogs).

2. **Increased probability of arrest.** The police can increase the expected cost of crime by increasing the probability of arrest (e.g., hiring more police officers).

3. **Increased probability of imprisonment.** The criminal justice system can increase the expected cost of crime by increasing the probabilities of conviction (e.g., hiring more investigators to gather evidence on crime).

4. **Increased severity of punishment.** The criminal justice system can increase the expected cost of crime by lengthening prison sentences (e.g., building more prison cells).

5. **Increased value of legal opportunities.** Society can increase the attractiveness of legal activity by increasing the job skills of potential criminals, thus increasing their legal wages. As the opportunity cost of crime increases, the net return on burglary decreases.

In Figure 22–5 the prevention-cost curve is negatively sloped. All of these preventive measures are costly, so the larger the number of crimes prevented (the fewer the burglaries committed), the higher the prevention cost. The prevention-cost curve increases in slope as the number of burglaries decreases, reflecting the assumption of

FIGURE 22–5   **The Optimum Number of Burglaries**

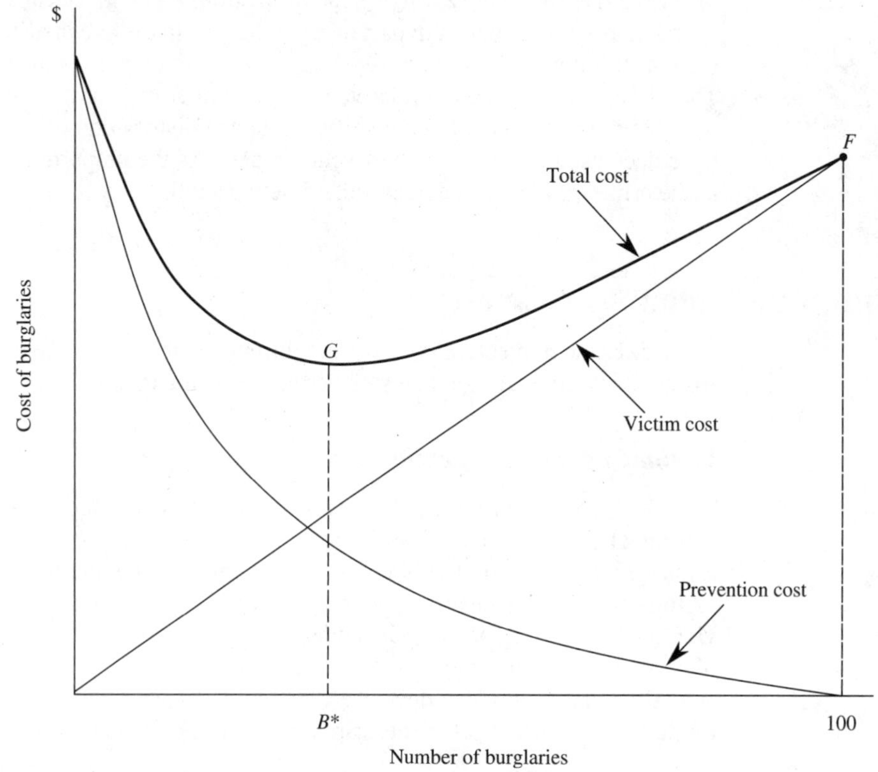

The total social cost of burglaries equals the sum of the cost incurred by victims and the cost of prevention. Victim cost increases at a constant rate if the cost per crime is constant. The prevention cost increases
rapidly as the number of burglaries decreases, a result of diminishing marginal returns. Total cost is minimized with B* burglaries (point G).

diminishing marginal returns to crime prevention: as prevention efforts increase and
the number of crimes decreases, it becomes progressively more difficult to prevent
more crime. For example, it is relatively easy to decrease the number of burglaries
from 100 to 99, but more difficult to decrease the number from 11 to 10.

The total cost of crime is the sum of the victim cost and the prevention cost.
In Figure 22–5, the total-cost curve is U-shaped, reflecting the trade-offs between
victim and prevention cost. Suppose that a city starts with zero prevention cost, so
it has 100 burglaries per day and the total cost of crime is the victim cost (point
F). The city could decrease the number of burglaries and decrease victim cost by
spending a small amount on prevention (e.g., hardening targets, lengthening prison
sentences, improving legal opportunities). By doing so, it would decrease the total
cost of crime: starting from point *F,* the savings in victim cost would exceed the
increase in prevention cost, so the city would move down the total-cost curve. The
total cost of crime is minimized at point *G*, so the optimum crime rate is *B**.

How does the city persuade burglars to commit the optimum number of burglaries (*B**)? The city would use its crime prevention resources to decrease the net

return to burglary to the point at which burglars commit B^* burglaries per day. In other words, the city picks the point on the burglary-supply curve and invests resources to bring the net return down to the necessary level.

Marginal Cost and Variation in Optimum Crime Levels

The optimum crime rate can also be derived from the marginal-cost curves underlying the total-cost curve in Figure 22–5. In Figure 22–6, the lower horizontal line shows the marginal victim cost for burglary, defined as the increase in victim cost per additional burglary (the slope of the total victim cost curve in Figure 22–5). This horizontal cost curve reflects the assumption that the cost per burglary victim is constant. The negatively sloped curve shows the marginal prevention cost, defined as the change in prevention cost per unit change in the number of crimes (the slope of the prevention-cost curve in Figure 22–5). It is negatively sloped because there are diminishing returns to crime prevention: the first unit of crime prevention (decreasing the number of crimes from 100 to 99) has a relatively low marginal cost; the last unit of crime prevention (decreasing the number of crimes from 1 to 0) has a high marginal cost.

The optimum amount of crime is shown by the intersection of the marginal-victim-cost curve and the marginal-prevention-cost curve. Starting with 100 burglaries, the marginal victim cost for burglary exceeds the marginal cost of prevention,

FIGURE 22–6   Marginal Victim and Prevention Costs and the Optimum Crime Level

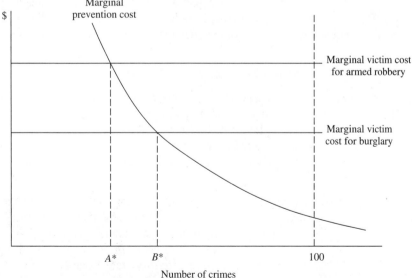

The optimum crime level is where the marginal victim cost equals the marginal prevention cost (B^* for burglaries and A^* for armed robberies). The optimum number of robberies is smaller because robbery has a higher victim cost.

so it is sensible to deter the 100th crime. Prevention is efficient as long as the marginal victim cost exceeds the marginal prevention cost, so the optimum burglary rate is B^*.

The marginal-cost curves explain why optimum crime rates vary across crimes. Suppose burglary and armed robbery have the same prevention cost, but different victim costs: the victims of armed robbery are often injured during the crime, so armed robbery has a higher marginal victim cost. In Figure 22–6, the optimum crime rate for robbery (A^*) is less than the optimum crime rate for burglary: more resources are invested in robbery prevention because the savings in victim cost per robbery are higher. Optimum crime rates also differ because of differences in prevention cost: crimes with higher marginal prevention costs have higher optimum crime rates, everything else being equal.

The same arguments can be used to explain why crime rates are higher in some central-city areas. These areas have large concentrations of poor and unemployed people, so the opportunity cost of crime is relatively low and the number of potential criminals is relatively large. Given the plentiful supply of criminals, the marginal prevention cost is relatively high. If the marginal victim cost is the same throughout the metropolitan area, the optimum crime rate is higher in the central city.

Crime Prevention Activities

This section discusses some of the details of crime prevention, exploring the effects of various "carrot" and "stick" approaches to preventing crime. The first part of the section discusses carrot policies: by increasing the value of legal opportunities, the government rewards people who choose legal activities over crime. The second part of the section shows how potential victims can protect themselves from crime. The final four parts examine stick policies: by increasing the likelihood and severity of punishment, the government deters crime by penalizing criminals.

Increasing the Value of Legal Opportunities

One approach to preventing crime is to increase the value of legal opportunities. This can be accomplished in a number of ways, including education, job training, and government employment. Chapter 13 (Poverty and Public Policy) describes several programs that provide education and training to the poor. The discussion generated three general conclusions about the effects of the various antipoverty policies on crime rates:

1. Because crime rates are lower among teenagers who stay in school longer and get better grades, programs that increase the amount of schooling and increase scholastic achievement decrease crime rates. For example, the Perry Preschool Programs increased high school completion rates and decreased arrest rates: compared to a control group, program participants had higher high school completion rates (67 percent versus 49 percent) and lower arrest rates (by a margin of 40 percent).

2. Some of the youth job-training programs (e.g., Job Corps and Youth Employment Demonstration Projects) increase earnings and decrease crime rates.

3. The job-training programs for ex-addicts and ex-offenders have had mixed results. For example, the National Supported Work Demonstration decreased the crime rates of ex-addicts, but had relatively small effects on ex-offenders.

What is the relationship between unemployment and crime? Freeman (1983) summarizes the evidence from dozens of studies of the relationship and comes to two basic conclusions. First, although there is a positive relationship between crime and unemployment, the relationship is relatively weak. Second, the crime rates of first-time offenders are relatively sensitive to the unemployment rate. This conclusion is consistent with the results of Fleisher (1966) and Phillips, Votey, and Maxwell (1972), both of whom found a strong relationship between youth unemployment and crime rates. A similar conclusion was reached by the National Bureau of Economic Research (NBER) study of youth unemployment (discussed in Chapter 12): teenage crime rates were higher in cities with fewer legal opportunities.

Victims as Crime Fighters

Potential victims can discourage crime by decreasing the thief's expected benefit. There are two strategies for decreasing the expected loot: hardening the target and decreasing the market value of the stolen property.

Hardening the Target.   The potential victim can harden the target by investing in protective devices. Alice's options for bike protection are listed in Table 22–4. If she does not spend any money on protection, there is a 30 percent chance that her $100 bike will be stolen, so her expected loss from theft is $30 (0.30 times $100). If she locks her bike with a flimsy lock, the probability of theft drops to 10 percent; if she locks her bike with a sturdy lock, the probability drops to 2 percent. If she hires an armed guard, the probability of theft is zero.

What is the optimum level of protection? Alice's objective is to minimize the total cost of protecting her bike, equal to the sum of protection cost and the expected loss from theft. She minimizes total cost with the flimsy lock: her protection cost is

TABLE 22–4   Protective Measures for $100 Bicycle

Protective Action	Protection Cost	Probability of Theft	Expected Theft Cost	Total Cost
No protection	$ 0	0.30	$30	$30
Flimsy lock	11	0.10	10	21
Sturdy lock	24	0.02	2	26
Armed guard	80	0.00	0	80

$11 and the expected loss is $10, for a total cost of $21. Although a sturdy lock would decrease the probability of theft, the marginal benefit of the additional protection (the $8 decrease in the expected cost) is less than the marginal cost (the $13 increase in protection cost). Alice tolerates a 10 percent chance of having her bike stolen because the marginal cost of additional protection exceeds the marginal benefit.

The optimum level of protection depends on the value of the item being protected. If Alice replaces her $100 bike with a $200 bike, she will upgrade her protection to a sturdy lock: the switch to the more expensive bike doubles the expected loss from theft, so the marginal benefit of the sturdy lock ($16) exceeds its marginal cost ($13). In general, people with more property to protect spend more money on protection.

How do people and firms harden crime targets? Most people lock their cars and houses, and some install burglar alarms. Purchasers of expensive car-stereo systems can buy plastic covers that make the stereos look cheap and unattractive. Most businesses keep their valuables in safes, and install alarms to deter robbers. Convenience stores keep their money in timed safes so clerks (and thieves) have access to a limited amount of cash.

Protection and Insurance.   How does insurance affect Alice's spending on protective measures? Suppose that she insures her $100 bicycle against theft, and there are no costs associated with filing a claim (no transactions cost and no deductible payment). If so, the total cost of leaving her bike unprotected is zero: every time her bike is stolen, she collects $100 from her insurance company and then buys a new bike. Therefore, Alice will leave her bike unprotected.

This is the **moral-hazard problem**. If Alice buys insurance, she reduces her own protective measures and is more likely to be victimized. The moral-hazard problem explains why many people do not lock their cars. According to the FBI, 80 percent of stolen cars are left unlocked, and 40 percent have the keys in the ignition. The moral-hazard problem also explains why most insurance policies have deductibles: the deductible increases the property owner's expected loss from theft, encouraging the owner to invest in protective measures. Recently, some insurance companies have tried to control the moral-hazard problem by providing free home-security systems to their policyholders.

Market Value of Loot.   Potential victims can also decrease the resale value of stolen property. As the resale value of the stolen property decreases, the net return from theft decreases, discouraging crime. A potential victim can decrease the likelihood of being victimized by making his property less valuable to criminals.

The resale value depends on how easily the loot can be identified as stolen property. A person who purchases stolen property is subject to prosecution for receiving stolen goods. Given the risks associated with buying stolen goods, a consumer is willing to pay less for a good that is easily identified as "hot." The more readily the stolen goods can be identified, the lower the resale value. The typical criminal sells his loot to a fencing operation and is paid between 20 percent and 50 percent of the legal market value of the goods.

Suppose that Natasha can steal either a hundred-dollar bill or an original painting with a legal market value of $100. What will she steal? The resale value of the painting is less than $100 because the purchaser of the painting could be arrested for the possession of stolen property. In contrast, the "resale" value of the cash is equal to its face value: given the number of hundred-dollar bills in circulation, it would be impossible to find and punish the person who "buys" the stolen hundred-dollar bill. Therefore, Natasha will steal the cash, not the painting.

How do potential victims facilitate the identification of stolen goods? In the Wild West, ranchers branded their cattle to discourage cattle rustling. More recently, ranchers have experimented with implanting microchips into cow hides to identify and locate stolen cattle. Many communities have developed programs under which residents mark their possessions with identification numbers (social security numbers, driver's license numbers) to discourage burglary. Participants in Operation Identification place warning labels in conspicuous places to inform potential burglars that "all items of value have been marked for ready identification."

The Police

The primary responsibility of the police is to arrest criminals. In the 1970s, the arrest ratio, defined as the number of arrests divided by the number of index crimes, was about 0.16 (Wilson, 1985). In other words, only about 16 percent of index crimes led to an arrest. From the criminal's perspective, the probability of being arrested for a crime is about 0.16. Changes in the arrest ratio affect crime rates. One rule of thumb is that the elasticity of property crime with respect to the probability of arrest is about -0.50: a 10 percent increase in the arrest ratio decreases the number of crimes by about 5 percent (see Ehrlich, 1972; Wilson and Boland, 1976; Bartel, 1979; Witte, 1980).

Police Patrol.   The police spend a lot of time patrolling streets and sidewalks. The idea behind patrol is that the police should be in a position to respond quickly when crime occurs. Does patrol deter crime? A number of studies have shown that car patrol does not have a significant effect on crime rates. In a famous experiment in Kansas City, the city increased patrolling activity in some neighborhoods and decreased patrolling in others. There were no significant changes in either arrest ratios or crime rates in any of the neighborhoods, suggesting that patrolling does not decrease crime. Other experiments have come to the same conclusion (Sherman, 1983).

Why doesn't car patrol work? One reason is that crime victims are slow to report crimes to the police. According to Sherman, the typical victim takes about 50 minutes to report the crime to police. Suppose that an increase in patrolling could decrease the response time of police (defined as the period of time between receiving a report of the crime and arriving on the scene) from 10 minutes to 2 minutes. If the typical victim takes 50 minutes to report the crime, the police could arrive on the crime scene 52 minutes after the crime is committed instead of 60 minutes. In either case, the criminal's trail is already cold, so the improved response time is unlikely to increase the arrest ratio. On the other hand, if the victim took only 1 minute to report the crime, an increase in patrolling could make a difference: the police would arrive 3 minutes after the crime instead of 11 minutes and would have a better chance of capturing the criminal.

What about foot patrol? A number of studies have shown that foot patrol can increase arrest ratios and deter crime. Police on foot patrol are constantly gathering information about the people and businesses in their territories. The foot-patrol officer knows who is arguing with whom, who is suddenly living beyond his means, and whose children are running amok. As a result, the foot-patrol officer is better equipped to prevent crimes and to solve crimes once they occur.

Police Investigation.   In addition to arresting criminals, police gather information for public prosecutors and the courts. The success of investigations is measured by the **clearance rate**, defined as the fraction of arrests that result in convictions. According to Forst (1983) about 32 percent of felony arrests result in conviction. The most important investigative task is to find eyewitnesses to the crime. One rule of thumb is that if the police provide two eyewitnesses to a crime, a conviction is virtually guaranteed.

Under the traditional investigative system, crimes are investigated by police detectives rather than patrol officers. The patrol officer usually makes the arrest, prepares a report on the crime, and then hands over the investigation to a detective.

Some police forces have experimented with alternative investigative systems. Under a **community service system**, each police officer is assigned a small territory and is responsible for both making arrests and investigating crimes. Instead of simply filing a report about the crime, the arresting officer finds eyewitnesses and gathers other evidence for prosecutors. The idea behind this system is that the local patrol officer has a great deal of information about his territory that would be useful in the investigation. There is some evidence that the community service approach increases clearance rates.

Other cities have experimented with different incentive systems. Under the traditional system, police rewards are based on the number of arrests, not on clearance rates or local crime rates. If police were rewarded for increasing clearance rates and decreasing crime rates, they might have a greater incentive to follow up arrests by gathering information and finding eyewitnesses. The city of Orange, California, has experimented with a system under which police salaries are tied to crime rates (see Reynolds, 1986).

The Court System

Forst (1983) shows how the court system handles a typical set of 100 felony arrests. His results are summarized in Figure 22–7. Only 9 of 100 felony arrests result in a prison sentence longer than a year. The process by which the 100 arrests are whittled down to nine imprisonments is as follows:

1. **Juvenile cases.** About one third of the offenses are committed by juveniles and are handled by the juvenile justice system. Little is known about the disposition of these cases.

FIGURE 22–7   Typical Disposition of 100 Felony Arrests, 1974–1984

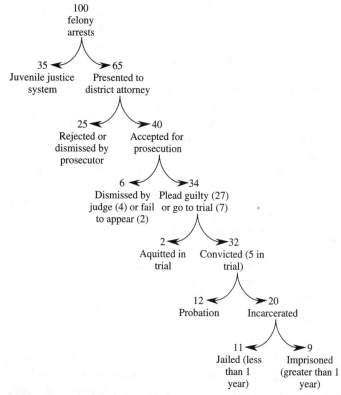

SOURCE: Brian Forst, "Prosecution and Sentencing," Chapter 10 in *Crime and Public Policy,* ed. James Q. Wilson (San Francisco: Institute for Contemporary Studies, 1983).

2. **Dismissed by prosecutor.** Of the 65 cases presented to the district attorney, 25 are dropped: most cases are dropped because of weak evidence; a small number of cases are dropped because the offense is trivial. Only about 1 percent of cases are dropped because of violations of rules concerning arrest procedures and evidence.

3. **Dismissed by judge.** Of the 40 cases accepted by the district attorney, 4 are dismissed by the judge, usually because the evidence is insufficient or the offense is trivial.

4. **Disappearing defendant.** Two cases are eventually dropped because the defendant disappears after being released on bond, personal recognizance, or third-party custody.

5. **Plea bargaining.** Of the 34 remaining cases, 27 of the defendants plead guilty, usually to a lesser charge.

6. **Trial acquittal.** Of the seven cases that go to trial, two result in acquittal and five result in a guilty verdict.

7. **Probation.** Of the 32 defendants found guilty (27 from plea bargains and 5 in trials), 12 receive probation (supervised release).

8. **Jail versus prison.** Twenty convicts are incarcerated. Eleven serve time in jails (receiving sentences of less than one year), and nine are imprisoned (receiving sentences of more than one year).

Plea Bargaining.   As shown in Figure 22–7, of the 32 cases that result in conviction, only 5 cases are actually decided by a trial. The other 27 cases are resolved through the **plea-bargaining process**.

The district attorney has broad powers to negotiate with the accused over the criminal charge and the resulting punishment. Under the plea-bargaining process, the district attorney reduces the criminal charge and the accused pleads guilty to the lesser charge. The plea bargain generates benefits for both sides: the district attorney gets a certain conviction, and the defendant receives a relatively light sentence. In addition, both parties avoid the cost of a criminal trial.

Table 22–5 provides a simple example of the plea-bargaining process. Suppose that Bonnie is accused of armed robbery, a crime that carries a three-year prison sentence. Given the evidence in the case, both Bonnie and the district attorney (DA) agree that there is a 50 percent chance that a criminal trial will produce a guilty verdict. Therefore, the expected penalty from the armed robbery charge is 1.5 years (3 years times 0.50). The alternative to a trial on the robbery charge is a plea of guilty to petit larceny, a crime that carries a one-year prison sentence.

Should Bonnie accept the plea bargain? Suppose that a criminal trial would cost Bonnie $1,000 in legal fees, but the plea bargain would cost only $200. She would be better off with a guilty plea for two reasons. First, she saves $800 in legal costs ($1,000 − $200). Second, the expected prison sentence is shorter (1 year versus 1.5 years). If the DA offers this plea bargain, Bonnie will accept it.

Should the district attorney offer the plea bargain or pursue a trial on the charge of robbery? Suppose that a criminal trial would cost taxpayers $2,000, but the plea bargain would cost only $300. From the perspective of law-abiding citizens who wish to see Bonnie punished for her crime, the plea bargain produces good news and bad news. The good news is that the plea bargain saves taxpayers $1,700. The bad news is that the plea bargain decreases Bonnie's expected prison time by half a year. If society is willing to give up half a year of punishment to save $1,700, the district attorney should offer the plea bargain.

TABLE 22–5   Plea Bargaining

	Armed Robbery	*Petit Larceny*
Penalty	3 years	1 year
Probability of conviction	0.50	1.0
Expected penalty	1.5 years	1.0 year
Court costs	$2,000	$300
Defense costs	$1,000	$200

Under what circumstances will Bonnie and the DA not agree to a plea bargain, but instead bring the case to trial? Suppose that both sides are optimistic about their chances of winning the court battle. Bonnie assumes that the probability of a guilty verdict is very low (10 percent), so the expected penalty from a robbery trial is 0.30 years, compared to a certain penalty of 1 year under the proposed plea bargain. She will demand a trial if the decrease in expected punishment (0.70 years) is worth at least $800 (the increase in legal cost if the case goes to trial). If the DA assumes that the probability of a guilty verdict is very high (90 percent), the expected penalty from a trial is 2.7 years, compared to a certain penalty of 1 year under the proposed plea bargain. The DA will seek a trial if the extra 1.7 years in expected punishment is worth at least $1,700. In this example, Bonnie's case will go to trial because the two parties disagree about the likely outcome of the trial.

Proof of Guilt.   In any justice system, two types of errors are inevitable. First, some innocent people are found guilty and punished for crimes they did not commit (a **false positive result**). Second, some guilty people are found innocent and escape punishment (a **false negative result**).

The U.S. courts have developed a set of rules that place the burden of proof on the shoulders of the prosecutors. To convict a person of a crime, the state must prove the person's guilt "beyond a reasonable doubt." Under the reasonable-doubt rule, the accused is presumed innocent until proven guilty, and close cases are decided in favor of defendants. The rule decreases the frequency of false positives (fewer innocents are convicted), but increases the frequency of false negatives (more guilty people are acquitted). In other words, the courts err on the side of innocence rather than guilt.

Other court systems err on the side of guilt rather than innocence. If the accused is presumed guilty until proven innocent, the burden of proof is on the shoulders of the accused. Under this type of rule, close cases are decided in favor of the state. The adoption of this rule would increase the number of false positives (more innocents are convicted) and decrease the number of false negatives (fewer guilty are acquitted).

The Principle of Marginal Deterrence

The penalties for various crimes are determined by legislators, prosecutors, and judges. Legislatures pass laws that establish minimum and maximum penalties, providing guidelines for prosecutors and judges. In the plea-bargaining process, the prosecutors negotiate with suspects over criminal charges and penalties and then pass on their recommendations to judges, who usually accept the plea bargains. If a case goes to trial and the defendant is found guilty, the presiding judge sets the penalty.

In determining the penalties for different crimes, legislators and judges are guided by the **principle of marginal deterrence**. According to this principle, the penalty for a particular crime should depend on the seriousness of the crime, with greater penalties for more serious crimes.

A Numerical Example.   The principle of marginal deterrence can be explained with a simple example. Suppose that a state initially has a one-year penalty for burglary and a two-year penalty for armed robbery. Robbery carries a greater penalty because robbery has a higher social cost: the victims of robbery are often injured or killed, while the victims of burglary simply lose their property.

Emil is a career criminal who must decide whether to commit a robbery or a burglary. He will commit the crime that provides the larger net benefit. His options are shown in Table 22–6. Robbery generates a greater expected loot ($2,000 versus $1,700), but also carries a higher expected cost ($1,600 versus $800). The expected net benefit of burglary is $900 compared to $400 for armed robbery, so Emil picks burglary rather than robbery.

The state's penalties for robbery and burglary provide a marginal deterrent for robbery, the more serious crime. In deciding on the level of crime, Emil weighs the marginal benefit and marginal cost associated with upgrading from burglary to robbery. The marginal benefit of upgrading is the increase in the expected loot ($300). The marginal cost is the increase in the expected prison cost ($800). Since the marginal benefit is less than the marginal cost, Emil sticks with burglary. Society deters Emil from the more serious crime by imposing a larger penalty on robbery.

Suppose that the state passes a law that equalizes the penalties for burglary and robbery at two years. The increase in the burglary penalty decreases the expected net benefit from burglary to $100 ($1,700 − $1,600), but does not affect the net benefit from robbery. Since the net benefit of robbery now exceeds the net benefit of burglary, Emil switches to robbery. The equalization of penalties eliminates the marginal deterrent: the marginal benefit of moving from burglary to robbery is still $300, but the marginal cost of upgrading (the increase in the expected penalty) is zero. If Emil receives the same penalties for the two crimes, he will commit the more lucrative crime. The equalization of penalties eliminates the marginal deterrent effect, so Emil switches to the crime with a higher social cost.

The General Effects of Equalizing Penalties.   Figure 22–8 shows the effects of increasing the burglary penalty on the number of burglaries and robberies. Suppose that initially the two crimes have the same net return (R'). Given the two supply curves, there are B' burglaries and A' armed robberies. When the state increases the

---

TABLE 22–6   **Marginal Deterrence**

	Armed Robbery	Burglary (1 year)	Burglary (2 years)
Expected loot	$2,000	$1,700	$1,700
Probability of punishment	0.10	0.10	0.10
Prison sentence	2 years	1 year	2 years
Annual opportunity cost of prison	$8,000	$8,000	$8,000
Expected prison cost	$1,600	$800	$1,600
Net benefit	$400	$900	$100

FIGURE 22–8   Response to an Increase in the Burglary Penalty

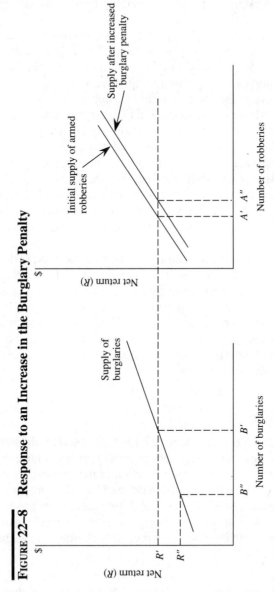

In the initial equilibrium, both burglary and robbery have a net return of R', so there are B' burglaries and A' robberies. A decrease in the net return of burglaries to R'' decreases the number of burglaries to B'' (movement down the supply curve) and increases the number of robberies to A'' (shift of the supply curve and unchanged net return to robbery). The increase in robberies is less than the decrease in burglaries because some burglars "go straight."

penalty for burglary, the net return drops to R'', decreasing the number of burglaries to B''. The decrease in the net return to burglary causes some criminals to upgrade to robbery, so the robbery supply curve shifts to the right. The net return to robbery is still R', so the number of robberies increases to A''. Because the increase in the burglary penalty weakens the marginal deterrent, some criminals upgrade to the more serious crime.

The increase in the burglary penalty decreases the total number of crimes: the decrease in the number of burglaries (from B' to B'') exceeds the increase in the number of robberies (from A' to A''). This occurs because the increased penalty causes some burglars to stop committing crimes. In other words, only some of the burglars who change their behavior shift to robbery.

Is society better or worse off under the higher burglary penalty? It depends on the social cost of the two crimes. Because victims are often injured or killed in robberies, the social cost of robbery exceeds the social cost of burglary. According to Phillips and Votey (1979) the social cost of the typical armed robbery is about $5,400 and the social cost of the typical burglary is only about $900. In Figure 22–8, the increase in the number of robberies is about one fourth the decrease in burglaries. If the social cost of robbery is six times the social cost of burglary, the total social cost of crime increases. In this case, the increase in the burglary penalty increases the social cost of crime.

There are two lessons for crime fighters. First, because stiffer penalties provide a marginal deterrent, an increase in the penalty for one crime causes some criminals to upgrade to a higher level crime. Second, policymakers could use this approach to estimate the effects of changes in penalties on the social cost of crime. To do so, they would need information on the social cost of different crimes and the criminals' responses to the change in penalties. The principal questions are: how many criminals would be deterred; how many would upgrade to a higher-level crime; and how many would downgrade to a lower-level crime?

The Prison System

The prison system has four functions. The first is the **rehabilitation** function, which is based on the idea that society can use education and counseling to persuade convicts to "go straight." The second function is **deterrence**: by punishing convicts, society makes the threat of punishment credible, discouraging other people from committing crime. The third function is **incapacitation**: prisons isolate criminals from their potential victims, decreasing crime by taking criminals out of circulation. A final function is **retribution** or revenge: law-abiding citizens like to see criminals punished for their actions.

The Rehabilitation Function.   According to the popular view, society can rehabilitate convicts. The purpose of education and counseling programs is to provide convicts with the skills and the desires to become lawful citizens. The success of a particular rehabilitation program is measured by its effect on the **recidivism rate**, defined as the percentage of convicts that are arrested for another crime after they leave prison. The overall recidivism rate is about 80 percent: four fifths of convicts are arrested after they leave prison.

Do rehabilitation programs work? According to Wilson (1975) there have been over 200 studies of rehabilitation programs, none of which has been able to demonstrate that rehabilitation decreases recidivism rates. The studies evaluated the effects of several types of rehabilitation schemes, including education and job-training programs, work-release programs, and counseling programs. The rehabilitation programs did not affect the recidivism rates of either juveniles or adults. Given the results of these studies, there is good reason to be pessimistic about the prospects for using rehabilitation to reduce crime.

Why doesn't rehabilitation work? First, it is difficult to change the antisocial attitudes that make criminals relatively receptive to crime. Second, by the time a criminal reaches the rehabilitation stage (i.e., by the time the criminal is imprisoned), he is firmly committed to crime. If the probability of being imprisoned for a particular crime is 2 percent, the typical criminal has committed 50 crimes by the time he is imprisoned. Third, it is difficult to make legal opportunities more profitable than crime: crime pays, and it is difficult to increase the job skills of an adult criminal.

The **parole system** is based on the principle of rehabilitation. Under the parole system, a convict stays in prison until the parole board declares that he is rehabilitated. The rehabilitated convict is released and serves the remainder of his prison term under the supervision of a parole officer. A parolee cannot get married or own a car, and must receive the approval of his parole officer before borrowing money or changing residence.

Most parole boards have large caseloads and base most parole decisions on simple rules of thumb. One popular rule is that a convict is released after serving either three years or one third of the prison sentence, whichever is shorter. Studies of the parole system have generated mixed results. In some states, parolees have lower rates of recidivism than convicts who serve out their entire sentence. In other states, there is no measurable difference between the recidivism rates of parolees and other convicts.

The Deterrence Function.   A number of studies have shown that the threat of imprisonment decreases crime rates. An increase in either the probability of imprisonment or the length of the prison term increases the expected cost of crime, decreasing the number of crimes.

There is evidence that an increase in the *certainty* of punishment provides a greater deterrent than an increase in the *severity* of punishment. In other words, an increase in the probability of imprisonment deters more crime than an increase in the length of the prison term. For example, Bartel (1979) estimates that the elasticity of the supply of crime with respect to the probability of punishment is about -0.30: a 10 percent increase in the chance of imprisonment decreases the crime rate by 3 percent. On the other hand, the elasticity of supply with respect to the length of imprisonment is close to zero.

Why don't longer prison sentences deter crime? Although an increase in the penalty may discourage crime by increasing the expected cost of crime, it may simultaneously encourage crime for three reasons:

FIGURE 22–9   Effects of Increased Punishment on Crime

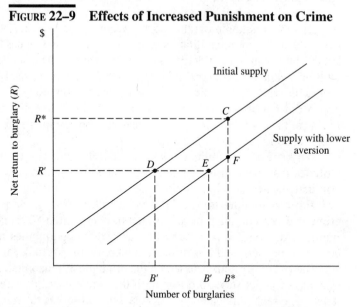

The increase in the severity of punishment decreases the net return from R^* to R', causing a move from C to D. If a longer prison term hardens the criminal, her aversion to crime will decrease, shifting the supply curve to the right and causing a move from point D to E: crime rises close to its original level (B'' is close to B^*). If the criminal also learns more in prison, she will have a higher probability of success when she gets out, causing a move from E to F (increasing the crime rate to its original level).

1. **Hardening the criminal.** Perhaps a long prison sentence hardens the convict, making antisocial behavior more likely. In Figure 22–9, a longer prison term decreases the net return to burglary from R^* to R', causing movement down the initial supply curve (from point C to D) and decreasing the number of crimes from B^* to B'. If criminals are hardened by longer prison terms, their anguish cost decreases, shifting the supply curve to the right and causing a move from point D to E. The net effect is a small decrease in the crime rate (from B^* to B'').

2. **Prison schooling**. If prison allows a criminal to learn the tricks of the trade from other criminals, a longer prison term means a more educated and skillful criminal. The postprison probability of success increases, increasing the net return from crime. In Figure 22–9, the prison-schooling effect causes a move from point E to F, restoring the original crime level (B^*).

3. **Discount rates.** If criminals are "present-oriented," they are more concerned with instant gratification than the long-term consequences of crime (imprisonment). The perceived cost of an additional year in prison (four years instead of three) is small relative to the benefits of today's crime. In formal terms, if criminals have large discount rates, the perceived cost of an additional year of imprisonment is relatively small in

present-value terms, so the additional year has a relatively small deterrent effect.

The Incapacitation Function.   The third function of the prison system is to take criminals out of circulation. An obvious way to reduce crime is to lock up potential criminals. The practical policy issue is whether the benefit of incapacitation (the decrease in crime) exceeds the cost (the cost of running the prison). If each prisoner costs the state about $18,000 per year, the question is whether a one-year prison term decreases the social cost of crime by at least $18,000. If the victim cost per burglary is $900, incapacitation is worthwhile if the burglar would have committed at least 20 burglaries per year. If the victim cost per armed robbery is $5,400, incapacitation is worthwhile if the robber would have committed four robberies per year.

Wilson and Boland (1976) estimate the effects of increased prison sentences on crime rates. They estimate the effects of a mandatory two-year prison sentence on felony crime rates. Underlying their computations (shown in Table 22–7) are the following assumptions:

1. **Probability of conviction.** The probability of being convicted for a felony crime is 10 percent.
2. **Base sentencing policy.** The basis for comparison is a world in which no convicted felons spend time in prison.
3. **Mandatory sentence.** The new sentencing policy is that every person convicted of a felony spends two years in prison.
4. **Incapacitation effect**. The rehabilitation and deterrence effects of prisons are ignored. The changes in crime rates are caused exclusively by the incapacitation effect.

As shown in Table 22–7, the switch to the mandatory two-year sentence decreases crime rates by different amounts, depending on the number of crimes the typical criminal commits. If the typical criminal commits five crimes per year, the change to two-year sentences decreases the crime rate by 50 percent. If the typical

---

TABLE 22–7   **Incarceration and Crime Rates**

Crimes per Offender	Percent Reduction from Two-Year Sentence
5	50.0
10	66.7
20	80.0
50	90.9

SOURCE: James Q. Wilson and Barbara Boland, "Crime," in *The Urban Predicament,* ed. William Gorham and Nathan Glazer (Washington, D.C.: Urban Institute, 1976).

convict commits 20 crimes per year, the decrease in crime is 80 percent. The table shows that the more prolific the criminal, the stronger the incapacitation effect.

To achieve the crime reductions listed in Table 22–7, society would have to spend more on police, courts, and prisons. To increase the probability of conviction to 10 percent, more would have to be spent catching and prosecuting criminals. If all convicts are sent to prison for two years, prison expenditures must increase. Would the additional spending be worthwhile? If the typical criminal commits a large number of offenses, the reduction in crime would be relatively large, so the benefits of the incapacitation program may exceed its cost.

Illegal Commodities and Victimless Crime

The fact that a product is illegal does not prevent people from consuming it. Simon and Witte (1982) estimated the sales volume of a number of illegal goods and services. Their upper-bound estimates for 1974 are as follows: $11.6 billion was spent on heroin, $9.1 billion on cocaine, $5.2 billion on marijuana, $2.2 billion on illegal gambling, $3.2 billion on loansharking, $14.8 billion on prostitution, and $16.7 billion on other illegal goods. These figures suggest that, on average, households spent about $785 per year on illegal goods and services.

Why are some goods outlawed? First, lawmakers assume that consumers are irrational about some products: a gambler is unable to make rational choices in the heat of a gambling frenzy, and a drug user is incapable of rational thought in the middle of a drug trip. Second, the consumption of certain goods is assumed to be contagious. Society protects itself from a drug "epidemic" for the same reasons that it protects itself from a polio epidemic. Third, drug addiction is often passed from parent to child, through either physiological or psychological means. By outlawing certain drugs, the government protects children from drug dependence. Fourth, lawmakers assume that drug use leads to unemployment, poverty, and welfare dependence.

Product Illegality and Production Costs

A firm selling an illegal product differs from a lawful firm in two ways. First, there are large penalties if the illegal activity is discovered by the police. The participants may be fined or imprisoned, and the assets of the firm may be seized. Second, contracts with illegal enterprises are not legally enforceable, so creditors cannot be certain that they will be paid for services rendered. These two characteristics make the production cost of the illegal firm relatively high.

The threat of punishment increases wages. To compensate for the risk of illegal activity, the firm must pay its workers a wage premium. Just as a coal miner is paid more than a person in a safe, clean job, a worker in an illegal enterprise is paid more than a person in a legal job. In addition, the firm pays a relatively high wage to prevent "squealing." If workers earn relatively high wages, they have more to lose if the firm's illegal activities are discovered, so workers have greater incentive to conceal those activities.

The threat of punishment also affects the way that a firm organizes its production process. To maintain secrecy, the firm controls the flow of information about its activities. One way to control information is to segment the work force into small work groups and limit the information that passes from one group to another. For example, heroin passes through many groups on the way from the poppy field to the consumer (importer, processor, wholesaler, distributor), and each group has little knowledge of the activities of the other groups in the chain. These evasion techniques add to the production cost.

The illegal activity also has a relatively high capital cost. A loan to an illegal enterprise is relatively risky for three reasons. First, contracts are not legally enforceable, so lenders can never be certain that they will be repaid. Second, given its desire for secrecy, the illegal firm cannot provide the lender with financial information. Since the lender cannot assess the profitability of the illegal enterprise, the loan is relatively risky. Finally, given the risk of confiscation, the illegal firm does not have any real collateral, so the lender may be unable to collect if the borrower defaults on the loan. Because a loan to an illegal enterprise is relatively risky, the lender charges a relatively high interest rate, so the production cost is relatively high.

Product Illegality and Price

Figure 22–10 shows the effect of product illegality on the market for drugs. Suppose that a particular drug is suddenly declared illegal. The cost of producing and distributing the drug increases, shifting the supply curve to the left: at every price, less is supplied. The illegal status of the drug also affects its demand curve. The total cost of consuming the illegal drug equals the sum of the market price and the expected penalty for consuming the drug. For example, if there is a 2 percent chance of a $1,000 penalty for drug consumption, the expected penalty is $20 per dose (0.02 times $1,000). When the product is declared illegal, the demand curve shifts downward by the expected penalty. The penalty for drug consumption is like a tax: it shifts the demand curve by the amount of the implicit tax.

If enforcement efforts are concentrated on the supply side of the drug market, the prohibition of drugs increases the market price. In Figure 22–10, the shift of the supply curve is larger than the shift of the demand curve, reflecting the assumption that the expected penalty for the production and sale of drugs is large relative to the expected penalty for consumption. The price rises from P' to P'', and the equilibrium quantity decreases from K' to K''. By declaring the drug illegal, the government increases the price and decreases the quantity consumed.

What are the implications for the consumers of illegal goods? Consumers pay higher prices for the illegal goods and services. The typical heroin addict, for example, pays about $60 per day for his habit, about 30 times the amount he would pay if heroin were legal. The same analysis applies to other types of illegal goods. The patrons of loansharks pay higher interest rates because the loanshark must be compensated for the risk of imprisonment and the cost of concealing his activities. Similarly, gamblers face lower odds (lower expected returns) because bookies face higher risks and incur a large concealment cost.

FIGURE 22–10   **Effects of Increased Punishment on Crime**

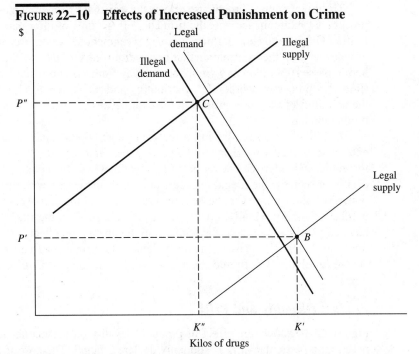

When a commodity is declared illegal, the cost of producing and selling it increases, shifting the supply curve upward. Consumer penalties increase the net cost of consuming the good, shifting the demand curve downward. The equilibrium moves from point *B* to *C*. The supplier penalty is large relative to the consumer penalty, so the supply shift is larger than the demand shift, and the price increases from *P'* to *P''*. The equilibrium quantity decreases from *K'* to *K''*.

Drugs and Property Crime

There is a positive correlation between drug use and criminal activity. According to Wilson (1975), between 25 percent and 67 percent of property crime is committed by drug addicts. Despite this high correlation, the causal link between drug consumption and crime is not fully understood. Although there is evidence that some addicts support their drug habits with property crime, it is unclear just how much addict crime is committed solely to support drug habits.

Will the enforcement of drug laws increase total property crime? In Figure 22–10, the illegality of drugs increases price and decreases the quantity consumed. The increase in price is relatively large because (1) the leftward shift of the demand curve is relatively small and (2) the demand curve is relatively steep (the price elasticity of demand for drugs is relatively low). Because the price rises by a relatively large amount, total expenditures on drugs (price times quantity) increase. If drug addicts support their habits with property crime, the increase in total expenditures increases property crime.

Silverman and Sprull (1977) estimate the effects of changes in drug prices on property crime. They estimate that the price elasticity of demand for heroin is about −0.27, so a 50 percent increase in the price of heroin would decrease the quantity of heroin demanded by about 13 percent and increase total drug expenditures by about

30 percent. Because only a portion of property crime is drug-related, the resulting increase in property crime (14 percent) is less than the increase in drug expenditures.

There are two implications from this analysis. First, there is often a trade-off between drug control and property crime. Because a supply-side policy increases total expenditures on drugs, property crime is likely to increase. Although drug-enforcement policies decrease drug consumption and thus decrease the social cost associated with drug abuse, they also increase property crime. The difficult policy question is whether the benefit (the decrease in the social cost of drug abuse) exceeds the cost (increased property crime). The second implication is that demand-side policies do not have the same trade-offs. Since a demand-side policy simply shifts the demand curve downward, decreasing both the price and quantity of drugs, it decreases total expenditure on drugs and thus decreases drug-related property crime.

Summary

1. The facts on crime are collected by the FBI (from local police departments) and the Justice Department (from victimization surveys).
2. Victimization rates vary with income, place of residence, and race. Victimization rates are generally higher for the poor, racial minorities, and the residents of central cities.
3. The direct costs of crime include injury cost and property losses. The indirect costs include protection cost and the cost of the criminal justice system. According to one study, the total cost of crime in 1983 was $2,331 per household.
4. The optimum amount of crime is where the marginal victim cost equals the marginal protection cost. Crimes differ in victim and prevention costs, so optimum crime rates vary.
5. A rational person commits a property crime if the net return on crime is large enough to offset her underlying aversion to crime.
   a. The expected benefit depends on the monetary value of the loot and the probability of success.
   b. The expected cost depends on the probability of imprisonment, the opportunity cost of prison time, and the length of the prison sentence.
   c. The opportunity cost of crime is the income forgone in a legal job.
   d. The net return is the expected benefit (the expected loot less the expected cost) minus the money that could be earned in a legal job.
   e. Crime is rational if the net return exceeds the anguish cost.
6. The supply curve for crime shows the relationship between the net return and the number of crimes. Society determines the net return to crime, thus picking a point on the supply curve.
   a. Investments in education and job training increase the value of legal opportunities.
   b. Potential victims can decrease the expected benefit of crime by hardening the target or decreasing the resale value of the loot.

c. The police can increase the expected cost of crime by arresting more criminals.

d. The courts can increase the expected cost of crime by increasing the likelihood and severity of punishment.

7. The supply curve shifts as a result of demographic and social changes.

 a. As the share of the population in the crime-prone years increases, the supply curve shifts to the right.

 b. Social changes that increase the underlying aversion to crime shift the supply curve upward.

8. Police are responsible for arresting criminals and investigating crimes.

 a. The arrest ratio is the fraction of crimes that lead to an arrest, currently about 0.16. The elasticity of crime with respect to the probability of arrest is about -0.50.

 b. The success of police investigation is measured by the clearance ratio, the fraction of arrests that lead to conviction. The most important investigative task is to find eyewitnesses to the crime.

 c. Although an increase in car patrols decreases the police response time, it does not affect arrest rates and crime rates because victims are slow to report crimes. Foot patrol is more effective because the police gather information about people and potential criminals on their beats.

9. The courts are responsible for determining guilt and setting penalties.

 a. About 9 in 100 felony arrests result in prison sentences. Many cases are dropped because the offense is trivial or the evidence is insufficient. About one third of arrests lead to convictions, but most convicts receive probation or short jail terms.

 b. Most criminal cases are resolved through plea bargaining: the district attorney reduces the criminal charge and the accused pleads guilty to the lesser charge. From the perspective of society, plea bargaining is efficient if the benefit (the savings in court costs) exceeds the cost (the decrease in the punishment of convicts).

 c. Two types of errors are inevitable in the criminal justice system: a false positive occurs when an innocent person is found guilty, and a false negative occurs when a guilty person is found innocent. In the United States, the state must prove the case beyond a reasonable doubt, which decreases the number of false positives and increases the number of false negatives.

10. According to the principle of marginal deterrence, penalties should be scaled to the severity of the crime, thus providing a marginal deterrent for more serious crimes. An increase in the penalty for a particular crime causes some criminals to switch to other crimes. For example, an increase in the penalty for burglary causes some criminals to upgrade to robbery, others to downgrade to larceny, and others to abandon crime.

11. The prison system has four purposes: rehabilitation, deterrence, incapacitation, and retribution.

 a. Contrary to popular opinion, rehabilitation is relatively ineffective in reducing crime.

    b. Deterrence works. An increase in the certainty of punishment provides a greater deterrent than an increase in the severity of punishment.

    c. Incapacitation is an efficient policy if the prisoner would commit a large number of crimes if he were free.

12. Illegal goods are relatively expensive because firms must compensate their workers and lenders for extra risks and must spend money on concealment.

13. Policies that decrease the supply of illegal drugs increase their prices. If drug addicts support their habits with property crime, an increase in total expenditures increases total property crime, partly offsetting the benefits associated with decreased drug abuse.

Exercises and Discussion Questions

1. Consider Waivah, a potential burglar who weighs the benefits and cost of burglary. Fill in the blanks in the following table:

Loot	$1,000
Probability of success	0.70
Expected loot	_____
Probability of being imprisoned	0.03
Wage per day	$20
Workdays per year	100
Forgone income per year	_____
Loss of freedom per year	$3,000
Opportunity cost per year	_____
Length of prison term	2 years
Expected penalty cost	_____
Expected benefit from burglary	_____
Daily income if employed	_____
Net return from burglary	_____

2. Consider Boris, whose benefit-cost analysis of burglary is shown in Table 22–3. Compute the values of the following variables such that Boris is indifferent between burglary and a legal job. In computing the threshold value for each variable, assume that the values of the other variables are the same as in Table 22–3.

    a. The probability of success (P_s).

    b. The value of the loot.

    c. The probability of imprisonment (P_i).

    d. The opportunity cost per year (C).

    e. The length of the prison sentence.

3. Consider a city with a wealthy area and a poor one. The two areas have the same horizontal MVC (marginal-victim-cost) curve and the same negatively

sloped MPC (marginal-prevention-cost) curve. The two curves intersect at a crime rate B^*. The crime rate in the wealthy area is B_w and the crime rate in the poor area is B_p. Given the current allocation of police between the two areas, $B_w < B^* < B_p$.

a. Use a graph to depict the current situation.

b. Is the current allocation of resources efficient? If not, how should resources be reallocated? Put some numbers on your graph and use the graph to show that the reallocation of resources will generate net gains for society.

c. Suppose that the two areas have the same MVC curve but different MPC curves. Depict a situation in which a higher crime rate in the poor area $(B_p > B_w)$ is efficient.

4. The city of Evilville suffers from two types of crimes, marijuana consumption and burglary. Suppose that you must decide how to allocate the city's crime-fighting resources between the two types of crime. The marginal-prevention-cost (MPC) curves are linear, and for a given crime rate, the marijuana MPC is twice the burglary MPC. The marginal-victim-cost (MVC) curves are horizontal. Under what conditions will the optimum number of marijuana crimes be less than the optimum number of burglaries? Illustrate your answer with a graph.

5. Suppose that your city has a fixed budget to allocate among 10 police precincts. You are responsible for allocating the budget.

a. Your allocation decisions should be guided by some crime-fighting objective. What is your objective?

b. What information would you collect, and how would you use it?

6. Suppose that Alice purchases an insurance policy for her bike. Complete the following table, assuming that her policy has a $20 deductible.

Protective Action	Protection Cost	Probability of Theft	Expected Theft Cost	Total Cost
No protection	$0	0.30		
Flimsy lock	11	0.10		
Sturdy lock	24	0.02		
Armed guard	80	0.00		

7. Recall the Bonnie example, shown in Table 22–5. You are negotiating with the DA over the length of the prison term for petit larceny. Suppose that Bonnie's opportunity cost of prison time is $8,000 per year. What is the maximum larceny term she will accept? In other words, what larceny term will make her indifferent between facing a criminal trial on armed robbery and a plea bargain for larceny?

8. Consider the following quote from Monty, a former district attorney who was recently elected the governor of a state in which the only crimes are burglary and robbery. "I'll stop the let's-make-a-deal approach to criminal

justice and replace the plea-bargaining process with a set of required penalties, one for burglary and one for robbery."

  a. Outline a strategy for determining the set of penalties. What information would you collect, and how would you use it?

  b. Is this a wise policy? Is it efficient?

9. Critically appraise: "The social cost of robbery is about six times the social cost of burglary. Given the principle of marginal deterrence, the length of the prison term for robbery should be six times the length of the prison term for burglary."

10. Consider the analysis of marginal deterrence shown in Figure 22–8. Under what circumstances (what values for the social cost of burglary and robbery) would the increased penalty for burglary decrease the total social cost of crime?

11. Consider a city in which there are only two types of crimes, burglary and armed robbery. Choose one of the words in each set of parentheses to make the following statement correct and then explain your choices: an increase in the penalty for burglary will decrease the total social cost of crime if

  a. The supply curve for burglary is relatively (*steep, flat*).

  b. The cross-elasticity of the supply of armed robbery with respect to the net return on burglary is relatively (*small, large*).

  c. The social cost of burglary is (*small, large*) relative to the social cost of armed robbery.

12. In the city of Swiftsure, there is only one crime, armed robbery. The city recently decided to double the probability of imprisonment from 10 percent (10 percent of armed robberies result in a prison sentence) to 20 percent. Because the city has a fixed prison capacity, it also cut the average prison sentence in half, from 3 years to 1.5 years.

  a. Would you expect these changes in the city's crime policy to increase, decrease, or not affect the city's crime rate?

  b. Would you expect these changes to increase, decrease, or not affect the total cost of crime (the sum of victim and prevention costs)?

13. Suppose that Gotham City doubles the required prison sentence for burglary (its only crime). Consider the following quote from Robin: "If my assumptions are correct, the longer prison sentence will increase the crime rate."

  a. What are Robin's assumptions?

  b. Use a graph to illustrate his prediction.

14. Consider a city with the following characteristics:

  i. The supply curve of heroin is vertical (perfectly inelastic) at 200 kilos.

  ii. The initial price is $40. The price elasticity of demand is -0.25.

  iii. The city will spend $500 on a drug policy to shift the supply curve to the left by 5 percent. The drug policy will not shift the demand curve.

  iv. The heroin market generates two types of social cost. First, consumption of heroin generates a social cost of $150 per kilo: the citizens of the city are willing to pay $150 for every one-kilo reduction of heroin. Second, heroin consumers support their habits with property crime.

   a. Is the drug program efficient?

   b. Choose the word in parentheses that makes the statement correct, and explain your choice: "As the price elasticity of demand for heroin increases in absolute value, the efficiency of the drug policy (*increases, decreases*)."

15. Consider the following statement: "Our drug policy is inefficient. We should legalize drugs and tax drug producers. We can set the tax at a level such that we have the same equilibrium drug consumption. By doing so, we will save all the money we currently spend on the enforcement of drug laws and the prosecution and punishment of drug dealers." What are the advantages and disadvantages of this policy, which combines legalization and taxation?

16. A number of insurance companies recently started offering free burglar alarms with their homeowner insurance policies. Evaluate the merits of such a policy. Would you expect such firms to make more or less money than firms that do not provide alarms?

17. Sympacity is considering a policy under which every victim of crime would be compensated for victim cost. The city would cover the property losses from crime and would also compensate victims for injuries suffered as a result of crime. Evaluate the efficiency and equity effects of the city's policy.

18. The property losses from business fraud (white-collar crime) totaled $600 per household in 1983, compared to losses of $90 for robbery, $93 for burglary, and $56 for auto theft. Yet white-collar crime receives less attention than other types of property crime. Why do you suppose white-collar crime receives such little attention?

19. During the 1970s, the crime rate of women increased five times faster than the crime rate of men. Why?

References and Additional Readings

Crime Facts

Chaiken, Jan M., and Marcia Chaiken. "Crime Rates and the Active Criminal." In *Crime and Public Policy*, ed. James Q. Wilson. San Francisco: Institute for Contemporary Studies, 1983. Discusses recent trends in crime rates.

U.S. Department of Justice. *Criminal Victimization in the United States*, 1989. Washington, D.C.: U.S. Government Printing Office, 1989.

————. *Sourcebook of Criminal Justice Statistics*, 1986. Washington, D.C.: U.S. Government Printing Office, 1987.

U.S. Federal Bureau of Investigation. *Crime in the United States, 1990*. Washington, D.C.: U.S. Government Printing Office, 1991. Data from the *Uniform Crime Reports*.

The Cost of Crime

Gray, Charles M., and Mitchell Joelson. "Neighborhood Crime and the Demand for Central City Housing." Chapter 3 in *The Costs of Crime*, ed. Charles M. Gray. Beverly Hills, Calif.: Sage Publications, 1979. Explores the effects of crime on property values.

Reynolds, Morgan. *Crime by Choice: An Economic Analysis*. Dallas: Fisher Institute, 1986. Estimates the cost of personal and property crimes.

Thaler, Richard. "Note on the Value of Crime Control—Evidence from the Property Market." *Journal of Urban Economics* 5 (1978), pp. 137–45. Examines the effects of crime rates on property values.

The Rational Criminal

Cobb, William. "Theft and the Two Hypotheses." In *The Economics of Crime and Punishment*, ed. Simon Rottenberg. Washington, D.C.: American Enterprise Institute, 1973.

Deutsch, Joseph; Simon Hakim; and J. Weinblatt. "A Micro Model of the Criminal's Location Choice." *Journal of Urban Economics* 22 (1987), pp. 198–208.

Gunning, J. Patrick Jr. "How Profitable Is Burglary?" In *The Economics of Crime and Punishment*, ed. Simon Rottenberg. Washington, D.C.: American Enterprise Institute, 1973.

Herrnstein, Richard J. "Some Criminogenic Traits of Offenders." In *Crime and Public Policy*, ed. James Q. Wilson. San Francisco: Institute for Contemporary Studies, 1983. Discusses the personal traits that predispose some people to crime, that is, the traits that cause some people to have a relatively low aversion to crime.

Krohm, Gregory. "The Pecuniary Incentives of Property Crime." In *The Economics of Crime and Punishment*, by Simon Rottenberg. Washington, D.C.: American Enterprise Institute, 1973.

Sesnowitz, Michael. "Returns to Burglary." *Western Economic Journal* 10, no. 4 (1972), pp. 477–81.

Crime, Demographics, and Culture

Blumstein, Alfred; Jacqueline Cohen; and Harold Miller. "Demographically Disaggregated Projections of Prison Population." *Journal of Criminal Justice* 8 (1980), pp. 1–26. Predicts that crime rates decline as the relative number of teenagers decreases.

Fox, James A. *Forecasting Crime*. Lexington, Mass: D. C. Heath, 1978. Predicts crime rates on the basis of the age distribution and racial composition of the population.

Schapiro, Morton Owen, and Dennis A. Ahlburg. "Why Crime Is Down." *American Demographics* 8 (1986).

Wilson, James Q. "Crime and American Culture." *The Public Interest* 70 (Winter 1983), pp. 22–48.

Unemployment and Crime

Cook, Philip J., and Gary A. Zarkin. "Crime and the Business Cycle." *Journal of Legal Studies*, 14 (1985), pp. 115–28. Found that robbery and burglary rates rise by a small amount during recessions.

Fleisher, Belton. *The Economics of Delinquency*. Chicago: Quadrangle Books, 1966. Suggests that an increase in the unemployment rate increases the juvenile crime rate.

Freeman, Richard B. "Crime and Unemployment." In *Crime and Public Policy*, ed. James Q. Wilson. San Francisco: Institute for Contemporary Studies, 1983. Reviews dozens of studies of the relationship between crime and unemployment. Concludes that there is a negative, but weak, relationship between the crime rate and the unemployment rate, and that the link between the crime rate and sanctions (expected punishment) is stronger. Speculates that an improvement in labor-market conditions may deter first-time offenders.

Orsagh, Thomas, and Ann D. Witte. "Economic Status and Crime: Implications for Offender Rehabilitation." *Journal of Criminal Law and Criminology* 72 (1981), no. 3. Found little evidence of a significant relationship between unemployment and crime.

Phillips, Llad; Harold Votey; and Harold Maxwell. "Crime, Youth, and the Labor Market." *Journal of Political Economy* 80 (1972), pp. 491–504. Suggests that the crime rates of 18- and 19-year-old males are sensitive to labor-market conditions: the lower the labor-force participation rate, the higher the crime rate.

Wilson, James Q. "Crime and Unemployment." *The Public Interest* 79 (Spring 1985), pp. 3–8. Discusses the relationship between unemployment rates and crime rates.

Victim as Crime Fighter

Balkin, S., and J. F. McDonald. "The Market for Street Crime—An Economic Analysis of Victim-Offender Interactions." *Journal of Urban Economics* 10 (1981), pp. 390–405. A discussion of the subtle interactions between potential victims and criminals.

Clotfelter, Charles D. "Explaining Unselfish Behavior—Crime and the Helpful Bystander." *Journal of Urban Economics* 8 (1980), pp. 196–212. Discusses altruistic behavior of witnesses to crime.

———. "Urban Crime and Household Protective Measures." *Review of Economics and Statistics* 59 (1977), pp. 499–503. Discusses the effects of increased crime rates on the protective measures of potential victims.

Clotfelter, Charles D., and Robert D. Seeley. "The Private Costs of Crime." In *The Costs of Crime*, ed. Charles M. Gray. Beverly Hills, Calif.: Sage Publications, 1979, pp. 213–32. Discusses the private and social costs of private protection measures.

Wilson, James Q., and Barbara Boland. "Crime." Chapter 4 in *The Urban Predicament*, ed. William Gorham and Nathan Glazer. Washington, D.C.: Urban Institute, 1976, pp. 179–230. Discusses how potential victims protect themselves from crime.

Police Issues

Carr-Hill, R., and N. Stern. "An Econometric Model of the Supply and Control of Recorded Offenses in England and Wales." *Journal of Public Economics* 2 (1973), pp. 289–318. Concludes that an increase in police and enforcement expenditures per capita increased reported (not actual) crime per capita.

———. "Theory and Estimation in Models of Crime and Its Social Control and Their Relations to the Concepts of Social Outputs." In *The Economics of Public Services*, ed. Martin Feldstein and Robert Inman. London: Macmillan, 1977. Discusses the issue of how to measure the output of crime enforcement.

Hakim, S.; A. Ovadia; E. Sagi; and J. Weinblatt. "Interjurisdictional Spillover of Crime and Police Expenditure." *Land Economics* 55 (1979), pp. 200–212.

Johnson, T. G.; B. M. Swallow; and B. J. Deaton. "Does Crime Prevention Pay?—An Analysis of Local Government Crime Prevention Expenditures." *American Journal of Agricultural Economics* 66 (1984).

Kelling, G. L.; T. Pate; D. Dieckman; and C. E. Brown. *The Kansas City Preventative Patrol Experiment: A Technical Report.* Washington, D.C.: The Police Foundation, 1974. Suggests that increases in patrol activity do not affect crime rates.

Levine, James. "The Ineffectiveness of Adding Police to Prevent Crime." *Public Policy* 23 (Fall 1975), pp. 523–45.

Mehay, Stephen. "Inter-Governmental Contracting for Municipal Police Services—An Empirical Analysis." *Land Economics* 55 (1979), pp. 59–72.

Phillips, Llad, and Harold Votey. "Crime Control in California." *Journal of Legal Studies* 4 (1975), pp. 327–50. Estimates the effects of enforcement expenditures on crime. An increase in the number of law enforcement personnel increases the probability of conviction.

Pogue, Thomas F. "Effect of Police Expenditures on Crime Rates." *Public Finance Quarterly* 3 (1975), pp. 14–44. Finds no relationship between police spending and crime rates.

Reynolds, Morgan. *Crime by Choice: An Economic Analysis.* Dallas: Fisher Institute, 1986.

Sherman, Lawrence. "Patrol Strategies for Police." In *Crime and Public Policy,* ed. James Q. Wilson. San Francisco: Institute for Contemporary Studies, 1983. Discusses the efficacy of alternative police patrol strategies.

Thaler, Richard. "Econometric Analysis of Property Crime—Interaction between Police and Criminals." *Journal of Public Economics* 8 (1977), pp. 37–51.

Wilson, James Q. *Thinking about Crime.* New York: Basic Books, 1975. Chapter 5 (The Police and Crime) discusses the efficacy of patrol in deterring crime and contrasts the traditional patrol approach to the community service approach.

Evidence of Deterrence

Bartel, Ann P. "Women and Crime: An Economic Analysis." *Economic Inquiry* 42 (1979), pp. 29–51. The probabilities of arrest and conviction have significant deterrent effects on female property crime. The decrease in the number of preschool children accounts for over half of the increase in female property crime between 1960 and 1970.

Craig, Steven G. "The Deterrent Impact of Police: An Examination of a Locally Provided Public Service." *Journal of Urban Economics* 21 (1987) pp. 298–311. Discusses the effects of changes in clearance rates on the crime rate and the reporting rate.

Ehrlich, Isaac. "The Deterrent Effect of Criminal Law Enforcement." *Journal of Legal Studies* 1 (1972), pp. 259–76.

———. "Participation in Illegitimate Activities." *Journal of Political Economy* 81 (1973), pp. 521–65.

Goldberg, I., and F. C. Nold. "Does Reporting Deter Criminals?—An Empirical Analysis of Risk and Return in Crime." *Review of Economics and Statistics* 62 (1980), pp. 424–31. Discusses the effects of increased reporting rates on the return on crime and the probability of being victimized.

Mathur, V. K. "Economics of Crime—Investigation of the Deterrent Hypothesis for Urban Areas." *Review of Economics and Statistics* 60 (1978), pp. 459–66. Discusses the deterrent effects of increases in the certainty and severity of punishment.

Myers, S. L. "Crime in Urban Areas, New Evidence and Results." *Journal of Urban Economics* 11 (1982), pp. 148–58. Examines the effects of increased penalties and increased income on crime rates.

Phillips, Llad. "Crime Control: The Case for Deterrence." In *The Economics of Crime and Punishment*, ed. Simon Rottenberg. Washington, D.C.: American Enterprise Institute, 1973.

Sjoquist, David L. "Property Crime and Economic Behavior: Some Empirical Results." *American Economic Review* 63 (1973), pp. 439–46. Found that an increase in the probability of arrest decreased the crime rates for burglary, robbery, and larceny.

Tullock, Gordon. "Does Punishment Deter Crime?" *The Public Interest*, Summer 1974, pp. 103–111.

Viscusi, W. Kip. "The Risks and Rewards of Criminal Activity: A Comprehensive Test of Criminal Deterrence." *Journal of Labor Economics* 4 (1986), pp. 317–40.

Wilson, James Q., and Barbara Boland. "Crime." Chapter 4 in *The Urban Predicament*, ed. William Gorham and Nathan Glazer. Washington, D.C.: Urban Institute, 1976, pp. 179–230. Overview of crime and crime prevention, including a summary of deterrent studies. Estimates that the elasticity of supply of burglaries with respect to the probability of arrest is -0.50.

Witte, Ann D. "Estimating the Economic Model of Crime with Individual Data." *Quarterly Journal of Economics* 94 (1980), pp. 57–84. Estimates deterrent effects and finds that the increased certainty of punishment (larger probability of punishment) has a larger deterrent effect than increased severity (larger penalty).

Wolpin, V. "A Time Series Cross-Sectional Analysis of International Variation in Crime and Punishment." *Review of Economics and Statistics* 62 (1980), pp. 1417–23. Compares the crime rates of the United States, Japan, and the United Kingdom.

Economics of the Courts

Forst, Brian. "Prosecution and Sentencing." In *Crime and Public Policy*, ed. James Q. Wilson. San Francisco: Institute for Contemporary Studies, 1983. Discusses how the criminal justice system processes a typical set of 100 criminal cases.

Landes, William. "The Bail System: An Economic Approach." *Journal of Legal Studies* 2, no. 1 (1973), pp. 79–105.

Rhodes, W. M. "Economics of Criminal Courts—Theoretical and Empirical Investigation." *Journal of Legal Studies* 5 (1976), pp. 311–430.

Schlesinger, Steven R. "Criminal Procedures in the Courtroom." In *Crime and Public Policy*, ed. by James Q. Wilson. San Francisco: Institute for Contemporary Studies, 1983. Discusses the bail system and the exclusionary rule.

Stepan, Jan. "Possible Lessons from Continental Criminal Procedure." In *The Economics of Crime and Punishment*, ed. Simon Rottenberg. Washington, D.C.: American Enterprise Institute, 1973.

Optimum Penalties

Becker, Gary S. "The Case for Fines." *Journal of Political Economy* 76, no. 2 (1968), pp. 168–217.

Dickens, William T. "Crime and Punishment Again: The Economic Approach with a Psychological Twist." *Journal of Public Economics* 30 (1985), pp. 97–107. Discusses the effects of psychological factors in the deterrent effect of increased penalties.

Stigler, George. "The Optimum Enforcement of Laws," *Journal of Political Economy* 78 (May 1970), pp. 526–36. Discusses the principle of marginal deterrence.

Wilson, James Q. *Thinking about Crime.* New York: Basic Books, 1975. Chapter 8 advocates several reforms of the sentencing procedure, including (1) centralized sentencing management and uniform sentences, (2) some form of confinement for every crime (certain punishment), (3) a shortening of prison and jail sentences. In other words, he advocates short but certain punishment.

Rehabilitation

Evans, Robert. "The Labor Market and Parole Success." *Journal of Human Resources* 3, no. 2 (1968), pp. 201–11.

Glaser, Daniel. "Supervising Offenders Outside of Prison." In *Crime and Public Policy*, ed. James Q. Wilson. San Francisco: Institute for Contemporary Studies, 1983. Discusses parole, halfway houses, counseling programs, and employment assistance.

Martinson, Robert. "What Works—Questions and Answers about Prison Reform." *The Public Interest* 35 (Spring 1974), pp. 22–54. Reviewed the results of 231 studies of the effects of rehabilitation programs on recidivism rates. Concluded that rehabilitation has no appreciable effect on recidivism.

Incapacitation

Greenberg, David F. "The Incapacitative Effects of Imprisonment: Some Estimates." *Law and Society Review* 9 (Summer 1975), pp. 541–80.

Greenwood, Peter. "Controlling the Crime Rate through Imprisonment." In *Crime and Public Policy*, ed. James Q. Wilson. San Francisco: Institute for Contemporary Studies, 1983. Discusses the trade-offs associated with selective incapacitation.

Shinnar, Reuel, and Shlomo Shinnar. "The Effects of the Criminal Justice System on the Control of Crime." *Law and Society Review* 9 (Summer 1975), pp. 581–611.

Wilson, James Q. "Dealing with the High-Rate Offender." *The Public Interest* 72 (Summer 1983), pp. 52–71.

Wilson, James Q., and Barbara Boland. Chapter 4 in *The Urban Predicament*, ed. William Gorham and Nathan Glazer. Washington, D.C.: Urban Institute, 1976, pp. 179–230. Estimates the incapacitation effect for different values of crimes per offender.

Prison Reform

Blumstein, Alfred. "Prisons: Population, Capacity, and Alternatives." In *Crime and Public Policy*, ed. James Q. Wilson. San Francisco: Institute for Contemporary Studies, 1983. Discusses alternative strategies for dealing with prison congestion, including new construction and selective incapacitation.

Conley, J. "Economics and the Social Reality of Prisons." *Journal of Criminal Justice* 10 (1981), pp. 25–35.

DiIulio, John J. "Prison Discipline and Prison Reform." *The Public Interest* 89 (Fall 1987), pp. 71–90.

Engel, Kathleen, and Stanley Rothman. "Prison Violence and the Paradox of Reform." *The Public Interest* 73 (Fall 1983), pp. 91–105.

Drugs and Property Crime

Becker, Gary S. "Should Drug Use Be Legalized?" *Business Week*, August 17, 1987, p. 22.

Clague, Christopher. "Legal Strategies for Dealing with Heroin Addiction." *American Economic Review* 63, no. 2 (1973), pp. 263–69.

Moore, Mark. "Controlling Criminogenic Commodities: Drugs, Guns, and Alcohol." In *Crime and Public Policy*, ed. James Q. Wilson. San Francisco: Institute for Contemporary Studies, 1983. Discusses the roles of drugs, guns, and alcohol in criminal activity.

———. "Policies to Achieve Discrimination of the Effective Price of Heroin." *American Economic Review* 63, no. 2 (1973), pp. 270–77.

Silverman, L. P., and N. L. Sprull. "Urban Crime and the Price of Heroin." *Journal of Urban Economics* 4 (1977), pp. 80–103. Discusses the interactions between drug policies and property crime.

Wilson, James Q. *Thinking about Crime*. New York: Basic Books, 1975. Chapter 7 discusses the relationship between heroin addiction and property crime and examines the British system of legalized heroin.

Organized Crime

Allsop, Kenneth. *The Bootleggers: The Story of Chicago's Prohibition Era*. New Rochelle, N.Y.: Arlington House, 1970.

Buchanen, James. "A Defense of Organized Crime." In *The Economics of Crime and Punishment*, ed. Simon Rottenberg. Washington, D.C.: American Enterprise Institute, 1973.

Reuter, Peter, and Jonathan Rubinstein. "Fact, Fancy and Organized Crime." *The Public Interest* 53 (Fall 1978), pp. 45–67.

Rottenberg, Simon. "The Clandestine Distribution of Heroin, Its Discovery and Suppression." *Journal of Political Economy* 76 (January 1968), pp. 78–90.

Rubin, Paul. "The Economic Theory of the Criminal Firm." In *The Economics of Crime and Punishment*, ed. Simon Rottenberg. Washington, D.C.: American Enterprise Institute, 1973.

Schelling, Thomas C. "Economics and Criminal Enterprise." *The Public Interest* 7 (1967), pp. 114–26.

Miscellaneous

Gordon, David. "Capitalism, Class, and Crime in America." *Review of Radical Political Economy* 3, no. 3 (1971), pp. 51–75.

Kates, Don B., Jr. "The Battle over Gun Control." *The Public Interest* 84 (Summer 1986), pp. 42–52.

Katzman, Martin. "The Economics of Defense against Crime in the Streets." *Land Economics* 19 (1968), pp. 431–40.

Phillips, Llad, and Harold Votey. *Crime and Public Policy*. Beverly Hills, Calif.: Sage Publications, 1979.

Shoup, Carl. "Standards for Distributing a Free Governmental Service: Crime Prevention." *Public Finance* 19 (December 1964), pp. 383–401. Discusses the trade-off between efficiency and equity in the distribution of crime-fighting resources.

Simon, Carl P., and Ann D. Witte. *Beating the System: The Underground Economy*. Boston: Auburn House, 1982.

Thurow, Lester. "Equity vs. Efficiency in Law Enforcement." *Public Policy* 18, no. 4 (1970), pp. 451–59.

Toby, Jackson. "Crime in the Schools." In *Crime and Public Policy*, ed. James Q. Wilson. San Francisco: Institute for Contemporary Studies, 1983.

Wright, James D. "Second Thoughts about Gun Control." *The Public Interest* 91 (Spring 1988), pp. 23–39.

Tools of Microeconomics

Tools of Microeconomics

This appendix provides a review of some of the microeconomic tools that are used throughout the text. The first part reviews the model of supply and demand. The second and third parts show how to use indifference-curve analysis to explore the decisions of consumers and workers. The fourth part reviews the notion of marginal decision making.

Model of Supply and Demand

The most frequently used model in economics is the model of supply and demand. Economists use supply and demand curves to show how prices are determined in markets and to predict the effects of changes in the market on equilibrium prices.

The Market Demand Curve

The **market demand curve** shows the relationship between the price of a particular good and the quantity of the good purchased by consumers. To draw the market demand curve, we change the price and observe how consumers respond, assuming that everything else that affects the consumption of the good remains fixed. In Figure A–1, the market demand for shirts shows that an increase in the price of shirts from $20 to $30 decreases the quantity demand from 260 (point *c*) to 200 (point *e*). According to the **law of demand,** an increase in price decreases the quantity demanded, *ceteris paribus* (Latin for "everything else remaining the same"). Therefore, the demand curve is negatively sloped.

What sort of changes would cause the market demand curve to shift to the right or left? A change in any one of the variables held fixed in drawing the demand curve would cause the entire curve to shift.

1. **Income.** In the jargon of economics, a **"normal" good** is defined as a good for which there is a positive relationship between income and

698   *Appendix*

FIGURE A–1   **Market Demand Curve**

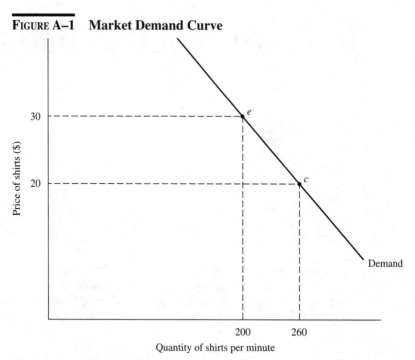

The demand curve shows the relationship between price and quantity demanded, *ceteris paribus* (everything else equal).

consumption: an increase in income increases the quantity of the good demanded. In Figure A–2, an increase in income would shift the market demand curve for a normal good to the right, from D' to D''. In other words, an increase in income means that a larger quantity will be demanded at a given price of shirts. For an **"inferior" good,** there is a negative relationship between income and consumption: an increase in income decreases the quantity of the good demanded. In Figure A–2, an increase in income would shift the market demand curve for an inferior good to the left, from D'' to D'.

2. **Price of a substitute.** An increase in the price of a substitute good will shift the demand curve to the right. Suppose that the curve shown in Figure A–2 is the demand curve for cotton shirts. An increase in the price of polyester shirts would shift the demand curve for cotton shirts to the right: at every price, more cotton shirts would be demanded. This is sensible because an increase in the price of polyester shirts will cause some polyester consumers to switch to cotton shirts.

3. **Price of a complement.** An increase in the price of a complementary good will shift the demand curve to the left. If the curve shown in Figure A–2 is the demand curve for cotton shirts, an increase in the price of pants will shift the demand curve to the left (from D'' to D'): at every

FIGURE A–2 Shifting the Market Demand Curve

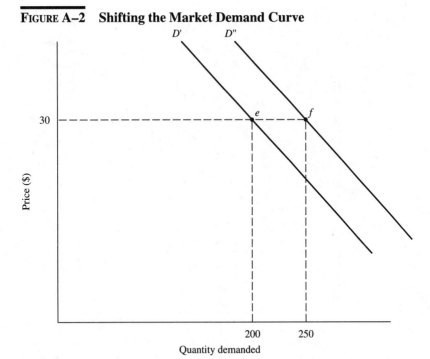

The demand curve shifts as a result of a change in income, a change in the price of a related good, or a change in the number of people in the relevant market area.

price, fewer cotton shirts will be consumed. This is sensible because an increase in the price of pants increases the cost of a dress outfit (shirt and pants), so consumers will demand fewer outfits and thus fewer shirts.

4. **Number of people.** One of the variables held fixed in drawing the market demand curve is the number of people in the relevant market area. In Figure A–2, an increase in the number of people will shift the demand curve to the right, from D' to D'': at every price, more shirts will be demanded.

The Market Supply Curve

The **market supply curve** shows the relationship between the price of a particular good and the quantity of the good supplied by firms. To draw the market supply curve, we change the price and observe how producers respond, assuming that everything else that affects the production of the good remains fixed. In Figure A–3, the market supply for shirts shows that an increase in the price of shirts (from $20 to $30) increases the quantity supplied from 100 (point *b*) to 200 (point *e*). According to the **law of supply,** an increase in price increases the quantity supplied, *ceteris paribus.* Therefore, the supply curve is positively sloped.

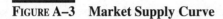

FIGURE A–3   **Market Supply Curve**

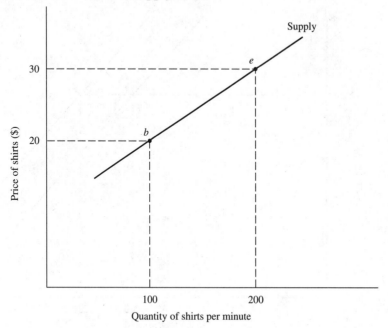

The supply curve shows the relationship between price and quantity supplied, *ceteris paribus.*

What sort of changes would cause the market supply curve to shift? A change in any one of the variables held fixed in drawing the supply curve would cause the entire curve to shift.

1. **Input prices.** An increase in the price of an input used to produce a particular good will increase the cost of production, causing firms to supply a smaller quantity at each price. In Figure A–4, the supply curve for cotton shirts would shift to the left (from S'' to S') if (a) the price of labor increased, (b) the cost of cotton increased, or (c) the cost of shirt-making machinery increased.

2. **Production technology.** A technological innovation that decreases the cost of production will shift the market supply curve to the right: at each price, firms will supply a larger quantity because it is less costly to produce the good. In Figure A–4, a cost-saving innovation in the production of shirts would shift the supply curve from S' to S''.

Elasticities of Demand and Supply

Economists use two simple formulas to measure the responsiveness of consumers and producers to changes in price. The **price elasticity of demand** for a particular good is defined as the percentage change in quantity demanded divided by the

FIGURE A–4 Shifting the Market Supply Curve

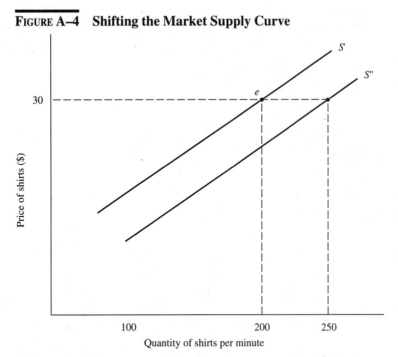

The supply curve shifts as a result of a change in input prices or a change in production technology.

percentage change in the price of the good. The demand elasticity measures the responsiveness of consumers to changes in price: the larger the computed elasticity (in absolute value), the more responsive are consumers to a change in price. Similarly, the **price elasticity of supply** for a particular good is defined by the percentage change in quantity supplied divided by the percentage change in price. The supply elasticity measures the responsiveness of producers to changes in price: the larger the computed elasticity, the more responsive are producers to a change in price.

Market Equilibrium

An **equilibrium** is a situation in which there is no tendency for things to change over time. In the market for shirts, equilibrium means that there is no tendency for the price of shirts to change over time: tomorrow's price will be the same as today's price. At the equilibrium price, firms produce the quantity of shirts that consumers want to buy: the quantity demanded (by consumers) equals the quantity supplied (by producers). Once the market reaches the equilibrium price, there is no tendency for the price to change because there is neither a shortage nor a surplus of shirts.

We can use demand and supply curves to depict the market equilibrium. In Figure A–5, the demand curve shows the negative relationship between the price of shirts and the quantity of shirts demanded: an increase in price decreases the quantity of shirts demanded. The supply curve shows the positive relationship between

FIGURE A–5   **Market Equilibrium and Disequilibrium**

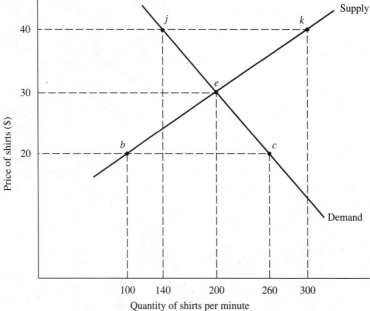

At the market equilibrium (point *e*, with price = $30 and quantity = 200), the quantity supplied equals the quantity demanded. At a price less than the equilibrium price (e.g., $20), there is a shortage: the quantity supplied (100 at point *b*) is less than the quantity demanded (260 at point *c*). At a price exceeding the equilibrium price (e.g., $40), there is a surplus: the quantity supplied exceeds the quantity demanded.

the price of shirts and the quantity of shirts supplied: an increase in price increases the quantity of shirts supplied. The market equilibrium is shown by the intersection of the supply and demand curves. At a price of $30, the quantity supplied (from the supply curve) equals the quantity demanded (from the demand curve), so there is neither a shortage nor a surplus of shirts: consumers want to buy 200 shirts, which is exactly the quantity that producers want to sell.

Shortage or Surplus

If the price is less than the equilibrium price, there will be a shortage of shirts. For example, if the price is $20, the market will be at point *c* on the demand curve (consumers would like to buy 260 shirts) and point *b* on the supply curve (producers are willing to sell only 100 shirts). In this case, there is a **shortage** or an excess demand of 160 shirts: the quantity demanded (260) exceeds the quantity supplied (100) by 160 shirts. Because consumers want to buy more shirts than firms are willing to supply, we would expect the price of shirts to increase over time: tomorrow's price will be higher than today's price.

An increase in the price of shirts will cause the market to move upward along both the supply and demand curves. An increase in the price of shirts allows firms in the shirt industry to outbid other industries for the inputs required to produce shirts (machines, labor, land, raw materials), so the output of the shirt industry will increase. In other words, the market moves upward along the supply curve: as the price increases, the quantity supplied increases. On the demand side, the increase in price decreases the quantity of shirts demanded: the market moves upward along the demand curve. In combination, the movements along the supply curve and the demand curve narrow the gap between the quantity supplied and the quantity demanded. The market continues to move upward along the two curves until the shortage is eliminated. This occurs at point *e,* where the quantity supplied equals the quantity demanded at a price of $30.

If the initial price exceeds the equilibrium price, there will be a surplus of shirts. For example, if the price is $40, the market will be at point *j* on the demand curve (consumers would like to buy 140 shirts) and point *k* on the supply curve (producers are willing to sell 300 shirts). In this case, there is a **surplus** or an excess supply of 160 shirts: the quantity supplied (300) exceeds the quantity demanded (140) by 160 shirts. Because producers want to sell more shirts than consumers are willing to buy, we would expect the price of shirts to decrease over time: tomorrow's price will be lower than today's price.

As the price decreases, the market moves downward along both the supply and demand curves. A decrease in the price of shirts means that the shirt industry will be outbid by other industries for some of the resources used to produce shirts (machines, labor, land, raw materials), so the output of the shirt industry will decrease. In other words, the market moves downward along the supply curve: as the price decreases, the quantity supplied decreases. On the demand side, the decrease in price increases the quantity of shirts demanded: the market moves downward along the demand curve. In combination, the movements along the supply curve and the demand curve narrow the gap between the quantity supplied and the quantity demanded. The market will continue to move downward along the two curves until the surplus is eliminated. This occurs at point *e,* where the quantity supplied equals the quantity demanded at a price of $30.

Market Effects of Changes in Demand or Supply

A change on either side of the market will change the equilibrium quantity and price. Figure A–6 shows the effect of an increase in the demand for shirts. The initial equilibrium is shown by point *e*: price is $30 and quantity is 200 shirts per minute. Suppose that the demand for shirts increases, shifting the market demand curve to the right. As explained earlier, this increase in demand could be caused by an increase in income, a change in the price of a related good, or an increase in population. At the initial price, there is a shortage of shirts, so the equilibrium price will increase.

We could also use the supply and demand curves to show the market effects of a change in supply. In Figure A–7, a rightward shift of the supply curve would generate a surplus of shirts at the original price: the quantity supplied will exceed the quantity demanded. The new equilibrium (shown by the intersection of the demand curve and the new supply curve) has a lower price and a larger quantity.

FIGURE A–6   The Market Effects of an Increase in Demand

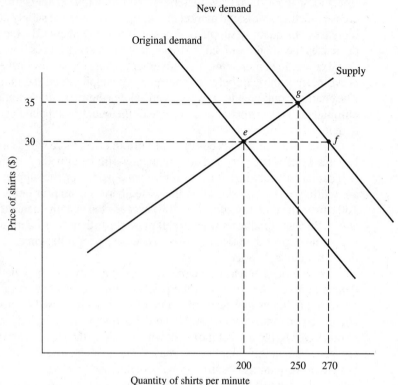

Quantity of shirts per minute

An increase in the demand for shirts shifts the demand curve to the right. At the initial price ($30) there is a shortage: the quantity demanded (point f) exceeds the quantity supplied (point e). The resulting increase in price causes the market to move upward along the supply curve and the new demand curve until equilibrium is restored at point g.

Theory of Consumer Choice

This part of the appendix provides an overview of indifference-curve analysis, which is used in *Urban Economics* to analyze consumers' choices among alternative goods. This material has been written for students who have not studied indifference-curve analysis in other courses, but could also be used as a refresher for students with more experience in economic analysis.

A consumer must decide how to allocate a fixed budget among a large number of consumer goods. Indifference-curve analysis is based on the notion that the consumer has an objective (to maximize his satisfaction or "utility") and a budget constraint (a fixed income to spend on consumer goods). The consumer's problem is to find the affordable consumption bundle that maximizes his utility. The analysis of the consumer-choice problem can be divided into two parts. An **indifference curve** summarizes the consumer's subjective preferences about alternative consumer goods. The **budget line** shows the limits (constraints) imposed on the consumer.

FIGURE A–7   The Market Effects of an Increase in Supply

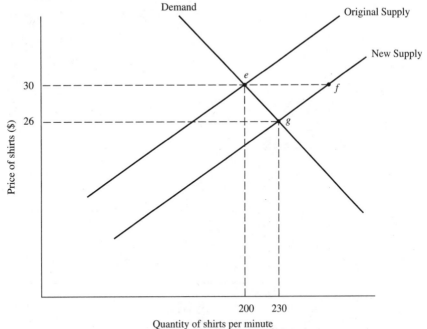

An increase in the supply of shirts shifts the supply curve to the right. At the initial price ($30), there is a surplus: the quantity supplied (point *f*) exceeds the quantity demanded (point *e*). The resulting decrease in price causes the market to move downward along the demand curve and the new supply curve until equilibrium is restored at point *g*.

Constructing an Indifference Curve

The simplest way to explain the notion of an indifference curve is to construct one. Suppose that Mary gets satisfaction or utility from consuming hamburgers and hot dogs. Figure A–8 shows the quantity of hamburgers on the horizontal axis and the quantity of hot dogs on the vertical axis. To construct an indifference curve, we pick a point (e.g., point *C,* with two hamburgers and five hot dogs) and pose two questions:

1. Which combinations of hamburgers and hot dogs would Mary prefer to the combination at point *C*? In other words, which combinations would generate a higher level of satisfaction or utility?
2. Which combinations of hamburgers and hot dogs would Mary consider to be inferior to the combination at point *C*? In other words, what combinations would generate lower utility?

Once we've established the combinations that are superior to point *C* (those that generate higher utility) and inferior to point *C* (lower utility), the remaining combinations are equivalent to point *C* in the sense that they generate the same level of satisfaction or utility. If we connect these combinations, we have an indifference curve. Mary will be indifferent among all the combinations along the indifference curve.

FIGURE A–8   Indifference Curve and Marginal Rate of Substitution

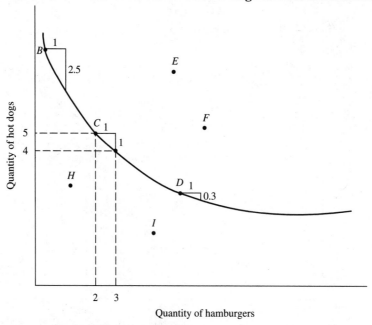

The indifference curve shows the different combinations of hamburgers and hot dogs that generate the same utility level.

The indifference curve that passes through point *C* divides the combinations of hamburgers and hot dogs into three groups.

1. **Superior combinations.** All combinations above the indifference curve generate more satisfaction (higher utility) than combination *C*. For example, Mary would prefer point *E* or *F* to point *C*.

2. **Inferior combinations.** All combinations below the indifference curve generate less satisfaction (lower utility) than combination *C*. For example, Mary would prefer point *C* to point *H* or point *I*.

3. **Equivalent combinations.** All combinations along the indifference curve generate the same satisfaction (the same utility) as combination *C*. For example, Mary would be indifferent between combinations *B*, *C*, and *D*.

Because indifference curves show the subjective preferences of consumers, the shapes of indifference curves vary from one consumer to another. Nonetheless, the indifference curves of all consumers share two characteristics: they are negatively sloped and convex.

Why are indifference curves negatively sloped? If the two commodities are "goods" (more of the commodity is better), not "bads" (more of the commodity is worse), the indifference curve will be negatively sloped. In other words, if we give Mary an additional hamburger, we must take away some hot dogs to restore her original utility level. The slope of the curve is the **marginal rate of substitution** (MRS) between the two goods. It shows the rate at which Mary is willing to substitute one good for another. In Figure A–8, if Mary starts at point C and we give her one more hamburger, we must take away one hot dog to keep her on the same indifference curve. Therefore, the marginal rate of substitution near point C is 1.0. Mary is willing to trade one hot dog for one hamburger, so her subjective trade-off between the two goods is 1.0.

The slope of the indifference curve decreases (in absolute value) as the quantity of hamburgers increases. In other words, the indifference curve becomes flatter as Mary's hamburger consumption increases. In Figure A–8, the slope (the rise over the run) near point B is 2.5: if we give Mary one more hamburger, we must take away 2.5 hot dogs to keep her on the same indifference curve (to keep her utility constant). Therefore, the MRS near point B is more than twice the MRS near point C. The MRS near point D is 0.30: if we give Mary one more hamburger, we must take away only 0.30 hot dog to keep her utility constant.

Because the slope of the indifference curve decreases as hamburger consumption increases, the indifference curve is convex to the origin. The convexity results from the assumption of diminishing marginal utility. The marginal utility of hamburgers is defined as the increase in Mary's utility per additional hamburger. Suppose that as Mary's hamburger consumption increases, the marginal utility of hamburgers decreases. As we move down Mary's indifference curve (increasing hamburgers and decreasing hot dogs to keep her utility constant), we must take away progressively fewer hot dogs to keep her at the same utility level because she gains progressively less utility per additional hamburger. At the same time, as Mary's hot-dog consumption decreases, the marginal utility of hot dogs increases, so a given decrease in the number of hot dogs has a larger effect on her utility level. Therefore, it takes progressively fewer hot dogs to offset a given increase in utility from an additional hamburger. The combined effect of decreasing marginal utility of hamburgers (as hamburger consumption increases) and increasing marginal utility of hot dogs (as hot-dog consumption increases) means that the subjective trade-off between hamburgers and hot dogs decreases. In other words, the indifference curve becomes flatter and the marginal rate of substitution decreases.

An Indifference Map

An **indifference map** is a set of indifference curves. To construct an indifference map, we pick several starting points and then draw indifference curves through each point. In Figure A–9, the starting points $J, K,$ and L generate indifference curves $I_1, I_2,$ and I_3. As Mary moves from any point on the indifference curve I_1 to any point on I_2, her utility increases. To show that her utility is higher along I_2, all we need to show is that she prefers one point on I_2 to one point on I_1. Point K (on I_2) is obviously better than point J (on I_1) because K provides more hot dogs and more hamburgers. Under the assumption that both commodities are "goods," she will prefer the combination with larger quantities of both commodities (shown by point K). In general, Mary's utility increases as she moves in the northeasterly direction to higher indifference curves (from I_1 to I_2 to I_3, and so on).

FIGURE A–9   Indifference Curve Map

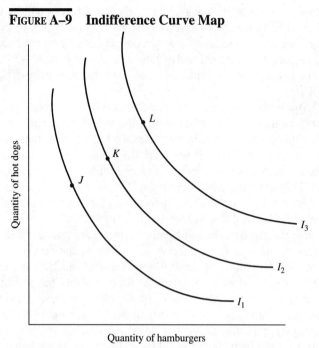

An indifference map shows a set of indifference curves, with utility increasing as we move northeasterly to higher indifference curves.

The Budget Set and Budget Line

Mary's ability to purchase hamburgers and hot dogs is limited by her income and the prices of the two goods. Mary's **budget set** includes all the combinations of hamburgers and hot dogs that she can afford, given her income and the prices of hamburgers and hot dogs. Figure A–10 shows Mary's budget set as the shaded area. The budget set is drawn under the following assumptions:

1. Mary's income is $120, and she spends all of her income on the two goods.
2. The price of a hamburger is $3 and the price of a hot dog is $2.

Given these numerical assumptions, Mary can afford all the combinations in the shaded area.

The **budget line** shows all the combinations of hamburgers and hot dogs that exhaust Mary's budget. In Figure A–10, the budget line is the line connecting points *M* and *N*. Point *M* is the combination that occurs if Mary spends her entire budget on hot dogs: if the price is $2 and she spends her entire $120 budget on hot dogs, she will get 60 hot dogs. Point *N* is the combination that occurs if Mary spends her entire budget on hamburgers (40 hamburgers from spending $120 on $3 hamburgers). If Mary spends some money on each good, she can reach the points between *M* and *N*. For example, she could reach point *Q* (20 hamburgers and 30 hot dogs) by splitting her budget equally between the two goods.

FIGURE A–10 **Budget Set and**
Budget Line

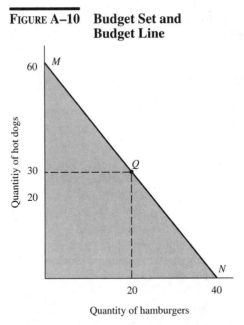

The budget set shows all the affordable combinations of
hamburgers and hot dogs, and the budget line shows the
combinations that exhaust the budget.

The slope of the budget line is the **market trade-off** between hamburgers and
hot dogs. It shows the rate at which the consumer can trade hamburgers for hot dogs,
given the market prices of the two goods. Starting from point *M,* if Mary gives up
one hamburger, she frees up $3 that can be spent on hot dogs. If the price of hot
dogs is $2, the $3 will buy 1.5 hot dogs, so the slope of the budget line is −1.5: the
"rise" is 1.5 hot dogs and the "run" is 1 hamburger. In general, the slope is equal
to the price of hamburgers (the good on the horizontal axis) divided by the price of
hot dogs (the good on the vertical axis). If the prices of the two goods do not change
as Mary changes her consumption pattern, the budget line will be a straight line
(the slope will be constant).

Changes in the prices of the two goods will change the budget line. In Figure A–11, a decrease in the price of hamburgers from $3 to $2 will shift the line
from *MN* to *MT*. The original vertical intercept (point *M*) is still in the budget set: if
Mary spends her entire budget on hot dogs, she will be unaffected by the decrease in
the price of hamburgers. The horizontal intercept moves from *N* (40 hamburgers) to
T (60 hamburgers) because at the lower price, a given budget buys more hamburgers.
If Mary buys some hamburgers and some hot dogs (she chooses some point between
the horizontal and vertical intercepts), she can afford more combinations because
she spends less per hamburger. The same argument applies to a decrease in the price
of hot dogs, shown in Figure A–11 as a shift from *MN* to *RN* (the price of hot dogs
decreases from $2 to $1.50).

FIGURE A–11   **Changes in Prices Shift the Budget Line**

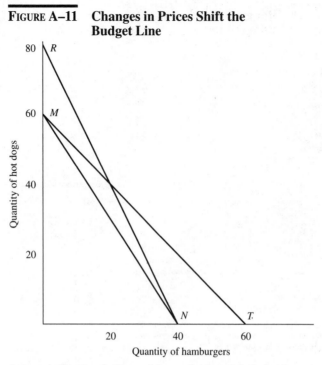

A change in the price of either good changes the slope of the budget line.

How does an increase in income affect the budget line? For a given set of prices, an increase in income increases the size of the budget set and shifts the budget line outward. In Figure A–12, an increase in Mary's income from $120 to $180 shifts the budget line from MN to ST. She can now afford to buy 90 hot dogs if she buys only hot dogs (point S, given a price of $2) or 60 hamburgers if she buys only hamburgers (point T, given a price of $3). If she spends half of her income on each good, she can buy 30 hamburgers and 45 hot dogs (point U).

Maximizing Utility

The consumer's objective is to maximize utility, subject to the budget constraint. In other words, Mary will choose the affordable combination of hamburgers and hot dogs that generates the highest utility. In graphical terms, Mary will choose a point on the highest feasible indifference curve.

In Figure A–13, Mary will choose point V (22 hamburgers and 27 hot dogs) and will achieve the utility level associated with indifference curve I_5. Why does she choose point V instead of point $W, X,$ or Y?

Point W: Mary doesn't choose this point for two reasons. First, it is not on the budget line, so it does not exhaust her budget. Second, it is on

FIGURE A–12 **Changes in Income Shift the Budget Line**

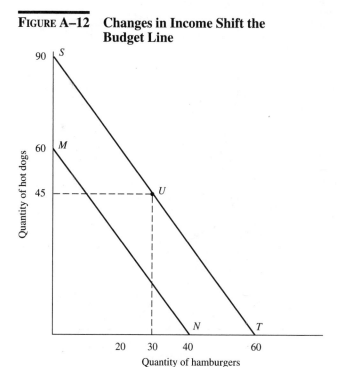

An increase in income shifts the budget line to the right.

a lower indifference curve (and thus generates less utility) than point *V*.

Point *X*: Although point *X* exhausts Mary's budget, *X* lies on a lower indifference curve than *V*, so it generates less utility than *V* (another point on the budget line). Starting from point *X*, Mary could reallocate her budget and buy more hamburgers and fewer hot dogs. As she moves down her budget line, she moves to progressively higher indifference curves, ultimately reaching point *V* and indifference curve I_5.

Point *Y*: Although point *Y* generates a higher utility level (it's on a higher indifference curve), it lies outside Mary's budget set, so she cannot afford it.

At point *V*, Mary reaches the highest indifference curve possible, given her budget set. The indifference curve touches—but does not pass through—the budget line. In other words, the indifference curve is tangent to the budget line. If the indifference curve cut through the budget line at some point (e.g., at point *X*), Mary could increase her utility by reallocating her budget between the two goods. A tangency occurs at the utility-maximizing combination.

FIGURE A–13   Consumer Maximizes Utility at Tangency of Indifference Curve and Budget Line

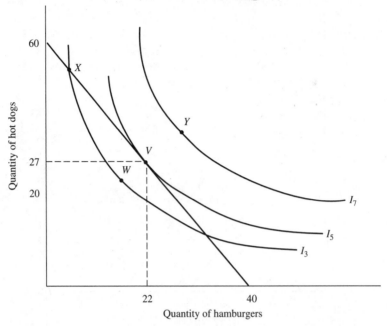

To maximize utility, the consumer finds the combination of hamburgers and hot dogs at which an indifference curve is tangent to the budget line, meaning that the marginal rate of substitution equals the price ratio.

What is the economic interpretation of the tangency condition? At the tangency, the slope of the indifference curve (the marginal rate of substitution) equals the slope of the budget line (the price ratio). Therefore, the consumer's subjective trade-off between the two goods (the consumer's MRS) equals the rate at which the two goods can be traded off in the consumer's budget (the price ratio). At any other combination, the MRS would be unequal to the price ratio, so the consumer could reallocate her budget and increase her utility. For example, starting from point *X*, Mary's indifference curve suggests that she is willing to give up about six hot dogs to get one hamburger (the slope of the indifference curve (the MRS) is about 6.0). Given the prices of the two goods, the price ratio is 1.5: Mary must give up only 1.5 hot dogs to get one hamburger. Therefore, she will increase her utility by reallocating her budget to consume more hamburgers and fewer hot dogs. She will continue to reallocate her budget until the MRS equals the price ratio (until the slope of the indifference curve equals the slope of the budget line). This occurs at point *V*, where MRS = 1.5.

Changes in Price and Income

How do changes in prices affect the utility-maximizing consumption bundle? As shown in Figure A–11, a decrease in price changes the shape of the budget set and the slope of the budget line. The consumer will find the highest indifference curve within the new budget set, going to the point at which an indifference curve is tangent to the new budget line. The consumer is likely to change the consumption of both goods. The **law of demand** states that (a) an increase in the price of a good will decrease the consumption of that good and (b) a decrease in price will increase the consumption of the good.

How do changes in income affect the utility-maximizing consumption bundle? As shown in Figure A–12, an increase in income shifts the budget line outward, providing the consumer with more budget options. The consumer will find the highest indifference curve within the new budget set, finding the point at which an indifference curve is tangent to the new budget line. The consumer is likely to change the consumption of both goods. A good is considered "normal" if an increase in income increases consumption of the good (and if a decrease in income decreases consumption). A good is considered "inferior" if consumption is negatively related to income (an increase in income decreases consumption and a decrease in income increases consumption).

Theory of Worker's Choice

Indifference-curve analysis can also be used to explore a worker's choice between leisure time and labor time (income-earning time). In this case, the two items that generate satisfaction or utility (the two "goods") are leisure time and income. People get utility from leisure activities (relaxing, reading, bowling, watching movies, playing sports) and also from the consumer products that can be purchased with wage income. The trade-off is obvious: the more leisure time you take, the less income you earn, so the smaller the quantity of consumer products you can purchase.

Indifference Curves for Worker

The worker's preferences concerning leisure time and income are summarized in indifference curves. The slope of an indifference curve equals the marginal rate of substitution between leisure and income. In other words, the slope indicates the rate at which the worker is willing to trade off income and leisure time. Figure A–14 shows three indifference curves, with leisure time on the horizontal axis and income on the vertical axis.

Budget Line for Worker

The worker has a fixed number of hours to allocate between leisure time and income-earning time. The budget line (*BC* in Figure A–14) shows the rate at which he can trade leisure hours for income. The slope of the budget line is the wage: a one-hour decrease in leisure time increases income by the hourly wage. In Figure A–14, we assume that the worker has 100 hours per week to allocate between leisure time and income-earning time, and the wage is $4 per hour. The horizontal intercept (point *C*) is the maximum leisure time (100 hours). As leisure time decreases, income

FIGURE A–14   Worker's Choice between Leisure and Income

To maximize utility, the worker finds the combination of leisure time and income at which an indifference curve is tangent to the budget line, meaning that the marginal rate of substitution equals the wage.

increases by $4 per hour, from $40 at point *D* (90 hours of leisure and 10 hours of labor) to $120 at point *E* (70 hours of leisure and 30 hours of labor), and so on.

How would a change in the wage affect the budget line? A decrease in the wage would decrease the slope of the budget line, causing it to pivot downward. At point *C*, labor time and income are zero, so a decrease in the wage has no effect. As leisure time decreases (work time increases), a given reduction of leisure time (a given increase in labor time) generates less labor income. Therefore, the decrease in the wage decreases the slope of the budget line. For example, if the wage drops to $3 per hour, the income earned from 10 hours of work (90 hours of leisure) would decrease from $40 to $30, so the budget point associated with 90 hours of leisure would drop by $10.

Maximizing Utility

The worker will maximize utility at point *E* because it is the combination of leisure and income that lies on the highest feasible indifference curve. The indifference curve is tangent to the budget line, so the worker's subjective trade-off between leisure and income (the marginal rate of substitution) equals the wage. At the optimum combination, the marginal rate of substitution will equal 4.0 (the slope of the budget line). For any other point along the budget line, the worker could reallocate his time and increase his utility. For example, starting with point *F,* the marginal rate of substitution is about 9.0, meaning that the worker is willing to give up $9 of income to get one more hour of leisure time. Because he gives up only $4 for every additional hour of leisure time, he will move down the budget line toward point *E.* He will continue to trade income for leisure until his subjective trade-off (the MRS) equals the wage, meaning that he will stop at point *E.*

How would an increase in the wage affect the amount of leisure time? An increase in the wage has two effects on the worker's choice between leisure and labor time. The first is the income effect: an increase in the wage means that the worker has a higher real income. The worker will consume more of all "normal" goods, including leisure. Therefore, the income effect provides upward pressure on leisure time and downward pressure on work time. The second effect of an increase in the wage is the substitution effect, or the opportunity-cost effect. An increase in the wage increases the opportunity cost of leisure time: given the higher wage, each hour of leisure time causes a larger reduction of income. As the opportunity cost of leisure time increases (as the benefit of work time increases), the worker will tend to spend less time on leisure and more time working. In other words, the substitution effect provides downward pressure on leisure time and upward pressure on labor time. It is not possible to predict, on theoretical grounds, which effect will dominate, so it's impossible to predict whether an increase in the wage will increase or decrease labor time.

Marginal Decision Making

The marginal principle provides a general rule for making decisions.

> **The Marginal Principle:** *Pick the level of an activity at which the marginal benefit of the activity equals its marginal cost.*

If the marginal benefit of some activity exceeds the marginal cost, you will be better off if you do more of the activity. You should continue to increase the level of an activity as long as the marginal benefit exceeds the marginal cost.

To explain the marginal principle, consider a problem facing Betty the beautician. Suppose that on a particular day, Betty must decide whether to keep her beauty shop open for an extra hour, meaning that her shop would be open for 10 hours instead of 9. To use the marginal principle, Betty must compare the marginal benefit of staying open to the marginal cost: if the marginal benefit exceeds the marginal cost, it will be sensible to remain open for the extra hour.

Marginal Benefits and Costs

On the benefit side, the **marginal benefit** of remaining open is the revenue generated during the extra (tenth) hour. The total benefit of operating the beauty shop is the revenue from beauty treatments, so the marginal—or incremental—benefit is the increase in total revenue from the tenth hour of operation. For example, if Betty expects to give five treatments at a price of $8 each during the tenth hour, the marginal benefit of remaining open is $40.

On the cost side, the **marginal cost** of remaining open is the extra cost incurred during the tenth hour. The costs associated with operating the beauty shop include the monthly rent and the costs of electricity to power and light the shop. To use the marginal principle, Betty must determine which of her costs increase when she remains open for the extra hour. In this case, keeping the shop open for an extra hour increases electricity costs and Betty's opportunity cost. The rent on the beauty shop is irrelevant to the decision because the monthly rent is independent of the number of hours the beauty shop is open.

Using the Marginal Principle

Once Betty has estimated the marginal benefit and cost of operating the beauty shop, she can make a decision about whether to remain open for an additional hour. Suppose that Betty's opportunity cost is $25 per hour. In other words, the value of her time in the next-best use is $25 per hour. If the cost of electricity is $5 per hour, the extra cost for the tenth hour (the marginal cost of remaining open) is $30. If the marginal benefit (the additional revenue from treatments) is $40, the extra hour is clearly profitable: the marginal revenue exceeds the marginal cost by $10.

The marginal principle suggests that Betty should keep the beauty shop open as long as the marginal benefit exceeds the marginal cost. She could use the same marginalist logic for the 11th, 12th, and 13th hour. Eventually, the marginal benefit will be less than the marginal cost, and then Betty can close the shop and go home. For example, suppose that the marginal benefit drops to $32 for the 11th hour (she does only four treatments during the 11th hour) and then drops to $24 for the 12th hour (three treatments during the 12th hour). In this case, the marginal benefit of the 12th hour ($24) is less than the marginal cost ($30), so she should remain open for only 11 hours. To maximize her welfare, the beautician picks the number of hours (11) at which the marginal benefit ($32) is just above the marginal cost ($30).

It is worth noting two important ideas underlying the marginal principle. To use the marginal principle, Betty must be careful how she measures her costs.

1. Betty ignores the **fixed costs** of the beauty shop, defined as costs that do not vary with the time she remains open. For example, her monthly rent is fixed, so she ignores this cost in calculating the marginal cost. A common error in economic analysis is to include fixed costs in the calculation of marginal cost.

2. Betty includes the **opportunity cost** of her time. Although Betty does not receive an hourly wage, the labor cost associated with remaining open equals the opportunity cost of her time. A common error in economic analysis is to include only explicit monetary costs in the computation of costs.

Index